Lecture Notes in Computer Science 9338

Commenced Publication in 1973
Founding and Former Series Editors:
Gerhard Goos, Juris Hartmanis, and Jan van Leeuwen

More information about this series at http://www.springer.com/series/7408

Floor Koornneef · Coen van Gulijk (Eds.)

Computer Safety, Reliability, and Security

SAFECOMP 2015 Workshops
ASSURE, DECSoS, ISSE, ReSA4CI, and SASSUR
Delft, the Netherlands, September 22, 2015
Proceedings

 Springer

Editors
Floor Koornneef
University of Technology
Delft
The Netherlands

Coen van Gulijk
University of Huddersfield
Huddersfield
UK

ISSN 0302-9743   ISSN 1611-3349 (electronic)
Lecture Notes in Computer Science
ISBN 978-3-319-24248-4   ISBN 978-3-319-24249-1 (eBook)
DOI 10.1007/978-3-319-24249-1

Library of Congress Control Number: 2015948709

LNCS Sublibrary: SL2 – Programming and Software Engineering

Springer Cham Heidelberg New York Dordrecht London

Printed on acid-free paper

Springer International Publishing AG Switzerland is part of Springer Science+Business Media
(www.springer.com)

Preface

It has become a tradition to organize workshops in conjunction with the annual SAFECOMP conferences. This year, we accepted proposals for 5 domain-specific high-quality workshops. This resulted in 5 workshops where safety and safety-related security formed the core content. This volume presents the proceedings of these workshops at the Delft University of Technology on September 22, 2015, preceding the SAFECOMP 2015 conference from 23 to 25 September. The SAFECOMP 2015 proceedings can be found in LNCS volume 9337.

The workshops allow for deep immersion into dedicated topics. This year's workshops are sequels to earlier workshops, which shows that the workshops are relevant to the scientific society that deals with safety in programmable industrial systems. The workshops maintained high-quality standards and were organized by well-known chairs and respected Program Committees. The workshops constitute a valuable addition to the SAFECOMP conference and the scientific society surrounding it. This year's workshops were the following:

- ASSURE 2015 - Assurance Cases for Software-Intensive Systems, chaired by Ewen Denney, Ibrahim Habli and Ganesh Pai;
- DECSoS 2015 - EWICS/ERCIM/ARTEMIS Dependable Cyber-physical Systems and Systems-of-Systems Workshop, chaired by Erwin Schoitsch and Amund Skavhaug;
- ISSE 2015 - International Workshop on the Integration of Safety and Security Engineering, chaired by Laurent Rioux, John Favaro, and Sanja Aaramaa;
- ReSA4CI 2015 - International Workshop on Reliability and Security Aspects for Critical Infrastructure Protection, chaired by Silvia Bonomi and Ilaria Matteucci;
- SASSUR 2015 - International Workshop on Next Generation of System Assurance Approaches for Safety-Critical Systems, chaired by Alejandra Ruiz, Tim Kelly and Jose Luis de la Vara.

This year 36 papers were accepted, resulting in 3 full-day and 2 half-day challenging workshops. The authors are from Austria, Canada, France, Germany, Hungary, Italy, Ireland, Japan, the Netherlands, Norway, Portugal, Singapore, Slovakia, Spain, Sweden, the UK, and the USA. Similar to the SAFECOMP conference, the workshops provide a truly international platform where academia and industry meet.

It has been an honor and pleasure for us, as the SAFECOMP 2015 program chairs, to work with the workshop chairs and the authors. We thank the workgroup chairs, authors, the members of workshop Program and Steering Committees and the Local Organizing Committee for doing a great job and for their pleasant cooperation. We also thank Saba Chockalingam and Yamin Huang for their contribution in formatting and completing the proceedings.

September 2015

Floor Koornneef
Coen van Gulijk

Organizing Committee

EWICS TC7 Chair

Francesca Saglietti   University of Erlangen-Nuremberg, Germany

General Chair

Pieter van Gelder   Delft University of Technology, the Netherlands

Program Co-chairs

Floor Koornneef   Delft University of Technology, the Netherlands
Coen van Gulijk   University of Huddersfield, UK

Workshop Chair

Frank Ortmeier   Otto von Guericke Universität Magdeburg, Germany

Finance Chair

Erika van Verseveld   Delft University of Technology, the Netherlands

Publicity Chair

Sandra Koreman   schetsboek.com, the Netherlands

ASSURE 2015

The 3rd International Workshop on Assurance Cases for Software-Intensive Systems

Ewen Denney[1], Ibrahim Habli[2], and Ganesh Pai[1]

[1] SGT/NASA Ames Research Center, Moffett Field, CA 94035, USA
{ewen.denney, ganesh.pai}@nasa.gov
[2] Department of Computer Science, University of York, York YO10 5DD, UK
ibrahim.habli@york.ac.uk

1 Introduction

Software-intensive systems play a key role in high-risk applications. Increasingly, regulations, standards, and guidelines now mandate and/or recommend that assurance cases be developed as part of the process for certification/approval of such systems, e.g., in defense, aviation, automotive, and healthcare systems. An assurance case is a reasoned argument, supported by a body of evidence, that a system exhibits certain behavior in a defined environment. Typically, assurance cases focus on a particular property—e.g., safety, security, or more generally, dependability—and are developed in a phased manner at the system level, with relations to the system development activities, i.e., requirements development, design, implementation, verification, and deployment. Ultimately, assurance arguments will form a core part of the assurance case for the wider system.

This volume contains the papers presented at the 3rd International Workshop on Assurance Cases for Software-intensive Systems (ASSURE 2015), collocated this year with the 34th International Conference on Computer Safety, Reliability, and Security (SAFECOMP 2015), in Delft, the Netherlands. As with the previous two editions of ASSURE, this year's workshop aims to provide an international forum for presenting emerging research, novel contributions, tool development efforts, and position papers on the foundations and applications of assurance case principles and techniques. The workshop goals are to: *i*) explore techniques to create and assess assurance cases for software-intensive systems; *ii*) examine the role of assurance cases in the engineering lifecycle of critical systems; *iii*) identify the dimensions of effective practice in the development/evaluation of assurance cases; *iv*) investigate the relationship between dependability techniques and assurance cases; and, *v*) identify critical research challenges towards defining a roadmap for future development.

2 Program

ASSURE 2015 began with an invited keynote talk by Pippa Moore of the UK Civil Aviation Authority (CAA). Nine papers were accepted this year, covering four themes that address the workshop goals: *foundations*, *methodology and patterns*, *tool support and tool demonstrations*, and *applications*. Papers under the 'foundations' theme considered topics such as formalizing the structure of assurance arguments, and the representation of confidence. The 'methodology and patterns' theme included papers that dealt with argument patterns addressing security and safety, as well as lifecycle approaches for safety and dependability. Papers concerning domain-specific model-based tools for safety argumentation, systems for safety condition monitoring, and building blocks for assurance cases comprised the 'tool support and tool demonstrations' theme, whereas the 'applications' theme mainly dealt with medical device assurance. Similar to the previous year's workshop, ASSURE 2015 concluded with a panel discussion, where researcher and practitioner panelists discussed the role of argumentation in certification and safety risk management.

3 Acknowledgments

We thank all those who submitted papers to ASSURE 2015 and congratulate those authors whose papers were selected for inclusion into the workshop program and proceedings. For reviewing the submissions and providing useful feedback to the authors, we especially thank our distinguished Program Committee members. Their efforts have resulted in an exciting workshop program and, in turn, a successful third edition of the ASSURE workshop series. Finally, we thank the organizers of SAFE-COMP 2015 for their support of ASSURE 2015.

ASSURE Program Organizers

Ewen Denney	SGT/NASA Ames Research Center, USA
Ibrahim Habli	University of York, UK
Ganesh Pai	SGT/NASA Ames Research Center, USA

ASSURE Program Committee

Robin Bloomfield	City University, UK
Jérémie Guiochet	LAAS-CNRS, France
Richard Hawkins	University of York, UK
David Higham	Delphi Diesel Systems, UK
Michael Holloway	NASA Langley Research Center, USA
Paul Jones	Food and Drug Administration, USA
Tim Kelly	University of York, UK
Yoshiki Kinoshita	Kanagawa University, Japan
John Knight	University of Virginia, USA
Andrew Rae	Griffith University, Australia
Roger Rivett	Jaguar Land Rover Automotive, UK
Christel Seguin	ONERA, France
Mark-Alexander Sujan	University of Warwick, UK
Kenji Taguchi	AIST, Japan
Alan Wassyng	McMaster University, Canada
Sean White	Health and Social Care Information Centre, UK

ASSURE Additional Reviewers

Katrina Attwood	University of York, UK
Oleg Lisagor	University of York, UK
Mark Nicholson	University of York, UK
Makoto Takeyama	Kaganawa University, Japan
Ian Whiteside	Avaloq Innovation, UK

DECSoS 2015

Introduction ERCIM/EWICS/ARTEMIS Workshop on Dependable Embedded and Cyber-Physical Systems and Systems-of-Systems at SAFECOMP 2015

European Research and Innovation Initiatives in the Area
of Cyber-Physical Systems and Systems-of-Systems
(selective overview)

Erwin Schoitsch[1] and Amund Skavhaug[2]

[1] AIT Austrian Institute of Technology GmbH, Vienna, Austria
erwin.schoitsch@ait.ac.at
[2] NTNU, Trondheim, Norway
Amund.Skavhaug@ntnu.no

1 Introduction

The DECSoS workshop at SAFECOMP follows already its own tradition since 2006. In the past, it focused on the conventional type of "dependable embedded systems", covering all dependability aspects as defined by Avizienis, Lapries, Kopetz, Voges and others in IFIP WG 10.4. To put more emphasis on the relationship to physics, mechatronics and the notion of interaction with an unpredictable environment, the terminology changed to "cyber-physical systems" (CPS). Collaboration and co-operation of these systems with each other and humans, and the interplay of safety and security are leading to new challenges in verification, validation and certification and qualification respectively.

In a highly interconnected world of highly automated systems, a finite number of independently operable and manageable systems including so-called "legacy systems" is networked together for a period of time to achieve a certain higher goal as constituent systems of a "system-of-systems" (SoS). Examples are the smart power grid with power plants and power distribution and control, smart transport systems (rail, traffic management with V2V and V2I facilities, air traffic control systems), advanced man-ufacturing systems ("Industry 4.0"), mobile co-operating autonomous robotic systems, smart buildings up to smart cities and the like.

Society as a whole strongly depends on CPS and SoS - thus it is important to consider dependability (safety, reliability, availability, security, maintainability, etc.), resilience, robustness and sustainability in a holistic manner. CPSs and SoS are a targeted research area in Horizon 2020 and public-private partnerships such as ECSEL

(Electronic Components and Systems for European Leadership), which integrates the former ARTEMIS (Advanced Research and Technology for Embedded Intelligence and Systems), ENIAC and EPoSS efforts, where industry and research ("private") are represented by the industrial associations ARTEMIS-IA (for ARTEMIS, embedded intelligence and systems), AENEAS (for ENIAC, semiconductor industry) and EPoSS (for "Smart Systems Integration"), and the public part is represented by the EC and the national public authorities of the member states which take part in the ECSEL Joint Undertaking. Funding comes from the EC and the national public authorities ("tri-partite funding": EC, member states, project partners).

2   ARTEMIS/ECSEL: The European Cyber-physical Systems Initiative

This year the workshop is co-hosted by the ARTEMIS projects:

- CRYSTAL ("Critical Systems Engineering Factories", http://www.crystal-artemis.eu),
- ARROWHEAD1 ("Ahead of the Future", http://www.arrowhead.eu/),
- EMC2 ("Embedded Multi-Core systems for Mixed Criticality applications in dynamic and changeable real-time environments", http://www.artemis-emc2.eu/) and
- R5-COP ("Reconfigurable ROS-based Resilient Reasoning Robotic Cooperating Systems", http://www.r5-cop.eu/)

and will as well present work from ARTEMIS projects, which has been finished recently:

- MBAT ("Combined Model-based Analysis and Testing of Embedded Systems", http://www.mbat-artemis.eu) and
- nSafeCer ("Safety Certification of Software-intensive Systems with Reusable Components", http://www.safecer.eu).

ARTEMIS was one of the European, industry-driven research initiatives and is now part of the ECSEL PPP. The current ARTEMIS projects will, however, be continued according to the ARTEMIS rules, but managed by the ECSEL JU. The six co-hosting ARTEMIS projects are described briefly:

MBAT was targeting at achieving better results by combining test and analysis methods. The MBAT project strongly fostered the development of high-quality embedded systems in the transportation sector at reduced costs (in short: higher quality embedded systems at lower price). Higher quality embedded systems in turn increases the overall quality and market value of the transportation products. Therefore, close co-operation with related projects was envisaged, especially with those of the ARTEMIS Safety & High-reliability Cluster (e.g. CESAR, MBAT, SafeCer, iFEST, R3-COP, CRYSTAL).

nSafeCer aimed at increased efficiency and reduced time-to-market together with increased quality and reduced risk through composable certification of safety-relevant embedded software-intensive systems in the industrial domains of automotive and construction equipment, avionics, and rail. nSafeCer provided support for efficient reuse of safety certification arguments and prequalified components within and across industrial domains. This addresses the overarching goal of the ARTEMIS JU strategy to overcome fragmentation in the embedded systems markets.

R5-COP focuses on agile manufacturing paradigms and specifically on modular robotic systems. Based on existing and newly developed methods for a formal modelling of hardware and software components, R5-COP will support model-based design, engineering, validation, and fast commissioning. Using existing interface and middleware standards R5-COP will strongly facilitate integration of components from various suppliers.

CRYSTAL, a large ARTEMIS Innovation Pilot Project (AIPP), aims at fostering Europe's leading edge position in embedded systems engineering by facilitating high quality and cost effectiveness of safety-critical embedded systems and architecture platforms. Its overall goal is to enable sustainable paths to speed up the maturation, integration, and cross-sector reusability of technological and methodological bricks in the areas of transportation (aerospace, automotive, and rail) and healthcare providing a critical mass of European technology providers. CRYSTAL will integrate the contributions of previous ARTEMIS projects (CESAR, MBAT, iFEST, SafeCer etc.) and further develop the ARTEMIS RTP (Reference Technology Platform) and Interoperability Specification.

ARROWHEAD, a large AIPP addressing the areas production and energy system automation, intelligent-built environment and urban infrastructure, is aiming at enabling collaborative automation by networked embedded devices, from enterprise/worldwide level in the cloud down to device level at the machine in the plant. The goal is to achieve efficiency and flexibility on a global scale for five application verticals: production (manufacturing, process, energy), smart buildings and infrastructures, electro-mobility and virtual market of energy.

EMC2 is up to now the largest ARTEMIS AIPP with EMC2 bundling the power for innovation of 100 partners from embedded industry and research from 19 European countries and Israel with an effort of about 800 person years and a total budget of about 90 million Euro. The objective of the EMC2 project is to develop an innovative and sustainable service-oriented architecture approach for mixed criticality applications in dynamic and changeable real-time environments based on multi-core architectures.

It provides the paradigm shift to a new and sustainable system architecture which is suitable to handle open dynamic systems:

- Dynamic Adaptability in Open Systems, scalability and utmost flexibility,
- Utilization of expensive system features only as Service-on-Demand in order to reduce the overall system cost,
- Handling of mixed criticality applications under real-time conditions,
- Full scale deployment and management of integrated tool chains, through the entire lifecycle.

The AIPPs ARROWHEAD and EMC2 are addressing "Systems-of-Systems" aspects in the context of critical systems, whereas SafeCer, MBAT and CRYSTAL are devoting their major efforts towards creating a sustainable eco-system of a CRTP

(Collaborative Reference Technology Platform) based on an ARTEMIS common IOS (Interoperability Specification).

3   This Year's Workshop

The workshop DECSoS 2015 provides some insight into an interesting set of topics to enable fruitful discussions during the meeting and afterwards. The mixture of topics is hopefully well balanced, with a certain focus on cyber security & safety co-analysis and on modelling, simulation and verification. Presentations are mainly based on the ARTEMIS/ECSEL projects mentioned above and on basic research respectively industrial developments of partners companies and universities.

The session starts with Introduction to the ERCIM/EWICS/ARTEMIS DECSoS Workshop setting the European Research and Innovation scene. Safety & Cyber security co-analysis and engineering are addressed in the first session (two from project EMC2, one from ARROWHEAD). Robotics reconfiguration testing (R5-COP), motion control certification and collision avoidance are topics in the session on robotics and motion control. Contract modelling and verification in railway applications (MBAT), multi-core motor drive control in aerospace (EMC2) and robustness testing with a Flexray bus tester supporting automated safety certification (nSafeCer) are contributions in the Modelling and Verification session. Two particular papers are presented in the last session on dependability: a perfectly scalable real-time system for automotive vehicle engine and behavior test (EMC2) on the one hand and a students' lab experiment on how to build dependable Cyber-Physical Systems with redundant consumer single-board Linux computers on the other hand.

As chairpersons of the workshop, we want to thank all authors and contributors who submitted their work, and want to express our thanks to the SAFECOMP organizers who provided us the opportunity to organize the workshop at SAFECOMP 2015 in Delft. Particularly we want to thank the EC and national public funding authorities who made the work in the research projects possible. We do not want to forget the continued support of our companies and organizations, of ERCIM, the European Research Consortium for Informatics and Mathematics with its Working Group on Dependable Embedded Software-intensive Systems, and EWICS, the creator and main sponsor of SAFECOMP, with its working groups, who always helped us to learn from their networks.

We hope that all participants will benefit from the workshop, enjoy the conference and accompanying programmes and will join us again in the future!

Erwin Schoitsch   Amund Skavhaug
AIT Austrian Institute of Technology GmbH   The Norwegian University
Safety & Security Department   of Science and Technology
Vienna, Austria   Trondheim, Norway

Acknowledgements: Part of the work presented in the workshop received funding from the EC (ARTEMIS/ECSEL Joint Undertaking) and the partners National Funding Authorities through the projects nSafeCer (295373), MBAT (269335), R5-COP (621447), CRYSTAL (332820), ARROWHEAD (332987) and EMC2 (621429).

DECSoS Program Organizers

Erwin Schoitsch	AIT Austrian Institute of Technology, Austria
Amund Skavhaug	Norwegian University of Science and Technology, Norway

DECSoS Program Committee

Bettina Buth	HAW Hamburg, Germany
Francesco Flammini	Ansaldo STS Italy, University "Federico II" of Naples, Italy
Janusz Gorski	Gdansk University of Technology, Poland
Denis Hatebur	Universität Duisburg-Essen, Germany
Willibald Krenn	AIT Austrian Institute of Technology, Austria
Dejan Nickovic	AIT Austrian Institute of Technology, Austria
Frank Ortmeier	Otto-von-Guericke-Universität Magdeburg, Germany
Matthieu Roy	LAAS-CNRS, France
Francesca Saglietti	University of Erlangen-Nuremberg, Germany
Christoph Schmitz	Zühlke Engineering AG, Switzerland
Erwin Schoitsch	AIT Austrian Institute of Technology, Austria
Rolf Schumacher	Ing.-Büro Softwaretechnik, Germany
Amund Skavhaug	NTNU, Norway

ISSE 2015

2nd International Workshop on the Integration of Safety and Security Engineering

Laurent Rioux[1], John Favaro[2], and Sanja Aaramaa[3]

[1] THALES Research & Technology
1, av Augustin Fresnel, 91767 Palaiseau Cedex, France
laurent.rioux@thalesgroup.com
[2] Intecs S.p.A. Via Umberto Forti 5, 56121 Pisa, Italy
john.favaro@intecs.it
[3] Department of Information Processing Science,
University of Oulu P.O. Box 3000, 90014 Finland
sanja.aaramaa@olou.fi

1 Introduction

As safety-related systems are increasingly opened up to the outside world through innovations in communication and value-added services, the need for introducing security engineering practices into the process has emerged. Exacerbating the problem is that the safety and security have the potential to interact with each other in mission critical systems in ways that are often subtle and difficult to analyze separately. Observations of this phenomenon has led to increasing interest in developing joint approaches to safety and security engineering, culminating in their integration in a unified approach.

At the First International Workshop on the Integration of Safety and Security Engineering (ISSE 2014) in Florence, Italy, a forum was established for sharing ideas and experience from research and practice. Keynote speakers from prominent standardization committees reported on the status of current standardization efforts. A roundtable discussion brought out concerns and priorities within ongoing industrial initiatives.

2 Workshop Format

Building upon the foundation laid by its predecessor, ISSE 2015 transitions to a full conference format. The selected papers bring the latest pertinent results from integrated safety and security engineering research and practice to the community. Methodologies (*A Combined Safety-Hazards and Security-Threat Analysis Method for Automotive Systems*), tools (*Safety and Security Assessment of Behavioral Properties Using Alloy*), and techniques (*Sequential and Parallel Attack Tree Modelling*) are all represented.

Novel approaches are combined with existing standard approaches (*Combining MILS with Contract-Based Design for Safety and Security Requirements*). New perspectives on domain-specific application areas are provided (*Security Analysis of Urban Railway Systems: The Need for a Cyber-Physical Perspective*). In summary, ISSE 2015 brings the issues brought out in its predecessor workshop into a full research context, establishing the basis for further progress in future editions of ISSE.

3   Acknowledgements

The ISSE 2015 workshop was supported by the following projects:

- **Multi-Concerns Interactions System Engineering (MERgE)**. The ITEA 2 project MERgE (www.merge-project.eu) aims to develop and demonstrate innovative concepts and design tools to address multi-concerns interactions in systems, targeting the elaboration of effective architectural solutions with a focus on safety and security.
- **Safety and Security Modelling (SESAMO)**. The recently completed ARTEMIS JU SESAMO project (www.sesamo-project.eu) addressed the root causes of problems arising with convergence of safety and security in embedded systems. The project delivered a complete methodology described in publicly available deliverables, together with fully elaborated and analyzed building blocks for use in the construction of safety and security related systems. An extensive tool chain was produced that supports all aspects of the combined methodology.

ISSE Program Organizers

ISSE Program Committee

ReSA4CI 2015

Introduction to the Safecomp 2015 Workshop: Reliability and Security Aspects for Critical Infrastructure Protection

Silvia Bonomi[1] and Ilaria Matteucci[2]

[1] Dipartimento di Ingegneria Informatica Automatica
e Gestionale "Antonio Ruberti"
Università degli Studi di Roma "La Sapienza"
Via Ariosto 25, 00185, Roma, Italy
[2] IIT-CNR, Via G. Moruzzi, 1 Pisa, Italy
bonomi@dis.uniroma1.it, ilaria.matteucci@iit.cnr.it

1 Overview

The ReSA4CI workshop aims at providing a forum for researchers and engineers in academia and industry to foster an exchange of research results, experiences, and products in the area of reliable, dependable, and secure computing for critical systems protection from both a theoretical and practical perspective. The ultimate goal of the ReSA4CI workshop is to envision new trends and ideas about aspects of designing, implementing, and evaluating reliable and secure solutions for the next generation critical infrastructures.

Critical Infrastructures (CIs) present several challenges in the fields of distributed systems, dependability and security methods and approaches crucial for improving trustworthiness on ICT facilities. The workshop aims at presenting the advancement on the state of art in these fields and spreading their adoption in several scenarios involving main infrastructures for modern society. Indeed, CIs are at the hearth of any advanced civilized country. These infrastructures include among others: finance and insurance, transportation (e.g. mass transit, rails and aircrafts), public services (e.g., law enforcement, fire and emergency), energy, health care. Hence, their destruction or disruption, even partially, may, directly or indirectly, strongly affect the normal and efficient functioning of a country. The global scope and massive scale of today's attacks necessitate global situational awareness, which cannot be achieved by the isolated local protection systems residing within the IT boundaries of individual institutions. This leads to foster the investigation of innovative methodologies for gathering, processing and correlating huge amounts of data understanding anomaly behaviors and learning automatically always-evolving cyber threats with the final aim to prevent and/or mitigate their consequences.

The workshop is at its second edition. The first one has been held in Florence on September 9th, 2014, co-located with the SAFECOMP 2014 conference, and it was able to attract 20-30 participants that actively took part to the event by questioning the speakers and participating to emerging discussions.

2 Workshop Program

The program of ReSA4CI 2015 consists of 5 high-quality papers, covering the above-mentioned topics, grouped as follows:

1 Session 1: Security and Dependability Analysis of CI

- Jonas Wäfler and Poul Heegaard. "How to use Mobile Communication in Critical Infrastructures: a Dependability Analysis".
- Kateryna Netkachova, Robin Bloomfield, Peter Popov and Oleksandr Netkachov. "Using Structured Assurance Case Approach to Analyse Security and Reliability of Critical Infrastructures".

2 Session 2. Evaluation methodologies for CI

- Andrea Ceccarelli and Nuno Silva. "Analysis of Companies Gaps in the Application of Standards for Safety-Critical Software"
- Marco Tiloca, Francesco Racciatti and Gianluca Dini. "Simulative evaluation of security attacks in networked critical infrastructures"
- Szilvia Varro-Gyapay, Dániel László Magyar, Melinda Kocsis-Magyar, Katalin Tasi, Attila Hoangthanh Dinh, Ágota Bausz and László Gönczy. "Optimization of reconfiguration mechanisms in Critical Infrastructures"

Each paper was selected according to at least three reviews produced mainly by Program Committee members and a little percentage of external reviewers. Selected papers come from several countries around the world. In addition, we are glad to host Dr. Palmer Colamarino from RHEA Group. He has a huge expertise in the domain of Critical Infrastructure protection, the core topic of our Workshop, and he will give a talk highlighting main challenges and research issues in the field.

3 Thanks

We would like to thank the SAFECOMP organization committee and collaborators for their precious help in handling all the issues related to the workshop. Our next thanks go to all authors of the submitted papers who manifested their interest in the workshop. With their participation the second edition of the Workshop on Reliability and Security Aspects for Critical Infrastructure Protection (ReSA4CI 2015) becomes a real success and an inspiration for future workshops on this new and exciting area of research. Special thanks are finally due to PC members and additional reviewers for the high quality and objective reviews they provided.

4 Acknowledgements

This workshop has been supported by the TENACE PRIN Project (n. 20103P34XC), about the degree of maturity of the Italian critical infrastructures to provide solutions to protect them and by the SESAMO EU project, (Grant Agreement No. 295354), about the convergence of safety and security in embedded systems at architectural level.

Additional Reviewer: Luca De Cicco, Institut Mines-Telecom, France

ReSA4CI Program Organizers

Silvia Bonomi	University of Rome La Sapienza, Italy
Ilaria Matteucci	Consiglio Nazionale delle Ricerche (IIT-CNR), Italy

ReSA4CI Program Committee

Valentina Bonfiglio	University of Florence, Italy
Francois Bonnet	Japan Advanced Institute of Science and Technology, Japan
Andrea Ceccarelli	University of Florence, Italy
Michele Colajanni	Univerity of Modena and Reggio Emilia, Italy
Barbara Gallina	Malardalen University, Sweden
Joaquin Garcia-Alfaro	Institut Mines, France
Felicita Di Giandomenico	ISTI-CNR, Italy
Karama Kanoun	LAAS, France
Paolo Masci	Queen Mary University of London, UK
Federica Paci	University of Southampton, UK
Marinella Petrocchi	IIT-CNR, Italy
Marco Platania	Johns Hopkins University, USA

Additional Reviewer

Luca De Cicco	Institut Mines-Telecom, France

SASSUR 2015

4th International Workshop on Next Generation of System Assurance Approaches for Safety-Critical Systems

Alejandra Ruiz[1], Jose Luis de la Vara[2], and Tim Kelly[3]

[1] TECNALIA, Spain
[2] Universidad Carlos III de Madrid, Spain
[3] University of York, UK
alejandra.ruiz@tecnalia.com, jvara@inf.uc3m.es,
tim.kelly@york.ac.uk

SASSUR 2015 is the 4th edition of the International Workshop on Next Generation of System Assurance Approaches for Safety-Critical Systems. As in the previous editions, the workshop is intended to explore new ideas on compositional and evolutionary safety assurance and certification. Safety assurance and certification are amongst the most expensive and time-consuming tasks in the development of safety-critical systems. The increasing complexity and size of these systems requires new approaches to constructing and managing system assurance artefacts, e.g. model-based assessment approaches offering increased automation, and strategies for explicit and managed reuse.

The topics of interest in the workshop include, among others, industrial challenges for cost-effective safety assurance and certification, cross-domain product certification, compliance management, evolutionary approaches for safety and security assurance, assurance case-based approaches, evolution of standards, mixed-criticality system assurance, and the safety assurance on adaptive systems. Systems and situations such as the wider use of autonomous air vehicles and its regulation, recent incidents with autonomous cars, regulation changes for medical devices, national authorities' request for information and comments on new assurance standards, and potential security threats in safety-critical systems all motivate the need for new, and cost-effective forms of assurance.

The program of SASSUR 2015 consists of six high-quality papers, covering the workshop topics. We have divided these papers into two categories based on their focus and the topics that they cover:

– *Safety Assurance Processes*

1. "Evaluation of a systematic approach in variant management for safety-critical systems development", by Michael Käßmeyer, David Santiago Velasco Moncada, and Markus Schurius.
2. "The Role of CM [Configuration Management] in Agile Development of Safety-Critical Software", by Tor Stålhane and Thor Myklebust.

3. "Is Incremental Safety Assurance Sound?", by Valentin Cassano, Silviya Grigorova, Neeraj Singh, Morayo Adedjouma, Mark Lawford, Tom Maibaum, and Alan Wassyng.

– *Verification & Validation Techniques*

1. "Approaches for Software Verification of an Emergency Recovery System for Micro Air Vehicles", by Martin Becker, Markus Neumair, Alexander Söhn, and Samarjit Chakraborty.
2. "Dependability Arguments Supported by Fuzz-Testing", by Uwe Becker.
3. "Multidirectional Modular Conditional Safety Certificates", by Tiago Amorim, Alejandra Ruiz, Christoph Dropmann, and Daniel Schneider.

Acknowledgements. We are grateful to the SAFECOMP organization committee and collaborators for their support in arranging SASSUR. We also thank all the authors of the submitted papers for their interest in the workshop, and the steering and programme committees for their work and advice. This year we also acknowledge the European Software Agency and especially Jean-Loup Terraillon for accepting our invitation to give the keynote presentation. Finally, the SafeAdapt project has supported the workshop.

SASSUR Program Organizers

Alejandra Ruiz	TECNALIA, Spain
Tim Kelly	University of York, UK
Jose Luis de la Vara	Universidad Carlos III de Madrid, Spain

SASSUR Steering Committee

John Favaro	Intecs, Italy
Huascar Espinoza	TECNALIA, Spain
Fabien Belmonte	RATP, France

SASSUR Program Committee

Michael Armbruster	Siemens, Germany
Paolo Barbosa	Universidade Estadual da Paraiba, Brazil
Ronald Blanrue	EADS/Eurocopter, France
Markus Borg	Lund University, Sweden
Marc Born	ikv++, Germany
Daniela Cancila	CEA, France
Ibrahim Habli	University of York, UK
Sunil Nair	Simula Research Laboratory, Norway
Jurgen Niehaus	SafeTrans, Germany
Paolo Panaroni	Intecs, Italy
Ansgar Radermacher	CEA, France
Mehrdad Sabetzadeh	University of Luxembourg, Luxembourg
Kenji Taguchi	AIST, Japan
Martin Wassmuth	EADS, Germany
Gereon Weiß	Fraunhofer ESK, Germany
Ji Wu	Beihang University, China

Sponsors

EWICS TC7

Delft University of Technology

University of Huddersfield

Conference Partners

Austrian Association for Research in IT

Austrian Association for Research in IT
Österreichische Vereinigung für IT-Forschung

Austrian Institute of Technology

Advanced Research & Technology
for EMbedded Intelligence
and Systems

European Network of Clubs
for Reliability and Safety
of Software

European
Network of
Clubs for
REliability and
Safety of
Software

European Research Consortium
for Informatics and Mathematics
(ERCIM)

ERCIM
European Research Consortium
for Informatics and Mathematics

European Safety
and Reliability Association

VDE-ITG

Gesellschaft für Informatik e. V.

International Federation
for Information Processing

NASA

LAAS-CRNS

Austrian Computer Society

ResilTech

Safety Critical Systems Club

Verband Österreichischer
Software Industrie

Contents

International Workshop on the Integration of Safety and Security Engineering (ISSE 2015)

Assurance Cases for Software-Intensive Systems (ASSURE 2015)

Informing Assurance Case Review Through a Formal Interpretation of GSN Core Logic

Victor Bandur[✉] and John McDermid

University of York, Heslington, UK
{victor.bandur,john.mcdermid}@york.ac.uk

Abstract. A formalization of a logical subset of Goal Structuring Notation (GSN) arguments is presented. The aim is to reveal the conditions which must be true in order to guarantee that an argument thus formalized is internally consistent. These conditions justify a number of systematic questions which must be answered in the affirmative if a standard safety argument based on natural language is to be believed to be free from inconsistencies. The relevance of these findings to the combination of GSN and controlled natural language with first-order logic semantics is discussed.

Keywords: GSN · Formalization · Assurance cases · Logic

1 Introduction

In practice, the core of assurance arguments is based on natural language, even if formalisms are used in some aspects of the corresponding system development. One of the tenets of computer science is that precision of expression can be achieved through the use of formalized languages. Despite the need for precision and lack of ambiguity in assurance arguments, the two have not yet been successfully brought together. In this work we focus on the popular Goal Structuring Notation (GSN) [6] for assurance argument structuring to investigate how full formalization of an assurance argument might look, what can be learnt from this and what can be done to bridge the gap between logical formality and practical assurance argumentation.

Our approach takes the view that the structure of the argument should be such that the logic which binds the various elements of the argument together could be formally verified and can not be compromised by reasoning flaws or by inconsistencies in the information upon which the argument relies. The argument should nevertheless rely on inputs from various sources, be they formal verification, testing or review by experts. This can be seen as formal assurance argumentation *modulo* engineering expertise. Our proposal draws inspiration from a hypothetical question: *What if a fully formal assurance argument were made about a refinement-driven development?*

A fully formal assurance argument is not what is desired in practice. Rather, the results of formal scrutiny of parts of the system (automatic code verification

© Springer International Publishing Switzerland 2015
F. Koornneef and C. van Gulijk (Eds.): SAFECOMP 2015 Workshops, LNCS 9338, pp. 3–14, 2015.
DOI: 10.1007/978-3-319-24249-1_1

with the aid of logical property annotations, formalization inside a theorem prover *etc.*) are usually offered as evidence in support of the overall argument. That is not to say, however, that with sufficient modelling, it is impossible to offer a fully formal assurance argument for certain types of system, but this is normally impractical. The value of such fully formal arguments lies in what they can teach us about composing natural language arguments. We show that in a formal setting the argument comes with a number of proof obligations regarding its consistency. We believe that these obligations remain valid for informal assurance arguments, and that discharging them – albeit informally, but nevertheless with extreme objectivity – leads to increased confidence in the correctness of the informal argument.

The rest of this work is structured as follows. First we give a high-level overview of the role that formalization currently plays in assurance argumentation. Then we begin the technical discussion with an introduction to the fundamental GSN elements which form the backbone of our formal treatment (Sect. 3) and continue with the formalization proper (Sect. 4). Argument consistency in the formal setting is then discussed (Sect. 5), followed by a discussion of the relevance of our findings to assurance arguments based on natural language, and future work (Sect. 6).

2   Formalization in Assurance Argumentation

The question of what roles formalization can play in assurance argumentation has been asked in the literature, but answers furnishing a general approach are not common. At the most abstract end, Rushby [9] proposes a formalization of the top-level structure of safety cases. His approach recognizes that the experience of seasoned engineers should not be ignored or discarded in favour of a fully formal safety argument. He argues that, since review is an accepted element of safety argumentation, a "formal safety case" should make use of the outcomes of such reviews, and that these results should be used as axioms of the formal framework of the safety case. This allows the top-level argument to make claims that are contingent on the favourable outcomes of such reviews. The argument structure can thus be formalized, but its axioms come from judgment proclaimed through the established review process. A far more detailed formal structuring of the system development and safety argumentation process is proposed by Hall *et al.* [7], which also integrates existing methods for safety assessment, but at much finer resolution regarding the roles of the various steps of, and inputs to, the process as a whole. At the least abstract end, but still allowing for qualitative assessments, Giorgini *et al.* [4] similarly formalize the overall structure of the argument, but allow for some flexibility in the logic used to make the case, through notions of full and partial satisfaction and denial of goals. In the work of Basir *et al.* [2] we find the role of safety arguments reversed, with the argument used to abstract and elucidate detailed mechanized proofs.

At both extremes, the formalism proposed forms a method for evaluating the soundness and completeness of the overall argument. Between the extremes we find that formalisms are not used for the sake of the argument itself, but rather as a means of increasing the "strength" of a particular item of evidence offered in support of a goal, *e.g.* a Z system model *vs.* a UML model, annotation-based automatic code verification *vs.* implementation testing *etc.* However, the logic of the argument, which links all the goals and evidence together, is under no formal constraints, and is thus subjective. Such reasoning has been shown to have fallen prey to common logical fallacies in a number of important safety cases [5].

Formal approaches sometimes appear in *retrospective* safety cases [3], where a safety case must be created for a legacy system that has been in use for a long time, and which has exhibited an unanticipated failure or fault. In the particular instance cited above, the use of formal methods yields the potential modes of failure of the system, rather than proving that (the model of) the system is correct with respect to its specification. The authors argue that the use of formal methods in this capacity makes it possible to discover more failure modes than manual inspection would reveal. The resulting information is then used as the starting point of risk analysis applied to each failure mode thus observed. Finally, it is the results of these risk analyses that feed into the resulting safety case, making the use of formal methods a means to an end. In such retrospective safety cases it is expected that the original system documents can no longer be located. This introduces a large amount of uncertainty in the process of creating a safety case. The systematic identification of failure modes through the use of formal methods alleviates this problem somewhat. Nevertheless, the logic of the resulting safety case is not formalized.

3   Fundamental GSN Elements and Notions

Natural language is prone to errors in meaning and logic. Worse, embedding natural language in a structured notation such as GSN does not ameliorate this problem. The structure of GSN does nothing to enforce logical soundness, and so the incorrect use of natural language, combined with faulty reasoning, can compromise such arguments. Fully formal arguments can therefore serve as an ideal "gold standard" of argument soundness, against which the soundness of natural language arguments can be evaluated. We consider this view to be correct for the following reason. The key GSN elements *Goal* and *Assumption* constrain the types of statement that can (or should) be made inside these elements to statements of (what is believed to be) fact. Such statements correspond to the type of statement that can be made in a fully formal setting, claims which are either true or false (in a correct formal argument, all claims made as goals are demonstrably true in the model). Because of this, reasoning inside natural language GSN arguments follows the same pattern as reasoning with full formality, that is, natural deduction of facts from supporting facts, inside a defined context and under explicitly stated assumptions. What makes this difficult is the use of natural language, but we believe that a "soundness checklist" derived from formal natural deduction, which can be applied to the structure of an informal argument, can increase confidence that the argument is sound. Of course this rests on the meaning of the natural language statements as understood by the readers of the argument, which in turn crucially depends on these statements being as precise as possible (we return to this issue at the end of the paper).

The following technical notions are fundamental to our formalization. The definitions vary in the literature, but we use the following without compromising correctness. A *condition* is a logical statement which contains free variables and which is either true or false for the different valuations of those variables. Conditions can also be regarded as definitions or axioms. A condition is said to *define* those sets of values which make it true. A *theory* is a collection of axioms, lemmas and other theorems. It defines a number of *alternative* entities, all of which satisfy the theory (its *models*, in the model-theoretic sense). For this reason, they are all considered equivalent with respect to what the theory means to capture. For instance, a theory containing the definition, "A set S of integers such that the size of S is at most 10" is satisfied by *any* subset of the integers which contains at most ten integers. A theory is very seldom satisfied by a single entity, and indeed this is not the intent of the formal approach. A *context* in what follows is taken to be a theory.

Context *refinement*[1] is the act of taking a given context and strengthening its set of conditions such that the total number of entities which it defines is strictly smaller. In the case of the set S above, the defining condition can be strengthened as follows: "A set S of integers such that the size of S is at most 10, and which does not contain the number 5." This then eliminates, from all those sets which satisfied the initial condition, all those which contain the number 5. The intent of refinement is that through several refinement steps it is possible to converge on a single system, the implementation. At each step of the refinement, a *commitment* is made to a particular path toward the ultimate system. In a formal argument these commitments legitimize claims about the implemented system at the top of the argument, because the argument concerns a specific concrete system, which is viewed at different levels of abstraction as one moves up the argument structure. It is not incorrect to claim at the top of the argument a property which is shown to be true farther down.

4 Semantics

We focus on a subset of GSN which forms the logical core of the notation. It is comprised of the elements *Goal, Assumption, Context, IsSupportedBy* and *InContextOf*. This set is chosen because its elements correspond very closely to the basic elements of formal reasoning: theorems, axioms, deduction laws and theories. The structuring elements of GSN can also be included in a discussion such as this, but here they are not perceived to add to the expressivity of the formalization (an arguable exception is the *Strategy* element, which is discussed later.) The fundamental starting point of a formal semantics for this subset of GSN is the meaning of so-called "goals". A GSN goal is a statement that is

---

[1] The notion of refinement used here is based on the notion from the Z [11] and B [1] methods for systematic software development.

believed to be true. The goal statement is not meant to be *taken* as being true, but is rather *postulated* to be true, with the rest of the argument serving the purpose of convincing the reader that the goal is true – that it is a *theorem*. Formally, therefore, GSN goals are here taken to be logical postulates, or propositions, to be proven true by the rest of the argument.

The next fundamental element to consider is the connection between GSN goals. The *IsSupportedBy* relationship depicted in Fig. 1a is meant to convey that if the goal G_1 is shown to be true, then the goal G is also true. In the absence of any other elements, the truth of G is *only* contingent on the truth of G_1. Formally, this is here taken to mean that G_1 logically entails G:

$$G_1 \vdash G$$

The use of logical entailment instead of the more specific logical implication makes it possible to argue in any logic without imposing any constraints on the GSN argument structure. Basir *et al.* [2] also associate logical entailment with the *IsSupportedBy* relationship. The general form of this construct is depicted in Fig. 1b, where the top-level goal G is supported by n sub-goals, G_1 to G_n. Naturally, its meaning is taken to be that all the sub-goals G_1 to G_n together logically entail the top-level goal:

$$G_1, \ldots, G_n \vdash G$$

In general a statement can not be determined to be true or false without a context. In a refinement-oriented system development effort, the theory is the system model at a given level of refinement. The purpose of a model verification effort is to determine whether desired properties are in fact theorems of the model. The second type of connection found in a GSN argument, the *InContextOf* connection, makes it possible to explicitly state the context in which a statement is made. These four elements, namely *Goal*, *IsSupportedBy* and *InContextOf* connections, and *Context* are sufficient to compose a formally analyzable GSN argument. An example is shown in Fig. 1c. It states that in the context Γ, the formula G is logically entailed by the sub-formulae G_1 to G_n:

$$\Gamma, G_1, \ldots, G_n \vdash G$$

We consider such an argument to be "correct" if it is possible to prove the top-level goal true. Short of this, and argument is considered to be "incorrect", owing for example to internal inconsistencies or insufficient information. It is now possible to state the fundamental condition for the correctness of a GSN argument of this form:

> *The GSN argument is correct if, and only if, it is possible to formally prove the sequent,*
> $$\Gamma, G_1, \ldots, G_n \vdash G$$

This condition reveals a number of possible ways in which the argument, as stated, can be flawed.

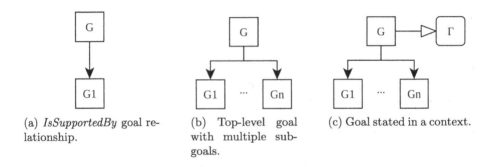

(a) *IsSupportedBy* goal relationship.

(b) Top-level goal with multiple subgoals.

(c) Goal stated in a context.

Fig. 1. Fundamental GSN logical elements.

For instance, the information contained in the argument structure may be incomplete, making it impossible to prove the sequent. This does not mean that G as stated is not a theorem, but that there simply is insufficient information to demonstrate that it is. A proof attempt in this case will reveal a statement that is clearly not provable from the premises. Usually this is valuable information that reveals, at times directly, what information is missing in the argument. Once this information is shown to exist, it can be incorporated in the argument structure as an extra supporting goal and the proof reattempted. Formally it is possible that the iteration of this prove-and-assert cycle will reveal the complete set of supporting goals for G. In practice it may not be feasible to link all the necessary information together, even though the information may exist. A separate "sufficiency" argument may justify an axiomatic (*i.e.* without further proof) inclusion of the necessary information in the goal structure.

A second type of flaw in the argument can be that G as stated is in fact not a theorem. A proof attempt in this case will reveal a sequent in which the goal is either clearly false, or clearly contradicts the premises. Depending on the logic and proof calculus used, at this point the premises may be either the G_i themselves, or, due to manipulation, may be modified forms of what is contained in the original antecedent of the sequent, $\Gamma, G_1, \ldots, G_n$. In either case, it is the fact that the proof attempt reaches a state where a clear contradiction exists between the current goal and its premises that indicates that the original G is in fact not a theorem. If the proof attempt reaches a state where it seems impossible to make any progress, but a contradiction is not apparent, it does not necessarily indicate that G is not a theorem, but rather that further lemmas must be developed from Γ and the G_i in support of G.

Yet another flaw in the argument may be that there is a contradiction at the starting point, in the antecedent clauses G_i. It may not be immediately apparent that the G_i contain a contradiction. But in this situation the proof attempt will go through a number of manipulations, both of the conclusion as well as of the premises, and will eventually arrive at an inference step with a false premise. Of course the goal can be proven at this point, but the fact remains that a contradiction in the original premises of the goal has been revealed.

5 Argument Consistency

This section elaborates on the issue of internal consistency (freedom from contradiction) introduced by the use of the *Context* and *Assumption* elements. The constraints imposed in this regard by the GSN standard are mainly structural in nature, and ensure that elements are connected in a way which makes sense, but they are not enough to prevent the construction of self-contradictory arguments.

We begin with a formal justification for a rule of GSN which is not always adhered to, namely context inheritance. GSN allows the association of context with any goal. However, in a fully formal setting, there must be a precise correspondence between contexts. Figure 2a represents the familiar *IsSupportedBy* relationship between two goals, but now each goal has its own context. The formal statement of the goal relationship remains logical entailment under context Γ. In the presence of context Γ_1, the two goals must have compatible "vocabularies", that is, the entities (free variables) referenced by G must be a subset of those referenced by G_1. But if this is the case, and context Γ_1 has a set of axioms that is unrelated to the axioms of Γ, then the goal G_1 may be true, but it will bear no relation to goal G, since it is true in an unrelated context.

The best option, which is embodied in the inheritance rule, is for context Γ_1 to *refine*, in an non-degenerate way, context Γ. Degeneracy would arise if the refinement Γ_1 is contradictory to Γ, so that no entity satisfies Γ_1. In the formal illustration here, context refinement corresponds exactly to system model refinement, the fundamental formal modelling technique of evolving a model through gradual introduction of more and more detail. The increasing level of detail makes it possible to claim and prove properties about the high-level system which can only be accomplished by reasoning over the finer details of a more concrete version of the model. The key to refinement is that if context Γ_1 refines context Γ, then everything that is true in Γ_1 is allowed to be true by Γ. Refinement establishes the correspondence necessary between contexts to allow the desired relationship of G_1 to G to be demonstrated. The full soundness condition for this argument then incorporates the context refinement condition:

$$\Gamma \sqsubseteq \Gamma_1 \ (\textit{Context } \Gamma_1 \textit{ refines context } \Gamma), \qquad \Gamma_1 \vdash G_1, \qquad \Gamma, G_1 \vdash G$$

In addition to context, the other GSN element that raises questions of argument consistency is *Assumption*. A GSN fragment with the example structure so far used may contain a number of assumptions, as illustrated in Fig. 2b. As ever, assumptions are simply taken as true statements. In a fully formal setting, if given without justification, any such assumptions can only be taken as additional axioms of the theory, or tier of model refinement, under consideration. Formally, this is considered an enrichment of the context. The argument, therefore, corresponds to the following sequent:

$$\Gamma, G_1, \dots, G_n, \Phi_1, \dots, \Phi_m \vdash G$$

The soundness condition for the GSN argument is similar to that for the argument of Fig. 1c, namely that the corresponding sequent must have a formal

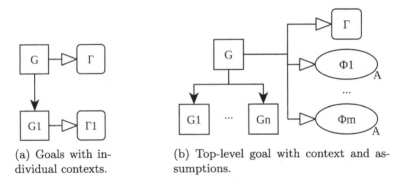

(a) Goals with in-
dividual contexts.

(b) Top-level goal with context and assumptions.

Fig. 2. Contexts and assumptions.

proof. Naturally, with the addition of further assumptions comes the possibility
of introducing inconsistencies. Depending on the size of the system model and
argument in question, the assumptions can be checked for mutual consistency
before the complete argument proof is attempted. Consistency of the assumptions means that their conjunction is true for at least one valuation of their free
variables. By free variables we mean labels in the GSN elements which refer to
aspects of the system model or wider context; they can be treated as free variables in the normal formal sense. Let $\mathbf{v}$ be the vector of all free variables of the
assumptions $\Phi_1, \ldots, \Phi_m$. Then it must be possible to show,

$$\exists \mathbf{v} \bullet \Phi_1 \wedge \ldots \wedge \Phi_m$$

Additional assumptions can be not only mutually contradictory, but they
may contradict the context to which they are added. Let Γ' be all the axioms
(including, if necessary, defining axioms) of the context Γ, and $\mathbf{v}'$ the union of
$\mathbf{v}$ and the free variables of the formulae of Γ. Then similarly it must be possible
to show,

$$\exists \mathbf{v}' \bullet \Gamma' \wedge \Phi_1 \wedge \ldots \wedge \Phi_m$$

Sub-goals can have not only context, but also their own assumptions, as
illustrated in Fig. 3. A setup such as this is even more prone to inconsistencies,
but it is one of the most common, as it is the most general argument structure
which also accommodates the crucial element of context refinement. According to
our stance on the relationship of the contexts $\Gamma_1, \ldots, \Gamma_n$ to Γ, n ways of refining
context can be identified from G to each of $G_1, \ldots, G_n$. We have also stated that
any statement which is true in a context Γ', where $\Gamma \sqsubseteq \Gamma'$, is allowed to be
true by the context Γ. Nevertheless, Γ can be refined in different, potentially
contradictory ways. For instance, assume that Γ states $x \geq 0$, for some quantity
x. This can be refined in Γ_1 to $x = 1$, and in Γ_2 to $x = 2$, meaning that the
trivial goal $x = 1$ can be asserted in the context Γ_1, which is contradictory to the
trivial goal $x = 2$ that can be asserted in Γ_2 (unlike a case-split on the value of
x, which can not be made across different contexts). These two trivial goals are

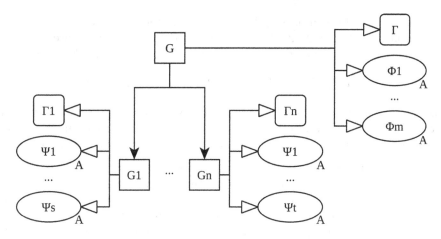

Fig. 3. Context and assumptions at several levels.

only illustrative of the contradictions that can arise among the goals $G_1 \ldots G_n$, which may be very subtle. This possibility forces us to insist that the contexts $\Gamma_1 \ldots \Gamma_n$ be *mutually consistent*:

It must not be possible to prove the sequent,

$$\Gamma_1, \ldots, \Gamma_n \vdash false$$

Even if the contexts satisfy this condition, they are not guaranteed to bear the correct refinement relation to Γ. As stated earlier, in a valid argument, contexts at lower levels in the argument must refine, somehow, the context above. This condition alone does not enforce this relationship. Each of the $\Gamma_1, \ldots, \Gamma_n$ can independently refine different aspects of Γ, or conversely, can break the refinement relationship and *generalize* Γ instead. If they are taken together to form a new context $\{\Gamma_1, \ldots, \Gamma_n\}^2$, it is possible to guarantee that the refinement relationship is not broken by showing that the new context itself refines Γ:

For mutually consistent contexts $\Gamma_1, \ldots, \Gamma_n$, it must be the case that,

$$\Gamma \sqsubseteq \{\Gamma_1, \ldots, \Gamma_n\}$$

If the argument is a case split, *e.g.* argument over a functional decomposition, then this refinement relationship trivially holds.

This condition can be generalized to account for the various assumptions placed on the subgoals. If consistent, and under the same non-degeneracy requirement imposed earlier, the set of assumptions $\Psi_1, \ldots, \Psi_j$ of a goal G_i in $G_1, \ldots, G_n$ will constrain the context Γ_i of that goal further, such that $\Gamma \sqsubseteq \{\Psi_1, \ldots, \Psi_j, \Gamma_i\}$.

---

[2] The context $\{\Gamma_1, \ldots, \Gamma_n\}$ is formed by combining all the definitions and axioms of the constituent contexts, many of which may be redundant.

The *complete* set of assumptions, then, attached to the goals $G_1, \ldots, G_n$, if consistent, constrain the context $\{\Gamma_1, \ldots, \Gamma_n\}$ and define *one* new context for *all* the goals $G_1, \ldots, G_n$, denoted $\{\Gamma_1, \ldots, \Gamma_n, \Psi_1, \ldots, \Psi_s, \ldots, \Psi_1, \ldots, \Psi_t\}$ such that,

$$\Gamma \sqsubseteq \{\Gamma_1, \ldots, \Gamma_n, \Psi_1, \ldots, \Psi_s, \ldots, \Psi_1, \ldots, \Psi_t\}$$

This aggregation reduces the structure of the argument to that shown in Fig. 2a (but with n subgoals), and the soundness condition remains essentially the same, albeit with the mutual consistency requirements on context and assumptions.

Other GSN Elements. There are three other fundamental GSN elements which can not be used in a fully formal argument, in the sense that the information contained in them can not be used *ad literam* to enable or facilitate the proof of a goal from its sub-goals. They are the *Justification*, *Strategy* and *Solution* elements. The role of the *Justification* and *Strategy* elements in a natural-language GSN argument is to guide the reader of the argument through the logic or reasoning approach of the authors. In a fully formalized argument this type of guidance is not necessary: the argument is structured strictly in accordance with the laws of the logic used and its deduction calculus, such that logical inference *is* the strategy. Nevertheless, these elements can be understood as follows in a formal argument.

In the formalization proposed here, the argument represented by a bundle of *IsSupportedBy* connections originating at a goal is justified by two things:

- An "AND" decomposition of the goal into a number of sub-goals which, if all proven true, provide sufficient evidence that the parent goal is true.
- The claim itself is justified by the soundness of the logic, which guarantees that it is impossible to arrive at a false conclusion from true premises.

Approaching arguments formally means that in every instance of this relationship, the strategy for supporting a parent goal is an "AND" decomposition into a complete set of sub-goals, justified by the soundness of the logic's deduction rules. In the formal setting this is intentionally the same at each level of the argument, so we omit *Justification* and *Strategy* from the semantics. However, strategy elements may be attached to formal GSN arguments in an informal capacity in order to capture application-specific information or guidance. For example, they can contain helpful hints or insights on using a particular verification tool on that part of the argument, such as what tactics or rules to use in order to move past a proof step. We do not elaborate on the formal role of *Solution* elements, other than to note that Takeyama's position that they justify turning the supported goal into an axiom [10] (necessarily subject to expert review), is a sensible approach for the purpose of formalization, and is also in accordance with Rushby's principle that expert opinion should be incorporated into any such formalization.

6 Conclusions

We have presented a fully formal interpretation of a subset of GSN which is based on notions from model-based system development. Our work fits the long-term agenda of developing a full semantics for GSN which will enable the automatic verification of GSN arguments for correctness. Fundamentally similar work by Takeyama [10] goes a long way in this direction, but as most assurance argumentation is not carried out formally, it is crucially important to review how such formalization can benefit the informal approach, hence our hypothetical question. The specific step proposed here is to understand what it is that a GSN argument represents formally. This reveals a number of conditions, dictated by strictly formal logic, which must be checked in order to ensure that the argument is self-consistent. The use of natural language makes it impossible to check arguments automatically against these conditions, but they can form the basis of a battery of informal but systematic tests to which arguments *must* be subjected. For instance, the conditions mandate that the following informal judgments must be true:

1. Goals must be decomposed in such a way that it is possible to relate them to the relevant subgoals, assumptions and context without further implicit assumptions.
2. Context elements at all levels of the argument must bear the correct refinement relationship to the context elements directly above.
3. Context elements across the same level must not refine the parent context in contradictory ways.
4. Assumptions on any given element must not be contradictory.
5. The assumptions on any given goal must not contradict the context assumed for that goal.

In practice, arguments in natural language may make "bigger leaps" than a formal argument. For instance, a formal argument is adequate if it provides a proof of a given claim, otherwise it is deficient in some way, as described earlier. In natural language arguments, the question of adequacy is much more complicated, especially in the presence of these large leaps, and we do not claim to address this through formalization. But the intent of these judgments is nevertheless appropriate.

If the argument elements currently given in natural language are instead expressed in an increasingly rigorous form, such as controlled natural language or a fully formal language, then automatic verification becomes possible. These conditions are only necessary for the internal consistency of an argument: just as violation of any of the formal conditions by a formal argument would render it inconsistent, so violation of these informal but unambiguous conditions by an argument based on natural language brings its correctness into question. Additional conditions come with the introduction of other GSN elements, such as *Away Goals*.

We see three viable avenues for investigation starting with the formal perspective proposed here. First, the complete set of GSN elements must be treated in this manner and further correctness conditions revealed. Second, the use of a form of controlled natural language inside the GSN elements themselves must be investigated. For ease of integration with GSN, the flavour of controlled natural language chosen should have a formal semantics in logic, as in the case, for example, of IBM International Technology Alliance Controlled English [8]. With a formal semantics for both argument structure and the information contained within individual statements, it becomes possible to mechanize and automatically verify argument claims and structure. Third, our perspective is based on the application of classical logic to system development, where detail is added incrementally through refinement. We have simply made use of the notion of logical deduction, leaving open the choice of logic and using classical logic only as an illustration. It may be far better to use a specialized modal logic instead, depending on the system domain targeted.

Acknowledgments. The authors would like to thank the anonymous reviewers for their helpful comments. This work is part of a larger project carried out for IBM UK and DSTL.

References

1. Abrial, J.R.: The B-Book: Assigning Programs to Meanings. Cambridge University Press, Cambridge (2005)
2. Basir, N., Denney, E., Fischer, B.: Deriving safety cases from automatically constructed proofs. In: Proceedings of the 4th International Conference on System Safety, IET (2009)
3. Eriksson, L.-H.: Using formal methods in a retrospective safety case. In: Heisel, M., Liggesmeyer, P., Wittmann, S. (eds.) SAFECOMP 2004. LNCS, vol. 3219, pp. 31–44. Springer, Heidelberg (2004)
4. Giorgini, P., Mylopoulos, J., Nicchiarelli, E., Sebastiani, R.: Reasoning with goal models. In: Spaccapietra, S., March, S.T., Kambayashi, Y. (eds.) ER 2002. LNCS, vol. 2503, p. 167. Springer, Heidelberg (2002)
5. Greenwell, W.S.: A taxonomy of fallacies in system safety arguments. Technical report. NASA (2006). (available from the NASA Technical reports server): http://ntrs.nasa.gov/archive/nasa/casi.ntrs.nasa.gov/20060027794.pdf
6. GSN Working Group: Goal structuring notation. http://www.goalstructuringnotation.info Accessed on 27–06–2015
7. Hall, J.G., Mannering, D., Rapanotti, L.: Arguing safety with problem oriented software engineering. In: High Assurance Systems Engineering Symposium, pp. 23–32. IEEE (2007)
8. Mott, D.: Summary of ITA controlled english, https://www.usukita.org/papers/5658/CE_summary_04b.doc, ITA Technical Paper (2010) Accessed on 29–06–2015
9. Rushby, J.: Formalism in safety cases. In: Dale, C., Anderson, T. (eds.) Making Systems Safer, pp. 3–17. Springer, Heidelberg (2010)
10. Takeyama, M.: A note on "D-Cases as proofs as programs", AIST Technical report AIST-PS-2010-007. http://cfv.jp/cvs/introduction/pdf/PS2010-007.pdf
11. Woodcock, J., Davies, J.: Using Z. Specification, Refinement, and Proof. Prentice-Hall, Upper Saddle River (1996)

Representing Confidence in Assurance Case Evidence

Lian Duan[1]([✉]), Sanjai Rayadurgam[1], Mats P.E. Heimdahl[1],
Oleg Sokolsky[2], and Insup Lee[2]

[1] University of Minnesota, Minneapolis, USA
{lduan,rsanjai,heimdahl}@cs.umn.edu
[2] University of Pennsylvania, Philadelphia, USA
{sokolsky,lee}@cis.upenn.edu

Abstract. When evaluating assurance cases, being able to capture the confidence one has in the individual evidence nodes is crucial, as these values form the foundation for determining the confidence one has in the assurance case as a whole. Human opinions are subjective, oftentimes with uncertainty—it is difficult to capture an opinion with a single probability value. Thus, we believe that a distribution best captures a human opinion such as confidence. Previous work used a doubly-truncated normal distribution or a Dempster-Shafer theory-based belief mass to represent confidence in the evidence nodes, but we argue that a beta distribution is more appropriate. The beta distribution models a variety of shapes and we believe it provides an intuitive way to represent confidence. Furthermore, there exists a duality between the beta distribution and subjective logic, which can be exploited to simplify mathematical calculations. This paper is the first to apply this duality to assurance cases.

Keywords: Opinion triangle · Beta distribtion · Subjective logic

1 Introduction

Certain safety critical systems must be demonstrated to be safe and certified or approved by some regulatory body before they are allowed to be taken into operation or sold to the general public. Typical examples are avionics software for civil aviation and complex medical devices. Developing an assurance case (of which a safety case is a subset) is one approach to documenting and demonstrating that a system has been adequately analyzed and is free from critical hazards (i.e., the system is adequately safe). The UK Ministry of Defence describes a safety case as *"A structured argument, supported by a body of evidence that provides a compelling, comprehensible and valid case that a system is safe for a given application in a given operating environment"* [1].

This work has been partially supported by NSF grants CNS-0931931 and CNS-1035715.

F. Koornneef and C. van Gulijk (Eds.): SAFECOMP 2015 Workshops, LNCS 9338, pp. 15–26, 2015.
DOI: 10.1007/978-3-319-24249-1_2

For an assurance case, the confidence (and uncertainty) that the reviewers—as well as creators—have in the evidence and the case itself is crucially important; how much trust can we put in the assurance case? To address this issue, researchers have proposed different approaches. Hawkings et al. proposed the use of a separate confidence case arguing why the assurance case can be trusted [2]. Others used Bayesian (Belief) Networks (BN) where nodes representing confidence are quantified using a doubly-truncated normal distribution [3,4] that then can be used to compute the confidence in the various claims in the case. Finally, Ayoub et al. used a belief mass based on Dempster-Shafer theory [5] that can be used similarly to the truncated normal distribution mentioned above.

Although these approaches allow the exploration of confidence and uncertainty in assurance cases, we in this paper argue that there may be a more intuitive way to capture the confidence and uncertainty associated with evidence and compute the confidence and uncertainty associated with claims relying on that evidence. The beta distribution, a more versatile distribution, allows for a better representation of human opinion. The beta distribution can also be tied to the idea of subjective logic [6] to aid in the quantification of confidence. Finally, the beta distribution can be represented as a point on an opinion triangle (and vice versa) [6] to allow an alternate way of capturing and visualizing the concept of confidence and uncertainty. Like the doubly-truncated normal distribution approach, the beta distribution with subjective logic approach allows for the combination of confidence in various evidence nodes in an assurance case, ultimately arriving at the confidence in the top-level claim. We are the first to propose using the beta distribution, with its correspondence to the opinion triangle, to represent confidence in evidence and compute the resultant confidence in claims supported by this evidence in an assurance case.

The remainder of the paper is organized as follows: Sect. 2 gives relevant background information and briefly touches upon some related work. Section 3 shows, through a few examples, how subjective logic operators and the beta distribution can be used to represent confidence in assurance cases. Section 4 offers some closing thoughts and anticipated future work.

2   Background and Related Work

An assurance case is a structured logical argument. Generally, it has a top-level claim supported by evidence and the arguments that connect the two. Confidence in an assurance case can viewed as confidence of two separate components—the confidence one has in the individual evidence nodes and the confidence one has in the argumentation used to combine the evidence nodes to ultimately demonstrate the validity of a top-level claim. Hawkins et al. took a qualitative approach through the use of a separate, but associated, confidence case [2]. Previous approaches to quantification of confidence and uncertainty have used the doubly-truncated normal distribution for the nodes in a Bayesian Network (BN) [3,4] or a Dempster-Shafer theory based triple of (belief, disbelief, and uncertainty) [5,7]. Duan et al. provide a general survey that summarizes various approaches to confidence in assurance cases [8]. Whether implied or explicitly stated, calculations are prudent and can aid in assessing confidence for a top-level claim. There has been debate among law scholars (in the US) about whether or not "probable cause" can and should be quantified. Kerr argues that it should not be [9], since quantification can, ironically, lead to less accurate values. However, his argument is for the legal domain and assumes the use of a single probability value for probable cause.

Bayesian Network Approaches. A Bayesian Network (BN) or Bayesian Belief Network (BBN) is a directed acyclic graph, usually similar in structure to an assurance case. BNs provide an easy to read solution to combining qualitative and quantitative data [10]. The qualitative information is encoded in the graphical connections between nodes (links) that indicate the flow of information. The graphical connections aid in informing users how information "nodes" are connected with each other and how they may be combined during evaluation. The quantitative information is encoded in the nodes themselves. Though the nodes of a BN when used for assurance cases are usually the evidence nodes, they also can include elements that are usually found in the links of an assurance case— e.g., whether or not the arguments are well developed, or how much trust one has in the manufacturer. One possible approach to quantifying such information is through the use of a probability value. How one determines this probability value is an area of active research and a non-trivial issue.

The popular AgenaRisk software [11] quantifies the confidence of a node in an assurance case by modeling the confidence using a doubly-truncated normal distribution, truncated to the interval $[0, 1]$ [4]. This method allows for the modeling of a variety of shapes of distributions, from an (approximate) uniform distribution, to the standard Gaussian distribution, to a narrow spike, or, if the mean were near the extremes (0 or 1), a sloped shape. However, there are a couple of shapes that the truncated normal cannot approximate, such as a curve where the mean and mode are not equal (a skewed Gaussian), a true uniform distribution, or a true power distribution.

Hobbs and Lloyd use AgenaRisk to quantify and combine trustworthiness in nodes of an assurance case [12]. They use logical-OR and logical-ANDs, as well as the more realistic Noisy-OR and Noisy-AND [13], among others. Denney et al. also have looked at quantifying confidence in assurance cases with a doubly-truncated normal distribution, extending the work of Fenton and Neil [3]. Since these researchers are using AgenaRisk, they are still using the truncated normal distribution and are subject to the same limitations.

Dempster-Shafer Approaches. The Dempster-Shafer theory based approach starts with the idea of an opinion, represented by a mass. As our opinion increases positively, mass increases. This opinion can be bounded by a lower bound, belief, and an upper bound, plausibility. An opinion can fall anywhere in this range. Dempster-Shafer differs from traditional probability in that it has a separate value for uncertainty. In traditional probability, there is a view that if one has 0.8 confidence, then one has 0.2 uncertainty. Dempster-Shafer might look at this as, for example, one has 0.8 confidence, 0.1 lack of confidence, and 0.1 uncertainty, taking the view that lack of confidence is not necessarily the same thing as uncertainty. Dempster-Shafer theory also provides a variety of methods to combine evidence based on different situations. A Dempster-Shafer opinion can be applied to an evidence node in an assurance case. The methods for combining disparate evidence also can be used to combine opinions in an assurance case, ultimately arriving at an opinion for the top level claim.

Cyra and Gorski developed their own plot of opinion versus confidence based on linguistics and mapped their plot onto Jøsang's opinion triangle [7]. They used Toulmin's argumentation structure [14] to combine the confidence nodes. Their approach was adapted into a tool [15] which has been adopted by over 30 institutions in areas of healthcare, security, and public administration self-assessment standards [16].

Beta Distribution. The beta distribution is a continuous version of the binomial distribution. When one has two options (e.g., heads or tails in a coin flip, or trust or distrust for an assurance case node), the binomial distribution is generally used. When one desires a continuous distribution for the binomial distribution, the beta is used. The beta distribution has finite range, most often between 0 and 1, which makes it ideal when dealing with probabilities. The beta distribution is a second order distribution, so it is used to describe a probability of probabilities. In statistics, the beta distribution is a popular choice for prior information, due to its scalability, variety of shapes, and finite boundaries [17].

The doubly-truncated normal distribution does not allow for situations where the mean and mode are different, and only can approximate the uniform and power distributions. By using only a doubly-truncated normal distribution, previous researchers are committing themselves to the distribution of every opinion being symmetrical. For instance, if the peak of a doubly-truncated normal distribution is at 0.8, the probability of an opinion at 0.7 and 0.9 would be exactly equal. While this may be true some of the time, one cannot say it will be true all of the time. Additionally, the doubly-truncated normal distribution can never truly equal 0 at a confidence value of 100 %. In some circumstances, such as with testing, it is not realistic to ever have 100 % confidence.

Merkle represents confidence using mixtures of beta distributions [18]. His approach seeks to model confidence that has been elicited, and represents a realistic view of what real confidence values would look like. His use of a beta distribution to represent confidence supports our view of the same.

The beta distribution is not a new concept in the realm of assurance cases. Bishop et al. use it in their work [19] to represent a "typical distribution" about an expert's belief. They, however, turn their focus to estimating conservative claims about dependability.

Subjective Logic and the Opinion Triangle. In standard logic, there is either true or false, with no ambiguity. There is absolute certainty and thus probability is an appropriate measure for situations such as flipping a coin or

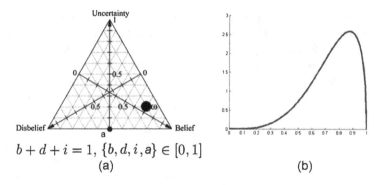

$$b + d + i = 1, \{b, d, i, a\} \in [0, 1]$$

(a)   (b)

Fig. 1. Jøsang's opinion triangle

throwing a pair of dice. Jøsang argues that when humans are a factor, there is never full certainty [6]. As such, we should use subjective logic, which deals with the realm of opinions.

An opinion in subjective logic is represented by a four element tuple: belief (b), disbelief (d), uncertainty (u), and relative atomicity (a). The first three are located on the vertices of an opinion triangle (see Fig. 1(a)) and are constrained by the boundaries of that triangle and each other. The three must have values between 0 and 1 and must sum up to 1. The relative atomicity, representing the *a priori* belief, is a known quantity with no uncertainty, so it is bounded to the base of the triangle. In Fig. 1(a), the opinion is $(0.7, 0.1, 0.2, 0.5)$. Jøsang's work offers a direct mapping between his opinion triangle and the beta distribution, making it appropriate for use in assurance cases [6]. In Fig. 1(b), we see an example of how the opinion in Fig. 1(a) would be represented by a beta distribution. When one has multiple opinions, one can combine them in a variety of ways using addition, multiple, and subtraction.

Jøsang has continued working on and expanding the uses of subjective logic, but not in the assurance case area. Specifically, he has looked at multi-nomial opinions via the Dirichlet distribution [20], trust networks using subjective logic [21], and, with Whitby, reputation systems using the beta distribution [22]. Ettler and Dedecius apply subjective logic to a hierarchical model derived from a condition monitoring system [23]. The hierarchical model has a structure similar to assurance cases and consists of similar components—leaf nodes that can be evaluated and combined to ultimately arrive at the top level. How their work continues will be of interest to us as the two areas share some commonalities. Han et al. use subjective logic and the beta distribution to fuse evidence that has a subjective bias or uncertainty [24]. Their work, though not related to assurance cases, represents another use for subjective logic and the beta distribution.

3   Application to Assurance Cases

Jøsang's subjective logic deals with opinions held by a person. We argue that a person's level of confidence can be viewed as an opinion, and thus Jøsang's opinion triangle is an appropriate way of representing the confidence one has in an evidence node of an assurance case. Jøsang provides a direct, easy, and intuitive mapping from the opinion triangle to the beta distribution, as well as multiple operators for combining opinions based on different situations.

Subjective logic intuitively makes more sense than standard logic when one is describing human opinions. The idea of uncertainty being a separate entity in subjective logic, different from belief and disbelief, is also intuitively appealing. A logical question would be—what does full uncertainty mean? One could answer "knowing nothing." One also could answer "being fully split between two options." Both might be viewed as full uncertainty. Jøsang specifies a difference. The former would be represented by an opinion of $(0.0, 0.0, 1.0)$, meaning one has no opinion whatsoever. For an assurance case, we can think of this as a situation where a reviewer has no experience or knowledge of anything—a completely blank slate. This opinion would be represented as $beta(1.0, 1.0)$, a uniform distribution where every value is equally likely. The latter would be represented by an opinion of $(0, 5, 0.5, 0.0)$, or having exactly equal arguments for both belief and disbelief. For an assurance case, we can think of having exactly equal and opposite information to contribute to a split opinion. This opinion would be represented in a beta distribution with a spike, or discontinuity, at 0.5. Such an example highlights exactly the importance of treating uncertainty—the lack of information—as a separate entity. Cyra and Gorski took the view that when one has high uncertainty, no decision can be made [7]. When one has high disbelief, one can reject a piece of evidence. But when there is high uncertainty, that uncertainty can be belief or disbelief. As such, no action can or should be taken.

Realistically, though, it is unlikely that either opinion will exist in the real world, which is part of the appeal of using a distribution, specifically the beta distribution, to represent confidence. The beta distribution can accommodate a variety of shapes (Fig. 2) while Jøsang's work ties the beta distribution into subjective logic. For future work, operators in subjective logic then can be used and represented as a beta distribution. The beta distribution parameters also can be used and manipulated to better represent confidence.

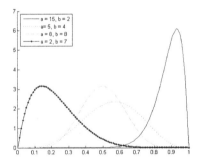

Fig. 2. Sample beta distribution shapes

3.1   Node Example

Elicitation of opinions from domain experts is still an active area of research. It is our view that distributions should be used when representing confidence instead of a single probability value. Human opinion is subjective in nature, and fraught with uncertainty. A single probability value cannot be expected to encompass all the nuances that comprise an opinion. Thus, a distribution more accurately represents a person's beliefs. A distribution models a probability of probabilities—at each confidence value, what is the probability that this confidence value is the one true confidence value for this person? When there is no uncertainty, we have a single value. When we have uncertainty, we have a distribution.

It makes intuitive sense to be able to provide an opinion triangle and have an expert simply point to where his/her opinion lies on such a triangle. This opinion then can be mapped onto a beta distribution to confirm that the distribution is an accurate representation of their opinion. Going in the other direction is possible with the aid of a parameter finder/best-fit program for the beta distribution. An expert can be asked to draw out a plot that best represents their opinion, and this plot then can be mapped onto the opinion triangle to see if it matches up to what the expert expected.

Suppose we want to quantify the confidence for an evidence node, specifically, software testing results. The software has been tested (and the test passed) by two different companies to the same test adequacy criterion, such as MC/DC [25]. This criterion is rigorous, but not perfect, so intuitively one expects the "peak" of the beta distribution to be fairly high, for example, around 0.8. The standard of testing, in this case, would affect where the peak belief or disbelief would be; however, the companies themselves would affect the variance of the distribution. Company A has documented and accounted for all of their testing meticulously, and has communicated all information clearly. Company B has had poor documentation and communication, increasing our uncertainty in their work. So intuitively, we would expect the beta distribution representations of our confidence in these companies' testing to have similar peaks, but one has a wider spread than the other. A sample plot is seen in Fig. 3—Company A's distribution is represented with a "–o" line while Company B's distribution is represented with a "–+" line. The two curves have peaks approximately at the same confidence value, as we would expect since both companies have tested to the same criterion; however, Company B's plot has a lower peak value and a higher variance due to the higher uncertainty we have in their testing.

3.2   Assurance Example

Figure 4 shows a sample assurance case, in GSN notation, based on an x-ray backscattering machine that might be used at an airport. For illustrative and clarity purposes, this assurance case is extremely simple.

We have a top-level claim that all causes of overradiation have been eliminated. For purposes of this example, "all causes" is actually just two causes—software errors and timer interlock errors. Each cause of overradiation has two

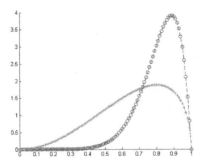

Fig. 3. Confidence distribution for two testing companies

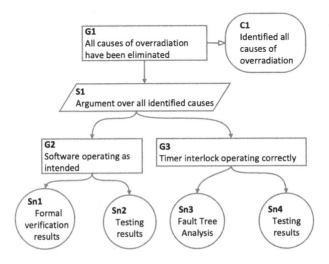

Fig. 4. Example assurance case

supporting evidence nodes. In Fig. 5, the assurance case has been modified to a fault tree analysis-based format to represent how the components could be combined via subjective logic operators in an intuitive way. Since we are dealing with *opinions* on nodes, the most appropriate operator for combining evidence is the consensus operator. Though testing results for the timer interlock or software are empirical, there are always external factors that can affect an opinion on the specific evidence node as mentioned in the previous section. When to use the empirical data by itself, versus an opinion on the result itself, will be the subject of a future work. The consensus operator for two opinions $\pi^A = b^A, d^A, u^A$ and $\pi^B = b^B, d^B, u^B$ is:

$$b^{A,B} = \frac{(b^A u^B + b^B u^A)}{\kappa}, \ d^{A,B} = \frac{(d^A u^B + d^B u^A)}{\kappa}, \ u^{A,B} = \frac{(u^A u^B)}{\kappa}$$
$$\text{where } \kappa = u^A + u^B - u^A u^B \text{ such that } \kappa \neq 0 \ [6]$$

After applying the consensus operator to an individual's opinion about the evidence nodes, we receive an intermediary opinion about whether or not

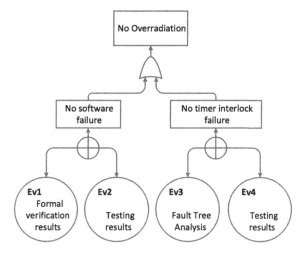

Fig. 5. Logical argument for example assurance case

software or timer components will fail. We use the logical-OR operator on our intermediary opinions to arrive at a final opinion about the claim. For overradiation to occur in a x-ray backscattering machine, both the software and the timer interlock needs to fail. Thus, for no overradiation to occur, just one of the two components needs to operate correctly—a logical-OR relationship. Such a redundancy system necessarily increases our confidence in the top level claim.

From this logical argument, the next step is to assign opinion values to the evidence nodes. There has been considerable research into the elicitation of opinions, as seen in works by Renooji [26], Druzdel and van der Gaag [10], O'Hagan [27], and van der Gaag et al. [28], but it is beyond the scope of this work to address such issues in detail. Instead, we have assigned personal opinions based on an informal survey of experts and what would give interesting and informative results (Table 1). With no prior information of any type, the relative atomicity of all nodes will be 0.5. The opinions are then mapped to their equivalent beta values based on Jøsang's work.

Table 1. Opinion and corresponding beta values.

Software Node	Opinion Values	Beta Parameters
Ev1 - Formal Verification	$\pi(0.7, 0.2, 0.1)$	$\alpha = 8.0, \beta = 2.0$
Ev2 - Testing	$\pi(0.5, 0.2, 0.3)$	$\alpha = 2.67, \beta = 1.67$
Hardware Node		
Ev3 - Fault Tree Analysis	$\pi(0.3, 0.5, 0.2)$	$\alpha = 2.5, \beta = 3.5$
Ev4 - Testing	$\pi(0.9, 0.05, 0.05)$	$\alpha = 19, \beta = 2$

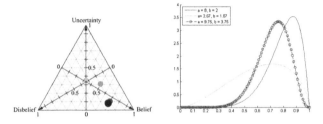

Fig. 6. Opinion triangle and beta distribution showing software node consensus

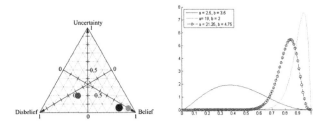

Fig. 7. Opinion triangle and beta distribution showing hardware node consensus

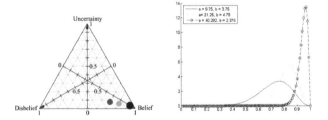

Fig. 8. Opinion triangle and beta distribution showing logical-OR for overradiation node

Figure 6 shows the opinion triangle and beta distributions for the two pieces of evidence that support the software node (Ev1 and Ev2) and the consensus of their opinions. The two smaller dots, in red and blue, represent the two opinions on Ev1 and Ev2. The larger black dot (partially covering the blue dot) represents the consensus opinion. Similarly, the red and blue lines represent the corresponding beta distribution of the opinions, while the black circled line represents the consensus beta distribution.

Figure 7 shows the opinion triangle and beta distributions for the two pieces of evidence that support the hardware node (Ev3 and Ev4) and the consensus of their opinions. Lastly, Fig. 8 shows the opinion triangle and beta distributions for logical-OR opinion of the two sub-claims—or the expected confidence for the no overradiation claim.

4   Conclusions

The use of a distribution to represent confidence in assurance cases makes intuitive sense and we claim that the beta distribution is the most appropriate one to use. The beta distribution can assume a variety of shapes and exists only on a finite range. The non-trivial mathematics that typically is associated with the beta distribution are eliminated with the use of Jøsang's subjective logic that maps the beta distribution onto an opinion triangle. The opinion triangle is not a new concept to assurance cases, but it is used in a new context here; additionally, it can be an alternative way of eliciting opinions.

We believe that such a novel use of subjective logic and the beta distribution to represent confidence will be of great benefit to assurance case evaluation and review. The next step is to explore more in depth how to combine different confidence values. We have started some of the work here with the use of the consensus and logical-OR operator, but there are many more situations and many more operators that can and will need to be used. Additionally, while subjective logic has provided a variety of operators that have been well thought out already, the assurance case domain is unique and a "pre-made" operator might not fit what we need. Such situations will need to be examined in future work.

References

1. Safety management requirements for defence systems. Defence Standard 00–56 4, Ministry of Defense (2007)
2. Hawkins, R., Kelly, T., Knight, J., Graydon, P.: A new approach to creating clear safety arguments. In: Advances in Systems Safety (2011)
3. Denney, E., Pai, G., Habli, I.: Towards measurement of confidence in safety cases. In: 2011 International Symposium on Empirical Software Engineering and Measurement (2011)
4. Fenton, N., Neil, M., Caballero, J.G.: Using ranked nodes to model qualitative judgements in Bayesian networks. In: IEEE Transactions on Knowledge and Data Engineering (2007)
5. Ayoub, A., Chang, J., Sokolsky, O., Lee, I.: Assessing the overall sufficiency of safety arguments. In: Safety-Critical Systems Club (2013)
6. Jøsang, A.: Artificial reasoning with subjective logic. In: Proceedings of the Second Australian Workshop on Commonsense Reasoning (1997)
7. Cyra, L., Górski, J.: Supporting expert assessment of argument structures in trust cases. In: 9th International Probability Safety Assessment and Management Conference PSAM (2008)
8. Duan, L., Rayadurgam, S., Heimdahl, M., Ayoub, A., Sokolsky, O., Lee, I.: Reasoning about confidence and uncertainty in assurance cases: a survey. In: Software Engineering in Health Care (2014)
9. Kerr, O.: Why courts should not quantify probable cause. In: Klarman, S., Steiker (eds.) The Political Heart of Criminal Procedure: Essays on Themes of William J. Stuntz. GWU Law School Public Law Research Paper No. 543 (2012)

10. Druzdzel, M.J., van der Gaag, L.C.: Elicitation of probabilities for belief networks: combining qualitative and quantitative information. In: UAI 1995 Proceedings of the Eleventh Conference on Uncertainty in Artificial Intellingence (1995)
11. AgenaRisk. http://www.agenarisk.com/products/free_download.shtml
12. Hobbs, C., Lloyd, M.: The application of Bayesian belief networks to assurance case preparation. In: Achieveing Systems Safety: Proceedings of the Twentieth Safety-Critical Systems Symposium (2012)
13. Cozman, F.: Axiomatizing noisy-or. In: Proceedings of the 16th European Conference on Artificial Intelligence (2004)
14. Toulmin, S.: The Uses of Argument. Cambridge University Press, Cambridge (1958)
15. NOR-STA. https://www.argevide.com/en/products/free_trial
16. Górski, J., Jarzębowicz, A., Miler, J., Witkowicz, M., Czyżnikiewicz, J., Jar, P.: Supporting assurance by evidence-based argument services. In: Ortmeier, F., Daniel, P. (eds.) SAFECOMP Workshops 2012. LNCS, vol. 7613, pp. 417–426. Springer, Heidelberg (2012)
17. Choi, W., Kurfess, T.R., Cagan, J.: Sampling uncertainty in coordinate measurement data analysis. Precis. Eng. **22**, 153–163 (1998)
18. Merkle, E.: The disutility of the hard-easy effect in choice confidence. Psychon. Bull. Rev. **16**(1), 204–213 (2009)
19. Bishop, P., Bloomfield, R., Littlewood, B., Povyakalo, A., Wright, D.: Towards a formalism for conservative claims about the dependability of software-based systems. IEEE Trans. Softw. Eng. **37**(5), 708–717 (2011)
20. Jøsang, A., Haller, J.: Dirichlet reputation systems. In: Proceedings of the 2nd International Conference on Availability, Reliability and Security (2007)
21. Jøsang, A., Hayward, R., Pope, S.: Trust network analysis with subjective logic. In: 29th Australasian Computer Science Conference (2006)
22. Whitby, A., Jøsang, A., Indulska, J.: Filtering out unfair ratings in Bayesian reputation systems. In: Proceedings fo the Workshop on Trust in Agent Societies, at the Autonomous Agents and Multi Agent Systems Conference (2004)
23. Ettler, P., Dedecius, K.: Probabilistic reasoning in service of condition monitoring. In: Proceedings of the 11th International Conference on Condition Monitoring and Machinery Failure Prevention Technologies (2014)
24. Han, S., Koo, B., Hutter, A., Stechele, W.: Forensic reasoning upon pre-obtained surveillance metadata using uncertain spatio-temporal rules and subjective logic. In: 2010 11th International Workshop on Image Analysis for Multimedia Interactive Services (WIAMIS), pp. 1–4 (2010)
25. Chilenski, J., Miller, S.: Applicability of modified condition/decision coverage to software testing. Softw. Eng. J. **9**, 193–200 (1994)
26. Renooij, S.: Probability elicitation for belief networks: issues to consider. Knowl. Eng. Rev. **16**, 255–269 (2001)
27. O'Hagan, A.: Eliciting expert beliefs in substantial practical applications. J. Roy. Stat. Soc. Series D (Stat.) **47**, 21–35 (1998)
28. van der Gaag, L.C., Renooij, S., Witteman, C., Aleman, B.M.P., Taal, B.G.: How to elicit many probabilities. CoRR abs/1301.6745 (2013)

Safe & Sec Case Patterns

Kenji Taguchi[✉], Daisuke Souma[✉], and Hideaki Nishihara[✉]

National Institute of Advanced Industrial Science and Technology,
Information Technology Research Institute,
Software Analytics Research Group, Tsukuba, Japan
{kenji.taguchi,d-souma,h.nishihara}@aist.go.jp

Abstract. Many industrial sectors, which manufacture safety intensive systems e.g., automotive, railway, etc., now face technical challenges on how to integrate and harmonize critical issues on safety in addition to security for their systems. In this paper, we will explore a new way of reconciling those issues in an argument form, which we call Safe & Sec (Safety and Security) case patterns. They are derived from process patterns identified from our literature survey on research and standards. Safe & Sec case patterns in this paper will provide practitioners a wide perspective and baseline on how they could provide an assurance framework for their safety intensive systems with security focus.

Keywords: Safety · Security · Integration · Safety cases · Cybersecurity cases · Patterns

1 Introduction

Many industrial sectors, which manufacture safety intensive systems e.g., automotive, railway, etc., now face technical challenges how to integrate and harmonize critical issues on safety in addition to security for their systems. After the stuxnet incident, any safety intensive systems, even not linked to any network are under the imminent threats for security vulnerabilities. We could now assume that any safety-related hazardous events (such as car crash, derailing, etc.,.) could be caused by hardware/software failures and/or malicious attacks, thereby we need to identify and analyze potential hazards and/or threats, their combinations and their associated risks in a systematic way, and build a new assurance framework which ensures both safety and security.

In this paper, we will explore a new way of reconciling those critical issues on safety and security in an argument form, which we call Safe & Sec (Safety and Security) case patterns. We must emphasize that we do not intend to discuss the very nature and/or differences between security and safety, and the aim of the paper is to show some argument patterns derived from different viewpoints when treating safety and security in the system development life-cycle. We present them in a more general form than argument patterns used in GSN (Goal Structuring Notation) by T. Kelly [11], so we call them *case patterns*.

© Springer International Publishing Switzerland 2015
F. Koornneef and C. van Gulijk (Eds.): SAFECOMP 2015 Workshops, LNCS 9338, pp. 27–37, 2015.
DOI: 10.1007/978-3-319-24249-1_3

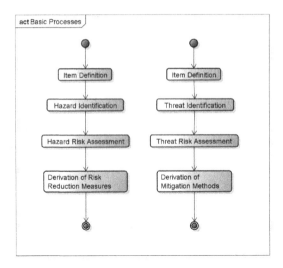

Fig. 1. Basic processes

We must admit that this work is still at the stage of the proof of concept and needs further elaboration and justification based on real case studies. We do hope that this work will provide some insight on how to deal with safety and security in an argument form.

This paper is structured as follows: the next section presents process patterns on interactions between safety and security, typically found in existing standards and literatures. The third section presents Safe & Sec case patterns based on those process patterns. The fourth section compares our work with related work. Finally the fifth section concludes this paper.

2   Safe & Sec Process Patterns

Interplays between safety and security fall into broad range of issues found in the whole system life-cycle. We only focus on early stages in the system life-cycle and only deal with hazard identification/threat identification, risk assessment and derivation of safety/security requirements, which we call risk reduction measures and mitigation methods respectively.

We will show the following process patterns in this section:

– Basic
– Subordinate
– Interrelated
    • Uni-directional Referencing
    • Independent
    • SafSec

First of all, we present two types of basic processes, each of which represents that of safety and security respectively in Fig. 1. The Item Definition includes preliminary architecture of the target system, the Hazard Identification to identify potential hazards, the Hazard Risk Assessment to assess the risk involved in hazards identified based on some safety risk metrics (e.g., ASIL in ISO 26262 [9] for automotive systems), and finally the Derivation of Risk Reduction Measures to derive safety requirements. The security side has identical activities paraphrased in security terms instead.

We think that it is not too bold to assume that this is the basic safety/security process in the initial phase of safety/security related activities in the system lifecycle.

2.1 Subordinate Process Pattern

This process pattern in Fig. 2 shows that all activities on the security side is subordinate to their counterparts in safety. For instance, threat identification may be included in hazard identification, and so on. The typical example of this process pattern can be found in the research project SEISES [2], in which safety standards for airworthiness and security are integrated to provide a seamless assurance framework.

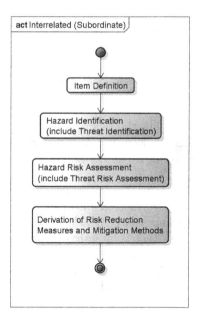

Fig. 2. Subordinate process pattern

2.2 Uni-Directional Reference Process Pattern

This process pattern is called the uni-directional reference process pattern depicted in Fig. 3. In this process pattern, the Threat Identification activity refers to identified hazards, but not vice versa. In this diagram, the reference relationship is indicated by the dashed line with an open-headed arrow and the stereotype << reference >> attached above the line.

This process pattern is drawn from the avionic security standard DO-326A [15], where safety related activities do not refer to any work products produced in the security life-cycle.

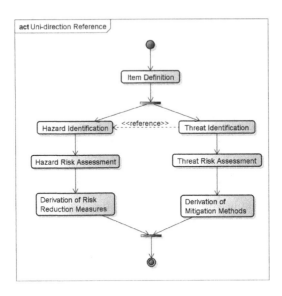

Fig. 3. Interrelated (Uni-directional reference) process pattern

It might look too extreme, but this is a typical view, which shows that safety concerns are predominant over security. We can also point out that this type of view is implicitly adopted in a railway standard for the open transmission systems; IEC 62280 [7].

Looking at some existing research on integration of hazard analysis and threat analysis, there are some works which fit into this type of process. Fault Trees (FT) [8] and its security counterpart Attack Trees ([12,17]) are of particular interest to researchers due to their syntactic similarities. For instance, Steiner [19] proposed a combination of Fault Trees with attacks, in which attacks appear as a cause of some fault. IEC 62280 also includes an example FT diagram, which mixes faults and attacks (in the Figure D.1 in the Annex D).

We could not find any literature on bi-directional reference process pattern. However, we think two processes referencing bi-directionally would be plausible, since it places the same value to safety and security.

2.3   Interrelated (Independent) Process Pattern

Figure 4 shows that safety and security processes are independent but converged on the trade-off analysis activity. The trade-off analysis could be carried out in several ways. For instance, Born [5] proposed a process in the concept phase

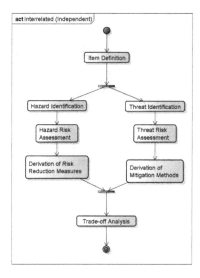

Fig. 4. Interrelated (Independent) process pattern

in ISO 26262 where the interference analysis is carried out on derived functional safety requirements and security requirements. The aim of this interference analysis is to identify potential feature interaction between functional safety requirements and security requirements. For instance, timing constraints on a functional safety requirement may be interfered by time-consuming encryption mechanism on a security requirement, thereby they need to be re-considered. The work is based on the research output of the FP7 research project SESAMO (SEcurity and SAfety Modelling) [18].

2.4 Interrelated (SafSec) Process Pattern

This process pattern in Fig. 5 is based on the SafSec standard/guideline sponsored by UK MOD and carried out by Praxis [13,14]. The main aim of the SafSec is the double/simultaneous certification of a security standard (in this case, CC [10] and a safety standard (in this case Defence standard 00-56 [20]). The SafSec standard/guideline demonstrates compliance with both standard using the common terminology for safety and security, and uses a dependability case for assurance.

   In this process pattern, after hazard analysis and threat analysis are carried out separately, their results are converged as losses. The loss is the coined term used in the SafSec, which represents both hazard and threat.

   In the next sections, we will show case patterns based on those process patterns presented in this section.

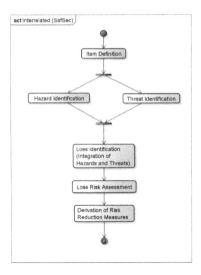

Fig. 5. Interrelated (SafSec) process pattern

3 Safe & Sec Case Patterns

In this section, we will present several case patterns following the process patterns presented in the previous section.

3.1 Independent Case Pattern

The first case pattern treats safety and security independently which reflects the process pattern in Fig. 1.

This is rather naive view of safety and security, but we do not exclude this pattern. This is mainly because it would show some case in real world where a safety case and a security case would be separately mandated in an industrial sector. For instance, in the automotive domain, ISO 26262 [9] requires a safety case and SAE J3061 [16], a new cybersecurity guideline for automotive would require a cybersecurity case [4] and currently none of these appears to require any seamless integration of the two cases.

3.2 Subordinate Case Pattern

From the safety point of view, security is a part of safety. This view is plausible as long as part of safety hazards are caused by security threats, and no-safety related security issues including privacy are ignored. This view appears to be predominant in the safety critical systems community. This type of case pattern is depicted in Fig. 6, which corresponds to the process pattern in Fig. 2. Each goal addresses safety issues but includes security part in them.

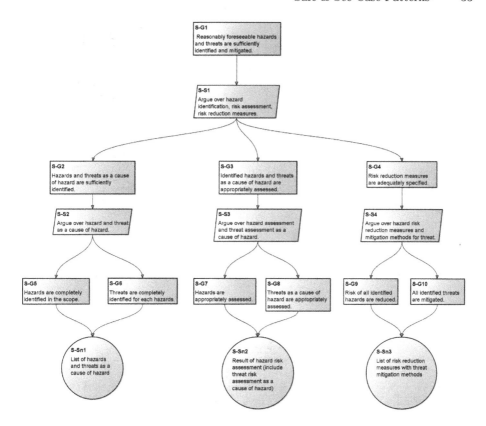

Fig. 6. Subordinate case pattern

3.3   Uni-Directional Reference Case Pattern

Even though two different cases of different system attribute (in this paper, safety and security) are separately built; they may be referencing each other. As was already presented, the security standard for airworthiness, DO-326A includes security development as part of safety assessment and system development (Fig. 2-3 on page 14 [15]). In that figure, some outcomes in the safety assessment process flows to security risk assessment but not vice versa (e.g., Aircraft Failure conditions). This means that the reference relationship is supposed to be uni-directional from safety to security in an argument form as well.

   This case pattern is given in Fig. 7. This case pattern consists of two sub-arguments and the left argument represents a safety case and the right argument represents a security case. The solution UR-Sn1 in the left (safety) argument is remotely referenced by the context UR-C1 in the right (security) argument.

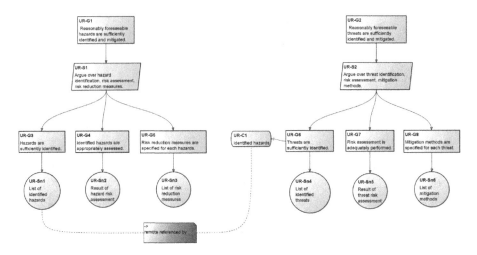

Fig. 7. Interrelated (Uni-directional reference) case pattern

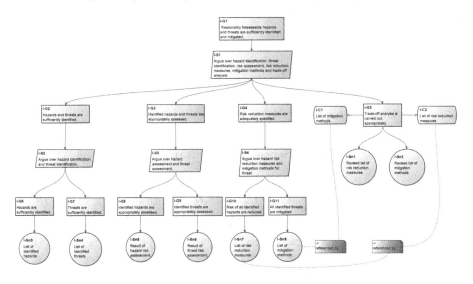

Fig. 8. Interrelated (Independent) case pattern

3.4   Interrelated (Independent) Case Pattern

This case pattern corresponds to the process pattern in Fig. 4. In this case pattern, the right-most argument represents the trade-off analysis part which remotely refers the context I-Sn8 for the list of mitigation methods and the context I-Sn7 for the list of risk reduction measures.

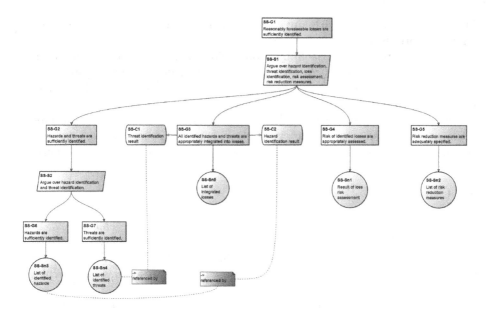

Fig. 9. Interrelated (SafSec) case pattern

3.5 Interrelated (SafSec) Case Pattern

We show the SafSec case pattern in Fig. 9, which corresponds to the Fig. 5. In this case pattern, the results of hazard analysis and threat analysis are referenced when they are integrated into losses.

In the SafSec standard/guideline [13, 14], a GSN diagram is provided to show how compliance with Common Criteria [10] and Defence standard 00-56 [20] is achieved. It must be noted that our SafSec case pattern is very simplied and the sub-arguments about the target system and assurance requirements in the original SafSec goal structure do not appear in our Interrelated (SafSec) case pattern.

4 Related Work

There are so many works related to safety cases so we just omit them from this paper. There are several research works which enhance assurance cases for security. Alexander, et. al., proposed an assurance case for security with the use of practices about safety cases [1]. In the paper it was pointed out that approaches to the goal descriptions are similar between safety and security. Thus the authors proposed a security case described with GSN and discussed about its advantages. Goodenough, et. al., showed security cases and their patterns [6]. In the article, security assurance was the main focus and structured security cases typically depicted as diagrams were discussed. Common argument structures for security were formalized to patterns and several expected benefits are explained.

These works do not deal with any interactions between safety and security in an argument form in Fig. 8.

The closest to our work is [3] by Bloomfield, et. al. They call their assurance cases *Security Informed Safety Cases*. They build a safety case first and analyze impact of security on the safety case. This work would be classified under the subordinate case pattern in our classification.

Our Safe & Sec case patterns do not support any detailed analysis on interactions between safety and security but provide a wide spectrum of thoughts on how we can build a case which integrates issues raised from safety and security.

5   Conclusion

In this paper, we presented several case patterns, which we call Safe & Sec case patterns derived from process patterns which integrate safety and security activities at the early stage of the system life-cycle. We hope this work would be the first step stone when building a case which assures issues on interplays between safety and security concerns.

Our future work includes more thorough survey on current practices and literature on interplays between safety and security. For instance, as was mentioned previously, the bi-directional reference process pattern (and its case pattern) is plausible but could not find any existing practice or literature. So there could be more patterns which we could add to our work.

There are on-going standardization activities on security in several industrial sectors such as automotive, medical devices amongst a few. Most of them do not seem to take a thorough consideration into harmonization of their safety counterparts. We hope our work on this Safe & Sec case patterns would provide some insight into how to harmonize them.

References

1. Alexander, R., Hawkins, R., Kelly, T.: Security assurance cases: Motivation and the state of the art. Department of Computer Science, University of York, Technical report (2011)
2. Bieber, P., Blanquart, J.P., Descargues, G., Dulucq, M., Fourastier, Y., Hazane, E., Julien, M., Léonardon, L., Sarouille, G.: Security and safety assurance for aerospace embedded systems. In: Proceedings of the 6th International Conference on Embedded Real Time Software and Systems, ERTS 2012, pp. 1–10 (2012)
3. Bloomfield, R., Netkachova, K., Stroud, R.: Security-informed safety: if it's not secure, it's not safe. In: Gorbenko, A., Romanovsky, A., Kharchenko, V. (eds.) SERENE 2013. LNCS, vol. 8166, pp. 17–32. Springer, Heidelberg (2013)
4. Boran, L.: Automotive cyber-security. In: Escar Europe (2013)
5. Born, M.: An approach to safety and security analysis for automotive systems. In: SAE 2014 World Congress and Exhibition (2014)
6. Goodenough, J., Lipson, H.F., Weinstock, C.B.: Arguing security - creating security assurance cases. Technical report SEI/CMU (2014)

7. IEC 62280:2014: Railway applications - Communication, signaling and processing systems -Safety related communication in transmission systems (2014)

8. IEC61025: Fault tree analysis (FTA) (2006)

9. ISO26262:2011: Road Vehicle - Functional Safety -, Part 1 to Part 9 (2011)

10. ISO/IEC 15408: Common Criteria for Information Technology Security Evaluation (2012)

11. Kelly, T.: Arguing Safety - A Systematic Approach to Safety Case Management. Ph.D. thesis, Department of Computer Science, University of York (1998)

12. Kordy, B., Piètre-Cambacédès, L., Schweitzer, P.: Dag-based attack and defense modeling: Don't miss the forest for the attack trees. Comput. Sci. Rev. 13–14, 1–38 (2014). http://dx.doi.org/10.1016/j.cosrev.2014.07.001

13. Praxis: SafSec: Integration of Safety & Security Certification, SafSec Methodology: Guidance Material (2006)

14. Praxis: SafSec: Integration of Safety & Security Certification, SafSec Methodology: Standard (2006)

15. RTCA DO-326A: Airworthiness Security Process Specification (2014)

16. SAE: Cybersecurity Guidebook for Cyber-Physical Automotive Systems

17. Schneier, B.: Attack Trees. Dr. Dobbs Journal (1996)

18. SESAMO. http://sesamo-project.eu/

19. Steiner, M., Liggesmeyer, P.: Combination of safety and security analysis - finding security problems that threaten the safety of a system. In: Workshop DECS (ERCIM/EWICS Workshop on Dependable Embedded and Cyber-Physical Systems) (2013)

20. UK Ministry of Defence: Defence standard 00–56: Safety management requirements for defence systems (2004)

A Comprehensive Safety Lifecycle

John Knight[(✉)], Jonathan Rowanhill, M. Anthony Aiello,
and Kimberly Wasson

Dependable Computing LLC, Charlottesville, USA
{john.knight, jonathan.rowanhill, tony.aiello,
kim.wasson}@dependablecomputing.com

Abstract. CLASS is a novel approach to the safety engineering and management of safety-critical systems in which the system safety case becomes the focus of safety engineering throughout the system lifecycle. CLASS expands the role of the safety case across all phases of the system's lifetime, from concept formation and problem definition to decommissioning. Having the system safety case as the focus of safety engineering and management only has value if the safety case is properly engineered and appropriately consistent with the system. To achieve these properties, CLASS requires that a system and its safety case be regarded as a single composite entity, always linked and always correctly representing one another. CLASS introduces new techniques for the creation, approval and maintenance of safety cases, a rigorous analysis mechanism that allows determination of properties that relate to defect detection in subject systems, and a set of software support tools.

Keywords: Safety case · Software assurance · System lifecycle

1 Introduction

The *Comprehensive Lifecycle for Assuring System Safety* (CLASS) is a safety-engineering system lifecycle based on the subject system's safety case. CLASS extends the *Assurance Based Development* software concept [1, 2] to the system lifecycle level. CLASS encompasses system development, approval, operation, maintenance and decommissioning, and integrates with the safety-management system.

The goal of CLASS is to ensure that all engineering elements in the system lifecycle are justified by and contribute to the assurance of system safety. As in Assurance Based Development, the concept is to make assurance a primary objective in the system lifecycle, since functionality without assurance in a safety-critical system is of marginal value. By design, CLASS process elements are derived from desired system properties explicitly thereby obviating the need for indirect evidence.

CLASS is structured as a *meta* process that embodies a broad range of techniques, an *instantiation* mechanism that tailors the meta process to the specific details of a given application, and a *repository* that provides a wealth of resources such as argument patterns, support tools, process patterns and guidance to support rigorous development. In this paper, we present the rationale for and overall design of CLASS.

© Springer International Publishing Switzerland 2015
F. Koornneef and C. van Gulijk (Eds.): SAFECOMP 2015 Workshops, LNCS 9338, pp. 38–49, 2015.
DOI: 10.1007/978-3-319-24249-1_4

2 CLASS Principles

Specific artifacts are used to define many existing software development methodologies. For example, in *test driven development, tests* guide system development; in *requirements driven development, requirements* are refined to system implementation; and in *enterprise architecture, architectural patterns* that demonstrate useful system properties guide development.

Each of these methodologies involves *synchrony* between a non-functional, analytic product (tests, requirements, architecture) and the functional system. This synchrony is a co-informing relationship: the functional system informs the analytic product, and the analytic product informs the functional system. Furthermore, the two must not contradict each other, but are instead extrapolations of one another. Finally, the analytic products must be coherent, just as the pieces of the functional system are coherent.

These concepts have been adopted as a guiding principle for CLASS. In CLASS, the non-functional, analytic product is the *safety case*, and the notion of synchrony that is inherent in these advanced software development methodologies is a fundamental principle of CLASS.

In view of the importance of synchrony in the CLASS approach, we define the term as follows:

Synchrony. A safety case and the system about which it argues have the property of synchrony if all elements of the safety case are current for the subject system and all analytic products are coherent.

Failure of assurance can result from a failure of synchrony. In that case, there is an underlying error in the safety case, implementation, or both, such that synchrony does not hold between the two in a given system instance.

The principles upon which CLASS is built are:

- **Composite Entity**. The subject system and the associated safety case are treated as a single, *composite* entity, the *System and Safety Case Pair* (SSCP).
- **Synchrony**. Synchrony between the subject system and the associated safety case is maintained whenever they should be synchronized. Timing of synchronization is determined by analysis. Synchrony will not be continuous– synchrony has to be broken in a planned way in order to permit concurrent development of the system and the safety case.
- **Assured Properties**. The CLASS lifecycle process structure precludes the introduction of safety defects to the extent possible. Assurance of this process property is by analysis.
- **Monitoring**. CLASS undertakes necessary and flexible monitoring of itself and system artifacts in order to ensure that crucial process properties and state are maintained. Necessary sensors and monitoring algorithms are determined by analysis. Monitoring can include any aspect of the CLASS process and state (including the subject system) over time. CLASS monitoring enables properties that follow from the definition of the process to be assured.

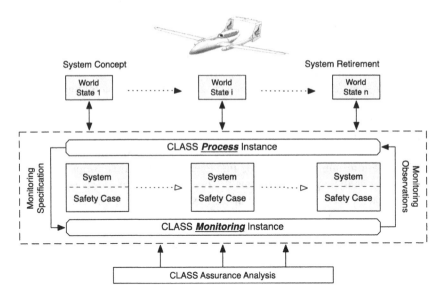

Fig. 1. CLASS instance outline

An outline of a CLASS instance in operation is shown in Fig. 1. The subject system moves through a series of world states from initial concept and problem definition to retirement, throughout which the CLASS instance operates continuously. At all times during the system lifecycle, the system and its safety case are treated as a composite entity. Assurance analysis of the composite entity indicates how properties of the subject system will derive from the process and provides details of the necessary monitoring of the process and the state.

The three major components of CLASS, the meta process, the instance process, and the resource repository, are significantly interwoven. We discuss these three components separately in the next three sections but note that the interweaving cannot be discussed easily in this linear presentation.

3   The CLASS Meta Process

The CLASS meta process, referred to as *metaCLASS*, provides a variety of support for the SSCP throughout the lifecycle. Figure 2 illustrates the basic metaCLASS instantiation mechanism and the major outputs of the associated CLASS instance, referred to as *instanceCLASS*.

Also shown in Fig. 2 is the *Safety Information Repository* (SIR). The SIR is a structure that holds the safety case and all related assets that result from the creation and use of an instanceCLASS for a subject system. The SIR is created as part of the instantiation process and is a lifetime entity, *i.e.*, the SIR accompanies the system throughout the system's lifetime. The SIR provides all of the artifacts needed to support the instanceCLASS as changes become necessary during the system's lifetime.

MetaCLASS is composed of two basic components:

- **Development Component**. The development component of metaCLASS along with the CLASS Resource Repository (CRR) supports creation of instanceCLASS processes, both initially and over the system lifecycle.
- **Update Component**. The update component of metaCLASS along with the CRR supports updates of instanceCLASS processes over the system lifecycle.

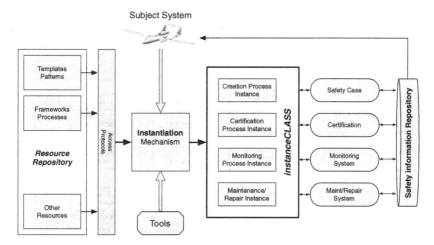

Fig. 2. Primary elements of CLASS instantiation including the safety information repository

3.1   Development Component

An instanceCLASS is needed for any project using CLASS, and each instanceCLASS is created from metaCLASS using resources from the CRR. Once the instanceCLASS is created and the necessary activities needed for the system safety case are initiated, metaCLASS remains in operation and available to provide lifecycle support. Additional resources can be obtained from the CRR at any point.

MetaCLASS provides access to the CRR using a set of access protocols designed to facilitate the location of useful resources and appropriate use of those resources.

As an example of an access protocol, consider the resources needed for approval or certification. In an aviation context, the resources needed for approval will be influenced by the application type (ground or airborne), the criticality level of the system, the overall system requirements, and so on. The role of the access protocols in this case is to provide a means of locating the right versions of standards, process support entities, tools, regulatory mechanisms and so on.

3.2   Update Component

The update component of metaCLASS is responsible for ensuring that all instance-CLASSs remain properly synchronized over time with all available resource information. The resource update mechanism in CLASS is shown in Fig. 3. The issues that force interaction between instanceCLASS and metaCLASS arise from the temporal dimension of SSCP support. The problem that the update component is designed to address has two components:

- **Meta Resource Updates**. Updates to resources within the CRR and the availability of new resources within the CRR need to be communicated to all instanceCLASSs that might have an interest in those resources, e.g., an instanceCLASS that was derived from those resources. This communication is especially important for defects that are detected and repaired in the CRR. As an example, consider the possibility of a defect in an argument pattern being detected. All safety cases relying on that pattern would need to be checked and possibly updated.

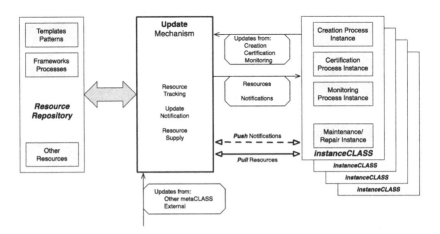

Fig. 3. CLASS resource update mechanism.

- **Instance Resource Updates**. Necessary updates to CRR resources might be detected by an instanceCLASS that was using those resources. The CRR needs to be informed of such updates and then instanceCLASSs derived from those resources need to be informed. As an example, again consider the possibility of a defect in an argument pattern being detected by an instanceCLASS. Correcting that defect in the CRR and all other derived instanceCLASSs is crucial.

Effecting an update to either the CRR or the resources being used by an instanceCLASS in an unsynchronized manner could disrupt ongoing activities. Conversely, the CRR, metaCLASS and all instanceCLASSs need to be informed promptly of an update. To accommodate these requirements, the CLASS update mechanism is divided into a *Notifications* element and a *Resources* element.

A notification includes the details of an update but is merely to notify all interested processes of the update. Processes can then decide on the relevance and importance of the update. Notifications are "pushed" to all interested processes. The Resources element of the update component provides the mechanism for interested processes to acquire updated resources. Resources are "pulled" by the interested processes and so the installation of an update in under the control of the processes.

4   The CLASS Instance Process

4.1   InstanceCLASS Information Flow

The CLASS instance process, referred to as *instanceCLASS*, includes a wide variety of types of information. Figure 4 is organized around these items of information and their flows through an instanceCLASS.

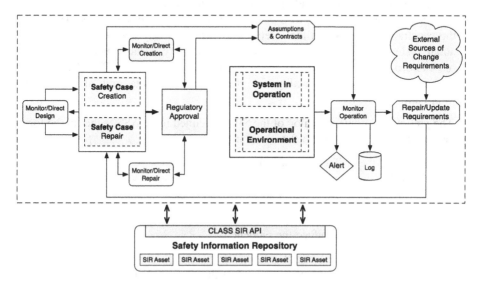

Fig. 4.   CLASS instance information flow.

The key elements of the information flow structure are:

- Approval assets and shared information for and from audits flow between developers and the approval agency.
- The evolving safety case design flows to and from a variety of sources and sinks intended to inform and consult all system stakeholders.
- Details of process activities flow to the process monitoring system.
- Specification of essential state monitoring activities flow from the safety case design to the state monitoring system.
- Assets flow to the SIR as they are completed and from the SIR for reference later in the lifecycle.

4.2   Safety Information Repository

The *Safety Information Repository* (SIR) is a *source* and a *sink* for all of the information that flows in a CLASS instance. The SIR expands the concept of a safety case to include all relevant information that might have value across the lifecycle.

The role of the SIR in the overall CLASS architecture is shown in Fig. 2. The information flow of the subject system, the associated instanceCLASS, and the SIR is shown in more detail in Fig. 4.

As examples of the role of the SIR, consider: (a) the safety case itself and (b) the results of state monitoring of the subject system:

- The safety case has to be accessible and available for update and repair at any point during the subject system's lifecycle. The SIR provides this storage and access facility for the safety case and all associated information.
- State monitoring is designed to check on the conformance of the subject system to the constraints upon which the safety case was built. Any deviations raise issues about system and safety case consistency and validity. Details of the monitoring record need to be available in an accessible and predefined form. The SIR provides this storage and access facility for the monitoring data and all associated information.

The preliminary content catalog of the SIR as defined in CLASS, either in the form of the actual artifacts or links to the actual artifacts, is:

- A directory of the artifacts contained within the SIR.
- The system's safety case.
- Source artifacts used to create the system's safety case including:

  - All items of evidence.
  - Tools needed to reproduce the evidence.
  - Safety arguments.

- All artifacts associated with the approval of the system via the safety case.
- Logs of system maintenance.
- Logs of system monitoring.

As shown in Fig. 4, the SIR has an API that supports access and management of the SIR. For any lifecycle activity that involves safety-related information, processes that use the SIR through the API will be available. The details of the SIR content, the API access mechanism, the necessary tool support and the associated access process will be elaborated as CLASS is applied.

5   The CLASS Resource Repository

The CLASS Resource Repository (CRR) supplies resources that metaCLASS uses to build and maintain an instanceCLASS. The expectation is that the CRR will provide resources of many types and permit a great deal of reuse across projects.

The CLASS Resource Repository cannot be unique, i.e., there cannot be a single CRR that provides resources to all projects. Any organization that is using CLASS will require organization-specific elements in the CRR. All instantiations of the CRR should be (though need not be) derived from a central facility so as take advantage of the common base of resources. Nevertheless, a tailoring mechanism is required to permit a generic CRR to be adapted to the needs of a specific organization.

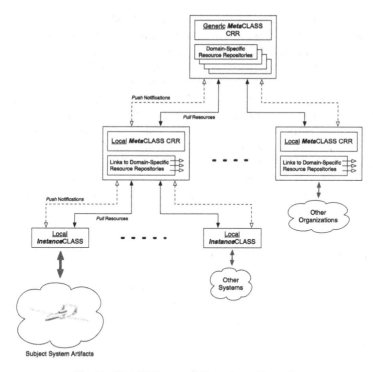

Fig. 5. CLASS Resource Repository hierarchy.

To accommodate the various modifications necessary within the CRR and to permit flexible use of those modifications, CLASS defines a hierarchy of CRRs. The CLASS CRR hierarchy is illustrated in Fig. 5. The hierarchy begins with a *generic* CRR used by metaCLASS. Along with the specific content designed to support CLASS, this generic CRR includes domain specific resource repositories that are provided by other sources.

Examples of this type of repository are:

- Standards and documentation repositories maintained by regulatory and standards bodies.
- GSN pattern libraries maintained by organizations such as universities and research organizations.
- Software libraries that provide common services such as those available from system software and middle-ware vendors.

At the next layer of the hierarchy are a set of *local* CRRs, each designed to support the metaCLASS operated by a specific organization, such as an aerospace system supplier. Each local CRR is adapted from the generic CRR to support the particular organization. Within a given organization, each instanceCLASS is created from the local CRR. As shown in Fig. 5, a set of instanceCLASSs within an organization are derived from the organization's local CRR.

The CLASS Resource Repository is not static. As shown in Fig. 3, updates or additional materials derived from external sources might be entered into the CRR over time. Other changes to the CRR might be motivated by either resource demands or determination of defects in resources as a result of their use.

As discussed in the context of the update component of metaCLASS, no matter what the cause, changes in the CRR must be handled carefully. Enhanced resources might not be of immediate value to existing instanceCLASSs, and the decision about their adoption must be the responsibility of the individual instanceCLASS. Declining adoption of a new or enhanced resource entirely by the CRR might be preferable. Similarly, defects identified in resources by an instanceCLASS must be made available to other instanceCLASSs in order to protect the latter from the effects of the identified defect. Nevertheless, each instanceCLASS must be able to exercise explicit individual control over the action taken when resources are updated.

6   The CLASS Analysis Framework

The CLASS analysis framework is designed to analyze CLASS *itself* so as to provide justification for rigorous statements about properties of the *subject system* that result from the tools and techniques used in CLASS. The goal of the framework is:

- to enable examination of CLASS based on a list of desired properties of the subject system, and
- to determine the extent to which CLASS can ensure these properties, *i.e.*, the extent to which CLASS precludes the introduction of defects that could make a property false.

If the framework can show that CLASS avoids the introduction of or enables significant reduction in a class of defects, then that result translates immediately into a property of the desired system, i.e., elimination or limitation of a class of defects.

The basic approach used in the analysis framework is use of the *Filter Model* introduced by Steele and Knight [3]. Based on the Filter Model, CLASS itself is treated as a safety-critical system. In other words, allowing a defect to be introduced into or allowing a defect to remain in a subject system is considered an *accident*.

The Filter Model was introduced to analyze approval processes and associated standards. The model derives a mapping between the detailed content of a standard and the intent of that detail; a mapping that is universally absent from standards. Applying the model to CLASS yields the mapping between process elements in CLASS and the associated intent. With that mapping, the content of a CLASS instance can be adjusted and so that properties of systems built with CLASS can be inferred.

Treating the *development* process as a safety-critical system (entirely separately from the system under development), i.e., the Filter Model principle, allows the application of all of the techniques used in safety engineering to the *process* and thereby to reduce the residual *development* risk associated with an instanceCLASS. Techniques that can be applied include hazard identification, hazard analysis, fault-tree analysis, failure-modes-effects-and-criticality analysis, and so on.

As an example, suppose that installing the subject system with inconsistent software components is defined to be a development hazard. Fault-tree analysis could be applied to this hazard to identify process events that could cause the hazard. Changes to both the process and the process monitoring system could then be developed to reduce the associated development risk to an acceptable level.

The overall concept upon which the analysis framework rests is illustrated in Fig. 6. This analysis permits much of an instanceCLASS process to be mapped to properties of the subject system. By analyzing CLASS in this manner, everything undertaken in CLASS leads to rigorous statements about the subject system and the necessary evidence to support the associated claim. Thus, the framework feeds directly and immediately into the safety case for the subject system. This mapping essentially eliminates the need for indirect evidence, because the process is enabling strong statements to be made about the system itself.

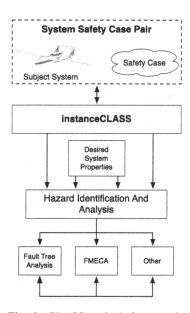

Fig. 6. CLASS analysis framework.

7   The CLASS Approval Process

CLASS addresses approval as a vital part of the entire lifecycle, from system concept formation and problem definition to system decommissioning, and bases approval on the system safety case. This explicit attention to approval across all of the lifecycle phases is manifested in the following considerations:

- The development phase of the lifecycle must ensure that artifacts developed support approval throughout the remainder of the lifecycle.

- The operation and maintenance phases of the lifecycle must support approval of revised versions of the subject system irrespective of the cause of the revision.
- The primary focus of approval will be with the lifecycle phase following development and preceding deployment. The focus must be supported by both artifact structures and processes that maximize the value and minimize the cost of approval to all of the system stakeholders, including the regulating agency.

Although the safety case is the basis of approval, the entire approval process is informed by the likely need to meet the requirements of a regulating agency. In the case of aviation systems, for example, the regulating agency involved is the Federal Aviation Administration (FAA). CLASS provides a framework within which adequacy of protection of the public interest as defined by the FAA can be determined. CLASS is designed specifically and deliberately to ensure that elements of CLASS can be adjusted to meet the needs of the FAA.

In CLASS, the safety case combines and structures many items that would normally be identified and elicited separately as part of existing approval mechanisms. By definition, the safety case documents the rationale for belief in the adequacy of the safety of the subject system, and maintenance of the safety case across the complete lifecycle facilitates the requisite approval activities.

Since the CLASS analysis framework allows indirect evidence about the subject system to be minimized or eliminated, the majority of the doubts about the properties of a system that are engendered by indirect evidence are avoided. The CLASS monitoring mechanism provides a high level of confidence that the expected properties established by the analysis framework will be true and either remain so or alert system stakeholders to violations. Thus, the starting point for approval is a safety case for the subject system with properties established by direct evidence in which stakeholders and certifiers can have high confidence.

CLASS approval is composed logically of two significant audit phases that are expected to be accomplished by experts from the regulating agency. The audit phases are:

- **Process Audit**. By design, CLASS attempts to preclude faults in a wide variety of categories. Provided CLASS is used properly, faults in certain explicit categories should be either eliminated or reduced to a tolerable level. The details of the categories of faults that are precluded together with all the associated evidence for the subject system are documented explicitly in the safety case. Despite the role of both the analysis framework and the monitoring system, an audit is required to *confirm* to the extent possible that the claimed properties of the subject system are present.
- **Safety Case Audit**. By definition, the safety case describes the rationale for belief in the safety of the subject system. Thus the second audit need not examine the product. Rather, the safety of the subject system should be argued in a compelling manner by the safety case. The second audit is of the safety case. Many aspects are examined in the audit including a variety of simple yet important properties. The main emphasis of the safety case audit is the assessment of the degree to which the safety argument has the essential properties of being *comprehensive, valid*, and *compelling*. The approach to audit in CLASS is based on previous work by Graydon et al. [4].

8 Conclusion

Safety cases are being used in practice and many benefits accrue from the approaches used in current practice. The goal of CLASS is to take the use of the safety-case concept to its practical limit by making the safety case the focus of the product lifecycle.

The present design of CLASS has explored the role of process rigor derived from the safety case, system approval based on a safety case within the larger framework of the system lifecycle, the provision of rich resource libraries to support lifecycle development and analysis, and the analysis of the lifecycle itself using the concepts of the filter model. The result is a comprehensive approach to system safety that integrates all phases of the lifecycle and provides safety assurance across those phases.

Acknowledgments. This work was supported in part by NASA Contract NNL13AA08C.

References

1. Graydon, P., Knight, J., Strunk, E.: Assurance based development of critical systems. In: 37th IEEE International Symposium on Dependable Systems and Networks, Edinburgh, Scotland (2007)
2. Graydon, G., Knight, J.: Process synthesis in assurance based development of dependable systems. In: 8th European Dependable Computing Conference, Valencia, Spain (2009)
3. Steele, P., Knight, J.: Analysis of critical system certification. In: 15th IEEE International Symposium on High Assurance Systems Engineering Miami FL (2014)
4. Graydon, P., Knight, J., Green, M.: Certification and safety cases. In: International System Safety Conference, Minneapolis, MN (2010)

An Approach to Assure Dependability Through ArchiMate

Shuichiro Yamamoto[✉]

Strategy Office, Information and Communications Headquarters,
Nagoya University, Nagoya, Japan
syamamoto@acm.org

Abstract. This paper describes a method to create assurance cases for the Open Dependability through Assuredness (O-DA) standard of The Open Group (TOG) based on ArchiMate. ArchiMate provides Enterprise Architecture (EA) models to describe Business, Application and Technology Architectures. Although O-DA shows the necessity of agreeing on the assuredness of EA using assurance cases, O-DA does not mention how to create assurance cases for EA. In this paper, an assurance case pattern is proposed to argue the assuredness for these three kinds of architectures modelled by ArchiMate.

Keywords: Assurance case · O-DA · Archimate · ADM · Assuredness · EA

1 Introduction

This paper describes a method to create assurance cases for the Open Dependability Assuredness (O-DA) standard of The Open Group (TOG) based on ArchiMate. ArchiMate provides Enterprise Architecture (EA) models to describe Business, Application and Technology Architectures. Although O-DA shows the necessity of agreeing on the assuredness of EA using assurance cases, O-DA does not mention how to create assurance cases for EA. In this paper, an assurance case pattern is proposed to argue the assuredness for these three kinds of architectures modelled by ArchiMate.

Section 2 describes related work on argument pattern approaches for assurance cases. The O-DA standard, the assured architecture development method (AADM), and ArchiMate are also briefly described. Section 3 describes an assurance case pattern which is proposed to formalize the argument decomposition structure from ArchiMate models. In Sect. 4, an example case study using the pattern is presented. Discussions on the effectiveness and appropriateness of the D-Case pattern are shown in Sect. 5. Our conclusions are presented in Sect. 6.

2 Related Work

This section describes the related work on the assurance case, ODA (Open dependability through Assuredness, and the Assured ADM.

© Springer International Publishing Switzerland 2015
F. Koornneef and C. van Gulijk (Eds.): SAFECOMP 2015 Workshops, LNCS 9338, pp. 50–61, 2015.
DOI: 10.1007/978-3-319-24249-1_5

2.1 Assurance Case

The safety case, the assurance case, and the dependability case are currently the focus of considerable attention for the purpose of providing assurance and confidence that systems are safe. Methods have thus been proposed for representing these using Goal Structuring Notation (GSN) [1–5]. GSN patterns were originally proposed by Kelly and McDermid [2]. In the absence of any clearly organized guidelines concerning the approach to be taken in decomposing claims using strategies and the decomposition sequence, engineers have often not known how to develop their arguments. It is against this backdrop that the aforementioned approaches to argument decomposition patterns—architecture, functional, attribute, infinite set, complete (set of risks and requirements), monotonic, and concretion—were identified by Bloomfield and Bishop [6]. When applying the architecture decomposition pattern, claims of the system are also satisfied for each constituent part of the system based on system architecture. Despotou and Kelly [7] proposed a modular approach to improving clarity of safety case arguments. Hauge and Stolen [8] described a pattern based safety case approach for the Nuclear Power control domain. Wardzinski [9] proposed an approach for assurance in the vehicle safety domain based on the assumption that hazardous sequences of events. An experimental result of argument patterns was reported by Yamamoto and Matsuno [10]. Argument pattern catalogue was proposed based on the format of design patterns by Alexander, Kelly, Kurd and McDermid [11]. In their paper, Alexander and others showed a safe argument pattern based on failure mode analysis. Graydon and Kelly [12] observed that argument patterns capture a way to argue about interference management. Ruiz and others [13] proposed an assurance case reuse system using a case repository. Denney and Pai [14] proposed a Formal Basis for Safety Case Patterns. They formalized pattern refinements such as (1) Instantiating parameters (2) Resolving choices (3) Resolving multiplicities, and (4) Unfolding loops. These are refinement rules of parameterized argument patterns.

Hawkins and others proposed a Model-Based Assurance Case development approach by weaving reference information models and GSN argument patterns [15]. They used a script language to define precise weaving procedures. Gallina and others [16] proposed a Safety Case Line approach to develop ISO 26262 compliant safety cases based on Product Line Engineering by using GSN extensions. Lin [17] showed how a safety case pattern can be applied to a manufacturers' development process as reusing strategies for building a new safety argument. These approaches assumes specific adaptation mechanisms to generate assurance cases for reusing GSN patterns.

Assurance cases have been extended to handle modular architectures [18]. Yamamoto and others proposed the d* framework to introduce responsibility of modules in assurance cases [19–21].

2.2 Open Dependability Through Assuredness

The Open Group Real Time & Embedded Systems Forum focuses on standards for high assurance, secure dependable and complete systems [22]. At the heart of this O-DA (Open Dependability through Assuredness) standard, there is the concept of modeling dependencies, building assurance cases, and achieving agreement on accountability in the event of actual or potential failures. Dependability cases are necessary to assure dependable systems [22]. The DEOS process was proposed to manage dependability of complex systems by using dependability cases [23–25]. The DEOS process is an integrated iterative process containing the change accommodation cycle and the failure response cycle.

Complex systems, especially where the boundaries of operation or ownership are unclear, are often subject to change: objectives change, new demands are made, regulations change, business partners are added, etc. So when the failure of the system can have a significant impact on lives, income or reputation, it is critical that a process is in place to identify these changes and to update the architecture by using the assurance cases and the agreements on accountability. It is also critical that a process is in place to detect anomalies or failures, to understand the causes, and to prevent them from impacting the system in the future.

The O-DA standard outlines the criteria for mitigating risk associated with dependability of complex interoperable systems. It also outlines individual accountability. The Open Group announced the publication of the Dependability through Assuredness™ Standard (O-DA) published by The Open Group Real-Time & Embedded Systems Forum [26].

O-DA will benefit organizations relying on complex systems to avoid or mitigate the impact of failure of those systems. O-DA includes the DEOS process mentioned before. The Change Accommodation Cycle and the Failure Response Cycle that together provide a framework for these critical processes. O-DA brings together and builds on The Open Group vision of Boundaryless Information Flow. These concepts include O-DM (Open Dependency Modeling) and Risk Taxonomy of The Open Group Security Forum, and Architecture models of The Open Group ArchiMate® Forum. However, the relationship between O-DA and ArchiMate concepts has not yet been clear.

2.3   Assured ADM

TOGAF [27] is The Open Group Architecture Framework. TOGAF Architecture types include business, data, application and technology architectures.

Business architecture describes business strategy, governance, organization, and key business processes. Data architecture describes the structure of an organization's logical and physical data assets and data management resources. Application architecture describes a blueprint for the individual applications to be deployed, their interactions, and their relationships to the core business processes of the organization. Technical architecture describes the logical software and hardware capabilities that are required to support the deployment of business, data, and application services. This includes IT infrastructure, middleware, networks, communications, processing, and standards. Architecture Development Method (ADM) is the core of TOGAF. Constituents of ADM phases are Preliminary, Architecture Vision, Business Architecture, Information Systems Architectures, Technology Architecture, Opportunities and

Solutions, Migration Planning, Implementation Governance, Architecture Change Management, and Requirements Management.

Table 1 summarizes AADM issues according to ADM phases. This paper focusses on the assurance case development in the B, C, and D phases, respectively.

Table 1. Issues of assured ADM

ADM phase	AADM
Preliminary	(1) Architecture repository to store evidence and assurance case, (2) Dependability board to agree on priority among claims
A. Architecture vision	(1) Dependability scope definitions, (2) Quantitative evaluation index, (3) Capability evaluation of dependability, (4) Dependability parameter
B. Business architecture	(1) Dependability principle definition (2) BA assurance case development (3) BA assurance case review
C. Information system architecture	(1) IA assurance case development, (2) IA assurance case review
D. Technology architecture	(1) TA assurance case development, (2) TA assurance case review
E. Solution	(1) Integration of BA, IA, TA assurance case, (2) Integrity confirmation
F. Transition	(1) Operation management assurance case development, (2) Value analysis of operation assurance case
G. Implementation	(1) Evidence development for assurance case, (2) Process evidence development method, (3) Exhaustive relationship validation between claims and evidences, (4) Operational assurance case review
H. Architecture change management	(1) Evidence management of operational assurance case, (2) Confirmation of measure for claim failures, (3) Risk management by assurance case, (4) Failure analysis by assurance case
Requirements management	Traceability management of assurance case

2.4 ArchiMate

The ArchiMate language [28] defines three layers. The **Business Layer** provides products and services to external customers, which are realized in the organization by business processes performed by business actors. The **Application Layer** describes application services which are realized by (software) applications to support the Business Layer entities. The **Technology Layer** offers infrastructure services (e.g., processing, storage, and communication services) that are realized by computers and communication hardware and system software to support applications.

3   Assurance Case Patterns for Architecture

3.1   Dependability Argument and ArchiMate

A dependability argument constitutes the intra-dependability of Architecture layers and the inter-dependability of layer interactions. It is necessary to assure the intra dependability by using assurance cases for the business, application, and technology layers. It is also necessary to assure the inter dependability by using assurance cases for the interactions between the business, application and technology layers.

The decomposition pattern is based on the description in Table 2.

Table 2. Assurance case pattern for ArchiMate

Hierarchy	Description
Root goal	The root goal states that the ArchiMate model shall satisfy dependability principles
Concepts and relationships	Root goal is decomposed by concepts and relationships of ArchiMate notations
Category of concepts and relationships	Second level goals are decomposed by categories of concepts and relationships of ArchiMate notations
Category instances of concepts and relationships	Third level goals are decomposed by instances of concepts and relationships of ArchiMate notations
Risk mitigation for Instance risks	Fourth level goals are decomposed by risks for the corresponding instances and are supported by evidence to mitigate risks

This pattern generally describes the transformation from an ArchiMate model to an assurance case. An ArchiMate model consists of model elements and relationships between elements. Therefore, the top goal of the assurance case for ArchiMate model is decomposed into two sub-goals.

The first level sub-goal claims state that concept elements and relationships of the ArchiMate model satisfy dependability principles. Figure 1 shows the decomposition of the top goal into two sub-goals.

The second level sub-goal claim states that category of elements and their relationships among ArchiMate model satisfy dependability principles.

The third level goals are decomposed by instances of concepts and relationships of ArchiMate notations.

The fourth level goals are decomposed by risks for the corresponding instances and are supported by evidences to mitigate risks. Therefore, the fifth level of the assurance case consists of evidences for the fourth level goals.

3.2   Assurance Case Derivation from ArchiMate Model

It is necessary to derive assurance cases from ArchiMate descriptions to assure architectures described in ArchiMate. An assurance case derivation method from ArchiMate model is as follows.

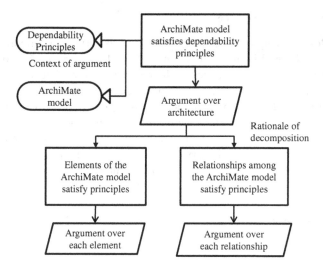

Fig. 1. Assurance case structure of ArchiMate diagrams

For each ArchiMate model A = <Concept Set, Relationship Set> , Concept Set and Relationship Set are defined as follows.

Concept Set = {< Name, Cc > | Cc is a Concept category of ArchiMate}
Relationship Set = {< Name, Cr > | Cr is a Relationship category of ArchiMate}
Then, the following four sets are calculated.
Concept Category (A) = {C | < x, C > is in Concept Set of A}
Relationship Category (A) = {C | < r, C > is in Relationship Set of A}
Concept Instance (C, A) = {x | < x, C > is in Concept Set of A}
Relationship Instance (C, A) = {r | < r, C > is in Relationship Set of A}

Based on the above sets, the GSN model D is derived by the following steps. The root goal can simply be developed such that ArchiMate model A satisfies dependability principles. The second level goals are derived by Concept and Relationship. The third level goals are derived by using Concept Category(A) and Relationship Category(A). The fourth level goals are derived by using Concept Instance(C, A) and Relationship Instance(C, A). Fifth level goals are derived by analyzing instance risks. The derivation shall be conducted by eliciting risks for each instance element of A.

The assurance case decomposition hierarchy in Table 2 for ArchiMate can be constructed by the above method. The steps of the method show the systematic assurance case derivation procedure from an ArchiMate model.

4   Example Study

The example study was conducted to evaluate the effectiveness of the proposed assurance case pattern for a realistic business application named Driving Diagnosis Service.

4.1   Driving Diagnosis Service

A gasoline sales company provides a driving diagnosis service to support safe driving by the analysis of car driving information with a cloud service. The on-board car devices gather all the information such as the number of immediate slowdowns, idling time, and the quantity of injection. When a car enters the gas station and stops the engine, the on-board device sends the car driving information to the communication device at the gas station by using a wireless network. When the car driving information is sent to the cloud server through the network from the communication device at the gas station, the driving diagnosis service analyzes the car driving information and provides the driving report to the drivers through smart phones.

The service can make a precise decision on the quality of the car driving technique of drivers. The gasoline sales company provides motor vehicle insurance that varies the payment according to the driving technique levels by collaborating with an insurance company.

4.2   BA in ArchiMate

The business architecture of DDS (Driving Diagnosis Service) described in ArchiMate is shown in Fig. 2. The figure shows an application process of the driving diagnosis insurance service. The process is initiated by an event of the application of DDS by a driver.

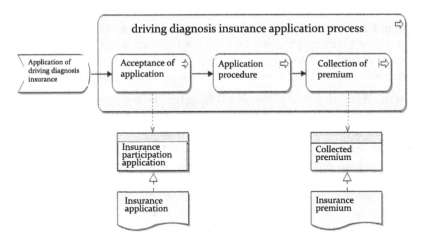

Fig. 2. Business architecture example of DDS

The assurance cases derived for the BA in Fig. 2 by using the above assurance case pattern are shown in Figs. 3, 4, and 5. Figure 3 shows the top level assurance case for assuring DDS. The top level assurance case decomposes the top level goal into two sub-goals, G_2 "process elements are dependable," and G_3 "relationships among process elements are dependable."

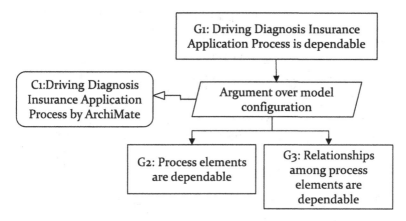

Fig. 3. Top level assurance case for BA

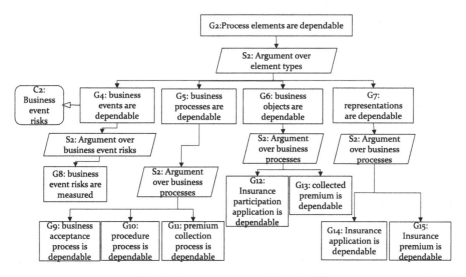

Fig. 4. Assurance case sub-tree for G2

Figures 4 and 5 are assurance cases for G_2 and G_3, respectively. In Figs. 4 and 5, risks and evidence are omitted for simplicity.

5   Discussion

In this section, we discuss on the effectiveness, applicability, generality, and limitations of the proposed method.

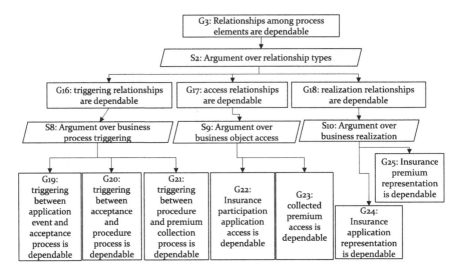

Fig. 5. Assurance case sub tree for G3

5.1 Effectiveness

The case study on the DDS was executed to evaluate the effectiveness of the derivation method proposed in Sect. 3. The result showed the derivation from the BA for DDS in ArchiMate to assurance case is easy and traceable. This showed the effectiveness of the derivation method. Although the derivation was only described for BA, it is clear the same results can be derived for AA and TA of DDS.

5.2 Applicability

The applicability of the derivation pattern from ArchiMate to assurance case is also clear by the above discussions. The proposed derivation pattern can be applicable for BA, AA, and TA described in ArchiMate. Any architectures in ArchiMate contain elements and relationships among elements. Therefore, the decomposition hierarchy defined by Table 2 can be applied to AA and TA models of ArchiMate.

5.3 Generality

The proposed method to derive assurance cases from ArchiMate described in Sect. 3 can be extended to any models represented in graph structures. Every graph G can be represented by nodes and relationships among nodes. Nodes and their relationships may have categories. It is necessary to validate every instance of nodes and relationships according to the sort of categories, if we validate the G.

For example, GSN can be described by a graph structure. GSN nodes are categorized into claim, context, strategy, and evidence nodes. GSN relationships are also categorized into claim-context, strategy-context, strategy-claim, and claim-evidence relationships. An assurance case pattern for assuring the validity of GSN descriptions can be derived by the method in Sect. 3, as shown in Fig. 6.

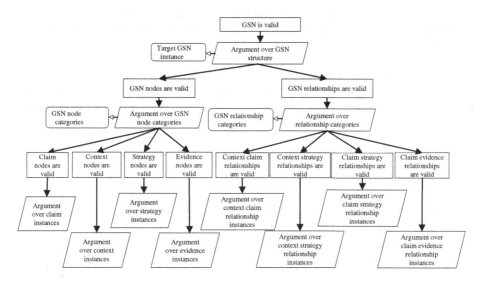

Fig. 6. Assurance case for GSN

The pattern example omits claims and evidence for validating each instance of nodes and relationships of GSN descriptions. The GSN pattern can be used to validate GSN descriptions. The example shows the generality of the derivation method proposed in Sect. 3. It is obvious that the derivation method can be applied to any model represented by graphs, such as UML and BPMN.

5.4 Limitations

This paper only examines the effectiveness of the proposed method for a simple example architecture described by ArchiMate. More evaluations are necessary to validate the proposed method. This paper only examines the B phase of AADM for the applicability of the proposed method, although the method can be applied to phases C and D. Other AADM phases shall also be evaluated.

6 Conclusion

In this paper, an assurance case pattern is proposed to derive the argument decomposition structure from ArchiMate models. The method solves O-DA issues for assuring business, application, and technology architecture of TOGAF. An example case study using the proposed pattern is also shown for the Driving Diagnosis Service in the insurance domain.

Discussions based on the case study showed the effectiveness and appropriateness of the proposed methods. The proposed method can resolve the issues of B, C, and D in Table 1.

Future work includes the formalization of assurance case derivation process from ArchiMate models and the development of solutions for the issues other than B, C, and D in Table 1.

Acknowledgment. This work was supported by KAKENHI (24220001). This work has been conducted as a part of "Research Initiative on Advanced Software Engineering in 2015" supported by Software Reliability Enhancement Center (SEC), Information Technology Promotion Agency Japan (IPA).

References

1. Kelly, T.: A Six-Step Method for the Development of Goal Structures, York Software Engineering (1997)
2. Kelly, T., McDermid, J.: Safety Case Construction and Reuse using Patterns. In: Daniel, P. (ed.) Safe Comp 97, pp. 55–69. University of York, New York (1997)
3. Kelly, T.: Arguing safety: a systematic approach to managing safety cases, Ph.D thesis, Department of Computer Science, University of York (1998)
4. McDermid, J.: Software safety: where's the evidence? In: SCS 2001: Proceedings of the Sixth Australian workshop on Safety critical systems and software, pp. 1–6. Australian Computer Society, Inc., Darlinghurst, Australia (2001)
5. Kelly, T., Weaver, R.: The goal structuring notation – a safety argument notation. In: Proceedings of the Dependable Systems and Networks 2004 Workshop on Assurance Cases (2004)
6. Bloomfield, R., Bishop, P.: Safety and assurance cases: past, present and possible. In: Future, Safety Critical Systems Symposium, pp. 9–11, Bristol, UK (2010)
7. Despotou, G., Kelly, T.: Extending the concept of safety cases to address dependability. In: proceedings of the 22nd International System Safety Conference (ISSC), Providence, RI USA (2004)
8. Hauge, A.A., Stølen, K.: A pattern-based method for safe control systems exemplified within nuclear power production. In: Ortmeier, F., Lipaczewski, M. (eds.) SAFECOMP 2012. LNCS, vol. 7612, pp. 13–24. Springer, Heidelberg (2012)
9. Wardziński, A.: Safety Assurance Strategies for Autonomous Vehicles. In: Harrison, M.D., Sujan, M.-A. (eds.) SAFECOMP 2008. LNCS, vol. 5219, pp. 277–290. Springer, Heidelberg (2008)
10. Yamamoto, S., Matsuno, Y.: An evaluation of argument patterns to reduce pitfalls of applying Assurance Case. In: ASSURE 2013 (2013)
11. Alexander, R., Kelly, T., Kurd, Z., McDermid, J.: Safety cases for advanced control software: safety case patterns, Technical report, University of York (2007)
12. Graydon, P.J., Kelly, T.P.: Assessing software interference management when modifying safety-related software. In: Ortmeier, F., Daniel, P. (eds.) SAFECOMP Workshops 2012. LNCS, vol. 7613, pp. 132–145. Springer, Heidelberg (2012)
13. Ruiz, A., Habli, I., Espinoza, H.: Towards a case-based reasoning approach for safety assurance reuse. In: Ortmeier, F., Daniel, P. (eds.) SAFECOMP Workshops 2012. LNCS, vol. 7613, pp. 22–35. Springer, Heidelberg (2012)

14. Denney, E., Pai, G., Pohl, J.: AdvoCATE: an assurance case automation toolset. In: Ortmeier, F., Daniel, P. (eds.) SAFECOMP Workshops 2012. LNCS, vol. 7613, pp. 8–21. Springer, Heidelberg (2012)
15. Hawkins, R., Habli, I., Kolovos, D., Paige, R., Kelly, T.: Weaving an assurance case from design: a model-based approach. In: HASE 2015, pp. 110–117 (2015)
16. Gallina, B., Gallucci, A., Lundqvist, K., Nyberg, M.: VROOM & cC: a method to build safety cases for ISO 26262-compliant product lines. In: SAFECOMP 2013 (2013)
17. Lin, C.L.: Applying safety case pattern to generate assurance cases for safety-critical systems. In: HASE2015, pp. 255 – 262 (2015)
18. Bate, I., Kelly, T.: Architectural considerations in the certification of modular systems. Reliab. Eng. Syst. Saf. **81**, 303–324 (2003)
19. Yamamoto, S., Matsuno, Y.: d* framework: Inter-Dependency Model for Dependability, DSN 2012 (2012)
20. Saruwatari, T., Yamamoto, S.: Definition and application of an assurance case development method (d*). Springer Plus 2.1. **4**(6), 1–8 (2013)
21. Saruwatari, T., Yamamoto, S., Matsuno, Y.: A comparative study of d*framework and GSN, ISSRE2013, pp. 315–320 (2013)
22. Jackson, D., et al., Software for dependable systems– sufficient evidence?, National Research Council (2008)
23. DEOS project (2013). http://www.crest-os.jst.go.jp
24. DEOS project, JST White Paper DEOS-FY2011-WP-03 (2011). www.dependable-os.net/ja/topics/file/White_Paper_V3.0J.pdf
25. Tokoro, M.: Open Systems Dependability: Dependability Engineering for Ever-Changing Systems. CRC Press, Boca Raton (2012)
26. Real-Time and Embedded Systems, Dependability through Assuredness™ (O-DA) Framework, Open Group Standard (2013)
27. Josely, A., et al.: TOGAF® Version 9.1 A Pocket Guide. Van Haren, Zaltbommel (2011)
28. Josely, A., et al.: ArchiMate®2.0: A Pocket Guide, The Open Group. Van Haren8 Publishing, Zaltbommel (2013)

Tool Support for Assurance Case Building Blocks

Providing a Helping Hand with CAE

Kateryna Netkachova[1,2(✉)], Oleksandr Netkachov[1,2], and Robin Bloomfield[1,2]

[1] Centre for Software Reliability, City University London, London, UK
{Kateryna.Netkachova.2,
Oleksandr.Netkachov,R.E.Bloomfield}@city.ac.uk
[2] Adelard LLP, London, UK
{kn,reb}@adelard.com

Abstract. This paper presents a tool for structuring arguments in assurance cases. The tool is designed to support the methodology of Claims-Arguments-Evidence (CAE) Building Blocks that provides a series of archetypal CAE fragments to help structure cases more formally and systematically. It assists with the development and maintenance of structured assurance cases by providing facilities to manage CAE blocks and partially automate the generation of claim structures. In addition to the tool, new visual guidelines called "Helping hand" is provided to assist in applying the building blocks. The tool has been implemented on the Adelard ASCE platform. The target users are assurance case developers and reviewers. The tool and associated methodology can also be useful for people learning how to structure cases in a more rigorous and systematic manner.

Keywords: Claims · Argument · Evidence · CAE building blocks · Helping hand · ASCE tool · Support

1 Introduction

Over the past ten years there has been a trend towards an explicit claim-based approach to safety justification and considerable work has been done on developing and structuring assurance cases [1–3]. However, the practice of how to structure and present cases is very varied. There are lots of different styles with different expressiveness and these many approaches make it difficult to compare cases and hard to provide a more rigorous semantics. To address these issues and provide a more rigorous approach to architecting cases, we have defined specific rules that restrict the type of argument structures and developed a collection of building blocks for assurance cases that help construct cases more formally and systematically [4].

During the development of CAE building blocks, we reviewed a wide range of cases from the defence, medical, financial and nuclear sector and the proposed set of building blocks were able to capture most of what was being expressed. We wish to deploy these CAE building blocks, evaluating their use and improving the methodology.

F. Koornneef and C. van Gulijk (Eds.): SAFECOMP 2015 Workshops, LNCS 9338, pp. 62–71, 2015.
DOI: 10.1007/978-3-319-24249-1_6

The tool presented in this paper is designed to aid the research and practice of developing structured formal and semi-formal assurance cases. There are other products [5, 6] available to assist in the structured assurance case development. What makes our tool unique is support for the CAE blocks as self-contained reusable configurable components. It is a purpose-built tool designed specifically for the building blocks methodology, therefore, it was essential to integrate it with a widely-used assurance case software to make an impact. We implemented it on top of ASCE [7], which is a market-leading tool for the development and maintenance of assurance cases across a wide range of industries. ASCE is a commercial product but it is available free of charge for academic research purposes.

The paper is structured in the following way. The concept of CAE building blocks needed to understand the idea and a new "helping hand" guidance are introduced in Sect. 2. The software tool, which is the main focus of the paper, along with its technical information and implementation details are described in Sect. 3. Some early experience with the tool and the future directions of work are outlined in Sect. 4.

2   CAE Building Blocks and the "Helping Hand"

2.1   Building Blocks Concept

CAE building blocks are a series of archetypal CAE fragments, derived from an empirical analysis of real cases in various domains. They are created using a standardised structure for combining CAE and are part of a stack of resources that we are developing to support authors of assurance cases. These resources comprise the basic concepts of claims, argument, evidence; building blocks with a set of specific CAE structures; templates created out of the blocks to address particular classes of problems, and the overall assurance case created using blocks and templates. The stack of CAE resources is shown in Fig. 1, where arrows indicate the instantiation of elements to produce an assurance case. The approach can be extended to support GSN notation [3] as well. In that case, GSN elements will be used instead of CAE and GSN patterns will be constructed out of the building blocks in a similar way as the CAE templates. This extension will be implemented in due course.

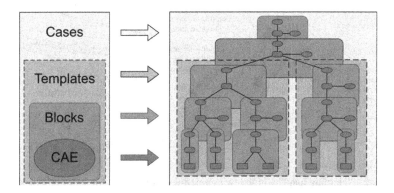

Fig. 1. Schematic of the stack of CAE resources (left) instantiated into a specific case (right)

The block structure contains enhancements to the classical CAE approach [1, 2]. One enhancement is to how arguments are addressed: a special side-warrant element is introduced to explain and assist in a structured way whether the top-level claim can be deduced from the subclaims and under which circumstances the argument is valid. The five basic CAE building blocks that we have identified are:

- Decomposition – partitions some aspect of the claim
- Substitution – refines a claim about an object into another claim about an equivalent object
- Concretion – gives a more precise definition to some aspect of the claim
- Calculation or proof – used when some value of the claim can be computed or proved
- Evidence incorporation – incorporates evidence that directly supports the claim

The summary and the structure of these basic block are provided in the Appendix A. Additional information and guidance can be found in the paper [4].

2.2 "Helping Hand" for CAE Building Blocks

In order to support the teaching and deployment of CAE Building Blocks, we have created a visual guidance shown in Fig. 2. We call it a "helping hand" as it is designed to help people structure assurance cases in an easier and more intuitive way by providing a "cheat sheet" on a hand with some hints and questions to answer. Instead of wondering what to do next and how to better expand the case, this approach shifts the question to an easier one: "which block is best to use?" and helps to find the answer by following the provided guidance.

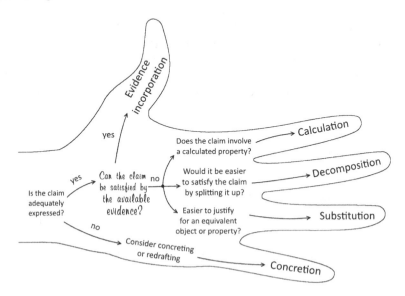

Fig. 2. "Helping hand" – high level guidelines for applying the building blocks

3 Tool Description

The main focus of this paper is on the software tool that assists in using CAE building blocks within the existing assurance case development processes. The tool we have developed provides facilities for creating and managing block-based argumentation to help create more formal, structured and maintainable assurance cases.

The usage of CAE Building Blocks is not isolated and in order to be effective our tool should be integrated with the current processes and other tools used for the creation and management of cases. To address this, we implemented it on top of the ASCE platform, which is a widely-used powerful graphical and narrative hypertext tool for the development, review and maintenance of assurance cases. The detailed description of the ASCE tool can be found in the help file [8]. Below we only highlight the features of ASCE that are used by our tool and needed to understand the rest of the paper.

- Graphical editor for creating and arranging arguments
- Support for different notations, including CAE
- A content editor for editing the narrative content of nodes in a HTML format
- Functionality to validate the resulting network against the logical constraints of the notation being used
- Extensibility allowing support for specific applications and integration with other technologies

The extensibility feature is particularly important for us as it is used to incorporate our tool into the existing ASCE environment. The integration is performed through the use of the ASCE mechanism of plugins and a customised "schema" file.

Therefore, the implementation of the tool involved two major activities: supporting the Building Blocks methodology and integrating it into the ASCE tool. Each of them is described in Sects. 3.1 and 3.2 below. The interaction between ASCE and both parts of our tool is schematically shown in the sequence diagram provided in Fig. 3.

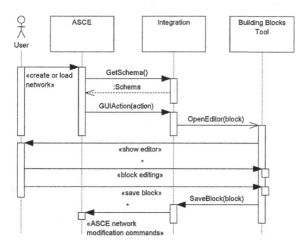

Fig. 3. Interaction sequence diagram

3.1 Tool Support for CAE Building Blocks

The Building Blocks tool is developed as a DHTML application. The graphical user interface (GUI) components are created using HTML5, CSS3 and JavaScript. The structure of the GUI controls follows the Model-View-Controller architectural pattern: every control has a model containing its internal state, HTML view reacting to any changes of that model and controllers reacting to the user events and modifying the model based on them. Examples of the GUI for the decomposition and concretion blocks are provided in Fig. 4.

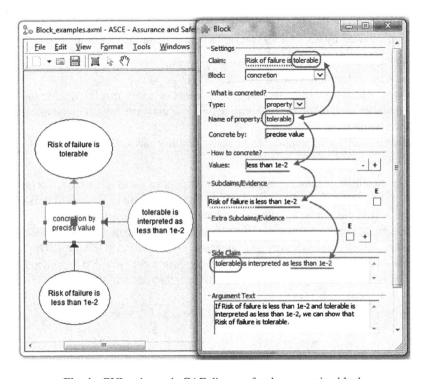

Fig. 4. GUI and sample CAE diagram for the concretion block

Most of the fields are completed automatically to save the user unnecessary typing. For example, the top claim is parsed to locate the name of the object. As soon as the values are completed, the subclaims titles, argument and side-warrant text are generated. One of the design choices we made is the ability to grade the formality, e.g. the side-warrant can be formulated informally or it can be generated by the tool in a more formal way (math based side-warrant). All the inputs are editable and the users are free to alter the text of the subclaims, side-warrants, etc. the way they want. The OK button at the bottom of the dialog is used to apply the block. Of course, it is not a one way write as the tool supports the evolution of CAE structures. If the users decide to change their minds and delete or modify the nodes, this is reflected back in the tool. In that case the automatically created text is regenerated, while any custom modifications are preserved (no user data is lost). A sample CAE structure and the tool GUI with dependencies between auto-generated text values shown in red are provided in Fig. 4.

In terms of the implementation details, the following JavaScript libraries are used by the GUI components: jQuery for DOM querying and manipulating, Backbone for implementing the Observer pattern, Lo-Dash for general-purpose object model queries. The standard HTML controls such as inputs and checkboxes are wrapped by the MVC triads to keep GUI control set consistent. In addition to those wrappers, there are custom application-specific controls, such as ListControl, which iterates over the collection of items, rendering each of them into an independent row. The class diagram for the tool is provided in Fig. 5.

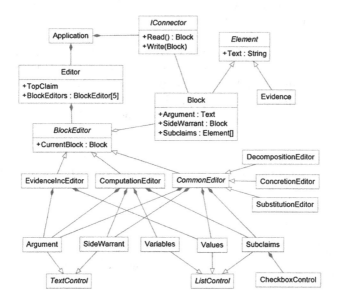

Fig. 5. UML class diagram for the tool

All classes of the tool are grouped into three main packages:

- Block model - classes that represent Block elements
- GUI - user-interaction controls and Block editors, constructed from these controls
- Application engine - manages instantiation of Block editors, contains dependency injection points for connector used for the integration with ASCE

The classes representing CAE Building Block elements (claims, argument, side-warrant etc.) and links are included in the Block model package. This package also contains rules for checking whether the model is well-formed by following the rules of the CAE normal form, specifically:

- Claim nodes may only be connected to argument nodes
- Argument nodes may only be connected to claim and evidence nodes
- Each argument node may only have one outbound link to a claim node

- Each claim is to be supported by only one argument
- Argument nodes must be supported by at least one subclaim or evidence node
- Evidence nodes represent the bottom of the safety argument and are not supported
- A claim, subclaim or evidence may support more than one argument

All modules within the packages conform to the CommonJS Modules specification. To load these modules the execution environment should contain the implementation of the CommonJS "require" function. The next section describes the integration part, where this function is implemented by using the Windows Scripting Host components.

3.2 Integration with ASCE

The extensible architecture of ASCE allows users to implement new features on top of the core functionality of ASCE using additional schemas and plugins. The developer documentation is freely available and can be found at [9, 10]. Basically, ASCE plugins are written as XML files which contain a mixture of configuration information, user interface and code. The recommended approach is to use HTML forms with event handlers created in one of the Windows Scripting compatible languages (VBScript or JScript). The GUI approach used for our tool is suitable for this type of integration, so we implemented the tool as an ASCE plugin that runs in the Web browser component. The two major integration tasks we had to solve involved:

1. *Implementation of CommonJS API in the plugin using Windows Scripting Components*: As was mentioned above, ASCE uses Windows Scripting while our tool is

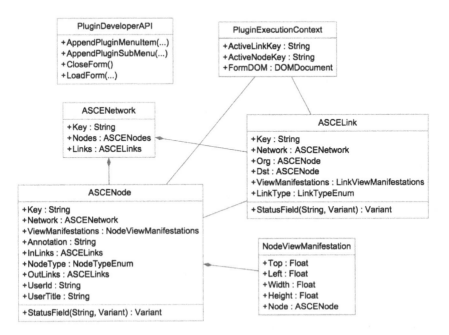

Fig. 6. Class diagram showing ASCE COM components

built using CommonJS architecture. In order to use CommonJS with ASCE, we had to implement CommonJS interfaces using objects available in Windows Scripting.

2. *Implementation of the converter between the object models of the building blocks and ASCE*: Specific classes of the ASCE tool that are used by the converter are shown in the Fig. 6.

Additionally, we also created a new ASCE schema file with a few custom node properties used to store the block settings.

4   Conclusions and Future Directions

In this paper we have presented a software tool for structuring assurance cases using CAE Building Blocks. The tool is integrated in the ASCE environment through the use of additional schemas and plugins. Additionally, we have introduced a high level guidance – a "helping hand" – to assist in the case structuring process. The tool and the methodology are going through a progressive, iterative approach to deployment and will continue to evolve. At the moment, CAE notation forms the basic blocks of the approach. However, it can be extended to other graphical and tabular notations and their tool support in the future.

We have already deployed the prototype tool and the methodology on a number of projects. Some of the completed tasks include drafting of guidance for the IAEA on the assessment of dependability of nuclear I&C systems important for safety, drafting of templates for arguing about statistical testing as part of the EU Harmonics project, developing cases to address probabilistic modelling of critical infrastructure and particular how one addresses model doubt. We have also used CAE Blocks on a professional Masters level course at City University London on Information Security and Risk in an Assurance Case module.

The experience to date has shown the utility of the building blocks. However, there is more research and development to be done. For example, we need to explore composition of blocks into reusable domain-specific fragments or patterns, using GSN notation elements [3] and a related formal basis [11]. We also plan on looking into links to challenge and review checklists generated from the blocks, enhancing the default evidence incorporation block to be a composite block for trusted evidence and providing more support for the formal aspects of assurance cases. This is a very active and growing area with a number of research trends on argumentation, confidence and model based approaches and we plan to continue our research in this direction. In addition we will reflect on how the experience of CAE Blocks can further support Assurance Case workflows as well as what impact they might have on standardisation activities.

Acknowledgement. We acknowledge support from the Artemis JU SESAMO project (number 295354) and the UK EPSRC funded Communicating and Evaluating Cyber Risk and Dependencies (CEDRICS) project which is part of the UK Research Institute in Trustworthy Industrial Control Systems (RITICS).

A Appendix Basic Building Blocks for Assurance Casesf

Structure	Description
	Decomposition block This block is used to claim that a conclusion about the whole object or property can be deduced from the claims or facts about constituent parts.
	Substitution block This block is used when a claim needs to be given a more precise definition or interpretation. The top claim *P(X, Cn, En)* can be replaced with a more precise or defined claim *P1(X1, Cn, En)*, *Cn* and *En* are configuration and environment.
	Concretion block This block is used when a claim needs to be given a more precise definition or interpretation. The top claim *P(X, Cn, En)* can be replaced with a more precise or defined claim *P1(X1, Cn, En)*, *Cn* and *En* are configuration and environment.
	Calculation block This block is used to claim that the value of a property of a system can be computed from the values of related properties of other objects. Show that the value *b* of property *Q(X, b, E, C)* of system *X* in env *E* and conf *C* can be calculated from values $Q_1(X_1,a_1,E,C),Q_2(X_2,a_2,E,C),....,Q_n(X_n,a_n,E,C)$
	Evidence incorporation block This block is used to incorporate evidence elements into the case. A typical application of this block is at the edge of a case tree where a claim is shown to be directly satisfied by its supporting evidence.

References

1. ISO/IEC 15026-2: Systems and software engineering – Systems and software assurance – Part 2: Assurance case (2011)
2. Bishop, P.G., Bloomfield, R.E.: A methodology for safety case development. In: Safety-critical Systems Symposium 98, Birmingham, UK, February 1998, ISBN 3-540-76189-6
3. Kelly, T.: The goal structuring notation-a safety argument notation. In: Proceedings of the DSN 2004 Workshop on Assurance Cases (2004)
4. Bloomfield, R.E., Netkachova, K.: Building blocks for assurance cases. In: IEEE International Symposium on Software Reliability Engineering Workshops (ISSREW), pp. 186–191 (2014). doi:10.1109/ISSREW.2014.72
5. Denney, E., Pai, G., Pohl, J.: AdvoCATE: an assurance case automation toolset. In: Ortmeier, F., Daniel, P. (eds.) SAFECOMP Workshops 2012. LNCS, vol. 7613, pp. 8–21. Springer, Heidelberg (2012)
6. Aiello, M., Hocking, A., Knight, J., Rowanhill, J.: SCT: a safety case toolkit. In: IEEE International Symposium on Software Reliability Engineering Workshops (ISSREW), pp. 216–219 (2014). doi:10.1109/ISSREW.2014.99
7. Adelard LLP: Assurance and Safety Case Environment (ASCE), Accessed 29 June 2015. http://www.adelard.com/asce/
8. Adelard LLP, Assurance and Safety Case Environment (ASCE) Help File, Accessed 29 June 2015. http://www.adelard.com/asce/
9. Emmet, L.: Introduction to plugin and schema development for ASCE, Accessed: 29 June 2015. http://www.adelard.com/asce/plugins/developer-documentation/4.1/w1873v01c_ASCE_v4_plugin_API_docs.doc
10. Emmet, L.: API documentation for ASCE v4.1, Accessed 29 June 2015. http://www.adelard.com/asce/plugins/developer-documentation/4.1/w2082v02a_ASCE_plugin_developer_documentation.doc
11. Denney, E., Pai, G.: A formal basis for safety case patterns. In: Bitsch, F., Guiochet, J., Kaâniche, M. (eds.) SAFECOMP. LNCS, vol. 8153, pp. 21–32. Springer, Heidelberg (2013)

Safety.Lab: Model-Based Domain Specific Tooling for Safety Argumentation

Daniel Ratiu, Marc Zeller$^{(\boxtimes)}$, and Lennart Killian

Siemens Corporate Technology, Munich, Germany
{daniel.ratiu,marc.zeller,lennart.killian}@siemens.com

Abstract. Assurance cases capture the argumentation that a system is safe by putting together pieces of evidence at different levels of abstraction and of different nature. Managing the interdependencies between these artefacts lies at the heart of any safety argument. Keeping the assurance case complete and consistent with the system is a manual and very ressource consuming process. Current tools do not address these challenges in constructing and maintaining safety arguments. In this paper we present a tooling prototype called Safety.Lab which features rich and deeply integrated models to describe requirements, hazards list, fault trees and architecture. We show how Safety.Lab opens opportunities to automate completeness and consistency checks for safety argumentation.

Keywords: Model driven engineering · Safety-critical systems · Assurance cases · Tooling

1 Introduction

Product based safety argumentation needs a holistic view over the system and links heterogeneous artefacts from different development stages (requirements specification, system design, implementation, verification & validation) [15]. In the current practice, these artefacts are maintained in different heterogeneous and loosely integrated tools if at all. The content of referenced artefacts from within the argumentation is opaque and the references are only at a high granularity level, e.g. entire documents (see Fig. 1-left).

Developing assurance cases is not new, but is still imature in industrial practice [2]. Building assurance cases is entirely manual and with low tool support. Checking that the safety argumentation is complete and consistent with the system model is expensive and mostly a manual process done through reviews. Moreover, the costs are amplified during the evolution of the system when the safety argumentation needs to be evolved in order to keep up with the changes.

Model-based engineering promotes the use of models in all development phases from requirements to code and deployment. This means that adequate and rich models are used to describe different aspects of the system. Rich models spanning various abstraction levels of dependable systems allow to precisely define the interdependancies of the model artefacts on different level concerning

© Springer International Publishing Switzerland 2015
F. Koornneef and C. van Gulijk (Eds.): SAFECOMP 2015 Workshops, LNCS 9338, pp. 72–82, 2015.
DOI: 10.1007/978-3-319-24249-1_7

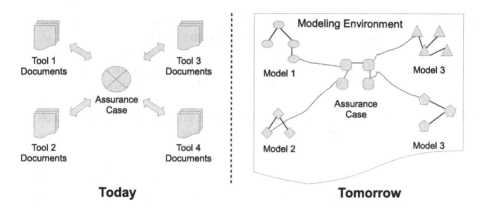

Fig. 1. Safety argumentation is today (left) coarse granular, based on documents managed by different tools. This limits the automation opportunities in building, quality assuring and reviewing assurance cases. Model-based safety argumentation (right) puts together fine granular elements of deep models. This increases the automation and enables advanced consistency checks.

a particular safety feature. Tracing these interdependencies through the model as well as the development process lies at the heart of any safety argument. Such models ease the development, increase the quality and enable a systematic reuse. This opens new possibilities to build and maintain assurance cases which involve different disciplines and directly reference fine granular model elements (see Fig. 1-right). Furthermore, having a deep integration of artefacts in a tool, eases the development and verification of assurance cases by increasing automation for building models and continuously checking their consistency.

However, in industrial practice model-based development is currently only applied to isolated sub-systems (e.g. model-based testing or software modules). The overall system development and safety assessment are mainly based on multiple specification and analysis documents. *Our long term goal is to move away from documents-based development and analysis of safety critical systems to a model-based world in which semantically rich models are used to describe the system characteristics in an appropriate manner.*

In this paper, we present our experiments to build a model-based tool that supports development of safety cases and linking them to models developed in early process phases. Based on these deep models we present a set of automatic consistency checks between the safety argument structure and the structure of the models of the developed product.

Language Engineering as Technological Basis: Our work uses language engineering technologies, which refer to defining, extending and composing languages and their integrated development environments (IDEs). Language workbenches [3] are tools that support efficient language engineering. Our implementation relies on the JetBrains MPS[1] language workbench, which, unlike most other language

---

[1] https://www.jetbrains.com/mps/.

workbenches, uses projectional editing. Projectional editing makes it possible to easily combine models defined in different languages and notations [4].

One of the biggest projects developed using this technology is mbeddr [1], a stack of extensible domain specific languages for model driven engineering of embedded systems. Siemens is involved in the mbeddr project by building commercial extensions for controls software development. Our work presented here is part of our investigations on how can we extend the mbeddr technology stack to enable deeply integrated safety engineering.

Structure of this paper: In the next section we present our vision for the next generation of model-based tools for the development of assurance cases for safety critical systems. Subsequently we describe tooling for a set of safety-domain specific modeling languages and how are they integrated in order to achieve a gapless landscape of models. We present how we integrate these languages with requirements, architectural design, and safety analyses in order to provide a holistic view over the safety of the system. We conclude the paper with related work and presenting our plans for future work.

2   Long-Term Vision for Safety Argumentation Tooling

2.1   Use of Rich and Domain Specific Models

The input for safety analyses are models which capture safety relevant characteristics of the system. These models are at different abstraction levels and captured using different notations like text, tables or diagrams. Unfortunately, in practice these models are captured only implicitly in tools providing weak structuring and consistency enforcements mechanisms like spreadsheets in MS Excel, "boxes and lines" drawn in MS Visio or plain natural language text written in MS Word. Hence, constructing and maintaining assurance cases are currently manual tasks which are performed mostly based on documents and with only spare tool support. The structure of artefacts referenced from assurance cases varies from a domain to another. For instance, the certification of trains is different from the certification of cars or medical equipment. Current tools are mostly agnostic with respect to the business domain. Domain specific structures are encoded with the help of modeling conventions if at all.

Safety.Lab targets to use domain specific models in order to fulfill the specific needs of engineers working in specific business units.

2.2   Integration of System Design and Safety Analysis

A lot of safety argumentation relevant information is redundant and replicated across different views, many times in different tools. Common practice today is that weak and high-granular traceability links are present between development artefacts. A deep integration between system design and safety analysis is essential for the development of safety-critical systems because safety conditions such as hazards and failure modes are often an outcome of unintended system functionalities and behaviours in a given environment.

The goal of Safety.Lab is to work with deeply integrated models in which the artefacts are integrated with each other and referenced from the assurance case. Functional system requirements are used as input in safety assessment and this lead to a set of hazards and failure modes that the system needs to deal with. These hazards must be mapped to the design and checked that indeed they are addressed. Thereby, Safety.Lab aims to minimize redundancies between artefacts and avoid inconsistencies in the safety argumentation and between the safety argumentation and the system model.

2.3 Support the Construction of Assurance Cases

Safety assurance documents gather together heterogeneous information from different development stages. A safety case includes the system's safety concept which is build in an early stage of the development and is based as input for further development. During later development stages a variety of evidence is produced (e.g. test cases, FMEA tables, fault trees). This evidence is used to support safety arguments which explain that the system is sufficiently safe.

Safety.Lab takes advantage of the deep models and modern IDE techniques in order to support engineers building the safety cases. Building of safety cases still remains a manual process but with modern IDE support.

2.4 Support the Evolution of Assurance Cases

Systems are evolving due to refinement and modification during the development and consequently the assurance cases must also evolve. Thereby, it must be enforced that changes in the system design lead to proper adaptions in the safety analyses and assurance cases. Before changes are implemented, we need to estimate the impact of such changes on the safety of the system. Performing change impact analysis is currently a manual process and thereby very time-consuming. Many times the costs are so high that changes are avoided and only work-arounds are provided.

Safety.Lab aims to take advantage of rich models and their integration in order to help engineers to keep their models consistent with the assurance case and assess possible inconsistencies due to changes.

3   Safety.Lab

In this section we, present our tool Safety.Lab as a first step towards realizing our long-term vision of a fully model-based construction of critical systems including their assurance cases. Our tool is based on a deeply integrated set of languages that address early phases in the development process for safety critical systems. Our presentation is illustrated with a running example about the braking function of a car.

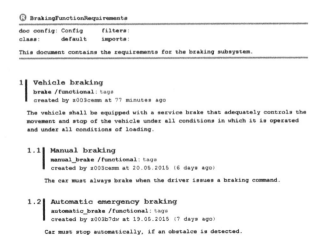

Fig. 2. A fragment of a requirements model.

System-level functional requirements. Functional requirements represent the input in our process and are documented using a domain specific language (DSL) for describing requirements. The requirements DSL integrates natural language text with model fragments [13] (due to the lack of space, we present in this paper only requirements as prose text and simple meta-data). In Fig. 2 we illustrate an example high-level functional requirement about the braking function of a car. The braking function has two sub-functions: manual brakes triggered by the driver and emergency braking triggered by the onboard-computer in case when an obstacle is detected to be too close to the car.

Hazards analysis. The next process step that we support is hazards analysis. Input for the hazards analysis are the functional requirements. In our example, from the set of functional requirements about braking we identify two hazards: unintended braking and braking omission. The set of hazards along with their attributes (severity, controllability, exposure) are captured using a domain specific language with tabular notation. The reference to the functional requirement that is used as basis for the hazards analysis is a first class modeling construct rather than a trace link.

In Fig. 3 we illustrate how Safety.Lab models a list of hazards. The table field "BrakingFunctionRequirements" is a first-class reference to the requirements module which contains the functional requirements of braking function.

High-level safety requirements. Safety requirements are derived based on the hazards analysis. Each hazard leads to one or more safety requirements which are captured using an extension of the requirements DSL. This extension allows each safety requirement to reference the hazard it addresses and contains its integrity level which is automatically derived (based on ISO26262) based on the attributes of the corresponding hazard.

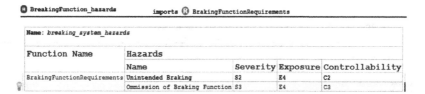

Fig. 3. Hazards list for the braking function

ⓡ BrakingFunctionSafetyRequirements

doc config: Config   filters:
class: default   imports:
Abstract:

1 | **Avoid accident by missing braking function**
braking_function_ommission / safety_req; ASIL D hazard: Ommission of Braking Function: tags
created by z003b7dw at 19.05.2015 (3 months ago)

If human driver intends to brake the car with a force higher than the one computed by the automatic braking, he should
be able to override the automatic braking.

2 | **Avoid unintended braking**
unintended_braking / safety_req; ASIL B hazard: Unintended Braking: tags
created by z003b7dw at 19.05.2015 (3 months ago)

Unintended braking must be avoided.

Fig. 4. Safety requirements example

The safety requirements for our braking example are illustrated in Fig. 4. The hazards analysis lead to two safety requirements for avoiding unintended braking and for preventing accidents caused by missing braking function. These requirements have ASIL B and D.

(Sub-)system architecture. The high-level architecture is used to structure the system such that the requirements can be satisfied. During the design phase the integrated safety analysis helps to find tailored solutions the mitigate threats originating from the relevant failure modes within the system. Architectural decisions are thus motivated by the need to address safety requirements. In our example (Fig. 3), we have two channels to implement the braking functionality - this is required (cf. ISO26262) by the ASIL D of one of our safety requirements (Fig. 5).

Safety analysis. For example, fault trees are used to analyze possible fault propagation at sub-system level that can lead to a hazard on the system level. The fault tree represents a view (propagation of faults between different sub-systems) on the system architecture. In Fig. 6 we illustrate an example of a fault tree for the "ommision of braking" hazard.

Safety Case. Goal Structuring Notation (GSN) [6] is a modeling language for capturing safety arguments. GSN has a diagramatic notation; the safety argument is structured by a set of individual elements (claims, evidence and contextual information) as well as the relationships between these elements

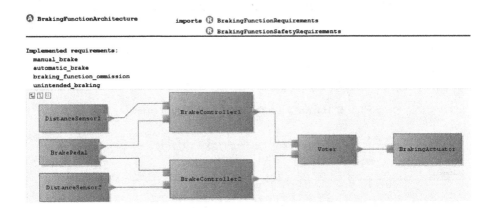

Fig. 5. Braking subsystem architecture. This particular architecture is motivated by the requirements which are directly referenced.

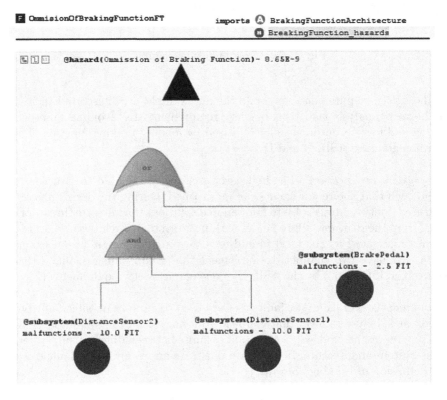

Fig. 6. Example of propagation of faults accross different subsystems. The subsystems are directly referenced as sources for the basic events. The top event is dirrectly linked to one of the hazards.

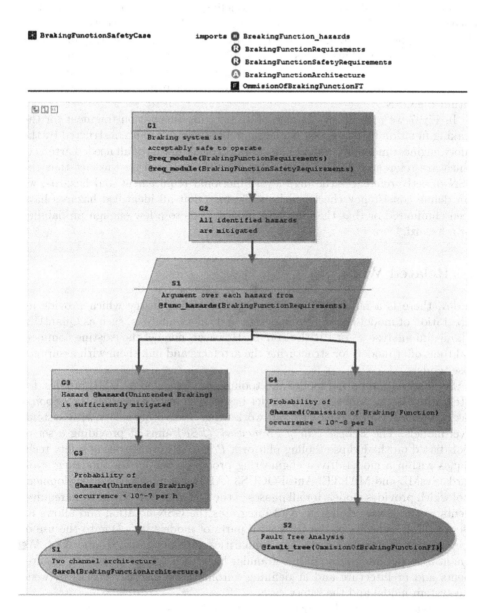

Fig. 7. Each element of the GSN directly references elements from the system model. Thereby, navigating between argumentation and the system model is directly supported. Furthermore, when the system evolves, we can increase the automation of consistency checks that the argumentation is consistent with the implemented changes.

(i.e. how claims are supported by other claims and by evidences). From the point of view of Safety.Lab, GSN is another modeling language whose elements reference other models from the modeling environment. A GSN represents a view over the system under development which summarizes information already present in the product model. This opens the possibility to define advanced consistency checks for the entire model since the structure of the GSN should be consistent with the structure of the product models whose elements are referenced from within the GSN.

In Fig. 7 we present an example of a safety argumentation fragment for the braking function by using a GSN diagram. This safety case is constructed by the safety engineer manually. Safety.Lab supports deep linking of all needed artefacts which are referenced by the safety argumentation. Based on the fact that the GSN directly references the high-level functional requirement and hazards, we can define consistency checks such as the fact that all identified hazards have been eliminated or that the fault tree indeed leads to a low enough probability for a hazard.

4 Related Work

Today, there is a number of tools in research and industry which provide an integration of model-based system design and safety analysis, such as QuantUM [7], medini analyze [8] or PREEvison [9]. However, none of the existing commercial tools offer models for structuring the artefacts and link them with assurance case models.

Sophia is a conceptual model and tooling, implemented as UML profiles, for integrating safety analyses with model based systems engineering [12]. Sophia has substantial overlapping with our work when integrating safety with system-level models. The *Eclipse Safety Framework (ESF)* aims at providing a set of tools based on the Eclipse tooling platform *PolarSys* for integrating safety techniques within a model-driven engineering process based on the modeling standards SysML and MARTE. AutoFOCUS3 (AF3) is a model based development tool which provides models for all phases of the system development from requirements to the low-level design. AF3 integrates the GSN notation and allows its users to link elements of the GSN with parts of models [14]. Due to the use of deep models, Safety.Lab has many similarities with Sophia, ESF and AF3. We aim at a deeper integration of fine granular hazards list, fault trees with requirements and architecture and at defining automatic consistency checks between the system model and the safety case.

Various large research project aim at delivering a tooling environment for the model-based development of safety-critical systems. For instance, the CHESS environment the SafeCer tools framework [11], the OPENCOSS platform [10]. Since all these tools are results of research projects only parts of the developed concepts are actually implemented.

A different approach for the model-based development of assurance cases is presented in [5]. In this approach, a weaving model is used, which allows integration between assurance case, design and process models, in order to automatically generate assurance cases. However, a tool to support this approach is not presented yet. Furthermore, Safety.Lab is focused on deep integration of artefacts as basis for advanced consistency checks. Assurance cases are manually created and linked to other artefacts and not automatically generated.

5   Conclusion and Future Work

Our long term goal is to get a holistic and deeply integrated product model that allows mechanized reasoning about safety qualities of software intensive systems. We use models to describe the system across several abstraction layers and to model the safety aspects of the system. In our vision, the safety arguments models will put together fine granular model elements from the system. In this way, the consistency and completeness of safety cases can be checked automatically by using the information from within development models.

In the future, we plan to work along three directions. Firstly, to extend Safety.Lab in the direction of mbeddr and link safety arguments with code modules or tests. Secondly, we plan to evaluate our tooling with real-world projects from the Siemens business units. Thirdly, we plan to investigate the use of richer models (e.g. state machines, contracts) in order to capture the semantics of requirements and of other artefacts.

References

1. Voelter, M., Ratiu, D., Kolb, B., Schaetz B.: mbeddr: Instantiating a Language Workbench in the Embedded Systems Domain. J. Autom. Softw. Eng. **20**(3), 339–390 (2013)
2. Langari, Z., Maibaum, T.: Safety cases: a review of challenges. In: International Workshop on Assurance Cases for Software-intensive Systems (2013)
3. Fowler, M.: Language Workbenches: The Killer-App for Domain Specific Languages? (2005). http://www.martinfowler.com/articles/languageWorkbench.html
4. Voelter, M.: Language and IDE modularization and composition with MPS. In: Lämmel, R., Saraiva, J., Visser, J. (eds.) GTTSE 2011. LNCS, vol. 7680, pp. 383–430. Springer, Heidelberg (2013)
5. Kelly, T., Hawkins, R.D., Habli, I., Kolovos, D., Paige, R.F.: Weaving an assurance case from design: a model-based approach. In: 16th IEEE International Symposium on High Assurance Systems Engineering (2015)
6. Kelly, T., Weaver, R.: The goal structuring notationa safety argument notation. In: Workshop on Assurance Cases Dependable Systems and Networks (2004)
7. Beer, A., Kühne, U., Leitner-Fischer, F., Leue, S., Prem, R.: Analysis of an Airport Surveillance Radar using the QuantUM approach, Technical report, University of Konstanz (2012)
8. Kath, O., Schreiner, R., Favaro, J.: Safety, security, and software reuse: a model-based approach. In: 4th International Workshop in Software Reuse and Safety (2012)

9. Adler, N., Hillenbrand, M., Mueller-Glaser, K.D., Metzker, E., Reichmann, C.: Graphically notated fault modeling and safety analysis in the context of electric and electronic architecture development and functional safety. In: 23rd IEEE International Symposium on Rapid System Prototyping (RSP) (2012)

10. OPENCOSS Consortium, Deliverable D3.3, Integrated OPENCOSS platform (2015)

11. SafeCer Consortium, Deliverables D3.1.3, CTF Platform Prototype (2012)

12. Cancila, D., Terrier, F., Belmonte, F., Dubois, H., et al.: SOPHIA: a modeling language for model-based safety engineering. In: 2nd International Workshop On Model Based Architecting and Construction Of Embedded Systems: ACES-MB (2009)

13. Voelter, M., Tomassetti, F.: Requirements as first class citizens. In: Dagstuhl Workshop on Model-based Development of Embedded Systems (2013)

14. Voss, S., and Carlan, C., Schaetz, B., Kelly, T.: Safety case driven model-based systems construction. In: 2nd International Workshop on Emerging Ideas and Trends in Engineering of Cyber-Physical Systems (2013)

15. Panesar-Walawege, R.K., Sabetzadeh, M., Briand, L. Coq, T.: Characterizing the Chain of Evidence for Software Safety Cases: A Conceptual Model Based on the IEC 61508 Standard. In: Third International Conference on Software Testing, Verification and Validation (2010)

A Safety Condition Monitoring System

John Knight[1(✉)], Jonathan Rowanhill[2], and Jian Xiang[1]

[1] Department of Computer Science, University of Virginia, Charlottesville, USA
{jck,jx5c}@virginia.edu
[2] Dependable Computing LLC, Charlottesville, USA
jonathan.rowanhill@dependablecomputing.com

Abstract. In any safety argument, belief in the top-level goal depends upon a variety of assumptions that derive from the system development process, the operating context, and the system itself. If an assumption is false or becomes false at any point during the lifecycle, the rationale for belief in the safety goal might be invalidated and the safety of the associated system compromised. Assurance that assumptions actually hold when they are supposed to is not guaranteed, and so monitoring of assumptions might be required. In this paper, we describe the Safety Condition Monitoring System, a system that permits comprehensive yet flexible monitoring of assumptions throughout the entire lifecycle together with an alert infrastructure that allows tailored responses to violations of assumptions. An emphasis of the paper is the approach used to run-time monitoring of assumptions derived from software where the software cannot be easily changed.

Keywords: Safety argument · Safety assumption · Safety condition monitoring

1 Introduction

The *Comprehensive Lifecycle for Assuring System Safety* (CLASS) is a safety-engineering system lifecycle that extends the Assurance Based Development software concept [1, 2] to the system level. CLASS encompasses system development, approval, maintenance, and decommissioning. An important element of CLASS is a system for *monitoring* safety assumptions. In this paper, we present the overall design of the monitoring system together with details of one complex part of the system, sensor technology for monitoring run-time assumptions in software where the software cannot be easily changed.

The safety analysis that is undertaken when developing a new, safety-critical system is *predictive*. The goal is to provide an estimate of the residual risk that remains as a result of the system's design, the planned operational context, and the planned mission profiles. In classical safety analysis, a variety of techniques are used to provide an estimate of the residual risk and associated variance. For safety-critical systems, decisions about deployment and continued operation are based, in part, on assessment of whether the estimated residual risk value and variance exceed that which is determined to be acceptable.

Inevitably, all safety analyses depend upon expectations about: (a) the system being analyzed, (b) the way that the system was built and approved, and (c) the way that the system will be used. Essentially, *predictions* are made about various aspects of the

© Springer International Publishing Switzerland 2015
F. Koornneef and C. van Gulijk (Eds.): SAFECOMP 2015 Workshops, LNCS 9338, pp. 83–94, 2015.
DOI: 10.1007/978-3-319-24249-1_8

system, and its development and use. Then *assumptions* are made that these predictions are correct. Predications are in areas such as:

- Conduct and reporting of *development processes* and analysis.
- Details of the *context* within which the system will operate, including ranges of input variables.
- Failure *rates* and failure *semantics* of physical and software components.
- *Physical capabilities* such as strengths of elements, wear resistance, and corrosion resistance.
- *Computing capabilities* such as computing rates, data transmission rates, and data generation rates.
- *Human performance* in areas such as operator fault rates and response times.
- *Maintenance* timing and expected application of maintenance procedures.

Assumptions about topics such as these are often stated explicitly in safety arguments or are implied by statements such as operational limitations. Irrespective of the source, all assumptions become part of the rationale for belief in a safety goal. In the event that an assumption is false or becomes false once the system is deployed, the rationale for belief in a goal within a safety argument might be invalidated.

In summary, the effectiveness of any safety-engineering activity, and in particular the effectiveness of CLASS, relies upon two conditions:

- That the detailed lifecycle (development, approval, maintenance, and decommissioning) process activities are conducted as defined.
- That the assumptions used in the safety analysis of the subject system (and therefore the assumptions contained both explicitly and implicitly in the system safety case) are true throughout the lifecycle of the subject system.

These two conditions imply predicates on the activities and state of a system throughout the lifecycle. These predicates must maintain their assumed values, and the role of monitoring is to check the values of the predicates. For purposes of discussion, we refer to these predicates as *lifecycle invariants* or simply as *invariants*.

We note that these invariants are *not* system safety requirements, although violation of an invariant could lead to a system hazard. System safety requirement derive from the need to avoid hazardous states during operation. Invariants derive from the logical basis of the basic safety argument. Leveson [3] and by Habli et al. [4] have presented related ideas.

A fundamental aspect of CLASS is to support selective monitoring of both conditions. The application of monitoring has to be selective in order to control overhead, and has to be adjustable over time to control measurement granularity. Monitoring in CLASS plays two roles:

- *Process Monitoring.* Process monitoring supports monitoring of adherence to the processes and procedures employed throughout the lifecycle.
- *State Monitoring.* State monitoring supports monitoring of adherence to the system state assumptions made about the system artifacts in the lifecycle analysis.

The CLASS Safety Condition Monitoring System (SCMS) implements invariant monitoring and is identical for all invariants; only the platform, the sensors, and the alerts that are used are different. The structure of the system is shown in Fig. 1.

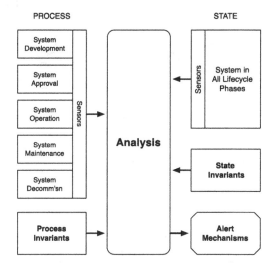

Fig. 1. CLASS safety condition monitoring system

2   Monitoring System Design

Frequently, development environments for safety-critical systems and the systems themselves are distributed, consisting of a number of components operating independently. Each such component often implements more than one service. Such system architectures lead to the need to: (a) monitor a number of different system elements, and (b) to integrate the results of analyses in order to ascertain the state of complex conditions. The monitoring system accommodates this system architecture by operating as a distributed system with the various elements of the system communicating in a manner determined by the structure and details of the invariants being monitored.

As an example, the distributed structure of an SCMS and how the SCMS might be integrated into a simple avionics architecture is shown in Fig. 2. In this example: (a) sensors monitor a variety of applications, (b) predicates local to each application are evaluated, (c) predicates distributed across the applications are evaluated, and (d) data needed elsewhere in the SCMS (other instances) is transmitted as necessary.

The design of the monitoring system is shown Fig. 3. The design assumes that all requisite sensors have been deployed through the relevant environments with which the system has to operate. During development, these environments would include, minimally, asset libraries used in the system's development, the subject system's design and analysis documentation, the process and workflow definitions, and the various assets in use for development. After deployment, these environments would include the system's operational, maintenance, and decommissioning environments.

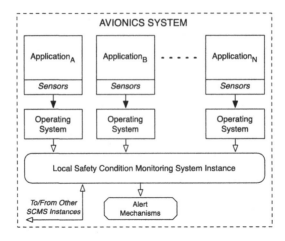

Fig. 2. Example CLASS monitoring system in a hypothetical avionics system.

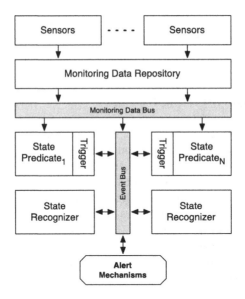

Fig. 3. The monitoring system design

2.1   Event Bus

Central to the design of the monitoring system is the *Event Bus* (see lower center of Fig. 3). The Event Bus accepts event notifications from any part of the monitoring system and delivers those notifications to any destination within the system. The purpose of the Event Bus is to provide a comprehensive, asynchronous notification mechanism. Thus changes sensed within one part of the monitoring system that require action elsewhere result in event generation, transmission, delivery and processing.

2.2 Monitoring Data Repository

Sensor data will arrive at intervals determined by the monitoring system but no polling of sensors is assumed. Separate scheduling and timing control is provided either by the host operating system or the sensors themselves. Sensor data is placed into the *Monitoring Data Repository* as the data becomes available. As appropriate, events are generated by agents within the data repository to signal the availability of sensor data.

Clocks within the system are treated as sensors so that logical timing information is maintained within the Monitoring Data Repository. The passage of time that triggers sensing is made known to the remainder of the monitoring system as necessary by the generation of events.

2.3 State Predicates

The *state predicates* codify the safety conditions, and the monitoring system forms all predicates so that the assumed value is always *true*. Thus, evaluation of a state predicate to false indicates that a safety condition has been violated. State predicates are documented using the standard operators from predicate and propositional logic with data values from the Monitoring Data Repository, including time.

State predicates have to be evaluated when suitable data is available for their evaluation and when evaluation is meaningful. A predicate referred to as a *trigger* controls each state predicate (see Fig. 3). A trigger encodes details such as: (a) arrival of relevant data in the data repository, (b) arrival of time for evaluation, and (c) system state as determined by other state predicates requiring evaluation of the subject state predicate. The evaluation of a state predicate to *false* causes the predicate to generate a *token* that is transmitted to the state recognizers.

2.4 State Recognizers

The *state recognizers* encode the alert semantics that the system stakeholders require for violations of any of the system's invariants. The *state* of interest is any sequence of invariant violations that requires some action. Possible actions include:

- **No Action**. There might be circumstances in which system stakeholders decide that violation of an invariant does not impact the system's safety.
- **Indicate the Violation to a System Operator**. Alerting an operator will allow human intervention should that be indicated for the invariant violation.
- **Change Monitoring Parameters**. Violation of an invariant might be best handled by more extensive or more detailed monitoring of the state. Thus, an action that might be required is adjustment of the parameters controlling a subset of the sensors or adjustment of the trigger(s) for one or more state predicates.
- **Modify the State of the System**. A violation might be sufficiently serious that the preferred response to a violation is to modify the development state or the operating state of the subject system, such as suspending development or shutting down all or part of the system.

- **Record Details of the Violation**. The response to violation of an invariant might depend upon prior violations. To accommodate such sequential actions, a necessary action might be merely to record details of a violation so as to modify the action taken on future violations of invariants.

To deal with the variety of actions that might be required from a state recognizer, the state recognizers are designed as *finite-state machines* and the actions they must take are defined with regular expressions. Inputs to the finite-state machines are the tokens generated by the state predicates. Each token that is generated is supplied to the subset of finite-state machines that have registered an interest in the type of token.

Every action arises from a transition in a finite-state machine and is implemented as an event. Each action event is sent to the required destination.

An example of a simple finite-state machine is shown Fig. 4. The example is for a UAS that has a mission operational restriction of remaining below FL 300 and at speeds less than 200 knots in order to limit exposure of onboard equipment to environmental stress. The safety argument's validity depends upon the assumptions that these limits are respected. Systems analysis has determined that:

- A single violation of either assumption warrants a warning to the UAS operator.
- Two violations of the assumptions during a single mission warrant a warning to the UAS operator and the UAS maintenance engineers.
- A third violation during a single mission requires that the UAS descend and slow down under autonomous control.

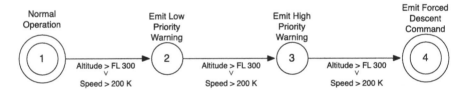

Fig. 4. A monitoring system state recognizer example

The finite-state machine implements these policies. Changes of state of the machine occur as a result of tokens that are generated by the state predicates. The state predicates are defined in terms of the altitude and speed data supplied to the monitoring system by sensors on the aircraft. The triggers for the state predicates are initiated by events generated from the Monitoring Data Repository as new data arrives from the UAS sensors.

3   Sensors

In all lifecycle phases, the necessary monitoring system sensors might have to measure a wide variety of signals with diverse characteristics and respond to demands to start sensing, stop sensing or change the sensing frequency. In this section, we summarize the characteristics of sensors and examine one particularly challenging type of sensor; sensors needed for software systems that cannot be modified easily.

3.1 Sensor Characteristics

The sensors used by the monitoring system in any particular circumstance have to be tailored to the specific application of interest and to the associated invariants. In general, sensors have to cover both periodic and aperiodic measurement, and have to handle a wide range of sampling frequencies, data types and data volumes. All sensors operate with the same basic interface to the associated monitoring repository.

Process invariants are tied closely to:

- **Process** - the various processes used throughout the lifecycle. Processes must be executed as expected if appropriate value is to be obtained.
- **Workflows** - the workflows used by each process. Workflows have to be executed by the expected entity (human, machine, or combination) and in the expected way.
- **Reuse** - the actions associated with use of the asset libraries, such as argument pattern, process pattern, and software libraries. Reuse of assets must be based upon appropriate selection and instantiation.
- **Updates** - updates to the asset libraries. If defects are detected in an asset after the asset has been used, one or more revisions to the subject system's artifacts might be required.

Sensors for process monitoring are merged into the tools and resources used to manage the various process elements. Process templates are defined in the *Business Process Model and Notation* 2 (BPMN2) [5]. BPMN2 is a graphical language that is easily read by humans and is executable on a wide range of common workflow engines. BPMN2 processes consist of activities that must be performed by particular roles and can involve humans or be automated. They follow partially ordered sequences and are often separated by decision points that execute flow control. Process monitoring sensors can be integrated relatively simply into BPMN2 specifications.

State monitoring requires sensors that capture data from the system artifacts and could include state information about development activities, approval activities, operational activities, maintenance activities and so on. Sensed data could be a record of human action as observed by a computer system, details of component failures or performance, calculated values within a software component, etc.

Many, perhaps most, state sensors will be implemented in software, and the sensor implementation will need access to the state so that the requisite data can be captured. As an example of state sensing, in the next section we discuss details of the monitoring system' approach to a particularly difficult type of state sensor, the state of software that cannot be easily modified.

3.2 Sensors and Unmodifiable Software Systems

In general, a sensor that samples data from a software system necessitates the introduction of additional software into the system, i.e., modifying the subject software. Such a modification usually requires access to the subject software's source code and subsequent rebuilding of the system. Modifications of this type might not be desirable, might be inconvenient, or might not be possible for several reasons including:

- **Inaccessible Source Code**. In some cases, the source code of an element of the system software might not be accessible. The source code for reusable libraries and software obtained from independent suppliers is frequently unavailable and so required sensors have to be installed in a different way.
- **Temporary Requirement**. A circumstance might arise in which monitoring an element of the state for which no sensor exists becomes necessary. This situation might arise if, through exceptional circumstances such as an emergency, concern arises that the system might need to operate outside of the planned environment. Introducing a sensing capability without having to modify the source code and rebuild the software is highly desirable in such a case.
- **Change in Data Demand**. Sensors would typically be installed as part of system development, and sensing rates would be determined and set as part of the design. Unplanned changes in sensing parameters might arise if field observations indicate the need. Again, modifying the sensing parameters such as the sampling rate without modifying the source code is highly desirable.

We characterize these situations as needing to modify software that is not easily modified. Though unusual, we expect such situations to arise, and the monitoring system deals with the difficulties of this type using *dynamic binary translation*. In effect, the binary version of the software is modified dynamically during execution to effect the desired change without having to modify the source code. Assurance of desired system properties is achieved by relying on formalism to a large extent.

Dynamic binary translation operates by executing the subject software in an application *virtual machine*. The translator is an execution-time fetch-execute loop that fetches a fragment of the binary program, examines and optionally modifies the fragment, and then executes the fragment. For monitoring system sensing, this translator can modify the binary by inserting sensing instructions into a fragment as part of the fetch-execute loop. Modern dynamic binary translation systems add very little overhead to the program. The monitoring system uses a specific system called *Strata* [6]. Strata does not require adaptation for a particular application. Rather, Strata uses formal specifications of the desired changes to machine instructions to generate sensing instructions.

Software invariants in safety arguments span a wide range of application semantic levels and application timeframes. At the highest level of abstraction, invariants are based upon quantities that are closely related to real-world entities such as aircraft operating parameters related to flight dynamics. At the lowest level of abstraction, invariants are based upon machine-level detail arising from the implementation.

For practical purposes, the software-state monitoring task can be divided into three semantic levels corresponding to:

- The *model* level, i.e., the application specification level. Software at this level derives from the application of tools such as MathWorks Simulink® that synthesize the associated high-level-language software.
- The *source-code* level, i.e., the level of the data structures and algorithms within the application. Outside of synthesis, software at this level derives from custom code developed by application engineers.

- The *binary-code* level, i.e., system implementation level. Software at this level derives from libraries and possibly other reused assets.

From the perspective of sensor changes in software that is hard to modify, the model-based-development level is the most complex of these semantic levels, and we discuss the use of dynamic binary translation for that case and give an example of the process.

The sensing technique for model-based development is shown in Fig. 5. High-level-language source code is generated for the subject model by synthesis. The monitoring system supports models specified in Simulink® running under Linux on Intel X86 platforms. For Simulink®, the synthesis is provided by MathWorks tools that generate C. The source code is compiled and linked to form the binary program.

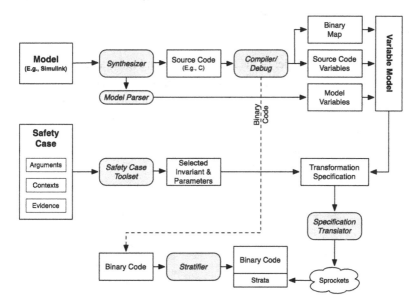

Fig. 5. Monitoring system sensing technique for model-based development.

For the monitoring system, the binary program is further processed by a utility called the *Stratafier* that installs Strata in the binary program. The semantics of the resulting program are unmodified although a modest overhead is introduced. Separately: (a) the Simulink® model is processed to extract the details of the variables used in the model, (b) the C code is processed to extract the variables used in the C program, (c) the binary program is processed to determine the locations of variables in the binary program, and (d) a *variable model* is built.

The variable model links the three sets of variables. The link between a Simulink® variable and the associated variable in C is derived from the naming convention that Simulink® uses in the generated code. The link between a variable in C and the associated memory and instructions in the binary program is derived from the symbol information placed in the binary file by the compiler.

The invariants are determined from the safety case arguments and contexts. The execution-time actions that Strata takes to effect the necessary sensing (machine instruction insertion and modification) are defined by specifications derived from the invariants and the variable model. These specifications are defined using Strata's translation specification infrastructure and are translated into Strata *sprockets*, low-level commands that control Strata during execution.

3.3 An Example of Sensing in a Simulink® Model

To illustrate the ideas outlined in the previous section, we present an example based on a hypothetical anti-lock braking system (ABS). In the example, we assume a requirement has arisen for temporary sensing of the vehicle speed (variable Vehicle Speed in the model) after deployment and that installing the sensor using dynamic binary translation is the preferred approach.

Part of the Simulink® model of the ABS is shown in Fig. 6, and part of the C code synthesized from the Simulink® model that includes an assignment to the C variable VehicleWithABS_B.Vs corresponding to the Simulink® variable Vehicle-Speed is shown in Fig. 7. The associated machine instructions are shown in Fig. 8. Based on a symbolic specification for the required sensing, Strata inserted a branch to a predefined instruction sequence that transmitted the value of the register holding the vehicle speed to the monitoring data repository.

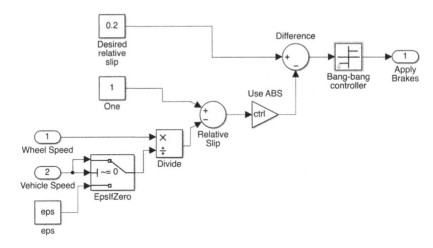

Fig. 6. Part of a hypothetical ABS defined using Simulink®.

Inevitably, dynamic binary translation will disturb the timing characteristics of a system and impact real-time performance. Various techniques can be used to mitigate the effects of the timing disturbance including: (a) using models to predict worst-case execution time (WCET) of monitored software given the WCET of the unmonitored software, (b) selective monitoring for much of the system's operating time could be

```
 VehicleWithABS.c    ×   +
136        VehicleWithABS_X.WheelSpeed1_CSTATE =
137          VehicleWithABS_P.WheelSpeed1_LowerSat;
138      }
139    }
140
141    VehicleWithABS_B.Ww = VehicleWithABS_X.WheelSpeed1_CSTATE;
142
143    /* Gain: '<Root>/Vehicle speed (angular)' */
144    VehicleWithABS_B.Vs = 1.0 / rtP_Rr * VehicleWithABS_B.Vehiclespeed_o1;
145
146    /* Integrator: '<Root>/Stopping distance' */
147    rtb_Ff = VehicleWithABS_X.Stoppingdistance_CSTATE;
148
149    /* Fcn: '<Root>/Relative Slip' */
150    VehicleWithABS_B.slp = 1.0 - VehicleWithABS_B.Ww / ((real_T)
151      (VehicleWithABS_B.Vs == 0.0) * 2.2204460492503131e-16 + VehicleWithABS_B.Vs);
152
153    /* Lookup_n-D: '<Root>/mu-slip friction curve' */
154    rtb_Ff = look1_binlxpw(VehicleWithABS_B.slp, rtP_slip, rtP_mu, 20U);
155
156    /* Gain: '<Root>/Weight' */
157    rtb_Ff *= rtP_m * rtP_g / 4.0;
158
159    /* Gain: '<Root>/-1//m' */
160    VehicleWithABS_B.um = -1.0 / rtP_m * rtb_Ff;
161
162    /* ModelReference: '<Root>/ABS Controller' */
163    ABS_Controller_oem(&(VehicleWithABS_DW.ABSController_DWORK1.rtm),
164                       &VehicleWithABS_B.Ww, &VehicleWithABS_B.Vs,
165                       &VehicleWithABS_B.ABSController,
```

Fig. 7. Part of the synthesized code for the hypothetical ABS.

```
402d5b:    48 8b 05 7e 82 21 00    mov     0x21827e(%rip),%rax    # 61afe0 <_DYNAMIC+0x390>
402d62:    48 8b 50 08             mov     0x8(%rax),%rdx
402d66:    48 8b 05 53 81 21 00    mov     0x218153(%rip),%rax    # 61aec0 <_DYNAMIC+0x270>
402d6d:    48 89 50 10             mov     %rdx,0x10(%rax)
402d71:    48 8b 05 40 82 21 00    mov     0x218240(%rip),%rax    # 61afb8 <_DYNAMIC+0x368>
402d78:    f2 0f 10 08             movsd   (%rax),%xmm1
402d7c:    f2 0f 10 05 f4 2f 01    movsd   0x12ff4(%rip),%xmm0    # 415d78 <gblInportContinuous+0x28>
402d83:    00
402d84:    f2 0f 5e c1             divsd   %xmm1,%xmm0
402d88:    48 8b 05 31 81 21 00    mov     0x218131(%rip),%rax    # 61aec0 <_DYNAMIC+0x270>
402d8f:    f2 0f 10 08             movsd   (%rax),%xmm1
402d93:    f2 0f 59 c1             mulsd   %xmm1,%xmm0
402d97:    48 8b 05 22 81 21 00    mov     0x218122(%rip),%rax    # 61aec0 <_DYNAMIC+0x270>
402d9e:    f2 0f 11 40 18          movsd   %xmm0,0x18(%rax)
402da3:    48 8b 05 36 82 21 00    mov     0x218236(%rip),%rax    # 61afe0 <_DYNAMIC+0x390>
402daa:    48 8b 40 10             mov     0x10(%rax),%rax
402dae:    48 89 45 f0             mov     %rax,-0x10(%rbp)
402db2:    48 8b 05 07 81 21 00    mov     0x218107(%rip),%rax    # 61aec0 <_DYNAMIC+0x270>
402db9:    f2 0f 10 48 10          movsd   0x10(%rax),%xmm1
402dbe:    48 8b 05 fb 80 21 00    mov     0x2180fb(%rip),%rax    # 61aec0 <_DYNAMIC+0x270>
402dc5:    f2 0f 10 40 18          movsd   0x18(%rax),%xmm0
```

Fig. 8. Part of the binary code for the hypothetical ABS.

disabled thereby eliminating the disturbance to real-time processing, and (c) static translation of the binary, where possible – static binary translation allows traditional WCET techniques to be applied.

4   Conclusion

Monitoring safety conditions is important, because belief in safety goals frequently depend upon them. We have presented the Safety Condition Monitoring System

(SCMS), a system designed to provide comprehensive, lifecycle monitoring of safety conditions. A key feature of the monitoring system is its ability to sense software state using dynamic binary translation without requiring any modifications to the subject software.

Acknowledgments. This work was supported in part by Dependable Computing LLC and in part by NASA Contract NNL13AA08C.

References

1. Graydon, P., Knight, J., Strunk, E.: Assurance based development of critical systems. In: 37th IEEE International Symposium on Dependable Systems and Networks, Edinburgh, Scotland (2007)
2. Graydon, G., Knight, J.: Process synthesis in assurance based development of dependable systems. In: 8th European Dependable Computing Conference, Valencia, Spain (2009)
3. Leveson, N.: A systems approach to risk management through leading safety indicators. Reliab. Eng. Syst. Saf. **136**, 17–34 (2015)
4. Denney, E., Pai, G., Habli, I.: Dynamic safety cases for through-life safety assurance. In: 37th IEEE International Conference on Software Engineering (NIER), Florence, Italy (2015)
5. Object Management Group, Business Process Model and Notation (BPMN) Version 2. http://www.omg.org/spec/BPMN/2.0/PDF/
6. Hiser, J., Nguyen-Tuong, A., Co, M., Rodes, B., Hall, M., Coleman, C., Knight, J., Davidson, J.: A framework for creating binary rewriting tools. In: 10th European Dependable Computing Conference, Valencia, Spain (2014)

Error Type Refinement for Assurance of Families of Platform-Based Systems

Sam Procter[1]([✉]), John Hatcliff[1], Sandy Weininger[2], and Anura Fernando[3]

[1] Kansas State University, Manhattan, KS, USA
{samprocter,hatcliff}@ksu.edu
[2] United States Food and Drug Administration, Silver Spring, MD, USA
sandy.weininger@fda.hhs.gov
[3] Underwriters Laboratories, Chicago, IL, USA
anura.s.fernando@ul.com

Abstract. Medical Application Platforms (MAPs) are an emerging paradigm for developing interoperable medical systems. Existing assurance-related concepts for conventional medical devices including hazard analyses, risk management processes, and assurance cases need to be enhanced and reworked to deal with notions of interoperability, reuse, and compositionality in MAPs.

In this paper, we present the motivation for a framework for defining and refining error types associated with interoperable systems and its relevance to safety standards development activities. This framework forms the starting point for the analysis and documentation of faults, propagations of errors related to those faults, and their associated hazards and mitigation strategies—all of which need to be addressed in risk management activities and assurance cases for these systems.

Keywords: Interoperable medical systems · Hazard analyses · Faults · Errors · Reusable components and assurance

1 Introduction

Modern medical devices are increasingly network-aware, and this offers the potential to use middleware infrastructure to form systems of cooperating components. Initial integration efforts in industry are focused on streaming device data into electronic health records and integrating information from multiple devices into single customizable displays. However, there are numerous motivations for moving beyond this to frameworks that enable devices to automate clinical workflows, provide clinical "dashboards" that fuse multiple physiological data streams to provide composite health scores, generate alarms / alerts derived

This work is supported in part by the US National Science Foundation (NSF) (#1239543), the NSF US Food and Drug Administration Scholar-in-Residence Program (#1355778,#1446544) and the NIH / NIBIB Quantum Program.

© Springer International Publishing Switzerland 2015
F. Koornneef and C. van Gulijk (Eds.): SAFECOMP 2015 Workshops, LNCS 9338, pp. 95–106, 2015.
DOI: 10.1007/978-3-319-24249-1_9

from multiple physiological parameters, provide automated clinical decision support, realize "closed loop" sensing and actuating scenarios, or even automatically construct and execute patient treatments.

Emerging Computational Paradigms and Dependable Architectures: In previous work, we have introduced the notion of a *medical application platform*. As defined in [6] a MAP is "a safety- and security-critical real-time computing platform for: (a) integrating heterogeneous devices, medical IT systems, and information displays via a communication infrastructure, and (b) hosting application programs (i.e., *apps*) that provide medical utility [beyond that provided by the individual devices] via the ability to both acquire information from and control integrated devices... and displays."

Platform-based approaches to integrated systems have a number of benefits, but they also introduce a number of safety and security challenges not addressed by current medical safety standards. While conventional approaches to development and deployment of safety-critical systems typically involve assessment and certification of complete systems, with a platform approach there is a need for (a) reuse of risk management artifacts, supporting hazard analyses, and assurance cases for both infrastructure implementations and components, and (b) compositional approaches to risk management, assurance, and certification.

Reliability Analysis and the Assurance Case Paradigm: In development and deployment of medical devices and other safety-critical systems, hazard analyses play a key role in achieving safety. A hazard is often defined as "a source of harm," and system hazard analyses focus on identifying how hazards may arise in the context of system development and execution. The results of hazard analyses are typically reflected in an assurance case for a safety critical system. For example, an assurance case will often argue that appropriate hazards have been identified and that each hazard has been designed out, its risks controlled, or it has been otherwise dealt with in a manner that will result in an acceptable level of residual risk. A hazard analysis may proceed in a "bottom-up" fashion as in a Failure Modes and Effects Analysis (FMEA) which considers how each component may fail and how effects of component failure may propagate forward and outward to the system boundary, giving rise to hazards; alternatively, a hazard analysis may proceed in a "top-down" fashion as in a Fault Tree Analysis (FTA) which starts from hazardous state or event at the system boundary and reasons in a backward fashion to determine events and failures within the system that could cause the top-level unwanted event [5]. Concepts that cross-cut most hazard analyses are the notions of *fault*: the root cause of a component's failure to satisfy its specification and *error*: the deviation from a component's specified behavior [12][1]. In a bottom-up analysis, consideration of possible faults initiates the analysis and leads to an enumeration of the ways in which a component may produce errors (e.g., corrupted values, inappropriate timing of message transmittal, inability to perform a requested service, etc.) that

---

[1] Though these definitions are sourced from the AADL EM standard document, we note that they align well with, e.g., the taxonomy in [4].

may end up propagating outward to the system boundary and exposing hazards. In a top-down analysis, the analyst works backward through causality chains, considering how different types of errors could flow through the system, until faults that correspond to root causes are identified.

Certification, Standards, and Regulation: To support the development, assurance, and certification of integrated medical systems, including systems built using platform concepts, the Association for the Advancement of Medical Instrumentation (AAMI) and Underwriters Laboratories (UL) are developing the 2800 family of standards for safe and secure interoperable medical systems. It has been proposed that AAMI / UL 2800 will provide a framework for specifying system and component-level safety and security requirements and guiding vendors in constructing objective evidence and assurance cases that demonstrate that their components, architectures, and integrated clinical systems comply with those requirements. 2800 is proposed to be organized as (a) a base "general" standard that provides architecture- and application-independent requirements and (b) "particular" standards that introduce application and architecture specific requirements by inheriting and refining the standard. It has been proposed that particular standards will specify how the generic risk management process and notions of faults, errors, failures, hazards, etc., in the base standard are specialized and allocated to the associated architectures, component kinds, and clinical applications. Vendor assurance cases that are used to demonstrate compliance with particular standards must provide evidence that their implementations account for, mitigate, or otherwise achieve an acceptable level of residual risk for the error types inherited through the standard hierarchy.

Reuse and Modularization: In this standards framework, there is a significant need for a flexible nomenclature framework for faults/errors. Interoperable systems include components produced by different vendors. When risk management and assurance case artifacts are reused among vendors as systems are composed from components, component vendors need to be able to disclose what types of errors may propagate out of their components and what types of errors their components mitigate. There needs to be a standard vocabulary with a consistent semantic interpretation for faults and errors to ensure proper composition. Some errors are relevant to some types of components but not others (e.g., those associated with failure to achieve message transmittal in accordance with declared real-time and quality of service constraints are relevant to middleware but not to medical device components). Taxonomy mechanisms are needed to organize errors into categories according to kinds of components found in interoperable medical systems. Safety is ultimately expressed in terms of the notions of harm associated with a particular clinical application. Accordingly, there is a need to extend and specialize generic errors to specific clinical applications while providing a mechanism to facilitate traceability back to generic errors to support standard requirements that guide vendors to consider all appropriate generic error categories.

Our Contributions: The contributions of this paper are as follows:

- we identify overall goals for organizing and standardizing error types in the context of hierarchically organized standards for platform-based interoperable medical systems,
- we illustrate how the SAE standard Architecture and Analysis Design Language (AADL) Error Modeling framework, its open error type hierarchy, and its built-in error library can potentially support the desired notions of organization, extensibility, and refinement described above, and
- we describe how this open error type hierarchy would be used in the context of broader risk management, assurance case development, and certification regimes for platform-based interoperable medical systems.

2   Background

2.1   AAMI / UL 2800

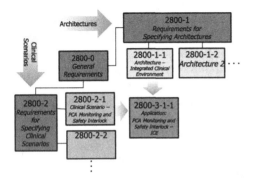

Fig. 1. The AAMI / UL 2800 Family of Standards

AAMI / UL 2800 aims to define safety and security requirements to support the paradigm of constructing integrated systems from heterogeneous interoperable components. These requirements address component interfaces, implementations of components, middleware and networking infrastructure, and architectures that constrain the interactions between components as they are integrated to achieve system safety objectives. The standard is not anticipated to prescribe specific technologies or interface specifications for achieving integration and interoperability. Instead, it is expected to provide a framework for specifying system and component-level safety requirements and guiding vendors in constructing evidence and assurance cases that demonstrate that their components, architectures, and integrated clinical systems comply with those requirements.

The structure for the 2800 family of standards aims to accommodate the following (sometimes conflicting) goals[2]:

- *Generality:* 2800 aims to provide safety requirements that are applicable to multiple architectures and a variety of clinical systems/applications.
- *Application Specificity:* Hazards and top-level system safety constraints, which typically drive risk management and safety assurance processes, are application specific. Thus, 2800 is expected to provide a framework for introducing specific standards that address particular systems/applications and state requirements on how vendors develop and assure specific systems.

---

[2] Some text in this section has been excerpted from unpublished communications as part of ongoing standardization efforts within the 2800 committee.

– *Architecture Specificity:* 2800 is expected to provide a framework for documenting architectures and the role that a specific architecture plays in (a) controlling potentially hazardous emergent properties by constraining interactions between components, and (b) providing safety-related services used to mitigate common errors.

To reconcile these potentially conflicting goals and to enable reuse of application- and architecture-independent requirements, 2800 is proposed to be organized into a collection of linked standards (see Fig. 1). The organization strategy is similar to that of IEC 60601 where a core set of requirements is refined along multiple dimensions to create requirements that are specialized to particular applications or implementation aspects. Specification-, application- and architecture-independent requirements are presented in the core *2800-0 General Requirements* standard while additional standards refine and extend core requirements for particular architectures (the *2800-1-x* series) or particular applications (the *2800-2-y* series). The *2800-3-x-y* series proposes to define application-specific requirements that are specialized for a particular architecture's approach to interoperability. The 2800 family's open, refinement-based approach allows for extension to address additional architectures and applications as new interoperability technologies and clinical needs arise. This enables manufacturers to specify an interoperable system's behavior but does not constrain how it should be implemented.

2.2 The Integrated Clinical Environment Architecture

The Integrated Clinical Environment (ICE) standard (ASTM F2761-2009 [3]) defines one particular architecture for MAPs. ASTM F2761 identifies an abstract "functional model" that includes components such the Supervisor, Network Controller, etc. with brief high-level descriptions of the role of these components within the architecture. Future implementation standards are envisioned that provide detailed implementation requirements and interface specifications for these components. 2800-1-1, currently being drafted, complements and provides guidance for the planned ASTM F2761 implementation standards by defining safety and security requirements for the ICE architecture. The Medical Device Coordination Framework (MDCF) is a prototype implementation of ICE jointly developed by researchers at Kansas State University and the University of Pennsylvania [9]. The MDCF provides a middleware substrate and associated services [8], tools for authoring apps, generating executable APIs [11], and performing risk management activities [10].

2.3 PCA Safety Interlock Scenario

We describe one example of the MAP approach—a PCA safety interlock scenario—here as a motivating example. After major trauma, hospital patients are often provided pain relief via patient-controlled analgesia (PCA) pumps. These allow a patient to press a button and request an analgesic (often an opioid narcotic) to manage pain. Standard safety mechanisms such as button timeouts fail to account for potential problems (e.g., opioid tolerance or human error), so various ways exist for an overdose to occur [7]. This can lead to respiratory depression and even death.

An ICE app can be used to implement a safety interlock that sets the PCA pump to a known safe state (i.e., infusion disabled) if—according to monitoring devices typically used in critical care situations—the patient shows signs of respiratory distress. While the exact set of monitored physiological parameters can vary, our example implementation uses the patient's blood-oxygen saturation (SpO_2), ratio of exhaled carbon-dioxide ($EtCO_2$) and respiratory rate (RR). After determining the respiratory health of the patient using some physiological model, the app can issue *enable* or *disable* commands to the pump. This app has been studied extensively in prior work, e.g., [2].

2.4   AADL's Error Model's Error Types

AADL enables the design of a system's architectural aspects including hardware and software components and the bindings between the two [13]. AADL adds a number of language annexes such as the error modeling annex, which enables the modeling of failure-related aspects of their systems [12]. One useful aspect of this error modeling annex is its error definition and propagation mechanisms derived from Wallace's fault propagation and transformation calculus [14].

In the AADL error model, errors are represented as error types, instances of which can be propagated between components over their existing ports and channels (i.e., those specified in the core AADL language). The error model comes with a pre-built type hierarchy—the *error library*—that is composed of five "root" types (`ServiceError`, `TimingRelatedError`, `ValueRelatedError`, `ReplicationError`, and `ConcurrencyError`) that can be refined (through a full type lattice, created via extension, renaming, and type sets) down to more specific errors. Consider Fig. 2, for example, which shows the hierarchy of the error library's `TimingRelatedError` (full hierarchies for the other types are available in [12]). The root type `TimingRelatedError` is a union of three types, including `ItemTimingError`, which is refined (through type extension) to both

```
1  --ErrorLibrary.aadl
2  TimingRelatedError: type set {ItemTimingError, SequenceTimingError,
       ServiceTimingError};
3  ItemTimingError: type;
4  EarlyDelivery: type extends ItemTimingError;
5  LateDelivery: type extends ItemTimingError;
6  SequenceTimingError: type;
7  HighRate: type extends SequenceTimingError;
8  LowRate: type extends SequenceTimingError;
9  RateJitter: type extends SequenceTimingError;
10 ServiceTimingError: type;
11 DelayedService: type extends ServiceTimingError;
12 EarlyService: type extends ServiceTimingError;
```

Fig. 2. AADL EM Base Error Types for timing related errors

EarlyDelivery and LateDelivery; i.e., if a single item (e.g., a message) has incorrect timing, it must be either early or late—it cannot be both, nor can it be neither. Finally, if the given root error types are insufficient for some purpose, completely new ones can be created.

3   Error Refinement

3.1   Supporting 2800 Goals

Developing a framework for error types within 2800 addresses multiple assurance-related needs: (a) libraries of error types to guide hazard analyses, risk management processes, and aspects of assurance case construction, (b) appropriate coverage and document traceability targets (embedded in error libraries) that vendors can trace to as part of their compliance obligations, (c) a common interpretation/semantics for errors across vendors in order to support interoperability, (d) machine-readable specification of error types for automation of hazard analyses, and (e) systematic specification of error types within formal architecture descriptions to provide the basis for fault-injection testing.

Addressing (d) and (e) are beyond the scope of this paper; we propose goals for addressing (a-c) across the 2800 hierarchy below.

Identifying Common Error Types: 2800-0 would provide a library of error types in an Informative Annex that supports the 2800 risk management process. The 2800-0 Risk Management requirements would specify that these error types should be considered in the initiating activities for bottom-up hazard analyses such as FMEA and would form the leaf nodes for top-down analyses such as FTA. Compliance requirements would specify that vendors should state how error types are accounted for in their analyses (e.g., they must use each error type or document why any that were left out were not applicable). Authors of standards that refine 2800-0 would be required to trace, via refinement mechanisms, newly introduced error types to those provided in the Informative Annex.

Allocation of Error Types to Common Component Categories Found in Interoperable Systems: 2800-0 would also identify Interoperability Component Categories—common categories found in interoperable medical systems, e.g., medical devices (which may be further subdivided by role, e.g., into sensors and actuators), communication infrastructure, application hosting components, health IT systems, network gateways, etc. In the 2800-1-x series, 2800-1-x authors would indicate how their architectural components align with 2800 Interoperability Component Categories. Based on this association, they would be required to specify how each component in the architecture accounts for the error types associated with that category. This "accounting" may involving refining the errors into more specific categories for the particular architecture.

Allocation of Error Types to Application Components and Hazards: In the 2800-2-x series, 2800-2-x authors would associate error types with specific devices or systems used in a particular application context. This would provide vendors seeking to comply with 2800-2-x a more precisely contextualized collection of errors, and a more accurate basis of accounting for appropriate "coverage" of errors associated with a particular context.

3.2 Refinement by Component Category

How can we leverage the concept of error refinement (via extension, renaming, or aggregation) from Sect. 2.4 given our goals from Sect. 3.1 (i.e., allocating error types to component categories and implementations)? We should focus on the "leaf" error types—i.e., the fully refined error model types. For example, authors of a 2800-1-x standard can decide whether a error type applies to a particular component role in the system architecture. If it does, they can extend it to one or more subtypes that better describe how the error might occur in a generic version of the component. If it does not apply, the standard can justify excluding it so that users of the architecture-specific error type library can understand the rationale. Consider Fig. 3, which shows our timing errors from Fig. 2 after their refinement to apps (different refinements would exist for other architectural elements, e.g., devices, networking components, supervisor components, etc.). Consider line 2 of Fig. 3: since early delivery of messages is impossible, we eliminate it from consideration by simply not extending it. We expect that MAP apps will receive two types of input: physiological data from patient monitoring devices (e.g., SpO_2 and $EtCO_2$) and commands to the application from other apps or clinicians. Lines 3 and 4 show that these two message types could both be late, and should be considered separately.

Of course, other types of components will have their own refinements. For example, the networking middleware (i.e., the in ASTM F2761) is agnostic to message types, so its refinements to, e.g., the `HighRate` error type would be generic to the types of messages being transmitted. We expect some real-time network controllers (such as MIDAS [8]) to provide guarantees against any particular component saturating the network, so errors refined to these network controllers would reflect this.

3.3 Refinement by Component Implementation

The behavior of medical devices and apps will vary considerably based on actual component implementation. For these components, the error types should be

```
1   --AppErrorLibrary.aadl
2   -- Ignore EarlyDelivery, since the network never holds messages
3   PhysioParamLate : type extends ErrorLibrary::LateDelivery;
4   ControlActionLate : type extends ErrorLibrary::LateDelivery;
5   PhysioParamFlood : type extends ErrorLibrary::HighRate;
6   ControlActionFlood : type extends ErrorLibrary::HighRate;
7   -- Ignore LowRate, since it's just an accumulation of delayed messages
8   -- Ignore RateJitter, since it's either EarlyDelivery (which we don't have) or
        LateDelivery
9   MissedPhysioParamDeadline : type extends ErrorLibrary::DelayedService;
10  MissedControlActionDeadline : type extends ErrorLibrary::DelayedService;
11  -- Ignore EarlyService since it's impossible
```

Fig. 3. Error types, refined for MAP Apps

further refined. The process specified in the previous section can be continued with our new architectural information, i.e., the actual architecture of a given component. Consider the error types from Fig. 3 (associated with *2800-2-1* and *2800-3-1-x*) as they might be applied to the PCA interlock app from Sect. 2.3. As the app uses three physiological parameters (SpO_2, $EtCO_2$, and RR) and one control action (PumpShutoff), the generic app error types can be refined to be specific to these parameters, as in Fig. 4. These fully refined error types are application specific and traceable to both the component's category (i.e., app) and the AADL EM library. The app's developer had a starting point for deriving hazards (i.e., Fig. 3) rather than the much more ambiguous starting position of the status quo.

3.4   Using Error Types in Hazard Analysis and Testing

Hazard analyses include reasoning about where errors originate, what failures may result, and how errors propagate through the system. While the error type framework can aid in a more consistent presentation of these concepts, when combined with formal architectural descriptions of systems, it can also enable automation of some hazard analysis steps. The AADL EM error propagation mechanisms (see Fig. 6) enable developers to specify how their components

```
1  --PCAInterlockErrors.aadl
2  SpO2Late : type extends AppErrorLibrary::PhysioParamLate;
3  EtCO2Late : type extends AppErrorLibrary::PhysioParamLate;
4  RRLate : type extends AppErrorLibrary::PhysioParamLate;
5  PumpShutoffLate : type extends AppErrorLibrary::ControlActionLate;
6  SpO2Flood : type extends AppErrorLibrary::PhysioParamFlood;
7  EtCO2Flood : type extends AppErrorLibrary::PhysioParamFlood;
8  RRFlood : type extends AppErrorLibrary::PhysioParamFlood;
9  PumpShutoffFlood : type extends AppErrorLibrary::ControlActionFlood;
10 -- Ignore MissedPhysioParamDeadline because we are just a subscriber
11 -- Ignore MissedControlActionDeadline because we are just a publisher
```

Fig. 4. Error types, refined for the PCA Interlock app

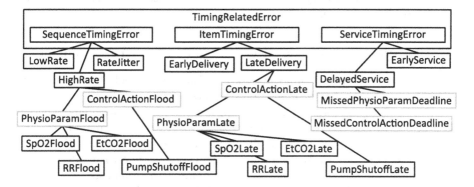

Fig. 5. A graphical view of the example error hierarchy, base types are in black (text given in Fig. 2), generic MAP app types are in red (Fig. 3), and PCA Interlock specific types are in blue (Fig. 4) (Color figure online)

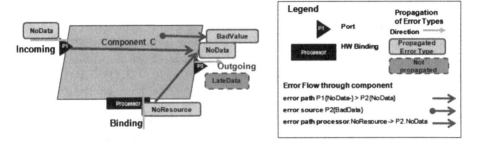

Fig. 6. An example of AADL's Error propagation, from [12]

create, propagate, transform and consume errors. In Fig. 6, for example, the outgoing `NoData` error type can result either from an incoming `NoResource` error (i.e., `NoResource` is *transformed* by the component into `NoData`) or it can simply be *propagated* from a predecessor component. The component is a *source* of the `BadValue` error type, meaning that it can produce the error even if its input is error-free. Note that both top-down and bottom-up analyses leverage AADL's error propagation mechanisms (Fig. 5).

There are two benefits to using the error types we have identified with the EM error propagation mechanism. First, component developers will know what kind of errors they'll receive simply as a function of declaring what kind of component they are creating (e.g., device, app, network controller, etc.). Second, they will also know what kind of errors they are allowed to propagate. In the assurance case arguing for a component's safety-related properties, they can explain how their component handles (or fails to handle) each incoming error, and under what conditions their component propagates particular errors. This explanation, unlike in the status quo, will not be narrative in form, but rather can be written in the much more precise, machine-readable format of the AADL EM error types. Tooling can leverage these precise specifications of error creation, propagation and compensation for a range of purposes, e.g., the hazard analysis report from [10] or even fault-injection testing [1].

3.5   Allocation of Related Concepts to 2800 Standard Documents

Table 1 provides examples of how the error type framework might be used in 2800. Table entry names that appear in square brackets represent standards content that complies with requirements in standards higher in the hierarchy, whereas names in parentheses represent requirements that are refined (made more specific to a particular application or architecture). The table is not exhaustive; other requirements may compel, for example, vendors to capture error-related propagation or mitigation properties on component boundaries (following the concepts but not necessarily the AADL tooling in Sect. 3.4), specify how errors at lower levels of abstraction (e.g., at the network or middleware layer) are manifested in terms of errors in application layers, and assign occurrence likelihood rankings to errors at particular points in the architecture.

Table 1. Examples of 2800 contents related to error type framework

2800-0: General Requirements	
Error Type Framework	Common categories of system and clinical process errors and semantics
System Topology	Common interoperability components kinds and allocation of 2800 errors
Risk Management	Requirements that vendors address 2800 error types in risk management
Testing	Requirements for fault injection testing to test for effectiveness of mitigation strategies
Assurance Cases	Requirements for arguing for safety in the presence of error handling and mitigation strategies
2800-1: Process/Requirements for Specifying Interoperability Architectures	
Traceability	Requirements that refining 2800-1-X standards map interoperability component kinds and errors to specified architectures
Arch. Specification	Requirements that refining 2800-1-X standards associate error types to standardized architectural viewpoints
2800-1-1: Safety and Security Requirements for ICE Interoperability Architecture	
[Traceability]	Map interoperability component kinds and refine error types to ICE Architecture components
[Arch. Specification]	Associate error types to standardized architectural viewpoints for ICE Architecture
(Risk Management)	Requirements that vendors address refined 2800-1-1 error types in risk management
(Testing)	Requirements for fault injection testing to test for effectiveness of mitigation strategies for refined 2800-1-1 error types
(Assurance Cases)	Requirements for arguing for safety in the presence of error handling and mitigation strategies for refined 2800-1-1 error types
2800-2: Process/Requirements for Specifying Clinical Scenarios	
Appl. Proc. Spec.	Requirements that refining 2800-2-X standards associate clinical error types to instantiations of common processes in the clinical application's context
Appl. Sys. Spec.	Requirements that refining 2800-2-X standards refine 2800-0 system error types to kinds of system components relevant to application
Appl. Proc. Mitigation	Informative Annex of common design / mitigation strategies for common clinical process error types.
2800-2-1: Safety/Security Requirements for PCA Infusion Monitoring and Safety Interlock	
[Appl. Proc. Spec.]	Associate clinical error types to instantiations of common processes in the clinical application's context.
[Appl. Sys. Spec.]	Refine 2800-0 system error types to kinds of system components relevant to application
(Testing)	Requirements for fault injection testing to test for effectiveness of mitigation strategies for refined 2800-2-1 error types
(Assurance Cases)	Requirements for arguing for safety in the presence of error handling and mitigation strategies for refined 2800-2-1 error types

4   Conclusion

Safety-critical medical systems are being developed using platform-based architectures that emphasize multi-vendor component reuse. Work is needed to adapt existing risk management and assurance case techniques to support this paradigm of system development. In this paper, we have argued that there is a need for a refinement-based framework that enables defining error types to support safety standards for interoperable systems.

We are working with the 2800 standards committee to align these concepts with the 2800 risk management processes. We are integrating the framework with our AADL-based risk management tooling environment for ICE apps [10] and collaborating with US Food and Drug Administration (FDA) engineers as part of the US National Science Foundation FDA Scholar-in-Residence program to ensure that the concepts are oriented to support regulatory submissions for MAP infrastructure implementations and apps. Although we have focused on the medical domain, the same motivation and solution strategy is relevant to other domains including avionics (e.g., the Open Group's Future Airborne Capability Environment[3]) and the industrial internet.

---

[3] https://www.opengroup.us/face/.

References

1. Arlat, J., Aguera, M., Amat, L., Crouzet, Y., Fabre, J.C., Laprie, J.C., Martins, E., Powell, D.: Fault injection for dependability validation: a methodology and some applications. IEEE Trans. Softw. Eng. **16**(2), 166–182 (1990)
2. Arney, D., Pajic, M., Goldman, J.M., Lee, I., Mangharam, R., Sokolsky, O.: Toward patient safety in closed-loop medical device systems. In: Proceedings of the 1st ACM/IEEE International Conference on Cyber-Physical Systems, pp. 139–148. ACM (2010)
3. ASTM International: ASTM F2761 - Medical Devices and Medical Systems - Essential safety requirements for equipment comprising the patient-centric integrated clinical environment (ICE) (2009). www.astm.org
4. Avižienis, A., Laprie, J.C., Randell, B., Landwehr, C.: Basic concepts and taxonomy of dependable and secure computing. IEEE Trans. Dependable Secure Comput. **1**(1), 11–33 (2004)
5. Ericson II, C.A.: Hazard Analysis Techniques for System Safety. Wiley, New York (2005)
6. Hatcliff, J., King, A., Lee, I., MacDonald, A., Fernando, A., Robkin, M., Vasserman, E., Weininger, S., Goldman, J.M.: Rationale and architecture principles for medical application platforms. In: 2012 IEEE/ACM Third International Conference on Cyber-Physical Systems (ICCPS), pp. 3–12. IEEE (2012)
7. Hicks, R.W., Sikirica, V., Nelson, W., Schein, J.R., Cousins, D.D.: Medication errors involving patient-controlled analgesia. Am. J. Health-Syst. Pharm. **65**(5), 429–440 (2008)
8. King, A., Chen, S., Lee, I.: The middleware assurance substrate: enabling strong real-time guarantees in open systems with openflow. In: 17th IEEE Computer Society symposium on Object/component/service-oriented realtime distributed computing (ISORC). IEEE (2014)
9. King, A., Procter, S., Andresen, D., Hatcliff, J., Warren, S., Spees, W., Jetley, R., Jones, P., Weininger, S.: An open test bed for medical device integration and coordination. In: Proceedings of the 31st International Conference on Software Engineering (2009)
10. Procter, S., Hatcliff, J.: An architecturally-integrated, systems-based hazard analysis for medical applications. In: 2014 Twelfth ACM/IEEE International Conference on Formal Methods and Models for Codesign (MEMOCODE), pp. 124–133. IEEE (2014)
11. Procter, S., Hatcliff, J.: Robby: towards an AADL-based definition of app architectures for medical application platforms. In: Proceedings of the International Workshop on Software Engineering in Healthcare. Washington, DC, July 2014
12. SAE AS-2C Architecture Description Language Subcommittee: SAE Architecture Analysis and Design Language (AADL) Annex, vol. 3, Annex E: Error Model Language. Technical report SAE Aerospace, June 2014
13. SAE AS5506B: Architecture Analysis and Design Language (AADL). AS-5506B, SAE International (2004)
14. Wallace, M.: Modular architectural representation and analysis of fault propagation and transformation. Electron. Notes Theor. Comput. Sci. **141**(3), 53–71 (2005)

EWICS/ERCIM/ARTEMIS Dependable Cyber-physical Systems and Systems-of-Systems Workshop (DECSoS 2015)

Qualitative and Quantitative Analysis of CFTs Taking Security Causes into Account

Max Steiner$^{(\boxtimes)}$ and Peter Liggesmeyer

Chair of Software Engineering: Dependability, University of Kaiserslautern,
Kaiserslautern, Germany
{steiner,liggesmeyer}@cs.uni-kl.de

Abstract. Component fault trees that contain safety basic events as well as security basic events cannot be analyzed like normal CFTs. Safety basic events are rated with probabilities in an interval [0,1], for security basic events simpler scales such as {low, medium, high} make more sense. In this paper an approach is described how to handle a quantitative safety analysis with different rating schemes for safety and security basic events. By doing so, it is possible to take security causes for safety failures into account and to rate their effect on system safety.

Keywords: Safety analysis · Security analysis · Quantitative combined analysis · Component fault trees · Attack trees · Security enhanced component fault trees

1 Introduction

Embedded systems are networked more and more, they evolve into cyber-physical systems, even if the initial design did not anticipate this. This networking creates new security problems that can lead to safety problems which have to be analyzed. The effects of such security problems are not taken into account in a traditional safety analysis. Thus consequences cannot be estimated correctly, which results in either insufficient or unnecessary and too expensive countermeasures.

This paper shows how to conduct a qualitative and quantitative safety analysis using component fault trees (CFTs), including the effects of security problems on system safety. In [16] the process as a whole was described. In this current paper the focus lies on the analysis of the security enhanced component fault trees (SECFTs). To achieve that, safety analysis methods of CFTs are extended to incorporate security problems as basic causes.

The paper is structured in the following way: After a short overview of related work, the overall analysis process is recalled. Then the foundations of an analysis are set by discussing rating scheme and calculation rules. And finally the qualitative and quantitative analysis procedure is shown using an example analysis of a generic patient controlled analgesia (GPCA) pump.

© Springer International Publishing Switzerland 2015
F. Koornneef and C. van Gulijk (Eds.): SAFECOMP 2015 Workshops, LNCS 9338, pp. 109–120, 2015.
DOI: 10.1007/978-3-319-24249-1_10

2   Related Work

The SECFTs used in this approach are CFTs [11] extended with additional elements from attack trees (ATs) [15] to model the effects of security attacks on the safety of a system. Based on established analysis methods for CFTs that are described in [18], adaptations were made to encompass the analysis of safety as well as security properties.

Other works concerning quantitative analysis of ATs like Mauw et al. [12] describe general calculating rules for predicates in ATs to compute the values for the (TE). Jürgenson and Willemson use those rules to calculate ratings in an AT in [10]. They use a combination of probabilities and costs/gain of the attacks. Fovino et al. propose in [6] a way how to combine quantitative analysis of (FTs) and ATs under the precondition that probabilities for all basic events (BEs) are available. But determining accurate probabilities for security attacks is often difficult or sometimes even not possible [17]. To circumvent that problem, Casals et al. use a scale with discrete values to rate security attacks in [5]. By those ratings they can compare different attack scenarios. The downside is that the accuracy is not as good as with probabilities for BFs in FTs.

Therefore, we decided to use a hybrid approach for the rating of the events to avoid the problem of assigning probabilities to security-related events. The overall process of the combined analysis was described in [7,16]. It is based on recommendations of standards as IEC 61025 [3] or IEC 60300–3–1 [2] to use a combination of inductive and deductive techniques to minimize the potential of omitted failure modes. Inductive techniques as failure mode and effects analysis (FMEA) [9] or hazard and operability study (HAZOP) [1] can be used to find the TEs. Deductive techniques as fault tree analysis (FTA) [3] are used to refine the analysis and to find causes and moreover combinations of causes that lead to the TE. The resulting graph is used to conduct qualitative and quantitative analyses.

The approach to introduce security aspects into safety analysis proposed in this work is based on CFTs. It extends the process described earlier by an additional step and modifies the analysis step [16]. After developing the CFT, it is extended by security attacks as additional causes that also could lead to the safety-related TE. Those security attacks are found by analyzing data flow and interface specifications, because most attacks are made at communication interfaces. Techniques such as STRIDE [8] and FMVEA [14] can be used to find possible attacks.

3   Analysis

To be able to conduct a quantitative analysis, a comprehensive rating of all of the events in a (SECFT) has to be available. Using a comprehensive rating for all events the individual impact of an attack on the occurrence of the (TE) can be determined.

3.1   Ratings

In component fault trees (CFTs) typical ratings for basic events (BEs) are probabilities or reliability values. These are used to calculate the respective values for minimal cut sets (MCSs) and the TE.

In an attack tree (AT) the same basic elements exist as in a CFT. Either Boolean or continuous values can be assigned to BEs. As Boolean values pairs such as *possible – impossible* or *expensive – not expensive* are used. Continuous values for BEs can be *costs to execute an attack*, *probability of success of a given attack* or *probability that an attack is actually conducted*.

A probability that an attack is successful could be determined from expert knowledge and experienced data just like failure probabilities. But even the success probability is difficult to determine. There is only a small portion of the data about successful attacks available. Most successful attacks are not published because companies fear the loss of trust of their customers.

The bigger problem is determining the probability that an attacker actually conducts an attack. First of all, this probability depends on different aspects: the attacker's motivation and experience, availability of assets/money, and accessibility of the system. And second of all, if this attack requires several distinct actions that are modeled as separate security events, these events are not independent, as it would be required for most calculation algorithms for CFTs.

Figure 1 shows an example of an attacker modeled as a component with two output ports out_1 and out_2. For the output port out_2 it is basically an AT which consists of 4 gates and 5 BEs. Two MCSs for out_2 are present which represent two different attack scenarios: $\{e_1, e_2, e_5\}$ and $\{e_3, e_4, e_5\}$.

If an attack is consisting of several actions an attacker has to perform, like the ones for output port out_2 in the example, these actions are not stochastically independent. If an attacker plans to attack a given system and that attack requires him to execute different actions (security events, sub-attacks), it is most likely that he will at least try all sub-attacks that are necessary to reach his goal. In terms of the given example this means if an attacker chooses to try BE e_1 and he succeeds, he most probably will also try e_2 and e_5. In general this means, in an AT the events in a MCS are not independent from each other.

Therefore, it makes more sense to assign a probability to a whole MCS, which represents the attack, instead of the BEs. The other rating values (other than probabilities) can be calculated for the MCSs from their respective BEs. For the TE the same conditions hold than for CFTs: ratings are calculated from BEs or MCSs.

A first result from a safety analysis based on SECFTs is the set of MCSs as they are all combinations of BEs that lead to the analyzed system failure. To decide which of these combinations have to be mitigated to reach a certain safety level, this set of MCSs has to be prioritized. And of course to decide whether a system is complying to a given safety level from a standard or a requirement, the TE rating of the CFT has to be calculated.

Instead of trying to assign probabilities to security events, it is a better idea to use a more coarse scale with only a few discrete values. IEC 61025 [3] states

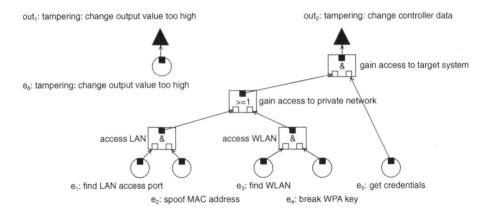

Fig. 1. Example attacker component.

for fault tree analysis that in case when probabilities cannot be assigned to BEs, a "descriptive likelihood of occurrence" can be used with values such as: "highly probable", "very probable", "medium probability", "remote probability", etc. Likelihood is defined as a qualitative probability for the occurrence of a security event. Security events are in most cases attacks conducted by an attacker. This likelihood can be used to rate security events in a SECFT.

The approach described in this paper can work with different numbers of distinct values. In the following a three-value scale is selected for simplicity. More fine-grained scales only make sense if more distinct values are needed explicitly. One has to keep in mind that assigning more precise numerical values might only add fictitious precision which can be misleading in the interpretation of the results. This also has to be considered when calculating values for combinations of events that are rated with likelihood values.

The values of that likelihood are determined from several indicators as: attack cost, attack resources, attacker motivation, accessibility, or attacker type. Casals et al. describe in [5] one possibility to determine likelihood values. The scale represents the likelihood of a security event to occur. To each value a numerical value is assigned for easier comparisons. From this follows that the likelihood would be mapped to integer values from the interval $[1, m]$, where $m \in \mathbb{N}$ is the number of discrete values.

One possibility to achieve a common rating, other than probabilities, is to use the likelihood for both safety and security events. The advantage of this approach is that values for all BEs can be determined relatively easy and comparisons of likelihood are easily performed. The disadvantage is that the accuracy coming from rating safety events with probabilities is lost.

To use the advantages of both, probabilities for safety events and likelihood for security events, an approach using a combination of both probability and likelihood is used. Hence in a SECFT there can be both likelihoods and probabilities for different events.

When MCSs are determined in a SECFT that includes safety as well as security events, there can be three types of MCSs as defined in the following:

Definition 1 *MCS types:*

1. *A safety MCS contains only safety events (BEs which occur due to random faults in the system).*
2. *A security MCS contains only security events (BEs which are triggered from outside the system by a malicious attacker or a random fault).*
3. *A mixed MCS contains safety events as well as security events.*

The TE will most certainly depend on safety as well as security events. Therefore a combination of both probabilities and likelihood is needed to calculate ratings for MCSs and TEs.

Events in a safety MCS are rated with probabilities. Therefore, the overall rating of a safety MCS is also a probability. Events in a security MCS are rated with likelihoods. So the overall rating of a security MCS is also a likelihood. In a mixed MCS however, there are both probabilities and likelihoods. As they are not directly comparable, the rating of a mixed MCS is a tuple consisting of the overall probability of all included safety events and the overall likelihood of all included security events. For TEs in a SECFT, the same holds as for mixed MCSs.

The next section will introduce the extensions for the calculation rules needed for a SECFT to handle the tuples of probabilities and likelihoods.

3.2   Calculation Rules for Likelihood and Probability Values in SECFTs

For the calculation of the ratings from Sect. 3.1 at least calculation rules for the gates AND, OR, and NOT are required. Other gates such as XOR or voter gates can be constructed from these three basic gates. Their calculation rules result from the combination accordingly.

Definition 2 (Likelihood of an AND-gate). *All subordinate events have to occur in order that the combined event occurs. Therefore, the event with the lowest likelihood determines the likelihood L of the combined event. This is explained by the fact, that if all events of an AND-gate have to occur, the one with the lowest likelihood also has to occur, which then determines the overall likelihood of the AND-gate.*

Definition 3 (Likelihood of an OR-gate). *At least one subordinate event has to occur in order that the combined event occurs. If there are alternatives to attack a system to trigger the same event, an attacker will execute the one that has the highest outcome while requiring the lowest effort. In other words he will execute the attack action with the highest likelihood.*

Definition 4 (Likelihood of a NOT-gate). *A subordinate event must not occur in order that the resulting event occurs. If the likelihood L is defined as an interval $[1, m]$ of integer values with $m \in \mathbb{N}$, the value of a NOT gate is defined as follows:* $L(\overline{A}) = (m + 1) - L(A)$

The outcome of AND, OR and NOT gates with independent input events A, B, or more general n independent input events X_i, is calculated as follows in Table 1 with $i, n, m \in \mathbb{N}$:

Table 1. Probability and likelihood calculation for AND, OR, and NOT-gates.

	probability	likelihood
AND	$P(A \wedge B) = P(A) \cdot P(B)$	$L(A \wedge B) = \min[L(A), L(B)]$
	$P\left(\bigwedge_{i=1}^{n} X_i\right) = \prod_{i=1}^{n} P(X_i)$	$L\left(\bigwedge_{i=1}^{n} X_i\right) = \min_{i=1}^{n}[L(X_i)]$
OR	$P(A \vee B) = P(A) + P(B) - P(A) \cdot P(B)$	$L(A \vee B) = \max[L(A), L(B)]$
	$P\left(\bigvee_{i=1}^{n} X_i\right) = 1 - \prod_{i=1}^{n}(1 - P(X_i))$	$L\left(\bigvee_{i=1}^{n} X_i\right) = \max_{i=1}^{n}[L(X_i)]$
NOT	$P(\overline{A}) = 1 - P(A)$	$L(\overline{A}) = (m + 1) - L(A)$

If the NOT gate is used it has to be considered that it has an unusual semantics in CFTs: The lower the probability/likelihood of occurrence of an event that is attached to a NOT gate, the higher is its effect on the TE, and vice versa. Whereas normally high probabilities of single events lead to a higher probability for the TE. From this follows that to reduce the TE probability/likelihood, an event or even a whole component that is connected via a NOT has to fail with high probability/likelihood.

To have a uniform rating scheme over all events in a CFT, all ratings of BEs are interpreted as tuples (P, L), where P is a probability and L a likelihood. For safety events there is no likelihood leading to $(P_e, -)$ with an undefined L_e, and for security events there is no probability value leading to $(-, L_e)$ with an undefined P_e. Undefined values will be ignored in the calculation of the rating.

This has to be explained further: The alternative to undefined values would be values that do not influence the order between the events. To achieve this, an *identity element* or *neutral element* for all possible gate-operations would be needed. This would mean in terms of probabilities, a value is needed, which is the identity element for addition and multiplication. Such a value does not exist because the identity element for the addition is 0, and the identity element for the multiplication is 1. The same problem arises for the likelihood operations: The identity element of the min-function is the maximum value, and the identity element of the max-function is the minimum value. These values exclude each other, so no value is selected and the undefined values are ignored during the calculation.

The tuple elements of a combination of events by logic gates are calculated independent of each other according to the rules established earlier. The following example illustrates this in more detail. Figure. 2 shows a high-level view of

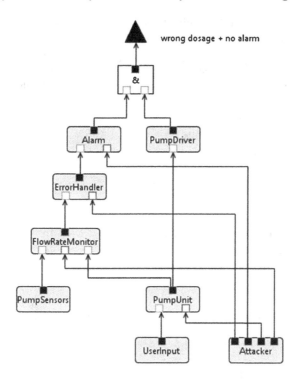

Fig. 2. High-level SECFT model of a generic infusion pump.

a SECFT of a generic patient controlled analgesia pump [4] with all modeled components. The security part is inspired from the security flaw of the infusion pump Hospira PCA3 that was published recently [13]. To include the attack, extra input ports were added to vulnerable components. The actual attack is modeled in component **Attacker**. Suitable ratings for all basic events were chosen. The required Safety Integrity Level for the individual components was estimated and used as order of magnitude for the rating of the safety events. The rating of the security events was chosen due to the simplicity of the physical access (attach an Ethernet cable) and telnet access (no authentication necessary to get root access). The likelihood for the security events in this example is a three-level scale of {low, medium, high} with corresponding values of {1,2,3}. The model has 7 MCSs. Their resulting ratings are shown in Table 2.

The rating of the TE can be calculated as a conservative estimate from a disjunction of all MCSs. The undefined values P_2 and $L_1, L_3, L_4, L_5, L_6, L_7$ are ignored in this calculation.

$$
\begin{aligned}
P_{TE} &= P\left(\bigvee_i MCS_i\right) \\
&= 1 - \prod_i(1 - P(MCS_i)), i \in 1,3,4,5,6,7 \\
&= 1.00000103975262 \cdot 10^{-7} \\
L_{TE} &= \max(L(MCS_2)) \\
&= \max(3) = 3
\end{aligned}
$$

Table 2. Minimal cut sets and ratings.

id	basic events	BE rating	MCS rating
1	PumpUnit.pump unit sets wrong values	10^{-7}	$(10^{-7}, -)$
2	Attacker.physical access the Ethernet interface of the pump	3 (high)	$(- , 3)$
	Attacker.access telnet service of the pump	3 (high)	
3	UserInput.user sets wrong values	10^{-6}	$(10^{-13}, -)$
	PumpUnit.check of user input fails	10^{-7}	
4	PumpDriver.pump driver fails	10^{-8}	$(10^{-15}, -)$
	Alarm.alarm fails	10^{-7}	
5	PumpDriver.pump driver fails	10^{-8}	$(10^{-15}, -)$
	ErrorHandler.error handler fails	10^{-7}	
6	PumpDriver.pump driver fails	10^{-8}	$(10^{-15}, -)$
	FlowRateMonitor.flow rate monitor fails	10^{-7}	
7	PumpDriver.pump driver fails	10^{-8}	$(10^{-15}, -)$
	PumpSensors.sensors provide wrong values	10^{-7}	

That results in a rating of $(P_{TE}, L_{TE}) = (1.00000103975262 \cdot 10^{-7}, 3)$ for the TE *wrong dosage and no alarm*.

3.3   Qualitative Analysis

The most important activity of a qualitative analysis in CFTs and SECFTs is the determination of MCSs. MCSs also are used to derive a coarse classification of the criticality of failure scenarios and BEs, and they allow to make statements about the general endangerment of the analyzed system. MCSs are also an important starting point for a following quantitative analysis. Based on the MCSs also a basic importance analysis of BEs and MCSs can be conducted.

This Section deals with necessary extensions of the qualitative analysis of CFTs to cope with additional security events in the SECFT. The first step of the analysis is the determination and analysis of the MCSs. The interpretation of a MCS is the same as in CFTs: a MCS is a minimal safety failure scenario (but possibly depending also on security attacks). A CFT (and therefore a SECFT as well) can be transformed into a set of MCSs that represents all failure scenarios which are relevant for the system. In general, a tree contains multiple MCSs corresponding to different failure scenarios.

In addition to size, an analysis of MCSs of a SECFT takes also the type of the MCSs into account. The result of a qualitative analysis are ordered lists of MCSs.

As discussed in detail in Sects. 3.1 and 3.2, ratings of safety and security events cannot be compared directly. Therefore, it makes sense to sort them according to safety events and security events. Then, one receives three lists of MCSs (Definition 1):

1. safety MCS
2. security MCS
3. mixed MCS

Safety MCSs are analyzed as usual: A qualitative analysis starts with an ordering according to the size of the MCS. The smaller a MCS the more critically it should be analyzed. This is explained by the fact that all events in a MCS have to occur, so that the TE occurs and the system fails. The lesser events have to occur, the more the TE depends on individual events. So events in smaller MCSs deserve more attention in an analysis. An especially critical case is a MCS with only one event – a single point of failure which itself can directly lead to the system failure.

Security MCSs are a more special case: In this case a system failure only depends on external influences and does not depend on failures of internal system components. Pure security MCSs are not more critical per se than pure safety MCSs, but the uncertainty of the modeling of an attack is relatively high. Depending on the threat scenario and the attacker type the likelihood value changes. Necessary tools become better available and cheaper over time which can make an attack more probable in the future. Also, the attacker type, the attacker's motivation and capabilities can and will change over time – potentially to the disadvantage of the system. This is why pure security MCSs should be avoided by adding suitable countermeasures which convert security MCSs to mixed MCSs.

Mixed MCSs on the other hand can be managed better: For the occurrence of the TE all events of a mixed MCS have to occur, which means regular safety events have to occur. These occurrences of safety events can be managed with the usual methods like redundancy or monitoring. The probability for a mixed MCS to cause the TE has an upper bound: the probability of the contained safety events. This way the criticality of security events can be mitigated by safety events with low probability. That means, the more statistically independent safety events a MCS contains the less probable it is to cause the TE.

To summarize the qualitative analysis of MCSs: There are three types of MCSs which differ in the level of controllability of their BEs. Controllability in this context means how much a failure scenario (a MCS) depends on faults of the system as opposed to external factors as e.g. attacks. In descending order according to their controllability these are: safety MCSs, mixed MCSs and security MCSs. Resulting from that, additionally to MCSs containing only one event (single points of failure) also plain security MCSs should be avoided by adding more (safety) BEs. Also, the more MCSs exist in a given SECFT, the more opportunities for the TE exist, which indicates a higher vulnerability of the system with respect to this TE.

Another goal of an analysis is to determine the importance of BEs. The importance shows how much of an impact a BE has on a TE. BEs that are part of more than one MCS are more important than the ones that are only part of one MCS. But the size of MCSs is also a factor. BEs in smaller MCSs are more important than the ones in larger MCSs. More accurate importance analysis is possible within a quantitative analysis.

3.4 Quantitative Analysis

A quantitative analysis is conducted if more accurate statements about the system safety are necessary than the results from a qualitative analysis, which are mainly the determination and preliminary ordering of MCSs. A quantitative analysis, therefore, has several goals [3, 18]:

- to determine the rating of the TE under consideration to compare it to the given requirements from standards or customers,
- to determine ratings of the individual MCSs to determine the MCS that has the biggest contribution to the TE (the most probable failure scenario),
- and derived from the previous ones: to determine where countermeasures would have the most effect.

A quantitative analysis of a SECFT starts with a quantitative evaluation of its MCSs. The first step here is to assign probabilities to safety events and likelihoods to security events. (During the assignment of likelihood values to security events it should be kept in mind that those security events belonging to the same MCS can influence each other.)

After the determination of the MCSs there are two possibilities to order them: according to size and type (see qualitative analysis in Sect. 3.3) or according to type and ratings (probability and likelihood). An ordering simply according to the ratings is not possible for all MCSs in general because of the incomparability of probabilities and likelihoods (see also Sect. 3.1). For each MCS a tuple rating (P, L) is calculated according to the rules described in Sect. 3.2. For probabilities this means the value for the MCS is the product of all probabilities of the contained events. (Under the precondition that all events are independent, which is usually given for safety events.) For the likelihood of a MCS the minimum of all likelihoods of the included events is determined.

Each type of MCSs can be ordered by itself. To compare two minimal cut sets MCS_1 and MCS_2 with tuple ratings (P_1, L_1) and (P_2, L_2), the ordering has to be prioritized either according to probability or to likelihood. The resulting ordered list of MCSs reflects the relative criticality of the represented failure scenarios. Higher ratings here correspond to a higher criticality and vice versa. To find out if the system complies with the given requirements, the list of MCSs is filtered according to the requirements (e.g.: "show me all MCSs with size ≤ 2", "$P > 10^{-7}$" or "$L \geq 2$(medium)"). The results are the failure scenarios that require countermeasures.

As mentioned earlier, requirements can define boundary values for MCSs in size or rating, but usually the main requirement is a boundary value for the rating of the TEs: "the system shall not fail with a probability more than . . . " The TE probability can be calculated as the sum of the probabilities of all MCSs if only AND and OR gates are used. This defines an upper bound for the probability:

$$P(TE) \leq \sum_{i=1}^{n} P(MCS_i), i, n \in \mathbb{N}, n \text{ number of MCSs} \qquad (1)$$

The other variant is to calculate $P(TE)$ using the binary decision diagram (BDD) algorithm which returns the exact probability value. To adapt the BDD algorithm to SECFTs only the BEs with an assigned probability value are considered for the calculation as already discussed in Sect. 3.2.

The likelihood of the TE $L(TE)$ is simply calculated as the maximum of the likelihoods of all MCSs as defined in the equations for the OR-gate:

$$L(TE) = L\left(\bigvee_{i=1}^{n} X_i\right) = \max_{i=1}^{n}[L(X_i)], i, n \in \mathbb{N}, n \text{ number of MCSs} \qquad (2)$$

With the described extensions of the calculation rules and the different types of MCSs SECFTs can be used to conduct safety analysis with additional consideration of security problems.

4   Conclusion

Based on SECFTs a qualitative and quantitative safety analysis is extended to include influences of security problems on the safety of a system. To avoid the problem how to assign probabilities to security events, a scale of discrete values (e.g. {low, medium, high}) is used to rate security events while retaining the higher accuracy of probabilities for safety events. Existing analysis techniques are extended to work with probabilities for safety events as well as discrete likelihoods for security events. As a result, a hybrid rating scheme is used to rank the different MCSs according to the tuple of probability and likelihood, and to calculate TE ratings that can be used to check the compliance of requirements.

Acknowledgement. The research leading to these results has received funding from the ARTEMIS Joint Undertaking under grant agreement n° 621429 (project EMC^2) and from the respective national funding authorities.

References

1. IEC 61882: Hazard and operability studies (HAZOP studies) – Application guide (2001)
2. IEC 60300-3-1: Dependability management - Part 3–1: Application guide; Analysis techniques for dependability; Guide on methodology, May 2005
3. IEC 61025: Fault tree Analysis (FTA) (2006)
4. Arney, D., Jetley, R., Zhang, Y., Jones, P., Sokolsky, O., Lee, I., Ray, A.: The generic patient controlled analgesia pump model. Website (2009). http://rtg.cis.upenn.edu/gip.php3
5. Casals, S.G., Owezarski, P., Descargues, G.: Risk assessment for airworthiness security. In: Ortmeier, F., Lipaczewski, M. (eds.) SAFECOMP 2012. LNCS, vol. 7612, pp. 25–36. Springer, Heidelberg (2012)

6. Fovino, I.N., Masera, M., Cian, A.D.: Integrating cyber attacks within fault trees. Reliab. Eng. Syst. Saf. **94**, 1394–1402 (2009)

7. Förster, M., Schwarz, R., Steiner, M.: Integration of modular safety and security models for the analysis of the impact of security on safety. Technical Report, Fraunhofer IESE, Technische Universität Kaiserslautern (2010). http://publica.fraunhofer.de/dokumente/N-151512.html

8. Hernan, S., Lambert, S., Ostwald, T., Shostack, A.: Uncover security design flaws using the stride approach. MSDN Magazine, November 2006. http://msdn.microsoft.com/en-us/magazine/cc163519.aspx

9. IEC/TC 56 Reliability and maintainability: IEC 60812: Analysis techniques for system reliability - Procedure for failure mode and effects analysis (FMEA), January 2006

10. Jürgenson, A., Willemson, J.: Computing exact outcomes of multi-parameter attack trees. In: Meersman, R., Tari, Z. (eds.) OTM 2008, Part II. LNCS, vol. 5332, pp. 1036–1051. Springer, Heidelberg (2008)

11. Kaiser, B., Liggesmeyer, P., Mäckel, O.: A new component concept for fault trees. In: 8th Australian Workshop on Safety Critical Systems and Software. Canberra, October 2003. http://dl.acm.org/citation.cfm?id=1082051.1082054

12. Mauw, S., Oostdijk, M.: Foundations of attack trees. In: Won, D.H., Kim, S. (eds.) ICISC 2005. LNCS, vol. 3935, pp. 186–198. Springer, Heidelberg (2006)

13. Scherschel, F.: Root-Shell im Krankenhaus: Hospira-Infusionspumpe mit Telnet-Lücke. Website (2015). http://heise.de/-2633529

14. Schmittner, C., Gruber, T., Puschner, P., Schoitsch, E.: Security application of failure mode and effect analysis (FMEA). In: Bondavalli, A., Di Giandomenico, F. (eds.) SAFECOMP 2014. LNCS, vol. 8666, pp. 310–325. Springer, Heidelberg (2014)

15. Schneier, B.: Attack trees. Dr. Dobb's Journal, December 1999. http://www.schneier.com/paper-attacktrees-ddj-ft.html

16. Steiner, M., Liggesmeyer, P.: Combination of safety and security analysis - finding security problems that threaten the safety of a system. In: ROY, M. (ed.) Proceedings of Workshop DECS (ERCIM/EWICS Workshop on Dependable Embedded and Cyber-physical Systems) of the 32nd International Conference on Computer Safety, Reliability and Security (2013). http://hal.archives-ouvertes.fr/hal-00848604

17. Verendel, V.: Quantified security is a weak hypothesis: a critical survey of results and assumptions. In: NSPW 2009: Proceedings of the 2009 Workshop on New Security Paradigms Workshop, pp. 37–50. ACM, New York, NY, USA (2009)

18. Vesely, W., Goldberg, F., Roberts, N., Haasl, D.: Fault Tree Handbook. U.S, Nuclear Regulatory Commission (1981)

Sequential Logic for State/Event Fault Trees: A Methodology to Support the Failure Modeling of Cyber Physical Systems

Michael Roth[✉] and Peter Liggesmeyer

Chair of Software Engineering: Dependability, University of Kaiserslautern,
Kaiserslautern, Germany
{michael.roth,liggesmeyer}@cs.uni-kl.de

Abstract. The society is nowadays increasingly controlled through embedded systems. The certification process of such systems is often supported by tree based approaches like fault trees. Nevertheless, these methodologies have some crucial drawbacks when it comes to dynamic systems. In the standard fault tree analysis it is not possible to model dependent events as well as timing behavior. To deal with these disadvantages state/event fault trees (SEFTs) were developed. However, this method is mainly restricted to academic problems due to its poor analysis procedures. To overcome this problem, this paper introduces a new qualitative analysis technique for SEFTs based on event sequences that can be identified out of their reachability graphs. To analyze these sequences an event sequence minimization schema similar to minimal cut sets of normal fault trees is proposed. Afterwards, a sequence algebra is used to further minimize these temporal expressions and transform them as far as possible into static ones.

Keywords: State event fault tree · Fault tree · Sequential logic · Reliability analysis · Cyber physical system

1 Introduction

Due to its effectiveness, fault tree analysis (FTA) is a widely accepted method to determine the failure behavior of safety critical systems. Since fault trees (FTs) are originally designed to model the failure behavior of mechanical as well as electrical parts it is hard to apply them on dynamic system parts, like e.g. software-controlled modules. This relies on the fact that they are not able to model dependencies or timing relations of the underlying system. FTs describe the failure relations via a hierarchical decomposition of the involved failure events through logical gates. This results in Boolean logic expressions. It is obvious that such simple Boolean formulas cannot describe temporal relations. Furthermore, modeling of dependent events leads to wrong evaluations, which is intolerable in modern systems where designs like warm stand-by situations are ubiquitous. In [8] Kaiser et al. introduced state/event fault trees (SEFTs) to overcome these

© Springer International Publishing Switzerland 2015
F. Koornneef and C. van Gulijk (Eds.): SAFECOMP 2015 Workshops, LNCS 9338, pp. 121–132, 2015.
DOI: 10.1007/978-3-319-24249-1_11

problems. SEFTs can be seen as a combination of state charts to model the temporal dependencies and fault tree similar gates to model the causal relations. The wide spread of standardized FTs could be mainly attributed to their variety of evaluation methods. It is possible to analyze FTs quantitatively as well as qualitatively. An often used qualitative analysis method is the minimal cut set (MCS) analysis. MCS analysis determines the smallest sets of events that trigger the tree's root by their simultaneous occurrence. The root node is also called top event (TE). By such a MCS analysis it is possible to identify the most critical events early in the life-cycle since there is no need for any quantification. This is easily possible by the length of the cut sets or via the involvement of a specific basic event in different minimal cut sets. The first measure identifies the most critical events by their participation in short cut sets whereas the second method identifies critical events by their frequent occurrence in different cut sets. This paper shows a quantitative analysis approach for SEFTs similar to the MCS analysis of standard fault trees. It is based on the reachability graph which represents a SEFT's state-space. Based on this reachability graph this work propose a subsequent sequential analysis that identifies pure failure event sequences through a differentiation of the involved events. A second innovation is given by the introduction of a sequential algebra which is able to deal with these pure failure event sequences by transforming them into temporal expressions. This approach could be seen as a further development of the ideas introduced in [12].

2   Related Work

FTs were first introduced in the 1960's by H. R. Watson [16]. In the last few decades FTs were consequently improved and adapted to changing requirements and domains. One way to do this, was by introducing new gates to adopt FTs to the growing demands of system engineering [3, 14]. The introduction of smarter gates, however, require more advanced analysis approaches, on the quantitative [9, 10, 13] as well as the qualitative [6, 17] side. The major drawback of these extended fault tree approaches remains however their inability to deal with repairable systems.

A technique that is especially developed for modeling temporal failure dependencies in dynamic systems is the so-called temporal fault tree (TFT) approach, introduced in 2001 by Palshikar [11]. TFTs are able to improve the temporal expressiveness of origin fault trees via special gates that are strongly related to the backward operators of linear temporal logic. Thus, it is possible to identify traces that trigger the TE of the tree. Especially their analysis procedures are very immature and it is necessary to spend additional effort in developing customized analysis techniques. To the best of our knowledge, there is no quantitative analysis approach available whereas the proposed qualitative analysis approaches are insufficient to analyze complex tree models.

The next kind of temporal fault trees are invented by Martin Walker [15]. In comparison to DFTs, this approach is more concerned about an accurate time model instead of modeling dependencies. Similar to the approach proposed in this paper, Walker's fault trees can be transformed into temporal expressions. These expressions can then be reduced by temporal laws. However, this approach focused on non-repairable systems, which is an assumption that is untenable in most of the today's technical environments. Other approaches to model the dynamic behavior of systems are Markov chains [4] or Petri-nets [2].

Another approach is proposed by Bozzano and Villaorita [1]. They use a symbolic model checker to determine ordering information of basic events. Therefore, it is necessary to describe the system as a formal model whereas its failure behavior is modeled as a static fault tree. The model checker determines event sequences of the tree's MCSs. In contrast to that, our approach uses only one model to produce similar event sequences. This is more intuitive, especially for people from the safety domain. The major drawback of this approach, however, is its suitability only for persistent failures which is equal to the non-reparability assumption of the most fault tree based approaches.

3   State/Event Fault Trees

This section gives a deeper introduction to SEFTs. SEFTs are, roughly spoken, a combination of state charts and fault tree gates which can be connected via so-called ports. A state chart exists out of states (Fig. 1a-V) and events (Fig. 1a-IV) connectable through edges that are called temporal connections (Fig. 1a-VII) because of their ability to express the timing information within a SEFT. These states and events can be connected via causal edges (Fig. 1a-VIII) with gates (Fig. 1a-VI) to express combinatorial failure-behavior. The gates are similar to the static gates of standard FTs drawn as rectangles with the difference that there exist state and event inlets and -outlets. This gives the modeling of failures completely new possibilities. To combine elements of one state chart (also called component) with those from another one an effective port concept is available. State ports (Fig. 1a-II) as well as event port (Fig. 1a-III) could be used as input (Fig. 1a-III.I,III.II) or output ports (Fig. 1a-II.I,II.II) of a component. Their connection with gates allow the application of pure causal relations between different components. Constructs like triggered events (Fig. 1a-VI.III) or guarded events (Fig. 1a-IV.IV), however, can also be used to express dependencies between two components. A triggered event could be understood as an externally controlled event. This means that one component triggers the switching process of a second one. Additionally, it is possible to use guarded events to model events that become enabled in case of the activation of a specific state. Typically, these state is a member of another component. To describe the inner relations in a component there exist different event types. The first class are immediate events (Fig. 1a-IV.V), which fire directly in case of their enabling and are mostly used as so-called initialize (init) events. One init event is mandatory in each state chart and defines its starting state. Another event class are timed events that could either fire after a deterministic timespan (Fig. 1a-IV.II) or after an exponentially distributed one (Fig. 1a-IV.I). As already mentioned before, there exist different types of gates in SEFTs. These gates are defined through the type of their inlets. Thus, there exist pure state gates (only state inlets), pure event gates (only event inlets) and, finally, mixed gates. An example of a state gate is an AND-gate. It is activated if all states connected to its inlets are activated. Other gates can be found in the gate dictionary of [8, Appendix]. It also defines temporal gates that are able to model dynamic behavior on their own. To get an overview of all modeling elements in SEFT see Fig. 1.

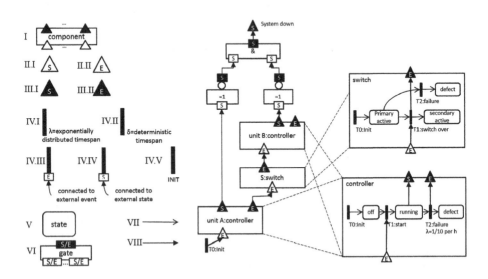

Fig. 1. SEFT elements Primary stand-by system modeled as SEFT

An example of a simple SEFT is depicted in Fig. 1b. Therein a primary stand-by system is showed that consists out of two redundant controller units, named *unit A* and *unit B*. The *switch* component is responsible for shifting the workload to the secondary unit (*unit B*) in case of a failure of the primary unit (*unit A*). The switch has also a failed state (*defect state*). If it fails, the system is not able to perform the switching process after a failure of the primary unit. This also leads to a system failure. The controllers are both modeled as a proxy of type controller that includes an *off state*, a *running state* and a *defect state*. Due to the assumption that a component can only fail under a specific workload there exists no direct transition between the *off state* and the *defect state*. Since there is the need of a trigger impulse from the component's environment to switch it on, the transition between the *off state* and the *running state* is modeled as immediate transition (*start transition*). The primary unit is directly connected with the initial event of the system by which it is transfered into its *running state* at system start. For the secondary unit these triggering relation is executed by the switch element through the *switch-over transition*. Due to simplicity reasons, all components are modeled without a repair strategy. The hazardous situation of the system is reached whenever both controllers are not in their running states, expressed by the negated event-out-ports connected via the AND-gate.

The gate's outlet represents the top element of the model that can be expressed by the boolean equation $\overline{unitA.running} \wedge \overline{unitB.running}$.

4 Sequence Logic of SEFTs

In the original design of SEFTs it is only possible to analyze them quantitatively by the use of the tool TimeNet [18]. Therefore it is necessary to translate an SEFT into a Petri-net, more precisely into a deterministic and stochastic Petri-net (DSPN). [12] proposes an multi-step approach which is able to analyze such a DSPN qualitatively as well, via a reduced reachability graph (RRG). A four step reduction process compresses the RRG afterwards. This results in an intuitive and understandable graph which represents the event sequences that lead to a hazardous reachability state graphically. If it comes, however, to much more complex system models it could be hard to evaluate their sequences manually. In this case it could be beneficial to transform them automatically into event sequences. We provide an recursive deep-first search algorithm to derive the event sequences from a RRG. This algorithm delivers event sequences starting from a RRG's initial state and ending in one of its top element afflicted nodes. In relation to the work of Liu et al. [9] we call the total set of sequences the standard event sequence set (SSS). The temporal relations in a standard event sequence are represented through the sequential operator $\rightarrow$ which expresses the situation that an event on its left side is in **direct** sequence to the event on its right side. The RRG of the primary stand by system results in a SSS with two sequences shown in (1).

$$System.Init \rightarrow A.start \rightarrow A.failure \rightarrow S.switchover \rightarrow B.start \rightarrow B.failure$$
$$System.Init \rightarrow A.start \rightarrow S.failure \rightarrow A.failure$$
$$(1)$$

Large state-spaces mostly deliver long standard event sequences that include a series of insignificant events. To be able to represent a SSS more user friendly, our approach distinguishes between different event classes: *failure events*, *repair events* and *other events*. By this it is possible to filter out complete sets of events. For evaluation proposes the SSS can be transformed into a so-called failure event sequence set (FSS). Thereby, only the events that are typed as failure events remain in the sequences. This can be done by a simple operation that connects the first failure event of a standard event sequence with the following one, disregarding events of other types in between. Thus, the original SSS of (1) can be transfered into the FSS of (2) under the assumption that every involved component has one failure event named *failure*.

$$A.failure \rightarrow B.failure$$
$$S.failure \rightarrow A.failure$$
$$(2)$$

It is imaginable to extend this classification schema into a structure similar to an inheritance hierarchy. This allows a more fine grained distinction between events, e.g. splitting up the failure events into safety and security related failure events. Thus, it is possible to build a cross domain model which could be of major interest for the certification process of upcoming systems.

To remove redundancies in the resulting event sequence set, we propose a set of mathematical reduction rules which are derived from Boolean logic. These rules are represented in Table 1. First of all, it is possible to use the *rule of minimization* to delete all sequences that represent detours in the graph. This results in a minimal event sequence set (MSS) which could be seen as the temporal counterpart to a MCS of a static fault tree.

Theorem 1. *A standard sequence is called minimal if it does not include any other sequence of the SSS. A sequence $S1$ includes the sequence $S2$ if all events of $S2$ represent a subset of the events of $S1$ and if these subset have the same ordering schema as the events of $S2$.*

Thus, it is obvious that a failure event sequence is always a minimization of its origin standard sequence. The sequence $System.Init \rightarrow A.start \rightarrow S.failure \rightarrow A.failure$ includes the sequence $S.failure \rightarrow A.failure$ as well as the sequence $System.Init \rightarrow S.failure \rightarrow A.failure$. Applying this rule to the SSS of (2) results in an unmodified sequence since all involved sequences are already minimal.

Further reductions can mainly be achieved though the use of the sequence algebra's *distributive law* by setting equal subsequences into brackets. This allows removing equal parts of different sequences by combining all members of a SSS

Table 1. Sequential logic inference rules

Distributive rule	$E1 \rightarrow (E2 \vee E3)$		$E1 \rightarrow E2 \vee E1 \rightarrow E3$
	$(E1 \vee E2) \rightarrow E3$	$\Leftrightarrow$	$E1 \rightarrow E3 \vee E2 \rightarrow E3$
	$E1 < (S1 \vee S2)$		$E1 < S1 \vee E1 < S2$
	$(S1 \vee S2) < E1$		$E1 < S1 \vee E1 < S2$
Associative rule	$(E1 \rightarrow E2) \rightarrow E3$	$\Leftrightarrow$	$E1 \rightarrow E2 \rightarrow E3$
	$(E1\ H\&\ E2)\ H\&\ E3$		$E1\ H\&\ E2\ H\&\ E3$
Commutative rule	$E1\ H\&\ E2$	$\Leftrightarrow$	$E2\ H\&\ E1$
	$E1 \vee E2$		$E2 \vee E1$
Idempotent rule	$... \rightarrow E1 \rightarrow E1 \rightarrow ...$	$\Leftrightarrow$	$... \rightarrow E1 \rightarrow ...$
	$... < S1 < S1 < ...$		$... < S1 < ...$
Rule of minimization	$S1 \vee S2$ iff $S1 \subseteq S2$	$\Leftrightarrow$	$S1$
Conjunction rule	$S1\ H\&\ S2$	$\Leftrightarrow$	$S1 < S2 \vee S2 < S1$
Rule of absorbtion	$S1\ H\&\ S2$ iff $S2 \subseteq S1$	$\Leftrightarrow$	$S1$
Illegal expressions	$... \rightarrow E1 \rightarrow ... \rightarrow E1 \rightarrow ...$; $... < S1 < ... < S1 < ...$		

via OR-gates since they represent independent paths that end in a critical system state. This rule could be used to eliminate the redundant starting sequence of both members of the SSS of (1). Thus, the subsequence $System.Init \rightarrow A.start$ can be bracket out resulting in the following expression:

$$
\begin{aligned}
System.Init \rightarrow A.start \rightarrow (A.failure \rightarrow S.switchover \rightarrow \\
B.start \rightarrow B.failure \vee S.failure \rightarrow A.failure)
\end{aligned}
\tag{3}
$$

Another reduction could be achieved by the use of the *conjunction rule*. It allows the reduction of two so-called temporal redundant expressions into a static one. The two sequences: $S1 : E1 \rightarrow E2$, $S2 : E2 \rightarrow E1$ can be combined via an AND operation since these two events are no longer in a temporal relationship. A first occurrence of $E1$ followed by an occurrence of $E2$ completes the sequence $S1$ whereas the vice versa situation completes $S2$. To express this relation, the static AND-gate seems to be insufficient due to the presence of events which have, in contrast to basic events of static fault trees, infinitesimal short occurrence times. Basic events of static fault trees could be understood as a transition of a failure free state to a fail state of the corresponding system part whereas events in a SEFT follows Definition 2.

Theorem 2. *An event is the occurrence of an observable thing that happen at a random point in time which, itself, has no duration.*

Thus, the formal AND-gate definition would never recognize the activation of the gate since there exist no point in time where both inlets are triggered simultaneously. For this reason a history-AND-gate (H&-gate) is proposed to overcome this problem. The H&-gate allows the detection of events and produces an event at its outlet whenever all input events have occurred at least once since the last occurrence of the output event. To be able to describe the H&-gate formally correct in our sequence algebra it is necessary to introduce a second temporal operator - the before/after-relation expressed by $<$. It describes the situation that its left sided expression has to occur before the expression on the right side. This allows the decomposing of a static expression that includes a H&-gate into a set of temporal ones. Two sequences separated by the before/after operator result in a set of sequences by a stepwise merging operation. This concept is exemplified in (4) for the sequences $S1 : E1 \rightarrow E2$ and $S2 : E3 \rightarrow E4$.

$$
\begin{aligned}
S1 < S2 = (E1 \rightarrow E2) < (E3 \rightarrow E4) \\
= E1 \rightarrow E2 \rightarrow E3 \rightarrow E4 \vee E1 \rightarrow E3 \rightarrow E2 \rightarrow E4 \vee E3 \rightarrow E1 \rightarrow E2 \rightarrow E4
\end{aligned}
\tag{4}
$$

This concept allows the use of the sequence algebra in both directions: either to reduce a SSS into a more compact static expression or to decompose a reduced static expression in its SSS. To hold the temporal expressions intuitive and comprehensible, the conjunction rule is only partially implemented in our analysis tool, the qualitative SEFT analyzer [12]. It only converts simple permutations into static expressions. This allows a reduction only if every permutation of a subsequence is available. Since the identification of permuted subsequences is an NP complete problem it is realized by a brute force approach. The algorithm starts with removing all equal sequences in the corresponding sequence set. Afterwards, it compares all sequence members with each other and retains only the sequences with equal member sets. This results in a sequence set with equal members but different sequences which claims that all remaining sequences are permutations of each other. Finally, a simple comparison of the total amount of sequences (*sequence count* with the faculty of the number of sequence members (*sequence member count*) is used to proof the existence of a complete permutation set (cf. Equation (5)). A successful proof allows the replacing of the sequence set by a H&-linked expression of the sequence members. Thereby, the member ordering does not play a role due to the *commutative rule* of the H&. In the SEFTAnalyzer is also a test class implemented which allows a maximal reduction of a given SSS. First evaluation results, however, confirm that a maximal reduction mostly ends in complex expressions that are hard to interpret.

$$sequence count \stackrel{!}{=} sequence member count! \tag{5}$$

The next rule which should be considered in more detail is the *rule of absorption*. By this rule it is possible to remove the input sequence $S1$ of a H&-gate ($S1$ H&$S2$) if $S1$ is included in $S2$. This rule represents the counterpart to the rule of minimization. Due to its AND relation of two sequences it is obvious that a H&-gate's outlet is triggered only if the longer sequence is completely executed. This means, however, that the shorter one is also entirely executed since it is included in the longer one. This allows disregarding of the included sequence. Against that, the minimization rule could be seen as a similar operation applied to an OR-gate. In case of an inclusion relation of both input sequences ($S1 \subseteq S2$), the gate is activated as soon as its shorter input sequences $S1$ is complete.

A strict application of this sequence algebra could end in so-called illegal expressions. Such expressions can be directly removed from the set of sequences since they could never be completely executed due to their logical inadequacies. The expression ($E1 \rightarrow E2$) < ($E2 \rightarrow E3$) for example ends in the sequence $E2 \rightarrow E1 \rightarrow E2 \rightarrow E3$ which can be neglected due to the fact that all repair strategies are eliminated during the development of the origin SSS. Thus, it is impossible that $E2$ fires at two different point in times. The remaining two sequences include subsequences of equal events ($E1 \rightarrow E2 \rightarrow E2 \rightarrow E3$) which can be simplified through the *idempotent rule* by removing equal sequencing events. This ends in the reduced sequence $E1 \rightarrow E2 \rightarrow E3$ which is, by the way, the only valid outcome of the given expression.

5   Evaluation

In this section we present the application of our approach with an example system. We decided to use a hypothetical dynamic system (HDS) which is already used in other case studies [7,9]. By the use of this system it is easy to compare the results of our approach with them of [9]. Since the origin version of the

HDS is modeled as a dynamic fault tree (DFT) there are some changes necessary to represent it as a SEFT. The HDS is a complexer version of the already
introduced primary stand-by system of Fig. 1b. It is extended by one additional
control unit. In case of the HDS, however, it is necessary that at least two controller units are available to ensure a working system. The third unit, named
unit C, is a cold stand-by part that take over the workload of one of the two
main controllers depending on which fails first. For this reason the *switch* has to
be extended by an OR-gate (for events) to be able to monitor failures of both
main units simultaneously.

To be able to apply our methodology to the HDS it was necessary to remodel
it as a SEFT without any loss of accuracy (cf. Fig. 2). The three controllers
therein are proxies of the controller element of Fig. 1b. The repair strategies
were omitted on purpose of comparability and simplicity. The inner structure
of the unknown components, like the switch and the voter, can be found on the
right side of Fig. 2. The *two out of three voter gate* (2oo3) has an activated outlet
whenever two of its three inlets are in a fail state, respectively in a not-working
state. This is modeled via a NOT-gate at the controllers *running state-out-port*.
Consequently, its TE can be expressed as the Boolean expression $(\overline{A} \wedge \overline{B}) \vee (\overline{A} \wedge \overline{C}) \vee (\overline{B} \wedge \overline{C})$ where $\overline{X}$ represents a controller which is not in its running state.
The origin version of the HDS can be found in [9] [Fig. 5].

We use the modeling tool ESSaRel [5] to build the SEFT model of the HDS
which is depicted in Fig. 2. The complete MSS analysis is done with an extension
of the SEFT-Analyzer tool [12] which is origin developed for state-space analysis

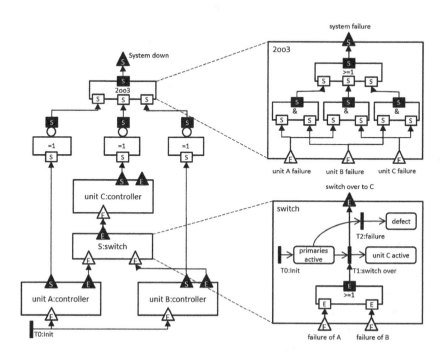

Fig. 2. SEFT model of the hypothetical dynamic system

of SEFTs. It uses the RRG of the model to extract its MSS. (6) shows a cutout of the raw sequence set of the HDS. There are 12 standard sequences in total for the model.

$$
\begin{aligned}
&I.\ System.Init \rightarrow A.start \rightarrow B.start \rightarrow A.failure \rightarrow \\
&\quad S.switchover \rightarrow C.start \rightarrow B.failure \\
&II.\ System.Init \rightarrow B.start \rightarrow A.start \rightarrow A.failure \rightarrow \\
&\quad S.switchover \rightarrow C.start \rightarrow B.failure \\
&III.\ System.Init \rightarrow A.start \rightarrow B.start \rightarrow A.failure \rightarrow \\
&\quad S.switchover \rightarrow C.start \rightarrow C.failure \\
&\qquad\qquad \vdots \\
&XII.\ System.Init \rightarrow B.start \rightarrow A.start \rightarrow S.failure \rightarrow \\
&\quad B.failure
\end{aligned}
\tag{6}
$$

A major reduction can be achieved by filtering out all non-failure events. In case of the given SEFT only the *.failure* events remains in the sequences. The resulting FSS is given afterwards in (7). This ends in six sequences in total due to the start sequence variation ($System.Init \rightarrow (A.start \rightarrow B.start \vee B.start \rightarrow A.start)$) which could be replaced by the static expression $System.Init \rightarrow (A.start\ H\&\ B.start)$ (conjunction rule). The substitution of the start sequence of every SSS ends in six duplicated failure event sequences (cf. I. and II. in (6)) where one sequence of every duplicate can be neglected (rule of minimization).

$$
\begin{array}{llll}
I. & A.failure \rightarrow B.failure & IV. & B.failure \rightarrow C.failure \\
II. & A.failure \rightarrow C.failure & V. & S.failure \rightarrow A.failure \\
III. & B.failure \rightarrow A.failure & VI. & S.failure \rightarrow B.failure
\end{array}
\tag{7}
$$

A comparison of (7) with the results of [9] (6) allows the assumption that the SEFT model of the HDS is defined correctly due to the equal results. A further simplification can be achieved through the application of the inference rules on the FSS. A stepwise adoption of the sequential logic laws is shown in the expression (8).

$$
\begin{aligned}
&(A.failure \rightarrow B.failure) \vee (A.failure \rightarrow C.failure)\vee \\
&(B.failure \rightarrow A.failure) \vee (B.failure \rightarrow C.failure)\vee \\
&(S.failure \rightarrow A.failure) \vee (S.failure \rightarrow B.failure) \\
=&(A.failure\ H\&\ B.failure) \vee (A.failure \rightarrow C.failure) \vee (B.failure \rightarrow C.failure)\vee \\
&(S.failure \rightarrow A.failure) \vee (S.failure \rightarrow B.failure) \\
=&(A.failure\ H\&\ B.failure) \vee ((A.failure \vee B.failure) \rightarrow C.failure)\vee \\
&(S.failure \rightarrow A.failure) \vee (S.failure \rightarrow B.failure) \\
=&(A.failure\ H\&\ B.failure) \vee ((A.failure \vee B.failure) \rightarrow C.failure)\vee \\
&(S.failure \rightarrow (A.failure \vee B.failure))
\end{aligned}
\tag{8}
$$

The sequential analysis of the model determines a total set of three independent failure sequences for the HDS. The first reduction in (8) has been achieved through the application of the conjunction rule. By applying the distributive law it is possible to achieve the second as well as the third simplification. This removes all temporal redundancies in the resulting temporal expression. There are also other reductions imaginable which ends in different solutions. The SEFT Analyzer, however, searches for the solution with the smallest sequence set. In case of two or more sequence sets of the same size, the tool searches for the solution with the shortest members. This is done by the determination of the average sequence length. But again, the main focus lays not in the maximum reduction of the expressions. As already discussed in the previous sections, our approach rather aims on maximal simplification of the expressions w. r. t. the understandability. For this reason not every inference rule is implemented in our tool.

6 Conclusion

In this paper we presented a qualitative approach to determine a compact and simplified sequence set of a SEFT. As a basis we use the state-space of the corresponding DSPN. We proposed a sequential logic for the failure event sequences which can be derived from the Petri-net's reachability graph. By a set of inference rules, it is possible to summarize the sequences to compact temporal expressions. This is helpful if it comes to complex state-spaces where it is hard to identify the important failure event sequences by hand. The sequential logic aims to remove the temporal redundancies in the sequence set what could be seen as the major benefit of the approach. Therefore, it uses specific rules that transform a temporal expression into a static one (distributive law, conjunction rule, etc.). In total, we presented seven temporal rules for the simplification of the event sequences and exemplified illegal expressions that have to be removed in the resulting sequence set. To evaluate the approach, we use an hypothetical example system which is already used in other dynamic fault tree approaches to validate their results. Due to the fact that this approach is tested only under academic conditions, we plan to apply it to larger systems as the next step. Therefore, we actually work on a methodology that determines the RRG of an SEFT without a DSPN–translation to restrict the state-space explosion. The analysis strategy shown in this paper extend the range of SEFT evaluation and could be helpful to push SEFTs a little further to real industrial use cases. We are of the opinion that SEFTs can strongly enrich the failure modeling of dynamic systems and can support the certification process of software-controlled systems as well as cyber physical systems.

References

1. Bozzano, M., Villafiorita, A.: Integrating fault tree analysis with event ordering information. In: Proceedings of the European Safety and Reliability Conference (ESREL) (2003)
2. Buchacker, K.: Combining Fault Trees And Petri Nets To Model Safety-Critical Systems, pp. 439–44. Society for Computer Simulation, International (1999)

3. Dugan, J.B., Bavuso, S.J., Boyd, M.A.: Dynamic fault-tree models for fault-tolerant computer systems. Trans. Reliab. **41**, 363–377 (1992)
4. Bechta-Dugan, J., Sullivan, K., Coppit, D.: Developing a low-cost high-quality software tool for dynamic fault tree analysis. Trans. Reliab. **49**, 49 (1999)
5. ESSaRel: Embedded systems safety and reliability analyser. http://www.essarel.de
6. Fussell, J.B., Aber, E.F., Rahl, R.G.: On the quantitive analysis of priority AND failure logic. IEEE Trans. Reliab. **25**(5), 324–326 (1796)
7. Gulati, R., Dugan, J.B.: A modular approach for analyzing static and dynamic fault trees. In: Proccedings of the Annual Reliability and Maintainability Symposium, Philadelphia, USA, pp. 57–63 (1997)
8. Kaiser, B., Gramlich, C.: State-event-fault-trees – a safety analysis model for software controlled systems. In: Heisel, M., Liggesmeyer, P., Wittmann, S. (eds.) SAFECOMP 2004. LNCS, vol. 3219, pp. 195–209. Springer, Heidelberg (2004)
9. Liu, D., Xing, W., Zhang, C., Li, R., Li, H.: Cut sequence set generation for fault tree analysis. In: Lee, Y.-H., Kim, H.-N., Kim, J., Park, Y.W., Yang, L.T., Kim, S.W. (eds.) ICESS 2007. LNCS, vol. 4523, pp. 592–603. Springer, Heidelberg (2007)
10. Long, W., Sato, Y., Horigome, M.: Quantification of sequential failure logic for fault tree analysis. Reliab. Eng. Syst. Saf. **67**, 269–274 (1999)
11. Palshikar, G.K.: Temporal fault trees. Inf. Softw. Technol. **44**, 137–150 (2002)
12. Roth, M., Liggesmeyer, P.: Qualitative analysis of state/event fault trees for supporting the certification process of software-intensive systems. In: Proceedings of the International Symposium on Software Reliability Engineering Workshops (ISSREW), pp. 353–358, Pasadena, CA (2013)
13. Tang, Z., Dugan, J.B.: Minimal cut set/sequence generation for dynamic fault trees. In: Proccedings of the Annual Reliability and Maintainability Symposium (RAMS), Charlottesville, USA, pp. 207–213 (2004)
14. Vesely, W.E., Goldberg, F.F., Roberts, N.H., Haasl, D.F.: Fault Tree Handbook (1981)
15. Walker, M.D.: Pandora: A Logic for the Qualitative Analysis of Temporal Fault Trees. PhD Thesis, University of Hall, UK (2009)
16. Watson, H.R.: Launch control safety study. Bell Labs (1961)
17. Yuge, T., Yanagi, S.: Quantitative analysis of a fault tree with priority AND gates. Reliab. Eng. Syst. Saf. **93**, 1577–1583 (2008)
18. Zimmermann, A., German, R., Freiheit, J., Hommel, G.: TimeNET 3.0 Tool Description. In: International Conference on Petri Nets and Performance Models (PNPM 1999), Zaragoza, Spain (1999)

Towards a Framework for Alignment Between Automotive Safety and Security Standards

Christoph Schmittner$^{(\boxtimes)}$ and Zhendong Ma

Department of Digital Safety & Security, AIT Austrian Institute of Technology,
Donau-City-StraßE 1, 1220 Vienna, Austria
{christoph.schmittner.fl,zhendong.ma}@ait.ac.at
http://www.ait.ac.at/departments/digital-safety-security/

Abstract. Modern automotive systems increasingly rely on software and network connectivity for new functions and features. Security of the software and communications of the on-board system of systems becomes a critical concern for the safety of new generation vehicles. Besides methods and tools, safety and security of automotive systems requires frameworks of standards for holistic process and assurance. As a part of our ongoing work, this paper investigates the possibility of a combined safety and security approach to standards in the automotive domain. We examine existing approaches in the railway and avionics domain with similar challenges and identify specific requirements for the automotive domain. We evaluate ISO 15408 as a potential candidate for a combined safety and security approach for complementing automotive safety standard ISO 26262, and discuss their points of alignment.

Keywords: Safety · Security · Standard · ISO 26262 · ISO 15408 · Common criteria · Automotive · ASIL · EAL

1 Introduction

State of the art automotive systems are becoming increasingly software dependent and interconnected. It is estimated that around 90 % of new features are enabled by programmable systems and connectivity, which transforms automotive from mechanical devices to complex cyber-physical systems where multiple networks interconnect up to 100 Electronic Control Units (ECU) within a vehicle [1]. Communications enable vehicles to interact with each other (V2V) and with the outside environment (V2I) for new functions and increase driver safety and comfort. The benefits are obvious, from applications such as remote tracking, unlocking the doors, remote diagnosis, over the air updates (OTA), to automated e-call in case of emergency.

The complexity of in-vehicle system of systems (SoS) and the interconnectivity are growing. While the number of ECU's is increased only by a factor of 1.45 over the last five years, the total size of application software is increased by a factor of 4.5 during the same period [1]. A survey showed that

© Springer International Publishing Switzerland 2015
F. Koornneef and C. van Gulijk (Eds.): SAFECOMP 2015 Workshops, LNCS 9338, pp. 133–143, 2015.
DOI: 10.1007/978-3-319-24249-1_12

in the next years connectivity will be a distinguishing feature for automotive systems. Consumers expect connectivity with their private devices and with the outside environment [18]. This will add additional complexity to the automotive system of systems, where currently up to 4 Km of wiring are used to connect up to 10 different types of on-board networks with multiple forms of outside connectivity [15]. Such connectivity enables new application classes for automotive systems, which includes eco/green/mobility, convenience, crash avoidance, safety awareness and emergency applications [17].

At such a scale of complexity and connectivity, serious security concerns arise in the automotive domain. Recent events and analysis demonstrated that the current ad-hoc approach towards security engineering in the automotive domain delivers sub-optimal results. A recent survey by the U.S. Senate showed that most car manufactures did not follow a structured and systematic approach towards security engineering [20]. While all responding car manufactures stated that their vehicles offer one or more wireless connections, only one of them was able to provide information on threats and vulnerabilities. Experimental analysis of systems like the wireless tire pressure monitoring system (TPMS) [13], the external automotive attack surfaces [3], surveys of potential security threats [21] and telematics unit [7] all support the conclusion in the survey. Furthermore, the capability and processes to address vulnerability and conduct security testing are also underdeveloped.

Being safety-critical, the automotive domain has a set of established safety standards, which are used to design safety-critical components and systems and ensure that all safety risks are reduced to a tolerable level. However, security for safety-critical systems is a relatively new challenge. As safety can no longer guaranteed if security fails, the question is how to take security into consideration in the existing safety standards. For adding security to safety in the automotive domain, it is worthwhile to look at similar issues in railway and avionics. As shown by a recent study [2] in the railway domain, where similar security challenges arise [19], solving them is not restricted to identifying a need for security and safety and defining new methods. Systematic approaches that address safety and security equally are needed. In the railway domain, the ISO 15408 (Information technology - Security techniques - Evaluation criteria for IT security (Common Criteria)) [12] and the IEC 62443 (Industrial communication networks - Network and system security - Security for industrial automation and control systems) [9] have the potential to address security. The author of the study [2] proposed to use IEC 62443 as a suitable addition to established safety standards. It was also proposed to add the requirements for security level 1 to the EN 5012x standards series. The avionics domain takes a different approach and started to develop its own security standards. The generic safety standard IEC 61508 [10] was extended with security related requirements in the second edition and there is ongoing activity to extend this in the third edition.

In the automotive domain, ISO 26262 [11] is the established safety standard. It is currently in revision. The focus is on the addition and identification of safety-cybersecurity interface points, points in the safety lifecycle for information exchange or combined activities and work products[1] with security. As a part of our ongoing work on safety and security co-engineering for the automotive domain, this paper investigates how to extend existing safety standards to address security concerns. Given the complexity of the problem, we envision a standard framework with several standards cover the whole area of safety and security. Our main contributions in this paper include:

- we identify requirements for suitable security standards for automotive safety, review and compare automotive safety standard ISO 26262 and security standard ISO 15408,
- we identify important work products and approaches in both standards for points of alignment,
- we propose an alignment of Automotive Safety Integrity Level (ASIL) and Evaluation Assurance Level (EAL), and discuss its feasibility.

In the following, Sect. 2 briefly discusses related work; Sects. 3 and 4 review the ISO 26262 and ISO 15408 standard, respectively; Sect. 5 presents our comparison and a proposal for alignment; Sect. 6 concludes the paper with a discussion of potential challenges and further steps.

2   Related Work

Automotive industry has a long history of following and implementing stringent safety requirements. With the rapid development and integration of ICT components, the need for a tighter coupling of safety and security for connected safety-critical systems becomes necessary. The issue has attracted attentions in recent years. Macher *et al.* [16] developed a security extended hazard analysis and risk assessment methodology for the automotive domain and reported that they were able to identify 34 % more hazardous situations in industrial use cases. Multiple studies demonstrated the different possibilities of interactions between safety and security [6,8,22]. A survey of safety and security for the industrial domain [14] listed 37 methods for co-engineering.

Furthermore, specific challenges for the safety engineering in the automotive domain have been identified in [5]. A domain independent approach towards a combined safety and security lifecycle is proposed in [4].

3   ISO 26262

ISO 26262 is a domain specific instantiation of IEC 61508, the generic safety standard [10]. It follows a risk based approach and is mainly based around safety integrity levels, safety goals and safety concepts.

Figure 1 gives an overview of the safety lifecycle defined in ISO 26262. Development of a new item starts in the concept phase with the item definition, initiation of the safety lifecycle, hazard analysis and risk assessment and definition

---

[1] A work product is the result of an activity related to a requirement.

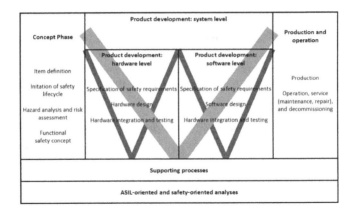

Fig. 1. Safety lifecycle according to ISO 26262

of the functional safety concept. During hazard analysis and risk assessment, potential hazards are identified and the risks are investigated. The risk rating depends on the driving situation in which a hazard occurs, the potential controllability of the situation and the severity of the caused harm. Depending on the risks, safety goals are defined. An automotive safety integrity level (ASIL) is assigned to each safety goal. ASIL ranges from D for the most stringent level of safety measures to A for the most lenient level of safety measures. For systems with lower risks, quality management activities are sufficient.

Based on the safety goals, functional safety requirements are derived and assigned to preliminary architectural elements. The functional safety concept is compromised of all functional safety requirements and describes the functionality to achieve the safety goal.

Next step is the product development on system level. During this step the technical safety requirements are specified, the system is designed, hardware and software of the item are integrated and tested, compliance and correctness of the safety goals and their implementation is validated and the functional safety is assessed. Complementary to the functional safety concept, the technical safety concept consists of all technical safety requirements and describes how the functional safety requirements are implemented in hardware or software. The system development includes hardware and software development. During the hardware development, hardware safety requirements are specified, the hardware is designed, observation of hardware architectural metrics in regard to fault handling is assessed and potential violation of safety goals due to random hardware failures are evaluated. The hardware development is concluded with integration and testing. In a similar manner software design starts with the specification of software safety requirements, the design of the software architecture, and the design and implementation of the individual software units. It is concluded by testing of the units, software integration and integration testing and verification of the software safety requirements.

Additional parts of ISO 26262 are concerned with production and operation and safety analysis for determining the ASIL. The final evidence for the functional safety of an item is the safety case which summarizes all work products from the ISO 26262. A particularity in the ISO 26262 is the Safety Element out of Context (SEooC). A SEooC is an element for which the final item and operating environment is not known during design and development. It is therefore developed using assumptions and hypothesis. This assumptions have to be confirmed in order to safely integrate a SEooC in a item. A SEooC can be verified, the validation occurs during the item development.

4   ISO 15048, Common Criteria

Comparing with most safety standards, the ISO 15048 follows a different approach. While safety defines a system lifecycle and an engineering approach, ISO 15048 focuses on the evaluation and assurance of the system security.

The Target of Evaluation (ToE) is evaluated based on security specifications with different levels of generality. A Protection Profile (PP) is a implementation independent specification of security requirements for a class of systems. A Security Target (ST) is the implementation specific specification of security requirements for a system. Since automotive protection profiles are more of an idea for future work, we will focus on the security target definition. An ST consists of the definition of the ST, the conformance claim to any protection profiles, the definition of the security problem and the security objectives, the extended components definition, the security requirements and the TOE summary specification. Figure 2 gives an overview about the contents of an security target.

An ST is intended as a specification of the security properties of a TOE and as a definition for the scope of the evaluation. It is not intended as a detailed or complete specification for the design or implementation of a system. It is explicitly mentioned in the ISO 15408: "This means that in general an ST may be part of a complete specification." [12].

The assumptions in the security problem definition (cf. Fig. 2) describe assumptions about the operating environment of a TOE. If a TOE is placed in operational situations where these assumptions are not true, the TOE may not be able to provide its security functionality. ISO 15408 differs between the Security Functional Requirements (SFR) and the Security Assurance Requirements (SAR). The SFRs are a formalized and implementation independent specification how the security objectives are achieved. The SARs describe how and to which strictness a TOE is evaluated. Evaluation assurance levels (EAL) describe seven sets of SARs with rising strictness. The TOE summary specification finally describes how a TOE implements the SFRs.

Using properly, ISO 15408 can increase software and hardware security assurance level. It provides the assurance by enforcing good and comprehensive documentation during the system design and development phase, including system specification, system internals, system tests, and development tools. It also forces

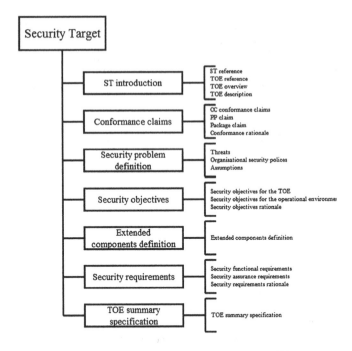

Fig. 2. Security target contents according to ISO 15408

a development team to take security as the main objective from the beginning of the project. It raises awareness of the security problems throughout the system's design and development phase, in which both security and non-security team members are invovled. The specification of PP, SFRs, and SARs, defined in accordance with ISO 15408 will provide comprehensive and clear specifications on the requirements of critical parts in the automotive system. Such an intensive practice can force the project team to identify ambiguities early on and solve the identified problems accordingly.

5   Comparison and Points for Interaction

To complement automotive safety standard ISO 26262 and to promote a combined approach to safety and security, we identified the following requirements for the evaluation of candidate security standards:

1. There should be an overlap in required work products for safety and security argumentation. It should be possible to build a holistic assurance case which reuses and extends existing work products for safety argumentation and combine them with security related work products.
2. Assurance levels between safety and security should be translatable. Verification activities for safety and security should be on a similar level. Strictness of required documentation, design, testing and verification should be similar between pure safety goals and security motivated safety goals.

3. Approaches and concepts from the ISO 26262 should be mirrored by the security standard. ISO 26262 supports some automotive specific approaches, like the Safety Element out of Context. Such approaches and concepts should be representable by the security standard.

Based on these requirements, we investigate the feasibility of using ISO 15408 to complement ISO 26262 for safety and security.

5.1 Work Products

Table 1 shows a comparison of work products from the two standards. It can be seen that for the required parts of a security target, existing work products from the ISO 26262 contain similar, or in some parts, overlapping content. However, it does not imply a complete overlap between safety and security work products. Numbers in the ISO 15408 column refer to part 1 of the standard. The reference to parts of ISO 26262 are given for each specific requirement.

Table 1. Work products from ISO 15408 and ISO 26262

ISO 15408	ISO 26262
A.4.1 ST reference and TOE reference	Part3–5: Item definition
A.4.2 TOE overview	
A.4.3 TOE description	
A.5 conformance claims	-
A.6.2 Threats	Part3–7.5.1: Hazard analysis and risk assessment
A.6.3 Organisational security policies	Part2–5: Overall safety management,
	Part2–5.5.1: Organization specific rules and processes for functional safety
	Part2–7: Safety management after release for production,
	Part2–7.5: Evidence of a field monitoring process
A.6.4 Assumptions	Only for Safety element out of Context
A7.2.1 Security objectives for the TOE	Part3.7.5.2: Safety Goals
A7.2.2 Security objectives for the operational environment	-
A7.3. Relation between security objectives and the security problem definition	Part3–7.5.3: Verification review of hazard analysis and risk assessment and safety goals
A.8 Extended components definition	-
A.9.1 Security functional requirements	Part3–8.5.1: Functional safety concept
A.9.2 Security assurance requirements	Part2–6: Safety management during development of the item,
	Part2–6.5.5: Confirmation plan
	Part6–11:Verification of software safety requirements
	Part6–11.5.1: Software verification plan
A.9.3 Security requirements rationale	
A.10 TOE summary specification	Part2–6.5.3: Safety Case

The table lists safety work products from ISO 26262 that are best suited to be extended with their security specific counterpart from ISO 15408. It will define a holistic assurance case, which integrates required parts for the safety case with the mandatory parts for a security target. For example, the item definition of

ISO 26262 contains mission, functional and non-functional requirements, dependencies between the item and its outside and already known safety requirements from familiar items. In addition, the boundaries, interfaces, elements, distribution of functions, operating scenarios and requirements from and on other items are described. The item description already contains most required parts of the TOE reference, TOE overview and TOE description. It needs to be extend with an overview of the included security features and the functionality of the item.

While the conformance claim has no direct counterpart in ISO 26262, the next row demonstrates how a safety work product may be extended. The goal of the hazard analysis and risk assessment is to identify and evaluate all hazards for an item and to formulate the safety goals to achieve the necessary risk reduction. The intention of ISO 15408 is similar, in which a list of all undesired actions from a threat agent may have negatively influence on one or more properties. Extending the hazard analysis and risk assessment with a list of potential threat scenarios that negatively influence the safety of the item can be used for safety and security argumentation.

5.2 Assurance Levels

ISO 15408 follows a strict assignment of measures to levels, while ISO 26262 has levels of highly recommend, recommend and methods without recommendation. The different EAL can be summarized as:

- EAL1: functionally tested
- EAL2: structurally tested
- EAL3: methodically tested and checked
- EAL4: methodically designed, tested and reviewed
- EAL5: semi-formally designed and tested
- EAL6: semi-formally verified design and tested
- EAL7: formally verified design and tested.

Since EAL and security in general relates mostly to software design, implementation and testing, we based our structuring of the ASIL mostly on the ASIL dependent requirements for this part of the complete system engineering. However, at the moment, there is no absolute direct translation and mapping. For example, formal methods are only recommend for the highest ASIL, while semi-formal methods are highly recommend for ASIL D and C.

Based on a examination of the ISO 26262 requirements, a translation between EAL and ASIL, based on their strictness and degree of formalism is proposed as following (Table. 2).

Similar to the conversion from SIL to ASIL, where the highest SIL is more critical than the highest ASIL, in a summarized translation, EAL7 would be out of reach. A more elaborate approach might be to build a specific set of SAR tailored according to the requirements from ISO 26262. ISO 15408 allows such an approach with the EALx+ specification. It describes a set of requirement which exceeds EALx in strictness in some parts but does not reach the next EAL. This would allow a more accurate translation.

Table 2. Comparison of integrity and assurance levels

ASIL		EAL
ASIL A	~	EAL3
ASIL B	~	EAL4
ASIL C	~	EAL5
ASIL D	~	EAL6

5.3   Automotive Domain Specific Concepts

Compared to the generic safety standard IEC 61508, the automotive domain has defined a few domain-specific concepts in ISO 26262. As described in [2], it becomes challenging to add security to safety if attack probabilities are to be considered. Probability estimation in ISO 26262 is based on the concept of "how frequently and for how long individuals find themselves in a situation where the aforementioned hazardous event can occur." In ISO 26262, this is defined to be a measure of the probability of the driving scenario taking place in which the hazardous event can occur (E = exposure) [11]. As shown in [16], the risk rating for ISO 26262 is therefore well suited for an integration of security threats. One can simply redefine exposure as probability that a driving scenario takes place in which a cyber attack is possible and therefor causes a hazardous event. The determined ASIL for security motivated safety goals can then be translated to an EAL for the corresponding security objective.

An important concept in the ISO 26262 is the SEooC. It enables supplier to develop components for different OEMs and to carry out safety engineering based on the assumed usage and operational environment of the component. ISO 15408 supports a similar concept with the dependency on the operational environment for security. The final assessment depends in both cases on the operational environment.

6   Conclusion

Automotive systems become increasingly software-intensive and interconnected. This makes security a burning issue and attracts many attentions in recent years. Cooperation between safety and security standards is urgently needed in the automotive domain. As a part of our on-going work on safety and security co-engineering, we investigate the possibility of a framework of standards that addresses safety and security in automotive domain in a holistic and co-operative way. We investigate domains with similar safety-critical requirements and evaluate ISO 15408 and ISO 26262 to find points that have the potential for combinations.

As a work-in-progress, out next step is to conduct more in-depth analyzes of existing automotive safety and security standards. Specifically, we will address the challenge of how to align and harmonize assurance levels on safety and security in different standards.

Acknowledgments. This research has received funding from the EU ARTEMIS Joint Undertaking under grant agreements no. 621429 / 332987 (EMC^2 / Arrowhead) and from the FFG (Austrian Research Promotion Agency) on behalf of BMVIT, The Federal Ministry of Transport, Innovation and Technology.

References

1. Abelein, U., Lochner, H., Hahn, D., Straube, S.: Complexity, quality and robustness-the challenges of tomorrow's automotive electronics. In: Design, Automation & Test in Europe Conference & Exhibition (DATE), pp. 870–871. IEEE (2012). http://ieeexplore.ieee.org/xpls/abs_all.jsp?arnumber=6176573
2. Braband, J.: Towards an IT security framework for railway automation. Toulouse, Febuary 2014. http://www.erts2014.org/site/0r4uxe94/fichier/erts2014_7c3.pdf
3. Checkoway, S., McCoy, D., Kantor, B., Anderson, D., Shacham, H., Savage, S., Koscher, K., Czeskis, A., Roesner, F., Kohno, T.: Comprehensive experimental analyses of automotive attack surfaces. In: USENIX Security Symposium (2011)
4. Schmittner, C., Ma, Z., Schoitsch, E.: Combined Safety and Security Development Lifecylce. Cambridge (2015)
5. Schmittner, C., Ma, Z., Gruber, T.: Standardization challenges for safety and security of connected. In: Automated and Intelligent Vehicles, Wien, November 2014
6. Eames, D.P., Moffett, J.D.: The integration of safety and security requirements. In: Felici, M., Kanoun, K., Pasquini, A. (eds.) SAFECOMP 1999. LNCS, vol. 1698, p. 468. Springer, Heidelberg (1999)
7. Dieter Spaar: Auto, ø"ffne dich! Sicherheitsluecken bei BMWsConnectedDrive. c't (5), pp. 86 – 90 (2015). http://heise.de/-2536384
8. Dong-bo, P., Feng, L.: Influence between safety and security. In: ICIEA 2007, pp. 1323–1325 (2007)
9. International Electrotechnical Commission: IEC 62443, Industrial communication networks - Network and system security - Security for industrial automation and control systems
10. International Electrotechnical Commission: IEC 61508: Functional Safety of Electrical / Electronic / Programmable Electronic Safety-Related Systems (2010)
11. International Organization for Standardization: ISO 26262 Road vehicles - Functional safety (2011)
12. International Standardization Organization: ISO 15408, Information technology - Security techniques - Evaluation criteria for IT security (Common Criteria)
13. Ishtiaq Roufa, R.M., Mustafaa, H., Travis Taylora, S.O., Xua, W., Gruteserb, M., Trappeb, W., Seskarb, I.: Security and privacy vulnerabilities of in-car wireless networks: a tire pressure monitoring system case study. In: 19th USENIX Security Symposium, Washington DC. pp. 11–13 (2010). https://www.usenix.org/legacy/event/sec10/tech/full_papers/Rouf.pdf
14. Kriaa, S., Pietre-Cambacedes, L., Bouissou, M., Halgand, Y.: A survey of approaches combining safety and security for industrial control Systems. Reliab. Eng. Syst. Saf. **139**, 156–178 (2015). http://linkinghub.elsevier.com/retrieve/pii/S0951832015000538
15. Leen, G., Heffernan, D.: Expanding automotive electronic systems. Comput. **35**(1), 88–93 (2002). http://ieeexplore.ieee.org/xpls/abs_all.jsp?arnumber=976923
16. Macher, G., Sporer, H., Berlach, R., Armengaud, E., Kreiner, C.: SAHARA: a security-aware hazard and risk analysis method. In: Proceedings of the 2015 Design, Automation & Test in Europe Conference & Exhibition, pp. 621–624 (2015)

17. Onishi, H., Mlinarsky, F.: Wireless technology assessment for automotive applications. In: Proceedings of the ITS World Congress (2012). http://www.octorange.com/English/Collaterals/Whitepapers/octoScope_WP_WirelessAutomotive_20120421.pdf

18. Kalmbach, R., Bernhart, W., Grosse Kleimann, P., Hoffmann, M.: Automotive landscape 2025 - opportunities and challenges ahead. Technical report, Roland Berger, Strategy Consultants, March 2011

19. Smith, J., Russell, S., Looi, M.: Security as a safety issue in rail communications. In: Proceedings of the 8th Australian Workshop on Safety Critical Systems and Software, vol. 33, pp. 79–88. Australian Computer Society, Inc. (2003). http://dl.acm.org/citation.cfm?id=1082058

20. Markey, E.J.: Tracking & Hacking Security & Privacy Gaps Put American Drivers at Risk. Technical report (2015)

21. Studnia, I., Nicomette, V., Alata, E., Deswarte, Y., Kaniche, M., Laarouchi, Y.: Survey on security threats and protection mechanisms in embedded automotive networks. In: 2013 43rd Annual IEEE/IFIP Conference on Dependable Systems and Networks Workshop (DSN-W), pp. 1–12. IEEE (2013). http://ieeexplore.ieee.org/xpls/abs_all.jsp?arnumber=6615528

22. Sun, M., Mohan, S., Sha, L., Gunter, C.: Addressing safety and security contradictions in cyber-physical systems. In: Proceedings of the 1st Workshop on Future Directions in Cyber-Physical Systems Security (CPSSW 2009) (2009). http://cimic3.rutgers.edu/positionPapers/cpssecurity09_MuSun.pdf

Reconfiguration Testing
for Cooperating Autonomous Agents

Francesca Saglietti[(✉)], Stefan Winzinger, and Raimar Lill

Lehrstuhl für Software Engineering (Informatik 11),
University of Erlangen-Nuremberg, Martensstr. 3, 91058 Erlangen, Germany
{francesca.saglietti,stefan.winzinger,raimar.lill}@fau.de

Abstract. In order to verify reconfiguration of interacting autonomous agents to be exclusively beneficial and never hazardous to cyber-physical systems, this article suggests a systematic approach based on incremental model-based testing and illustrates its application to cooperating mobile robots.

Keywords: Cyber-physical systems · Robots · Autonomous agents · Cooperation · Reconfiguration · CPN modelling · Incremental testing

1 Introduction

Cyber-physical systems increasingly tend to rely on the pro-active cooperative behaviour – or at least on the safe co-existence – of autonomous systems, e.g. mobile robotic agents, singularly developed and validated beforehand. The major purpose of systems-of-systems resulting from aggregation and cooperation of individual agents in a common environment is the provision of higher service performance or efficiency than can be expected from the mere union of their parts. In particular, such improvement may involve autonomous decision-making on proper counteractions to be activated upon detection of anomalous operational conditions by means of suitable reconfiguration strategies.

Evidently, the additional behaviour emerging from interaction of cooperating agents must be verified to be exclusively beneficial and never hazardous to the cyber-controlled physical world, especially in case of safety-relevant applications. For this purpose, the present article suggests a systematic approach to incremental testing of reconfiguration behaviour for cooperating mobile robots by defining objective metrics of structural coverage to be successively fulfilled by automatic test case generation.

The article is structured as follows: after this introduction, the stages characterizing individual and cooperative robot activities are presented and analysed in terms of potential fault and failure modes (Sect. 2). Successively, these stages are further considered in the light of reconfiguration strategies (Sect. 3). For the purpose of modelling and verifying increasing levels of reconfiguration, the selection of Coloured Petri Nets is justified in Sect. 4 and its application illustrated in Sect. 5 by means of an example inspired by a hospital logistics system involving cooperating trolleys. Finally, Sect. 6 proposes a novel structural testing concept based on the incremental generation of test

© Springer International Publishing Switzerland 2015
F. Koornneef and C. van Gulijk (Eds.): SAFECOMP 2015 Workshops, LNCS 9338, pp. 144–155, 2015.
DOI: 10.1007/978-3-319-24249-1_13

case sets targeted at covering all consecutive state pairs of corresponding CPN models capturing increasing degrees of reconfiguration.

2   Processing Stages

2.1   Individual Behaviour

The typical processing scheme of a robot deployed in a given environment is structured along the following successive stages.

- **Sensing.** Measurement of raw data by means of appropriate (e.g. electric, electro-magnetic or optical) sensors [1] concerning contextual information about environmental conditions (e.g. distance to next obstacle, external temperature, brightness, GPS-coordinates) or robot attributes (e.g. energy, internal temperature, speed).
- **Perception.** Interpretation of sensed data for the purpose of gaining insight about properties of the real world surrounding the perceiving robot such as to allow to represent it by means of environmental models providing a solid knowledge base for further decision-making, e.g. by visual pattern recognition algorithms for object identification.
- **Reasoning.** Application of decision-making algorithms based on pre-defined logic rules to the current perception of reality for the purpose of determining how to proceed, i.e. which actions to instantiate next, typically involving trade-off optimization w. r. t. alternative options.
- **Action.** Execution of action(s) previously identified during decision-making, where super-ordinate actions, e.g. *target next charging station*, may involve further sensing, perception and reasoning activities concerning corresponding sub-ordinate actions, e.g. in the above case the sub-actions *find shortest path*, *move*, *recharge* and *resume original mission*.

2.2   Cooperative Behaviour

In case each robot disposes of own local sensors, the initial sensing phase may be usually assumed to rely on exclusively individual behaviour of interacting agents, while all later processing stages (s. Figure 1) may involve cooperative behaviour:

- **Perception-based Cooperation.** Fusion of data sensed by multiple robots for the purpose of extracting more information than achievable by the sum of its parts, e.g. robots gathering visual information from different view angles such as to obtain consistent stereo-vision.
- **Reasoning-based Cooperation.** Coherent decision-making of robots working in a common environmental context, such that the global behaviour emerging from individual actions is beneficial to cooperation. For example, facing robots aiming at switching their position must avoid symmetrical evasive manoeuvre in order to exclude mutual blockades.

- **Action-based Cooperation.** Efficient and effective coordination of individual robot actions in order to achieve a common task. For example, the cooperative lifting of a heavy load requires synchronicity of movement and balanced application of forces in order to avoid tilting effects.

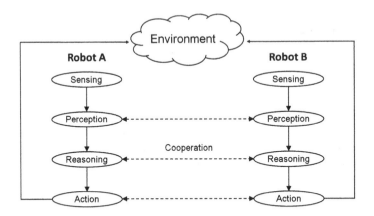

Fig. 1. Individual and cooperative processing stages

Evidently, each of these stages may be affected by specific faults or inaccuracies potentially jeopardizing the performance of the corresponding activity as well as that of later stages relying on it (s. Table 1). As sensing, perception and action represent classical challenges in robot design and construction which may rely on long research and industrial experience, in the following they are assumed to have been trained and verified before deployment with respect to a wide range of target environments.

On the other hand, the real challenges arising after robotic construction are felt to be especially related to the verification of *reasoning*, *cooperation* and *reconfiguration* tasks which depend on plant-specific design concepts and therefore must (and can only) be explicitly addressed in later testing phases.

While systematic testing of cooperative behaviour based on autonomous reasoning has been the subject of investigations on which we reported in the past [2, 3], the present article poses the focus of its considerations on the particular issue of testing *reconfiguration* of autonomous cooperating agents.

3 On-Line Fault and Anomaly Handling

3.1 Fault Detection and Fault Tolerance

In case the acceptable system behaviour can be specified in advance in a unique and precise way, classical fault tolerance approaches may be applied to enforce this behaviour (possibly allowing for some degree of degradation) even in the sporadic occurrence of component failures.

This can be achieved by activating during runtime appropriate counter-measures based on different redundancy classes:

- **fault masking**, where a majority is selected by comparison checking (voting) among *structurally redundant* components;
- **error recovery**, where a predefined acceptable state is (re-)established upon detection of an error by a *functionally redundant* component (acceptance test);
- **error correction**, where errors resulting from transmission or storage failures are corrected thanks to the *information redundancy* provided by additional data.

Table 1. Fault classes and failure modes

| Stage | Fault Classes / Failure modes | |
	Individual behaviour	Cooperative behaviour
Sensing	flawed sensor(s) resulting in - delivery of distorted data, - data delivery outside required time slots, - (partial) omission of data delivery.	----
Perception	inaccurate interpretation of sensed data by - inaccuracy of environmental model, - lack of significant sensed data, - inappropriate perception algorithm.	incorrect representation by inconsistent data fusion
Reasoning	incorrect decision-making due to - inadequate specification, - flawed design, - incorrect implementation.	conflicting decisions by non-concerted reasoning
Action	incapability of completing action due to - inappropriate use of instruments, - flawed instruments, - lack of energy resources, - environmental constraints.	inefficient / ineffective / unsafe behaviour by uncoordinated actions

3.2 Anomaly Detection and Reconfiguration

In general, the behavioural multiplicity of robotic applications, induced by varying missions and operational conditions, does not allow for the determination of one single target behaviour. Upon detection of anomalies preventing them from carrying out a standard functionality, robots must rather evaluate alternative procedures and select one of them on the basis of their current perception by reconfiguration, i.e. by adjusting their future physical and/or logical activities. Reconfiguration, therefore, goes beyond fault tolerance by permitting to adapt the behaviour to anomalous operational conditions; it includes the following classes:

- **Adjusted Sensing.** Upon detecting that sensed information does not offer acceptable quality, be it due to environmental conditions or to sensor defects, a robot may replace its current sensing technique by an alternative one revealing as more suitable under the present circumstances, e.g. by switching to infrared-based sensors if the light conditions are insufficient to rely on daylight camera sensors.

- **Adjusted Perception.** Upon detecting that the perception technique currently applied does not provide for satisfactory quality, a robot may switch to an alternative algorithm, e.g. a different image filtering technique for identifying object patterns.
- **Adjusted Reasoning.** Upon detecting that the targeted action cannot be carried out satisfactorily due to anomalous conditions, a robot may revise its reasoning stage under the constraints just identified, e.g. by adapting its current route planning to allow for an intermediate stop at the closest opportunity if recharging is required.
- **Adjusted Action.** Upon detecting that the targeted action cannot be carried out satisfactorily by means of the techniques currently applied, a robot may select an alternative physical or logical instrument to achieve the same task, e.g. by switching between continuous and discontinuous gait modes for moving depending on the conditions of the terrain and of the robot leg joints [4].
- **Adjusted Autonomy.** Upon detecting that an intended task cannot be carried out at an acceptable level of efficiency, a robot may temporarily transfer part of its autonomy to another entity, be it another robot or a central controller, e.g. by proceeding in a coordinated formation or *platoon* [5, 9].

The fault and anomaly handling strategies just mentioned are summarized in Table 2.

Table 2. On-line fault / anomaly handling strategies

	Technique	Examples
Fault Tolerance	fault masking by structural redundancy	N-version programming by majority voting
	error recovery by functional redundancy	recovery block programming by acceptance testing
	error correction by information redundancy	error-correcting codes, cyclic redundancy checks
Reconfiguration	adjustment of sensing instruments	switch between infra-red and daylight camera sensing
	adjustment of perception algorithms	change of filtering algorithms for object patterns identification
	adjustment of decision-making	route replanning for recharging or collision avoidance
	adjustment of action	adaptation of movement mode in case of joint failure
	adjustment of autonomy degree	platooning, delegation

4   Modelling Reconfiguration by Coloured Petri Nets

This section focuses on the representation of reconfiguration behaviour by an appropriate formal notation capable of capturing multiplicity of runtime behaviour including both time-varying, scenario-based operational properties and time-invariant, plant-specific design concepts.

4.1 Multiplicity of Runtime Behaviour

For the purpose of capturing multiplicity of runtime behaviour by appropriate models, the following scenario-dependent attributes must be taken into account:

Robots. Agents are characterized by current information on

- *sensing capabilities* providing in particular continuous feedback on their locations,
- *functional capabilities* reflecting the degree of acceptance of their performance,
- *energy resources* available.

Missions. Tasks are characterized by

- *required functional capabilities* to be provided by entrusted robots,
- *working area(s)* to be accessed /traversed to carry out the mission,
- *current processing status* (available, allocated, completed, degraded).

Environment. Working areas are characterized by

- *sensing and functional complexity*, concerning a. o. visibility or slipperiness,
- *resource consumption*, e.g. depending on path steepness,
- *mobility*, especially concerning the presence of obstacles hindering access.

4.2 CPN Modelling of Behaviour Allowing for Reconfiguration

Based on the positive experiences gained in the past w. r. t. non-reconfigurable robots [2, 3], the notation used in the following to capture both plant-specific reconfiguration concepts and multiple operational conditions is CPN (Coloured Petri Nets [6, 7]), a well-known extension of the more classical Place/Transitions Petri Nets [8]. The main advantage offered by CPN lies in its high compactness and scalability providing appropriate modelling elements to allow to represent both

- permanent, plant-specific reconfiguration concepts by the static CPN part, i.e. by the *net structure* consisting of CPN *places*, *transitions* and *arcs*, and
- time-varying, scenario-dependent information by the dynamic CPN part, i.e. by the *marking* capturing the momentary state by means of flowing CPN *tokens*.

5 Example

The following application is inspired by a robot-based logistics system for hospitals consisting of a number of trolleys moving autonomously along predefined lanes for the purpose of transporting household linen to predetermined places.

5.1   Requirements Concerning Regular Behaviour

Plant Topology. The plant is structured in concentric rings (s. Figure 2) partitioned into numbered segments, where

- for safety reasons at most one trolley can traverse a segment at any time;
- the two internal circular lanes are used for *clockwise* traffic movement (*inner lane*) and for *anticlockwise* traffic movement (*outer lane*);
- the two external circular lanes (*inner border* and *outer border*) are used as parking lots and partly also as battery-loading areas.

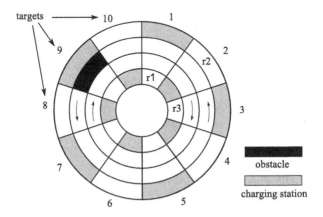

Fig. 2. Plant topology with initial robot positions, obstacle and mission targets

Mission Allocation. Missions are

- characterized by the target segments to be reached;
- allocated to idle trolleys providing the functional capabilities required;
- completed as soon as a border of their target segment is reached.

Robot Movement. Whenever possible, trolleys try to move towards their target:

- once a mission is assigned, the trolley entrusted with it determines its direction (*clockwise* or *anticlockwise*) such as to allow for the shortest path to its target;
- successively, the trolley moves forward by accessing segments as long as they are perceived to be free from obstacles;
- the energy required to traverse a segment amounts to 5 % of a full charge;
- upon reaching its target segment, the trolley moves to the right margin and stops.

5.2   Requirements Concerning Reconfiguration

Upon perception of particular internal anomalies or external anomalous conditions, robots can react by changing their current target behaviour as follows:

Reconfiguration Strategy 1 (R1): Battery Recharging. As soon as their energy level is sensed to be below a predefined threshold, robots will

- target the closest charging station to be encountered in their current direction;
- after conclusion of energy recharging, resume their mission.

Reconfiguration Strategy 2 (R2): Route Replanning. Upon perceiving an obstacle (passive object or human) immediately preceding them on their moving lane, robots

- move to the opposite traffic lane and
- change their moving direction accordingly.

Reconfiguration Strategy 3 (R3): Platooning [5, 9]. For reasons of safety, traffic efficiency and energy saving, if disposing of sufficient energy and entrusted with yet incomplete missions, queuing robots build formations by

- temporarily delegating decision-making to the front robot and following their predecessor, hereby reducing energy consumption to 2 % of a full charge per segment traversal;
- as soon as its energy level is under a predefined threshold, a formation-building robot will abandon the platoon to target the closest charging station (s. above), hereby giving rise to a splitting of the platoon;
- as soon as a formation-building robot reaches its target segment, it will abandon its platoon to stop at the margin, hereby giving rise to a splitting of the platoon.

5.3 CPN Models for Increasing Levels of Reconfiguration

The CPN model developed to represent the behaviour illustrated above is shown in Fig. 3. It consists of the following 3 *CPN places* to store state information:

- *MissionPool* captures information on the current mission state,
- *RobotPlatoons* captures information on the current lists of moving formations,
- *Areas* captures information on the current environmental conditions,

as well as of the following 7 *CPN transitions* reflecting generic atomic actions:

- *AssignMission* denotes entrusting a given robot with a given mission,
- *MoveForward* denotes accessing the next segment,
- *ChangeLane* denotes moving to the next closest traffic lane,
- *JoinPlatoon* denotes releasing of autonomy by following the preceding robot,
- *LeavePlatoon* denotes resuming of autonomy w.r.t. movement decisions,
- *Park* denotes moving to the right border to stop there,
- *Charge* denotes recharging the battery.

The CPN net structure G shown in Fig. 3 includes all 3 reconfiguration behaviours R1, R2, R3 mentioned before. By removing the 2 transitions *JoinPlatoon* and *LeavePlatoon* it can be easily degraded to a simplified CPN net structure G' representing the same regular behaviour without allowing for building formations. Assuming the common mission assignment shown in Table 3, these 2 net structures give rise to the following 4 different Coloured Petri Nets:

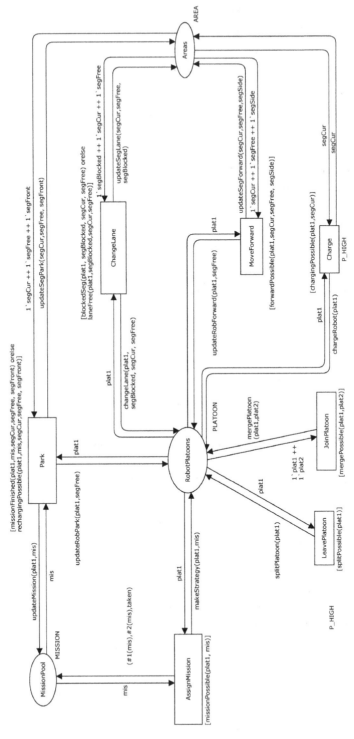

Fig. 3. CPN model of reconfigurable cooperating robots

- CPN0 based on net G', fully charged robots and no obstacles;
- CPN1 based on net G', robots charged for one third (33 %) and no obstacles;
- CPN2 based on net G', robots charged for one third (33 %) and an obstacle in segment #10 (outer lane);
- CPN3 based on net G, robots charged for one third (33 %) and an obstacle in segment #10 (outer lane).

Table 3. Series of CPN models capturing incrementing reconfiguration levels

	CPN0	**CPN1**	**CPN2**	**CPN3**
reconfiguration	no	R1	R1, R2	R1, R2, R3
net structure	G'	G'	G'	G
initial marking		r1: #1(inner parking lane)→#10 r2: #2 (outer parking lane)→#9 r3: #3 (inner parking lane)→#8		
	a full charge	33% of a full charge		
	no obstacles		obstacle in #10 (outer lane)	

The number of corresponding CPN entities is shown in Table 4, where events denote variable bindings enabling transition firing and state pairs denote pairs of consecutive markings.

Table 4. Size and complexity of CPN models considered

	CPN0	**CPN1**	**CPN2**	**CPN3**
# transitions	5	5	5	7
# events	23	42	70	1966
# states	454	1265	3581	17325
# state pairs	981	2508	7537	30824

Within the set of all state pairs of CPNi ($i \in \{1, 2, 3\}$) we may further distinguish the subset of Ri-state-pairs initiating reconfiguration Ri, more precisely:

- R1-state-pairs traversed by firing transition *Park* for charging purposes, i.e. when the parking segment differs from the mission target;
- R2-state-pairs traversed by firing transition *ChangeLange* upon sensing an obstacle on the next segment to be accessed by the robot considered;
- R3-state-pairs traversed by firing transition *JoinPlatoon*.

The number of the Ri-state-pairs ($i \in \{1, 2, 3\}$) is shown in Table 5.

Table 5. Number of state pairs involving corresponding reconfiguration levels

i	1	2	3
#Ri-state-pairs in CPNi	198	294	1448

6   Incremental Reconfiguration Testing

This section is devoted to the definition of a systematic procedure for the determination of CPN test cases targeted to the verification of the 3 reconfiguration strategies illustrated above. Hereby, a CPN test case is defined as an initial marking followed by a sequence of events occurring during its execution such as to represent behaviour from mission assignment to mission accomplishment. As Ri-state-pairs are defined to initiate reconfiguration, their coverage suffices to test the complete corresponding reconfiguration behaviour.

It is envisaged to reduce testing effort by avoiding to retest behaviour already verified beforehand. The testing procedure proposed for this purpose addresses increasing levels of reconfiguration; at each level, appropriate test cases must traverse all pairs of consecutive states involving corresponding reconfiguration behaviour. Evidently, the advantage of proceeding incrementally is the stepwise inclusion of anomalous operational conditions. In other words, after regular behaviour has been verified by extensive coverage of CPN0, additional reconfiguration testing requires further test cases covering Ri-state-pairs in CPNi for the purpose of addressing reconfiguration strategies Ri ($i \in \{1, 2, 3\}$).

Depending on the state transition graph generated by CPN Tools [7], appropriate test cases may be determined by analytical [10] or heuristic approaches [11, 12]. In the present case, appropriate test cases were analytically generated by *hot-spot prioritization* [10] based on the successive identification of test cases providing the maximum number of state pairs yet uncovered. Their number is shown in Table 6.

Table 6. Number of test cases required by different test coverage criteria

test coverage criterion in CPNi	i = 0	i = 1	i = 2	i = 3
# test cases covering all state pairs	133	270	614	3981
# test cases covering Ri-state-pairs	n.a.	111	239	1011

The incremental testing approach proposed reveals as beneficial in terms of testing effort, as it requires only 1494 test cases (the sum of the shaded entries in Table 6) instead of the 3981 test cases required by non-incremental reconfiguration testing.

7   Conclusion

In order to verify reconfiguration behaviour potentially emerging from interacting autonomous agents to be exclusively beneficial and never hazardous to cyber-physical systems, this article proposed a systematic approach based on incremental model-based testing and illustrated its application to cooperating mobile robots involving 3 different reconfiguration strategies.

The testing procedure derived is based on the automatic generation of test cases covering a series of CPN models capturing increasing degrees of reconfiguration. An exemplifying application confirmed both the practicality and the cost-effectiveness of the approach developed.

Acknowledgment. The authors gratefully acknowledge that part of the work presented was carried out within the European Research Programme ARTEMIS (Advanced Research and Technology for Embedded Intelligence and Systems), project R5-COP (Reconfigurable ROS-based Resilient Reasoning Robotic Co-operating Systems), agreement number 621447.

References

1. Bajd, T., et al: Robotics. In: Series: Intelligent Systems, Control and Automation: Science and Engineering, vol. 43, Springer, Heidelberg (2010)
2. Saglietti, F., Lill, R.: A testing pattern for automatic control software addressing different degrees of process autonomy and cooperation. In: Proceedings 19th IFAC World Congress, International Federation of Automatic Control (2014)
3. Lill, R., Saglietti, F.: Model-based testing of cooperating robotic systems using coloured petri nets. In: SAFECOMP 2013 Workshop Proceedings, LAAS-CNRS (2013)
4. Krishnan, V.L., et al.: Reconfiguration of four-legged walking robot for actuator faults. In: Proceedings of the Spring Simulation Multiconference (SpringSim 2010), ACM Digital Library (2010)
5. Klančar, G., Matko, D., Blažič, S.: Wheeled mobile robots control in a linear platoon. Journal of Intelligent and Robotic Systems, Vol. 54(5) (2009)
6. Jensen, K., Kristensen, L.M.: Coloured Petri Nets. Springer, Heidelberg (2009)
7. Jensen, K., Kristensen, L.M., Wells, L.: Coloured petri nets and CPN tools for modelling and validation of concurrent systems. In: International Journal on Software Tools for Technology Transfer (STTT), vol. 9, no. 3–4, Springer, Heidelberg (2007)
8. Murata, T.: Petri Nets: properties, analysis and applications. Proc. IEEE, **77**(4) (1989)
9. Bergenhem, C., Shladover, S., Coelingh, E.: Overview of platooning systems. In: Proceedings 19th World Congress on Intelligent Transportation Systems (ITS) (2012)
10. Wong, W.E., Lei, Y., Ma, X.: Effective generation of test sequences for structural testing of concurrent programs. In: Proceedings of the 10th IEEE International Conference on Engineering of Complex Computer Systems (ICECCS) (2005)
11. Lill, R., Saglietti, F.: Testing the cooperation of autonomous robotic agents. In: Proceedings of the 9th International Conference on Software Engineering and Applications (ICSOFT-EA), Scitepress Digital Library (2014)
12. Saglietti, F., Föhrweiser, D., Winzinger, S., Lill, R.: Model-based design and testing of decisional autonomy and cooperation in cyber-physical systems. to be published. In: Proceedings of the 41st Euromicro Conference on Software Engineering and Advanced Applications (SEAA), IEEE Xplore Digital Library (2015)

A Motion Certification Concept to Evaluate Operational Safety and Optimizing Operating Parameters at Runtime

Sebastian Müller[(✉)] and Peter Liggesmeyer

Lehrstuhl für Software Engineering: Dependability, Technische Universität Kaiserslautern,
67653 Kaiserslautern, Germany
{sebastian.mueller,liggesmeyer}@cs.uni-kl.de

Abstract. For technical systems, which perform highly automated or so-called autonomous actions, there exist a large demand to evaluate their operational safety in a uniform way at runtime based on the combination of environmental threats and the conditions of subordinated system modules. To guarantee a safe motion based on autonomous decisions we have introduced a universal and transparent certification process which not only takes functional aspects like environment detection and collision avoidance techniques into account but especially identifies the associated system condition itself as a key aspect for the determination of operational safety and for an automated optimization of operating parameters. Similar to a feedback loop possible constraints for environment perception of sensor components or the ability of actuator components to interact with their environment have to be taken into account to introduce a generalized safety evaluation for the entire system. Therefore, a model is derived to evaluate the operational safety for the autonomous driving robot RAVON from TU Kaiserslautern based on an integrated behavior-based control (IB²C).

Keywords: Condition monitoring · Safety · Autonomous vehicles · Conditional safety certificates · Modularity · Adaptive systems · Mobile robots

1 Introduction

In an industrial environment, technical systems act more and more autonomously to improve their efficiency in automation due to better adaption to environment and processes. Systems, which are able to make decisions autonomously, can react to a much greater range of unforeseeable situations and are in this sense able to expand their range of applications. Currently the capabilities from driving assistance systems become more and more extended. There is an ongoing trend towards entirely autonomous vehicles. In industrial processes, robot arms should act autonomously in the presence of human co-workers and work more and more closely with them together.

But many of these potential application areas are strongly limited due to questions of operational safety. For the introduction of autonomous systems they are in the light of unsolved liability issues but also for system performance aspects what is explained later of crucial importance.

© Springer International Publishing Switzerland 2015
F. Koornneef and C. van Gulijk (Eds.): SAFECOMP 2015 Workshops, LNCS 9338, pp. 156–166, 2015.
DOI: 10.1007/978-3-319-24249-1_14

In recent years when considering motion safety of autonomous systems the safety research was mainly focused on topics like environment detection or collision avoidance. The importance of the system condition itself as the counterpart to environmental aspects for the overall operational safety wasn't a focus of the safety researchers, even though changes in the conditions of components like sensors and actuators could have big influence on generating, processing and executing data in the autonomous system. With the general expression "condition" we want to summarize this uncertainty to handle data for different kinds of components. With terms like condition monitoring as self-diagnosis this expression is well established in the scientific community and provides the idea of a somehow "smart" component, which gives feedback about its own status.

But considering present autonomous cars they are mainly based on regular cars and require a lot of manual checks of safety related components, especially the mechanical ones. So in some cases safety related data is simply not available to the autonomous system. For most other safety relevant components the only distinction is drawn between a normal correct working data-processing component according to the specifications or a defect one. Obviously this is not the nature of real-world technical components especially as we talk about wear parts from mobile autonomous systems or components which are more or less degraded in their functionalities based on environmental aspects. This could be wear parts like chassis, steering and brakes or temporarily deterioration from sensors like stereo cameras through contamination with dust or through temporarily occurring fog in the surrounding area. So if we want to ensure the operational safety for the autonomous systems at runtime, the impact of such environmental aspects as well as the wear of components on component specific safety related functions should be displayed with a more detailed component condition as uncertainty rating.

The advantages of using more safety related data for the overall system safety and system performance are illustrated with an example of an expected idealized behavior of a regular car driver. Such a driver would probably consider for his driving behavior that the tires of his car are slightly worn in the sense of a safety related component condition. From a driver safety training he knows that the combination of bad tires, a wet surface and a high speed could lead to aquaplaning, which finally leads to a total loss of the reaction capability of his car to obstacles. Based on this knowledge he would hopefully consider such environmental aspects and ensure a sufficient reaction capability to obstacles due to limiting the top speed depending on environmental aspects. In this example the current driving speed should be seen as the only performance factor. So from a theoretical point of view the driver's intention would always be to drive as fast as possible. On the other hand the driver wants to ensure that the hazard to collide with obstacles is sufficiently low. So if the driver takes such additional safety related aspects into account, he could always provide a situation specific sufficiently low risk to collide with obstacles and could extent the system performance due to driving always the maximum allowed speed in each environmental situation. In reality this behavior is of course error-prone because of subjective decisions of the driver.

This example shows that also slightly degraded functions of components like the grip of the tires have to be considered for autonomous systems to ensure the overall system safety, because in combination with other factors like the wet surface the grip becomes even lower which finally leads to a catastrophic loss of control.

Another conclusion is that allowing a graceful degradation of performance like the top speed as a preventive measure of safety based on the detailed knowledge of component condition, the driver has always the ability to recover a specific safety level. As a result the system availability could be raised to an appropriate level.

This is especially appreciated for autonomous systems, where a high availability is required during operation. In such an application a fail-safe system would be unsatisfactory because in case of failures the system would always stop operating and give the control back to the driver. Due to economical reasons there is typically no other way to raise the system availability with additional redundant components.

To introduce the idea of graceful degradation of performance in autonomous systems the main question is how to determine the uncertainties for the operational safety at runtime. We believe that this safety evaluation has to be done bottom-up based on the component condition. Each component provides a certain basic function for the superordinate level in an autonomous system. The complex autonomous system behavior is than hierarchical derived from these basic functions. So to understand the extent of uncertainty in the autonomous system behavior we have to keep track of this function fusion and simultaneously evaluate uncertainties for each function.

To guarantee the optimal situational uncertainty rating for a function, this uncertainty evaluation should be supported with data or provided as a whole by the developer of this function or more general the component manufacturer, because he should have the maximum knowledge about it.

Without considering this knowledge of component conditions in a proper way for the safety evaluation the autonomous motion would either be unsafe or too conservative regarding the system design. For this reason there is a strong demand for an improved use of the scope of service of a component to increase the cost effectiveness and also to guarantee a safe motion considering more safety related aspects based on component conditions at runtime.

Clear and generally binding rules for the described evaluation of the overall motion safety are necessary. How could we ensure a safe motion or action based on the combination of environmental aspects and system condition? How should a consistent evaluation for the introduction of general and mandatory standards be displayed, which also take into account the different perspectives of the various participants like the system configurator, the sensor- or actuator manufacturer, the developer of evaluation software for sensor signals, the developer of the control or the safety engineers?

To overcome the simplification of component conditions we have introduced a certification concept, which enables more realistic description of components but also leads to much wider scope for specifications of system properties and analytical techniques for autonomous systems.

In Sect. 2 the requirements for safety evaluation for autonomous motions are shown. In Sect. 3 the state of the art for safety evaluation is shown. In Sect. 4 is based on the previous sections a new concept for safety certified motion presented.

2   Safety Evaluation Requirements for Autonomous Motions

The operational safety for technical systems is guaranteed through the verification of the proper condition and appropriate use [2]. Till now the operational safety for autonomous systems is reached due to strong limitations of the degrees of freedom, such as the limitation of the activity space, the velocity or the surveillance through an operator. The responsibility for the proper condition lies with the operator and the appropriate use is simply ensured by the limitation of degrees of freedom.

Regardless of these limitations the performance of autonomous systems rises potentially more and more because of various aspects. On the one hand the possibilities of environment detection rises because of a constantly improved measurement accuracy as well as improved self-diagnostic functions of sensors and sinking prices, which simply enable the use of more sensors. On the other hand the possibilities for evaluation of the dataset rises through better software algorithms and the constantly rising processing power according to Moore's law. Combining these technical trends the possibilities of autonomous systems increase to recognize their environment and to enhance their self-diagnostic for a better self-perception.

In comparison to systems, which are immobile, the safety evaluation for autonomous movements are far more complex. This is mainly based on the fact that we have not only to consider the system itself but also the environment and the interaction between system and environment. As an additional demand this safety evaluation has to be done at runtime due to several reasons.

One important argument for runtime analysis for modern technical systems are commonly the requirements, which should according to concepts like "industry 4.0" enable an integration of additional or modified components at runtime [2]. Therefore an open interface for the integration of components from various manufacturers is necessary and also an additional safety evaluation at runtime to analyze the impact of the afterwards added or modified components to the entire system.

Besides the demands from concepts like "industry 4.0", which don't have to be necessarily supported by autonomous systems in safety critical domains, the high hazard potential of autonomous motions itself is a main reason against considering the safety just at development time. While for a stationary system like a desktop-PC a blackout would be acceptable, for an autonomous motion it would not be allowed, because the consequences of a system failure would be less predictable and so potentially more hazardous.

A very detailed safety evaluation is needed whose complex fault model cannot be displayed in a sufficient way at development time. The extension of the fault models to the unforeseeable environment as well as the interrelation from the technical system to this, while considering the time dependent relationships, results in a too complex model where faulty assumptions or uncertainties cannot be excluded.

For the safety of the technical system the environment can be seen similar to the requirements of "industry 4.0" as a previously unknown component, which changes at runtime and influences the operational safety. In comparison to a technical component it has considerably more degrees of freedom and should interact concerning safety issues with the technical system similar to a feedback loop to lower existing threats.

A comprehensive view of all safety related components like sensors and actuators based on statistical data at development time can lead to strong deviations of the system behavior at runtime. So it would be best to reduce the possible fault model based on a runtime diagnosis to current hazards. Nevertheless, strict rules for the evaluation of operational safety as well as the definition of the evaluation scale should be determined at development time to limit the uncertainties in system behavior at runtime.

The term system behavior indicates already that the main reason for the safety evaluation is no longer only a passive evaluation of the motion situation rather an active influence of the motion behavior. Therefore fast reactions of the autonomous system to threats and short computation times of the operational safety at runtime are needed. Similar to the definition of safety evaluation rules, short computation times also demands for a maximal shift of the safety evaluation to the development time.

Thereby keeping in mind that the evaluation of the proper condition through the system itself at runtime is important. If the proper condition of components would be evaluated by a responsible person like the driver of a car, which is not autonomous, this information would not or only insufficient be available for the system. As stated in the previous section this safety related runtime information is an essential part for determining the autonomous behavior based on preventive measures of safety.

However, if the system has access to environment data and its own condition in the way described before, there is at the moment no uniform concept available to evaluate the operational safety in a standardized way. This limits the possibilities of autonomous decisions and increases possible liability risks. And because a modular concept for the safety evaluation is missing, an overall system operator like the manufacturer of autonomous vehicles takes the whole responsibility for all part systems, which can lead him to too conservative assumptions for the system performance. Furthermore, a missing unified frame concept leads to strong diversification in research for autonomous systems, which in case of safety issues is unfavorable.

According to that a concept is needed which guarantees independent from a specific function a safe motion for the autonomous system. For the transmission to concrete applications a component oriented approach is needed, which allows a transparent evaluation of the states of the entire system based on the classification of part components and the interaction to the environment at runtime. The modular structure needs precisely defined interfaces for responsibilities and functions of subcomponents. Subsystems should be certified regarding their safety level and depending on that the subordinate functional level. Based on this evaluation the motion control should be influenced according to safety benchmarks.

In the next section methods for the modular safety analysis as well as the determination of the overall system safety at runtime based on variable component conditions are introduced.

3   State of the Art for Safety Evaluation

When considering safety related aspects for safe autonomous motions we focused on three main topics: Firstly the state-of-the-practice for safety evaluation of technical systems is discussed. Secondly an innovative safety evaluation method for modular and adaptive systems is shown. Thirdly the available techniques for the determination of a safe motion based on runtime evaluation are explained in more detail.

In industrial environment fault trees are still state of the art to analyze technical systems in detail. For an undesired state of a system all possible causes are deductively derived in a hierarchical way according to their cause-event chain of effects based on Boolean logic. With the resulting fault tree it is then possible based on statistical data to calculate the probability of occurrence of the analyzed undesired state.

However a disadvantage of the standard fault tree is that only the causal relationships of fault propagation in the system are considered where each cause of a fault is only displayed once. If a safety engineer wants to analyze the failure emergence based on the real system architecture, he has to derive the cause-event chain based on causes in the real existing subcomponents. This requires a component oriented fault tree with the option to display similar faults repeated, according to their real occurrence within the system components.

Therefore, Kaiser [3] introduced the Component Fault Trees (CFT), which exactly fulfill these requirements. In Fig. 1 such a CFT is shown. In comparison to a standard fault tree for a CFT it is possible to display faults of the same kind in different components and derive from that a common cause fault based on the system architecture.

The fault propagation for the component model is again based on Boolean logic. However in another work from [4] it was pointed out that the use of CFT is not limited to the level of technical realization. CFT could also be used to describe the hierarchical connection of components and with a uniform interface specifications it could be used for an extended modularized description of system functions. The idea that components

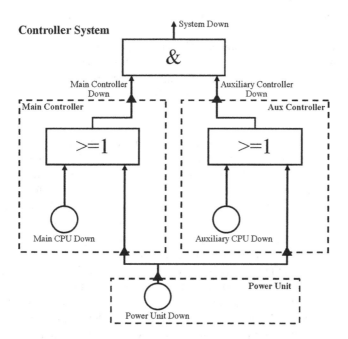

Fig. 1. Component Fault Tree

have related faults and that they could provide failure rates based on their internal logic and their input data is very important for the later on introduced concept based on component conditions.

An alternative approach for safety evaluation is the Failure Mode and Effects Analysis (FMEA) [5] where for each component the failure modes and the resulting effects on the system are systematically derived. The various failure modes are, as part of the quality management in the design- and development phase of a technical system, rated according their extent of damage, their probability of failure occurrence as well as the probability of fault detection during runtime. Later on the system is optimized based on these results. Within the modularized system function both evaluation methods FMEA and fault tree analysis can be beneficially matched to combine the bottom-up and top-down approach. The FMEA concept is well suited for the approach in Sect. 2 to shift most of the motion safety analysis to development time due to safety and computational reasons. If the resulting effects of different combinations of failure modes to the system safety are derived at development time, there is at runtime only the need to monitor the component conditions and their influencing factors and to conclude from that to the whole system safety.

Nevertheless the described analysis methods have in common that they were introduced for safety evaluation at development time. A simple transfer to runtime is for the FMEA not possible or in case of the CFT not suitable because of the complex evaluation model and the resulting long processing times. Because if we think about a runtime evaluation all system parameters would have to be evaluated in specified short intervals according to real time requirements as even minimal parameter variations could have impact on the entire system reliability.

With the "Condition-based fault tree analysis" (CBFTA) [6] a method to evaluate the condition of a system with a fault tree at runtime was introduced. Empirical data and runtime data are combined in a simplified fault tree to determine the condition of the entire system. Compared to the standard fault tree the probability rating of an occurring top level event based on a CBFT is more realistic. Nevertheless, with this condition-based fault tree the possibilities to analyze failure emergence and propagation are also limited because of the missing possibility to illustrate the system architecture and the top down approach.

As mentioned in the previous sections for a runtime analysis it is necessary to evaluate the current system condition based on the condition of subcomponents. An illustrative example for the modification of a useful signal during propagation through components depending on their conditions is the so called "health signal" [7]. This value is always given additionally to the sensor signal for processing in different component levels to determine the remaining reliability of the signal. The "health signal" seems to be an easy way to propagate a reliability guarantee through components at runtime. Based on this the impact of a less reliable signal could be easily determined, in each component, with a previous FMEA evaluated at development time. Obviously the ability of the "health signal" to guarantee their reliability is restricted to a single signal. So in the following a more sophisticated evaluation method called ConSerts is introduced.

This procedure allows to guarantee the reliability for arbitrary system functions, concentrates on the modular component idea and introduces an appropriate way to segregate the propagated reliability values based on guarantee/demand combinations.

With "Conditional Safety Certificates" (ConSerts) [8] it's possible to reduce the recalculation time during system changes to a minimum and to determine the entire system condition based on components and their conditions at runtime. System and safety specifications were as far as possible shifted to development time, so that at runtime only the component conditions have to be evaluated with Boolean logic.

The components are therefore linked with demand/guarantee combinations. For each component a "Conditional Safety Tree" based on Boolean logic is determined at development time with demands as input and guarantees depending on the Boolean logic as output. This means a component is able to provide guarantees to other components based on the existing guarantees from other components.

But ConSerts were introduced for stationary systems with a static functionality, where there are only a few modifications for the CST of a component at runtime mainly based on shared resources. Similar to the approach of "System of Systems" the main changes of safety properties of the entire system happen due to adding or removing subcomponents with specific safety properties. For the concept of safety certified motion the component model and the relationship of components is determined at development time and not changed at runtime. The changes happen inside the components because of the wear of components or environmental aspects, which influence components. As explained before if we change the safety evaluation from a stationary system to a dynamical and reactive one also the passive safety evaluation changes to an active influencing of system behavior according predefined safety regulations, which has to be considered additionally.

4   A Safety Certified Motion Sequence

The ConSerts are most suitable for the derived requirements stated in Sect. 2 for the certification of autonomous motions mainly because of their open and modular concept as well as their efficient runtime evaluation and bottom-up approach. For the safety evaluation of autonomous motion the environment as well as the interaction between system condition and environment at runtime have to be considered additionally. So the ConSert approach is extended in a way that the environment is rated at runtime similar to component conditions based on safety critical factors like distance and angle to unpredictable obstacles.

Based on CSTs a generally valid reaction to specific combinations of environment scenario and condition of sensor-/actuator components could be defined at development time. A fundamental finding is that the allocation of certificates for the safety evaluation of the nearer environment not only depends on the actual sensor signals but also from the condition of sensor components itself as well as the reliability rate for the obstacle detection. Consequently, the component which allocates certificates based on the environment analysis has to be subordinated to the sensor-/actuator components.

In the derived entire system in Fig. 2 are sensors and actuators as independent elements in separate component modules integrated. The additional benefit is that they introduce besides the propagation of a certain signal an evaluation level and could so provide additional information for the safety evaluation based on certificates. These could be safety relevant specifications of certain sensors or actuators, but also data from condition monitoring or interpretation of measurement results with firmware.

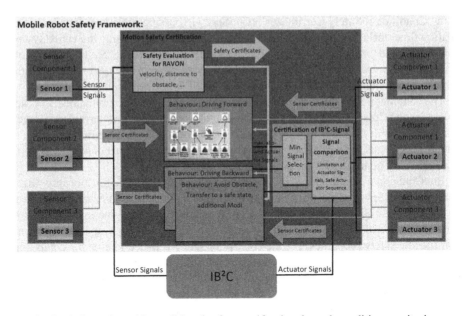

Fig. 2. Safe motion with conditional safety certification through condition monitoring

For a uniform presentation and safety evaluation of the entire system at development time a frame concept with the name "Mobile Robot Safety Framework" is introduced. This frame concept segregates the different components and emphasizes the separation of the regular control, in this case the behavior-based control (IB^2C) and the level of safety certification. The IB^2C network processes sensor signals based on the planning task and calculates adaptively the optimal actuator activation for a specific environmental situation. Concerning safety issues it's sometimes difficult to understand the actuator activation of an IB^2C network in specific situations. The "Motion Safety Certification" component doesn't consider those planning tasks. The main objective for this module is the safety evaluation based on sensor signals and the available certificates, which is according the actuator activation, dominantly overlaid to the regular IB^2C network. In case of a malfunction the causing component could be easily derived by analyzing the present certificates at that point of time.

The operational safety is guaranteed through the proper condition as well as the appropriate use. At development time the composition of components is proved based on the demand/guarantee combinations. With this at the point of commissioning from formal point of view the proper condition is guaranteed. During runtime the proper condition is proved based on certificates. If a component deteriorates the system reacts based on actions determined at development time. The appropriate use is checked at runtime based on the analysis of environment hazards and the interaction of system with the environment. The appropriate use is ensured through defined reactions to environmental aspects determined at development time. In Fig. 3 the safety evaluation mechanism based on runtime certificates is shown and explained in the following.

To ensure a sufficiently low risk to collide with obstacles the safety evaluation takes the conditions of sensors as the capability to detect obstacles into account. In combination with the detected obstacles the environmental situation is rated according their hazards. The effective remaining hazards from obstacles to the autonomous system is then rated based on the reaction capability of the autonomous system to the obstacles. Therefore the conditions of actuators in combination with properties of the driving mode (like current speed) are considered additionally. Based on this hazard analysis the current driving mode is influenced due to the limitations for the IB^{2}C-control or the execution of safe sequences. The adapted driving mode increases the reaction capability to obstacles and reduces the overall hazard of a collision.

The advantages of considering the conditions of components in contrast to distinct only correct working or defect components next to environmental aspects are stated in the following based on an autonomous vehicle with Fig. 3.

On the one hand there is the possibility of **compensation** of uncertainties to raise the whole system availability. If the reaction capability to hazards is low because of poor brakes it's possible to drive slowly forward if there is no obstacle detected in the closer surroundings and the sensors are in a good condition. The other way round if it's very difficult to detect obstacles because of fog, good actuator condition could enable slowly forward driving. In other words the more information about the component condition are available the more performance potential of the autonomous system can be used. As stated in Fig. 3 the driving mode influences like a **feedback loop** the reaction capability to hazards in combination with the condition of actuators for example a steering system. As a result with rising speed the reaction capability to hazards becomes lower and the entire safety evaluation becomes more critical. Also the **relevance** of safety aspects for the entire system safety becomes more visible considering bad sensors on the rear side while forward driving.

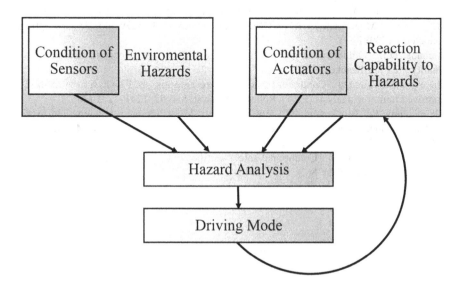

Fig. 3. Safety evaluation with feedback

5   Conclusion

With the concept of safety certified motions it's possible to bring the various disciplines with their specific knowledge such as the sensor-/actuator manufacturer, the developer of software (for example to evaluate sensor measurements), safety experts and the system configurator closer together. The uniform interface between them are the certificates. Each participant guarantees with specific certificates for a certain function. The determination of certificates for a specific functional scope or a component condition should be done similar to the admission of regular technical systems in cooperation with safety authorities to guarantee reliability. As a result a car manufacturer only has to think about a black box for a sensor component which provides reliable certificates according to his requirements. The effects of changing certificates in the system behavior at runtime are defined with the Conditional Safety Trees at development time. So all in all, a system is introduced whose safety concept is determined at development time and checked at runtime.

References

1. Adamy, J., Bechtel, P.: Sicherheit mobiler Roborter (Safety of mobile robots). at-Automatisierungstechnik/Methoden und Anwendungen der Steuerungs-, Regelungs- und Informationstechnik **51**(10), 435–444 (2003)
2. Liggesmeyer, P., Trapp, M.: Safety: Herausforderungen und lösungsansätze. In: Industrie 4.0 in Produktion, Automatisierung und Logistik. Springer Fachmedien Wiesbaden (2014)
3. Kaiser, B., Liggesmeyer, P., Maeckel, O.: A new component concept for fault trees. In: Australian Computer Society, I. (ed.): Proceedings of the 8th Australian Workshop on Safety Critical Systems and Software, vol. 33, pp. 37–46. Australian Computer Society, Canberra, Australia (2003)
4. Domis, D., Trapp, M.: Integrating safety analyses and component-based design. In: Harrison, M.D., Sujan, M.-A. (eds.) SAFECOMP 2008. LNCS, vol. 5219, pp. 58–71. Springer, Heidelberg (2008)
5. Stamatis, D.H.: Failure mode and effect analysis: FMEA from theory to execution. ASQ Quality Press, Milwaukee (2003)
6. Shalev, D.M., Tiran, J.: Condition-based fault tree analysis (CBFTA): A new method for improved fault tree analysis (FTA). Reliab. Eng. Syst. Saf. **92**, 1231–1241 (2007)
7. Kleinlützum, K., Brockmann, W., Rosemann, N.: Modellierung von anomalien in einer modularen roboter-steuerung. In: Berns, K., Luksch, T. (eds.) Autonome Mobile Systeme 2007, pp. 89–95. Springer, Berlin (2007)
8. Schneider, D., Trapp, M.: Conditional safety certification of open adaptive systems. ACM Trans. Auton. Adapt. Syst. **8**(2), 1–20 (2013)

Approach for Demonstrating Safety for a Collision Avoidance System

Thomas Gruber[✉] and Christian Zinner

AIT Austrian Institute of Technology GmbH, Donau-City-Strasse 1, Vienna, Austria
{thomas.gruber,christian.zinner}@ait.ac.at

Abstract. For many years, the Digital Safety and Security Department of the Austrian Institute of Technology has been developing stereo vision algorithms for various application purposes. Recently, these algorithms have been adapted for use in a collision avoidance system for tramways. The safety validation of such a system is a specific challenge as - like in the automotive domain - the rate of false positives cannot be lowered to zero. While automotive suppliers typically tackle with this problem by reducing the sensitivity of the system and validating it in hundreds of thousands of test kilometres, this paper presents an approach how it is possible to demonstrate safety with a carefully chosen functionality and less field test kilometres.

Keywords: Safety · Validation · Driver assistance system · Collision avoidance system · Stereo vision algorithm · Tramway · Tramcar

1 Introduction

Public transport providers operating tramway lines incur high cost in terms of casualties, material loss and also in image damage as a consequence of accidents. During the past years or almost decades, increased traffic safety awareness has caused authorities to take measures for road traffic safety, in particular for individual car traffic. But also public transport has reacted and lowered the rates of personal damage by targeted safety measures. As an example, the Wiener Linien[1] reduced the accident rate between 2010 and 2014 from 91 down to 63 events per million km, which corresponds to a decrease by 31 %. But there are still casualties and even fatalities through tramway accidents, and also material damage is considerable, for instance collisions with tramway depot gates during shunting.

According to statistics, between 80 and 90 % of the tramway accidents are caused by other road users: This leaves between 10 and 20 % of the hazardous cases for improvement, and driver assistance systems which detect and warn about imminent collisions can be an essential step forward towards more safety.

The potential of an automated collision warning or avoidance system lies mainly in two aspects:

---

[1] http://www.wienerlinien.at/eportal2/.

© Springer International Publishing Switzerland 2015
F. Koornneef and C. van Gulijk (Eds.): SAFECOMP 2015 Workshops, LNCS 9338, pp. 167–177, 2015.
DOI: 10.1007/978-3-319-24249-1_15

- The Shorter Reaction Time: While the driver typically has a reaction time of around one second, the system needs only a few tenths of a second.
- The Absence of Fatigue and Inattentiveness: The driver may be tired, distracted by a passenger, brood about private problems or - although prohibited - type on his smartphone. At 50 km/h, one second of inobservance corresponds to a "blind" drive of 14 m.

It is therefore obvious that an assistance system that warns the driver early or wakes him up from his daydream bears great potential for safety improvement. An intervening system, which activates the brake, can be even more beneficial.

In the automotive domain, driver assistance systems like collision avoidance systems have found their way into cars from the luxury class down to small cars with the expectation of improving road traffic safety. So the question arises why they are not yet used in tramways.

From a market perspective it is evident that the expected number of tramway driver assistance systems sold is smaller by several orders of magnitude compared to the figures in the automotive domain. In Vienna, as an example, Wiener Linien statistics for 2014[2] give a number of 519 tramcars while, according to Statistik Austria[3], there were 683.258 passenger cars registered in Vienna by end of 2014. Consequently, development cost for a tramway driver collision warning system must be considerably lower than in the automotive domain in order to be economic. One approach can be to simply re-use an automotive driver assistance system. Another one can be re-using sensory knowhow gained in a comparable or even in essentially other domains and porting the pre-developed algorithms with according adaptations and parameterizations for the specific application purpose on a COTS (commercial off-the-shelf) computer.

As will be described later in this paper, there are moreover essential differences between motorcars and tramways regarding technical properties. But also the risks for passengers vary between cars and trams, and finally the expectations with respect to the reliability of a professional driver in a tramway deviates from the one of a potentially unexperienced and less well trained private driver. These differences define limits for choosing the approach how the system is used and influence in particular its safety properties. In the following, the particularities of a tramway collision warning and avoidance system will be presented, based on the system currently (2015) being developed at AIT, and an approach will be drafted how safety of such a driver assistance system can be demonstrated.

2   State of the Art

2.1   Collision Warning and Avoidance Systems

Collision warning systems detect obstacles in front of the vehicle and warn the driver by acoustic or optic signals. Collision avoidance systems intervene additionally into the

---

[2] http://www.wienerlinien.at/media/files/2015/betriebsangaben_2014_151135.pdf.

[3] http://www.statistik.at/web_de/statistiken/energie_umwelt_innovation_mobilitaet/verkehr/strasse/kraftfahrzeuge_-_bestand/index.html.

vehicle control or braking systems. In the way they are devised today, these systems aim at compensating possible inattentiveness of the driver or occasional overestimation of his capabilities. But they do not exempt him from his duties and merely support him.

For obstacle detection, most of these systems use short range radar sensors in parallel to a mono camera or an ultrasonic or laser sensor. All these systems, however, come up with comparably unreliable obstacle detection, partly due to inherent weaknesses of the sensor technologies used, but also because even the definition of what is to be considered as an obstacle is fundamentally imprecise. Despite of these deficiencies, driver assistance systems have become a standard in luxury cars for a few years and collision warning and avoidance systems are today penetrating the market down to the middle-sized or even compact car class.

For tramways, however, there is to our knowledge no commercially available collision warning or avoidance system on the market yet. But there are prototypes under evaluation; [1] describes shortly two such systems. One of them is based or a collision warning system for motorcars using a radar sensor for obstacle detection and a video camera for determining the track layout, the other one is the system developed by AIT, which uses three cameras and a stereo vision algorithm for detecting both the obstacles and the track geometry. For this system, more details are given further below in this paper.

In addition, we found two papers proposing a collision avoidance system for tramways which was derived from an automotive system and is based on digital maps and a laser-scanner [2, 3].

2.2   Safety Validation Strategies for Collision Warning and Avoidance Systems

The sensors which the driver assistance systems are using are not very reliable in the sense that they more or less frequently signal potential collision objects where there are none. These false positives can cause unnecessary emergency brake activations. One important reason is that the spatial resolution of radar and ultrasonic sensors is comparably low.

On the other hand, not all relevant obstacles are detected (false negatives). Here the reflection properties for microwaves and sound waves of the objects to be detected by the respective sensors play an essential role. For this reason, continuous driver attention and - in case of a false negative - his immediate intervention are indispensable for safety.

In order to avoid nasty false positives with increased rear-end collision risk, these systems often fuse the output of different sensors, mostly radar or supersonic sensors and video cameras. This goes, however, at the cost of the false positives rate, and only a mediocre proportion of all actually relevant obstacles is eventually signalled. Figure 1 illustrates the failure of a collision avoidance system when the collision object doesn't reflect microwaves [4].

Collision warning and avoidance systems for the automotive domain have to be developed according to ISO 26262 [5]. These complex systems are, however, based on inherently incomplete models, and a complete verification is therefore infeasible. It is state of the art that for the overall system safety validation of driver assistance systems extensive field tests are conducted, typically in the magnitude of hundreds of thousands or millions of km. For fully autonomous driving, i.e. without driver controllability,

Fig. 1. Collision avoidance system not detecting an inflatable car dummy (Source: ÖAMTC (Österreichischer Automobil-, Motorrad- und Touring-Club))

the amount of required tests would be extreme, as Prof. Winner and W. Wachenfeld stated "More than 100 Mio km of road driving are required for fully automatic vehicle release" [6]. As for the undetected obstacles in our case, i.e. the false negatives rate, the controllability argument helps reduce the necessary amount of tests. Controllability means that the driver is constantly alert while driving and is able to take over control at any instant when the system fails to detect a potential collision.

False positives in an automatically intervening collision avoidance system, in contrast, induce the hazard of rear-end collisions. It is improbable that the private (non-professional) driver will be able to quickly interrupt an unnecessary automatic emergency braking action caused by a system failure, thus the controllability argument is certainly not fully applicable. Actually, in the automotive domain unintended braking is rated much more critical (ASIL C) than no braking (ASIL A or QM). Therefore the false positives rate has to be reduced to such an extent that the resulting rear-end collision risk is within the tolerable range, and system validation has to prove this by sufficiently extensive field tests.

When we consider tramways, there is an additional, non-negligible risk caused by false positives (unnecessary emergency braking), namely injury of passengers inside the vehicle. This risk doesn't apply to passengers in motorcars as they are supposed to have the safety belts fastened. For tramways, by contrast, this is the most important risk arising from false positives.

3   Stereo-Vision-Based Collision Warning/Avoidance System

For about a decade a research group in AIT has been developing stereo vision algorithms for different application areas [7, 8], among them an obstacle detection system prototype validated on an autonomous train [9] and an obstacle detection and route determination system for an autonomous off-road vehicle [10]. Recently, the algorithms have been adapted for a tramway driver assistance system [11].

The system consists of three parallel cameras mounted in a horizontal line, two of them in a distance of a bit less than 1 m from each other, and the third one between them, at about one third of the wide distance. The stereo vision algorithms running on a COTS computer receives the three camera signals. It computes the track geometry and detects obstacles within the clearance gauge of the train. Figure 2 illustrates typical results of the stereo vision algorithm: The clearance gauge (conic shape symmetric to the track) and smaller rectangles marking detected obstacles reaching into the clearance gauge.

Fig. 2. Tramcar clearance gauge and detected obstacles marked with rectangles

The technical structure of the stereo-vision-based collision warning/avoidance system is shown in Fig. 3.

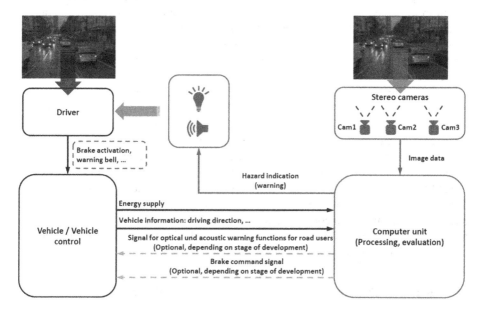

Fig. 3. Technical structure of the stereo-vision-based collision warning/avoidance system

Based on the result of the obstacle detection algorithm as shown in Fig. 2, the Computer unit evaluates whether the detected obstacles are within a hazardous distance. This is determined in the decision module and depends on the distance to the obstacle, which is computed by the stereo matching algorithm, and on the vehicle speed, which is calculated based on scene flow analysis.

The system can be configured to act as a merely warning system; in this case the warning is signalled by an acoustic (e.g. buzzer or bell) or an optical signal (warning lamp) or both; it is the responsibility of the driver to make the right decision, i.e. to decide whether to brake or not, and - if so - with which deceleration.

The alternative is an intervening system, where the system activates the brake via the Brake command signal (see lower dashed arrow in Fig. 3). Tramcars usually provide different levels of braking force; it is a safety-relevant design decision which brake type, i.e. which maximum deceleration is triggered by the driver assistance system.

4   Approach for Safety Demonstration

4.1   Applicable Functional Safety and Security Standards

In the area of tramcars and light rail vehicles it is - unlike in the railway domain - not clear which functional safety standard has to be applied for E/E/PE[4] systems. One of the first suggestions we got was surprisingly the application of the machine directive [12] and the IT security standard EN 27001 [13]. For the E/E/PE systems this would additionally imply the harmonized standard IEC 62061 [14]. We collected informal information from people involved in standardization, who confirmed that the regulation is currently not clear. Actually, there are national regulations like for instance in Germany BOStrab [15], and German public transport operators rely primarily on this legal act. But the trend goes towards the CENELEC railway norms [16–18], and so we decided for them, too.

As for security aspects, we can rely on the fact that the system has no physical or wireless connection to the outside world. Therefore cyber-attacks are unfeasible; a perpetrator would have to get physical access to the driver assistance system. And in this case he can cause damage or casualties more effectively by manipulating for instance the brakes. One kind of attack is, of course, conceivable: Influencing the system with high-power electromagnetic waves. Such an attack would, however, probably compromise the vehicle control systems as well and cause unpredictable effects. The stereo-vision system would most probably suffer some malfunction in the system logic and - as a consequence - the watchdog function would set the system into the safe state (collision avoidance system switched off and warning lamp turned on). So a detailed security management seems dispensable.

4.2   Under Which Conditions Is the System Safety-Critical?

The minimum safety goal is that the system does not decrease safety compared to a tramcar without this driver assistance system. When it comes to safety we have to distinguish two basic variants of the driver assistance system:

- Warning system, and
- Intervening system

Warning System. The mere collision warning system is generally accepted as safe because the system cannot cause any hazard; it only avoids or mitigates risks. One issue, however, needs to be considered: The potential learning process of the driver, i.e. his confidence in the system, may grow and reduce his attendance with the consequence that the false negatives rate of the system plays an increasing role.

---

[4] Electrical / Electronic / Programmable Electronic.

Generally, a professional driver, who passes extensive trainings, should be able to control himself. A respective instruction should be included in the learning material.

Intervening System. In a motorcar, where all passengers are supposed to have their seat belts fastened, an unnecessary emergency braking event does not pose a major additional risk to them[5]. The intervening tramway collision avoidance system, in contrast, is potentially safety-critical because passengers may be hurt when the tramcar suddenly brakes. Braking is, on the other hand, an absolutely normal manoeuvre. To get a clearer picture, we have to distinguish different deceleration levels with different associated injury risk for passengers. The following sub-chapter gives more details.

4.3   Tramcar Brake Systems and Their Influence on Passenger Safety

The Tramcars usually provide at least three brake types, among them the emergency brake, for which 4 levels are distinguished. Table 1 shows the deceleration limits and the brake response times as defined in EN 13452-1 [19].

Table 1. Theoretical dynamic limits of deceleration and brake response time

	Service brake	Emergency brake 1	Emergency brake 2	Emergency brake 3	Emergency brake 4	Safety brake
Minimum deceleration a_e in m/s^2	variable 0.. 1.2	1.2	1.2	2.8	2.8	1
Maximum response time t_e in s	1.5	1.5	2	0.85	0.85	2

This standard gives furthermore details on who may activate which type and level of brake and in which way.

- The service brake is the one which the driver applies usually in normal tramway line operation. The associated brake deceleration and jerk are considered safe. So if our system activates the service brake only it can still be considered safe.
- All emergency brake levels are considered safety-critical, but the benefit from avoiding or mitigating accidents is considered higher than the injury risk of passengers.
  - Level 1 is related to the dead man's handle,
  - level 2 is activated when a passenger pulls the red handle in the tramcar,
  - level 3 can be activated by the driver in a special position of the brake lever, and
  - level 4 is reserved for special purposes.
- The safety brake is activated when the driver pushes the emergency button

---

[5] The Automotive domain accepts quite high deceleration values for automatic braking. The standard for Adaptive Cruise Control (ACC) systems [20], for instance, proposes a deceleration limit of 3.5 ms^{-2} and a limit of 2.5 ms^{-3} for the jerk.

As one can see, the selection of a brake type for use in an intervening collision avoidance system is safety-relevant. Basically, the system is planned such that the driver can intervene also into the automatic brake activation through the assistance system, i.e. he can also reduce the imposed brake force and is then responsible for the effect.

In order to reduce risk, we furthermore considered different ways of automated brake activations:

- Activate only the service brake but so early that a standstill is possible with the service brake only.
- Activate the service brake early and, if the driver doesn't react, activate in addition emergency brake level 3.
- Another approach would be warning the driver early via the dead man circuitry. In case he shows no quick reaction the dead man function integrated in the vehicle activates emergency brake level 1.

The way of intervening, and if an automatic brake activation is desired at all, is moreover influenced by the requirements of individual public transport providers. It can be expected that first versions of the system are deployed as warning-only systems followed by moderately intervening systems.

4.4 Operation on a COTS Hardware with Safety Requirements

As mentioned earlier, the software is intended to run on a COTS computer for economic reasons. It is evident that the failure rate of such a hardware, which lies typically in the magnitude of 10^{-4} h^{-1} is not adequate for a safety-relevant system. The problem is no so much that hardware faults could result in additional unnecessary braking actions - these happen anyway, but rather that the system could stop working without the driver being informed about that. As a consequence, we planned to use an independent fail-safe watchdog, which sets the system into a safe state in case a fault is detected. This applies to hardware faults of the processor and the peripherals causing the system to stop working as well as to permanent failures of the software running on it like endless loops or deadlocks. The safe state is switching off the driver assistance system and signalling the failure to the driver with an acoustic or optic signal (or both).

For the intervening system, another safety requirement must be realized: The connection to the vehicle brake systems, whichever is used, must be constructed such that the system can never, not even in a faulty state, reduce or inhibit the driver's control over the brakes.

As for the cameras, we exploit the fact that the stereo vision matching algorithm runs twice, once for the camera pair with narrowest distance and in parallel for the pair with the widest distance. The fact that there is a dependence between the two image processing results allows for a mutual failure detection of the software algorithms as well as of the cameras including cabling.

4.5 Safety Argumentation for a Software with Inherent False Positives

The aforementioned CENELEC standards mandate that the software be developed according to EN 50128 [17]. The stereo-vision software, however, is the result of a long development process throughout years, integrating experience from different domains gained by trial and error. A continuously standard-conformant re-development of the software would be economically unfeasible.

Yet another point has to be mentioned: The CENELEC standards are intended for safety-relevant *control* systems in infrastructure-based railway signalling systems and on the rolling stock. They are reasonably not directly applicable to highly-complex stereo-vision-based assistance systems like ours. So our approach to demonstrate software safety is not primarily process-based, as EN 50128 prescribes, but our safety argumentation relies on logical considerations and an adequate safety validation by field tests.

The applicable approach in this case is to consider the image processing software as pre-validated and use the proven-in-use argument in conformance with EN 50128. This is in particular adequate to the problem as the remaining false positives rate is not mainly a result from flaws in the algorithm but from the inherently incomplete model of how an obstacle representing a hazard is defined.

4.6   Safety Validation

The proven-in-use argument implies that we have to conduct sufficient field tests with the software in the concrete target environment and system context. Apart from the functional validation of the system, field tests are also necessary to prove that the safety goal as stated earlier is met. We have to get confidence that the collision warning or avoidance system doesn't endanger safety. For this purpose we collect video data during field tests. This allows us to "play" with that data, and when we detect that a certain situation may result in a false positive, we can improve the algorithm. Furthermore the same collected data can then be used for the regression test.

Actually much of the video data is not very relevant because there are no people or vehicles around and the tram is running undisturbed straight forward. We can therefore concentrate the stored data focusing on interesting situations where the stereo algorithm can "see" something potentially relevant. Interesting situations are around the moments where our system detects something and when the driver brakes. This increases efficiency by reducing data volume as well as testing time.

5   Conclusions and Further Work

In the previous chapters we have drafted an approach for the demonstration of safety for the special case of a tramway collision avoidance system. The work is still ongoing (June 2015) and we hope to finalize it within the coming months. We are working in an area where previous experience or proven approaches are not yet available, in particular because the conditions for a tramcar with respect to safety differ from those applicable to a motorcar. Economic margins are much smaller due to the low number of tramcars. Neither can we simply use approaches taken in the automotive industry nor is our approach simply transferable to that domain.

Future work will bring more field experience and further improvement of the algorithms. We expect to determine a sound value for the - positive - safety improvement and look forward to publishing results.

With respect to test scenarios, we can try to get ideas from the automotive sector. ISO 15622:2010 [20], for example, provides guidance for test procedures for Adaptive Cruise Control (ACC) systems, which can be partly adapted to our problem domain.

We have yet another option for future research: A group in AIT is developing a method called VITRO [21, 22] for artificially generating test images, which can be used to produce scenario-based test data with defined scenario or situation coverage. This allows testing all conceivable situations with potential collision objects of different kind under various light conditions or track geometries.

References

1. Verband Deutscher Verkehrsunternehmen e.V. (VDV): State of the art of driver assistance systems for collision avoidance for tramcars and light rail vehicles. VDV Report 1520, Köln (2015)
2. Katz, R., Schulz, R.: Towards the development of a laser scanner-based collision avoidance system for trams. In: IEEE proceedings of the Intelligent Vehicles Symposium (IV), pp. 725–729 (2013)
3. Lages, U., Katz, R., Schultz, R., Krähling, M.: Collision avoidance system for trams using laserscanners. In: Proceedings of the 20th ITS World Congress; Tokyo (2014)
4. Österreichischer Automobil-, Motorrad- und Touring-Club (ÖAMTC): Sicher ganz sicher?. In: Auto Touring November 2013, pp. 28–30, Vienna (2013)
5. ISO 26262 Road vehicles - Functional safety, Part 1-10. International Organization for Standardization (ISO) (2011)
6. Winner, H., Wachenfeld, W.: Absicherung automatischen Fahrens, 6. FAS Tagung, Munich (2013)
7. Humenberger, M., Zinner, Ch., Weber, M., Kubinger, W., Vincze, M.: A fast stereo matching algorithm suitable for embedded real-time systems. Comput. Vis. Image Underst. **114**(11), 1180–1202 (2010)
8. Ambrosch, K., Zinner, Ch., Leopold, H.: A miniature embedded stereo vision system for automotive applications. In: Vortrag: IEEE 26th Convention of Electrical and Electronics Engineers, Eilat, Israel; 17.11.2010 - 20.11.2010. In: Proceedings of the IEEEI 2010, pp. 786–789, IEEE, Israel (2010). ISBN: 978-1-4244-8680-9
9. Weichselbaum, J., Zinner, Ch., Gebauer, O., Pree, W.: Accurate 3D-vision-based obstacle detection for an autonomous train. Comput. Ind. **64**(9), 1209–1220 (2013)
10. Kadiofsky, T., Rößler, R., Zinner, Ch.: Visual 3D environment reconstruction for autonomous vehicles. ERCIM News **95**, 29–30 (2013)
11. Lechleitner, C., Newesely, G., Zinner, Ch.: Die Straßenbahn lernt Sehen - Innovationen im Bereich Straßen- und Stadtbahnen; Vortrag: Schienenfahrzeugtagung, Graz; 07.09.2014 - 10.09.2014. In: ZEVrail Sonderheft Tagungsband 42. Tagung Moderne Schienenfahrzeuge, Georg Siemens Verlag, pp. 105–111 (2014). ISSN: 1618-8330
12. ISO 13849-1:2006 Safety of machinery – Safety-related parts of control systems – Part 1: General principles for design. In: International Organization for Standardization (ISO) (2006)
13. ISO/IEC 27001:2013: Information technology – Security techniques – Information security management systems - Requirements (2013)
14. IEC 62061:2005 Safety of machinery – Functional safety of safety-related electrical, electronic and programmable electronic control systems. In: International Electrotechnical Commission (2005)

15. Federal regulation of the Federal Republic of Germany: Verordnung über den Bau und Betrieb der Straßenbahnen (Straßenbahn-Bau- und Betriebsordnung - BOStrab) (1987, latest update 2007)
16. EN_50126-1: Railway application - The specification and demonstration of Reliability, Availability, Maintainability and Safety (RAMS). Part 1: Basic requirements and generic process. Comité Européen de Normalisation Électrotechnique (CENELEC) (1999/corr. 2010)
17. EN_50128: Railway applications – Communication, signalling and processing systems. Software for railway control and protection systems, Comité Européen de Normalisation Électrotechnique (CENELEC) (2011)
18. EN_50129: Railway applications - Communication, signalling and processing systems 002D. Safety related electronic systems for signalling. Comité Européen de Normalisation Électrotechnique (CENELEC) (2003 / corr. 2010)
19. EN 13452-1:2003: Railway applications - Braking - Mass transit brake systems - Part 1: Performance requirements, Comité Européen de Normalisation (CEN) (2003)
20. ISO 15622:2010: Intelligent transport systems - Adaptive Cruise Control systems - Performance requirements and test procedures, International Organization for Standardization (ISO) (2010)
21. Zendel, O., Herzner, W., Murschitz, M.: VITRO - Model Based Vision Testing for Robustness. Poster: ISR 2013, Seoul/Korea; 24.10.2013 - 26.10.2013. In: ISR 2013, IFR, Seoul (2013)
22. Zendel, O., Herzner, W., Murschitz, M.: VITRO - Vision Testing for Robustness, ERCIM News **97** 58–59 (2014)

Contract Modeling and Verification with FormalSpecs Verifier Tool-Suite - Application to Ansaldo STS Rapid Transit Metro System Use Case

Marco Carloni[1]([⊠]), Orlando Ferrante[1], Alberto Ferrari[1],
Gianpaolo Massaroli[2], Antonio Orazzo[2], and Luigi Velardi[2]

[1] Advanced Laboratory on Embedded Systems, Via Barberini, 50, Rome, Italy
{marco.carloni,orlando.ferrante,
alberto.ferrari}@ales.eu.com
[2] Ansaldo Signalling and Transportation Solutions,
Via Argine, 425, Naples, Italy
{gianpaolo.massaroli.prof644,antonio.orazzo,
luigi.velardi}@ansaldo-sts.com

Abstract. Motivated by the emergent research on mixed techniques of analysis and testing, we focus our attention on producing analysis results that can efficiently reduce the effort in testing a modern metro system. In particular, we promote contract-based design to formalize requirements and support different kind of analyses on hazards, coverage and signal independency. This work is carried out on the following three different levels: at the application level, the system under development is specified and modeled by the experts of the railway industrial domain; at the methodology level, the contract-based paradigm was adopted to join the application requirements with a rigorous formal view necessary for enabling an automated verification process; at the machinery level, the utilization of the FSV tool suite for aiding the design represents a twofold gain for its developers since, first, it provides a new occasion to validate and improve their technology for automatic analyses and, second, it lets them to identify the analysis technique of the equivalent model checking, to match the industrial need in reducing the effort of testing.

Keywords: Contract-based design · Requirement engineering · Technologies for formal methods · Embedded systems

1 Introduction

To cope with the complexity and the evolution of embedded system design a formally strong and innovative methodology is paramount. With Contract-based Analysis and Testing (CBA&T) we aim to find a solution to verify and validate the system under development in the early phases of the design flow. The final goal is to minimize the effort of testing along with identifying the parts of the system where testing is necessary but it can be mitigated if applied in combination with a formal verification technique.

© Springer International Publishing Switzerland 2015
F. Koornneef and C. van Gulijk (Eds.): SAFECOMP 2015 Workshops, LNCS 9338, pp. 178–189, 2015.
DOI: 10.1007/978-3-319-24249-1_16

This semi-formal verification approach is based on two necessary methodology ingredients: a correct unambiguous requirements formalization, that permits an univocal interpretation of the specifications, and a careful system partitioning, that allows a consistent definition of the interfaces through different layers of abstraction from the early conceptual view till the final implementation view. The contract theory [1] precisely hits the above two items.

In this work we describe and complete the application of Contract-based Design to the specifications of the ASTS CBTC system [2] performed as part of the MBAT European Project [3]. MBAT aims at exploiting synergies between formal analyses and testing for the verification and validation of complex embedded systems. We analyze a part of the on-board sub-system of the ASTS CBTC, which commands the passengers' doors of a metro train. Keeping in mind the goal of minimizing the expensive effort of the latest design steps, we model the system following a component-based approach and elaborate its requirements by formalizing them as contracts. Then, we identify the set of analyses to perform and the techniques to adopt for formally verifying the contracts against the model. We develop and use the ALES tool suite Formal Specs Verifier (FSV) [4, 5] to model the contracts and making the analyses. The main contributions of the paper can be summarized as follows (1) a ASTS workflow was identified for combining analysis and testing in order to leverage formal verification to reduce the effort of the testing phase (2) the contract-based theory was adopted to formalize the requirements and the FSV-BCL toolbox was further developed for modeling contracts as composition of graphical blocks (3) a formal analysis was derived to be executed using FSV-Formal Verification tool and (4) the results provided by FSV on the CBTC modeled system were collected to show the applicability of the workflow and the analyses.

This paper is organized as follows: Sect. 2 resumes related works on Contract-based design principles. Section 3 presents the railway use case and the functional models under analysis. In Sect. 4 the technology developed is briefly described. Section 5 is dedicated to the detail of how this technology is used for modeling the requirements as contracts, performing analyses and interpreting the collected results. Finally, Sect. 6 summarizes and comments the produced work.

2 Related Work

SPEEDS [6] and SPRINT [7] European projects defined theory, methodology and tools to support Contract-based Design (CBD). CBD methodology was proposed in [8] and [9] to facilitate the development of the work among different design groups. The definition of contract [1] relies on the concept of system/component interface in a component-based model. A system/component is a hierarchical entity that represents a unit of design and components are interconnected and communicate through ports carrying discrete or event values. The interface of a system/component is defined by its ports. Moreover, implementations and requirements can be attached to components. Requirements are expressed as contracts. Finally, a contract formalizes expectations between the system/component and its environment. In this context, the models are

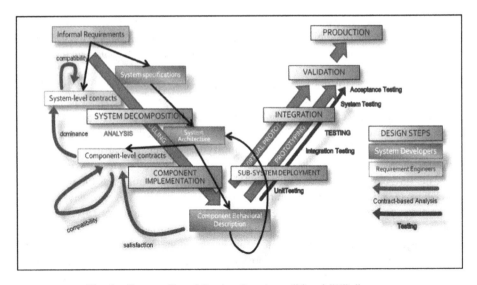

Fig. 1. Contract-Based Design flow in traditional "V" diagram.

"rich" - not only profiles, types, or taxonomy of data, but also models describing the functions, performances of various kinds (time and energy), and safety [2].

Formally, a contract C is represented as a pair of assertions (A, G), where A corresponds to the assumption, and G to the promise. The promise is an assertion on the behaviors of the system/component under the associated assumption on the behaviors of its environment. This Assume/Guarantee reasoning is used as verification mean for the design of the embedded systems. The contract (A, G) is satisfied by an implementation of the system M if during its operation the promise G under assumption A is not violated. Of course, a component's contract can be trivial, i.e. the universal assertion for the assumption and the empty assertion for the promise. The following three relations on contracts for checking consistency of the specifications throughout the design flow can be distinguished: *compatibility* ensures that when composing different contracts the resulting contract admits an implementation; *dominance* expresses substitutability for contracts: if a contract dominates another one, it can safely substitute it; and *satisfaction* allows checking whether a given implementation complies with a given contract. Compatibility, satisfaction and dominance together ensure a safe integration process of the component, effectively reducing test and validation efforts and improving the quality of the integrated system. The formal definitions of these contract relations are provided in [8–10]. The impact of the contract theory in the traditional system engineering "V" diagram is visually depicted in Fig. 1. In Contract-based Analysis only the left side of the diagram is considered. At the beginning, the team of the system developers and the team of the requirements engineers process the same informal document of requirements written in natural language to derive a common system interface. Then, the developers produce the design document of the system specifications; meanwhile the requirements engineers formalize the system functional requirements as contracts and check if there are some incompatibilities among them. During the system decomposition phase, the developers decompose the system identifying its first-level components and the relations among them through the definition of their interfaces. The second team takes the resulting system architecture as input for the modeling of the component-level contracts. The contracts are then allocated to the related components. At this level, in addition to the analysis of the compatibility relation, the dominance relation is checked with the aim of respecting the contracts defined at the above level of abstraction. In the component implementation phase, the developer team enriches the structural view of the system by specifying for each component the internal structure in terms of its atomic behavior or the interconnection of further sub-components. In the second case, the requirements team will produce the related contracts and the process will cycle until all the leaves of the system tree will be modeled. Finally, the satisfaction relation can be verified by processing the modeled system against its contracts.

3   Rapid Transit Metro System Use Case

The model provided by ASTS derives from Communication-Based Train Control (CBTC) technology, CBTC ensures that the trains stop at the right position at the stations, open and close the doors, leave the stations, keep the correct speed and the secure distance between the trains, and so on, by means of subsystems integrated in the trains, on the tracks, on the stations and in the control room, which have the capability to exchange real-time data in continuous way. The main system architecture is shown in Fig. 2.

The correct integration of these different sub-systems and the consequent proper operation of the final system in compliance with the given requirements, involves deep and extensive activities of verification & validation [11–14].

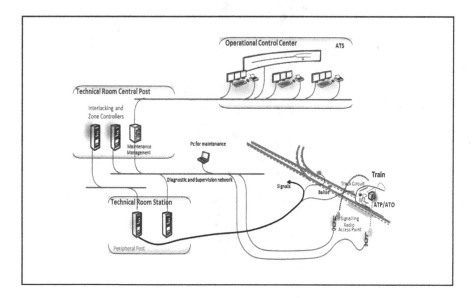

Fig. 2. CBTC overview – architecture.

In this work we focus on a sub-function, called *Determine Doors Opening Side*, of the system under development. The role of this combinatorial function is to determine on which side of the train its doors should open and on which side of the platform its screen doors should open, when a train is stopped at a platform. This safety check ensures that the driver does not select the wrong opening side of the doors.

Following the design methodology described in Sect. 2, this function was modeled in the MATLAB Simulink/Stateflow environment [15]. Figure 3 shows the top view of the model, constituted of seven inputs and nine outputs. For proprietary reasons the content of the model is not described. However since contracts rely on the component interface definition, the identification of the I/O ports is enough to describe the Contract-based analysis performed in Sect. 5.

4   Formal Specs Verifier (FSV)

ALES laboratory has recently started up the development of the Formal Specs Verifier (FSV) tool-suite [4] to meet the emerging industrial request of having an instrument that applies the methodology described in Sect. 2 for the verification of embedded systems. FSV is thought to be a dynamic platform for analysis and testing. Concretely,

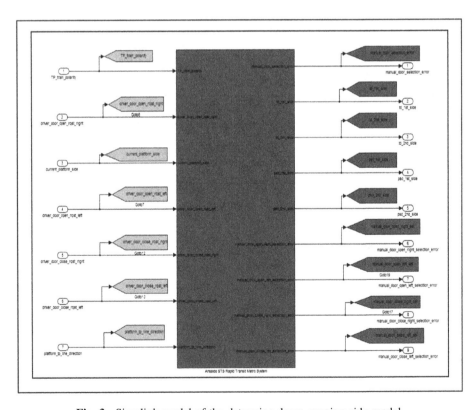

Fig. 3. Simulink model of the determine doors opening side model.

once the model is available in the FSV format, FSV offers the possibility to the user of applying traditional formal verification techniques on his/her system, such as model checking, and, at the same time, it encourages the ALES developers to think about, combine, and define new methods for efficiently achieving specific design needs. The present version of FSV supports a rich subset of the language constructs provided by MATLAB Simulink and Stateflow [15] with the aim of automatically processing the schematics modeled with this professional design software. This process translates the Simulink schematics in an equivalent internal model representation that is used to feed the following developed backend tools: FSV-Automatic Test Generation [5] and FSV-Formal Verification. In particular, FSV-Formal Verification takes as inputs the model of the system under development and a description of the requirements specification, i.e. the expected behavior. The requirements are formalized as contracts by modelling the assumptions and the promises using a user friendly graphical language called Block-based Contract Language (BCL). For this purpose, FSV provides the FSV-BCL toolbox that is a Simulink implementation of BCL. Once the designer has selected the contract to be verified, FSV-Formal Verification automatically checks if this contract is not violated. When the implemented component behaves correctly with respect to a contract specification we say that the component satisfies that contract. Checking satisfaction, therefore, amounts to making sure that a component will provide the stated promises when used in a context that does not violate the assumptions. If the contract is violated the tool provides an executable counter-example, technically named harness model, composed by the original system model connect to a tool-generated input trace. The trace exercises the model provoking the undesired behavior. Being confident that the requirement was correctly specified and formalized then we can conclude that the model is flawed and needs to be corrected. On the contrary, if the check performed by FSV gives a positive answer then the model can be considered correct and used in the next design steps.

5 Requirements, Formalization and Analysis

In this section we use the technology of Sect. 4 to perform the Contract-based Analysis (CBA) on the modeled functions of Sect. 3.

5.1 Formalization of the ASTS Requirements

The first block of requirements, related to the first function under investigation, is specified in natural language and belongs to the independency category (Table 1). In applying the contract formalization, the first step consists in finding out the signals included in each requirement; signal labels are included in brackets after the relevant text object. For clarity and brevity in description, in the next we illustrate the work done only on the RI01requirement. Table 2 details RI01 translated in the contract formalization: the assumption is done on the input signals to check the set of admissible values, while the promise is done on the output signals to verify that the model respects the stated requirement. Thanks to the capability offered by our developed tool FSV-BCL, we are able to replace the effort of writing for all the analyzed requirements the formal notation of Table 2, necessary for machine processing, with a user-friendly graphical composition of pattern blocks. FSV takes care of the automatic translation from the user graphical notation to the machine notation. Figure 4 shows the top view of the model of Contract CI01. The green inputs to the assumption block are linked to some of the input signals of the model from Fig. 3; the red inputs to the promise block are linked to some outputs of the same model; the logic inside the assumption and promise blocks was modeled using the FSV-BCL library; the "A" and "P" blocks are used to set the expected logic value. In this particular case there are two different tonalities of green and red because some inputs and outputs signals are duplicated since they come from two equal models of the same system. This is justified by the adopted analysis technique to verify independency among some I/O signals. This technique is described in the next section.

Table 1. Independency.

Req. ID	Natural Language Description
RI01	the output signals: the first platform side to be opened (psd_1st_side) and the second platform side to be opened (psd_2nd_side) are independent from the input signals: train's polarity (TP_train_polarity), the driver has commanded the doors on the right side of the train to open (driver_door_open_rqst_right), the driver has commanded the doors on the left side of the train to open (driver_door_open_rqst_left), the driver has commanded the doors on the right side of the train to close (driver_door_close_rqst_right), the driver has commanded the doors on the left side of the train to close (driver_door_close_rqst_left).
RI02	the two operations of the first train side to be opened (td_1st_side) and the second train side to be opened (td_2nd_side) are independent from the following facts: platform is in the line direction (platform_tp_line_direction); the driver has commanded the doors on the right side of the train to open (driver_door_open_rqst_right), the driver has commanded the doors on the left side of the train to open (driver_door_open_rqst_left), the driver has commanded the doors on the right side of the train to close (driver_door_close_rqst_right), the driver has commanded the doors on the left side of the train to close (driver_door_close_rqst_left).
RI03	the four operations of the manual door open right selection (manual_door_open_right_selection_error), the manual door open left selection (manual_door_open_left_selection_error), the manual door close right selection (manual_door_close_right_selection_error), the manual door close left selection (manual_door_close_left_selection_error) are independent from the following fact: platform is in the line direction (platform_tp_line_direction).

Table 2. Independency contract CI01.

Contract ID		Formal Language Description
CI01	ASSI01	TP_train_polarity in {"positive","negative","unspecified"} && current_platform_side in { "left","right", "left_then_right", "right_then_left","none"} && platform_tp_line_direction in {"TRUE", "FALSE"} && driver_door_open_rqst_right in {"TRUE", "FALSE"} && driver_door_open_rqst_left in {"TRUE", "FALSE"} && driver_door_close_rqst_right in {"TRUE", "FALSE"} && driver_door_close_rqst_left in {"TRUE", "FALSE"}.
	PRMI01	psd_1st_side(TP_train_polarity, driver_door_open_rqst_right, driver_door_open_rqst_left, driver_door_close_rqst_right, driver_door_close_rqst_left) = psd_1st_side && psd_2nd_side(TP_train_polarity, driver_door_open_rqst_right, driver_door_open_rqst_left, driver_door_close_rqst_right, driver_door_close_rqst_left) = psd_2nd_side

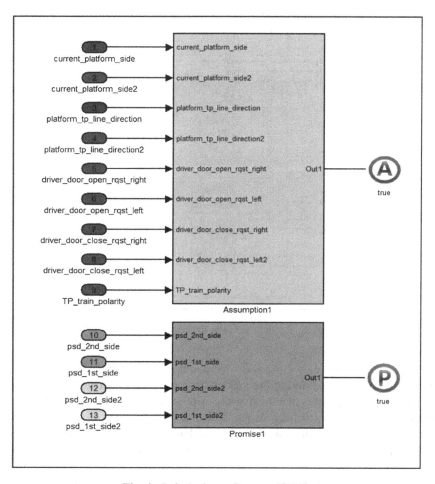

Fig. 4. Independency Contract (CI01).

5.2   Reduction Rules Analysis

Reduction Rules Analysis on the requirements of the independency category completes
the analyses already started in [2], where safety and reachability categories were
considered. In this analysis we want to prove independency of some system outputs
from some inputs such that the effort spent during the dynamic testing phase can be
reduced once we state that the required rules are verified [16]. In Fig. 5 the concept of
reduction rule is sketched. With the intention of testing requirements Req2 and Req3 in
Fig. 5, we have to consider all the possible combinations of the inputs (i3, i4 and i5)
involved into these requirements both with all the possible values for the other inputs
(up to i7) which contribute to the definition of the output o1. On the contrary, as far as
concerns the other inputs (i8, i9, etc.) generating the outputs o2 and o3, if the system
has been correctly designed, their behavior will not impact on the generation of the
output o1.

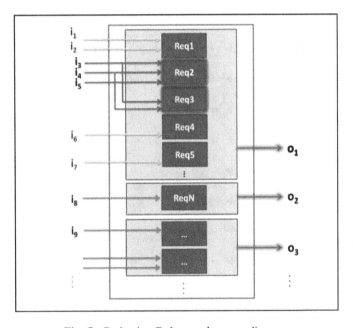

Fig. 5. Reduction Rules: explanatory diagram.

This consideration allows a priori of discarding specific input combinations by
fixing some input values during the generation and execution of tests, saving hence
time and costs. The point is that the hypothesis of input/output independence has to be
verified to ensure the correctness of the reduction of the number of tests. To achieve
this result we adopt the equivalent model checking technique, consisting in the following steps: first, duplication of the part of the model under analysis with its relative
inputs, second, restriction to a fix value for each input of the cloned part which is
supposed not to affect the output under test (e.g.: i8, in Fig. 5), third, construction of the

contracts that state the equivalence between the outputs of the two models, using FSV-BCL, as the contract reported in Fig. 4. In synthesis, each reduction rule is modeled as a contract and the resulting input model for FSV-Formal Verification is represented in Fig. 6. FSV is able to process all the contracts in one shot in order to formally check their satisfaction and consequently verify the effectiveness of the reduction rules.

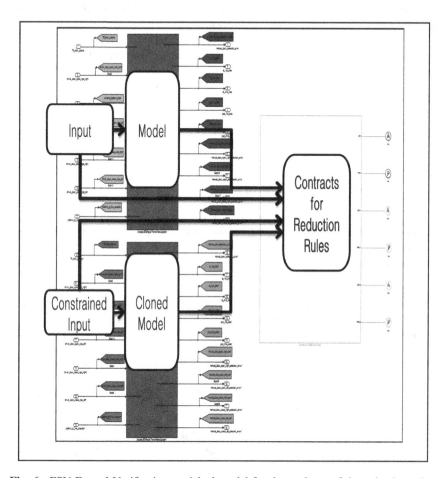

Fig. 6. FSV-Formal Verification: enriched model for the analyses of the reduction rules.

6   Conclusion and Future Work

In this work, we made use of the contract-based design methodology for analyzing a specific part of the ASTS CBTC system for the door control of a train arriving at the metro stop. The methodology was successfully stressed both in the project management and in the design development. At project level, the team who developed the system model was different from the one who formalized and modeled the requirements. Both teams worked independently under some agreed assumptions and promises.

At design level, we formalized the related requirements as contracts for accomplishing reduction rule analysis using FSV, a tool suite that ALES is presently developing for the verification of the embedded systems. FSV aided us to automatically verify the contract satisfaction against the modeled system through the equivalent model checking technique. In the future, we will continue to work on the formal analysis of large systems and, in particular, to tackle the well-known state explosion problem that limits the use of the model checking technique by compensating it with the adoption and the refinement of our methodology.

Acknowledgements. The research leading to these results was partially funded by the EU ARTEMIS Joint Undertaking under grant agreement no. 269335 (project MBAT) and the Italian Ministry of Education, University and Research (MIUR).

References

1. Benveniste, A., Caillaud, B., Nickovic, D., Passerone, R., Raclet, J.-B., Reinkemeier, P., Sangiovanni-Vincentelli, A., Damm, W., Henzinger, T., Larsen, K.: Contracts for System Design (2012)
2. Carloni, M., Ferrante, O., Ferrari, A., Massaroli, G., Orazzo, A., Petrone, I., Velardi, L.: Contract-Based analysis for verification of communication-based train control (cbtc) system. In: Bondavalli, A., Ceccarelli, A., Ortmeier, F. (eds.) SAFECOMP 2014. LNCS, vol. 8696, pp. 137–146. Springer, Heidelberg (2014)
3. MBAT: Combined Model-based Analysis and Testing of Embedded Systems, Accessed 2011-2014. http://www.mbat-artemis.eu/home/
4. Ferrante, O., Benvenuti, L., Mangeruca, L., Sofronis, C., Ferrari, A.: Parallel NuSMV: A NuSMV extension for the verification of complex embedded systems. In: Ortmeier, F., Daniel, P. (eds.) SAFECOMP Workshops 2012. LNCS, vol. 7613, pp. 409–416. Springer, Heidelberg (2012)
5. Marazza, M., Ferrante, O., Ferrari, A.: Automatic Generation of Failure Scenarios for SoC., Tolouse, Embedded Real Time Software and Systems (2014)
6. SPEEDS Consortium In: SPEculative and Exploratory Design in Systems Engineering, Accessed 2010. https://speeds.eu.com/
7. SPRINT Consortium: D2.1 SPRINT Requirements (2011)
8. Benveniste, A., Caillaud, B., Passerone, R.: Multi-viewpoint state machines for rich component models. In: Press, C. (ed.): Model-Based Design for Embedded Systems, November 2009
9. Benvenuti, L., Ferrari, A., Mangeruca, L., Mazzi, E., Passerone, R., Sofronis, C.: A contract-based formalism for the specification of heterogeneous systems. Forum on Specification & Design Languages (FDL 2008), September 2008
10. Ferrante, O., Mignogna, A., Sofronis, C., Mangeruca, L., Ferrari, A.: Contract based design chain integration: An automotive domain case study. In: Applied Simulation and Modelling, ACTA Press (2011)
11. De Nicola, G., di Tommaso, P., Rosaria, E., Francesco, F., Pietro, M., Antonio, O.: A Grey-Box approach to the functional testing of complex automatic train protection systems. In: Dal Cin, M., Kaâniche, M., Pataricza, A. (eds.) EDCC 2005. LNCS, vol. 3463, pp. 305–317. Springer, Heidelberg (2005)

12. De Nicola, G., di Tommaso, P., Esposito, R., Flammini, F., Orazzo, A.: A hybrid testing methodology for railway control systems. In: Heisel, M., Liggesmeyer, P., Wittmann, S. (eds.) SAFECOMP 2004. LNCS, vol. 3219, pp. 116–129. Springer, Heidelberg (2004)

13. De Nicola, G., di Tommaso, P., Esposito, R., Flammini, F., Marmo, P., Orazzo, A.: ERTMS/ETCS: working principles and validation. In: Proceedings of the International Conference on Ship Propulsion and Railway Traction Systems, SPRTS 2005, Bologna, Italy, pp. 59–68 (2005)

14. Donini, R., Marrone, S., Mazzocca, N., Orazzo, A., Papa, D., Venticinque, S.: Testing complex safety-critical systems in SOA context. In: Proceedings of the 2008 International Conference on Complex, Intelligent and Software Intensive Systems (CISIS), Barcelona, Spain (2008)

15. MathWorks. In: Simulink - Simulation and Model-Based Design. http://www.mathworks.com/products/simulink

16. Bonifacio, G., Marmo, P., Orazzo, A., Petrone, I., Velardi, L., Venticinque, A.: Improvement of processes and methods in testing activities for safety-critical embedded systems. In: Flammini, F., Bologna, S., Vittorini, V. (eds.) SAFECOMP 2011. LNCS, vol. 6894, pp. 369–382. Springer, Heidelberg (2011)

Towards Verification of Multicore Motor-Drive Controllers in Aerospace

Stylianos Basagiannis$^{(\boxtimes)}$ and Francisco Gonzalez-Espin

United Technologies Research Centre, 4th Floor Penrose Wharf, Cork, Ireland
{basagis,gonzalfj}@utrc.utc.com

Abstract. It is a known fact that development of models on the design stage of a product, constitutes a highly important stage proving early evidence of error absence for the proposed artifact. Meanwhile, advances in the embedded systems domain push for rapid architecture product changes based on current state-of-the-art solutions. Multicore systems have exhibit enormous benefits due to parallelization of task execution, increasing availability of resources in multiple domains such as the automotive and telecommunication. Such a premise creates the need to invest into new verification methodologies that will re-assure the safe and efficient transition of new solutions like multicores, especially in the demanding aerospace world. In this paper we describe current challenges and trends on the development of safe and efficient methods for power controllers' verification in multicore-based hardware platforms, such as motor-drive applications. We outline current industrial practices and describe common toolsets, workflows and techniques used in the aerospace domain. Then our discussion focus on formal verification techniques that could provide efficient solutions for verifying power control algorithms in aerospace applications. We conclude with remarks about an ongoing verification effort for power control of a multicore-based motor drive towards producing certification evidence.

Keywords: Aerospace · Motor-drives · Multicore · Power control · Safety · Verification

1 Introduction

In the most challenging domain of aerospace applications where certification proof is needed from system till component level, model based design and formal verification techniques is considered a necessity in the product's lifecycle. The development of new methodologies for automating verification and accelerating certification is currently an important agenda being pursued by major aerospace companies operating in highly regulated environments [1]. Whether it is a single avionics sub-system or an integrated aerospace platform, the related embedded firmware and hardware plays a critical role in safety and performance, increasing the importance of attaining evidence that the system will behave as desired throughout its operational profile.

© Springer International Publishing Switzerland 2015
F. Koornneef and C. van Gulijk (Eds.): SAFECOMP 2015 Workshops, LNCS 9338, pp. 190–200, 2015.
DOI: 10.1007/978-3-319-24249-1_17

An emerging approach that could help achieve this goal is model-based certification, where system designer is supported by automated tool assisted model-based verification approaches that span through the complete system lifecycle from development till operation. Formal verification, hybrid system analysis and testing are all likely to form part of this approach. In the specific stages where formal verification constitutes a finite-time operation it may successfully complement the model based techniques for interim verification of the product. Meanwhile the rising trend of multicore architectures into 'everywhere' computing industry is already a reality. General-purpose multicore processors are being accepted in all segments of industry as the need for more performance and general-purpose programmability has grown.

But is the aerospace domain ready to adapt multicore devices ? Aerospace regulations such as the ARP4754A [23] and DO-178B [4] urge aerospace industries to certify their products to a certain acceptable degree of assurance. In the multicore case, controlling access to the shared resources like memory and proving that no conflict will occur when the device has to execute a critical operation, is the major challenge. Currently, model-based design tools and techniques primarily allow control engineers to design their control strategy in mature simulation environments, such as in Simulink. In a later stage, control artifact is coded either using tool-aided single-core code generation (e.g. through Math-Works Embedded coder or HDL Coder) or by manual coding activities, leaving open questions of producing certifiable, conflict-free native code for multicore systems.

This paper aims to describe design and verification advances towards the establishment on model-based certification (MBC) principles, in order to support compositional "design-for-certification" methods of safety-critical aerospace systems. As multicore solutions become an attractive power-efficient solution, we focus on evaluating their usage into future aerospace applications provided that all regulations should be respected. Thus, it is of paramount importance that validated frameworks and workflows will be in place and tested for their applicability, in verifying conflict-free parallel execution of motor-drive operations. Additional modelling techniques to overcome the foreseen model complexity challenge in multicore artifacts should also be inspected. Those can include new (i) model transformation mechanisms for model integration within the certification framework, (ii) combination of random simulation and statistical model checking, (iii) partitioning and smart model-slicing for compositional verification, (iv) reusability of verified models and (v) model-based pattern identification in order to reduce and prune the resulted state space and so on.

Rest of the paper is organized as follows: in Sect. 2 we define the problem area of multicore certification concerning the aerospace domain. Later on, in Sect. 3 we present the state of the practice related to model-based design techniques and tools and describe modelling solutions being used when developing critical systems. As a use-case, in Sect. 4 we focus on a power control strategy for a multicore-based motor drive, depicting basic power control operations. Verification framework of the motor-drive power control is presented describing anticipated results and challenges that we face. Finally we conclude this paper with remarks and ongoing research activities.

2   Problem Definition and Challenges

The increasing concern of society on CO_2 emission and the air traffic market expectations, with a grow at 5 % per year until 2020, has made the aerospace industry to look for alternative technologies to decrease energy consumption while reducing design, operation and maintenance costs [16]. One of the alternatives proposed for achieving this target is based on the increase of electrical power in the mix of power generation, distribution and consumption in the aircraft. But the latter require also an evolution in the computational power even at the component level of aerospace devices, boosting additional prognostic and processing services. Aerospace research and development efforts face great challenges to enter new markets, as qualification and certification requires exuberant effort [2], both in time and cost. System verification and certification are the main problems to be solved [10] especially when the system has to comply with a variety of FAA and avionics regulations [3,7,12–14]. In addition to that, current certification practices do not support reusability of existing designs, implementations, and already certified components. On the other hand, the ever increasing list of regulations including international standards such as DO-178C and ARP-4754 for aerospace recommended practices, force additional delays to the development cycles of aerospace products. Current challenges towards multicore certification can be summarized as follows:

- Research challenges in the area of multicore model based certification and verification techniques include complexity of the system under-certification, scalability of the verification process or accuracy of the derived results when using hybrid verification techniques
- Aerospace systems and components will always require software certification following the guidelines of DO-178B/C in order to manage Safety Integrity Levels (SILs) activities and objectives during the implementation
- Process models in current aerospace development cycles follows a traditional development V cycle that progress linearly from requirements through design and code to integration and final testing, forced to be completed in a top-down approach
- Verification processes mainly focus on test coverage of functional requirements, and traceability enablers following each high-level software requirement to it(s) low level requirements. For the multicore case, low-level requirements verification challenges have to be mapped into device safety requirements in a bottom-up manner
- From current state of the practice toolsets, their is no or minimum support for automated generation of certifiable multicore code

It should be also noted that product development cycles in safety critical domains involve a large number of diversified engineers working into different components of the same device. To this end, when considering the development, integration -and later on- testing of the developed prototype, embedded systems engineers, control engineers, systems architects and firmware/software developers need to jointly assess their own requirements towards high level system requirements. Thus, when incorporating a new multicore architecture to be the basis of a product, overall verification and certification of the new artifact will have to overcome time-consuming requirements traceability and validation processes. We argue that an automated traceability framework allowing tool integration and model intra-collaboration should be in place, in order to enable traceability of requirements among the different engineers and along the lifecycle.

3 Model Based Design for Aerospace Verification

Formal methods and model-based certification have matured considerably in the last decade attracting in this way a great interest from aerospace companies. Regulation standard DO-178B [4] has treated the use of automated formal verification as a supplement for the certification of software products. Its successor though, DO-178C, specify detail guidelines on how these techniques can enhance and improve testing while minimizing the overall cost. Recent experiences from previous studies [1,8] adopted by major aerospace companies have shown that the application of model-based certification and formal verification can be a practical and cost-effective solution against the certification requirements. Developing new methodologies that will combine and in some cases replace testing processes throughout the development cycle of the product, is certain to become a research area that will help to advance further current certification practices. As it has been mentioned earlier model-based certification, analysis, validation and verification tools and techniques for the aerospace domain, have to take into consideration the regulations and guidelines. Moreover, those enablers/tools should take into account the end-user applications aimed to be serviced at the end by the device. It is obvious thus, in the multicore case, that single core performance characteristics needs not only to be respected, but also, considerably outperformed by the new platform.

For example, considering a highly integrated motor drive actuator, requirements are derived from different groups of specifications, both having a same criticality factor. As shown in Fig. 1, a prototypical certification framework has to be directly combined with requirements traceability at all product development stages. Requirements elicitation and traceability functionality is considered to be of paramount importance for generating certification evidence for the safety and robustness of the developed artifact. In general, requirements can be gathered through:

System Requirements: High level requirements that include integration and communication constraints of the system components

Component Requirements: Device specific requirements and constraints for performance and safety of the device

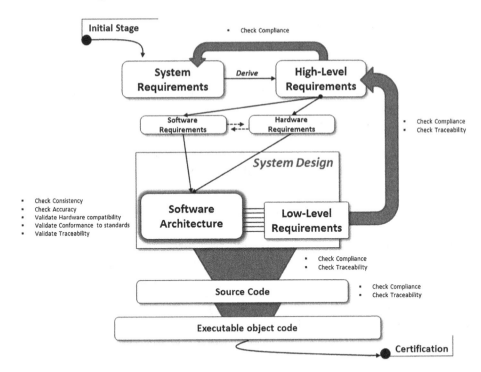

Fig. 1. Certification framework enabling traceability of requirements

Regulation Requirements: Requirements obtained by DO-178C and ARP-4754A for an embedded device that wish to be certified for safe and secure usage in the aerospace domain

In the the case of verifying a power controller of a motor drive actuator, different tools and techniques can be used to categorize and decompose the requirements, specifying domain-driven characteristics where is possible. Domain-specific modelling approaches can utilize mature and standard tools for requirements capturing such as Unified Requirements Modelling Language (UML), Systems Modelling Language (SysML), Embedded Systems Modelling Language (ESML), Systems Description Language (SDL), Architecture Analysis and Design Language (AADL) and Architecture Description Language (EAST-ADL) that offers an integrated approach based on UML/SysML- and so on [5,6,9]. Selected model-based approaches should also include co-simulation options for component interaction, resource allocation, hardware configuration, scheduling policies and other aspects that will be relevant for the system designer, the control and the software engineer.

Upon selection of system modelling tools, the core control modules of the motor drive needs to be designed and implemented. The current trend in the motor-drive domain is model development of power control modules using some of the most popular model-based suites (e.g. MathWorks Simulink). Using model-based tools early in the design phase of a product cycle and having a clear definition of the architecture and requirements of the product to be developed on the previous step, will not only reduce the cost of building separate analysis models but also, aid in the consistency of the models with the software or hardware realization. At this point, formal verification tools [15] will immediately applied in order to provide automatic proofs of correct, exhaustive verification or counterexamples in case an error has been detected. The latter incident can prove fundamental in such analysis, as the designer will be able to refine and improve his model in order to overcome the error detected by verification where analytical analysis and testing could not reveal it. Moreover, early detected errors and producing exhaustive verification results will be the major advantage introducing the cost of certification.

4   Verification of Motor-Drive Power Control Applications

In order to achieve verification of the multicore-based motor-drive power control, formal verification techniques and tools has to be reviewed, down-selected and applied. We aim to use SPIN model checker [15] as the primary verification tool. Furthermore, integration of model-based design and verification toolsets should enable also multilayered analysis and verification process on the design phase of the product that, according to the complexity of the system, the designer will have the flexibility to switch to different analysis techniques favorably to accuracy and time-finite analysis completion [11].

4.1   Motor-Drive Power Control

In the aerospace domain, current trend for motor-drive power control evolutions is governed by the More Electric Aircraft (MEA) initiative [16–18]. MEA main objective is to progressively substituting the hydraulic, pneumatic and mechanical power by electrical power. In the MEA scenario, the hydraulic actuators are replaced by electro-mechanical ones. An electro-mechanical actuator is based on an electrical motor attached to the mechanical surface to be displaced (e.g. a flap). In order to achieve the required actuation action, the electrical motor interfaces the electrical power distribution network with a power electronics device. The power electronics device can be controlled by an embedded controller, which hosts the control algorithms and the operation logic providing the correct operation and safety according to mission profiles [19]. Figure 2 shows the basic architecture of the electro-mechanical actuator, where the embedded controller represents the multi-core platform presented in this paper. The controller receives the sensing stage output, processes the data, and generates a control action that allows the power electronics stage to process the energy at the input to feed the electrical motor.

The typical control architecture of the motor drive is shown in Fig. 3, where the PI blocks represent the proportional + integral control action, the block to dq is the Park transformation, and the block abc to is the Clarke transformation, according to 1, 2 and 3 respectively. The block dq to is the inverse

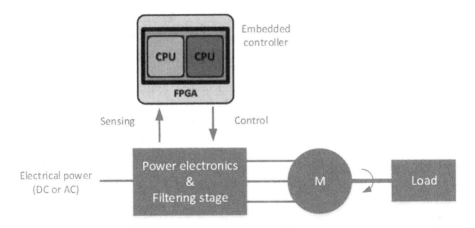

Fig. 2. Basic electro-mechanical actuator

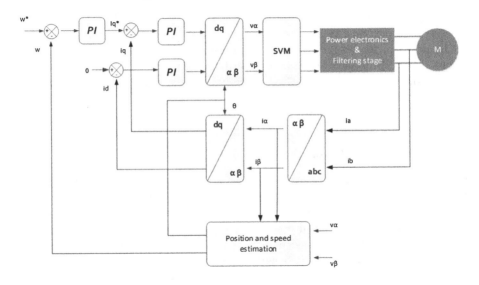

Fig. 3. Simplified schematic of a field oriented control of an electrical motor

of 3. Finally, the block related to the position and speed estimation could be implemented through different algorithms depending upon performance and complexity requirements [20].

$$y(t) = K_p \cdot x(t) + K_i \int x(t)dt \tag{1}$$

$$T_{dq} = \begin{bmatrix} \cos(\omega t) & \sin(\omega t) & 0 \\ -\sin(\omega t) & \cos(\omega t) & 0 \end{bmatrix} \tag{2}$$

$$T_{\alpha\beta} = \frac{3}{2} \begin{bmatrix} 1 & -\frac{1}{2} & -\frac{1}{2} \\ 0 & \frac{\sqrt{3}}{2} & -\frac{\sqrt{3}}{2} \end{bmatrix} \qquad (3)$$

The power electronics stage is composed of semiconductors devices switching at a frequency higher than the fundamental one (i.e. depending upon the rotational speed of the machine and the number of poles). In order to obtain the switching pattern, the space vector modulation (SVM) is a well-known modulation strategy [21] with a wide application to motor drives. The basic switching pattern depends upon the required output voltage at the terminals of the converters. The time that the switches stay at a certain position allows the modulation strategy to achieve that target.

Based on a multicore motor-drive, we aim to validate different modulation strategies that will be executed in conjunction with advanced prognostic and health management services for the motor's operational status. In more detail, critical tasks containing power control instructions for the motor can be dedicated to the FPGA, while additional data analytics and prognostic services can be allocated to the Cortex A9 cores. Scheduling mechanisms based on real-time information have to be in place to ensure mutual exclusion of the cores to the shared resources, while ensuring that the FPGA registers will contain up-to-date prognostic information originated by the cores.

4.2 Verification Approach

The majority of our efforts for addressing verification of the designed power motor control strategies is depicted in the use-case shown in Fig. 4. Based on a formal framework, we model the cores functionality of a multicore architecture derived from the real platform that is composed of two A9-Cortex hard coded units and an FPGA programmable logic component, provided by Xilinx [22]. Our engineering approach to design and analyze complex hardware designs is based upon decomposing the artifact into sub-designs of atomic message dispatch, each of which has to be verified in an independent manner. Using abstraction-based modeling techniques of control modules, we transform control strategies and allocate tasks to cores keeping motor operation execution to the FPGA. Using model-based design simulation results, we can extract time estimates of the task execution, composing the effectively a scheduler mechanism to assure shared resource access within the platform. Crucial part of the verification is based upon the creation of abstraction models in PROMELA, the input language of the SPIN model checker. PROMELA models will be exhaustively verified for deadlock detection of the task scheduling mechanism; in the meantime verification will include also time estimation of the task execution, assuring that certain performance requirements will be met upon implementation.

Overall goal for the model-based certification and verification will be to test-in practice the usefulness of the framework. Taking into account that a variety of heterogeneous models will be developed from the first steps of the requirements of the power system, analysis and verification results will be evaluated and drive the

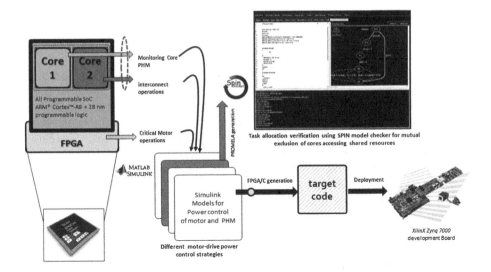

Fig. 4. Motor-drive multicore based use-case verification

overall process of the certification of the product, both at the component and the system level. With respect to the aerospace regulations, automatic verification and certification of systems compliance to a series of properties (e.g. detecting conflicting constraints or shared process deadlocks) will be executed and at the end documented. Results can prove the correctness of the software embedded in the controllers of the power control device, certifying not only the product itself but more importantly the new processes followed for the completion of the certification.

5   Conclusions and Look Ahead

Automated verification and fast certification is currently important milestones pursued by major aerospace companies for certifying their products. Whether it is a single aerospace device or an integrated aerospace platform, embedded components verification will play a critical role in safety, thus, placing an increased importance on its confidence to behave as desired. One of the technology enablers that will help to ensure efficient and complete testing during all the stages of the product development is model-based certification. Aforementioned technique will provide automated tool-assisted model-based techniques that will span in the complete development cycle for early and accurate early detection prior to the testing of the product. On the other hand, formal verification must be utilized towards this end. As multicore architectures tend to expand today it is presaged that a transfer of multicore devices will be placed in the aerospace domain [8]; such a premise will state the multicore analysis and verification a prerequisite for its safer and verified transition. As a look ahead, ongoing research activities will focus on evaluating and developing new abstraction modeling techniques, compiler re-design and certification as well as, standardization efforts of current multicore solutions towards achieving higher TRL levels with increased assurance levels.

Acknowledgments. This work is supported by the EMC^2 ARTEMIS project: *Embedded Multi-Core systems for Mixed Criticality applications in dynamic and changeable real-time environments.* UTRC is supported jointly by the European Commission and the Irish Development Agency (IDA), Project Number: 621429.

References

1. Bhatt D., Madl G., Oglesby D., Schloegel K.: Towards scalable verification of commercial avionics software. In: Proceedings of the AIAA Infotech@Aerospace Conference, April 2010
2. Dutertre, B., Stavridou, V.: A model of non-interference for integrating mixed-criticality software component. In: Weinstock, C., Rushby, J. (eds.) DCCA, vol. 112, pp. 301–316 (2008)
3. RTCA Inc., Document RTCA/DO-178B. Federal Aviation Administration, January 11, Advisory Circular 20–115B (1993)
4. Paulitsch, M., Ruess, H., Sorea, M.: Non-functional avionics requirements communications in computer and information. Sci. **17**, 369–384 (2009)
5. Durrieu, G., Laurent, O., Seguin, C., Wiels, V.: Formal proof and test case generation for critical embedded systems using scade. In: Jacquart, R. (ed.) BIS. IFIP AICT, vol. 156, pp. 499–504. Springer, Cambridge (2004)
6. Alur, R., Kanade, A., Ramesh, S., Shashidhar, K.: Symbolic analysis for improving simulation coverage of simulink/stateflow models. In: Proceedings of EMSOFT, pp. 89–98 (2008)
7. DO-178B, Software Considerations in Airborne Systems and Equipment Certification. Requirements and Technical Concepts for Aviation, (This document is known as EUROCAE ED-12B in Europe) Washington, DC, December 1992
8. Nowotsch, J., Paulitsch, M.: Leveraging multicore computing architectures in avionics. In: European Dependable Computing Conference, pp. 132–143 (2012)
9. Knapp, A., Merz, S.: Model checking and code generation for UML state machines and collaborations. In: Proceedings of 5th Workshop on Tools for System Design and Verification (FM-TOOLS 2002), Report 2002–11, p. 6 (2002)
10. Rushby J.: Formal methods and the certification of critical systems, Technical report SRI-CSL-93-7, 4551, Computer Science Laboratory, SRI International, Menlo Park, CA (1993)
11. Amjad, H.: Verification of AMBA using a combination of model checking and theorem proving, electronic notes in theoretical computer science. In: Proceedings of the 5th International Workshop on Automated Verification of Critical Systems (AVoCS 2005), vol. 145, pp. 45–61 (2006)
12. DOD-HDBK-763 Human Engineering Procedures Guide, 27 February 1987
13. EUROCAE: European Organisation for Civil Aviation Equipment. http://www.eurocae.org
14. FAA: Federal Aviation Administration. http://www.faa.gov
15. Hollzman, G.: The model checker SPIN. IEEE Trans. Soft. Eng. **23**(5), 279–295 (1997)

16. Roboam, X., Sareni, B., Andrade, A.D.: More electricity in the air: toward optimized electrical networks embedded in more-electrical aircraft. IEEE Ind. Electron. Mag. **6**, 6–17 (2012)
17. Roboam, X.: New trends and challenges of electrical networks embedded in "more electrical aircraft". In: 2011 IEEE International Symposium on Industrial Electronics (ISIE), pp. 26–31 (2011)
18. Rosero, J.A., Ortega, J.A., Aldabas, E., Romeral, L.: Moving towards a more electric aircraft. IEEE Aerosp. Electron. Syst. Mag. **22**, 3–9 (2007)
19. Wenping, C., Mecrow, B.C., Atkinson, G.J., Bennett, J.W., Atkinson, D.J.: Overview of electric motor technologies used for more electric aircraft (MEA). IEEE Trans. Ind. Electron. **59**, 3523–3531 (2012)
20. Boldea, I.: Control issues in adjustable speed drives. IEEE Ind. Electron. Mag. **2**, 32–50 (2008)
21. Holmes, D.G., Lipo, T.A.: Pulse Width Modulation for Power Converters. Principles and Practice. Wiley-Interscience, New York (2003)
22. Xilinx Zynq-7000 All Programmable SoC ZC702 Evaluation Kit. http://www.xilinx.com/products/boards-and-kits/ek-z7-zc702-g.html
23. Guidelines for Development of Civil Aircraft and Systems ARP4754A. http://www.sae.org/technical/standards/arp4754a

FlexRay Robustness Testing Contributing to Automated Safety Certification

Erwin Kristen[✉] and Egbert Althammer

Digital Safety and Security Department, AIT Austrian Institute of Technology GmbH,
1220 Donau-City-Straße 1, Vienna, Austria
{erwin.kristen,egbert.althammer}@ait.ac.at

Abstract. Software development work flows for safety relevant software require that each artefact is tested by at least one test case. An automatic overnight test case execution process supplying the newest results every morning makes this time-consuming process more efficient.

This paper describes a tool framework consisting of the BusScope, the TCBP (Test Case Batch Processor) and WEFACT (Workflow Engine For Analysis, Certification and Test). It manages all necessary steps: initialization of the test objects, execution of the test cases by applying test patterns and test evaluation to find the test verdict – Passed or Failed. It supports automation of the certification process by managing requirements and collecting evidences for the safety case.

A demonstrator, a steering actuator of a steer-by-wire application with redundant components, implemented on a real hardware and software platform, shows the proposed fully automated test case execution.

The demonstrator was developed in the EU-funded research project SafeCer (Research partly funded by ARTEMIS-JU Call 2011 project no. 295373 (nSafeCer)).

Keywords: Safety · Certification · Automated certification · Flexray · Safecer · Robustness testing

1 Motivation

This chapter introduces the reader into the engineering domain of safety relevant systems, the challenges to ensure safety and how scientific research can help to find solutions for a suitable safety certification process.

1.1 Why Research in Safety Certification Is Indispensable

A central goal of mankind is to find ways to let tedious and monotonous work be done by machines. A well-known example would be the invention of the steam engine, which freed people from heavy labour and introduced both an industrial and a technological revolution. Other ones followed such as electricity, and private mobility (pushed by the combustion engine and the availability of private vehicles). In many cases every

F. Koornneef and C. van Gulijk (Eds.): SAFECOMP 2015 Workshops, LNCS 9338, pp. 201–211, 2015.
DOI: 10.1007/978-3-319-24249-1_18

technological revolution creates new types of dangers to life and limb, lot of them unexpected in the first time. Necessarily new regulations and construction methods are defined to make the new technologies safer.

To avoid any risk of injury in advance, all new technological inventions and systems must be considered regarding harmfulness first before release to commercial usage. In general every new technology product contains the potential to be unsafe and should be classified as a safety relevant system. Safety relevant systems need additional precautions to prevent harm by the system itself.

A new safety relevant application which gets more and more attention is the autonomous acting vehicles for future mobility. These vehicles do not need a human driver anymore who controls the vehicle. They take reasonable decisions to prevent accidents in case of a dangerous situation and they navigate autonomously on the road. To release these types of vehicles, all safety relevant aspects must be analysed in advance. And the complete product life cycle must be adapted by handling it as a high safety relevant system.

1.2   Outline of the Paper

This paper documents a safety related research work, realized in the research project SafeCer [1]. The goal of the project was to define a seamless and consistent work process flow for the certification of safety relevant systems.

Section 2 gives an overview of the process for the certification of safety relevant systems. Additionally, the researched process extensions from SafeCer are explained in a theoretical way.

Section 3 describes a demonstrator of a test bed to perform automatic test execution, an important process part in the safety certification process.

Section 4 shows the tool framework used in this research work. The tools of the framework are under development by AIT and are introduced in the following list:

- **BusScope:** The BusScope test platform analyses the data on the FlexRay bus in the data and time domain according a verification description. On the other hand the BusScope test platform simulates on the same FlexRay bus test patterns to observe the reaction of the test object by analysis.
- **TCBP:** The BusScope test platform is controlled by the TCBP (Test Case Batch Processor) which coordinates the complete test case execution process flow.
- **WEFACT:** WEFACT (Workflow Engine For Analysis, Certification and Test) controls the processing of the test, e.g. it provides the test case input files for each test case and collects the evidence for the safety case.

Section 5 describes the test cases examples of the BOLDI demonstrator including the test case definition and the test case results.

Section 6 provides the conclusions and gives an outlook for future work for the BOLDI demonstrator.

2   The Safety Certification Process

Companies involved in the design of safety relevant systems must meet safety process requirements which are defined in the functional safety standards (e.g. IEC 61508 in a general form and ISO 26262 for the automotive domain) and must align their business processes according to the mandatory given regulations.

Figure 1 shows the activity pattern for the development flow of safety relevant systems. As we can recognize there are some activities (the green ones) that are included in any development process for safety relevant systems while some other activities (the blue ones) are specifically added to describe SafeCer specific activities [1].

- **Contract Definition:** Each artefact (component, design, function and feature) is supplied with a contract which describes the necessary actions and precautions to guarantee a given safety level. The contract is part of the artefact description.
- **Certificate Preparation:** The precautions (both by hardware and by software) and the actions (both for implementation and for tests) must be prepared for the full life cycle of the artefact according to the contract.
- **Argumentation:** By documentation and/or with test methods the actions and precautions defined in the contract must be augmented for a successfully safety certification of the desired artefact.

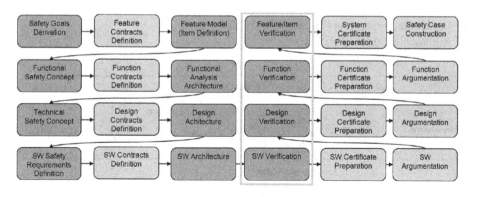

Fig. 1. Development flow activity pattern

3   The BOLDI Demonstrator

The activity patterns, which are covered by the yellow box in Fig. 1, are demonstrated by the test bed demonstrator. In SafeCer it is named BOLDI (Bus OnLine DIagnosis) demonstrator [3]. The BOLDI demonstrator supports efficient robustness testing [4] of FlexRay bus systems. It shows a system validation process for an electronic controlled steering actuator, used for steer-by-wire applications. The goal of the demonstrator is to show a tool framework to perform test case deduction from the requirements, the test preparation, the test processing and finally the test result evaluation to find a validation verdict as an input for a safety case.

Let us reduce the activity pattern configuration from Fig. 1 to the simpler, one line process model description as shown in Fig. 2.

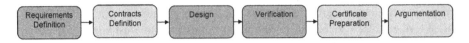

Fig. 2. SafeCer process model activity pattern

The BOLDI demonstrator focuses on the confirmation of the challenge number one defined in SafeCer: reduction of the cost of qualification, certification and verification - by a high automated validation process at the test bed. The challenge joins the following two SafeCer objectives:

- Reduce the cost of system design.
- Shorten the lead-time for re-validation and re-certification.

Figure 3 shows the instantiation of the SafeCer process model activity pattern for the BOLDI demonstrator and the associated tools of the tool framework. The design activity denotes the electronic steering actuator from the BOLDI demonstrator.

- Requirements definition (WEFACT)
- Contract definition (WEFACT)
- Verification (TCBP, BusScope)
- Certificate Preparation (TCBP, WEFACT)
- Argumentation (WEFACT)

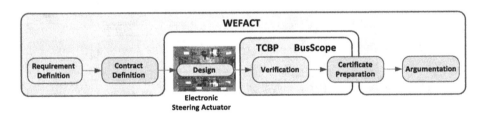

Fig. 3. Instantiation of the SafeCer process model activity pattern

Figure 4 shows the setup of the BOLDI demonstrator in a carrying case. It consists of a FlexRay cluster of four FlexRay nodes, a mechanical steering actuator, the BusScope test equipment, a computer unit with a display and an Ethernet connection.

4   The Tool Framework

In the following sub chapters the tools of the tool framework, BusScope, the TCBP and WEFACT are presented in detail.

Fig. 4. BOLDI demonstrator in carrying case

4.1 BusScope

The BusScope test platform analyses the data on the FlexRay bus in the data and time domain according to a verification description. On the other hand the BusScope test platform simulates on the same FlexRay bus test pattern to observe the reaction of the test object by analysis.

In the BOLDI demonstrator the BusScope generates test pattern on the FlexRay bus according to the definitions in the test case script files. The BusScope supports test case types both in the data and the timing domain. Additionally, the BusScope traces all data on the FlexRay bus to form the input for the test case verdict evaluation. The BusScope test platform is controlled by the BusScope Control Host.

4.2 TCBP

On the BusScope Control Host the TCBP is installed and coordinates the complete test case execution process flow in four steps, PARSE, INIT, RUN and EVAL which are illustrated in Fig. 5 and are described in detail in Table 1.

Table 1. TCBP steps

Step	Comment
PARSE	Parses all configuration script files of the test case.
INIT	Initializes the test object to bring the test object in a defined state.
RUN	Runs the test pattern on the test object and records all relevant data for the test report.
EVAL	Explores the test report to find the test case verdict "PASSED" or "FAILED".

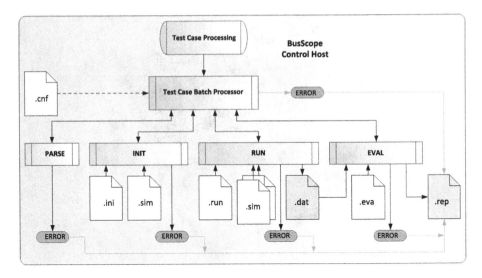

Fig. 5. TCBP test process steps

These steps are controlled by a configuration script file set (".cnf", ".ini", ".sim", ".run", ".eva") which is provided for each test case. The trace file (".dat") contains the measured signal values of the RUN step which is evaluated in the EVAL step. The report file (".rep") collects the test results and the error messages.

4.3 WEFACT

WEFACT [2] has the goal to facilitate validation, verification (V&V) and certification of safety relevant systems in a modular (component based) manner.

Figure 6 illustrates the WEFACT framework which provides a flexible infrastructure for defining and executing V&V processes. External resources – external processes, tools and standards – are integrated into the WEFACT framework by well-defined interfaces.

The safety case is the central output of WEFACT. It summarizes the information of the V&V process and provides a basis for the certification of the Artefact Under Test (AUT).

The validation plan (V-plan) consists of the requirements for the AUT as well as the V&V activities which are necessary in order to satisfy those requirements. A V&V activity is the application of a V&V method by means of an appropriate V&V tool. It is possible to integrate various external tools such as simulation tools.

Positive results of the V&V activity are used to establish evidence for the requirements, while negative results are fed back to the developer team.

The WEFACT framework is implemented in IBM Rational DOORS® and extends the basic DOORS functionality by implementing a work flow for the V&V processes, e.g. for V&V activity processing and safety case generation.

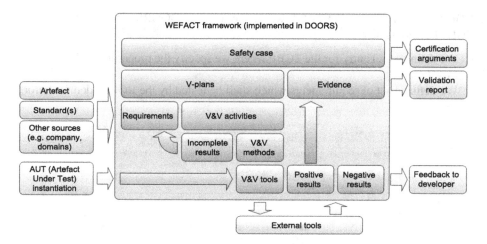

Fig. 6. WEFACT framework

TCBP Tool Server. WEFACT was adapted for the BOLDI demonstrator by providing the V&V tool integration for TCBP. This was realized by implementing a TCBP tool server which is based on the message queuing (MQ) technology and which supports the automatic execution of the tool.

Once started the TCBP tool server periodically polls the input queue of the MQ server. When a V&V activity is processed which uses the TCBP, an appropriate message is generated and put on this queue. The TCBP tool server decodes the message and automatically downloads the TCBP configuration script file set from the document repository and starts the TCBP. After the TCBP has finished, the TCBP tool server uploads the TCBP report file to the document repository, creates an overall result using the verdict created by the TCBP, generates an appropriate message and puts in the output queue. WEFACT polls the output queue and updates the status of the V&V activity according to the overall result stated above.

ID	V&V methods and V&V tools		Method/Tool	Responsibility	Tool Invocation Strin	Tool Integration Level
VV189	TCBP		Tool	Erwin Kristen	java -jar TCBPToolServer.jar <input>	Automatically executed external tool
VV156	BusScope		Tool	Erwin Kristen	BusScopeGUI.exe	Manually executed external tool

Fig. 7. Tool entry for the TCBP

DOORS Elements. In WEFACT we define a set of DOORS elements to start the BOLDI demonstrator.

- We define a tool entry for the TCBP where we specify the properties of the tool, see Fig. 7.
- We define a set of requirements which shall be tested by the BOLDI demonstrator, see Fig. 8.

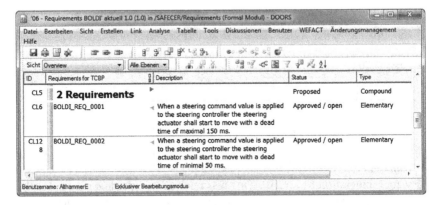

Fig. 8. Requirements for the BOLDI demonstrator

- We define a V-plan which contains the V&V activities which shall verify the requirements, see Fig. 9. For each test case we define one V&V activity. A V&V activity entry contains (a) the links to the requirements for the BOLDI demonstrator, (b) the link to the TCBP tool entry and (c) the parameters for the test case execution, e.g. the TCBP configuration script file set.

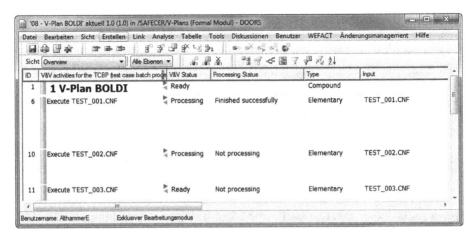

Fig. 9. V-plan for the BOLDI demonstrator

Test Automation. Using the elements defined above, we are now able to automate the execution of the test cases using the WEFACT functions for processing V&V activities.

5 Test Case Examples

This chapter documents test case examples deployed in the BOLDI demonstrator. The test cases focus on the steering actuator control mechanism and verify the specified function both in the data and the timing domain.

5.1 Test Case Definition

In the steering actuator control application the BusScope transmits command frames on the FlexRay bus. The frames include the target steering angle (SET) value which the steering mechanism shall approach.

The electronic control units receive the steering angle command and drive the motors of the steering mechanism until the SET value is reached. This is performed with a delay, because the command must be interpreted and the motors must operate to reach the SET value.

The following requirements describe the specified function:

Dead Time Requirements

- When a steering command value is applied to the steering controller, the steering actuator shall start to move with a dead time of maximal 150 ms.
- When a steering command value is applied to the steering controller, the steering actuator shall start to move with a dead time of minimal 50 ms.

Steering Actuator Moving Speed Requirements

- The requested steering angle shall be reached with a maximal average speed of 30 angular degrees per second.
- The requested steering angle shall be reached with a minimal average speed of 10 angular degrees per second.

Angle Deviation Requirement

- When the set angle is reached the maximal angle deviation shall be equal or smaller than 2 angular degrees.

Figure 10 shows the SET value and the measured steering angle (ACTUAL) value signal waveform which fulfils the given five requirements (numbers ① – ⑤). The red line is the SET value signal. The value of the signal is normalized to 100. In this case the SET value for the steering angle was 30 angular degrees.

The blue line shows the ACTUAL value over the time. The signal starts with a dead time of 100 ms (see requirements 1 and 2), and then the signal rises with an average speed of 20 angular degrees per second (see requirements 3 and 4) till the requested angle is reached with a tolerance of 1 angular degrees (see requirement 5). The same behaviour is shown when the SET value returns to 0 angular degrees.

In these examples the BOLDI demonstrator is commanded to apply three test cases by moving the steering actuator mechanism for 10°, 20° and 30° steering angle.

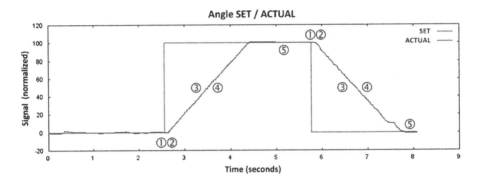

Fig. 10. SET and ACTUAL value signal waveform

5.2 Test Case Results

The expected test results for all three tests are that the EVAL signal may never excess the upper and lower borders (grey coloured areas). Additional the #VERDICT string in the report file must be PASSED.

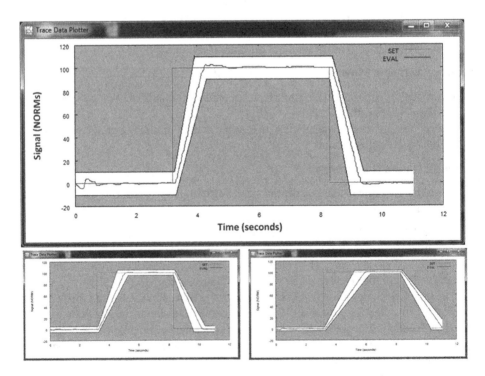

Fig. 11. Test case results for 10°, 20° and 30° steering angle

Figure 11 shows the three test result graphics each for 10°, 20° and 30° steering angle.

6   Conclusions and Future Work

Using the implemented tool framework as described in the realm of this paper, the test cases for FlexRay robustness testing are processed fully automated without any manually interaction by the test engineering team. Especially for iterated test cycles the automated test process reduces the cost of system design.

Furthermore, when the test case definition is already available in an early development phase, some design decisions can be proven in advance by early test runs. A design, pre-proven in this way, reduces and assures design quality, too.

In case of a design change or design expansion needs a re-validation to ensure that no requirement is violated by the design change. An automated test process helps to shorten the lead-time for re-validation and re-certification.

The SafeCer challenge number one, the reduction of the cost of qualification, certification and verification, is therefore successfully demonstrated.

A concept for the future usage of the BOLDI demonstrator could be a laboratory equipment and demonstration unit for education and training purposes.

References

1. SafeCer, Safety Certification of Software-Intensive Systems with Reusable Components. http://www.safecer.eu/
2. Schoitsch, E., Althammer, E., Eriksson, H., Vinter, J., Gönczy, L., Pataricza, A., Cstertán, G.: Validation and certification of safety-critical embedded systems - the DECOS test bench. In: Gorski, J. (ed.) SAFECOMP 2006. LNCS, vol. 4166, pp. 372–385. Springer, Heidelberg (2006)
3. Bruckmüller, F., Kristen, E., Kubinger, W.: FlexRay demonstrator for certification. In: Computer Safety, Reliability, and Security; 32nd International Conference, SAFECOMP 2013, pp. 151–158. Springer, Berlin Heidelberg New York (2006). ISBN: 2-907-801-09-0
4. Kropp, N.P., Koopman, P.J., Siewiorek, D.P.: Automated robustness testing of off-the-shelf software components. In: FTCS 1998 Proceedings of the Twenty-Eighth Annual International Symposium on Fault-Tolerant Computing, p. 230. IEEE Computer Society, Washington DC (1998). ISBN: 0-8186-8470-4

Towards Perfectly Scalable Real-Time Systems

Peter Priller[(✉)], Werner Gruber, Niklas Olberding, and Dietmar Peinsipp

ITS Research and Technology, AVL List GmbH, Graz, Austria
{peter.priller,werner.gruber,niklas.olberding,
dietmar.peinsipp}@avl.com

Abstract. Verification and Validation (V&V) systems used in automotive engineering typically face two potentially contradicting design constraints: real-time capability versus scalability. While there has been substantial research on deterministic timing behavior [1, 2], the software of such systems is usually designed statically to satisfy requirements available at design time only. If those requirements change due to new V&V applications, a complete redesign might be necessary. This paper suggests a design methodology and architecture as a step towards perfectly scalable real-time systems, i.e. systems with deterministic timing behavior and the ability to be structurally modified even at run-time, including the ability to add, re-configure, re-connect or remove existing components without affecting timing correctness of the remaining system. A component model is introduced which allows to easily extract signal dependencies of software components instantiated by the run-time system, as well as to control and manage changes in system composition automatically. As an additional benefit, modularization allows component isolation equivalent to sand boxing of modern general-purpose operating systems, thus improving system robustness. We conclude with an outlook on how to extend scalability from multi-core to many-core hardware platforms.

Keywords: Scalable software system · Real-time system · Automotive testing · Reconfiguration

1 Introduction

By a perfectly scalable real-time system we mean hard- and software of a time-deterministic computational system, satisfying a set of time constraints comprised of guaranteed upper-bound response time, specific cycle time etc., which can be adapted to different applications (within a defined range) easily by simple (re)configuration at run-time, without the need for redesign or re-build. In this paper we suggest a software architecture and runtime for such a system called COBRA (COmponent Based Runtime Architecture), applied to the domain of automotive test systems, typically comprised of a plurality of real-time I/O, control, simulation and automation tasks. We assume sufficient hardware support by hardware parallelization, which is available in current multi-core solutions, and concentrate on industrial PC platforms powered by e.g. INTEL Xeon series CPU's.

© Springer International Publishing Switzerland 2015
F. Koornneef and C. van Gulijk (Eds.): SAFECOMP 2015 Workshops, LNCS 9338, pp. 212–223, 2015.
DOI: 10.1007/978-3-319-24249-1_19

The following sections are structured as follows: Sect. 2 summarizes our vision of a future automotive testing system and some of its consequences, followed by a short overview on current technologies to achieve configurability and scalability for embedded real-time systems in Sect. 3. In Sect. 4 we outline a proposed architecture. Section 10 focusses on communication network aspects, followed by first results of applying a prototypical implementation to a typical automotive test application (Sect. 11). The paper ends with an outlook on derived research topics in Sect. 12 and conclusions in Sect. 13.

2 Challenges for Next Generation Automotive Test Systems

Commoditized systems based on x86/x64 and PCI still provide a very cost-efficient and performant hardware platform with lots of choices of mature real-time and general-purpose operating systems and frameworks available.

A typical automotive V&V application as depicted in Fig. 1 includes a large set of systems, aggregating

- data acquisition systems collecting data from typically several hundreds of sensors (speed, torque, pressure, temperature, vibration, gas or fluid flow, ...)
- actuators including dynamometers exerting torque/speed at vehicle shafts, combined with valves, pumps, linear motors, conditioning systems etc. to effect the unit under test (UUT) directly or indirectly by emulating specific environment conditions
- communication between sensors and subsystems, typically via analog and digital signals, automotive networks like CAN or FlexRay, standard Ethernet and real-time Ethernet like EtherCAT etc., and wireless connectivity like IEEE 802.11 and 802.15.x becoming more and more important.

Fig. 1. Vehicle test bed for automotive V&V

Software of such a test system is typically a heterogeneous and complex combination of mixed criticality real-time tasks, taking care of communication and data handling, signal processing, process monitoring, simulation, verification and validation and overall test automation, as well as storage and system control. In automated testing, test cases will be executed sequentially, typically requiring to reconfigure parts of the system, activating diverse signal flows through the system, alternative simulation models, or modifying test profiles, as an example. In order to be able to do this during run-time (e.g. while the engine is running), parts of the real-time system need to continue operation, while others might need to be modified, deleted or created in a deterministic way, without effecting the remaining system.

Next-generation test systems need to support flexibility in configuration, parameterization, and diagnostics, while at the same time delivering high performance and robustness. Therefore, the suggested architecture supports fine-granular configuration changes on level of individual instances of software components, without impacting function or time determinism of the remaining application.

With the approach of the connected powertrain we expect to see a further significant increase of complexity in V&V systems for simulation and data processing requirements, as described in [3], as well as security oriented challenges. For example, to test a hybrid control strategy considering GPS and V2x information, the vehicle test bed will need to simulate appropriately these signals on a test bed, requiring high-performance scenario simulation and signal emulation. As a prerequisite, we assume hardware providing sufficient resources like processor cores, main memory and I/O bandwidth, which appears to become available in upcoming hardware generations (e.g. INTEL i7 Broadwell and beyond). As an additional constraint, we want a system architecture to be efficient, minimize the computation overhead during runtime, and to allow implementation of systems with minimal resource requirements.

3   Reconfigurable Real-Time Systems

Reconfigurable systems have been a research topic for some time (e.g. [4]), also for automotive systems (e.g. [5]), and are commercially deployed in solutions from small toy-like "intelligent bricks" [6], to mainframe or server-farms running large scale business applications. However, reconfiguration of real-time systems, especially allowing such reconfiguration during operation, i.e. at run-time, without interrupting the rest of the system, with a wide range of adaptability spanning from single CPU to multi-core/multi-CPU systems, are rare.

Some work has been published on optimizing resource scheduling for reconfigurable systems, suggesting new scheduling strategies and resource management for underlying operating systems. In [7], Steiger et al. focus on establishing a component and system architecture able to run on standard, commercially available real-time operating systems (RTOS), taking re-configurable hardware into account.

Some proposals discuss HW/SW co- synthesis (e.g. CRUSADE, see [8]) to achieve re-configurability. While heterogeneous systems comprised of GP-CPU's and configurable hardware like FPGA can be highly optimized to achieve challenging performance goals for specific applications, re-configuration might require re-design and thus might become a complex task. Especially in our domain of automotive verification and validation (V&V), large sets of test cases and configurations might be required to be executed in short time, requiring frequent re-configuration also during tests without effecting run-time behavior of the remaining system, as described in [9].

4   Architectural Considerations

4.1   General

Assuming simple AMP (asynchronous multi-processing) RTOS design, a methodology for automated distribution of configurations to multiple CPU cores is suggested. For sake of performance and simplicity, only in-machine parallelism is exploited. Distributed systems networked via standard communication links suffer latencies one or more orders of magnitude higher than inter-CPU communication, and are therefore less appropriate for our intended use.

V&V applications typically require high cyclic runtime performance with cycle rates of 10 kHz and above, and might be running hundreds of tasks. Therefore our architecture defines as a first step a central, offline configuration analysis and optimization, comparable to a just-in-time compile step done on the target system before runtime. This helps to minimize runtime overhead inevitably required by online management described in [5], as well as a need for interface negotiation, respectively search & discovery, self-configuration, self-optimization or even self-optimization. It is not intended to support dynamic load balancing, but to avoid load imbalance to begin with.

4.2   Identify Dependencies to Achieve Scalability

A software architecture matching these requirements must support run-time compose-ability while at the same time allowing high performance, scalable and therefore parallelizable, robust software-execution of (a multitude of) real-time tasks. Composing tasks to form a system can be straightforward, as long as enough resources are available and all tasks run independently. However, there may be several sources of explicit or implicit coupling, which might defy the purpose, and need to be taken care of. For a clear definition of what constitutes a task, and at which point interaction with the rest of the world occurs, the notion of component was proposed e.g. in [4]. In COBRA, a component includes coding for the intended behavior and collections of objects it requires for its operation, like data-ports for data exchange and message-ports for communication with other components. It is important that these objects cannot be created by the component itself, but must be requested from the runtime system. This allows controlling, managing and thereby optimizing execution from a system-global view, as will be shown below. As an additional layer of isolation, requested and created data ports cannot be interconnected ("wired") by the component itself. In fact, the component has no knowledge about the other components it is wired to. Component have no way to modify the overall system, cannot act outside their own boundaries. This approach mimics aspects of sandboxing available to browsers or operating-systems using kernel-mode functionality for process isolation [10]. In order to achieve perfect scalability, dependencies between components (both class and instance) need to be identified, in order to be managed. Dependencies like data flow (example: input of component B depends on output of component A), required resources etc. are explicitly declared in a configuration based on component manifests, and is processed during system configuration. Analysis of data dependencies results in detection of data paths and is therefore used to generate the sequence of execution. Data paths found to be independent are perfect candidates to be mapped to parallel computing resources like multiple CPU cores. Thus, any identified independent data path forms a sequence called Trigger-Sequence (TS). By definition a TS is the smallest possible sequence of components to run in order to satisfy all data dependencies of its members, therefore in can be called atomic. As we assume a consistent data flow through this path, all components along it are to be executed with the same cycle time, in the sequence given by the data path. Signal flow analysis of an application results in a set of one or more TS, and each TS is in turn an ordered collection of references to components, which need to be executed in this very sequence.

In Fig. 2, an example for a simple signal flow implemented in the test system is depicted: C_i denotes software components, V_i labels variables, which underpin the channels connecting in- and out ports of components. In this example, C_1 might represent software importing an external value, e.g. sampled via an ADC, while C_4 and C_5 represent software handling outputs, e.g. messages sent on a CAN bus to the unit under test. If there are no other constraints, several alternatives for valid TS would be possible, e.g. the sequence $\{C_1, C_2, C_3, C_4, C_5\}$.

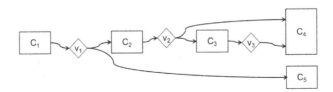

Fig. 2. A simple signal flow

In cases where signal flow forms a loop (example: Fig. 3), the extraction of TS will need additional information in order to be able to cut it in a linear sequence. As has been shown by Olberding [11] this can be done by considering component behavior (feed-through characteristic). For nested loops, iterative solver algorithms are described. Each TS has its cycle time specified, which is static and for the sake of simpler scheduling defined from a discrete set of frequencies (e.g. 10/100/1000/10000 Hz). Running a sequence once per cycle time requires execution of all of its members in the specified order within that time. From here on, each TS can be treated like a cyclic task. Driven by this analogy, we apply the principles as described for software tasks in [12] now to TS. Each one will be statically assigned a run-time priority based on RMS, resulting in equal priorities for all TS of the same cycle time, and higher priorities for TS of shorter cycle times.

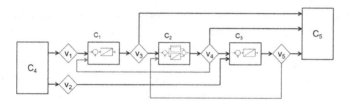

Fig. 3. Nested signal flow: controller for a two-mass spring damper system

As no other data dependencies exist, each TS can be executed independently from other TS, as long as it honors the timing requirement of its members. This makes TS a perfect candidate for parallelization: it can be assigned to any core for execution, assuming a consistent timing (synchronization) across all cores. For a real system however, such assignment of a TS to a core needs to fulfill rules like

- the core shall provide sufficient computation resources
- the core shall provide all required system resources, e.g. access to interrupts, I/O,..., which is in fact often a constraining factor in asymmetric systems
- strategic considerations like functional safety, which might require TS driving redundant signals to be deliberately assigned to different cores

In order to guarantee sufficient computing resources before assigning a TS to a core, the system needs to be aware of the execution time of the TS and available computation time on its cores. This can be done in providing WCET for each component, and appropriate bookkeeping across all TS and cores. However, realistic WCET values might be hard to determine, and overly pessimistic values would lead to inefficient use of hardware resources. In certain cases WCET estimation might allow a reasonable approximation, see [13]. For the execution platform we assume current hardware based on x86/x64 multi-core/multi-CPU architecture in standard PC/PCI architecture, supported by a suitable RT OS like INtime™ [14], offering virtual memory management and pre-emptive multi-tasking in a AMP system.

5 Modifying Systems in Runtime

Reconfiguration of a system includes re-wiring of ports of components, changing parameters and thus behavior in components, but also more structural change like adding or deleting components. In order to allow exchange of one or more components, without impacting the remainders, a copy-modify-switch-delete strategy is implemented. Beside the actual switch-over, which needs to be done with highest priority after the associated TS has finished, all other steps are not time critical and can therefore be done at idle priority level. Modifiability without affecting the residual system is limited by non-symmetric properties (see Sect. 12) and potentially the need to transfer component-inherent information like signal history or state.

6   Mapping of Software to Hardware

A perfectly scale-able system shall be able to distribute and map its tasks to the executing hardware automatically, i.e. without human intervention. This assumes the underlying hardware is accurately enough described, including execution capabilities, and available hardware resources. As hardware changes between system boots might be possible, an analyze, discover and register mechanism runs at least during system startup, storing properties like number and type of cores, power modes, RAM, IO, DMA, interrupts, peripheral configuration etc. in a registry available to the configuration and mapping algorithms. This is used by a constrained-based solver to find a valid (in later versions: optimal) mapping pattern between the applications to run (in the granularity of TS) and available hardware, satisfying described dependency constraints.

7   Inter-process Communication and Run-Time Dependencies

Shared memory has proven to be a very versatile architecture for inter-process communication, also for cyclic operation. Without taking cache into account, shared memory allows random access to values at constant time, independent of data size, which is why it is used in COBRA to connect data between components. In order to allow re-wiring between value producing components and value-consuming components, and more importantly, to manage exact timing when a value is written and when it is read, a port is used as mediator. Ports are solely managed by the runtime system. Components access the ports from the "inner" side, while a runtime management controls the outside. Non-cyclic communication between components and the runtime system in COBRA is based on synchronous and asynchronous message-passing.

8   Component Development Considerations

COBRA relies on strongly componentized software to allow compose-ability to a perfectly scalable system. Explicit declaration of dependencies allows even to use components from different software versions in a common configuration, enabling partial and "hot" updates of systems. This however requires rigid interface management, verified and ensured by the runtime system.

9   Robustness Considerations

Automotive test systems govern devices like combustion engines and high-power electrical drives, posing potential hazards to humans or facility, and are therefore subject to functional safety regulations. Typically, not all parts of e.g. automation, simulation and control software are certified to higher safety integrity levels (SIL), which is why an additional dedicated safety system monitors and controls the whole test setup including the V&V system described in Sect. 2. As mentioned in Sect. 4, COBRA contributes to system dependability by providing a sandbox-like isolation of (potentially buggy) components in at least three aspects:

- all system resources are managed centrally by the run-time system; components can only access and use resources as described in the system configuration description, which needs to be carefully verified before being applied. Malicious component to component interaction is thereby minimized.
- Component execution is highly deterministic as is fully described in the TS.
- In case a component exceeds its specified runtime causing a cycle time violation (e.g. spinning thread), it can be easily identified and consequently be de-activated. As the signal flow is clearly defined and represented in the TS, the impact of such a scenario is obvious as well, and limited to components directly depended on the malfunction component, but not more.

10   Parallelized, Mixed Criticality Aware Networking

Another important aspect in V&V relates to networking between test system and the UUT, respectively its one or more electronic control units (ECU, also called xCU). One of the goals of the joined European research project EMC2 [15] is leveraging multi-core CPU's also for ECU's in cars, allowing to consolidate different modules and functions within a single system, thus reducing complexity, costs and weight of vehicles. However, this requires to be able to deal with multiple applications of diverse (mixed) criticality in one system, quite similar to the challenges we face in the testing system. Current work focusses on how to provide communication for mixed-criticality applications on multicore automotive control units to the relating tasks of the V&V systems via unified, standardized, low latency real-time capable networks (CAN, CAN-FD, automotive Ethernet).

Time-determinism (e.g. cyclic real-time requirements), data consistency and synchrony will be have to be addressed, considering specific design constraints of automotive systems (robustness, safety requirements, cost efficiency, etc.), implementing on hardware platforms and software frameworks with standards like AUTOSAR and protocols like XCP. We suggest a multi-platform capable "connectivity manager" (see Fig. 4) to control connections for described multiple endpoints in different tasks and diverse contexts, managing various life-cycles, timing requirements, criticality and underlying protocol as well as software architectures, which we plan to publish later in the project.

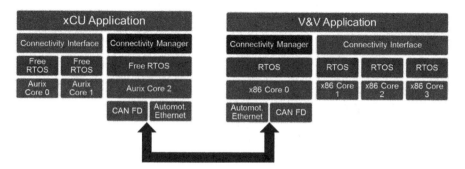

Fig. 4. Proposed connectivity manager handling networking in complex AMP-based V&V systems for automotive control units

11   Example: Four-Wheel Test Application

In order to validate the scalability of the proposed COBRA architecture, a simple all-wheel test application based on the setup depicted in Fig. 1 was configured, combining four sets (one per wheel) of input and output components and a computationally reasonably intensive model-based controller component. This results in a structure shown in Fig. 5(a) and (c), potentially a good candidate for distribution to several cores. Each of the four instances of the model-based controller (with a design based on [16]) is supposed to govern one axle/dyno of the vehicle under test.

The test was done on a PC equipped with two CPU's with quad core each (type: INTEL Xeon E5607), 24 GB RAM, INtime 4.20.14 running on 5 cores, Windows 7 64 bit running on the remaining cores. Note that one core was exclusively used for system management including clocking, synchronization and timing and general housekeeping (marked "Task System" in Fig. 5). Measurements were done using Microsoft's PerfMon tool with an INtime plugin from tenAsys to measure consumed CPU cycles, expressed in per cent of overall cycles. This provides a first overview; for a more detailed analysis we work on a tool providing exact invocation and runtime measurements.

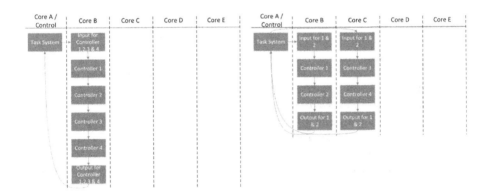

a) Test application on a single core   b) Test application on two cores

c) Test application on four cores

Fig. 5.   Scaling a four-wheel test application for a one, two and four core system

As the result (Table 1) indicates, the scaling effect follows pretty much the expected parallelization benefit (considering the limited resolution of the measurement method). The steep incline of CPU load of the management core in relation to the number of execution cores appears to be caused by the RTOS and is currently being analyzed together with the vendor in more detail.

Table 1. Comparing CPU load values (in % of overall cycles) for three parallelization scenarios

Number of executing cores	1	2	4
Core A (management node)	6 %	11 %	19 %
Execution Core B	71 %	38 %	18 %
Execution Core C		36 %	18 %
Execution Core D			18 %
Execution Core E			18 %

12 Outlook

Further research is suggested to deal with some "foes of perfect scalability" which have been identified so far.

- Complex dependencies of components (e.g. nested loops in signal paths with only direct feed-through components, or dependencies between components based on e.g. states or resources rather than signal paths)
- Non-linear scaling effects due to system asymmetry (e.g. hardware resources dedicated to certain cores only; or data access via levels of cache vs. main memory)
- As described, configurations may be changed during run-time, which potentially could cause a TS to grow. As there is currently no TS migration from one core to another supported, imbalances (which could be seen as fragmentation of executing cores) might occur
- Assuming non-symmetric properties like cache hit/miss or access to low-level DMA, system clock etc., can we find the *optimal* distribution of TS to cores, for example also considering data locality and size?
- COBRA relies on a central management of system configuration, which for combined or highly complex systems might become a bottleneck. Parallelization and therefore distributing control over several CPU's might solve this issue. However it requires mechanisms to ensure consistency, like encapsulating configuration modifications like transactions, followed by synchronization.
- The proposed strategy is based on static models (descriptions) of hardware and software, therefore a feed-forward method. Further research to include feed-back strategies, e.g. adjusting WCET values to current measurements, or to the specific hardware used, need to be considered.

13   Summary and Conclusion

In this paper an architecture for highly scale-able real-time systems is proposed, applicable to complex combinations of measurement, control, simulation, communication and automation tasks as required in automotive verification and validation testing. The underlying software component model allows highly flexible system composability, with ridged means of resource control for the system management. Explicit declaration of resources and dependencies allows amongst other benefits to extract graphs of data and resource dependencies. In a next step, so-called Trigger Sequences (TS) are computed, to partition complex configurations into independent, thus parallel executable pieces. Finally these TS can be automatically distributed for execution on multi-core CPU's. A first analysis of complex V&V systems indicate that the proposed method allows to identify and exploit enough parallelism even to utilize upcoming many-core hardware platforms sufficiently. However, potential issues like resource asymmetry, cache-interdependence, inaccurate execution time information and system fragmentation caused by unthrifty reconfigurations at runtime have been identified and require additional research.

Acknowledgements. Research leading to these results has received funding from the ARTEMIS Joint Undertaking under grant agreement 621429 (project EMC2) and financial support of FFG *Basisprojekt* "Next Generation Simulation" of the Austrian Federal Ministry for Transport, Innovation and Technology.

References

1. Audsley, N., Burns, A., Richardson, M., Tindell, K., Wellings, A.J.: Applying New Scheduling Theory To Static Priority Pre-emptive Scheduling (1993)
2. Burns, A.: Preemptive Priority-Based Scheduling: An Appropriate Engineering Approach (1994)
3. Geneder, S., Pfister, F., Wilhelm, C., Arnold, A.: Development of connected powertrains at the power test bed. ATZ Worldw. **116**, 14–19 (2014)
4. Stewart, D.B., Volpe, R.A., Khosla, P.K.: Design of dynamically reconfigurable real-time software using port-based objects. IEEE Trans. Softw. Eng. **23**, 759–776 (1997)
5. Anthony, R., Rettberg, A., Chen, D., Jahnich, I., Boer, G., Ekelin, C.: Towards a dynamically reconfigurable automotive control systen architectur. IFIP Int. Fed. Inf. Process. **231**, 71–84 (2007)
6. Salemi, B., et al.: Modular Self-Reconfigurable Robot Systems (2007)
7. Steiger, C., Walder, H., Platzner, M.: Operating systems for reconfigurable embedded platforms: Online scheduling of real-time tasks. IEEE Trans. Comput. **53**, 1393–1407 (2004)
8. Dave, B.P.: CRUSADE: Hardware/software co-synthesis of dynamically reconfigurable heterogeneous real-time distributed embedded systems. In: Proceedings of the Design, Automation and Test in Europe Conference and Exhibition 1999, pp. 97–104 (1999)
9. Prisching, D., Paulweber, M., Rinner, B.: Configuring Complex Multi-Sensor Test Bed Systems. TCMC (2003)
10. Prevelakis, V., Spinellis, D.: Sandboxing applications. In: Proceedings of the USENIX Technical Annual Conference Free Track, pp. 119–126 (2001)

11. Olberding, N.: Erweiterung einer echtzeitfähigen Ablaufumgebung für den Anwendungsfall Co-Simulation (2014). (in German)
12. Prisching, D., Rinner, B.: Thread-based analysis of embedded applications with real-time and non real-time processing on a single-processor platform (2000)
13. Pfragner, M., Priller, P., Prisching, D., Rinner, B.: Performance Estimation in complex Automation Systems (2006)
14. TenAsys: INtime RTOS Family. http://www.tenasys.com/tenasys-products/intime-rtos-family/overview-rtos
15. Home - Artemis EMC2. http://www.artemis-emc2.eu/
16. Gruenbacher, E., Langthaler, P., Steinmaurer, G., Del Re, L., Kokal, H.: Adaptive inverse torque control of a diesel engine using adaptive mapping update (2003)

Dependable Cyber-Physical Systems with Redundant Consumer Single-Board Linux Computers

Øyvind Netland[1(✉)] and Amund Skavhaug[2]

[1] Department of Engineering Design and Materials, Trondheim, Norway
oyvind.netland@ntnu.no
[2] Department of Engineering Cybernetics, Trondheim, Norway
amund.skavhaug@itk.ntnu.no

Abstract. There are a large number of small and inexpensive single-board computers with Linux operating systems available on the market today. Most of these aim for the consumer and enthusiast market, but can also be used in research and commercial applications. This paper builds on several years of experience with using such computers in student projects, as well as the development of cyber-physical and embedded control systems. A summary of the properties that are key for dependability for selected boards is given in tabulated form. These boards have interesting properties for many embedded and cyber-physical systems, e.g. high-performance, small size and low cost. The use of Linux for operating system means a development environment that is familiar to many developers, and the availability of many libraries and applications. While not suitable for applications were formally proven dependability is necessary, we argue that by actively mitigating some of the potential problems identified in this paper such computers can be used in many applications where high dependability is desirable, especially in combination with low-cost. A solution with redundant single-board computers is presented as a strategy for achieving high dependability. Due to the low cost and small size, this is feasible for applications were redundancy traditionally would be prohibitively too large or costly.

Keywords: Dependability · Cyber-physical systems · Linux · Single-board computer · Redundancy

1 Introduction

Since the release of the Raspberry Pi in 2012 [1], a large number of similar single-board computers has been released. Most of these have hardware very similar to what are used in smart phones, which means high computation power, low power consumption, small size and low cost. In this paper, we will use the name consumer-grade single-board Linux computer (CSBLC) to reference such computers, due to the lack of a commonly used name. This definition includes all development board type computers that are widely available and used. As the name implies, only boards capable of running Linux are included, i.e. not Arduino and other boards that use microcontrollers without a real operating system.

© Springer International Publishing Switzerland 2015
F. Koornneef and C. van Gulijk (Eds.): SAFECOMP 2015 Workshops, LNCS 9338, pp. 224–234, 2015.
DOI: 10.1007/978-3-319-24249-1_20

A typical CSBLC uses an ARM CPU in the range from a single core with 700 MHz to 1.8 GHz quad cores, and RAM between 500 MB and 2 GB. Due to the graphical nature of smart phones, they tend to have connectors for graphical user interfaces and powerful graphical processing units for processing HD video. In this respect, they are similar to regular desktop computers and can often be used as a low-powered alternative for these.

CSBLCs usually have low-level I/O signals, such as UART, I2C, SPI, GPIO etc., available for the user. This makes them attractive for use in embedded and cyber-physical systems that have to interface with low-level electronic components. Figure 1 illustrates how CSBLCs can be considered a hybrid between desktop computers and lower level microcontrollers.

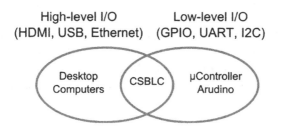

Fig. 1. I/O capabilities of CSBLCs

This paper considers a cyber-physical system [2] or embedded control system that interacts with the real world with sensors and actuators. It is also assumed that the system communicates with users or with other parts of a distributed system via a network connection, either wired or wireless. Dependability, safety and security are often mentioned as challenges for such systems [2–4], both because these are systems we rely on, and that repairs can be challenging in a distributed and/or remotely located system.

Dependability can be defined as a system's ability to deliver a service that can be justifiable trusted, and can be divided into the attributes of availability, reliability, safety, integrity, and maintainability [5]. CSBLCs are not considered suitable for systems that have formal dependability demands, or where a failure has catastrophic consequences. However, this does not mean that they cannot be dependable when used correctly, especially when a combination of high dependability and low cost is desirable. Linux as an operating system is suitable for embedded development [6] that is a well-known environment with good support communities and commonly used libraries and development tools. All these factors contribute to reducing the development cost.

We have used CSBLCs in the development of a system for remote inspection and maintenance of offshore wind turbines [7]. This is an example of a system where a failure is not catastrophic, since the turbine will continue to work. However, dependability is still of importance, since functionality is lost if the system fails, and difficult access makes repairs expensive.

The experience that this paper builds on is the previously mentioned development with CSBLCs and the supervision of multiple master student projects using CSBLCs. The most important advantages and disadvantages for dependability of using such devices are described, and how the disadvantages can be mitigated. Redundancy is suggested as a method for increasing dependability, and a solution suitable for CSBLCs with sensors and actuators for interacting with the real world is described.

2   Dependable CSBLCs

2.1   Hardware

CSBLCs are not specifically designed for dependability. However, since most of the users are relatively inexperienced, and the boards encourage for experimenting with connecting different sensors and electronic components, they must be durable enough to survive rough treatment. Due to an abundance of competing products, it would be difficult for an unreliable board to survive in the market. Manufacturers would therefore have to have reliability in mind, for it to be a viable commercial product.

The ARM CPUs that are commonly found in CSBLCs are low powered chips. Devices like Raspberry Pi and Beaglebone Black have no heat sinks and the CPU still do not feel warm to the touch. Operating at such low temperatures is in general beneficial for the reliability of electronics. In addition, no cooling fans that can fail are needed, and it is easier to encapsulate the system.

2.2   Software and Development

Most CSBLCs support at least one of the leading Linux distributions, as Ubuntu, Arch and Debian. This is a significant advantage for a developer that is used to work within these environments, which will result in shorter development time and thus costs. Linux is a well-used environment that many developers are comfortable with, and it has a large collection of libraries and tools that are widely used and extensively tested.

Most default distributions contain a large number of software packets, including a full graphical desktop with applications. Large portions of this will not be used by embedded systems, thus there will be large amount of unused code and programs that bring no benefit to the system. There can also be several services running in the background that are not used. This is disadvantageous for the dependability. Best-case is that memory and CPU resources are wasted [8], while worst case is that there is a fault in this otherwise unused code that cause a failure in the system, or used as leverage for breaking into the system. When it comes to dependability, it is beneficial that the software is as small as possible. This also has an effect on the system's ability interact with the real world in real-time, which will be discussed in more detail in Sect. 3.

To reduce this problem it is important to remove as much of the unused programs as practically possible. An extreme variant of this would be to build your own Linux system from open source programs, but this is likely to be very time consuming, and not necessarily without its own problems.

2.3   Concerns Regarding Dependability

Some common properties with CSBLCs that can be a concern for the dependability is listed below:

- Most CSBLCs use a 5V power supply, from either a power jack or USB, without any protection circuits. The power supply is connected directly to an on-board power management chip that generates the different lower voltage levels needed by the CPU and peripherals. This chip can be damaged by reverse voltage, over-voltage, or over-current, which could happen, either if an incorrect power supply is connected during development or if there is a fault in the power supply while in use.
- On CSBLCs, many of the individual pins of the CPU are exposed as I/O headers, which is something that is not seen on other consumer computers. The advantages of this are obvious, since direct access to headers with I/O signals makes it easy to interact with other electronic components. Unfortunately, there are no protection circuits between the headers and the CPU pins, and any voltage outside the commonly used 0-3.3 V range, or in some cases 0-1.8 V range, will likely damage the board. Developers that are used to significantly more tolerant devices with low-level microcontrollers, as the Arduino, have to be more careful when handling CSBLCs.
- Most CSBLCs use an ARM CPU, which is a different architecture than desktop computers (x86 or x86-64). This means that all software must be ported to this architecture. Linux have supported ARM for a long time, and can be considered stable. However, drivers are often a problem, since driver development for ARM often is normally prioritized lower than for x86 and x86-64. Our experience has been that especially USB WiFi drivers have been problematic for ARM devices. Some USB WiFi devices do not have drivers for ARM at all, while others can be unstable. Unstable WiFi drivers can reduce the availability of CSBLCs that depend on WiFi for communication with users or other parts of a distributed system.
- SD or mirco SD cards are often used as storage media for CSBLCs. These are inexpensive and widely available devices, but can be a problem for reliability. There are significant quality differences between SD cards, thus it is important to use one that is known to be reliable. In addition, the physical SD socket can be vulnerable to vibrations and similar. Some CSBLCs have onboard eMMC instead for or in addition to SD cards. This is preferable for dependability, as eMMC memory usually have longer expected life. Read and write speeds are usually higher as well.

2.4 Practical Experience with CSBLCs

Our experience with CSBLCs comes from several years of development with different such computers, and with supervising multiple master student projects using them. The findings presented here are some example observations from this, but since dependability related events were not systematically registered, this is not guaranteed to be a complete list.

We have observed a large number of failures due to faults during software and hardware development with CSBLCs. Software faults are normally easy to recover by flashing the SD card or eMMC memory to a known working state, while hardware faults, especially incorrect wiring of I/O signals, can often do fatal damage to the computer. We have seen multiple fatal failures, e.g. only two of ten Beaglebone Black computers survived being used in multiple master projects over a period of one and a half years.

Exactly how the eight computers were damaged is unknown, but incorrect wiring of I/O wires or power supply is the most likely explanation.

Such failures during development are expected, especially since a large portion of the developers was relatively inexperienced students. These errors do not describe the dependability of the computer systems themselves, but their susceptibility to failures due to incorrect handling. Therefore, we have not focused on these types of error in this paper.

Failures occurring during normal operation, not development, are of more concern for dependability. We have only experienced one such failure that did permanent damage, when two Beaglebone Black computers both failed while being left on over a weekend. The two computers were set up in a redundant configuration, and only shared a few signal wires. They had separate switched power supplies that were connected to the power outlet. Since the two boards were damaged during the same period, it is likely that both have a common cause, which could be from the shared power outlet or the shared I/O signals.

In addition, we have seen multiple problems with CSBLCs losing their wireless network connection and failing to reconnect. This is probably caused by unstable wireless drivers and a failure of the system to reconnect. To resolve this problem would normally be simple, except if the wireless network connection is the only method of communicating with the computer.

2.5 Dependability of Selected CSBLCs

We have selected twelve of the most popular CSBLCs from the comprehensive list in [9], and presented a summary of key properties related to dependability in Table 1. Different models of the same board and producer have been grouped for readability. Boards that we have experience with ourselves has been marked with a '*'.

The table can be used as a reference when considering any of these devices, and consist of information from [9] and the web sites for the different board. More specific information for evaluating whether the different computers are suitable for an application can also be found at these sources. An "unknown" power protection means that specific information regarding this was not found, which in most cases is expected to mean "none".

2.6 Security

Security of a system is its availability for authorized actions only, confidentiality and the absence of unauthorized system alterations [5]. Since cyber-physical systems usually have some type of network connection, they are vulnerable to unauthorized access and eavesdropping. This makes it important to consider security, and communication should be encrypted, for confidentiality. Each end of the communication should be able to identify the other party securely for authorization.

Table 1. Properties that are relevant for dependability of selected CSBLCs.

Name	CPU	Cooling	Power protection	Storage options	WiFi
Banana Pi	ARM A7	None	Unknown	SD, SATA	USB
*Beaglebone	ARM A8	None	None	Micro SD, eMMC	USB
Cubieboard	ARM (various)	None	Unknown	Micro SD, eMMC, SATA	Model dependent
Intel Galileo	x86	None	Unknown	Micro SD	USB
Marsboard	ARM (various)	None	Unknown	Micro SD, eMMC, SATA	Onboard
*Odroid	ARM (various)	Model dependent	Yes	Micro SD, eMMC module	USB
OLinuXino	ARM (various)	None	Unknown	Micro SD, eMMC (some models)	USB
*Pandaboard	ARM A9	None	None	SD	Onboard
Pcduino	ARM (various)	None	Unknown	Micro SD, eMMC	USB
*Raspberry Pi	ARM (various)	None	None	SD or Micro SD	USB
UDOO	ARM	None or passive	Unknown	Micro SD, SATA (some models)	USB
Wandboard	ARM A9	None	Unknown	Micro SD, SATA (some models)	Model dependent

Correct implementation of secure communication is notoriously difficult, which is demonstrated by the constant flow of software security updates in commonly used software. One of the advantages of using Linux is that a large number of open source libraries are available, among them different security and encryption libraries. These libraries have been used, improved, and hardened over long periods, and although there is no guarantee that they are without faults, they are likely more secure than a custom solution.

3   Real-Time Performance

A real-time computer system must be able to guarantee a response within a specified time constraint or deadline [10]. We divide this in hard, firm and soft real-time. If a hard real-time deadline is missed, it will result in a, possibly catastrophic, system failure. For firm and soft real-time, a missed deadline will only reduce the overall quality of the system. The differences between the two are that the results from a soft real-time task still have some value after the deadline, while the results from a firm task are useless.

Real-time performance is important when interacting with the real world, as cyber-physical systems often will do. A real-time operating system provides guaranties that a task with a high priority will be executed in a timely manner even if other lower priority tasks are running. The ability to react to external events is also important, e.g. to have a known response time to a change in a sensor value.

Most operating systems, including Linux, are not considered real-time operating systems. It is possible to assign priorities to a task in Linux, but even the highest priority can be prevented from running by a system call, interrupt etc. The probability of this will increase the busier the CPU is. This means that the ability to perform a specific task at a specific time is highly dependent on how many other processes and services that are running on the system. Linux distributions on desktop computers and on CSBLC, often have an overwhelming amount of software, thus the probability that something can interfere with a time-critical task can be higher than acceptable. Two commonly used strategies for improving the real-time performance of Linux is presented here.

3.1   Real-Time Addition to Linux

Although Linux itself is not a real-time operating system, there are multiple methods for adding real-time capabilities to Linux. There are two strategies for this, which are described in detail in [11]. The first strategy is to alter the Linux kernel to give it better real-time capabilities, the most common being the RT_PREEMPT patch. The second is to have a real-time microkernel that runs between the hardware and the Linux kernel [12]. Xenomai is an example of the second of these two that has official support for both Raspberry Pi and Beaglebone. Using Xenomai (or a similar solution) require the use their API for accessing the real-time capabilities of the microkernel, and real-time access to the I/O, require custom developed real-time I/O drivers. Both of these will increase development time.

3.2   Slave Microcontroller

The other possible method for achieving necessary real-time properties is to "outsource" the real-time tasks to a slave microcontroller. Since only a few, known tasks will run on the slave, the feasibility of reaching the assigned deadlines can be determined analytically. This also have the added benefit of using the I/O pins of the slave microcontroller, which often will be more tolerant than the I/O pins of the CSBLC.

Disadvantages with this approach are that there will be some time delay from the communication between the CSBLC and the slave microcontroller, and that two devices instead of one will have to be considered during the development.

4 Increased Reliability with Redundancy

By having two or more redundant computers that are able to do the same task, the dependability can be increased. Figure 2 illustrate how two computers, with shared or computer-specific sensors and actuators can be organized in a 1oo2 architecture. This is intended to provide redundancy for one system or for one node in a distributed system. There could in addition be redundancy from several nodes being able to do the same tasks, but this is not considered here.

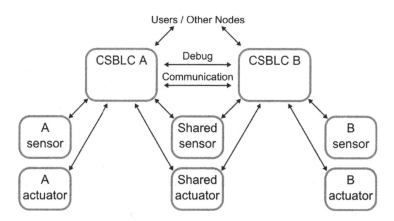

Fig. 2. Redundancy solution with two CSBLCs and individual and shared sensors and actuators

CSBLCs make it possible to implement redundancy at a low-cost and with a small physical size. The use of redundancy can to some degree, and if implemented correctly, compensate for assumed lower dependability of CSBLCs.

4.1 Computer Redundancy

The system described in Fig. 2 show two (1oo2) CSBLCs that are identical aspects of the same system. Internally they would have to share the responsibility of their tasks, e.g. with a typical active/standby method were both collect information from the sensors, but only one of the computers control the actuator at any given time. A user or another node in the distributed system can then communicate with either of the two computers and get the same information. If one of the CSBLCs, or the computer-specific resources are unavailable, it can instead be accessed from the other. A similar solution could be designed with more than two CSBLCs if even better redundancy is required.

To be able to share responsibility, the two CSBLCs will have to communicate, preferably through a reliable channel with minimal latency. Most CSBLCs have multiple UART signals, and one can be used as a dedicated communication channel between the two that will be operational as long as both computers are available. Network communication can be down or have delays, thus it is considered a less suitable solution. Busses as I2C and SPI are generally not suitable for communication between two Linux computers due to lack or limited support in the Linux kernel for acting as a slave on the bus.

Most CSBLCs use a console UART as the main terminal of the system, meaning that through this interface you can follow messages from the kernel during boot, and access a Linux terminal as root. In a redundant solution, each of the CSBLCs can use an UART to listen to the console UART of the other, for debugging purposes. This is a valuable ability if one of two remote computers is unavailable. The problem can be found and possibly solved remotely. For security reasons, the access to the UART debug should be limited to only the root user; otherwise, it could be used as a method of gaining root access without permission.

4.2   Resource Redundancy

A redundant pair of CSBLCs that interact with resources, as sensors and actuators, has to be organized so all information and actuation options are available to both computers. In Fig. 2, two possible solutions for resources are shown, either computer-specific or shared. Computer-specific sensors or actuators mean that each of the computers has its own. For sensors, this requires two of the same type and at the same location for observing the same phenomena, e.g. two temperature sensors next to each other. For actuators this requires two that can be used to generate the same effect, e.g. two heating elements in the same location. Both computer-specific sensors and actuators can be used interchangeably in case of a failure.

Computer-specific actuators can be difficult to implement, e.g. two motors that perform the same motion. Figure 3 illustrates a simplified method of how this can be achieved. If such a solution is used it is important that only one motor tries to move or hold the position at the time, while the other motor remain inactive. The active motor has to turn the inactive one, thus this solution is not suitable for motors that require high torque to turn when inactive, e.g. a motor with a high ratio gearbox. Stepper motors are suitable for this solution, because only a very small torque is needed to rotate a motor that is not turned on. It is also possible to have a solution where the motor gears can be disconnected from the common gear when not used. If it is difficult to rotate one motor with the other, this will be necessary. However, this will introduce new possible failures, e.g. failure to connect or disconnect a motor.

It will not always be practical to have computer-specific resources, either because of cost constraints, or because it is difficult to implement. A shared resource can be used instead. The downside is that there will be no backup if this resource fails. For some actuators it could also be challenging to make a driver that can be controlled by two different computers.

Fig. 3. Two motors both acting on the same common gear

4.3   Common-Cause Failures

To have effective redundancy, the number of possible common-cause failures should be minimized. This means single failures that are capable of causing failures in all parts of a redundant system. Some possible common-cause failures that have not been considered in this limited description are listed here. How these can be addressed will depend on the application and is outside the scope of this paper.

- If a common power-supply is used, a failure will cause both computers to fail. In addition, over voltage or current can damage both computers.
- If both computers use the same network, or connect to the same wireless access point, then an error can make both inaccessible.
- Any electrical contact between the two computers can cause a failure to propagate from one computer to the other.
- A failure in one computer that causes it to send uncontrollable commands to its resources can cause problems that the other computer is unable to mitigate.
- A failure in a shared resource will be a common-cause failure.

5   Conclusion

Single-board Linux computers aimed for the consumer market have high computing capacity in spite of their small size and low cost. Since their capabilities include low-level I/O signal and busses, they are suitable for interacting with other electronic devices and for use in control systems. The Linux operating system can simplify development with a many well-tested development tools, libraries, and applications.

A table with a summary of the properties that are considered especially relevant for dependability of specific single-board computers has been presented and can be used as a reference. These computers are often not considered for use in systems with high dependability requirements, due to an, often unfounded, assumption that they cannot be reliable enough. We argue that this often is not the case, and that high reliability can be achieved by addressing potential problems, as the ones mentioned in this paper. However, in applications where failures have particularly large consequences, or there are specific or formalized requirements for documentation of all hardware and software, a system based on these computers is not advisable.

One method for increasing the reliability is to use multiple, redundant single-board computers. Redundancy is an especially useful technique for these types of computers since they are small, inexpensive and can be seen as a single and possibly replaceable component. The outline of a 1oo2 redundancy solution with redundant control computers and individual or shared resources has been presented. The low-cost and small size of these single-board Linux computers make it possible to use redundancy for increased dependability in applications where a traditional redundant solution would be too expensive or physically too large.

References

1. BBC News, The Raspberry Pi computer goes on general sale, 29th February 2012. http://www.bbc.com/news/technology-17190918
2. Sha, L., Gopalakrishnan, S., Liu, X., Wang, Q.: Cyber-Physical systems: a new frontier. In: 2008 IEEE International Conference on, Sensor Networks, Ubiquitous, and Trustworthy Computing, IEEE (2008)
3. Schneider, D., Armengaud, E., Schoitsch, E.: Towards trust assurance and certification in cyber-physical systems. In: Bondavalli, A., Ceccarelli, A., Ortmeier, F. (eds.) SAFECOMP 2014. LNCS, vol. 8696, pp. 180–191. Springer, Heidelberg (2014)
4. Miclea, L., Sanislav, T.: About dependability in cyber-physical systems. In: 2011 9th East-West Design and Test Symposium (EWDTS), pp. 17–21. IEEE (2011)
5. Avižienis, A., Laprie, J.C., Randell, B., Landwehr, C.: Basic concepts and taxonomy of dependable and secure computing. IEEE Trans. Dependable Secure Comput. $1(1)$, 11–33 (2004). IEEE
6. Lehrbaum, R.: Using Linux in Embedded and Real-Time Systems. In: Linux Journal, vol. 2000, no. 75es, Belltown Media (2000)
7. Netland, Ø., Jenssen, G.D., Schade, H.M., Skavhaug, A.: An experiment on the effectiveness of remote, robotic inspection compared to manned. In: 2013 IEEE International Conference on Systems, Man and Cybernetics, pp. 2310–2315. IEEE (2013)
8. Kruger, C.P., Hancke, G.P.: Benchmarking internet of things devices. In: 2014 12th IEEE International Conference on Industrial Informatics (INDIN), pp. 611–616. IEEE (2014)
9. Wikipedia.: Comparison of single-board computers. Accessed 9th June 2015. http://en.wikipedia.org/wiki/Comparison_of_single-board_computers
10. Burns, A., Wellings, A.: Real-time systems and programming languages: Ada 95, real-time Java, and real-time POSIX. Addison Wesley, Boston (2001)
11. Vun, N., Hor, H.F., Chao, J.W.: Real-time enhancements for embedded linux. In: 2008 14th IEEE International Conference on Parallel and Distributed Systems, pp. 737–740. IEEE (2008)
12. Barabanov, M., Yodaiken, V.: Real-time linux. Linux J. **23** (1996)

International workshop on the Integration of Safety and Security Engineering (ISSE 2015)

A Combined Safety-Hazards and Security-Threat Analysis Method for Automotive Systems

Georg Macher[1,2](✉), Andrea Höller[1], Harald Sporer[1],
Eric Armengaud[2], and Christian Kreiner[1]

[1] Institute for Technical Informatics, Graz University of Technology, Graz, Austria
{georg.macher,andrea.hoeller,sporer,christian.kreiner}@tugraz.at
[2] AVL List GmbH, Graz, Austria
{georg.macher,eric.armengaud}@avl.com

Abstract. Safety and Security appear to be two contradicting overall system features. Traditionally, these two features have been treated separately, but due to increasing awareness of mutual impacts, cross domain knowledge becomes more important. Due to the increasing interlacing of automotive systems with networks (such as Car2X), it is no longer acceptable to assume that safety-critical systems are immune to security risks and vice versa.

This paper presents the application and method description of a novel approach for combined safety hazard and security threat analysis. In this paper we present a detailed description of the SAHARA method and an application of this method for an automotive system. We analyze the impact of this novel method and highlight the impacts of security threats on safety targets of the system. The paper describes the experiences gained at application of the method and how safety-critical contribution of successful security attacks can be quantified.

Keywords: ISO 26262 · HARA · STRIDE · Automotive systems · Safety/Security co-engineering

1 Introduction

Embedded systems are already integrated into our everyday life. For the automotive industry embedded systems components are responsible for 25 % of vehicle costs, while the added value from electronics components ranges up to 75 % for electric and hybrid vehicles [17]. The complexity of embedded systems has grown significantly in recent years. Current premium cars employ more than 90 electronic control units (ECU) with close to 1 Gigabyte software code [2] implemented. This trend is also strongly supported by the ongoing replacement of traditional mechanical systems by modern embedded systems. This enables the deployment of more advanced control strategies, thus providing additional benefits for the customer and environment. At the same time, the higher degree

© Springer International Publishing Switzerland 2015
F. Koornneef and C. van Gulijk (Eds.): SAFECOMP 2015 Workshops, LNCS 9338, pp. 237–250, 2015.
DOI: 10.1007/978-3-319-24249-1_21

of integration and the safety- and security-criticality of the control application raise new challenges.

Future automotive systems will require appropriate systematic approaches to support dependable system engineering. This means, among other factors, applying combined approaches for system dependability features (such as safety and security). System dependability attributes have a major impact on product development and product release as well as for company brand reputation. Mutual impacts, similarities, and interdisciplinary values are in common and a considerable overlap among methods exists. Besides this, standards, such as ISO 26262 [4] in safety and Common Criteria [5] in security domain, have been established to provide guidance during the development of dependable systems and are currently reviewed for similarities and alignment. For this paper we employed an approach which classifies the probability and impact of security threats using the STRIDE approach [9] and safety hazards using hazard analysis and risk assessment (HARA). This SAHARA concept [8] quantifies the security impact on dependable safety-related system development on system level. Within this work we describe the SAHARA concept in more detail and show how the concept has been accomplished to an early development phase safety-hazards and security-threat analysis.

This paper is organized as follows: Sect. 2 assesses the relation to related works dealing with (automotive) safety and security related topics. In Sect. 3 provides a description of the applied SAHARA method and its accomplishment to an early development phase safety-hazards and security-threat analysis. The application of the method for an automotive battery management system (BMS) use-case is presented in Sect. 4. Finally, Sect. 5 concludes this work with an overview of the presented approach.

2   Related Work

Safety and security of control systems are challenging research domains inheriting continuous development and growing importance. For this reason, many researchers and industrial experts have recently made efforts to combine security and safety.

Although only safety standards, such as the road vehicles functional safety norm ISO 26262 [4] and its basic norm IEC 61508, exist in the automotive industry, several safety and security norms and guidelines have been established in aeronautics industry. In addition to DO-178C [19], which addresses aeronautics software safety, ARP4754 [14] provides guidance for system level development and defines steps for the adequate refinement and implementation of requirements. Safety assessment techniques, such as failure mode and effects analysis (FMEA) and functional hazard assessment (FHA), among others, are specified by ARP4761 [13]. Security concerns in aeronautics industry are tackled e.g., by the Common Criteria [5,21] approach respectively ED202 specification.

The common basic analysis method for the related works is hazard analysis and risk assessment (HARA) [4], which identifies and categorizes hazardous events of components of the system under development (SuD). It furthermore specifies high-level safety goals and measures related to the prevention or mitigation of the safety hazards in order to avoid unreasonable risk. These measures determine the criticality of the SuD and define requirements and strategies to be applied for the rest of the systems lifecycle. For more details on HARA we recommend ISO 26262 part 3 Annex B [4].

The work of Gashi et al. [3] focuses on redundancy and diversity, and their effects on safety and security of embedded systems. This work is part of the SeSaMo (Security and Safety Modeling for Embedded Systems) project which focuses on synergies and trade-offs between security and safety in concrete use-cases.

Security concerns of safety-critical systems are also focused by aerospace domain. Paulitsch et al. [10] outline issues in assessing the reliability of avionics software for safety and security perspectives. The authors aim at collecting evidence and finding indicators of effectiveness of existing safety-related and security-related processes in terms of effects on aircraft security.

A security-informed risk assessment is mentioned in the work of Bloomfield et al. [1]. Focus of this publication is a 'security-informed safety case' and the impact of security on an existing safety case. The authors mention the requirement of such an assessment methodology and describe a risk assessment process briefly, but neither provide guidance as how such an assessment is done, nor do they propose an approach to it.

Kath et al. [7] state model-based approaches as a promising approach to guarantee safety and security features. The authors present a model driven approach to security accreditation of service-oriented architectures in their work.

An overall security threat analysis of an unmanned aerial vehicle (UAV) is done by Javaid et al. [6]. Although their analysis summary calculates the likelihood, impact, and risk of a security threat analog to the SAHARA approach, this work does not focus on the impact of security threats on safety goals.

A threat analysis framework for critical infrastructures is proposed by Simion et al. [18]. This framework applies the same procedure as the SAHARA method, (1) identification and definition of threat attributes and (2) usage of attributes to characterize the threat potential. The authors also consider the required resources and attackers commitment for determining the threat attributes. Nevertheless, the SAHARA method is more focused towards the automotive domain and safety-critical automotive systems, which implies a completely different determination of threat attributes and potential threat impacts.

Some recent publications in the automotive domain also focus on security in automotive systems. On the one hand, the work of Schmidt et al. [15] presents a security analysis approach to identify and prioritize security issues, but solely provides an analysis approach for networked connectivity.

The work of Ward et al. [22], on the other hand, also mentions a risk assessment method for security risk in the automotive domain called threat analysis and risk assessment, based on HARA. This work identifies potential security attacks and the risk associated with these attacks. The work also describes how such a method has been developed based on the state-of-the-art HARA method. Nevertheless, the work does not combine hazard and threat analysis within one approach to acknowledge threats that may contribute to the safety-concept or lead to violation of safety goals.

The works of Roth et al. [12] and Steiner et al. [20] also deal with safety and security analysis, but focus on state/event fault trees for modeling of the system under development, while Schmittner et al. [16] present a failure mode and failure effect model for safety and security cause-effect analysis. This work categorizes threats also with the help of the STRIDE threat model in focus of an IEC60812 conform FMEA approach. Nevertheless this work characterizes the attack probabilities in a more complex way than the SAHARA method, which requires higher analysis efforts and more details of the SuD.

Raspotnig et al. [11] also combine safety and security methods for combined safety and security assessments of air traffic management systems. The approach of their publication relies on modeling misuse cases and misuse sequence diagrams within a UML behavior diagram, which implies a lot of additional modeling expenses for the early development phase.

The STRIDE threat model approach [9] developed by Microsoft Corporation can be used to expose security design flaws. This approach uses a technique called threat modeling. With this approach the system design is reviewed in a methodical way, which makes it applicable for integration into the HARA approach. Threat models, like STRIDE approach, may often not prove that a given design is secure, but they help to learn from mistakes and avoid repeating them, which is another commonality with HARA in safety domain.

Finally, the SAHARA concept [8] quantifies the security impact on dependable safety-related system development on system level. This concept classifies the probability and impact of security threats using the STRIDE approach [9]. Derived from the SAHARA concept, this method represents a systematic approaches towards concurrent safety and security development and is described in more detail in the next section.

3   SAHARA Approach

This section describes the basics of the SAHARA concept [8] and the derived method, which will be applied in the next section.

Due to the increasing impact of the internet of things also in the automotive domain, it is no longer acceptable to assume that safety systems are immune to security risks. Automotive engineers require appropriated systematic approaches and cross-domain knowledge of safety and security to appropriate support security-aware safety development. Therefore, the SAHARA method combines the automotive HARA [4] with the security domain STRIDE approach [9] to trace impacts of security issues on safety concepts on system level.

Threat modeling using STRIDE can be seen as the security equivalent to HARA. STRIDE is an acronym for spoofing, tampering, repudiation, information disclosure, denial of service, and elevation of privileges. Key concept of this

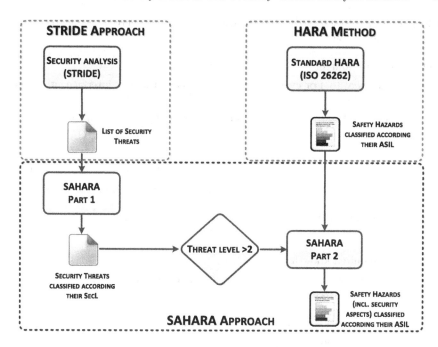

Fig. 1. Conceptual overview of the SAHARA method

threat modeling approach is the analysis of each system component for susceptibility of threats and mitigation of all threats to each component in order to
argue that a system is secure.

Figure 1 shows the conceptual overview of the novel SAHARA method. As
can be seen in the figure, an ISO 26262 conforming HARA analysis (right part
of the overview figure) can be performed in a conventional manner. Besides
this, attack vectors of the system can be modeled using the STRIDE approach
independently (left part of Fig. 1) by specialists of the security domain. The
two-stage SAHARA method then combines the outcome of this security analysis
with the outcomes of the safety analysis. Therefore, a key concept of the HARA
approach, the definition of automotive safety integrity level (ASILs) is applied
to the STRIDE analysis outcomes. Threats are quantified aligned with ASIL
analysis, according to the resources (R), know-how (K) required to exert the
threat, and the threats criticality (T). The second stage is the hand-over of
information of security threats that may lead to a violation of safety goals for
further safety analysis. This improves completeness of safety analysis in terms
of hazardous events initiated due to security attacks, related to the ISO 26262
requirement of analysis of 'foreseeable misuse'.

First step of the SAHARA approach to combining security and safety analysis
is to quantify the STRIDE security threats of the SuD in an analog manner as
done for safety hazards in the HARA approach. Therefore, we use the HARA
approach to quantify the STRIDE security threats of the SuD.

Table 1. Required Resource 'R' Classification - determination of 'R' value for required resources to exert threat

Level	Required resource	Example
0	no additional tool or everyday commodity	randomly using the user interface, strip fuse, key, coin, mobile phone
1	standard tool	screwdriver, multi-meter, multi-tool
2	simple tool	corrugated-head screwdriver, CAN sniffer, oscilloscope
3	advanced tools	debugger, flashing tools, bus communication simulators

Table 2. Required know-how 'K' Classification - determination of 'K' value for required know-how to exert threat

Level	Required know-how	Example
0	no prior knowledge (black-box approach)	average driver, unknown internals
1	technical knowledge (gray-box approach)	technician, basic understanding of internals
2	domain knowledge (white-box approach)	person with technical training and focused interests, internals disclosed

Table 1 classifies the **required resources -'R'** to threaten the SuDs security and gives some examples of tools required to successfully exert the security threat. Level 0 covers threats not requiring any tools at all or an everyday commodity, available even in unprepared situations. Level 1 tools can be found in any average household, while availability of level 2 tools is more limited (such as special workshops). Tools assigned to level 3 are advanced tools whose accessibility is very limited and are not wide-spread.

Table 2 does the same classification for the **required know-how -'K'**. Here level 0 requires no prior knowledge at all (the equivalent of black-box approach). Level 1 covers persons with technical skills and basic understanding of internals, representing the equivalent of gray-box approaches, while level 2 is tantamount to white-box approaches and represents persons with focused interests and domain knowledge.

An overview of the **criticality of a security threat -'T'** is given in Table 3. Level 0 indicates in this case a security irrelevant impact, such as raw data which can be visualized but whose meaning cannot be determined. The threat impact of level 1 threats is limited to annoying, maybe reduced, availability of services, but does not imply any damage of goods or manipulation of data or services;

Table 3. Threat criticality 'T' classification - determination of 'T' value of threat criticality

Level	Threat Criticality	Example
0	no security impact	no security relevant impact
1	moderate security relevance	annoying manipulation, partial reduced availability of service
2	high security relevance	damage of goods, invoice manipulation, non availability of service, possible privacy intrusion
3	high security and possible safety relevance	maximum security impact and life-threatening abuse possible

such threats belong to level 2. Level 3 threats imply privacy intrusion or impacts on human life (quality of life) as well as possible impacts on safety features.

$$
SecL = \begin{cases}
0 & \text{if } T = 0 \\
> 0 & \text{if } T = 3 \\
4 & \text{if } 5 - K - R + T \geq 7 \\
3 & \text{if } 5 - K - R + T = 6 \\
2 & \text{if } 5 - K - R + T = 5 \\
1 & \text{if } 5 - K - R + T = 4
\end{cases}
\tag{1}
$$

These three factors determine the resulting security level (SecL). The SecL determination is based on the ASIL determination approach and is calculated according to (1). A depiction of this SecL determination in matrix form is shown in Table 4.

The quantification of required know-how and tools instead of any likelihood estimation (e.g. of the attacks success or fail) is beneficial due to the fact that the classification of these factors is more common in the automotive domain and is more likely to remain the same over the whole life-time of the SuD. Besides this, the quantification of these two factors can be seen as equivalent to a likelihood estimation of an attack to be carried out. The quantification of the threats impact, on the one hand, determines whether the threat is also safety-related (threat level 3) or not (all others). An information which is handed over to the safety analysis method in the second stage of the SAHARA approach. On the other hand, this quantification enables the possibility of determining limits of resources spent to prevent the SuD from a specific threat (risk management for security threats). After this quantification these threats may then be adequately reduced or prevented by appropriate design and countermeasures.

In the case of safety-related security threats, the threat can be analyzed and resulting hazards evaluated according their controlability, exposure, and severity. This improves, as mentioned earlier in this document, the completeness

Table 4. SecL determination matrix - determination of the security level from R, K, and T values [8]

Required Resources 'R'	Required Know-How 'K'	Threat Level 'T'			
		0	1	2	3
0	0	0	3	4	4
	1	0	2	3	4
	2	0	1	2	3
1	0	0	2	3	4
	1	0	1	2	3
	2	0	0	1	2
2	0	0	1	2	3
	1	0	0	1	2
	2	0	0	0	1
3	0	0	0	1	2
	1	0	0	0	1
	2	0	0	0	1

of the required situation analysis of the HARA approach by implying factors of reasonably foreseeable misuse (security threats) in a more structured way.

4 Application of the Approach

This section describes the application of the SAHARA approach for an automotive battery management system (BMS). The BMS use-case is an illustrative material, reduced for training purpose of both students and engineers. Therefore, technology-specific details have been abstracted for commercial sensitivity and presented analysis results are not intended to be exhaustive.

BMS are control systems inside of high-voltage battery systems used to power electric or hybrid vehicles. The BMS consists of several input sensors, sensing e.g. cell voltages, cell temperatures, output current, output voltage, and actuators (the battery main contactors). Figure 2 depicts the general structure, main hardware components, and software modules of the high-voltage battery with BMS. The illustration shows the main features of a BMS:

- Power contactors - connection with vehicle HV system
- Interlock - de-energizing HV system when tripped
- CAN - automotive communication interface
- Relay - main contactor and output unit of the BMS
- Temperature sensors - feedback of actual cell temp
- Voltage/current sensors - feedback of actual cell voltages / current flows
- Fuse - protective circuit breaker in case of fault
- Cells - electro-chemical energy storage
- BMS controller - monitoring and control unit

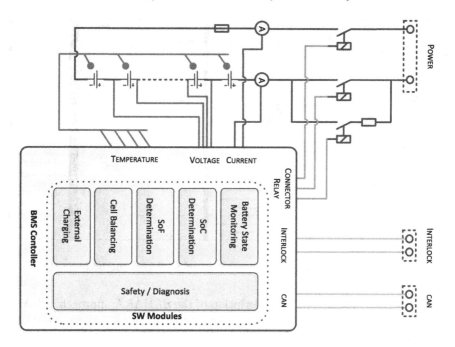

Fig. 2. Depiction of the general BMS use-case structure

Hazard description				Hazard classification				Safety goal description	
Hazard ID	Assumed Hazard	General Driving Situation	General Environment al Conditions	Severity 'S'	Exposure or Frequency 'E'	Controlability 'C'	Resulting ASIL	Safety Goal	Safe State
43	wrong estimation of driving / charging statues	parking	all	3	4	2	ASIL E	Estimate correct status of cycle (driving / charging)	Disconnect HV battery, driver warning
20	Short circuit outside of the battery	all	all	3	4	3	ASIL D	Manual main switch off must be possible	Disconnect HV battery, driver warning
11	Voltage shock of driver	Parking	all	3	4	3	ASIL D	Prevent from electric shock	Disconnect HV battery, driver warning
12	Voltage shock of driver	Driving	all	3	4	3	ASIL D	Prevent from electric shock	Disconnect HV battery, driver warning
23	failure to disconnect HV battery	accident	all	3	1	3	ASIL A	Prevent from electric shock	Disconnect HV battery, driver warning
25	unintende closing of HV connectors	accident	all	3	1	3	ASIL A	Prevent from electric shock	Disconnect HV battery, driver warning
26	unintende closing of HV connectors	repair	all	3	2	3	ASIL B	Prevent from electric shock	Disconnect HV battery, driver warning
44	HV battery filled with water	all	all	3	4	3	ASIL D	Prevent from electric shock	Disconnect HV battery, driver warning
50	HV system elements filled with water	any	car wash	3	3	3	ASIL C	Prevent from electric shock	Disconnect HV battery, driver warning

Fig. 3. Screenshot of a common HARA spreadsheet

The BMS is a safety related system intended for installation in series production passenger cars and therefore within the scope of ISO 26262. For this reason, ISO 26262 aligned development processes are required. For the scope of this work the focus is set on hazard analysis and risk assessment (HARA) to elaborate a functional safety concept, which has been done with the SAHARA approach.

Security Risk description					Security Risk classification				Security Goal
Security Hazard ID	STRIDE Function	Attack description	General Situation	attacker generated malfunction	Required Resources 'R'	Required Know-How 'K'	Threat Level 'T'	Resulting SecL	Security Goal
SH_1	Spoofing	spoofing of HV system ready signals	all	HV system ready without ensured overall system safety	2	2	3	1	Secure HV ready signal integrity
SH_2	Tampering	tampering of SoH	reselling	SoH is higher than in reality	3	2	2	0	no
SH_3	Tampering	tampering of SoH	reselling	SoH is higher than in reality	3	2	2	0	no
SH_4	Spoofing	spoofing actual sensor readings	all	extending safe operation areas of HV battery (temp, cell current, cell voltages)	1	1	3	3	ensure sensor signal integrity
SH_5	Denial of service	DoS communication with charger	charging	communication with charger jammed	3	2	3	0	no
SH_6	Denial of service	disconnecting of LV battery	all	immobilizing of driving functionality	1	1	2	2	prevent LV battery from being removed
SH_7	Denial of service	bypass manual emergency kill switch	all	emergency kill switch without function	1	2	3	2	enclosure emergency kill switch
SH_8	Denial of service	bypass battery fuse	all	replace fuse with non current limiting element	1	1	3	3	prevent HV battery fuse from being removed
SH_9	Spoofing	spoofing of HV isolation monitoring signals	all	HV system ready without ensured overall system safety	3	2	3	0	no

Fig. 4. Screenshot of application of SAHARA method

As already mentioned in the description of the SAHARA approach, a HARA safety analysis can be done in a conventional manner. Figure 3 shows a common spreadsheet approach for an ISO 26262 aligned HARA. As can be seen in this figure, a description of the hazard and the worst situation in which this hazard may occur is provided in a first step. This 'hazardous situation' is classified by an ASIL via severity, exposure, and controllability in step two. An high-level safety target (safety goal) and safety function (safe state) description concludes the conventional analysis.

In comparison, the SAHARA method, as an excerpt shows in Fig. 4, follows this concept. As first step the components of the system and their possible attack vector groups (taken from initial system design and STRIDE approach) used generate a list of possible attacks (see Fig. 4 column two and three). This list is refined with a general situation description in which this attack may be performed and the system service (high level service provided by the system, also from initial design phase) malfunction to which the attack will lead (see Fig. 4 column four and five). The first phase of the SAHARA method is concluded by the classification of the security risk by a SecL via resource, know-how, and threat level of the security attack. This SecL classification provides means for assigning adequate efforts to mitigate the security risk and also states high-level security requirements to close these attack vectors.

Figure 4 also shows a highlighting of threat levels 3. These security threats are handed over to the safety analysis for further analysis of their safety impact (step two of the SAHARA method).

An excerpt of the SAHARA analysis of the BMS use-case is shown in Fig. 5. The SAHARA of the BMS use-case covers 52 hazardous situations, quantifies the respective ASIL and assigns safety goals fully in line with the ISO 26262 standard. Additionally, 37 security threats have been identified using the STRIDE approach and quantified with their respective SecL. 18 security threats have

| Security Risk description | | | | | Security Risk | | | Security Risk related Safety goal description | | | | |
Security Hazard ID	STRIDE Function	Attack description	General Situation	attacker generated malfunction	Threat Level 'T'	Resulting SecL	Severity 'S'	Exposure 'E'	Controlability 'C'	Resulting ASIL	Safety Goal
SH_1	Spoofing	spoofing of HV system ready signals	all	HV system ready without ensured overall system safety	3	1	3	4	3	ASIL D	Prevent from electric shock
SH_4	Spoofing	spoofing actual sensor readings	all	extending safe operation areas of HV battery (temp, cell current, cell voltages)	3	3	2	4	3	ASIL C	Battery outgasing and fire shall be prevented
SH_5	Denial of service	DoS communication with charger	charging	communication with charger jammed	3	0	3	4	3	ASIL D	Battery outgasing and fire shall be prevented
SH_7	Denial of service	bypass manual emergency kill switch	all	emergency kill switch without function	3	2	3	4	2	ASIL C	Manual main switch off must be possible
SH_8	Denial of service	bypass battery fuse	all	replace fuse with non current limiting element	3	3	3	4	3	ASIL D	Battery outgasing and fire shall be prevented
SH_9	Spoofing	spoofing of HV isolation monitoring signals	all	HV system ready without ensured overall system safety	3	0	3	4	3	ASIL D	Detect short circuit and isolation faults, Prevent from electric shock
SH_12	Denial of service	bypass HVIL	all	bypass HVIL	3	2	3	4	3	ASIL D	Detect short circuit and isolation faults, Prevent from electric shock
SH_15	Denial of service	destroy battery containment	all	mechanical damage to battery containment	3	4	3	1	3	ASIL A	Prevent from electric shock
SH_17	Denial of service	bypassing of HV relais control signals	all	bypass HV relais control signals	3	2	3	4	3	ASIL D	Prevent from electric shock
SH_19	Spoofing	generating spoofed interlock signal for HV components	all	interlock spoofing	3	1	3	4	3	ASIL D	Prevent from electric shock

Fig. 5. Application of the SAHARA approach for the BMS use-case

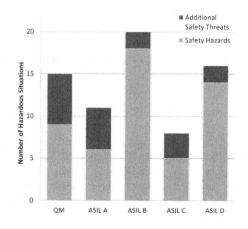

Fig. 6. Analysis of SAHARA approach for the BMS use-case - representation of safety hazards (identified with common HARA approach) plus additional hazards resulting from security threats (newly identified with SAHARA approach)

been classified as having possible impacts on safety goals and have therefore been further analyzed for their impacts on safety of the SuD. Figure 6 presents the number of hazardous situations which have been analyzed and quantified with ASILs and highlights the additional portion of additional safety hazards derived from security threats.

5 Conclusion

In conclusion, safety and security are two challenging research domains for future automotive systems. Although these two features have been treated separately it is becoming increasingly relevant to exploit commonalities and tackle safety and security development with concurrent methods.

This paper therefore presents an application of the SAHARA method for an automotive use-case. This safety-aware hazard analysis and risk assessment (SAHARA) approach combines the automotive HARA (hazard analysis and risk assessment) with the security domain STRIDE to trace impacts of security issues on safety goals on system level. The SAHARA approach is fully in line with the requirement of a HARA analysis from the automotive safety standard for road vehicles ISO 26262 [4] and implies a quantification scheme for security threats.

The feasibility and usefulness of the SAHARA approach for ISO 26262 aligned development has been demonstrated on a battery management system use-case. The application of the SAHARA approach identified 34 % more hazardous situations than the application of a traditional HARA approach. The applied approach conjointly combines concurrent safety and security co-development and supports the considerable overlap of in-place safety and security methods.

While the authors do not claim completeness of the analysis of the use-case (due to confidentiality issues), the benefits of the approach are already evident. First, the dependencies between safety and security analysis are made explicit and can be handed over from one domain to the other. Second, and maybe the most important, the proposed cooperative safety and security evaluation enables consolidation of the different system attributes in a consistent way and at an early design phase.

Acknowledgment. This work is partially supported by the INCOBAT and the MEM-CONS projects.

The research leading to these results has received funding from the European Unions Seventh Framework Programme (FP7/2007-2013) under grant agreement n 608988 and financial support of the "COMET K2 - Competence Centers for Excellent Technologies Programme" of the Austrian Federal Ministry for Transport, Innovation and Technology (BMVIT), the Austrian Federal Ministry of Economy, Family and Youth (BMWFJ), the Austrian Research Promotion Agency (FFG), the Province of Styria, and the Styrian Business Promotion Agency (SFG).

We are grateful for the contribution of the SOQRATES Safety AK experts and the expertise gained in SafEUr professional training.

Furthermore, we would like to express our thanks to our supporting project partners, AVL List GmbH, Virtual Vehicle Research Center, and Graz University of Technology

References

1. Bloomfield, R., Netkachova, K., Stroud, R.: Security-informed safety: if it's not secure, it's not safe. In: Gorbenko, A., Romanovsky, A., Kharchenko, V. (eds.) SERENE 2013. LNCS, vol. 8166, pp. 17–32. Springer, Heidelberg (2013)
2. Ebert, C., Jones, C.: Embedded software: facts, figures, and future. IEEE Comput. Soc. **42**(4), 42–52 (2009). ISSN: 0018-9162

3. Gashi, I., Povyakalo, A., Strigini, L., Matschnig, M., Hinterstoisser, T., Fischer, B.: Diversity for safety and security in embedded systems. In: International Conference on Dependable Systems and Networks, vol. 26, 06 2014
4. ISO - International Organization for Standardization. ISO 26262 Road vehicles Functional Safety Part 1–10 (2011)
5. van Tilborg, H.C.A., Jajodia, S. (eds.): Encyclopedia of Cryptography and Security. ISO/IEC 15408, 2nd edn. Springer, Heidelberg (2011)
6. Javaid, A.Y., Sun, W., Devabhaktuni, V.K., Alam, M.: Cyber security threat analysis and modeling of an unmanned aerial vehicle system. In: IEEE Conference on Technologies for Homeland Security (HST), pp. 585–590, November 2012
7. Kath, O., Schreiner, R., Favaro, J.: Safety, security, and software reuse: a model-based approach. In: Fourth International Workshop in Software Reuse and Safety Proceedings, September 2009
8. Macher, G., Sporer, H., Berlach, R., Armengaud, E., Kreiner, C.: SAHARA: a security-aware hazard and risk analysis method. In: 2015 Design, Automation Test in Europe Conference Exhibition (DATE), pp. 621–624, March 2015
9. Microsoft Corporation. The stride threat model (2005)
10. Paulitsch, M., Reiger, R., Strigini, L., Bloomfield, R.: Evidence-based security in aerospace. In: ISSRE Workshops 2012, 21–22 (2012)
11. Raspotnig, C., Katta, V., Karpati, P., Opdahl, A.L.: Enhancing CHASSIS: a method for combining safety and security. In: 2013 International Conference on Availability, Reliability and Security, ARES 2013, Regensburg, Germany, 2–6 September 2013, pp. 766–773 (2013)
12. Roth, M., Liggesmeyer, P.: Modeling and analysis of safety-critical cyber physical systems using state/event fault trees. In: SAFECOMP 2013 - Workshop DECS (ERCIM/EWICS Workshop on Dependable Embedded and Cyber-physical Systems) of the 32nd International Conference on Computer Safety, Reliability and Security (2013)
13. SAE International. Guidelines and Mehtods for Conductiong the Safety Assessment Process on Civil Airborne Systems and Equipment (1996)
14. SAE International. Guidelines for Development of Civil Aircraft and Systems (2010)
15. Schmidt, K., Troeger, P., Kroll, H., Buenger, T.: Adapted development process for security in networked automotive systems. In: SAE 2014 World Congress and Exhibition Proceedings, (SAE 2014-01-0334), pp. 516–526 (2014)
16. Schmittner, C., Gruber, T., Puschner, P., Schoitsch, E.: Security application of failure mode and effect analysis (FMEA). In: Bondavalli, A., Di Giandomenico, F. (eds.) SAFECOMP 2014. LNCS, vol. 8666, pp. 310–325. Springer, Heidelberg (2014)
17. Scuro, G.: Automotive industry: Innovation driven by electronics (2012). http://embedded-computing.com/articles/automotive-industry-innovation-driven-electronics/
18. Simion, C.P., Bucovtchi, O.M.C., Popescu, C.A.: Critical infrastructures protection through threat analysis framework. Ann. Oradea Univ. 1, 351–354 (2013)
19. Special Committee 205 of RTCA. DO-178C Software Considerations in Airborne Systems and Equipment Certification (2011)
20. Steiner, M., Liggesmeyer, P.: Combination of safety and security analysis - finding security problems that threaten the safety of a system. In: SAFECOMP 2013 - Workshop DECS (ERCIM/EWICS Workshop on Dependable Embedded and Cyber-Physical Systems) of the 32nd International Conference on Computer Safety, Reliability and Security (2013)

21. The Common Criteria Recognition Agreement Members. Common Criteria for Information Technology Security Evaluation (2014). http://www.commoncriteriaportal.org/
22. Ward, D., Ibara, I., Ruddle, A.: Threat analysis and risk assessment in automotive cyber security. In: SAE 2013 World Congress and Exhibition Proceedings, pp. 507–513 (2013)

Safety and Security Assessment of Behavioral Properties Using Alloy

Julien Brunel[✉] and David Chemouil

ONERA-DTIM, 2 Avenue Edouard Belin, BP 74025, 31055 Toulouse, France
{Julien.Brunel,David.Chemouil}@onera.fr

Abstract. In this paper, we propose a formal approach to supporting safety and security engineering, in the spirit of Model-Based Safety
Assessment, using the Alloy language. We first implement a system modeling framework, called Coy, allowing to model system architectures and
their behavior with respect to component failures. Then we illustrate
the use of Coy by defining a fire detection system example and analyzing some safety and security requirements. An interesting aspect of this
approach lies in the "declarative" style provided by Alloy, which allows
the lean specification of both the model and its properties.

1 Introduction

In the context of critical systems engineering, formal approaches have been used
for a long time with great successes. In particular, in order to support safety
analyses, an approach called Model-Based Safety Assessment (MBSA) [3] has
been proposed. The language AltaRica [1] and associated tools is one the main
techniques used in MBSA. It allows to model system architectures as a set of
communicating automata (one automaton per function or system, depending on
the level of abstraction retained for the system under study) and then to study
the impact of failure or erroneous events. Then, for instance, fault trees may
be generated, the impact of events can be simulated or some property can be
assessed exhaustively using a model-checker. Besides, some security properties
can also be addressed with the same kind of approach as the language is in fact
agnostic with respect to the nature of feared events.

Following earlier work, we propose here to address the question of safety
and security assessment using the Alloy language and the Alloy Analyzer free-
software tool. Alloy [9] is a formal modeling language amenable to automatic
analyses. Alloy has recently been used in the context of security assessment, for
instance to model JVM security constraints [11], access control policies [12], or
attacks in cryptographic protocols [10]. Besides, we proposed in earlier works a
study of the safety and security assessment of an avionic system supporting an
approach procedure [4–6].

Our motivation for relying on Alloy instead of, say, AltaRica is to take benefit
from the model-based aspect of Alloy and its expressiveness for the specification
of the properties to check. Indeed, Alloy allows to define metamodels easily,

© Springer International Publishing Switzerland 2015
F. Koornneef and C. van Gulijk (Eds.): SAFECOMP 2015 Workshops, LNCS 9338, pp. 251–263,
2015.
DOI: 10.1007/978-3-319-24249-1_22

which allows for instance to devise domain-specific metamodels. Here, as will be seen, we develop in Alloy a modeling framework called Coy which can be partly seen as the embedding of the general concepts of AltaRica into Alloy (ignoring concepts we do not need). Furthermore, with Alloy, the specification of the properties we check is expressed in relational first-order logic, with many features adapted to model-based reasoning.

With respect to our previous propositions around using Alloy for MBS&SA, we devise here a richer architectural framework and, more importantly, we formalize a notion of behavior so as to be able to check properties of the considered system along time.

Thus, this paper is organized as follows: in Sect. 2, we give a very brief account of Alloy. Then, in Sect. 3, we describe the Coy modeling framework that we implemented in Alloy to model system architectures and their behavior. We show how Alloy is well adapted to designing domain-specific metamodels and to getting some flexibility in the modeling of time and behavior. In Sect. 4, we illustrate our approach on a fire detection example that we model in Alloy following the Coy metamodel. In particular, we show how using Alloy allows to express "in one shot" properties ranging over a set of elements selected by navigating in the model structure.

2   Alloy in a Nutshell

Alloy is a formal modeling language that is well adapted to the following (non-exhaustive) list of activities: abstract modeling of a problem or of a system; production of a metamodel (model corresponding to a viewpoint); analysis of a model using well-formedness or formal semantic rules; automatic generation of an instance conforming to a model, possibly according to supplementary constraints; finding interesting instances of a model. Models designed in Alloy can deal with static aspects only, or integrate also dynamic aspects, so as to check behavioral properties.

We now give a brief glance at the main concepts of the language using a simple example. The most important type of declaration is that of a *signature* which introduces a structural concept. It may be seen as a class or entity in modeling parlance. A signature is interpreted as a set of possible instances; and it can also come with fields that may be seen, as a first approximation, as class attributes or associations.

```
sig Data { consumedBy : some System }
sig System {}
sig Criticality {
    concernedData : one Data,
    concernedSystem : one System
}
```

Here, we defined 3 concepts: Data, System and Criticality. Alloy advocates not to delve into unnecessary details and only give information on things we want to understand or analyze. Thus, here, a system is just defined to be a set of "things", but we do not say anything about the exact nature of its elements.

The keywords some or one give details on the multiplicity of the relation, as 1..* and 1 in UML. Here the field declarations mean that: every datum is consumed by at least one (some) system; every criticality concerns exactly one (one) data and one system. Other possible multiplicities are: lone which means at most one (0..1); and set which means any number (0..*).

Then, we can add constraints on possible instances of our model. For instance, we would like to state that every system consumes at least one datum. This can be done by writing additional facts (facts are axioms, so as few facts as possible should be stated in order to avoid over-specification):

```
fact {
    // every system consumes at least one datum
    all s : System | some consumedBy.s
    // for any system which consumes a given datum, the said datum and system
    // should belong to a same unique criticality
    all d : Data | all s : System | one c : Criticality |
        c.concernedData = d and c.concernedSystem = s
}
```

The . operator yields the join of two relations, matching the last column from the first one to the first column of the second one. Thus one may write d.consumedBy to get the systems consuming a data d, but also consumedBy.s to get the data consumed by the system s.

The formal foundation of Alloy is relational first order-logic, that is first-order logic extended with relational terms (including the transitive closure of a binary relation). Besides allowing navigation in models, this logic suffices to encode various models of time (*e.g.* to go from a linear to a tree view of time, or to give either an interleaving or a true-concurrency semantics).

Finally, although the language does not preclude unbounded verification in principle, in practice the Alloy Analyzer works only on *finite* models, reducing a given problem to a SAT instance the analysis of which is delegated to an off-the-shelf SAT solver. Then Alloy may be used to carry out some explorations (the command run builds instances that satisfy a given statement) or to check whether a given *assertion* is satisfied by all instances of the model (command check). Therefore, as analysis is sound but carried out on finite instances only, the Alloy Analyzer is able to find counter-examples *up to a certain bound* but it cannot prove the validity of an assertion. This is not a problem in our case because (1) the system architecture we consider is fixed in advance so its number of instances may not vary and (2) only time (*i.e.* the size of the time model) may be unbounded but, in our analyses, we do not aim at proving the absence of errors but rather that a bounded number of events does not lead to a feared situation (which induces that bounded time is sufficient).

3   The Coy Modeling Framework

We now present the Coy modeling framework, implemented as a metamodel in Alloy (*i.e.* a model where each signature is abstract and only instantiated in a second model corresponding to the system under study). We take inspiration in model-based safety assessment but our formalization is not specific to this sole family of properties.

As will be seen hereafter, Coy models essentially represent hierarchical structures of transition systems communicating instantaneously through data ports.

The overall structure of the framework is presented graphically in Fig. 1. Extension links are figured using black dashed arrows. As the metamodel contains n-ary relations with $n > 2$, the figure shows these after projection on parts of their domain (this is indicated using square brackets, as in conns[Port] for instance). Furthermore, the metamodel contains a Time signature: its purpose is that every signature field with Time as its last column can be conceptually seen as mutable field, *i.e.* its value may change (discretely) over time. Notice that the metamodel in Fig. 1 is projected over Time, hence it is not shown in the diagram.

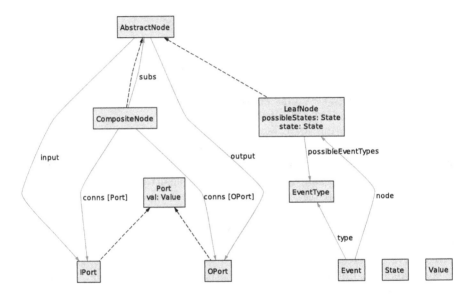

Fig. 1. Graphical depiction of the coy metamodel (projected over Time)

3.1   Composite Structure

Let us now delve into more details in the metamodel (in what follows, for the sake of readability, we do not show all Alloy facts enforcing the well-formedness of instance models or just classical properties). The basic architectural element is a *node*. Nodes are arranged hierarchically as a tree, so we use the classical *Composite* design pattern and devise a notion of AbstractNode which is inherited by signatures CompositeNode and LeafNode, the former pointing back to abstract nodes.

Every node comes with a set IPort of input ports and a set OPort of output ports. These sets are disjoint and every port belongs to a single node. Every port carries a value at every instant (possible values may differ for distinct ports).

Connections (between ports) are constrained so that they cannot cross a parent node boundary or many levels of composition. In other words, nodes are arranged as trees and connections can only happen between siblings or between a parent and a child. Furthermore, connected ports always carry the same value.

```
abstract sig Port { // a port carries one value at every instant
    val : Value one →Time }
abstract sig IPort, OPort extends Port {}
abstract sig AbstractNode { // input and output ports
    input : set IPort,
    output : set OPort }
abstract sig CompositeNode extends AbstractNode {
    // a composite node contains at least one sub−node
    subs : some AbstractNode,
    // port connections with siblings and between sub−nodes and this node
    conns : subs.@output →subs.@input +input →subs.@input
            +subs.@output →output,
} { // connected ports always carry the same value
    all t : Time, po, pi : Port | po→pi in conns implies po.val.t = pi.val.t
    // +other structural properties
    ... }
abstract sig LeafNode extends AbstractNode { ... }
```

3.2 Behavior

As Coy is mainly aimed at describing systems where atomic nodes are endowed with behavior, we now introduce a notion of state (for leaf nodes) and of events that may happen. One approach to deal with such models could be to rely on classical model-checkers, such as Spin [8] or NuSMV [7], the modeling languages of which are well-suited to describing transition systems. While this is of course a possibility, our aim with using Alloy is:

- to be able to easily adapt the Coy metamodel depending on the domain of study (e.g. to add a notion of connectors as in many architecture-description languages);
- as explained earlier, to change the model of time if need be (e.g. to go from a linear to a tree view of time, or to give either an interleaving or a true-concurrency semantics);
- and above all to allow the use of logic for specification, which brings two interesting aspects:
  1. it provides a single language to specify both models and expected properties;
  2. the logic allows for the expression of rather abstract properties (e.g. relying on under-specification) or to navigate through elements of a model to specify a given property in only one formula.

Thus, every leaf node is in one given state at any time (the set of possible states may vary for two different nodes). Besides, such nodes may undergo events. An event is an instance of an event type that happens at a certain instant and concerns a given node: this distinction between events and event types then allows to consider events of a certain type only, for instance to characterize their effects.

Notice also we impose the end-user to give, for any leaf node, the set of its possible states and the set of event types that concern it: this is a bit redundant from the theoretical point of view but it provides a sort of additional safety check akin to a poor man's typing that we deem important from a methodological point of view.

```
abstract sig LeafNode extends AbstractNode {
    possibleStates : some State,
    state : possibleStates one →Time,
    possibleEventTypes : set EventType,
}
abstract sig EventType {}
abstract sig Event { // event occurrence
    instant : one Time,
    node : one LeafNode,
    type : one EventType
} { type in node.possibleEventTypes }
```

Finally, as Alloy does not feature a native notion of time, we encode it by characterizing finite traces of instants. The fact accounting for this says how states change depending on events, at every instant.

```
fact traces { // if a node state changed, there was an event concerning this node
    all t : Time, t' : t.next, n : LeafNode {
        n.state.t ≠n.state.t' implies some e : Event {
            e.instant = t
            e.node = n } } }
```

4   Fire Detection Example

In this section, we provide an illustration of Coy with a fire detection system in facility such as, for example, an airport or a port.

4.1   Presentation of the System

The system consists of the following components: a *smoke detector* and a *heat detector*, which are part of the automatic *fire alarm system*; a manual *fire alarm pull station*; the *local firemen*, inside the facility; and the *city firemen*, in the nearest city.

The automatic fire alarm system, which is activated by either of the two detectors, directly calls the city firemen. The manual pull station, triggered by a human present on site, calls both the local and the city firemen.

We also represent two possible failures for each of the components: (1) the loss of a component: once a component is lost, it does not send any information, (2) an erroneous failure of a component: after this kind of failure, a component sends a corrupted data (in the case of a fire detector, for instance, it can be a false alarm or a false negative). Lastly, we represent three security threats: (1) intentional wrong activation of the pull station, (2) the deactivation of the smoke detector and (3) of the heat detector.

Notice that the loss of a component and the deactivation of the smoke detector (or of the heat detector) have the same effect on a component (the availability is not ensured) although they do not have the same nature (the former is a failure, the latter is a security threat). The same applies to an erroneous failure and the intentional wrong activation of the pull station, which both affect the integrity of the information. Nevertheless, it is important to distinguish between these failure and threat events in order to allow a pure safety analysis, a pure security analysis, and a combined analysis.

4.2   Coy Model

The Coy model of this system imports the Coy metamodel, declares signatures instances and relates them. Components of the system are modeled as Coy nodes. Figure 2 illustrates a particular instance of the fire detection model at a given instant. As can be seen, at this instant, all nodes are in the state OK and all ports yield a correct data (modeled by OKVal). The occurrence of an event of type failLoss (see the declaration of event types below) can be observed on the node pullStation.

Regarding the possible failures and threats mentioned above, we use the following event types, node states and possible values for the node ports.

```
one sig failLoss, failErr, threatBlock, threatPull extends EventType {}
one sig OK, Lost, Err extends State {}
one sig OKVal, LostVal, ErrVal extends Value {}
```

Then, we can declare the components and ports, as instances of the corresponding Coy concepts. For instance, here is the declaration of the fire pull station.

```
one sig pullStation extends LeafNode {} {
   input = none and output = oPullStation
   possibleStates = OK +Lost +Err and possibleEventTypes = failLoss +threatPull
}
```

The model also comprises axioms stating what happens to nodes depending on observed events. An interesting point here is that this description is declarative and does not depend on the effective nodes and ports. Concerning an event of type failLoss:

– the event can only occur on a node which is not in the state Lost,
– after the occurrence of the event, the node moves to the state Lost.

Here, we chose to model events of type **threatBlock** in the same way (the node also moves to the state Lost). So, they have the same effect (but they do not occur on the same components). In further analysis, if we want to distinguish between the effects of both kinds of events, we just have to use a specific node state and a specific port value corresponding to the occurrence of **threatBlock**.

The behavior of events of type **failErr** and **threatPull** are specified in a similar way.

```
fact behaviour {
  all e : Event | e.type in failLoss +threatBlock
      implies e.node.state.(e.instant) ≠Lost and e.node.state.(e.instant.next) = Lost
  all e : Event | e.type in failErr +threatPull
      implies e.node.state.(e.instant) = OK and e.node.state.(e.instant.next) = Err
}
```

The propagation of values is also described by an Alloy fact. For example, here is the description of the value propagation for leaf nodes with one input:

```
// leaf nodes w/ 1 input
all n : LeafNode, t : Time | {
    one n.output // tautology for this specific model, but useful if we extend it
    one n.input
} implies {
    n.state.t = OK implies n.output.val.t = n.input.val.t
    n.state.t = Err implies n.output.val.t = ErrVal
    n.state.t = Lost implies n.output.val.t = LostVal
}
```

4.3   Properties Verification

Now we can express the safety and security properties that we want to check as Alloy *assertions*. We have mainly expressed properties related to the consequence of some failures/threats or to the robustness of the system to a given number of failures/threats. For instance, the following assertion states that whenever the smoke detector is lost (and all other nodes are OK) then the firemen can still act.

```
assert smokeDetectorLoss {
  all t : Time | {
      all n : LeafNode − smokeDetector | n.state.t = OK
      smokeDetector.state.t = Lost
  } implies (localFiremen +CityFiremen).output.val.t = OKVal
}
```

The following assertion expresses that whenever the pull station is attacked, (and all other nodes are OK) then at least one firemen department is able to act.

```
assert pullStationThreatPull{
  all t : Time | {
      all n : LeafNode − heatDetector | n.state.t = OK
      heatDetector.state.t = Err
  } implies OKVal in (localFiremen +CityFiremen).output.val.t
}
```

Notice that the first-order quantifiers and the object-oriented syntax allows to navigate easily through the model and is convenient to state safety properties.

The following assertion expresses that whenever the smoke detector is erroneous and the pull station is attacked **threatPull**, then both local and city firemen are unable to act.

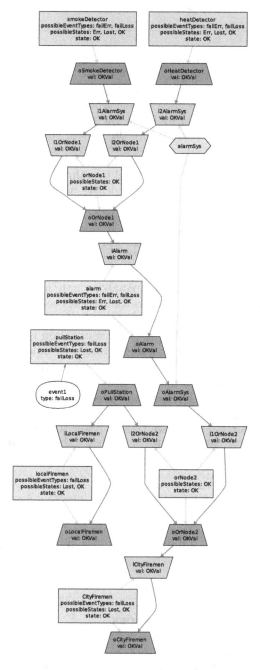

Fig. 2. Fire detection model example (see also Fig. 3 for following time steps); leaf nodes are beige rectangles, output ports are red trapeziums, input ports are green trapeziums and connections between ports are blue arrows (Color figure online).

```
assert smokeDetectorFailErrPullStationThreatPull {
  all t : Time | {
      all n : LeafNode − (smokeDetector +pullStation) | n.state.t = OK
      smokeDetector.state.t = Err
      pullStation.state.t = Err
    } implies OKVal not in (localFiremen +CityFiremen).output.val.t
}
```

The following assertions express the robustness of some parts of the system to possible failures/threats. We took benefit from the possibility to reason about a set cardinality in Alloy. Here, we count the number of events (corresponding to failures/threats) that occurred before the system enters a bad situation. For instance, the following assertion expresses that in order to make both local and city firemen unable to act properly, either the threat **threatPull** has occurred, or there has been at least two distinct failures/threats. Remark that it would have been also possible to reason independently about the number of failures and about the number of threats.

```
assert noSingleFailureThreatLeadsToFiremenNotOK {
  all t : Time | OKVal not in (localFiremen +CityFiremen).output.val.t
      implies some e : Event | e.type = threatPull and lt[e.instant, t]
          or let events = { e : Event | lt[e.instant, t] } | #events ≥ 2
}
```

In order to check assertions, Alloy Analyzer searches for counter-examples up to a certain bound (*i.e.* the counter-examples are such that their signatures have a cardinality less than the bound). The bound can be given by the user or chosen by the tool. In general, this bounded verification is thus incomplete: the tool may not find counter-examples whereas there are some. But in our case, the cardinality of all the signatures (**nodes**, **ports**, etc.) is fixed by the model itself. Therefore, the verification performed by Alloy Analyzer is complete.

The last four assertions have been validated by Alloy Analyzer (it does not find any counter-example).

The following assertion expresses that in order to make both local and city firemen unable to act, there has to be at least three failures/threats in the architecture.

```
assert noDoubleFailureThreatLeadsToFiremenNotOK {
  all t : Time | OKVal not in (localFiremen +CityFiremen).output.val.t
      implies let events = { e : Event | lt[e.instant, t] } | #events ≥ 3
}
```

This last assertion is not satisfied by the model. Alloy Analyzer exhibits a counter-example where the pull station and the city firemen are lost after two events (Fig. 2 shows the first time step of this counter-example, Fig. 3 shows the next time steps).

5   Conclusion and Future Work

In this article, we presented a framework, called Coy, to model and assess safety and security properties of behavioral models. We have chosen to embed it in Alloy so that we can benefit from its model-based features and its expressiveness for the specification of the properties to check. A Coy model essentially describes transition systems communicating through data ports (note that other means of communication, such as synchronization of transitions, are also possible).

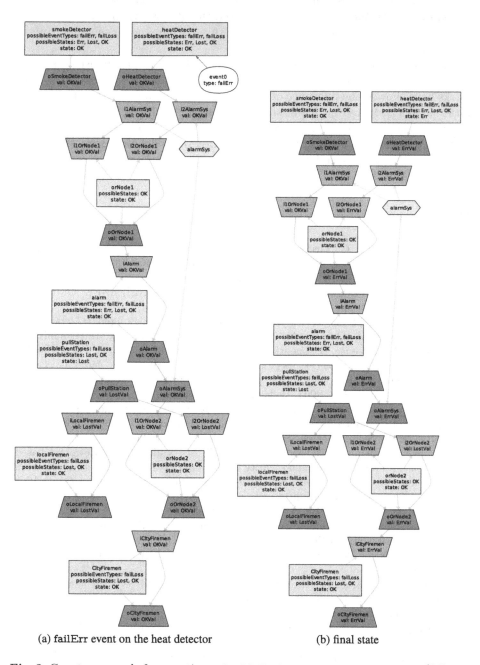

(a) failErr event on the heat detector   (b) final state

Fig. 3. Counter-example for assertion `noDoubleFailureLeadsToFiremenNotOK` (follow-up from Fig. 2)

We illustrated Coy through an example of a fire detection system, and showed it is suited to the specification of failures and threats propagation along the system. We were able to check properties over this system, and to generate counter examples for the violated properties.

In this work, the security aspects are not developed (we have just considered three threats that have the same kind of effects as failures). However, recent works have showed the relevance of Alloy to assess more advanced security properties [6,10,11]. Moreover, it was shown that using AltaRica, one can specify the effect of richer security threats over a system architecture [2] and check related security properties. This is in favor of using Coy to model and assess security of more complex systems architectures, where both concerns are rich and interact with each other.

References

1. Arnold, A., Point, G., Griffault, A., Rauzy, A.: The altarica formalism for describing concurrent systems. Fundam. Informaticae 40(2,3), 109–124 (1999)
2. Bieber, P., Brunel, J.: From safety models to security models: preliminary lessons learnt. In: Bondavalli, A., Ceccarelli, A., Ortmeier, F. (eds.) SAFECOMP 2014. LNCS, vol. 8696, pp. 269–281. Springer, Heidelberg (2014)
3. Bozzano, M., Villafiorita, A., Aakerlund, O., Bieber, P., Bougnol, C., Böde, E., Bretschneider, M., Cavallo, A., Castel, C., Cifaldi, M., Cimatti, A., Griffault, A., Kehren, C., Lawrence, B., Luedtke, A., Metge, S., Papadopoulos, C., Passarello, R., Peikenkamp, T., Persson, P., Seguin, C., Trotta, L., Valacca, L., Zacco, G.: Esacs: an integrated methodology for design and safety analysis of complex systems. In: Proceedings of ESREL 2003. Balkema publisher (2003)
4. Brunel, J., Chemouil, D., Mélédo, N., Ibanez, V.: Formal modelling and safety analysis of an avionic functional architecture with alloy. In: Embedded Real Time Software and Systems (ERTSS 2014), Toulouse, France (2014)
5. Brunel, J., Chemouil, D., Rioux, L., Bakkali, M., Vallée, F.: A viewpoint-based approach for formal safety and security assessment of system architectures. In: 11th Workshop on Model-Driven Engineering, Verification, and Validation (MoDeVVa 2014) hosted by MODELS 2014, vol. 1235 of CEUR-WS, pp. 39–48 (2014)
6. Brunel, J., Rioux, L., Paul, S., Faucogney, A., Vallée, F.: Formal safety and security assessment of an avionic architecture with alloy. In: Proceedings Third International Workshop on Engineering Safety and Security Systems (ESSS 2014), vol. 150 of Electronic Proceedings in Theoretical Computer Science (EPTCS), pp. 8–19 (2014)
7. Cimatti, A., Clarke, E., Giunchiglia, F., Roveri, M.: NUSMV: a new symbolic model verifier. In: Halbwachs, N., Peled, D.A. (eds.) CAV 1999. LNCS, vol. 1633, pp. 495–499. Springer, Heidelberg (1999)
8. Holzmann, G.J.: The model checker spin. IEEE Trans. Softw. Eng. 23(5), 279–295 (1997)
9. Jackson, D.: Software Abstractions: Logic, Language, and Analysis. The MIT Press, Cambridge (2006)
10. Lin, A., Bond, M., Clulow, J.: Modeling partial attacks with ALLOY. In: Christianson, B., Crispo, B., Malcolm, J.A., Roe, M. (eds.) Security Protocols 2007. LNCS, vol. 5964, pp. 20–33. Springer, Heidelberg (2010)

11. Reynolds, M.C.: Lightweight modeling of java virtual machine security constraints. In: Frappier, M., Glässer, U., Khurshid, S., Laleau, R., Reeves, S. (eds.) ABZ 2010. LNCS, vol. 5977, pp. 146–159. Springer, Heidelberg (2010)
12. Toahchoodee, M., Ray, I.: Using alloy to analyse a spatio-temporal access control model supporting delegation. Inf. Secur. IET **3**(3), 75–113 (2009)

Combining MILS with Contract-Based Design for Safety and Security Requirements

Alessandro Cimatti[1], Rance DeLong[2], Davide Marcantonio[1], and Stefano Tonetta[1]([✉])

[1] FBK-irst, Trento, Italy
{cimatti,marcantonio,tonettas}@fbk.eu
[2] The Open Group, Reading, UK
r.delong@opengroup.org

Abstract. The distributed MILS (D-MILS) approach to high-assurance systems is based on an architecture-driven end-to-end methodology that encompasses techniques and tools for modeling the system architecture, contract-based analysis of the architecture, automatic configuration of the platform, and assurance case generation from patterns. Following the MILS ("MILS" was originally an acronym for "Multiple Independent Levels of Security". Today, we use "MILS" as a proper name for an architectural approach and an implementation framework, promulgated by a community of interested parties, and elaborated by ongoing MILS research and development efforts.) paradigm, the architecture is pivotal to define the security policy that is to be enforced by the platform, and to design safety mechanisms such as redundancies or failures monitoring. In D-MILS we enriched these security guarantees with formal reasoning to show that the global system requirements are met provided local policies are guaranteed by application components. We consider both safety-related and security-related requirements and we analyze the decomposition also taking into account the possibility of component failures. In this paper, we give an overview of our approach and we exemplify the architecture-driven paradigm for design and verification with an example of a fail-secure design pattern.

Keywords: MILS · Contract-based design · Safety and security · Formal verification

1 Introduction

The *MILS architectural approach* [6] to the design and implementation of critical systems involves two principal phases: the development of an abstract architecture intended to achieve the stated purpose, and the implementation of that architecture on a robust technology platform. During the first phase, essential properties are identified that the system is expected to exhibit, and the contributions to the achievement of those properties by the architectural structure and by the behavioural attributes of key components are analyzed and justified.

© Springer International Publishing Switzerland 2015
F. Koornneef and C. van Gulijk (Eds.): SAFECOMP 2015 Workshops, LNCS 9338, pp. 264–276, 2015.
DOI: 10.1007/978-3-319-24249-1_23

Safety and security are more and more intertwined problems. The potential impact of security threats on safety-critical systems is increasing due to the interconnections of systems. Safety, security, and dependability are emergent behavioural properties of a system interacting with its environment. The MILS approach leverages system architecture to support vital system-level properties. The architecture reflects an intended pattern of information flow and causality referred to as the *policy architecture*, while key components of the architecture enforce *local policies* through specific behavioural properties. By reasoning compositionally over the components about the policy architecture and the local policies, many useful system-level properties may be established.

The *MILS platform* provides the technology for the concrete realisation of an abstract system architecture. A *separation kernel* [31,33], the underlying foundational component of the MILS platform, is used to establish and enforce the system architecture according to its configuration data.

The assurance of a system's properties depends not only on the analysis of its design but on the correct implementation and deployment of that design. The configuration of the separation kernel must faithfully implement the specified architecture. This is guaranteed by the *MILS platform configuration compiler* that is driven by a model of the architecture and the constraints of the target platform to synthesize viable and semantically correct configuration data corresponding to the specified architecture.

In this paper, we give an overview of the integration of the MILS approach with contract-based reasoning developed in the D-MILS project [1]. The approach relies on the OCRA tool [13] to formally prove that the global system requirements are met, provided local policies are guaranteed by application components. We consider both safety-related and security-related requirements and we analyze the decomposition also taking into account the possibility of component failures. We exemplify the architecture-driven approach on the Starlight Interactive Link example [5], extended with a safety mechanism in order to take into account the possibility of component failures.

The rest of the paper is organized as follows: in Sect. 2, we give an overview of D-MILS project; in Sect. 3, we detail how the MILS approach has been extended with a contract-based design of the architecture and the related tool support; in Sect. 4, we describe how we extended the Starlight example and the related analysis of contract refinement; in Sect. 5, we give an overview of the related work, while we conclude in Sect. 6.

2   Overview of D-MILS

The D-MILS concept extends the capacity of MILS to implement a single unified policy architecture to a network of separation kernels [28,29]. To accomplish this, each separation kernel is combined with a new MILS foundational component, the *MILS networking system* (MNS), producing the effect of a distributed separation kernel. In the D-MILS Project [1] we have employed *Time-Triggered Ethernet* (TTE) [32] as the MILS "backplane", permitting us to extend the

robustness and determinism benefits of a single *MILS node* to the network of
D-MILS nodes, referred to as the *distributed MILS platform*[1] [26, 27].

Since D-MILS systems are intended for critical applications, assurance of the
system's critical properties is a necessary byproduct of its development. In such
applications, evidence supporting the claimed properties must often be presented
for consideration by objective third-party system certifiers. To achieve assurance
requires diligence at all phases of design, development, and deployment; and, at
all levels of abstraction: from the abstract architecture to the details of configuration and scheduling of physical resources within each separation kernel and
within the TTE interfaces and switches. Correct operation of the deployed system depends upon the correctness of the configuration details, of the component
composition, of key system components[2], and of the D-MILS platform itself.
Configuration is particularly challenging, because the scalability that D-MILS is
intended to provide causes the magnitude of the configuration problem to scale
as well. The concrete configuration data and scheduling details of the numerous
separation kernels and of the TTE are at a very fine level of granularity, and
must be complete, correct, and coherent.

The only reasonable prospect of achieving these various aspects of correctness, separately and jointly, is through pervasive and coordinated automation as
embodied in the D-MILS tool chain. Inputs to the tool chain include, a declarative model of the system expressed in our own MILS dialect of the Architecture Analysis and Design Language (AADL) [18], facts about the target hardware platform, properties of separately developed system components, designer-
imposed constraints and system property specifications, and human guidance
to the construction of the assurance case. Components of the tool chain perform parsing of the languages [19], transformations among the various internal
forms [20, 21], analysis and verification [24], configuration data synthesis and
rendering [25], and pattern-based assurance case construction [22, 23]. Outputs
of the tool chain include, proofs of specified system properties, configuration
data for the D-MILS platform, and an assurance case expressed in Goal Structuring Notation (GSN) [2]. We say that D-MILS provides not only a robust and
predictable platform for system implementation, but also an end-to-end and
top-to-bottom method supported by extensive automation.

3   Architecture-Driven Integration of the MILS Approach and Contract-Based Design

In this paper we focus on the integration of the MILS architectural approach with
contract-based design and analysis. Both MILS and contract-based approaches

---

[1] Our D-MILS Platform is composed of the LynxSecure Separation Kernel from Lynx
Software Technologies, France, and TTE from TTTech, Austria.

[2] The D-MILS Project regards proof of component correctness to a specification as a
"solved problem" and focusses on the correctness of the composition of components'
specifications, and of the configuration of the D-MILS platform.

focus on architecture, and do so in a complementary way. MILS regards information flow policy as an abstraction of architecture, and seeks to maximize the correspondence between architectural structure and the desired information flow policy of a system, which may rely on the behavior of key components to enforce local policies that further restrict the maximal information flow permitted by the architecture. The contract-based approach employs formalization and a method to prove that the architecture decomposition represented in the set of contracts of the components is a proper refinement of the system requirements. Contracts specify the properties that the components individually, and the system as a whole, are expected to guarantee, and the assumptions that their respective environments must meet. Formal verification techniques are used to check that the derivation of the local policies from the system requirements is correct.

An architecture is only as valuable as the integrity of its components and connections. Recognizing the importance of integrity, MILS provides an implementation platform that can be configured to the "shape" of the architecture by initializing it with specific configuration data compiled to embody the global information flow policy.

The two methods are complementary and their combination yields a strong result. The contract-based method proves that the composition of components that satisfy their contracts will meet the system requirements, provided that their integrity is protected. The MILS platform guarantees the integrity of components and their configured connections, preventing interference that could cause a verified component to fail to satisfy its contract[3].

In Fig. 1, we show the approach applied to an abstract example. The system A is decomposed into subsystems B and C, and B in turn is decomposed into D and E. Each component is enriched with a contract (represented here by green scrolls). If the contract refinement is correct, we have associated with the architecture a formal proof that the system is correct provided that the leaf components (D, E, and C) satisfy their contracts. Namely, if D and E satisfy their contracts ($D \models P_D, E \models P_E$) and the contract refinement of B is correct ($\gamma_B(P_D, P_E) \preceq P_B$), then the composition of D and E satisfies the contract of B ($\gamma_B(D, E) \models P_B$). Moreover, if C satisfies its contract ($C \models P_C$) and the contract refinement of A is correct ($\gamma_A(P_B, P_C) \preceq P_A$), then the composition of B and C satisfies the contract of A ($\gamma_A(B, C) \models P_A$).

In MILS terms, the architecture defines three subjects (D, E and C) and prescribes that the only allowed communications must be the ones between D and E and between E and C. This is translated into a configuration for the D-MILS platform (taking into account other deployment constraints in terms of available resources), which in this example encompasses two MILS nodes.

3.1 Tool Support for Contract-Based Reasoning

In D-MILS, the architecture is specified in a variant of AADL, called MILS-AADL, similar to the SLIM language developed in the COMPASS project [7].

---

[3] For the purpose of our work we assume that components can be constructed and verified to satisfy their contracts.

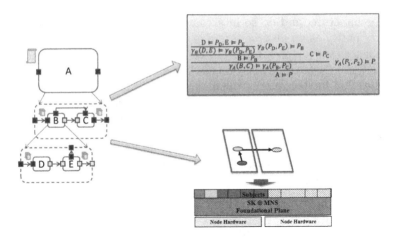

Fig. 1. The architecture is used for (1) formal reasoning to prove that the system requirements are assured by the local policies, (2) configuration of the platform to ensure the global information flow policy and the integrity of the architecture.

The COMPASS tool set has been extended in order to support the new language and to enrich the components with annotations that specify different verification properties such as contracts. The language used to specify the component contracts is the one provided by the OCRA tool [13]. It consists of a textual human-readable version of a First-Order Linear-time Temporal Logic. The logic has been extended in D-MILS to support uninterpreted functions, i.e. functional symbols that do not have a specific interpretation but are used to abstract procedures and the related results (such as CRC checksum or encryption), or to label data with user-defined tags (such as "is_high" or "low-level", etc.).

Such a very expressive language required the development of effective techniques to reason about the contracts. To this purpose the engine undertakes to prove the contract refinement. The refinement is first translated by OCRA into a set of entailment problems in temporal logic. nuXmv [11] translates this into a liveness model-checking problem with a classic automata-theoretic approach [37]. The resulting problem requires proving that a certain liveness condition can be visited only finitely many times along an (infinite) execution. This problem is in turn reduced to proving an invariant on the reachable states with the K-liveness techniques described in [17]. This has been extended to infinite-state systems and to take into account real-time aspects in [15]. Finally, the invariant is proved with an efficient combination of induction-based reasoning, explicit-state search, and predicate abstraction, extending the IC3 algorithm [9] to the infinite-state case, as described in [14].

4   Starlight Example

4.1   Architecture

In this section, we exemplify the approach on an example taken from the literature [5,12]. The Starlight Interactive Link is a dispatching device developed by the Australian Defense Science and Technology Organization to allow users to establish simultaneous connections to high-level (classified) and low-level networks. The idea is that the device acts as a switch that the user can control to dispatch the keyboard output to either a high-level server or to a low-level server. The user can use the low-level server to browse the external world, send messages, or have data sent to the high-level server for later use.

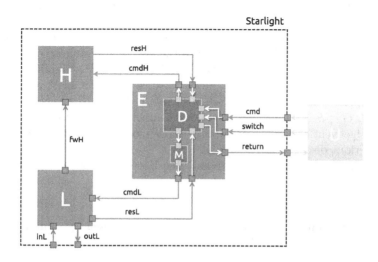

Fig. 2. Architecture of the D-MILS Starlight example.

Figure 2 shows the architecture of the Starlight Interactive Link as formalized in D-MILS. The components H and L represent respectively the high-level and low-level networks. The low-level network can exchange information with the external world. The component D represents the Starlight device, which receives commands from the user and dispatches the commands to H or to L based on an internal state. The state is changed with two *switch* commands, namely *switch_to_low* and *switch_to_high*. The original architecture has only the blue components, with D in place of E. We extended this architecture with a safety mechanism to make the system "fail-secure" with respect to failures of the dispatcher: the dispatcher is extended with a monitor M; the communication of the dispatcher to L is filtered by M that in case of failure of D blocks the communication. To avoid confusion we refer to the actual device that is filtered by M as the dispatcher (D), while to the component consisting of D and M as the extended dispatcher E.

4.2   System Contract

The architecture has been enriched with contracts that formalize the functional requirements to ensure that the system responds correctly to the user commands, and the security requirement that there is no leakage of high-level data. Here, we focus on the latter, which says:

Req-Sys-secure: No high-level data shall be sent by L to the external world.
  The architecture ensures Req-Sys-secure assuming the following requirement on the user:
Req-User-secure: The user shall switch the dispatcher to high before entering high-level data.
  Moreover, we consider the following safety requirement:
Req-Sys-safe: No single failure shall cause a loss of Req-Sys-secure.

We formalized the requirements of the system and of the components using OCRA contracts. In the following, we use the concrete syntax accepted by the tool. We briefly clarify the used notation: "and", "or", "not", "implies" are standard Boolean operators; "always", "never", "since", "in the past" are standard temporal operators of LTL with past also referred to with the mathematical notation G, $G\neg$, S, O; "last_data" is a built function to refer to the last data passed by the event of a event data port; italics names refer to ports or uninterpreted functions declared in the model.

The requirements Req-Sys-secure and Req-User-secure have been formalized into the FO-LTL formulas:

Formal-Sys-secure: never *is_high*(last_data(*outL*))
Formal-User-secure: always   ((*is_high*(last_data(*cmd*)))   implies   ((not *switch_to_low*) since *switch_to_high*))

Note that the formalization of Req-User-secure improves the informal requirement, which is not precise. A literal formalization would be:

Formal-User-secure-wrong: always ((*is_secure*(last_data(*cmd*))) implies (in the past *switch_to_high*))

but this is wrong, because we have to ensure that the last switch was a *switch_to_high*, without a more recent *switch_to_low*[4]. We can actually improve the informal requirement as:

Req-User-secure-new: Whenever the user sends commands with high data, she shall previously issue a *switch_to_high* and no *switch_to_low* since the last *switch_to_high*.

which is formalized by Formal-User-secure.

---

[4] As suggested by one of the reviewers, in an alternative model, we could use only one event data instead of two switch events and ensure that the last switch was low.

Note that while Req-Sys-secure is a requirement on the implementation of the Starlight system, Req-User-secure is actually a requirement on its environment (the user). This is reflected by the system contract specification, which sets Formal-Sys-secure as the guarantee and Formal-User-secure as the assumption of the system contract.

4.3   Component Contracts

The dispatcher ensures the system security requirement with the following local requirement:

Req-D-low-mode: The dispatcher shall send commands to L only if the last switch was a *switch_to_low* and the input command has been received after.

formalized into:

Formal-D-low-mode: always $(cmdL$ implies $(((\text{not } switch\_to\_high)$ since $switch\_to\_low)$ and $((\text{not } switch\_to\_low)$ since $cmd)))$

In order to fulfill requirement Req-Sys-safe, we also filter the commands to L by a monitor M, which has a requirement **Req-M-low-mode** identical to Req-D-low-mode, and formalized in the same way. Thus, D passes also the switches to the monitor and must ensure the following requirement:

Req-D-fw-switch: Whenever the dispatcher receives a *switch_to_high*, it shall pass it to M before doing any other actions and it sends a *switch_to_low* to M only if the last received switch was a *switch_to_low*.

formalized into:

Formal-D-fw-switch: always $((switch\_to\_high$ implies $((\text{not } (cmdH$ or $cmdL$ or $return$ or $monitor\_switch\_to\_low))$ until $monitor\_switch\_to\_high))$ and $(monitor\_switch\_to\_low$ implies $((\text{not } switch\_to\_high)$ since $switch\_to\_low)))$;

Finally, in order to make the refinement correct, we must require all components to not invent high data. We express this by requiring that D, M, and L only pass the data that they have received. Thus, for D, we require that:

Req-D-data: D shall pass to $cmdL$ only the data that has been received with last cmd.

formalized into:

Formal-D-data: always $((cmdL$ implies $((\text{in the past } cmd)$ and $(\text{last\_data}(cmdL) = \text{last\_data}(cmd)))))$

The requirements **Req-M-data** and **Req-L-data**, of M and L respectively, are analogous. Note that these formulas are actually guarantees of corresponding contracts, without assumptions (i.e. assumptions equal to *true*).

4.4   Analysis Results

Given the above contract specifications, OCRA can prove the system Req-Sys-secure assuming Req-User-secure is correctly refined by the contracts of D, M, and L (see [16] for more details on the technique). One can also show that by using Formal-User-secure-wrong instead of Formal-User-secure the refinement is not correct and yields a counterexample trace execution.

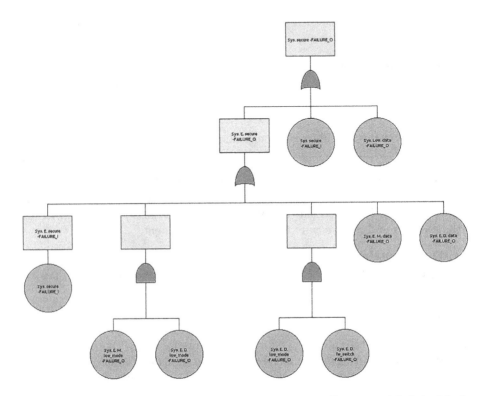

Fig. 3. Fault-tree generated from the contract refinement. Events are labeled with the name of the component instance followed by the name of the contract, followed either by FAILURE_O, which represents the failure of the component to satisfy the contract, or by FAILURE_I, which represents the failure of the component environment to satisfy the contract assumption.

In order to prove Req-Sys-safe, we use OCRA to produce a fault tree showing the dependency of the system failure on the failure of the components (see [8] for more details on the technique). The generated fault tree is exhibited in Fig. 3. It shows that neither Req-D-low-mode nor Req-M-low-mode are single points of failure. Instead, Req-D-data, Req-M-data, Req-L-data are single points of failure. While the failure of Req-L-data does not represent real threats since L never receives high data, the failure of Req-D-data and Req-M-data could result in D or M sending information that had been temporary stored in a buffer used for handling multiple requests or in a cache for improving performance. This can be solved for example by ensuring that such memories are deleted before every *switch_to_low* is completed.

5   Related Work

Security-by-contract is an approach proposed in [30] to increase the trust in code downloaded on mobile applications. The work proposes a framework where downloaded code can be checked according to a security contract. With respect to this work, there is no focus on the system architecture, the refinement of contracts, or safety analysis taking into account component failures.

Information flow contracts are supported in SPARK, a safety-critical subset of Ada [3,4]. The SPARK contracts are specified at software level on procedures. So, in principle, they are complementary to our approach, which focuses more on the system-level architecture. As for future work, we will consider to extend the approach with information flow contracts. Currently, the information flow can be specified only at coarse level with the connections in the architecture. To our knowledge, there are no works combining SPARK information flow contracts with safety analysis.

In [10], an avionic case-study architecture is formalized in Alloy and analyzed with respect to safety and security requirements. Similarly to our approach, first-order logic is used to formalize the requirements, although Alloy does not support temporal operators. The case study formalizes also security attacks that are not present in our example. Different to our approach, the failures and security attacks are explicitly modeled, while in our case we exploit a feature of OCRA to automatically inject the failures starting from the nominal contract specification. Our conjecture is that the same case study of [10] can be formalized in MILS-AADL or directly in OCRA with the possibility of checking contract refinement and performing contract-based fault-tree analysis.

Another case study on validation of safety and security requirements has been presented in [35], but it focuses on testing.

Fault trees and FMEA have been extended in [34,36] to consider also security aspects. Different to our approach and other model-based safety analysis techniques, these works are not based on the automatic generation of fault trees and FMEA tables from the system design.

6   Conclusions

In this paper, we briefly overview the approach to safety and security undertaken in D-MILS and we describe a small example of the D-MILS approach to the verification of the system architecture with respect to safety and security requirements. The example is based on the Starlight device that switches commands between high-level and low-level servers. The requirements of the system and its components have been formalized using OCRA contracts, their refinement has been verified and analyzed taking into account the failure of components. This is a preliminary application of the methodology, which will be further evaluated in the D-MILS project demonstrators. In the future, we would like to integrate contracts and their analysis with finer-grained information flow properties as do the SPARK contracts discussed in [3,4].

Acknowledgments. This work was performed on the D-MILS project ("Distributed MILS for Dependable Information and Communication Infrastructures", European Commission FP7 ICT grant no. 318772), with our partners fortiss, Verimag, RWTH Aachen, U of York, Frequentis, Lynx, TTTech, and INRIA, funded partially under the EC's Seventh Framework Programme.

References

1. D-MILS Project. http://www.d-mils.org/
2. GSN community standard. Technical report, Origin Consulting (York) Limited (2011)
3. Amtoft, T., Hatcliff, J., Rodríguez, E.: Precise and automated contract-based reasoning for verification and certification of information flow properties of programs with arrays. In: Gordon, A.D. (ed.) ESOP 2010. LNCS, vol. 6012, pp. 43–63. Springer, Heidelberg (2010)
4. Amtoft, T., Hatcliff, J., Rodríguez, E., Robby, Hoag, J., Greve, D.: Specification and checking of software contracts for conditional information flow. In: Hardin, D.S. (ed.) Design and Verification of Microprocessor Systems for High-Assurance Applications, pp. 229–245. Springer, New York (2010)
5. Anderson, M., North, C., Griffin, J., Milner, R., Yesberg, J., Yiu, K.: Starlight: interactive link. In: 12th Annual Computer Security Applications Conference, pp. 55–63 (1996)
6. Boettcher, C., DeLong, R., Rushby, J., Sifre, W.: The MILS component integration approach to secure information sharing. In: 27thAIAA/IEEE Digital Avionics Systems Conference, St. Paul, MN, October 2008
7. Bozzano, M., Cimatti, A., Katoen, J., Nguyen, V.Y., Noll, T., Roveri, M.: Safety, dependability and performance analysis of extended AADL models. Comput. J. **54**, 754–775 (2011)
8. Bozzano, M., Cimatti, A., Mattarei, C., Tonetta, S.: Formal safety assessment via contract-based design. In: Cassez, F., Raskin, J.-F. (eds.) ATVA 2014. LNCS, vol. 8837, pp. 81–97. Springer, Heidelberg (2014)
9. Bradley, A.R.: SAT-based model checking without unrolling. In: Jhala, R., Schmidt, D. (eds.) VMCAI 2011. LNCS, vol. 6538, pp. 70–87. Springer, Heidelberg (2011)
10. Brunel, J., Rioux, L., Paul, S., Faucogney, A., Vallée, F.: Formal safety and security assessment of an avionic architecture with alloy. In: ESSS, pp. 8–19 (2014)
11. Cavada, R., Cimatti, A., Dorigatti, M., Griggio, A., Mariotti, A., Micheli, A., Mover, S., Roveri, M., Tonetta, S.: The NUXMV symbolic model checker. In: Biere, A., Bloem, R. (eds.) CAV 2014. LNCS, vol. 8559, pp. 334–342. Springer, Heidelberg (2014)
12. S. Chong and R. Van Der Meyden, Using architecture to reason about information security (2014). arXiv preprint arXiv:1409.0309

13. Cimatti, A., Dorigatti, M., Tonetta, S.: OCRA: a tool for checking the refinement of temporal contracts. In: ASE, pp. 702–705 (2013)
14. Cimatti, A., Griggio, A., Mover, S., Tonetta, S.: IC3 modulo theories via implicit predicate abstraction. In: Ábrahám, E., Havelund, K. (eds.) TACAS 2014 (ETAPS). LNCS, vol. 8413, pp. 46–61. Springer, Heidelberg (2014)
15. Cimatti, A., Griggio, A., Mover, S., Tonetta, S.: Verifying LTL properties of hybrid systems with K-LIVENESS. In: Biere, A., Bloem, R. (eds.) CAV 2014. LNCS, vol. 8559, pp. 424–440. Springer, Heidelberg (2014)
16. Cimatti, A., Tonetta, S.: Contracts-refinement proof system for component-based embedded systems. Sci. Comput. Program. **97**, 333–348 (2015)
17. Claessen, K., Sörensson, N.: A liveness checking algorithm that counts. In: FMCAD, pp. 52–59 (2012)
18. Specification of MILS-AADL. Technical report D2.1, Version 2.0, D-MILS Project, July 2014. http://www.d-mils.org/page/results
19. D2.2 translation of mils-aadl into formal architectural modeling framework. Technical report D2.2, Version 1.2, D-MILS Project, February 2014. http://www.d-mils.org/page/results
20. Intermediate languages and semantics transformations for distributed mils - part 1. Technical report D3.2, Version 1.2, D-MILS Project, February 2014. http://www.d-mils.org/page/results
21. Intermediate languages and semantics transformations for distributed mils - part 2. Technical report D3.3, Version 1.0, D-MILS Project, July 2014. http://www.d-mils.org/page/results
22. Compositional assurance cases and arguments for distributed mils. Technical report D4.2, Version 1.0, D-MILS Project, April 2014. http://www.d-mils.org/page/results
23. Integration of formal evidence and expression in mils assurance case. Technical report D4.3, Version 0.7, D-MILS Project, March 2015. http://www.d-mils.org/page/results
24. Compositional verification techniques and tools for distributed mils–part 1. Technical report D4.4, Version 1.0, D-MILS Project, July 2014. http://www.d-mils.org/page/results
25. Distributed mils platform configuration compiler. Technical report D5.2, Version 0.2, D-MILS Project, March 2014. http://www.d-mils.org/page/results
26. Extended separation kernel capable of global exported resource addressing. Technical report D6.1, Version 2.0, D-MILS Project, March 2014. http://www.d-mils.org/page/results
27. Mils network system supporting TTEthernet. Technical report D6.3, Version 1.0, D-MILS Project, March 2014. http://www.d-mils.org/page/results
28. R. DeLong, Commentary on the MILS Network Subsystem Protection Profile. Technical report, Version 0.31, September 2011
29. DeLong, R., Rushby, J.: Protection Profile for MILS Network Subsystems in Environments Requiring High Robustness, Version 0.31, September 2011
30. Dragoni, N., Massacci, F., Walter, T., Schaefer, C.: What the heck is this application doing? - a security-by-contract architecture for pervasive services. Comput. Secur. **28**, 566–577 (2009)
31. Information Assurance Directorate, National Security Agency, U.S. Government Protection Profile for Separation Kernels in Environments Requiring High Robustness, Fort George G. Meade, MD 20755–6000, Version 1.03, June 2007

32. Kopetz, H., Ademaj, A., Grillinger, P., Steinhammer, K.: The time-triggered ethernet (TTE) design. In: 8th IEEE International Symposium on Object-oriented Real-time distributed Computing (ISORC), Seattle, Washington (2005)
33. Rushby, J.: The design and verification of secure systems. In: Eighth ACM Symposium on Operating System Principles, Asilomar, CA, December 1981, pp. 12–21 (1981). (ACM Operating Systems Review, Vol. 15, No. 5)
34. Schmittner, C., Gruber, T., Puschner, P., Schoitsch, E.: Security application of failure mode and effect analysis (FMEA). In: Bondavalli, A., Di Giandomenico, F. (eds.) SAFECOMP 2014. LNCS, vol. 8666, pp. 310–325. Springer, Heidelberg (2014)
35. Sojka, M., Krec, M., Hanzálek, Z.: Case study on combined validation of safety & security requirements. In: SIES, pp. 244–251 (2014)
36. Steiner, M., Liggesmeyer, P.: Combination of safety and security analysis - finding security problems that threaten the safety of a system. In: SAFECOMP Workshop DECS (2013)
37. Vardi, M.Y.: An automata-theoretic approach to linear temporal logic. In: Moller, F., Birtwistle, G. (eds.) LC 1995. LNCS, vol. 1043, pp. 238–266. Springer, Heidelberg (1995)

Security Analysis of Urban Railway Systems: The Need for a Cyber-Physical Perspective

Binbin Chen[1]([⊠]), Christoph Schmittner[2], Zhendong Ma[2], William G. Temple[1],
Xinshu Dong[1], Douglas L. Jones[1,3]([⊠]), and William H. Sanders[3]([⊠])

[1] Advanced Digital Sciences Center, Singapore, Singapore
{binbin.chen,william.t,xinshu.dong}@adsc.com.sg
[2] Austrian Institute of Technology, Donau-City-Strasse 1, 1220 Vienna, Austria
{christoph.schmittner.fl,zhendong.ma}@ait.ac.at
[3] Electrical and Computer Engineering Deptartment,
University of Illinois at Urbana-Champaign, Champaign, IL, USA
{dl-jones,whs}@illinois.edu

Abstract. Urban railway systems are increasingly relying on information and communications technologies (ICT). This evolution makes cybersecurity an important concern, in addition to the traditional focus on reliability, availability, maintainability and safety. In this paper, we examine two examples of cyber-intensive systems in urban railway environments—a communications-based train control system, and a mobile app that provides transit information to commuters—and use them to study the challenges for conducting security analysis in this domain. We show the need for a cyber-physical perspective in order to understand the cross-domain attack/defense and the complicated physical consequence of cyber breaches. We present security analysis results from two different methods that are used in the safety and ICT security engineering domains respectively, and use them as concrete references to discuss the way to move forward.

Keywords: Security analysis · Urban railway systems · Cyber-physical systems

1 Introduction

Information and communications technologies (ICT) play a vital role in helping railway operators improve their system safety and service reliability, provide higher transit capacity, and keep the costs of building, operating, and maintaining their infrastructure in check. For example, many urban transportation systems around the world have deployed some form of communications-based automatic train control (e.g., [1,2]). In those systems, multiple cyber components, including wireless communication, software-defined control logic, and near-real-time data visualization at control centers, have been introduced to replace their conventional physical counterparts. As another example, with smart phones becoming ubiquitous, transit operators (e.g., [3,4]) are introducing mobile apps

© Springer International Publishing Switzerland 2015
F. Koornneef and C. van Gulijk (Eds.): SAFECOMP 2015 Workshops, LNCS 9338, pp. 277–290, 2015.
DOI: 10.1007/978-3-319-24249-1_24

to provide consumers with information about train schedules, as well as push-notifications about emergency events or other relevant information.

While the benefits of *digitizing* urban railway systems are obvious, the potential implications of this evolution could be multi-faceted and profound, especially when it comes to the issue of security. For older railway systems, where train protection is based on track circuits and mechanical relay signaling, the security concerns reside primarily in the physical domain. In comparison, the ICT components used in newer automatic train control systems expose additional cyber attack surfaces, which could allow sophisticated attackers to combine cyber attack vectors with physical attack means to achieve malicious goals. This makes it difficult to assess the security of digitized urban railway systems using traditional approaches (e.g., safety analysis methods) that are most familiar to transit operators and other stakeholders. At the same time, security analysis approaches used in other ICT systems (e.g., enterprise networks) are also not readily applicable to urban railway systems, since cyber components can have complicated interactions with the physical assets, or even passengers (e.g., with a false notification through a mobile app).

In this work, we take a close look at two concrete examples of cyber-intensive systems used in urban railway environments—a communications-based train control (CBTC) system and a mobile transit information app—and use them to analyze the cyber-physical security challenges introduced by the digitization of urban railway systems. At the high level, we identify two key challenges:

- **Cross-domain Attack and Defense:** For a digitized urban railway system, with its many components that span a large geographic area in the physical domain and interconnect with each other in the cyber domain, attack and defense can manifest in multiple stages, involving both cyber and physical actions.
- **Physical-domain Consequences from Cyber Breaches:** Security breaches in the cyber domain, such as falsified information or malicious control logic, can have a complicated impact on the physical domain, which is also subject to an urban railway system's underlying design features, such as fail-safe mechanisms.

The evolution of urban railway systems requires the corresponding evolution of security analysis methodologies—in particular, the need for encompassing a systematic cyber-physical perspective. In the second part of this work, we make an initial attempt to apply existing security analysis approaches for the CBTC and mobile transit information app cases. We use these two examples to illustrate the implications of the two challenges mentioned above. In particular, we find that in the CBTC example, the Failure Modes, Vulnerabilities and Effects Analysis (FMVEA) approach [5], which originates from the safety engineering domain, provides a convenient starting point, since the primary concern in train signaling is avoiding "hazards" such as train collisions or derailments, regardless of whether they are caused by cyber or physical means. However, new extensions are needed to better model the complicated cross-domain multi-stage attacks. On the other hand, in the second example of a mobile transit information app where the delivery of accurate, relevant, and timely information is the key, we find attack tree analysis [6], which is used widely in ICT systems, can serve as a natural starting point, although further extension to better understand the physical consequences of cyber security breaches is necessary.

In summary, we analyze the cyber-physical security implications of the ongoing evolution of urban railway systems, present analysis results obtained from two different methods, and use them as concrete references to discuss the way to move forward. We begin by discussing features of urban railway systems and describing the two example cases in Sect. 2. In Sect. 3 we present our efforts to apply different methods to analyze the security risk in the two cases. In Sect. 4 we summarize our findings and provide additional recommendations for future work. We then conclude in Sect. 5.

2   Railway Security Risks and Implications

To provide safe, dependable, and efficient transportation service, a rail transport operator needs to coordinate dozens of different systems, including, e.g., the railway signalling system, fire detection/suppression system, ventilation system, traction power system, passenger information system, and fare collection system. The increasing reliance of such systems on ICT introduces cybersecurity risks with complex cyber-physical implications, as exemplified by the two scenarios we describe next.

2.1   Scenario 1: Risks in CBTC Systems

The train control/railway signaling system is a safety-critical system that lies in the core of a railway infrastructure. It can be implemented in diverse forms: from a purely manual form as in the early days, to a fully automatic form as in the communications-based train control (CBTC) systems that serve many cities today. Traditionally, fixed block signaling is used, where the track is divided

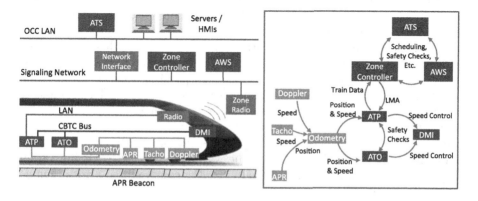

Fig. 1. An example CBTC system and its simplified data flow for LMA determination.

into physical sections, and no more than one train is allowed in each section. Today's urban railway systems increasingly use a moving block design, which gets rid of the fixed blocks so the block locations and lengths can be dynamically changed according to train location, weight and speed. One primary advantage of a moving block system is that the spacing between trains is reduced, allowing for higher capacity for transit operators.

Broadly speaking, a CBTC system [7] consists of trainborne systems, wayside systems, and a central management system, which are all connected continuously through high-speed data communication networks, as shown in the left subfigure of Fig. 1. They implement automatic train protection (ATP), automatic train operation (ATO), and automatic train supervision (ATS) functions. The right subfigure of Fig. 1 shows a simplified data flow diagram for some key CBTC operations. The train determines its position and speed based on data from onboard sensors (tachometer, Doppler) and data from the absolute position reference (APR) beacons located on the track. It submits train data (including position and speed) via the radio-based communication link to the wayside system, which is further connected with the central ATS system located at the operations control center (OCC). In a fully-automated CBTC system, zone controllers use the high-resolution train information to determine for trains their limit of movement authority (LMA), which describes the distance on the tracks until the next obstacle. A zone controller sends individual commands to each train under its control. The trainborne ATP and ATO systems then use the LMA information in conjunction with local train data to issue appropriate train control commands to the train, typically through some driver machine interface (DMI). Many CBTC systems also include auxiliary wayside systems (AWS), which implement auxiliary functionalities (e.g., interlocking) that can provide a "fall-back" signaling system if some other CBTC components become faulty.

Cyber-physical Challenges for Analyzing CBTC's Security Risk. By using radio-based digital transmission (instead of track circuits) to determine train location and perform train-trackside data communications, CBTC can increase the capacity, reduce the amount of wayside equipment needed, and improve the reliability. However, the new digital elements in CBTC — the passive APR beacons that provide accurate localization to trains, the trainborne and wayside systems that implement control logic in software, the radio-based communication system, and the central ATS at the OCC all present potential new attack surfaces. These components are interconnected, and engineered with various safety-enhancing mechanisms, e.g., physical access control, redundant data sources and networks, and fault-response procedures. This complexity makes it challenging to analyze the security level of such a system. In particular, an attacker can start from a physically less protected component (e.g., devices used by system maintenance staff), exploit a series of system vulnerabilities to compromise more critical ones, along the way leveraging or bypassing various safety-enhancing mechanisms, and finally use the compromised critical components to cause physical consequences.

2.2   Scenario 2: Risks in Mobile Transit Information Apps

The complicated coupling of different systems in an urban railway can lead to security implications with cascading effects. For example, while the public address (PA) or public information display (PID) systems do not directly impose safety issues, abusing those systems can potentially lead to overcrowding which could indirectly impact the passengers' safety. Also, for a rail transit operator, there are important non-safety-related security concerns: for example, whether an attack will cause interruption or degradation of service, leakage of information, loss of fare revenue, or damage to their reputation. This is the focus of our second risk scenario.

Traditionally in public transit systems, the operators at the operations control center and individual train stations broadcast traffic update information to commuters via the PID and PA systems. Beyond ordinary information such as train arrival times, those systems are also used to inform commuters of incidents, delays and even the crowdedness of certain routes, to advise them on alternative routes and means of transportation. Recently, urban rail systems have started to extend such information updates to mobile apps installed on commuters' mobile devices (e.g., [3,4]). For simplicity, we call them *PID apps* in this paper. PID apps can also push messages to end users regarding specific incidents, enabling commuters to plan adjustments to their route ahead of time. However, such extended PID or PA channels could be misused.

Cyber-physical Challenges for Analyzing PID Apps Security Risk. As Fig. 2 illustrates, the emerging adoption of PID apps has complicated the landscape of passenger traffic updates with additional channels and terminals that are much harder to properly secure. Although traditional PID/PA systems are clearly not immune from cyber threats, attackers would have to gain nontrivial physical access to well-guarded control rooms or direct connections with in-station PID or PA systems before they could launch attacks. These physical proximity requirements limit the time, venue, as well as scale of the attacks, and can easily expose attackers to monitoring systems and security personnel. On the other hand, the traffic update messages pushed to PID apps are potentially more susceptible to cyber attackers. The primary cause is that the communication channel for them is outside the premise and control of typical public transport

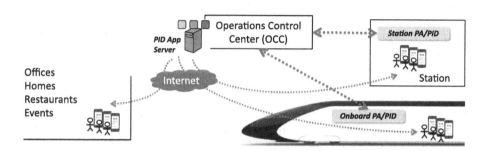

Fig. 2. Railway PA/PID systems, simplified from [8].

operators. The PID app server has to deliver the messages to the mobile apps via internet, which makes it a much more accessible target for cyber attackers than control servers well protected in the OCC. As we describe in Sect. 3.2, there are various vectors that cyber attackers can utilize to compromise the traffic update messages pushed to commuters' PID apps, with no or reduced reliance on physical access to the system.

In addition to examining cyber-physical intrusions, a systematic security analysis also needs to assess the physical consequence of possible cyber incidents in such systems. For example, announcing to all passengers that a certain train service has broken down, or that they can enjoy free rides on a certain route could cause abnormal and even unsafe crowding (e.g., stampeding) at stations or on trains.

3   Applying Existing Security Analysis Approaches

It is important to conduct a thorough and systematic analysis to understand the security postures of urban railway systems. There is a clear gap in this regard. In particular, in current railway safety standards like EN 5012X Series [9] for general railway systems and IEEE 1474 Series [7] for CBTC systems, security is still a lesser concern. Meanwhile, there is also a large body of research work and industrial experience to draw upon. On the one hand, there are well-established approaches for safety-critical system engineering (e.g., HAZOP [10] and FMEA [11]), and noticeable efforts (e.g., [5,12]) have been devoted to extending some of those methodologies to also consider the security aspect. On the other hand, security assessment methodologies for ICT systems have been studied and applied for a few decades (e.g., [6,13,14]), with several recent efforts focusing on cybersecurity issues of critical infrastructures (e.g., [15,16]).

3.1   Analysis of Scenario 1 with FMVEA Method

With the increasing awareness of the security implications for safety-critical systems, safety assessment methodologies and standards are being extended to explicitly take security into account. A recent example is the *Failure Modes, Vulnerabilities and Effects Analysis (FMVEA)* approach [5], which extends the well-established *Failure Mode and Effects Analysis (FMEA)* methodology [11] to include security related risks. Since safety remains the top concern for CBTC systems, we start our security analysis of Scenario 1 by using this safety engineering methodology extended with security features.

FMEA starts by dividing the studied system into elements. One then analyzes each of the elements one by one to identify potential failure modes. Afterwards, based on the functions of elements and their interactions, one rates the effects of each failure mode on the system's safety. For failure modes with intolerable system effects, one further identifies the causes. If enough information is available, one can further determine the risk based on the severity of the system effect and the probability of the causes. As its security generalization, FMVEA considers both failure modes and threat modes. While a failure mode describes

Table 1. Excerpt of FMVEA results for a CBTC system

Element	Failure / Threat Mode	Direct Effect	System Effect	Cause	S	P	ID
Train Odometry	APR beacon fails to send data	Train receives no data from APR beacon	Missing data can be detected through comparison with tacho, Doppler data and track geometry; the affected train switches to fail-safe state	Failure of hardware / software in APR Beacons	I	-	1
				Attacker jams or disables APR beacons	I	4	2
	Attacker manipulates data from APR beacon	Train receives wrong data from APR beacon	Wrong data can be detected through comparison with tacho data and track geometry; the affected train switches to fail-safe state	Attacker manipulates APR beacons	I	3	3
				Attacker installs additional APR beacons	I	3	4
Signaling Network	Attacker sends wrong LMA to train	Train receives wrong LMA	Train ATO and ATP detect inconsistent LMA; the affected train switches to fail-safe state	Attacker installs additional wireless transmitter to send manipulated LMA to train	I	3	5
	Attacker sends spoofed train data to wayside system	ATS slows down trains to adjust for additional train	OCC raises an alarm to investigate the event	Attacker installs additional wireless transmitter to send spoofed train data to wayside system	I	3	6
	Attacker blocks the authenticated LMA	Train ATO and ATP stop to receive LMA	All trains switch to fail-safe mode	Attacker gains access to signaling network and jams transmission	III	2	7

the manner in which a component fails, a threat mode describes the manner in which a component can be misused by a potential attacker. Failure causes are also extended to include vulnerabilities and intentional malicious actions. The risk of a mode is determined not only by the system attributes, but also by the properties of potential attackers.

FMVEA Based Security Analysis. We follow the FMVEA approach to conduct a systematic analysis of various failure and threat modes of a CBTC system. For each element in Fig. 1, potential failure and threat modes, their direct and system effects, and causes are identified. Due to space limitation, we report a selected subset of our FMVEA results in Table 1. Column S depicts the severity, and column P depicts the susceptibility against potential attacks, based on reachability and knowledge about the element.

As shown in the table, a potential threat mode for APR beacon is forged messages. This causes incorrect position data for the train, which would lead to an inconsistency between the position data from the APR beacon and the position data inferred from the tacho and track geometry. When such an inconsistency is detected, the train will send an alarm to the wayside system and switch to a fail-safe state. We also identify potential causes in order to assess the risks. For example, forged data from an APR beacon could be caused by manipulating an existing APR beacon or installing additional APR beaconing devices, both of which require cyber and physical actions.

Our FMVEA result shows that no single failure or threat mode *directly* leads to a safety hazard, due to the built-in safety-assured design features, specifically, redundancy checking and triggering of fail-safe mode under lost communication or inconsistent information. However, we do identify cases (e.g., case 6) where an attacker may be able to gradually influence measured position and speed to manipulate the system into a hazardous situation. Launching such an attack, however, requires access to the trainborne network and the manipulation of multiple measured values.

While our analysis does not identify major safety risks, there are multiple single events that can lead to degradation of functionality and system availability. For example, manipulations of the APR beacons in the tracks (see cases 1–4) can lead to missing or inconsistent data for the determination of the train position and cause a switch to a fail-safe mode. If an attacker is able to compromise the signaling network via direct access or via the installation of additional wireless antennas, she could cause the whole system to switch to a fail-safe mode (see case 7). The built-in safety-assured mechanisms makes such denial-of-service attacks easier to launch. This suggests some potential issue with the EN 50129 approach, which considers the overloading of the transmission system out-of-scope. While the EN 50129 approach is sound from a safety-centric perspective, its potential implications to the system's resilience and availability under malicious threat scenarios require systematic investigation.

Gaps in Analyzing Multi-stage Cross-domain Attacks. While the FMVEA approach helps an analyst to systematically consider failure and threat modes, their effects (i.e., physical consequences) and potential causes in an element-by-element manner, it does not provide support for the analysis of multi-stage cross-domain attacks. For example, consider a cyberattack on signaling network (case 7) that might cause critical incidents, the analysis does not include information about how such attacks could be launched. Also, in a multi-stage cross-domain attack an attacker may gain control of multiple elements. It does not readily provide the consequence analysis for such joined threat/failure modes.

3.2   Analysis of Scenario 2 with Attack Tree Method

Since the delivery of accurate, relevant, and timely information is the key for a mobile transit information app as described in our Scenario 2, we approach its analysis through the application of methods that have been more widely adopted in ICT systems security analysis context.

Assessment Methodologies used in ICT Security Domain. ICT security analysis methods are often used to identify potential weaknesses (e.g., software vulnerabilities) in the systems under inspection, and evaluate the likelihood of these weaknesses being misused by an assumed attacker to penetrate the system. Such analysis can also include assessing the consequences of successful attacks in terms of confidentiality, integrity, and availability. Here we take *attack tree* analysis [6] as an example: this is a widely-used technique to model attacker behaviour and deduce attack paths to a specific malicious goal, which is usually associated with a certain asset. In the railway security domain, the American Public Transportation Association [17] has recently proposed to use attack trees to analyze "narrow and deep" security questions in railway systems.

Attack Tree Based Analysis. Figure 3 shows an attack tree that illustrates a selected subset of possible attack vectors that can lead to the delivery of fake transit information to passengers. We focus on the information integrity here, since such fake messages can be used by attackers to mislead passengers into overcrowded stations, which could cause safety hazards, e.g., stampedes.

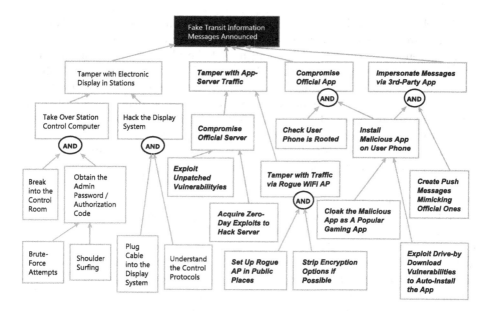

Fig. 3. An attack tree on announcing fake messages. *Branches are OR gates by default, unless marked as AND gates.* **Bold italics denote attacks from PID apps.**

The root node on top of the tree denotes the end goal of the threats, while the subsequent nodes along the branches represent the sub-attacks that attackers can launch to achieve the goal of the sub-attacks in the parent nodes. For instance, one of the ways attackers can push fake transit information to passengers is to compromise the official PID app, which in turn can be achieved by installing a malicious app on users' phones that are rooted. Furthermore, there can be various ways to install such a malicious app, e.g., by uploading it to app stores, or by exploiting a drive-by download vulnerability on victim users' phones.

The attack tree here includes both traditional threats to the electronic display boards in stations via physical attacks, as well as new threats brought in by PID apps (bold italics). As we can see, PID apps can potentially open up a larger attack surface for attackers to send fake transit information messages. With traditional display systems, in order to achieve this, the attackers would have to physically go to the station or control center, and manipulate either display board or server inside the control room. With modern CCTV monitoring systems, the chances of an attacker being caught and stopped is high. However, with PID apps in use, the attackers immediately gain access to such transit messages with much greater "convenience". For instance, they could sit at home and launch remote attacks against the official rail transit operator's PID server, or set up a rogue WiFi access point (AP) in a backpack when taking the train. Making matters worse, attackers have many other means to penetrate commuters' mobile devices directly and at a larger scale, e.g., by uploading a malicious app on Android or iOS app store, which may appear as an interesting game app, but surreptitiously push transit messages mimicking those from official PID apps.

Attack trees provide a convenient and intuitive way for security analysts to construct an overview on how attackers can take steps to achieve their goals. It is also a generic methodology that can model the blend of cyber and physical attacks in a unified way. For example, Fig. 3 models both traditional physical threats as well as emerging cyber threats, and how they may be exploited together by an attacker. With attack trees, one can also associate each individual attack step (regardless of whether it is cyber or physical) with some success probability (or more qualitative judgement about its likelihood). While it is much harder to obtain such quantitative data for security analysis as compared to fault analysis with fault trees, rough estimation based on empirical attacker models can help identifying more plausible attack paths. In particular, the overall attack success probability for the whole tree can be computed according to the logical (combinatorial) relationship among the different attack steps.

Note that the attack tree is only one example of the ICT security analysis methodologies available today. If necessary, more advanced security assessment tools are available, including, e.g., attack graph [13,14], ADVISE [15], CyberSAGE [18], attack-defense tree [19], etc. These tools support features such as automatic generation of likely attack scenarios based on vulnerability and system information, and more detailed modeling of attacker behavior and attacker/defender interactions.

Gaps in Analyzing Physical Consequences of Cyber Breaches. While attack tree analysis provides support for modeling multi-stage cross-domain attacks, it provides little aid and guidance in analyzing physical consequences of attacks, especially in terms of quantifying the severity of the consequences along with the likelihood of attack steps. We find that existing ICT security assessment methods generally lack in this aspect. They do not have mechanisms to analyze physical consequences of cyber breaches, nor do they provide support to incorporate such analysis results from other analysis methods. To meet the domain requirement of urban railway systems, it is important to extend ICT security analysis methodologies, such as attack trees, with the necessary mechanisms to have better capabilities of modeling physical consequences of cyber attacks.

4 Moving Forward

As illustrated in Sect. 3, the cyber-physical nature of modern railway systems presents new challenges for the analysis of their security posture. In particular:

- **Threat Prioritization.** Modern urban railway systems present large attack surfaces. In risk-driven analysis, security analysts need to understand what attacks are more likely to happen, considering factors like attacker motivation, skills, access, and traceability of the attacks.
- **Physical Consequences.** Attacks on railway systems often ultimately aim at the physical world. Security and safety analysts need to understand how cyber breaches can lead to various physical consequences.

Addressing the above challenges demands an integrative cyber-physical perspective. For example, if an attacker wishes to manipulate LMA commands in a covert way, she might consider different combinations of cyber and physical attack steps to find a better attack sequence. In fact, in a recently published railway security analysis exercise [17], the experts analyze different attack sequences for compromising a trackside programmable logic controller (PLC) and argue that a multi-stage cross-domain attack is among the most likely to happen since it reduces the traceability of malicious insiders. Supposing a cyber breach has been made, security analysts need a cyber-physical perspective to understand how relevant factors (e.g., safety-enhancing mechanisms and human behaviors) affect the outcomes of potential attacks, and how the consequences vary with time, location, and other physical context. One also need to consider non-safety-critical risks (e.g., degradation of service) together with safety-critical risks.

Existing approaches for security and safety analysis only partially fulfil such needs. In particular, while the FMVEA analysis in Sect. 3.1 provides a systematic way to examine individual components and reason about both the consequence (effect) and the likely cause, we see a clear need to further improve its support for analyzing more complicated causes (e.g., those spanning both cyber and physical domains and involving multiple stages) and consequences (e.g., those could be resulted from manipulation of multiple components in a coordinated manner). In comparison, while the attack tree analysis in Sect. 3.2 allows one to conveniently construct different possible combinations of attack sequences, it provides little aid and guidance in systematically analyzing the consequence of the attacks or exploring all potential attacks. Some safety standards for electronic systems (e.g., the automotive standards ISO26262 [20]) are already defined in a more extensible way that allows the inclusion of physical (such as mechanical) aspects. However, most existing ones (e.g., those from EN 5012X Series) often treat the physical aspect as "out of scope".

Hence, we need a cyber-physical integrative approach to address the two challenges in threat prioritization and physical consequences of cyber breaches. In particular, analyzing the security of urban railway systems requires the consideration of many different cyber and physical factors. Multiple approaches and techniques are often needed to fulfil the purpose, which calls for a framework to tie different parts in a consistent and meaningful way. Figure 4 illustrates a new framework that

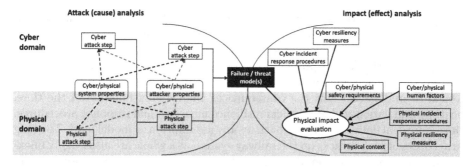

Fig. 4. Analyzing railway systems security with an integrative cyber-physical approach.

we are working on to integrate various security assessment results. The proposed framework is inspired by existing methods on risk analysis, such as [21]. As shown in the center of Fig. 4, the analysis will be anchored around a possible failure/threat mode induced by cyber breach (e.g., the manipulation of the LMA), or a set of such modes. The left hand side of Fig. 4 shows various attack sequences that lead to the cyber breach, which are enriched with more details about relevant information. Specifically, different attack steps are mapped to either cyber or physical domain. As shown by the dashed edges, each attack step further associates with various system and attacker properties, which can be integrated to estimate the overall attack likelihood. On the right hand side of Fig. 4, the physical consequences of the cyber breach are evaluated based on an impact model (e.g., through high-fidelity simulation) that considers physical context, as well as various cyber/physical procedures, measures, safety requirements, and human factors. A unified view of the cyber and physical domains, as provided in Fig. 4, can contribute to a more thorough security analysis of railway systems. It can also potentially enable the use of quantitative metrics to better understand the scenarios.

We envision such a framework can address the two challenges we highlight earlier by providing the capabilities for "cross-over" analysis for cyber-physical threats and multi-factor analysis for physical consequences.

Analysis of "Cross-over" Attacks in the Cyber and Physical Domain. Threats from physical attacks will continue to be of primary concern in urban transportation systems, especially in regions where control on weapons and explosives are relatively weak. Nevertheless, threats from the cyber space are increasingly yielding alternative and often complementary means to physical attacks.

Our new framework aims to provide an integrative way to analyze attacks, by explicitly associating attack steps to properties like requirement on attackers' proximity (physical or via a network), the knowledge or tools necessary to cause harm, and the level of attribution that may be possible to discourage an attack. For example, if a would-be attacker needs to be physically on a train at the time of the incident to disrupt a CBTC/signaling system, this scenario may be less risky than another scenario where an attacker remotely hacks into passengers' laptops or mobile phones and causes a train disruption. While our approach focuses on the threat modes, it also can be extended to model the typical operational processes and information flows in the system and analyze their implications on the system's security level (e.g., similar to [16]).

Multi-factor Analysis of Physical Consequences. Unlike cyber attacks on ICT systems that target information, attacks on urban railway systems often target passengers and physical assets, with an aim to cause safety hazards or widespread panics. Hence, our proposed framework incorporates detailed analysis of the physical impact of cyber breaches. High-fidelity modeling and simulation are needed to understand how the consequences change as a function of the time, location, and various cyber-physical resilience measures and response procedures. More empirical data is needed to back up any assumption or model used. The long term effects of such attacks on the railway system as a whole are also largely unexplored. We plan to incorporate realistic traffic models for human passengers in urban transit systems into our framework. This will strengthen security analysts' capabilities of understanding the consequences of such attacks [22]. In addition, we will develop methodologies and tools to incorporate empirical data, as well as advanced modeling and simulation techniques to estimate the potential physical consequences and correlated or cascading effects under different attack scenarios.

5   Conclusion

While the importance of cybersecurity in urban railway systems has become increasingly recognized, the exact roadmap to ensuring it is still largely an open problem. To shed some light into this topic, we examine two concrete examples of cyber-intensive systems in urban railway environments. One is a communications-based train control system, which is a modernized form of a classic safety-critical system. The other is a mobile app that provides transit information to commuters, which is a good example of how new information and communications technologies change the way critical information is propagated between systems and users. We use these two urban railway scenarios to illustrate the strengths of two widely adopted methods (FMVEA and attack trees), and potential gaps present in leveraging them to analyzing cybersecurity of urban railway systems. Our study highlights the need for a cyber-physical perspective in order to understand the cross-domain attack and defense, as well as complicated consequences of cyber breaches in physical domains.

To address the complex security engineering challenges in these safety-critical cyber-physical systems, we believe new security assessment methods and tools are needed. We outline a new framework for analyzing failure and threat modes that can link together attack and impact analysis, and embed the analysis in both cyber and physical domain contexts. We plan to further refine and apply this framework as part of our future work on urban railway security.

Acknowledgments. This work was supported in part by the National Research Foundation (NRF), Prime Minister's Office, Singapore, under its National Cybersecurity R&D Programme (Award No. NRF2014NCR-NCR001-31) and administered by the National Cybersecurity R&D Directorate, and supported in part by Singapore's Agency for Science, Technology, and Research (A*STAR) under the Human Sixth Sense Programme (HSSP). The work of Schmittner and Ma was partially funded by the European Commission through the project Creating an Agenda for Research ON Transportation sEcurity (CARONTE).

References

1. Ansaldo STS, "CBTC Communication Based Train Control". http://www.ansaldo-sts.com/sites/ansaldosts.message-asp.com/files/imce/cbtc.pdf
2. Siemens, A.G.: Trainguard sirius CBTC (2013). http://www.mobility.siemens.com/mobility/global/SiteCollectionDocuments/en/rail-solutions/rail-automation/train-control-systems/trainguard-sirius-cbtc-en.pdf
3. MyTransport.SG App. http://www.mytransport.sg/mobile/mytransport_mobile.html

4. Massachusetts Bay Transportation Authority Apps. http://www.mbta.com/rider_tools/

5. Schmittner, C., Gruber, T., Puschner, P., Schoitsch, E.: Security application of failure mode and effect analysis (FMEA). In: Bondavalli, A., Di Giandomenico, F. (eds.) SAFECOMP 2014. LNCS, vol. 8666, pp. 310–325. Springer, Heidelberg (2014)

6. Schneier, B.: Attack trees: modeling security threats. Dr. Dobb's J. **24**(12), 21–29 (1999)

7. IEEE Vehicular Technology Society, "IEEE Standard for Communications-Based Train Control (CBTC) Performance and Functional Requirements (1474.1-2004)" (2004)

8. Thales, INOV, "Secur-ed cyber-security roadmap for ptos". http://www.secur-ed.eu/wp-content/uploads/2014/11/SECUR-ED_Cyber_security_roadmap_v3.pdf

9. EN 50129, Railway applications–Communication, signalling and processing systems–Safety related electronic systems for signalling (2010)

10. Chudleigh, M., Catmur, J.: Safety assessment of computer systems using hazop and audit techniques. In: Proceedings of the Conference on Computer Safety, Reliability and Security (SAFECOMP) (1992)

11. IEC 60812, Analysis techniques for system reliability - procedure for failure mode and effects analysis (FMEA) (2006)

12. Winther, R., Johnsen, O.-A., Gran, B.A.: Security assessments of safety critical systems using HAZOPs. In: Voges, U. (ed.) SAFECOMP 2001. LNCS, vol. 2187, p. 14. Springer, Heidelberg (2001)

13. Sheyner, O., Haines, J., Jha, S., Lippmann, R., Wing, J.: Automated generation and analysis of attack graphs. In: Proceedings of the IEEE Symposium on Security and Privacy (2002)

14. Ou, X., Boyer, W., McQueen, M.: A scalable approach to attack graph generation. In: Proceedings of the ACM Conference on Computer and Communications Security (CCS) (2006)

15. LeMay, E., Ford, M., Keefe, K., Sanders, W.H., Muehrke, C.: Model-based security metrics using ADversary VIew Security Evaluation (ADVISE). In: Proceedings of the Conference on Quantitative Evaluation of SysTems (QEST) (2011)

16. Chen, B., Kalbarczyk, Z., Nicol, D.M., Sanders, W.H., Tan, R., Temple, W.G., Tippenhauer, N.O., Vu, A.H., Yau, D.K.: Go with the flow: toward workflow-oriented security assessment. In: Proceedings of the New Security Paradigms Workshop (NSPW) (2013)

17. APTA Standards Development Program, Securing Control and Communications Systems in Rail Transit Environments: Part IIIa (2014). http://www.apta.com/resources/standards/public-comment/Documents/APTASS_CC_WPSecuringCandCSystemsinRailTransitEnvironmentsPartIIIaPC4Q2014.doc

18. Vu, A.H., Tippenhauer, N.O., Chen, B., Nicol, D.M., Kalbarczyk, Z.: CyberSAGE: a tool for automatic security assessment of cyber-physical systems. In: Norman, G., Sanders, W. (eds.) QEST 2014. LNCS, vol. 8657, pp. 384–387. Springer, Heidelberg (2014)

19. Kordy, B., Mauw, S., Radomirović, S., Schweitzer, P.: Foundations of attack–defense trees. In: Degano, P., Etalle, S., Guttman, J. (eds.) FAST 2010. LNCS, vol. 6561, pp. 80–95. Springer, Heidelberg (2011)

20. ISO 26262, Road vehicles - Functional safety (2011)

21. Bowtie Method. http://www.caa.co.uk/bowtie

22. Legara, E.F., Monterola, C., Lee, K.K., Hung, G.G.: Critical capacity, travel time delays and travel time distribution of rapid mass transit systems. Physica A Stat. Mech. Appl. **406**, 100–106 (2014)

Sequential and Parallel Attack Tree Modelling

Florian Arnold[2], Dennis Guck[1]([✉]), Rajesh Kumar[1], and Mariële Stoelinga[1]

[1] Formal Methods and Tools, University of Twente, Enschede, The Netherlands
{d.guck,r.kumar,m.i.a.stoelinga}@utwente.nl
[2] Bayer Technology Services, Leverkusen, Germany
florian.arnold@bayer.com

Abstract. The intricacy of socio-technical systems requires a careful planning and utilisation of security resources to ensure uninterrupted, secure and reliable services. Even though many studies have been conducted to understand and model the behaviour of a potential attacker, the detection of crucial security vulnerabilities in such a system still provides a substantial challenge for security engineers. The success of a sophisticated attack crucially depends on two factors: the resources and time available to the attacker; and the stepwise execution of interrelated attack steps. This paper presents an extension of dynamic attack tree models by using both, the sequential and parallel behaviour of AND- and OR-gates. Thereby we take great care to allow the modelling of any kind of temporal and stochastic dependencies which might occur in the model. We demonstrate the applicability on several case studies.

Keywords: Attack trees · Security analysis · Sequential and parallel

1 Introduction

Modern institutions in the business, governmental and research sector have to rely more and more on highly complex socio-technical systems. The complexity in these systems arises from the continuous interplay between actors, IT-systems and the physical infrastructure. Sophisticated attacks against these systems try to exploit this complexity by targeting several components at once. For instance, an attacker can use a combination of malware and social engineering to steal important data, or simply steal the laptop. A most impressive example for this kind of socio-technical attacks is the famous Stuxnet attack [16].

Thus, the challenge for modern security engineering is to predict possible attack vectors and identify the severest vulnerabilities by taking a holistic view of the whole organization. This task requires to identify, model and quantify complex attack scenarios. The formal tool which is widely used in practice to satisfy these needs are attack trees.

Classical attack tree models allow to present multi-step attacks in a concise way while also offering a straight-forward analysis kit to compute important static metrics, such as the probability and execution costs of attack paths [15, 24]. These metrics allow security practitioners to take well-informed decisions with

© Springer International Publishing Switzerland 2015
F. Koornneef and C. van Gulijk (Eds.): SAFECOMP 2015 Workshops, LNCS 9338, pp. 291–299, 2015.
DOI: 10.1007/978-3-319-24249-1_25

respect to a systems vulnerability and can thus support the decision-making process to determine which countermeasures are most cost-efficient. However, static approaches fail to interpret results in the security context and have to be underpinned with many conditions and constraints. The result that a certain attack succeeds with 34 % is meaningless without a close definition of the precise scenario: What is the time frame of the attack, how many resources does the attacker have, and which attack vector does he choose?

Our Approach. To compute these metrics on attack trees, we deploy compositional aggregation, a powerful techniques that yields an efficient and flexible attack tree analysis framework. That is, we translate each attack tree element into a interactive Input/Output Markov Chain (I/O-IMC), which are basically continuous-time Markov chains, augmented with action labels that can be used for synchronization between various models. By parallel composing these individual I/O-IMCs, we obtain one I/O-IMC for the entire attack tree, which can then be analysed by standard stochastic model checking techniques [4]. However, we do not obtain the entire I/O-IMC in one step; rather we compose two I/O-IMCs at a time, and then deploy minimization techniques to ensure that our state spaces remain compact. In this way, we obtain an attack tree analysis framework that is efficient, flexible and extendible: if we choose to introduce a new attack tree gate, then we only have to provide the I/O-IMC translation for that gate. As we show here, we can easily handle sequential versions of the AND and OR gates. Also, we are capable of analysing trees with shared sub-trees, which is not the case for many other frameworks [8,12,20,21].

Related Work. The idea of attack tees (ATs) originates from threat logic trees [27] and they are formally introduced in [24]. ATs closely resemble fault trees, a popular model in reliability analysis [5]. ATs can be classified in *static* models, which do not take the evolution of time into account, and *dynamic* models which reason about the temporal evolution of an attack. Static ATs have been rigorously formalized in [18], and other static approaches refine the expressiveness like multi-parameter ATs [13]. Most approaches in the field of dynamic ATs are directed graph-based and evaluated with Markov models, for instance compromise graphs [19]. Piètre-Cambacédès and Bouissou [21] introduced an attack tree model based on Boolean logic driven Markov processes, while a computational model based on acyclic phase-type distributions was introduced in [3]. An overview about the diversity of ATs can be found in [14].

Petri-nets and its variants [11] such as GSPNs (Generalized stochastic petri-nets) [7] and SANs (Stochastic activity networks) [23] are another popular approach in security modelling [10,26]. Much of its popularity stems from its capability of exhibit concurrency and synchronization characteristics (though at the expense of complex graphical representation). Some other approaches are to model the system description and attacker behaviour via attack graphs [25] and adversary based security analysis [6,9,12]. Moreover, there exist formalisms such as SysML-Sec [1] which are aiming on integrating security engineers in all stages of the design and development process.

2   Attack Trees

An attack tree (AT) is a tree — or more generally, a directed acyclic graph — that describes how combinations of attack steps can lead to a system breach. The root node of an AT represents the goal of the attacker and can be reached via different branches, where each branch represents one possible attack scenario. The basic attack steps (BASs) are represented by leaves. Gates model how successful attack steps propagate through the system, and thereby form a logical sequence of individual steps within a complex scenario.

Gates. The classical attack tree model uses AND- and OR-gates to describe the conjunctive and disjunctive composition of their child nodes. That is, to succeed in an AND-gate, the attacker has to succeed in all of its child nodes, whereas the OR-gate requires the attacker to execute at least one child node successfully. The SAND- and SOR-gate are the sequential versions of the classical AT gates and model a temporal dependency between their child nodes. The SAND-gate represents attacks that are conducted in a specific order: only after the primary attack step (the first child node of the gate from the left-hand side) has been successful, the attacker will start with the next BAS. Similarly, a SOR-gate models that the attacker first executes the primary BAS, and only if that fails, he falls back to the next option.

Example 1. The attack tree depicted in Fig. 1 models an attack on a password protected file [21] with a sequential extension. The BASs in the leaves are annotated with a rate λ which specifies an exponentially-distributed execution time, as well as the BAS success probability p. The goal is to obtain a password by executing a *brute force attack* as well as a more sophisticated *password attack*, as modelled by the root node as a parallel OR-gate. For the *password attack* a sequential attack is executed as modelled by the SOR-gate, where the attacker

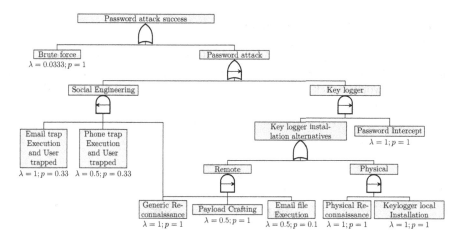

Fig. 1. Dynamic Attack Tree modelling the attack on password protected file.

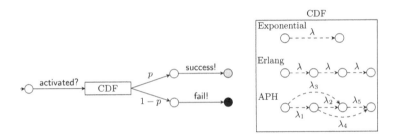

Fig. 2. Representation of a BAS.

first tries a *social engineering* approach and only when this fails he proceeds to install a *key logger*. The *social engineering* is a sequential execution as modelled by the SAND-gate, where the attacker first has to apply some *generic reconnaissance* which leads to a *phone trap* and finally an *email trap*, in case that all previous steps are successful. Note that the *generic reconnaissance* is a shared BAS; once it has been completed it can be used in both connected attack vectors.

Basic Attack Steps. Basic attack steps (BASs) represent individual steps within the execution of a more complex attack. We consider their success probabilities and execution times. That is, we equip each BAS with basic attack step information (BAI), consisting of (1) a probability $p \in [0, 1]$ that quantifies the attacker's overall success rate independent of execution time t; (2) The relationship between a successful attack and progressing time. The general assumption is that the chances of an attack success increases when the attacker is given a longer execution time. Thus, we are interested in the cumulative distribution function (CDF) $f(t) = \mathbb{P}[X \leq t]$ that represents the probability that the attack step is executed successfully within t time units. A graphical representation of a BAS is given in Fig. 2.

Sequential and Parallel Execution. Complex multi-step attacks are modelled by the composition of multiple BASs via gates. Whereas in classical attack tree models the description via AND- and OR-gates is sufficient, in a temporal context it is necessary to reason about sequential and parallel behaviour. Consider the password attack in Fig. 1 with the *key logger* attack. Obviously, one cannot intercept the password before having installed the key logger. This causal dependency induces a temporal order: certain steps can only be taken after other

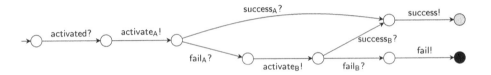

Fig. 3. A SOR-gate with children A and B.

steps have been successfully executed. In contrast to this sequential execution, other BASs can be executed independently from each other and, thus, can be executed at the same time if a sufficient number of attackers are involved. An example for this parallel execution is parallel execution of the *brute force* attack and the sophisticated *password attack*.

In [22] the authors introduced a trigger element to model the causal dependency between two or more actions. However, no existing model has so far offered a solution for the modelling of the sequential case for the OR-gate, depicted in Fig. 3. The sequential interpretations of the OR-gate is that the attacker starts with the execution of a first attack option. If he fails, he continues with the second option and so forth, until he runs out of options or succeeds in one. There are two challenges when using this gate in a model. From a practical point of view one needs to determine the attacker's preferred order of attack steps, whereas from an analysis point of view it is difficult to handle the inherent stochastic dependency.

Measures on ATs. Our framework can analyse ATs with respect to (1) probabilistic questions from static models, (2) time-dependent questions from dynamic models and (3) comprehensive questions from both models. For a static analysis the probability that the attack succeeds eventually given an unlimited amount of time can be computed by $\Pr(\Diamond \mathsf{Success})$, using model-checking syntax. The probability of an successful attack within a certain time horizon t can be analysed with $\Pr(\Diamond^{\leq t}\mathsf{Success})$, while the expected attack time is given by $\mathsf{ET}(\Diamond\mathsf{Success})$.

Compositional Aggregation. We exploit the compositional aggregation technique introduced for dynamic fault trees (DFTs) in [5]. The general idea is to have a modular framework, where each element of the AT is represented by the corresponding input/output interactive Markov chain (I/O-IMC). These models interact through synchronisation on their input and output signals. Thus, we compose the I/O-IMC models of the AT elements to obtain an I/O-IMC which represents the whole AT. To combat a state-space explosion, rather than composing the whole tree at once, we compose smaller sub-trees in a stepwise fashion and minimise the state space after each composition step. A graphical representation of the approach is given in Fig. 4.

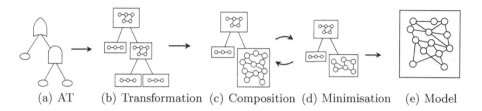

(a) AT   (b) Transformation (c) Composition (d) Minimisation   (e) Model

Fig. 4. Graphical overview of compositional aggregation for AT models.

3   Case Studies

We show the applicability of our approach by the means of two case studies from literature. They demonstrate that the use of I/O-IMCs accompanied by compositional aggregation techniques enable a highly-efficient analysis of the underlying attack tree. We use the ATCalc tool-chain[1], an extension of DFTCalc [2] with AT gates, to conduct our case studies.

Attack of a Password Protected File. The AT depicted in Fig. 1 models the attack of a password protected file and is described in Example 1. The parameters are based on the intrinsic difficulty, available resources, estimated skills and the level of protection as provided in [21].

Stuxnet Attack. The Stuxnet attack has been one of the most studied attack scenario given its serious implication on control systems of critical infrastructure. The goal of an attacker is to target the SCADA system, which hosts the industrial control system, and to reprogram the PLCs such that they slow down the centrifugal machines. The AT is presented in Fig. 5, and the rates and probabilities are based on [3,16].

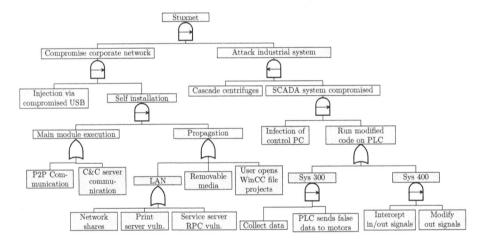

Fig. 5. Dynamic Attack Tree model of the Stuxnet attack.

Experimental Results. All experiments were computed on an Intel Xeon CPU E5335 at 2.00 GHz with 22 GB RAM under Linux. In order to derive valuable information about the system security, we perform a sensitivity analysis. We run the analysis multiple times, and in each run, we slightly change one of the BAS attributes while keeping the others fixed. We will observe the percentage change in probability of the attack goal caused by small changes in the attacks by using the Birnbaum importance measure [17].

---

[1] http://fmt.ewi.utwente.nl/puptol/atcalc/.

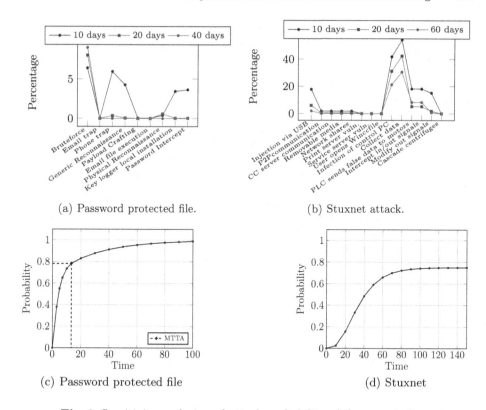

Fig. 6. Sensitivity analysis and attack probability of the case studies.

The sensitivity analysis is depicted in Figs. 6(a) and (b). In each analysis we double the mean time to attack of one BAS. The average runtime for one experimental run for each case study is: (1) 76.57 s for the password protected file; and (2) 113.61 s for Stuxnet. Figure 6(c) and (d) depict the probability of a successful attack over time. In the first case study, the attacker succeeds with about 61.9 % after one week while the mean time of an successful attack is 13.2 days. In the Stuxnet scenario, the attacker penetrates the root node with about 75 % after 130 and more days.

4   Conclusion

We presented a novel modelling approach for dynamic ATs and broadened the sequential expressiveness of attacks to the OR-gate. The complete approach is implemented in a prototypical tool, with which we showed the applicability of the analysis in two case studies. We firmly believe that the presented approach provides a substantial ground for the analysis of more complex and accurate attack scenarios for security engineering. Future work will focus on the integration of countermeasures within this framework as well as the determination of the correct order of sequential attacks based on the attackers profile.

Acknowledgements. This work has been supported by the EU FP7 project TREs-PASS (318003) and by the STW-ProRail partnership program ExploRail under the project ArRangeer (12238).

References

1. Apvrille, L., Roudier, Y.: SysML-Sec: a model-driven environment for developing secure embedded systems. In: SAR-SSI 2013, 8ème Conférence sur la Sécurité des Architectures Réseaux et des Systèmes d'Information, 16–18 Septembre 2013. Mont-de-Marsan, France, Mont-de-Marsan, France, September 2013
2. Arnold, F., Belinfante, A., Van der Berg, F., Guck, D., Stoelinga, M.: DFTCALC: a tool for efficient fault tree analysis. In: Bitsch, F., Guiochet, J., Kaâniche, M. (eds.) SAFECOMP. LNCS, vol. 8153, pp. 293–301. Springer, Heidelberg (2013)
3. Arnold, F., Hermanns, H., Pulungan, R., Stoelinga, M.: Time-dependent analysis of attacks. In: Abadi, M., Kremer, S. (eds.) POST 2014 (ETAPS 2014). LNCS, vol. 8414, pp. 285–305. Springer, Heidelberg (2014)
4. Baier, C., Katoen, J.: Principles of Model Checking. MIT Press, Cambridge (2008)
5. Boudali, H., Crouzen, P., Stoelinga, M.: A rigorous, compositional, and extensible framework for dynamic fault tree analysis. IEEE Trans. Dependable Secure Comput. **7**(2), 128–143 (2010)
6. Buckshaw, D.L.: Use of Decision Support Techniques for Information System Risk Management. John Wiley Sons Ltd, UK (2014)
7. Dalton, G., Mills, R., Colombi, J., Raines, R.: Analyzing attack trees using generalized stochastic petri nets. In: Information Assurance Workshop, 2006 IEEE, pp. 116–123, June 2006
8. Evans, S., Heinbuch, D.V., Kyule, E., Piorkowski, J., Wallner, J.: Risk-based systems security engineering: stopping attacks with intention. IEEE Secur. Priv. **2**(6), 59–62 (2004)
9. Ford, M.D., Keefe, K., LeMay, E., Sanders, W.H., Muehrcke, C.: Implementing the ADVISE security modeling formalism in Möbius. In: Proceedings of the 43rd International Conference on Dependable Systems and Networks (DSN), pp. 1–8 (2013)
10. Gupta, V., Lam, V., Ramasamy, H.G.V., Sanders, W.H., Singh, S.: Dependability and performance evaluation of intrusion-tolerant server architectures. In: de Lemos, R., Weber, T.S., Camargo Jr., J.B. (eds.) LADC 2003. LNCS, vol. 2847, pp. 81–101. Springer, Heidelberg (2003)
11. Haas, P.J.: Stochastic petri nets for modelling and simulation. In: Proceeding of the 36th Conference on Winter Simulation, pp. 101–112 (2004)
12. Ingolds, T.R.: Attack tree-based threat risk analysis. Technical report, Amenaza Technologies Ltd (2013)
13. Jürgenson, A., Willemson, J.: Computing exact outcomes of multi-parameter attack trees. In: Meersman, R., Tari, Z. (eds.) OTM 2008, Part II. LNCS, vol. 5332, pp. 1036–1051. Springer, Heidelberg (2008)
14. Kordy, B., Pietre-Cambacedes, L., Schweitzer, P.: DAG-based attack and defense modeling: Don't miss the forest for the attack trees. CoRR, abs/1303.7397 (2013)
15. Kordy, B., Pouly, M., Schweitzer, P.: Computational aspects of attack–defense trees. In: Bouvry, P., Kłopotek, M.A., Leprévost, F., Marciniak, M., Mykowiecka, A., Rybiński, H. (eds.) SIIS 2011. LNCS, vol. 7053, pp. 103–116. Springer, Heidelberg (2012)

16. Kriaa, S., Bouissou, M., Piètre-Cambacédès, L.: Modeling the stuxnet attack with BDMP: towards more formal risk assessments. In: Proceedings of the 7th International Conference on Risk and Security of Internet and Systems (CRiSIS), pp. 1–8, October 2012
17. Leemis, L.M.: Reliability: Probabilistic Models and Statistical Methods. Prentice Hall, Englewood Cliffs (1995)
18. Mauw, S., Oostdijk, M.: Foundations of attack trees. In: Won, D.H., Kim, S. (eds.) ICISC 2005. LNCS, vol. 3935, pp. 186–198. Springer, Heidelberg (2006)
19. McQueen, M., Boyer, W., Flynn, M., Beitel, G.: Quantitative cyber risk reduction estimation methodology for a small scada control system. In: Proceedings of the 39th Annual Hawaii International Conference on System Sciences (HICSS), vol. 9, p. 226, January 2006
20. Pieters, W., Davarynejad, M.: Calculating adversarial risk from attack trees: control strength and probabilistic attackers. In: Garcia-Alfaro, J., Herrera-Joancomartí, J., Lupu, E., Posegga, J., Aldini, A., Martinelli, F., Suri, N. (eds.) DPM/SETOP/QASA 2014. LNCS, vol. 8872, pp. 201–215. Springer, Heidelberg (2015)
21. Piètre-Cambacédès, L., Bouissou, M.: Attack and defense modeling with BDMP. In: Kotenko, I., Skormin, V. (eds.) MMM-ACNS 2010. LNCS, vol. 6258, pp. 86–101. Springer, Heidelberg (2010)
22. Piètre-Cambacédès, L., Bouissou, M.; Beyond attack trees: dynamic security modeling with boolean logic driven markov processes (BDMP). In: Dependable Computing Conference (EDCC), pp. 199–208, April 2010
23. Sanders, W.H., Meyer, J.F.: Stochastic activity networks: formal definitions and concepts. In: Brinksma, E., Hermanns, H., Katoen, J.-P. (eds.) EEF School 2000 and FMPA 2000. LNCS, vol. 2090, pp. 315–343. Springer, Heidelberg (2001)
24. Schneier, B.: Attack trees: modeling security threats. Dr. Dobb's J. **24** (1999)
25. Sheyner, O., Haines, J., Jha, S., Lippmann, R., Wing, J.: Automated generation and analysis of attack graphs. In: Proceedings of the 2002 IEEE Symposium on Security and Privacy, 2002, pp. 273–284 (2002)
26. Singh, S., Cukier, M., Sanders, W.H.: Probabilistic validation of an intrusion-tolerant replication system. In: Proceedings of the 2003 International Conference on Dependable Systems and Networks (DSN), pp. 615–624 (2003)
27. Weiss, J.: A system security engineering process. In: Proceedings of the 14th National Computer Security Conference, vol. 249, October 1991

International Workshop on Reliability and Security Aspects for Critical Infrastructure Protection (ReSA4CI 2015)

Analysis of Companies Gaps in the Application of Standards for Safety-Critical Software

Andrea Ceccarelli[1(✉)] and Nuno Silva[2]

[1] CINI-University of Florence, Florence, Italy
andrea.ceccarelli@unifi.it
[2] CRITICAL Software S.A., Coimbra, Portugal
nsilva@criticalsoftware.com

Abstract. The introduction of a new standard for safety-critical systems in a company usually requires investments in training and tools to achieve a deep understanding of the processes, the techniques and the required technological support. In general, for a new standard that is desired to be introduced, it is both relevant and challenging to rate the capability of the company to apply the standard, and consequently to estimate the effort in its adoption. Additionally, questions on the maturity in the application of such standard may still persist for a long time after its introduction. Focusing on prescriptive software standards for critical systems, this paper presents a framework for gap analysis that measures the compliance of a company's practices, knowledge and skills with the requirements of a standard for the development of safety-critical systems. The framework is exercised in a company to rate its maturity in the usage of the avionic standard DO-178B.

Keywords: Gap analysis · Standards · Certification · Safety-critical systems · Aerospace · DO-178B

1 Introduction

Companies working in safety-critical domains have mandatorily to comply with standards, regulating the system development, the techniques to be applied and the requirements to be fulfilled in the different lifecycle phases. A company working in compliance with a standard needs skills to exploit the required techniques, often with the support of tools developed within the company or from third parties. Several of such standards exist; for example, the DO-178B/C [2] is the mandatory international standards for software in the avionics domain while the European railway domain uses a set of standards to regulate railway equipment [7, 11]. When changing (certification) domain we can encounter several issues, such as different definitions, level of expectations, level of details of the required tasks, maturity level, tool qualification requirements [6, 10].

As a consequence, a company wanting to adopt a different standard, e.g., to enter the market in a new safety-critical domain, must necessarily (i) gain the skills, techniques and tools necessary to appropriately operate in compliance with the standard, (ii) have a

© Springer International Publishing Switzerland 2015
F. Koornneef and C. van Gulijk (Eds.): SAFECOMP 2015 Workshops, LNCS 9338, pp. 303–313, 2015.
DOI: 10.1007/978-3-319-24249-1_26

different mindset and (iii) acquire the necessary expertise. The question that is naturally raised is the required effort, both in time and cost, for the adoption of such new standard. Such effort can be considerable, if the company never worked with similar standards or domains.

Gap analysis is a renowned concept that finds application in several fields, including the area of safety critical systems, where new standards are being introduced [13]. Specifically to such area, gap analysis is part of the Software Process Improvement and Capability Determination (SPICE, [8]), to afford the process capability level evaluations of suppliers, which may result useful to select the cheapest supplier amongst those with sufficient qualification or to identify gaps between the supplier current capability and the level required by a potential customer. Similarly, the Automotive SPICE (ASPICE, [9]) starts from SPICE but is specific to the automotive industry. Furthermore, the Capability Maturity Model Integration (CMMI, [4]) includes the Standard CMMI Appraisal Method for Process Improvement (SCAMPI, [4]) that is aimed to appraise compliance of organization processes, activities and outcomes with CMMI; however evaluating performance lies outwith its scope [12]. CMMI compliance is not a guarantee of good performance per se, i.e., there is high variance in performance results within a maturity level [12].

In this paper we propose an intuitive, easily applicable methodology to support the introduction in a company of a new prescriptive standard for critical systems. The methodology traces the current status of knowledge available, identifies lacks and allows tracking the evolution of competences. Metrics are proposed to help spotting elements which may need further attention. Ultimately, the framework aims to estimate the required time to achieve an adequate level of confidence with techniques and tools that are relevant (for a specific company) to execute a specific standard. Noteworthy, our gap analysis is not necessarily related to a whole standard but it can be applied to part of it or to individual techniques and tools. Ultimately, we can note that it is specifically tailored for the characteristics of standards for critical systems. In the case study, the framework is applied to investigate the verification and validation phases of the DO-178B [2] standard in the company CRITICAL Software S.A.

2   Framework for Gap Analysis

We present the overall framework with the support of Fig. 1. It is structured in three main blocks: *Processes*, *Techniques and Tools*, and *Personnel*. The *standard* given as input to the first two blocks represents the standard under examination.

Processes. This block is devoted to the identification and matching of the processes. It contains (i) *internal processes*, that are defined and applied in a company (e.g., internal quality management systems, or internal processes that are required for having certifications like ISO 9001 [5] or CMMI [4]); and (ii) *standard processes*, that are instead the processes or requirements defined in standards (examples at a macro level are design, development, verification, validation, or integration processes).

For each standard, a corresponding traceability matrix must be created and populated; its aim is to check that *internal processes* are compliant to *standard processes*. One or more internal processes should be matched to each process of each individual standard.

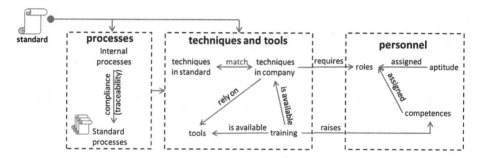

Fig. 1. Overall view of the gap analysis and introduction cost framework.

If the matching is not complete, there may be the necessity to review internal processes; otherwise, the applicability of the standard may be compromised.

The identification and matching of such processes are inputs to the block *Techniques and Tools*.

Techniques and Tools. Both standard processes and internal processes typically list recommended or mandatory techniques. A whole list of techniques in the standard (*techniques in standard*) and techniques available in the company (*techniques in company*) is required. The list of the techniques in standard needs to be compiled for each standard; the list of techniques in company needs to be compiled only once, and updated when a new technique is learnt. A traceability matrix can match techniques in company and techniques in standard, to identify the correspondence between the two or possible mismatches e.g., a technique discussed in a standard that has no correspondence among the techniques available in the company know-how. One or more techniques in company may be matched to each technique in standard. Techniques in standard and techniques in company must be also matched to, respectively, standard and internal process.

Tools are connected to the techniques in the company as they can support their execution. Similarly, *training* materials (e.g., slides from courses or tutorials), whenever available, are enlisted and mapped to the company tools and techniques. Noteworthy, techniques or tools not explicitly mentioned in internal processes may be available in the company and useful to support the execution of such internal processes: in this case, it is required to add such techniques or tools and create the appropriate connections to the internal processes.

It is fundamental to understand the confidence in using a technique or a tool, e.g., this can be done via a questionnaire, when done not on individual basis to rate the single worker, but as a collective exercise between expert workers.

Personnel. Our approach cannot be dissociated from the personnel that are operating in the company. In fact, the personnel is actually holding the background knowledge and is in charge of acquiring new knowledge. The *personnel* block relates the company's personnel to the know-how available on the listed techniques and tools. In fact, the block contains information on the personnel as the available *roles*, the desired *aptitude skills* for each specific role, and the required *competences*. Roles are matched directly to the techniques, while competences are matched to training. *Aptitude skills* [1] are instead soft skills as behavioral skills; they have an ancillary role in the framework but allow providing a more complete characterization of personnel.

The steps to be executed when using the framework are the same for gap analysis of standards already in use and for the introduction of a new standard. For simplicity, we refer only to this last case. We suppose that the standards $S_1, \ldots, S_{n-1}$ are already part of the framework, and that data on internal processes, techniques in the companies and personnel is already available. When a new standard S_n is introduced, the approach is the following.

Step 1. The list of standards is updated with S_n, and the corresponding traceability matrix of S_n w.r.t. internal processes is created. Considering for example the processes in the DO-178B standard, the process requirement "SW high level requirements comply with system requirements" can be matched to the hypothetical internal processes Verification Process and Requirements Analysis.

Step 2. The list of *techniques in standards* is updated with techniques that are mentioned in S_n; consequently, the match with *techniques in company* is updated. For example, the techniques "reviews, inspections, analysis" that are mentioned in several standards [3] could be matched to several company techniques, as reviews, inspections, HW/SW interaction analysis (HSIA), traceability analysis. If in S_n there is a technique with no matches amongst the list of techniques in company, it is sufficient to add the same exact name to such list. As a result, a very low rating on the maturity in using such technique will be assigned in step 4; this will be further discussed also in Sects. 3 and 4. Ultimately, tools are listed and matched to the techniques in company.

Step 3. The data acquisition process in this step allows gathering information on the confidence in using the techniques and tools.

Step 4. Data is analyzed, and gap analysis and learning time are computed.

In the case above, the standards $S_1 \ldots S_{n-1}$ are already part of the framework: this means that before S_n can be examined, it is required to populate the three blocks *processes*, *techniques and tools*, and *personnel* with information from the standards $S_1 \ldots S_{n-1}$ and from the company. This can be done iterating the above steps for the standards $S_1 \ldots S_{n-1}$, until the dataset is up-to-date.

3   Dataset Structure and Population

We comment on the most relevant elements of the dataset that is needed to populate in order to apply the methodology. The dataset is structured in tables and relations between tables. For brevity, we summarize on the three main areas of the dataset, which contain respectively (i) information on the standards, (ii) internal processes, and (iii) the definition and characterization of the personnel.

The *first area* contains three main tables: *standards*, *requirements*, *techniques in standards*. Table *standards* enlists the standards in use in the company including general information, for example release date, involved industrial domain, and emitting agency. Table *requirements* enlists the requirements described in each standard. It has to be remarked that the requirements in a standard usually contain the processes and suggest specific techniques: table *techniques in standards* enlists the techniques named in each standard. It is also possible to specify if a technique is a replacement or alterative to others that are mentioned in the standard. This is useful for the successive mapping with the second area, to favor the matching of techniques in standards with those applied in a company. Also, it has to be noted that many concepts in the standards are the same or similar but they are described using different terms.

The *second area* includes the table *company processes*, which describes the processes available in the company. Usually, these are described in the internal documentation of a company. Table *techniques in company* enlists the techniques available. Again, such list can be extracted from the internal documentation. Table *tools* contains the list of tools available in the company. To perform the gap analysis, it is also required to score the relevance of the technique and tool in the daily work, its frequency of use, the complexity from the point of view of the personnel, the experience of the team in using such technique, the *learning time* (learning time provides indication on how much training time and hands-on-the-job time is required to gather confidence in applying a specific technique). To achieve such scores, we propose a questionnaire that can be distributed between personnel expert in the area (e.g., V&V expert to comment on V&V standards) and acquire anonymous data. We propose the following entries and scores:

- *Relevance*: high relevance = 4, medium relevance = 3, limited relevance = 2;
- *Frequency of use*: often = 4, rarely = 3, never = 2;
- *Complexity*: complex = 4, affordable = 3, easy = 2;
- *Experience*: high experience = 4, medium experience = 3, low or no experience = 2;
- *Learning time*: less than 1 month = 0.5, ~ 1 month = 1, ~ 2 months = 2, ~ 3 months = 3, more than 3 months = 4.

The possibility to select the option *"unknown"* is offered, meaning that the expert filling the questionnaire was unable to decide on a rating. The questionnaire is supposed to be filled only by personnel expert on safety-critical processes, so that they can adequately judge on the techniques and tools, even when they had limited opportunities to get confident with them. Once all questionnaires are available, for each technique and tool we select the following values to be computed and added in the dataset: *average, standard deviation, mode,* and the *number of unknowns* (number of answers in which the "unknown" option was selected).

The *third area* is devoted to the identification of personnel. We propose the following minimum set of tables to describe the personnel, although our approach is open to improvements or adjustments in case companies offer different or enhanced characterizations of personnel. Table *roles* enlist the different roles. Roles are related to the techniques and tools, because it is expected that people having different roles are able to apply different techniques and tools, or take responsibility over different processes. Table *aptitude skills* is structured in [1] behavioral skills (for example, personal integrity, interpersonal skills), underpinning knowledge (knowledge on the system, required to successfully apply a technique), underpinning understanding (general knowledge on the area of work), statutory and legislation knowledge. Table *competences* lists the required competences as the number of years of experience, or the expertise in a specific topic or domain. Intuitively, the tables *competences* and *aptitude skills* are connected to table *roles*. A classification of the main personnel roles requested in critical software standards can be used as reference to populate table *roles*.

Relations between tables from the same or different areas allow connecting and extracting the relevant information from the dataset. For example, the dataset can be used to verify the matching between the standards requirements and company processes, or to differentiate techniques that are similar but used in a different way from domain to domain.

4 Metrics for Gap Analysis

4.1 Qualitative Analysis

Qualitative analysis is proposed to rapidly identify potential weaknesses and get an overall grasp on the results achieved.

Although several approaches can be envisioned, we propose in this paper an intuitive one, based on a simple binary tree that can be easily executed for each technique or tool.

The first four levels of the tree correspond to the attributes *relevance*, *experience*, *frequency of use*, *complexity*. The fifth level is a comment in natural language. Starting from the root, at each node, the left or right branch is selected if the score (extracted from the dataset) assigned to the attribute is below or above a given threshold. The leaves of the tree include conclusive judgments on the technique or tool under examination. As example, we discuss the binary tree that we also adopted in our case study. An extract is reported in Table 1. We suppose that the thresholds are set to 3 for *relevance*, *experience*, *frequency of use*, *complexity*. The final leaf includes a qualitative comment, resulting from the path of the tree, which may suggest the necessity of further investigation. In case this investigation results in the need of improving team experience, the estimation of the learning time can help to understand how long and expensive it will be to fill the identified gap.

4.2 Quantitative Analysis

The data acquired may contain information that is not grasped during the above analysis. We define the quantities Q_1, Q_2, Q_3 in order to seek the appropriate balance between complexity, relevance, frequency of use (called also *applied* below for simplicity) and team experience. The score 0 represents a balance between the different attributes; the higher such score is, the higher is the necessity of further investigating the technique or tool. Obviously different quantities could be identified and applied, without introducing any limitation to the applicability of the framework.

$Q_1 = (complexity)^2$ - *applied* × *experience*. This quantity intends to raise awareness of misalignment between difficulty and confidence. Intuitively, Q_1 is intended to heavily penalize complex techniques.

$Q_2 = (relevance + applied)$ - $(experience × 2)$. Q_2 aims to favor experience, evaluating if experience is sufficient w.r.t. the relevance and application of a technique/tool.

In other words, a small Q_2 means that the personnel feels confident with the application of the technique/tool, also considering its relevance in the safety-critical processes usually performed in the company.

Q_3 = (*relevance* × *complexity*) - (*applied* × *experience*). Intuitively, Q_3 compares the confidence in using a technique or tool to its relevance and complexity. Q_3 is a summarizing quantity that relates the four attributes. High values of Q_3 indicate gaps that are challenging and urgent to recover, because the technique/tool is identified relevant and complex to use, while confidence in its use is somehow limited.

4.3 Driving Conclusions

Whenever from the analysis above it emerges that the experience in some techniques or tools must be raised to achieve an adequate coverage of the (recommended) techniques in the standard, the learning time can estimate the time required to fill the gaps. The resulting *learning time* for all the identified gaps offers indications on the overall effort needed to acquire an adequate confidence in the usage of the standard. It has to be noted that once results are available, additional interviews with personnel may be required before drafting final conclusions, to achieve a full understanding of the questionnaire results, and to identify possible overlaps between techniques, thus defining a minimum set of techniques that is required to operate in compliance with the standard.

Table 1. The binary decision diagram.

Level 0	Level 1	Level 2	Level 3	Qualitative comment
Relevance	Experience	Frequency of usage	Complexity	
≥ 3	≥ 3	≥ 3	Any	Relevant, applied, and experienced
≥ 3	≥ 3	< 3	≥ 3	Relevant and large experience, but **not applied**, maybe because of **complexity.** May require further investigation.
...	...	...	...	...

5 Case Study: Gap Analysis for DO-178B

The framework was applied within CRITICAL Software S.A. on the (outdated) DO-178B standard for avionic systems. Both for space constraints and non-disclosure agreements with CRITICAL Software, we report only a synthesis on the procedure and the resulting analyses, that is here limited to the sections of the DO-178B devoted to verification and validation. It has to be noted that CRITICAL Software has long-term experience with DO-178B applied successfully in several projects for many years. Consequently, it is evident that the objective of this case study is not to identify lacks in CRITICAL Software processes, while it is to exercise the framework in a real context and show its potential.

For the population of the dataset, the list of techniques in standard was acquired from [3], and matched to company's techniques described in the documentation available at CRITICAL Software as processes, use cases, and V&V plans. Questionnaires were distributed and filled independently by eight experts at CRITICAL Software, operating as V&V, RAMS engineers or having managerial responsibilities, prevalently in the context of verification and validation and certification projects. The engineers had been selected with different experiences and expertise in order to make the questionnaires results more representative of the company level.

Step 1. Relating DO-178B processes and company's. Matching between standard's and company's processes was performed by manual inspection of the standard and the company internal processes.

Step 2. Relating DO-178B techniques and company's. For each verification and validation requirement in the standard processes, one or more techniques were identified at CRITICAL Software. Tools were also identified from ancillary material that is available at CRITICAL Software (these ranged from training material, to publications, leaflets, V&V plans for different projects, V&V reports, case studies and specific tools reports) as well as by directly interviewing the experts, and then matched to the company's techniques. Summarizing main results, at least one technique in company was matched to each verification and validation technique in the standard. For example the entry "reviews, inspections, analysis" [3] from the techniques in standard is matched to reviews, inspections, HW/SW interaction analysis (HSIA), traceability, static analysis from the techniques in company. Similarly, the "requirements-based testing" [3] enlisted amongst techniques in standard, is matched to coding/unit testing, system testing, functional testing and black box testing from techniques in company.

The techniques in the examples above present significant overlaps e.g., between functional and system testing. However such overlaps are not affecting the methodology as they can be analysed independently, offering summarizing results at step 4.

Step 3. Acquire data on confidence from personnel. The questionnaire was submitted and filled by eight people experts in the verification and validation of aerospace systems; data were acquired and processed.

Step 4. Data analysis. For most of the techniques, the standard deviation was computed below 0.5, showing that despite the limited number of questionnaires (eight), there was a high convergence of answers. Thus we preferred to use the average rather than the mode in our case study. We first comment individually on relevance, frequency of use, complexity and team experience, and then we compute the quantitative indicators.

Relevance and Frequency of Use. For these two quantities, the smallest scores were assigned to model checking/formal verification. The main reason is that these techniques have not been considered highly relevant for the company business up to now. Amongst testing, security testing was considered of little relevance and seldom applied. The reason is mostly due to the standards in use, which only sparingly require security testing.

Complexity. Lowest scores, i.e., less complex techniques, were assigned to reviews, inspections (e.g., Fagan, or walk-through), static analysis as traceability, code analysis, HW/SW interaction, and in general all testing techniques. Formal methods and modeling were instead acknowledged as the most complex techniques, with an average complexity of 3.8 (we remember from Sect. 3 that the maximum is 4). The number of *unknowns* was very limited, with at the highest 3 for formal methods.

Team Experience. Highest scores were assigned to reviews and inspections, Failure Mode and Effect Analysis (FMEA), fault trees, dependence diagrams, testing. In particular, although several kinds of testing are enlisted, team experience was high for all of them.

Quantitative Indicators. The two highest scores for Q_1 are 10.50 for formal methods and 10.87 for model checking. This is in line with the above observations. Similarly and not surprisingly, the lowest scores are assigned to reviews and inspections (lower than -10 in both cases), confirming that they were considered techniques with low complexity.

Most of the results for Q_2 are within the interval [-1.5; +1.5], i.e., in a near of 0. This means that there is a good balance between the relevance of a technique, its application, and the experience of the team. Few techniques are slightly outside such interval, although no techniques are significantly exceeding it. The highest number for Q_2 is assigned to safety analysis: the reason is that a proper and unified process for safety analysis does not exist, although the companies are constantly applying techniques that are part of safety analysis.

Regarding Q_3, we noticed that most of the techniques are in the interval [-7; +7]. For techniques outside such interval, relevant differences were identified between the couples [relevance; complexity] and [frequency of use; experience]. Most balanced scores, close to 0, are HW/SW interaction analysis (HSIA) and functional analysis (FFPA), considered in general with average scores of approximately 3 for all attributes.

Learning Time. The shortest learning time was assigned (i) amongst verification techniques, to reviews, inspections, traceability, static analysis, and (ii) amongst validation techniques, to coding/unit testing, regression testing, input-based testing, boundary value analysis, smoke testing, ad hoc testing. Longest learning time was assigned to formal methods, model checking, and (automatic) theorem proving.

Tools, related to the techniques above, were evaluated although no specific issues were identified. In general, some tools were identified as little relevant for a specific technique, but this was due to the fact that the tools list included also obsolete tools.

Concluding the analysis, as expected, no issues can be raised from the gap analysis of the DO-178B in CRITICAL Software. In general, the outcomes which suggest smaller confidence are those related to formal methods, model checking, and theorem proving, although other replacement techniques are used and this does not really constitutes a gap in what concerns the standard application. Mostly, it is relevant that a long learning time (above 3 months) is assigned to these techniques, meaning that it is considered not easy to acquire proficiency with them. However, this is mostly due to the fact that the company has a limited focus in such activities, thus having a limited number of people skilled in such area. The learning time indicates the effort required to train people on such topics. The real overall cost should also consider additional costs as tools licenses, subscriptions to courses, etc.; however, this is currently not included in the methodology and it is part of our future work.

As further observation, the fact that formal methods and modeling are not *-for the particular case study-* well ranked has at least three main reasons. First, engineers are often not prepared for these techniques from prior working experience. Second, formal methods and modeling are not yet widely accepted in industries, especially from customers. Last, formal methods and modeling are perceived more complex than others, and with limited easy-to-use tools support.

6   Concluding Remarks

This work provides a gap analysis to help understand the ability of a company to comply with a standard for safety-critical systems, and determine the actual level of knowledge and resources that can be reused instead of doing it in an *ad hoc* and less supported manner. The methodology is kept sufficiently intuitive in order to be applicable with limited effort and supporting tools; the analysis is relatively easy to perform provided that qualified personnel able to understand the standard is available.

Acknowledgments. This work has been partially supported by the European Project FP7-2012-324334-CECRIS and the TENACE PRIN Project (n. 20103P34XC) funded by the Italian Ministry of Education, University and Research.

References

1. IET, Competence Criteria for Safety-related system practitioners (2007)
2. RTCA DO-178B/EUROCAE ED-12B - Software Considerations in Airborne Systems and Equipment Certification, December 1992
3. Ceccarelli, A., Silva, N.: Qualitative comparison of aerospace standards: An objective approach. In: IEEE International Symposium on Software Reliability Engineering Workshops, pp. 331–336 (2013)
4. CMMI Product Team, CMMI for Development. Software Engineering Institute, CMU, Pennsylvania, Technical Report (2010)
5. ISO 9001:2008 Quality Management Systems (2008)
6. Esposito, C., Cotroneo, D., Silva, N.: Investigation on safety-related standards for critical systems. In: IEEE International Symposium on Software Reliability Engineering Workshops, pp. 49–54 (2011)
7. CENELEC EN 50126-1/EC:2006-05, Railway applications - The specification and demonstration of Reliability, Availability, Maintainability and Safety (RAMS) Part 1: Basic requirements and generic process (2006)
8. ISO/IEC 15504 Information technology - Process assessment (2004)
9. Verband der Automobilindustrie (VDA), Automotive SPICE - Process Assessment Model, 1st Edition (2008)
10. Duchi, F., Antunes, N., Ceccarelli, A., Vella, G., Rossi, F., Bondavalli, A.: Cost-effective testing for critical off-the-shelf services. In: Bondavalli, A., Ceccarelli, A., Ortmeier, F. (eds.) SAFECOMP 2014. LNCS, vol. 8696, pp. 231–242. Springer, Heidelberg (2014)

11. Ceccarelli, A., et al.: Design and implementation of real-time wearable devices for a safety-critical track warning system. In: High-Assurance Systems Engineering (HASE), pp. 147–154 (2012)

12. Margarido, I.L., Faria, J.P., Vidal, R.M., Vieira, M.: Towards a framework to evaluate and improve the quality of implementation of CMMI® practices. In: Dieste, O., Jedlitschka, A., Juristo, N. (eds.) PROFES 2012. LNCS, vol. 7343, pp. 361–365. Springer, Heidelberg (2012)

13. Gallina, B., et al.: Modeling a safety-and automotive-oriented process line to enable reuse and flexible process derivation. In: IEEE COMPSACW, pp. 504–509 (2014)

Simulative Evaluation of Security Attacks in Networked Critical Infrastructures

Marco Tiloca[1], Francesco Racciatti[2], and Gianluca Dini[2(✉)]

[1] Security Laboratory, SICS Swedish ICT AB,
Isafjordsgatan 22, 16440 Kista, Sweden
marco@sics.se
[2] Department of Ingegneria dell'Informazione,
University of Pisa, Largo Lazzarino 1, 56100 Pisa, Italy
f.racciatti@studenti.unipi.it, g.dini@iet.unipi.it

Abstract. ICT is becoming a fundamental and pervasive component of critical infrastructures (CIs). Despite the advantages that it brings about, ICT also exposes CIs to a number of security attacks that can severely compromise human safety, service availability and business interests. Although it is vital to ensure an adequate level of security, it is practically infeasible to counteract all possible attacks to the maximum extent. Thus, it is important to understand attacks' impact and rank attacks according to their severity. We propose SEA++, a tool for simulative evaluation of attack impact based on the INET framework and the OMNeT++ platform. Rather than actually executing attacks, SEA++ reproduces their effects and allows to quantitatively evaluate their impact. The user describes attacks through a high-level description language and simulates their effects without any modification to the simulation platform. We show SEA++ capabilities referring to different attacks carried out against a traffic light system.

Keywords: Security · Attack simulation · OMNeT++ · INET

1 Introduction

ICT is a fundamental component in monitoring and controlling critical infrastructures (CIs) such as electricity, railway and traffic systems. CIs are essential in the proper functioning of our daily life and their security is extremely important. In fact, a security infringement may have severe adverse consequences in terms of human being safety, service availability and business interests. In the past, CIs were somewhat secure as they had limited connectivity. However, the

---

(This work was carried out during the tenure of an ERCIM "Alain Bensoussan" Fellowship Programme. The research leading to these results has received funding from the *European Union* Seventh Framework Programme (*FP7/2007-2013*) under *grant agreement* n° 246016.)

F. Koornneef and C. van Gulijk (Eds.): SAFECOMP 2015 Workshops, LNCS 9338, pp. 314–323, 2015.
DOI: 10.1007/978-3-319-24249-1_27

increased connectivity to the Internet and the corporate network, as well as the use of commodity hardware, off-the-shelf protocols and software components make CIs no longer immune to cyber-security attacks.

In order to better understand the protection of CIs, it is important to analyze the security risks of such systems and develop appropriate solutions to protect them from malicious attacks. Unfortunately, addressing all the possible attacks is not viable, either from a practical or from an economical viewpoint. It is thus necessary to identify the attacks that have a more severe impact and focus on them. A possible approach to achieve this goal is via *simulation*. Simulations are important due to the fact that it is impractical to conduct security experiments on a real system, because of the scale and the cost of implementing standalone systems, as well as the potential risk of system downtime. On the other hand, although well consolidated, an analytical approach based on system theory does not provide a complete modeling of the ICT infrastructure [13].

In this paper, we present SEA++, a simulation tool aimed at quantitatively evaluating the impact of security attacks against the ICT infrastructure of a CI. We consider both cyber and physical attacks, where the former are addressed to messages, whereas the latter are addressed to nodes composing the infrastructure. A distinctive feature of our tool is that it allows us to simulate the effects of an attack by reproducing the events that the attack generates. This implies that we do not need to implement or port an attack, with clear advantages in terms of analysis time.

The tool is based on an off-the-shelf network simulator that we extend, but not modify, by integrating components for the processing of attack events. Good simulators are always the result of a large effort, and therefore any modification is preferably avoided. In particular, we use the INET Framework, an open-source model library for the OMNeT++ simulation environment, that contains networking models including those for the Internet stack, wired and wireless link layer protocols, and mobility [1,2]. Finally, our tool is also flexible, in that it allows us to describe attacks by means of a simple *attack specification language*. In order to simulate the effects of an attack, it is sufficient to provide a description of the events that it generates in that language.

The rest of the paper is organized as follows. In Sect. 2, we discuss related works. In Sect. 3, we illustrate the main concepts behind the simulation tools, briefly introduce the attack description language and sketch the simulator architecture. In order to show the tool capabilities and potentialities, in Sect. 4 we discuss a case study based on attacks against a traffic light control system. Finally in Sect. 5 we draw our conclusions.

2   Related Work

A number of different approaches to attack impact analysis have been presented so far. For instance, [10,12,15] discuss analytical models aimed at detecting and contrasting attacks, and rely on simulation to validate their own correctness and efficiency. In [3], Genge *et al.* presented AMICI, an assessment/analysis platform for multiple interdependent critical infrastructues. AMICI relies on simulation for the physical system components and an emulation testbed based on Emulab to recreate cyber components [5].

Wang and Bagrodia proposed SenSec, a framework that simulates the occurrence of security attacks in Wireless Sensor Networks (WSNs) by injecting events into real application simulators [14]. The framework NETA for simulation of communication network attacks based on INET has been presented in [7]. It relies on implementing *attacker nodes*, which can strike attacks when triggered at runtime through dedicated control messages. In [4], Queiroz *et al.* present SCADASim, a simulation tool to test the effect of attacks in SCADA systems.

Although it displays similarities with SenSec, NETA, and SCADASim, our simulation framework results more flexible and easier to use. In fact, SEA++ assumes that attacks have been successfully performed, and reproduces their effects on the network and application, rather than their actual performance. Also, SEA++ does not require the user to implement or customize any component of the simulation platform. This is particularly important for two reasons. First, it allows us to use off-the-shelf simulators. Second, good simulators are always the result of many man-years effort and therefore any modification is preferably avoided. In [6], we have presented ASF++, a framework akin to SEA++ but especially targeted to WSNs. A prototype implementation is available at [8]. In contrast, SEA++ provides a simulation framework for a conventional networking setting.

3   SEA++: Simulative Evalution of Attacks

The tool SEA++ is composed of the following three components. First, an *Attack Specification Language* (ASL) which allows the user to describe an attack to be evaluated, in terms of their practical and final *effects*. Second, an *Attack Specification Interpreter* (ASI) that converts the attack descriptions into configuration files for the attack simulation. Finally, an *Attack Simulator* that simulates the effects of specified attacks on the system under investigation, so making it possible to quantitatively evaluate their impact on the network and application.

Practically, the user first describes the effects of attacks to be evaluated by means of the high-level *Attack Specification Language*. Such descriptions can possibly be stored for later reuse. After that, the user runs the *Attack Specification Interpreter*, to convert the attack descriptions into an attack configuration file, which is provided as input to the *Attack Simulator*. Finally, the user runs the *Attack Simulator* and simulates the execution of the system affected by the described attacks. Note that the user is not required to further implement or customize any component of the *Attack Simulator*, with particular reference to application and communication modules.

3.1   The Attack Specification Language

The high-level *Attack Specification Language* allows users to describe attacks to be evaluated. It is worth noting that here we are not interested in how an attack can actually be mounted and carried out. Such an issue attains to the *feasibility* of the attack, i.e. the likelihood of a given threat to occur. Feasibility is the other dimension of risk assessment and is not the focus of SEA++. Instead, we are interested in evaluating the *impact* of successful attacks, i.e. their resulting consequences on the system. Practically, we quantitatively evaluate the effects of successful attacks. To fix ideas, let us consider a deception attack such as message injection. Then, we are not interested in how the adversary can inject fake messages in the system or in reproducing the actual message injection. Instead, our goal consists in understanding and evaluating what are the final effects of such messages on the network and application, once they have been successfully injected.

From this standpoint, we assume that the successful execution of an attack produces a sequence of *events* that takes place atomically. The ASL consists in a collection of *primitives* that allow us to specify the sequence of events related to a given attack. Primitives are organized into two sets, as described below.

(i) *Node primitives*, that account for physical attacks performed against nodes, and allow us to describe alterations in node behavior. In particular, the *node primitives* are:

- destroy(nodeID, t) removes node nodeID from the network at time t, preventing it from taking part in further communication.
- move(nodeID, pos, t) moves node nodeID to position pos at time t.

(ii) *Message primitives*, that account for cyber attacks, and allow us to describe actions on network messages, including eavesdropping, altering, injection and dropping. In particular, the *message primitives* are:

- drop(pkt) discards the packet pkt.
- create(pkt, fld, content, ...) creates a new packet pkt and fill its field fld with content. A single invocation makes it possible to specify the content of multiple fields.
- clone(srcPkt, dstPkt) clones packet srcPkt into packet dstPkt.
- change(pkt, fld, newContent) writes newContent into field fld of packet pkt.
- retrieve(pkt, fld, var) copies the content of the field fld of packet pkt into variable var.
- put(pkt, dstNodes, TX | RX, delay) puts packet pkt either in the TX or RX buffer of all nodes in the dstNodes list after a delay delay.

The ASL provides additional statements that allow us to specify the occurrence of a list of events described through *message primitives*. For instance, the statement `from T every P do {<list of events>}` specifies that the list of events takes place periodically, with period P, on the declared list of nodes since time T.

Also, the ASL allows us to specify the *conditional* occurrence of events described through *message primitives*, depending on specific conditions evaluated by nodes at runtime. For instance, the following statements specify that the list of events takes place on the declared list of nodes if condition is evaluated as TRUE.

```
from T nodes = <list of nodes> do {
  filter(<condition>) <list of events>
}
```

By means of the statements shown above, the ASL makes it possible to describe even complex attacks in a concise although clear way. For instance, let us consider a *wormhole attack* [11] starting at time 200 s, where node 9 tunnels MAC packets sent by node 5 to a remote area of the network containing nodes 10, 11 and 15. The attack can be described as follows:

```
dstList={10,11,15};
from 200 nodes ="9" do {
  filter(MAC.source==5 and MAC.type==DATA)
    put(packet,dstList,RX,0);
}
```

Note that we have used the *dot* notation packet.layer.field, in order to specify the field field of packet packet in the header of layer layer. It follows that the user must be aware of the actual specific network protocols that are adopted at each communication layer. Also, for each of them, the user must be aware of the packet header structure and fields, and the specific capabilities possibly offered by the simulation platform. For instance, the OMNeT++ platform [2] and the INET framework [1] considered by SEA++ provide a set of objects, namely *descriptors*, which allow us to handle packets of a given communication layer and conveniently access their header fields.

3.2   The Attack Simulator

The *Attack Simulator* module considers every node as implemented by a *Enhanced Network Node* module. The latter is in turn composed of an *Application* module, a *Communication Stack* module, and a *Local Event Processor* (LEP) module. The *Application* module may be composed of different sub-modules modelling the actual node application. Similarly, the *Communication Stack* module may include an arbitrarily complex combination of protocols for different communication layers, e.g. transport, routing and MAC. All sub-modules but LEP can be off-the-shelf.

The LEP module is responsible for the management of events related to attacks, and operates transparently with respect to the other components of the *Enhanced Network Node* module. In particular, the LEP module intercepts all application and network packets traveling through a node's communication stack. Then, depending on the considered attacks to be evaluated, it can inspect and alter packets' content, inject new packets, or even discard intercepted ones. Finally, the LEP module can also alter the node behavior at different layers, change its position in space, or even neutralize the node by making it inactive.

A system composed of multiple nodes is simulated by instantiating an *Enhanced Network Node* module for each node, and a single *Global Event Processor* (GEP)

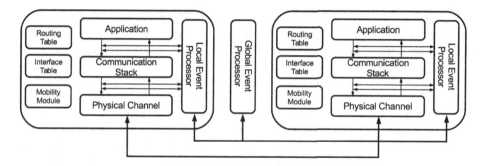

Fig. 1. The Attack Simulator architecture

module that connects all the *Enhanced Network Node* modules with one another. In particular, the GEP module is separately connected with every LEP module, so allowing them to synchronize and communicate with one another in order to implement complex distributed attacks, such as a wormhole attack. Figure 1 depicts the architecture of the *Attack Simulator* component, with reference to a system composed of two interconnected nodes.

3.3   Prototype Implementation for INET

We have implemented and released a prototype of SEA++. The *Attack Specification Interpreter* and *Attack Simulator* components are available at [9]. With reference to Fig. 1, as to the *Application* and *Communication Stack* modules we used INET [1], an off-the-shelf simulator for wired, wireless and mobile networks, based on the discrete-event simulation platform *OMNeT++* [2].

In the original INET architecture, network nodes are composed of different sub-modules. Also, nodes comprise a full communication stack composed by a transport, routing and MAC layer. INET provides the implementation of different communication protocols for each of such layers, as well as different network communication interfaces and physical channels. Thanks to the available communication stack, application running on the nodes can send/receive packets to/from the considered physical channel.

In our implementation of SEA++, we integrated the Local Event Processor and the Global Event Processor within the INET simulator. In particular, the Local Event Processor has been adapted to INET, in order to correctly manage simulation events and network packets. With reference to Fig. 1, the Local Event Processor intercepts incoming and outgoing packets traveling through a node's Communication Stack, between every pair of layers.

4   Case Study: A Traffic Light System

In this section, we consider a traffic light application scenario, and use SEA++ to evaluate the impact of two security attacks. In particular, we refer to the

T-intersection depicted in Fig. 2, including a secondary one-way road that intersects a main road. The vehicular traffic in the intersection is managed by means of three traffic lights, i.e. TL1 and TL2 on the main road, and TL3 on the secondary road. We assume that a single *Traffic Controller* node periodically sends control messages to the three traffic lights (every 2.5 s in our setting), with the intent to adapt their behavior to the experienced vehicular traffic. Furthermore, the three traffic lights periodically send a feeedback message to the Traffic Controller (every 0.2 s in our setting), reporting about the actual traffic light time experienced during the last time interval. So doing, the Traffic Controller can check the correct behavior of traffic lights, and possibly adjust them by means of additional control messages. We assume that the regular traffic light timing has a period of 10 s, and is set as $\{5s; 1s; 4s\}$. That is, the red light is on for 5 s, followed by the yellow light active for 1 second, after which the green light is on for 4 s before concluding the period. This is shown in the graph reported in Fig. 2, where values 5, 0 and -5 stand for green light on, yellow light on and red light on, respectively.

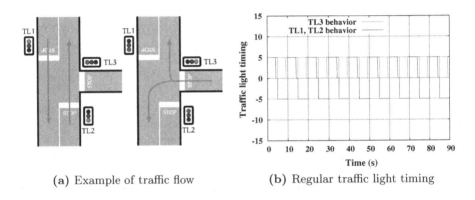

(a) Example of traffic flow   (b) Regular traffic light timing

Fig. 2. Traffic light scenario (Color figure online)

Hereafter, we consider an adversary who has managed to compromise the traffic light TL3, so being able to drop and alter feedback messages intended to the Traffic Controller. Also, the considered adversary is able to perform a number of attacks against the network. For instance, she can inject fake control messages intended to TL3. Having said that, the final goal of the adversary consists in altering the behavior of TL3, in order to create inconsistent traffic light configurations, which can be dangerous or prone to traffic stalemate, when both directions have red and green light, respectively. Besides, the adversary is insterested in concealing the effects of performed attacks to the Traffic Controller.

4.1 Attack Impact and Ranking

In the following, we consider two distinct attacks. In the first attack, namely *Injection*, the adversary regularly injects faked control messages intended to the traffic light TL3, specifying a traffic light timing $\{2s; 2s; 2s\}$. Then, upon receiving a fake control message, TL3 sets the traffic light period to 6 s, and starts to observe a traffic light timing $\{2s; 2s; 2s\}$, i.e. 2 s are assigned to each one of the red, yellow and green light. We refer to different *injection periods*, i.e. different time intervals between two consecutive transmissions of fake control messages. Note that, upon receiving a genuine control message from the Traffic Controller, TL3 starts again the regular traffic light period of 10 s, according to the regular traffic light timing $\{5s; 1s; 4s\}$.

In the second attack, namely *Bypass*, TL3 ignores *some* genuine control messages received from the Traffic Controller. Specifically, TL3 may bypass some control messages upon their reception, and instead set the traffic light period to 6 s and start to observe a traffic light timing $\{2s; 2s; 2s\}$. That is, 2 s are assigned to each one of the red, yellow and green light. We refer to different *Bypass intervals*, i.e. the number of control messages before the next one to be bypassed. Note that, in case a control message is regularly accepted and processed, TL3 starts again the regular traffic light period of 10 s, according to the regular traffic light timing $\{5s; 1s; 4s\}$.

In both attacks, TL3 keeps on regularly sending feedback messages to the Traffic Controller, although always specifying the *expected* regular traffic light timing, i.e. $\{5s; 1s; 4s\}$. As a consequence, the Traffic Controller is not able to recognize that the observed traffic light timing differs from the expected one.

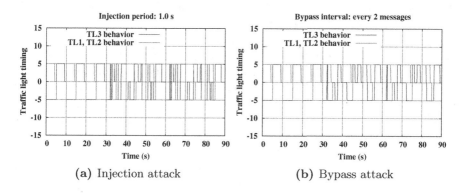

(a) Injection attack   (b) Bypass attack

Fig. 3. Traffic light timing under attack

Figure 3a and b report the behavior of the traffic light system when the *Injection* attack or the *Bypass* attack are performed. Specifically, Fig. 3a considers an *Injection period* of 1 s, whereas Fig. 3b considers a *Bypass interval* of 2 messages. In both cases, the considered attack starts at time $t = 30$ s and is then performed throughout the simulation experiment. The two lines in the graphs depict the evolution of the traffic light configuration over time, separately for the main and the secondary road. Besides, every overlap of the two lines denote a misbehavior due to the considered attack, i.e. the occurrence of an undesired configuration.

Table 1. Attack ranking

	Incorrect	GG	GY	YY	RR	Correct
Bypass (all messages)	51 %	14 %	17 %	3 %	17 %	49 %
Injection (Period 0.5 s)	41 %	11 %	14 %	3 %	13 %	59 %
Injection (Period 1 s)	36 %	9 %	12 %	3 %	12 %	64 %
Injection (Period 1.5 s)	35 %	9 %	9 %	3 %	14 %	65 %
Bypass (every 2 messages)	24 %	8 %	8 %	0 %	8 %	76 %
Bypass (every 3 messages)	9 %	1 %	6 %	0 %	2 %	91 %

Table 1 sorts the considered attacks according to their severity. In particular, attacks are sorted according to the amount of time that the system under attack experiences in a misbehavior state (see column *Incorrect*). Results are expressed as the percentage of time when the system observes a given traffic light configuration, while being under attack. In particular, the column *Incorrect* refers to all possible undesired configurations observed on the main and secondary road, i.e. Green-Green (GG), Green-Yellow (GY), Yellow-Yellow (YY) and Red-Red (RR). Separate results for each undesired configurations are reported in the relative dedicated columns. Finally, the *Correct* column refers to all possible licit configurations, i.e. Red-Green and Red-Yellow. We considered *Injection periods* 0.5 s, 1 s and 1.5 s for the *Injection* attack, and *Bypass intervals* 1, 2 and 3 messages for the *Bypass* attack.

As reported in Table 1, bypassing all control messages from the traffic controller results to be the most effective attack against the traffic light system. This suggests that this attack, especially when mounted at its maximum extent, is the one which deserves more to be addressed and counteracted. The *Injection* attack follows right after. In particular, as expected, the shorter the injection period, the more the attack is effective. Similarly, the *Bypass* attack is more effective when larger *Bypass intervals* are considered.

5   Conclusions

We have presented SEA++, a tool for simulative evaluation of attack impact based on the INET framework and the OMNeT++ platform. SEA++ allows the user to describe cyber-physical attacks and quantitatively evaluate their effects on the network and application. SEA++ does not require the user to modify any component of the simulation platform. As a case-study, we have showed the use of SEA++ to evaluate the impact of two different attacks on a traffic light management application scenario. In future work, we will integrate additional off-the-shelf simulators (e.g., Castalia, Simulink) to apply SEA++ to more complex systems such as smart grids and industrial plants. Finally, we intend to introduce the node primitive `disable` which complements `destroy` and disables every application activity of a node.

Acknowledgments. This work was supported by the EU FP7 Project SEGRID (Grant Agreement no. FP7-607109), and the PRIN Project TENACE (n. 20103P34XC) funded by the Italian Ministry of Education, University and Research.

References

1. INET Framework - OMNeT++. http://inet.omnetpp.org/
2. OMNeT++ Network Simulation Framework. http://www.omnetpp.org/
3. Genge, B., Siaterlis, C., Hohenadel, M.: AMICI: an assessment platform for multi-domain security experimentation on critical infrastructures. In: Hämmerli, B.M., Kalstad Svendsen, N., Lopez, J. (eds.) CRITIS 2012. LNCS, vol. 7722, pp. 228–239. Springer, Heidelberg (2013)
4. Queiroz, C., Mahmood, A., Tari, Z.: SCADASim-A framework for building SCADA simulations. IEEE Trans. Smart Grid **2**(4), 589–597 (2011)
5. Siaterlis, C., Garcia, A.P., Genge, B.: On the use of emulab testbeds for scientifically rigorous experiments. IEEE Commun. Surv. Tutorials **15**(2), 929–942 (2013)
6. Dini, G., Tiloca, M.: ASF: an attack simulation framework for wireless sensor networks. In: The 8th IEEE International Conference on Wireless and Mobile Computing, Networking and Communications (WiMob 2012), pp. 203–210 (2012)
7. Sánchez-Casado, L., Rodríguez-Gómez, R.A., Magán-Carrión, R., Maciá-Fernández, G.: NETA: evaluating the effects of NETwork attacks. MANETs as a case study. In: Awad, A.I., Hassanien, A.E., Baba, K. (eds.) SecNet 2013. CCIS, vol. 381, pp. 1–10. Springer, Heidelberg (2013)
8. Tiloca, M., Pischedda, A., Racciatti, F., Dini, G.: ASF++, An Attack Simulation Framework (2015). https://github.com/asfpp
9. Tiloca, M., Racciatti, F., Dini, G.: SEA++, a tool for Simulative Evaluation of Attacks (2015). https://github.com/seapp
10. Bonaci, T., Bushnell, L., Poovendran, R.: Node capture attacks in wireless sensor networks: a system theoretic approach. In: The 49th IEEE Conference on Decision and Control (CDC 2010), pp. 6765–6772 (2010)
11. Hu, Y.-C., Perrig, A., Johnson, D.B.: Packet leashes: a defense against wormhole attacks in wireless networks. In: The Twenty-Second Annual Joint Conference of the IEEE Computer and Communications (INFOCOM 2003), vol. 3, pp. 1976–1986 (2003)
12. Huang, Y.-L., Cárdenas, A.A., Amin, S., Lin, Z.-S., Tsai, H.-Y., Sastry, S.: Understanding the physical and economic consequences of attacks on control systems. Int. J. Crit. Infrastruct. Prot. **2**(3), 73–83 (2009)
13. Mo, Y., Kim, T.H.-J., Brancik, K., Dickinson, D., Lee, H., Perrig, A., Sinopoli, B.: Cyber-physical security of a smart grid infrastructure. Proc. IEEE **100**(1), 195–209 (2012)
14. Wang, Y.-T., Bagrodia, R.: SenSec: a scalable and accurate framework for wireless sensor network security evaluation. In: The 31st International Conference on Distributed Computing Systems Workshops (ICDCSW 2011), pp. 230–239 (2011)
15. Xu, Y., Chen, G., Ford, J., Makedon, F.: Detecting wormhole attacks in wireless sensor networks. In: Goetz, E., Shenoi, S. (eds.) Critical Infrastructure Protection. IFIP AICT, vol. 253, pp. 267–279. Springer, Heidelberg (2007)

Optimization of Reconfiguration Mechanisms in Critical Infrastructures

Szilvia Varró-Gyapay[2], Dániel László Magyar[1,2,3],
Melinda Kocsis-Magyar[2,3(✉)], Katalin Tasi[2,3],
Attila Hoangthanh Dinh[1,2,3], Ágota Bausz[2,3], and László Gönczy[1,3]

[1] Budapest University of Technology and Economics, Budapest, Hungary
{magyar.daniel.laszlo, dinh.attila, gonczy}@quanopt.com
[2] University of Pannonia, Veszprém, Hungary
gyapay@gmail.com,
{magyar.melinda, tasi, bausz}@quanopt.com
[3] Quanopt Ltd, Budapest, Hungary

Abstract. Recently, the protection of critical infrastructures became a core problem due to their importance in the everyday life and the attacks that may affect these systems. In order to ensure the safety and the efficient operation of such systems, a method together with an integrated framework is proposed to find a solution to the problem to deliver a system with cost-optimal operation by reconfiguration. Reconfiguration is possible via redundant structures of crucial resources while optimization aims at the minimization of the cost of the reconfiguration and the operational cost of the modified system. The method is illustrated by a SCADA control system case study.

Keywords: Redundancy · Reconfiguration · Optimization

1 Introduction

Due to the increasing demand for reliable systems with efficient operation, the simultaneous assurance of safety and optimality became a key problem in critical infrastructures. The delivery of the correct and cost-optimal operation of a system is crucial since unexpected external events may occur that can alter the parameters (e.g. cost of resource usage or supply) and also the structure of the system during their operation.

There exist several methods to describe how to improve the fault tolerance properties of a system or how to optimize the execution of a process. However, it is still an interesting question how to combine the best practices of these two fields.

This publication has been supported partially by the European Union and Hungary and co-financed by the European Social Fund through the project TÁMOP-4.2.2.C-11/1/KONV-2012-0004 - National Research Center for Development and Market Introduction of Advanced Information and Communication Technologies.

© Springer International Publishing Switzerland 2015
F. Koornneef and C. van Gulijk (Eds.): SAFECOMP 2015 Workshops, LNCS 9338, pp. 324–334, 2015.
DOI: 10.1007/978-3-319-24249-1_28

Our goal was to design a method that (i) provides a model-based solution for system reconfiguration in case of failure(s) (ii) by introducing redundancy for the crucial components (iii) such that it takes into account the cost of the reconfiguration and the operation of the delivered system to keep it minimal.

In our approach, at first the crucial components have to be identified. This will be based on the ontological representation of the infrastructure and the processes of the system. The aim of the ontology is to provide a metamodel-like representation of critical infrastructure protection (CIP) systems from which a formal model can be generated. This model is appropriate to capture reconfiguration and to support optimization of the operation of CIP systems according to dynamic changes. The ontology is motivated by the Security Ontology [1] and the ASTER data model [2].

In addition to the ontology model, we use Xtext language [7] to define the front-end infrastructure and process models that are transformed into mathematical models. Xtext is a framework for development of domain specific languages. In the current work, Alloy models and P-graphs provide the mathematical models for the analysis.

Alloy is a tool developed by the Software Design Group at MIT [9] that aims at the description and analysis of complex structure models by its expressive and flexible first-order logic based declarative language with relational algebra. P-graphs are the input models of Process Network Synthesis problems and algorithms that were developed to optimize process networks [6]. Alloy is responsible for the delivery of a sound model structure regarding to failures while Process Network Synthesis (PNS) methods [6] are used to deliver a reconfiguration solution with minimal cost.

The current paper focuses on an integrated method for the generation of a correct model with minimal cost of reconfiguration and system operation after dynamic changes.

Related Work. In [4] an error isolation and system recovery technique was proposed to satisfy optimization and fault tolerance needs simultaneously. The method used Alloy and PNS-based methods to analyze business processes with potential failures. The current paper focuses on a further development and extension presenting an integrated framework to tackle the optimization and reconfiguration problem. Another novelty of the current work is that the integrated framework provides not only the analysis of business processes as in [4] but also of critical infrastructures.

[3] proposed an approach to optimize fault tolerant architecture. Their solution is different from our one in the sense that they decide between the redundancy options based on the cost of the architecture according to the cost of the component structure not considering process activities.

[5] introduces on-line optimization for fault tolerant flight control. The aim of the method is to guarantee the correct operation of the flight control in case of actuator failures. Similarly to our solution, the presented optimization solution takes into account the remaining operational elements (actuators) and performs reconfiguration according to the given constraints, however it considers neither the cost of the reconfiguration nor the cost of the further operation after the reconfiguration.

[10] presents a new concept for automated reconfiguration control in SCADA systems based on fault isolation and service restoration within the power grid. This approach does not take into account the failures of the IT infrastructure of the SCADA system.

Structure of the Paper.   At first, related work is overviewed briefly. Then the approach and an integrated analysis tool is introduced. This part is followed by a case study to illustrate the approach through a SCADA example and finally, we conclude our work.

2   Proposed Solution

2.1   Structure and Workflow of the Integrated Analysis Tool

Figure 1 shows the structure of the integrated analysis tool which is capable to describe redundant infrastructure with behavior patterns and able to calculate the cost of the reconfiguration and the operational cost of the modified system if any error is occurred (or injected). The process consists of the following steps:

1. At first, the infrastructure and process models are defined in the Xtext grammar.
2. The definition of these models is followed by the generation of Alloy structures.
3. Then the models are imported by the integrated analysis tool and the Alloy code is run.
4. The Alloy tool generates feasible system structures (reconfiguration possibilities).
5. The operation costs of the system elements are added to the feasible structures in the integrated analysis tool, and they are transformed into a PNS model.
6. The PNS solver calculates the costs of the individual feasible solutions, and
7. The optimal solution is selected by integrated analysis tool.

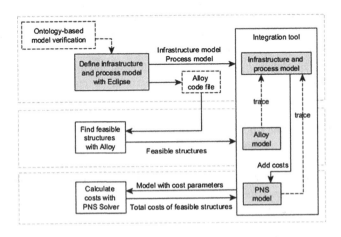

Fig. 1. The structure of the integration tool

2.2   The Model Definition Language

In order to model infrastructure with redundancy, dependencies and behavior patterns, an own grammar was defined for infrastructure and process description in Xtext language. The grammar consists of (see Fig. 2):

- a general ElementType concept which is used to describe the resources (for example servers or workstations),
- a Redundancy concept which is used to describe the redundancy structures, and
- an Activity concept which is used to describe the business process.

The main advantage of such a definition language is that it can be easily extended to support complex element models, deployment relation between HW and SW elements of the infrastructure and complex process models with alternative routes.

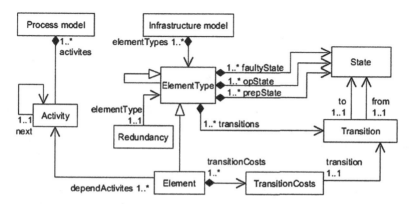

Fig. 2. The class diagram of the grammar

3   Case Study

In the following the operation of the integrated analysis tool is illustrated through an example SCADA system. SCADA systems are used to supervise critical infrastructures. Usually they contain at least one control center, several control units on the field site of the controlled infrastructure and the network between these elements.

The control center consists of at least one workstation used by a human operator in order to control the infrastructure such that workstations are redundant in most cases. Workstations can be used by operators to monitor and control the system.

The monitored data is collected and stored by servers that are redundant in most cases. In large systems there is a dedicated database server as well.

The local network in the control center is also redundant, and each workstation is connected to all of the servers.

The field sites are connected primarily to the servers through a field network that should be redundant as well. The field sites are equipped with RTUs and PLCs which are connected to the controlled/monitored unit of the actual infrastructure through actuators and sensors.

3.1   The SCADA System Model and the Control Process

In our example the controlled infrastructure is a power grid (see Fig. 3). For the sake of presentation, we use graphical notation to present the textual models.

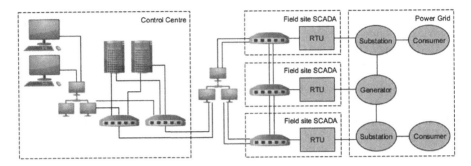

Fig. 3. The SCADA system model

The control center consists of two workstations, a local network, two switches and two redundant servers. The servers are configured to implement hot-standby redundancy.

The field network consists of the two switches in the control center, one router on every field site, and two parallel optical cables between the sites.

The field site SCADA consists of one router and one RTU on every field site. The RTU is connected to the actuators and sensors of the controlled infrastructure element.

In this example only the generators and substations of the power grid are equipped with RTUs while the consumers are not. On the consumer side, smart meters can be used to measure and control power consumption. The sample control process in Fig. 4 is used for demonstration purposes in the following: the operator sends a control message to a substation to change its state. The activities of the process are the following: (1) send control message, (2) process message, (3) issue command and (4) execute command.

The process activities are linked to those infrastructure elements which execute the activity representing the dependencies between the resources (or redundancy structures).

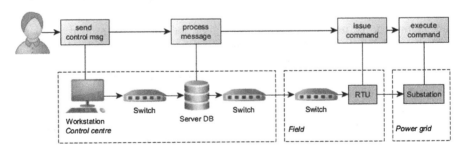

Fig. 4. The control process

Several errors may occur in this system. Typically the control center includes redundant infrastructure elements to assure that the system remains operational if any resource is failed. The redundancy also provides reconfiguration in the sense of load balancing between the operational elements and repairing of the failed one.

3.2 The Infrastructure and the Process Model

The infrastructure model is constructed in the model definition grammar (visualized as a P-graph hereafter). The internal behavior of a server element is represented by its internal states and transitions between them. This model describes the dependability of a resource representing the operational and faulty states [8]. Additional states are used to count the number of start and repair operations (see Fig. 5). These states are used later in the PNS model to ensure the existence of a transition in a reconfiguration structure. This behavior model is defined for each resource type. The definition of an element (e.g. server1) contains (i) dependency information that describes which process activity is completed by the element and (ii) the cost of the transitions.

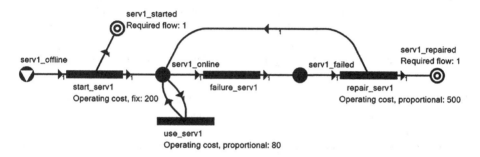

Fig. 5. Internal states of a server element

The redundancy structures are also defined within the grammar. The definition of the structure refers to element type information, number of redundant elements and the type of the redundancy structure (e.g. hot-standby). Dependent process activities are linked to the redundancy structure instead of individual elements.

The control process is also represented by the grammar. The definition contains the name of the control process, the initial activity and the chain of the activities. The graphical process model (see Fig. 6) is constructed by multiplying the activities (_using_server1, _using_server2) according to the redundant elements (server1, server2). This way the process model is extended with independent routes for each redundant resource modeling the reconfiguration possibilities.

3.3 The Alloy Model

Alloy is used for three purposes in the current workflow: for model verification, model construction and state space reduction. In order to create an Alloy metamodel the

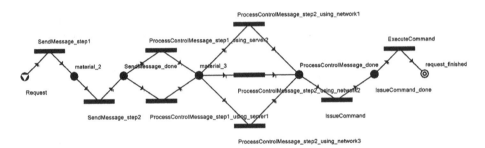

Fig. 6. Process model with redundancy structures

constraints and verification possibilities are discovered and built into the model. Then whenever an instance model is generated that satisfies the metamodel, these constraints are automatically checked.

The Alloy representations are generated by Eclipse from the Xtext model. The generation is based on an Alloy metamodel that contains the definitions of the element types, elements, activities and the process similarly to the Xtext grammar.

For model verification, only the predefined constraints are checked. For model construction, Alloy is used to deliver a model in which the number of resources is minimal and the process still can be completed. For state space reduction Alloy is used to find feasible structures regarding to the starting state of the system defined by constraints (expressing e.g., the presence of faults).

Infrastructure and Process Definition. Based on the generated Alloy structure, the defined model can be visualized and additional checks can be run for the reconfiguration scenario.

In order to ease the model construction, state types are assigned to the element states to make possible the construction of such models in which elements may have any number of operational and faulty states. These state types are used during the reconfiguration, e.g. one of the operational states has to be reached to complete the process.

The process definition in Alloy is very similar to the definitions used in the grammar. The process contains the activities connected by "next" transitions to each other.

Figure 7 shows the Alloy model generated from the Xtext models. For space consideration only the visualization theme (graphical notation) is summarized in Table 1.

After the definition of the metamodel, Alloy can be used to construct instance models as follows. The code below first defines a predicate with an empty body that always evaluates to true (example), then specifies a scope that bounds the search for instances, satisfying the constraints of the metamodel.

```
pred example{}run example for exactly 1 ElementType, 2 Element,
3 State, exactly 1 Redundancy, 3 Transition, 1 Activity, 1
Process
```

Table 1. Alloy visualization theme

Model element	Represents	Graphics
State	Internal state of an element	ellipse
FaultState	Fault state of an element (shall be repaired before usage)	red ellipse
InternalState	Optional state for counting the number of transitions	yellow ellipse
OperationalState	Online state of an element (can be used)	green ellipse
PrepareState	Offline state of an element (shall be started before usage)	blue ellipse
Transition	Transition between two states	white rectangle
Element	Container of an element	grey trapezoid
ElementType	Type reference of an element	grey house
Redundancy	Redundancy structure of elements	grey rhombus
Process	Business process	yellow rect.
Activity	Activities of the process	yellow rect.

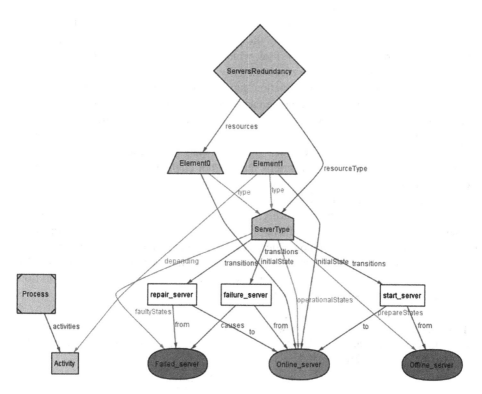

Fig. 7. The infrastructure model generated by Alloy

The Alloy tool delivers one or more feasible structures according to the states of the elements, e.g. for instance, all elements with FaultState are excluded from the structure. In the following the next step of the analysis is discussed.

3.4 The PNS Model

The integrated analysis tool is responsible for gathering all information about the defined infrastructure, control process and Alloy results. In order to deliver an optimal or near optimal solution for the underlying system the feasible structures generated by the Alloy tool are (i) traced back to the original model and (ii) they are extended by the cost parameters defined in the Xtext grammar. The P-graph representation is then generated by the integrated analysis tool using these cost parameters. Finally, the optimal cost of the P-graph is calculated by the PNS Solver and one solution can be chosen from the delivered possible solutions.

3.5 Results

The analysis in Alloy determines the possible reconfiguration steps, i.e. to alter the infrastructure from its initial (faulty) state-configuration to the set of reachable operational state-configurations that allows the processes to be executed. The result of the analysis is the reconfiguration workflow which is a directed graph of the steps. Each step of this workflow can be either (i) an activity of a process assigning an activity to an infrastructure element, or (ii) a transition that reconfigures a depending element to an operational state, so it can be used by an activity. Precedence constraints between steps are satisfied in the workflow, e.g. a depending element is reconfigured preceding its actual usage.

The workflow generation considers the initial state configuration; first unnecessary transitions are excluded, i.e. transitions that do not change the state of an element to operational state, then the required subset of transitions are included, i.e. transitions that repair a faulty dependent element or start an offline one. This process is carried out by the Alloy analyzer, and consists of a CNF (Conjunctive Normal Form) problem representation generation step and adherently finding a solution by using an off-the-shelf SAT solver on this representation. The measured average analysis runtime of a sample model like the presented one is shown in Table 2. The average runtime is linear for typical models. However, further evaluation of the average runtime of the workflow generation analysis is necessary for larger models.

Table 2. Average runtime of workflow generation analysis on a 2.19 GHz Intel Core i7 CPU under 1 GB memory limit, using MiniSat solver. Input model size is defined in the form: number of Activities/Elements/Transitions

	7a/8e/24t	14a/16e/64t	14a/24e/96t
CNF generation	1145.8[ms]	3434.9[ms]	5676.8[ms]
Analysis	75.4[ms]	180.50[ms]	264.8[ms]
Total	1221.2[ms]	3615.40[ms]	5941.6[ms]

The cost optimization of the feasible structures (representing reconfiguration possibilities) can be done using the PNS solver. The PNS model is built from the result of the Alloy analysis. This model contains a reconfiguration possibility for the failed elements. However, if there are redundancy structures in the model, one operating element is enough to complete the business task. PNS solver selects the optimal solution from the given possibilities with respect to reconfiguration cost and cost of the system operation. The cost parameters of each element are defined separately. The optimal solution describes the used elements in each redundancy structure and the reconfiguration actions to be performed (that is not discussed here in details for space consideration).

4 Conclusion and Further Work

The current paper introduced an approach and an integrated analysis tool (i) to model critical infrastructures with redundant resources and processes and (ii) to deliver a correct system with minimal operational and reconfiguration cost if an error occurs.

The main advantage of the proposed method and architecture is that the structure and also its dynamic behavior (both operational and repair activities) are modeled together. In the current implementation, dependencies and internal states of SCADA elements are modeled which can be extended in the future thanks to the modular structure of the tool and the definition language.

As a future work, the extendable Alloy representation can be used to check further requirements against the system and also the definition language or the Alloy models can be transformed into other analysis models.

References

1. Fenz, S., Ekelhart, A.: Formalizing information security knowledge. In: ASIACCS 2009, pp. 183–194 (2009)
2. Associazione Italiana Esperti Infrastrutture Critiche. Gruppo di Lavoro, Piano Sicurezza Operatore, Data Model (2013) http://www.infrastrutturecritiche.it/aiic/index.php?option=com_docman&task=doc_view&gid=536&tmpl=component&format=raw&Itemid=103
3. Adachi, M., Papadopoulos, Y., Sharvia, S., Parker, D., Tohdo, T.: An approach to optimization of fault tolerant architectures using HiP-HOPS. Softw., Pract. Exper. **41**(11), 1303–1327
4. Dinh, A.H., Magyar, D.L., Varró-Gyapay, S., Gönczy, L., Pataricza, A.: Optimization of Systems with Dynamic Structures, ASCONIKK, Information Security, pp. 11–18 (2014)
5. Zhong, L., Mora-Camino, F.: On-Line Optimization for Fault Tolerant Flight Control, Procedia Engineering, ISAA2013 **80**, 638–655 (2014)
6. Friedler, F., Tarjan, K., Huang, Y.W., Fan, L.T.: Combinatorial algorithms for process synthesis. Comput. Chem. Eng. **16**, S313–S320 (1992)
7. Xtext. https://eclipse.org/Xtext/
8. Avizienis, A., Laprie, J.-C., Randell, B., Landwehr, C.: Basic concepts and taxonomy of dependable and secure computing. IEEE Trans. Dep. Secur. Comput. **1**, 11–33 (2004)

9. Jackson, D.: Alloy: a lightweight object modelling notation. ACM Trans. Softw. Eng. Methodol. (TOSEM) **11**(2), 256–290 (2002)
10. Russell, K.J., Broadwater, R.P.: Model-based automated reconfiguration for fault isolation and restoration. In: 2012 IEEE PES Innovative Smart Grid Technologies (ISGT), IEEE (2012)

How to Use Mobile Communication in Critical Infrastructures: A Dependability Analysis

Jonas Wäfler$^{(\boxtimes)}$ and Poul E. Heegaard

Norwegian University of Science and Technology, 7491 Trondheim, Norway
{Jonas.Waefler,Poul.Heegaard}@item.ntnu.no

Abstract. Critical infrastructures, like the future power grid, rely strongly on a reliable communication infrastructure. Mobile communication seems an attractive candidate, as the entry costs are low and, provided the coverage, the new devices have immediate communication access upon installation. However, considering the long time-frame of this investment, it is important to think about the constraints in mobile networks and also potential challenges waiting in the future. In this study, which is based on the situation in Norway, we discuss four important future challenges: policy change, contract change, change of *Quality of Service* and network failure. We show that a clever use of mobile communication like multihoming or using a mobile virtual network operator may meet the challenges. In the second part, we quantify the availability of the different mobile communication usages with the help of analytical models and show that already a small increase of additional battery capacity in the mobile network improves the availability significantly.

Keywords: Mobile communication · Critical infrastructure · Battery backup · Smart grid · Availability · Interdependencies · Markov model

1 Introduction

Like other critical infrastructures, the future power grid is going to rely strongly on a reliable communication infrastructure. Intelligent electronic devices (IED) are going to be deployed throughout the power grid and are in need of a flexible communication platform [1]. The requirements concerning latency, availability and security [2,3] are very diverse and might be covered by either a flexible middleware framework for data communication like GridStat [4] or a mixture of different technologies. Among the considered technologies, mobile communication is regarded as a pragmatic choice for services like smart metering and monitoring in remote locations. It is a tempting candidate, because the entry costs are relatively low and, provided adequate coverage, the device has immediate communication access upon installation. However, there are many pitfalls to avoid, not least because of the long term nature of the investment.

The mobile networks conduct an access control based on the mobile device's subscription. A device is usually only allowed to use the network of the operator,

© Springer International Publishing Switzerland 2015
F. Koornneef and C. van Gulijk (Eds.): SAFECOMP 2015 Workshops, LNCS 9338, pp. 335–344, 2015.
DOI: 10.1007/978-3-319-24249-1_29

which issued the subscription. National roaming, i.e. the communication over networks of other operators, is technically possible but commonly not permitted. There are exceptions for special numbers like police and fire department and for special groups of customers, e.g. in Norway the regulator stipulated national roaming for a limited set of prioritized customers from rescue organizations [5]. If a utility wants to use a different operator because the reception has deteriorated or it changed the contract, it has to manually exchange the SIM card in the device, which may be very costly as the potential number of devices for smart metering and monitoring is very large.

An important property for the suitability of a communication infrastructure is its dependability. Only few public studies exist [6–8] as the access to data is usually restricted. The first two studies focus on operator internal incidents, the third one [8], however, takes a different approach: it is based on measurements done by mobile devices distributed over 300 different places in whole Norway. The logged connectivity to the different UMTS networks show the distribution of time between failures, down time and unavailability. This study measures the Quality of Service exactly how a user would perceive it.

In this paper we suggest several alternatives on how a power utility may use mobile communication; we single out the four main future challenges and analyze how the alternatives react to those. After this qualitative analysis we analyze the availability of the alternatives quantitatively based on measurement data from the study from [8]. And finally, we analyze the availability improvement when equipping the base stations in the mobile network with more battery capacity.

2   System Description

We consider the case, in which a company wants to roll-out a large number of mobile devices. These devices could be smart meters or monitoring devices inside the power grid. The study focuses on the implication of using mobile communication for these smart devices, this is done by concentrating on the communication between a single smart device and the company. The mobile communication is provided by two mobile network operators (MNO): *MNO A* and *MNO B*. It is assumed, that there is no national roaming agreement between *MNO A* and *MNO B*, i.e. subscribers of one network have no access to the other network. As in real networks, the two infrastructures are not completely independent and thus their failures manifest some dependencies. The reason is twofold. First, shared infrastructure or geographical collocation of infrastructure in certain parts of the network, e.g. *A* leases a communication line from *B* in rural and sparsely populated areas or *A* and *B* have their cables in the same ditch. Second, dependence on the same service like for example power supply. In both cases one failure can cause a failure in the two MNOs.

The MNOs are considered as black boxes, no internal state is known, the mobile device only knows whether a connection to an MNO is possible and, on a higher network level, if it has a connection to the power utility. It is assumed, that only the MNOs can fail, as they are the main focus of the study.

In order to connect to the mobile network any device needs a SIM card. On each SIM card there is a number (IMSI) which uniquely identifies each device. Part of this number is the mobile network code (MNC), which identifies the mobile company that issued the SIM card. Access control is based on the MNC, an MNO allows only connections from devices with its own MNC or with an MNC belonging to an MNO with a roaming agreement. In Norway, these roaming agreements are scarce and limited to foreign MNOs or mobile companies owning no or only a very limited network on their own.

2.1   Challenges

Any mobile solution faces challenges over its lifetime. In the following we list the challenges, which are in our opinion the most important once.

Challenge 1: Policy Change. Mobile communication depends on policies from the national regulator and also on policies from the MNO. The national regulator may for example forbid international roaming fees or impose national roaming; the MNO may change national and international roaming agreements.

Challenge 2: Contract Change. The contract between the subscriber and the MNO is subject to changes over time. Examples are an increase of the subscription fee above an acceptable price level, required services that are discontinued, bankruptcy of the MNO or its acquisition.

Challenge 3: Change of QoS. The *Quality of Service* (QoS) at a device may change over time. Examples are a reduced signal strength or increased blocking probability because of structural changes between the mobile device and the base station (e.g. new walls, new buildings) or changes in the usage pattern of the base station (e.g. increased number of subscribers).

Challenge 4: Network Failure. A network failure in this context is defined as service outage, i.e. communication from sender to receiver over this specific network is not possible. The mobile device always tries to connect to a base station of its prioritized MNO. If no base station of its prioritized MNO is available, it may try to connect to a base station of another MNO, but a connection is only established if a roaming agreement with that MNO exists.

The time granularity is very different and decreases from the first to the last challenge, i.e. the reaction time for the operator is getting shorter. Policy and contract changes have to be announced with a certain lead time and the operator can look for a solution well in advance. A change of QoS, however, may happen without notice and network failures usually come without warning and the system has to immediately react to mitigate the failure.

3   Usage Alternatives

The ordinary way is to buy regular SIM cards from an existing MNO, denoted in the following as *ordinary subscription*. This comes with a carrier lock-in:

a change of MNO can only be achieved by replacing the SIM card in each and every device. This is costly, as the number of devices is likely to be high and some of the devices may be located in remote areas or in places difficult to reach. Also a network failure has a strong impact, as a national roaming is usually not allowed, i.e. only the network of your own MNO can be used.

MVNO. The utility takes the role of a *mobile virtual network operator* (MVNO), buying a certain amount of services from an MNO. Utilities may collaborate nationally to reduce the operational costs.

The MNO can be changed by changing roaming agreements. There are already many MVNOs, so this is a proven solution and it can be implemented quickly by out-sourcing almost everything if desired. A precondition for this solution is that existing MNOs allow roaming by MVNOs. A policy change by the national regulator or the MNOs may therefore have an impact on this solution. An MVNO has usually only an agreement with one MNO and it may happen that no MNO can provide a satisfactory QoS for all the devices. In this case, changing the MNO does not help. This threat is higher for geographically wide spread utilities. In case of a network failure, this solution has the same weakness as the *Ordinary Subscription*, because the network cannot be changed on short notification but needs longer negotiations.

The MVNO may issue several series of SIM cards with different MNCs. It can then make individual roaming agreements for each MNC. This way some of the discussed problems can be mitigated.

Multihoming. Certain devices allow the use of multiple SIM cards. Using a SIM card from each MNO implements a national roaming without dependencies on policy changes by the regulator or the MNOs. An application on the device probes the different networks and chooses the one with the most favorable QoS. There is a carrier lock-in, however, by using several SIM cards the risk is minimized. Using a SIM card from an MVNO especially for utilities may increase the flexibility of this solution even more. A new MNO can only be used by inserting their SIM card. The cost per device is higher, as it needs multiple SIM card slots and multiple subscriptions per device.

International Subscription. Interestingly, users with a foreign subscription can have an advantage over those with a national subscription when the foreign MNO has roaming agreements with several national MNOs. In this case, the foreign subscription implements a national roaming.

The advantages are that it is very easy to implement and several mobile networks can be used, depending on the roaming agreements. The switchover to another network may be fast, depending on the network failure. International roaming depends strongly on the policies of the regulator and the MNOs that are in place. If the roaming costs are abolished for good, the MNOs may restrict roaming agreements or make international coalitions with roaming agreements.

But all depends strongly on what is de fined as legal by the European and the national regulator. Additionally, this solution leads again to a carrier lock-in.

4 Unavailability

The availability of the alternatives can be grouped in three classes.
A_{single}: only one single network is used, if it fails the connection fails as well;
$A_{standby}$: there is a standby network, which is used in the case of a failure in the primary one, the switchover time varies between the solutions;
A_{DMR}: (DMR: dual modular redundancy): two networks are used at the same time and a failure in one does not interrupt the connection.

The *ordinary subscription* and *MVNO* (with one MNC) are in the class A_{single} because they can only use the network of a single MNC, namely the one having issued the SIM card or the one having a roaming agreement, respectively. The solution *MVNO* (with multiple MNCs) is either in the class A_{single} or $A_{standby}$, depending on whether the MNC is fix or whether it can be changed dynamically in case of a network failure. *Multihoming* is in the class A_{DMR} if the SIM cards are used in parallel and in class $A_{standby}$ if one is in a standby state. The *international subscription* is in the class $A_{standby}$ because the device can only be connected to one network at a time and needs to reconnect in the case of a network failure.

We compute the unavailability U of the classes, given by $U = 1 - A$, where A is the availability defined as *"readiness for correct service"* [9].

4.1 Quantification of A_{single} and A_{DMR}

The mentioned study [8], contains data for our classes A_{single} and A_{DMR}. Additionally, it also contains the distributions for *time between failure* and *down time* when using a single net-

Table 1. Used parameters from study [8].

	Unavailability U	Failure rate $\lambda_{i,total}$ [s^{-1}]	Restoration rate μ_i [s^{-1}]
A_{single}	3.3×10^{-4}	1.11×10^{-5}	3.33×10^{-2}
A_{single}	5.0×10^{-3}	2.01×10^{-6}	4×10^{-4}
A_{DMR}	2.0×10^{-5}	–	–

work. Assuming the distributions to be negative exponential, the failure and restoration rates are computed with the approximated *mean time between failure (MTBF)* and *mean down time (MDT)* by $\lambda = 1/(\text{MTBF-MDT})$ and $\mu = 1/\text{MDT}$. The parameters are given in Table 1. The two networks have very different properties: *MNO A* has more failures than *MNO B*, but due to its short restoration time it has a lower overall unavailability.

4.2 Quantification of $A_{standby}$

There are no numbers for $A_{standby}$, however, we show how it can be computed with a Markov model and the given parameters. But first, we note, that the measurements in Table 1 indicate, that *MNO A* and *MNO B* are *not* independent, they are subject to common cause failures. In order to compute this common

cause failure rate the Markov model in Fig. 1 is
used. The round states are system up states and
the square states system down states. The state
of the whole system is defined by the states of
the two MNOs ($i_A : i_B$) with $i_A, i_B \in \{$ok,d,cf$\}$.
The states for each MNO are working (ok),
down (d) or down because of a common cause
failure (cf). Common cause failures from states
other than *(ok:ok)* are omitted for the sake of
readability; the introduced error is negligible,

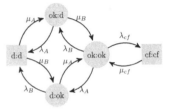

Fig. 1. Model for class A_{DMR}

as the *ok:ok* state has by far the highest state probability. The λ_is are computed
by $\lambda_i = \lambda_{i,total} - \lambda_{cf}$ in order to keep the total failure rates $\lambda_{i,total}$ constant
when varying λ_{cf}. Setting $\lambda_{cf} = 0$, i.e. making the networks independent, we
get an unavailability of 1.67×10^{-6}, i.e. around 12 times smaller than the measured unavailability in Table 1, showing that the networks are in fact dependent
as mentioned above.

Details about shared infrastructures and services in *MNO A* and *MNO B* are not known.
However, leased line and power incidents are possibly large contributors to failures [6], therefore,
we assume a restoration time of $\mu_{cf} = 2500s$,

Table 2. Common cause rates
after parameter fitting.

λ_{cf} [s^{-1}]	μ_{cf} [s^{-1}]
6.34×10^{-7}	4×10^{-4}

which is in the order of a longer mobile restoration time and a power outage
restoration [10]. Solving the model with the unavailability and rates given in
Table 1 yields a common cause failure rate λ_{cf} as listed in Table 2. The failure
rate λ_{cf} makes around 5 % of the total failure rate of *MNO A* $\lambda_{A,total}$ and around
30 % of *MNO B* $\lambda_{B,total}$.

Finally, the unavailability for A_{standby} is
computed by extending the state definitions to
($j_A : j_B$) with $j_A, j_B \in \{$ok, OK, d, D, cf, CF$\}$,
which yields the model depicted in Fig. 2.
Uppercase letters indicate that the mobile
device is currently using that network. E.g,
state ($ok : D$) means network B is used, but
down and network A is *ok*. It is a down state
(square), only after switching the network, leading to state ($Ok : d$) is the system up and running again.

In a business oriented setting it can be
advantageous to prefer one MNO over the other
because of special price models based for example on data volume. The other MNO is only
used if the preferred one is down. For that, the

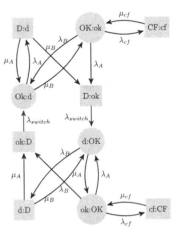

Fig. 2. Model for class A_{standby}

model in Fig. 2 is adjusted to always switch over
to the preferred network if it is working. i.e. if *MNO A* is preferred, adding a
new transition from *(ok:OK)* to *(OK:ok)* and marking the former state as down
state because of the unavailability during the switchover.

4.3   Discussion

The results of a steady-state analysis are given in Fig. 3. They show clearly the large difference in unavailability of the different solutions. Class A_{single} has two results depending on which MNO is chosen. The difference between the two MNOs is big because of the large difference in restoration time.

In the class A_{standby}, the unavailability is linearly increasing with the mean switching time. The unavailability is lower than the unavailability of A_{single} if the mean switching time is lower than 95 s or 1485 s for *MNO A* and *MNO B*, respectively. The first number is surprisingly small, it is explained by the very short average restoration time in *MNO A* of $1/\mu_A = 30\,s$. The switching time itself depends strongly on the used alternative and implementation. Two alternatives belonging to the class A_{standby} may, therefore, not necessarily have the same unavailability.

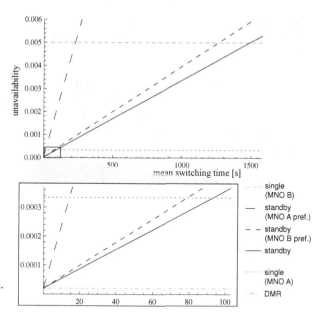

Fig. 3. Unavailability of the classes against switching time. Zoom-in for low values of switching time.

Preferring one MNO leads to a higher unavailability. *MNO B* is here the better choice of the two, as this solution benefits from the longer uptime of *MNO B* and the shorter restoration time of *MNO A*. Preferring one MNO creates additional interruptions, i.e. a lower mean time between failure (MTBF) and should be avoided. However, as stated above there might be other considerations that need to be taken into account. We consider the system as down during the switchover, if it is performed without downtime, then preferring *MNO B* has a lower unavailability than the standard standby class.

5   Improving Availability with Batteries

Today, batteries are available in some base stations. Depending on the MNO the number of equipped base stations as well as capacity varies strongly. In Norway there are discussions between the national regulator and MNOs about stipulating a required battery installation in base stations in mobile networks [11]. So far, installed batteries in the power grid were already included implicitly, because we used measurements of actual networks. In the following we study the effect of installing additional battery capacity.

Batteries allow the communication system to keep on working in case of a power failure, if it is bridgeable by battery. We assume that this is the case for $p\%$ of all failures, valid for both individual failures and common cause failures. The battery capacity is assumed to be negative exponentially distributed with mean $1/\lambda_{\mathrm{bat}}$. This assumption is justified by the variation of capacity due to different battery types, battery ages, working conditions and charging states.

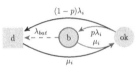

Fig. 4. Model for class A_{single} with limited battery capacity.

The extended models for the classes A_{single} and A_{DMR} are depicted in Figs. 4 and 5. The state definition is extended by the network state b, indicating that the network suffered a power failure and parts of it is running on battery. The dashed arrows indicate a transition caused by battery depletion. The model for A_{standby} is not depicted but is constructed as before by duplicating the model for A_{DMR}, adding an indication for which MNO is active and adding two new transitions with rate $\lambda_{\mathrm{switch}}$ between $ok{:}D$ to $OK{:}d$ and $D{:}ok$ to $d{:}OK$.

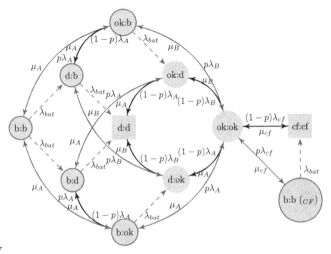

Fig. 5. Model for the class A_{DMR} with limited battery capacity.

5.1 Discussion

Figure 6(a) shows the results for the class A_{single} when using *MNO A*. The unavailability is most sensitive to a mean battery capacity in the order of the mean down time, i.e. $1/\mu_A = 30\,\mathrm{s}$. For the *MNO B* the plot would look similar, but shifted towards its mean down time of $1/\mu_B = 2500\,\mathrm{s}$.

Figure 6(b) shows the results for the class A_{DMR}. The two parameters λ_{cf} and μ_{cf} are set to the values used previously, noted in Table 2, which equals to a mean *common cause restoration time* of 2500 s. As expected are the absolute values lower than in the class A_{single}; the plot is in fact almost the same as for *MNO B*, except the y values are much lower. The reason being, that of the two down states in the model, the state *cf:cf* is responsible for the highest fraction

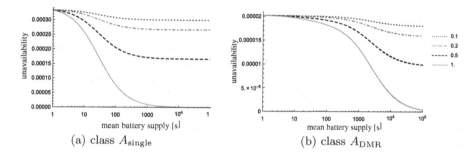

Fig. 6. Unavailability against battery capacity for different values of p.

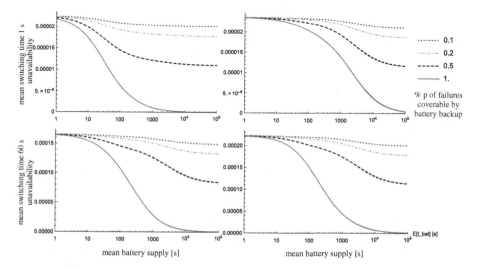

Fig. 7. Unavailability vs battery capacity for class A_{standby} with different values of p.

of the down time. The mean sojourn time for this state is given by $1/\lambda_{cf}$ and is equal to the restoration time in *MNO B*.

Figure 7 shows the results for the class A_{standby}. The simulation is done for two scenarios with different pairs for λ_{cf} and μ_{cf}. In scenario 1, $1/\mu_{cf}$ is chosen to be very short, i.e. 30 s, which corresponds to the restoration rate of *MNO A*. As before, λ_{cf} is given indirectly by the model in Fig. 1 by solving the steady state equations for it. In scenario 2, the two parameters λ_{cf} and μ_{cf} are set to the values used previously, i.e. $1/\mu_{cf}$ of 2500 s. Additionally, it is done for two different switching times. For a switching time of 1 s the difference between the two scenarios is big, i.e. the downtime caused by the common cause failure is dominant. When increasing the switching time to 60 s, however, the downtime caused by the switching itself becomes dominant and the difference between the two scenarios is minimal.

The numbers show that the availability gain can already be large for a small battery capacity bridging a time of 1–3 min. However, it depends strongly on the restoration times and switching times between the networks.

6   Conclusion

We list different alternatives of how to use mobile communication in this paper. By combining them, more are possible, but they are not fundamentally different to the presented ones. As the machine-to-machine communication (M2M) is likely to increase in the future, new technologies and especially new regulations may change the way mobile communication is used. For example, a decoupling of the SIM card and the operator by issuing carrier-free SIM cards would allow the switching between different networks and subscription contracts with only a short switching delay. This would inexpensively implement a virtual multihoming belonging to the availability class $A_{standby}$ as discussed above.

This study is based on the regulation status and availability statistics in Norway. Details might be different in other countries. If and how mobile communication should be used depends on what service is run over it and its requirements concerning availability, performance and costs. In this paper we only focused on future challenges, usage alternatives and the availability; performance and costs are important factors but were outside the scope.

References

1. International Energy Agency (IEA), Technology roadmap: Smart grids (2011)
2. Bakken, D.E., Bose, A., Hauser, C.H., Whitehead, D.E., Zweigle, G.C.: Smart generation and transmission with coherent, real-time data. Proc. IEEE **99**(6), 928–951 (2011)
3. Electric Power Research Institute (EPRI), The integrated energy and communication systems architechture, vol. IV, Technical analysis, Technical Report (2004)
4. Gjermundrod, H., Bakken, D.E., Hauser, C.H., Bose, A.: GridStat: a flexible QoS-managed data dissemination framework for the power grid. IEEE Trans. Power Deliv. **24**(1), 136–143 (2009)
5. Forskrift om prioritet i mobilnett, [Regulation about Priorities in Mobile Networks], FOR-2013-10-21-1241, NKOM, Norwegian Communication Authority (2013)
6. Følstad, E.L., Helvik, B.E.: Failures and changes in cellular access networks: a study of field data. In: Proceedings of DRCN, pp. 132–139 (2011)
7. Matz, S.M., Votta, L.G., Malkawi, M.: Analysis of failure and recovery rates in a wireless telecommunications system.: In: Proceedings of Dependable Systems and Networks (DSN), pp. 687–693 (2002)
8. Kvalbein, A.: Robusthet i norske mobilnett, [Robustness in Norwegian mobile networks], simula research laboratory, Technical Report (2013)
9. Avizienis, A., Laprie, J.C., Randell, B., Landwehr, C.: Basic concepts and taxonomy of dependable and secure computing. IEEE Trans. Dependable Secure Comput. **1**(1), 11–33 (2004)
10. Avbrotsstatistikk 2013, [Outage statistics 2013], NVE, Norwegian Water Resources and Energy Directorate (2014)
11. Sikkerhet og beredskap mot ekstremvær i telesektoren, [Security and preparedness for extreme weather situations in the telecommunication sector], Working Group Energi Norge and Telenor, Technical Report (2013)

Using Structured Assurance Case Approach to Analyse Security and Reliability of Critical Infrastructures

Kateryna Netkachova[1,2(✉)], Robin Bloomfield[1,2], Peter Popov[1],
and Oleksandr Netkachov[1]

[1] Centre for Software Reliability,
City University London, London, UK
{Kateryna.Netkachova.2,R.E.Bloomfield,P.T.Popov,
Oleksandr.Netkachov.1}@city.ac.uk
[2] Adelard LLP, London, UK
{kn,reb}@adelard.com

Abstract. The evaluation of the security, reliability and resilience of critical infrastructures (CI) faces a wide range of challenges ranging from the scale and tempo of attacks to the need to address complex and interdependent systems of systems. Model-based approaches and probabilistic design are fundamental to the evaluation of CI and we need to know whether we can trust these models. This paper presents an approach we are developing to justify the models used to assure CI using structured assurance cases based on Claims, Arguments and Evidence (CAE). The modelling and quantitative evaluation of the properties are supported by the Preliminary Interdependency Analysis (PIA) method and platform applied to a case study – a reference power transmission network enhanced with an industrial distributed system of monitoring, protection and control. We discuss the usefulness of the modelling and assurance case structuring approaches, some findings from the case study, and outline the directions of further work.

Keywords: Assurance cases · CAE building blocks · Critical infrastructures · Power transmission network · Preliminary interdependency analysis

1 Introduction

Reliable and resilient critical infrastructures are of vital importance to the society. Modern infrastructure components often depend on the information systems, which control their operation, monitor activities, provide real-time response to incidents and events. These information systems frequently become the target for cyber-attacks and can pose significant risks to the critical infrastructures (CI).

In this paper we present a systematic practical approach to justifying the models used to assure CI, taking into consideration the possibility of cyber-attacks. Building on the assurance case approach, we are creating a structured security-informed reliability case with the use of specially designed building blocks [1] that are based on the CAE notation [2, 3] and provide means for developing a more rigorous justification in assurance cases. The analysis of dependencies between elements of critical infrastructures as well as the

© Springer International Publishing Switzerland 2015
F. Koornneef and C. van Gulijk (Eds.): SAFECOMP 2015 Workshops, LNCS 9338, pp. 345–354, 2015.
DOI: 10.1007/978-3-319-24249-1_30

quantitative evaluation of reliability properties are performed using the Preliminary Interdependency Analysis (PIA) method and tool [4, 5].

The proposed approach addresses three key issues: considerantion of security attacks on the critical infrastructures, system model and assumption justification, and quantitative evaluation of reliability properties for the system under attack. We use the results of PIA to support decisions about the critical infrastructure. The PIA approach deals with the stochastic properties and addresses the aleatory uncertainty. There are also epistemic doubts arising from our lack of knowledge of the world e.g. about the systems being modeled, the attackers. These types of doubts are interrelated and both need to be taken into account in the decision making. In this research we explore how combining the CAE Assurance Case approach with the PIA modeling allows us to do that.

Our approach is demonstrated with aspecific case study – an advanced power transmission network – butit is not by any means confined to the power grids and can be used for a wide variety of industrial systems with complex topology and different functional, spatial and other stochastic dependencies between elements.

The paper is organized in the following way: In Sect. 2 we provide a brief overview of the main approaches used. Section 3 introduces the case study. Section 4 demonstrates how the approaches are applied to the case study to create a structured security-informed reliability case. Section 5 summarises the key findings and Sect. 6 concludes the paper indicating the directions of future research.

2   Overview of the Approaches

2.1   Structured Assurance Cases

An explicit claim-based approach to reasoning about safety, security, reliability and assurance, influenced by the basic model of argumentation developed by Toulmin [6], has been in use for many years. There are various solutions to structure assurance cases [3, 7, 8], and to increase rigour and confidence in them [9–11]. In this study we use a CAE approach, which provides an effective means for presenting and communicating cases. A graphical notation ASCAD [12] is used to describe the interrelationship of the claims, argument and evidence.

We extend the approach by developing a set of CAE building blocks that restrict the types of argument structures used in a case and help architect cases in a more systematic and rigorous way. Additional information on the building blocks including their definitions, application and guidance can be found in papers [1]. In this paper the building blocks are used to create a structured assurance case fragment for analysing reliability properties of power transmission system under cyber attack.

2.2   Preliminary Interdependency Analysis Method and Tool

Preliminary Interdependency Analysis (PIA) [4] is an analysis activity that helps to understand the range of possible interdependencies between the components of critical infrastructures. The objectives of PIA are to develop an appropriate service model for the infrastructures, and to document assumptions about resources, environmental impact, threats and other factors. PIA is used for both qualitative and quantitative assessment by accounting for both static (topology) and dynamic (behavioural) aspects of the modelled systems. The key concept of the PIA methodology is representing the system components as continuous-time state machines.

The simulation of the state machines by the PIA tool produces series of events that are then aggregated by a subroutine to calculate the metric of interest. Typically, the metrics are various "loss functions", e.g. the number of failed components, the duration of non-working state of a particular component or a combined characteristic of many components' states. Statistical analysis of the metric data is enabled by repeating the simulation multiple times.

3   Case Study

The case study is based on a reference topology of a Nordic32 electric power transmission system. The network consists of 32 substations operating at different voltage levels: 400 kV, 220 kV and 130 kV. Every substation is organised as a collection of bays. There are four different elements: a line, a transformer, a generator or a load. Each bay connects one of these elements with the bus bar of the substation. Bays also include protection and control units, which are responsible for switching on and off the connected elements. The control devices are typically used by operators or by a special purpose software (SPS) designed to undertake some of the operators' functions automatically and can both connect and disconnect the element from the bus bar. Each protection and control function (with respect to the individual bays) is available when the minimal cut set of equipment supporting the function is available. If the entire minimum cut set becomes unavailable, then the function itself also becomes unavailable.

A structure of the Nordic32 network and the architecture of one of the substations are shown in the Fig. 1. Other substations have similar architecture but with a different number of bays. The figure is only meant to provide a high-level overview, detailed discussion of the components is not necessary to understand the rest of the paper.

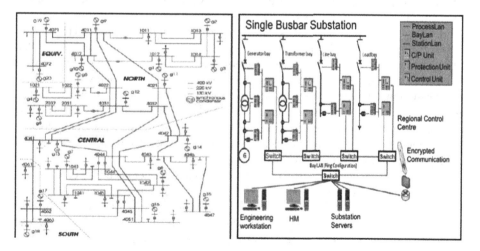

Fig. 1. Overview of Nordic32 system topology (left) and the architecture of a substation (right)

The substations are connected via a sophisticated information and communication technology (ICT) infrastructure, which includes a number of communication channels, control centres and data centres. Every substation has a Local Area Network (LAN), and a firewall protecting the LAN normally ensures that only legitimate traffic can pass through into the LAN from the rest of the world.

The modelled system can be studied with operational environment where only accidental failures are considered as well as those with cyber-attacks. In the later case, a model of Adversary is added in which the Adversary is tightly coupled with the assets. Further details about the case study and the various modeling assumptions can be found in papers [13, 14].

4 Analysis of the Case Study

In this study, our main focus is on the system's reliability. We need to provide assurance that the system's critical reliability properties are satisfied – this makes our top level claim. In order to support the top claim, we expand it in a more detailed case using the CAE building blocks structuring approach and eventually demonstrate that the properties are satisfied by using the results from the PIA method and tool. The assurance case is created with the ASCE tool [15].

4.1 Establishing the Environment

As was mentioned earlier, we need to take cyber-security into account when assessing the reliability of critical infrastructures. Cyber-attacks can pose various risks and thus the top claim is too general to be demonstrated by a convincing argument that it is valid. We need to define the claim more precisely by making the adverse environment explicit and considering specific cyber-attacks. This is done by using a Concretion block, and the concreted claim states that "the critical reliability properties of Nordic32 are satisfied under specific design-basis attacks". The instantiated block is shown in Fig. 2.

Making environment and attacks explicit in the claim highlights the need to consider various types of attacks, define them in terms of capability, frequency and justify that they adequately represent the possible attacks on the system. For our study, we analysed the effect of a single type of attack on system behavior: a cyber-attack via the firewall of a sub-station. The detailed model of Adversary and attack scenarios we developed are outside the scope of this paper and are described in recent publications [13, 16]. The justification of the models are performed in the side-warrant of the Concretion block. It can be supported by other documents and sources of attack information, e.g. scientific papers, insider knowledge, external expert analysis, and so forth.

At this point, the case could also be decomposed to consider each type of attacks in a separate branch. This could be useful if the case was going to be communicated to stakeholders who are particularly interested in different types of attacks, or if the case is likely to be changed in the future by introducing new types of attacks that could lead to different critical properties to be considered depending on the attacks.

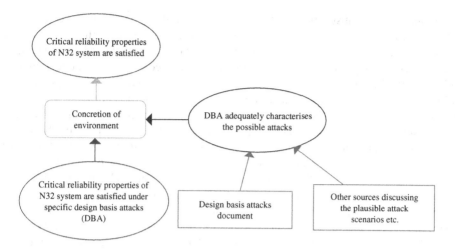

Fig. 2. Concretion making the attacks explicit in the claim

4.2 Substitution of a Model for the Real System

Once the top claim is concreted, the case continues with a Substitution block. For most complex systems, especially the critical ones, it is impossible to perform live analysis. Instead, a model of a system operating in a simulated environment is constructed. Therefore, we substitute the claim about the real Nordic32 system under its design-basis attacks by a model M(N32) under the simulated attacks M(DBA). PIA is used as a platform to create the model. The substitution is shown in Fig. 3.

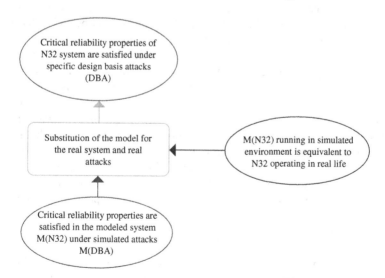

Fig. 3. Substitution of the model for the real system

When such a substitution is made, it is essential to justify that the model is adequate for the specific purpose it is being used for. We start with the side-claim stating that the modelled system running in simulated environment is equivalent to the real system operating in real life. "Equivalent" is of course context dependent and will need further justification. Therefore, the side-warrant is expanded to justify that all the models adequately represent the reality and that the PIA simulation platform itself is trustworthy. Each model is analysed separately: the model of the system should adequately represent the actual Nordic32 system, the model of the usage should be realistic and the model of the environment should be adequate. The latter includes the models of attacks identified at the previous stage of the analysis, as cyber-attacks are part of the overall adverse environment. The justifications are presented in Fig. 4, where the argument nodes of evidence incorporation blocks explain why the findings of the PIA report and research paper are taken as supporting the claim. There may also be further elaboration in terms of CAE, if needed. We used the IEEE research paper [16] as one of the evidence supporting the adequacy of the constructed models. The interaction of the models is considered within the validity of the platform as composing models together is part of the platform requirements. The expanded side-warrant structure with supporting evidence from PIA and other sources are shown in the Fig. 4.

4.3 Analysis of Critical Properties

At this stage, we expand the case further by considering specific reliability properties that are to be satisfied. In our case, these are the properties important from the customer point of view, concerning the power loss and availability of the service to consumers. The system must ensure that all consumers are connected to the grid most of the time (consumers should have 99 % or better availability of the supply) and the losses do not exceed 20 % of the nominal value. The property values should be calculated for individual consumers, not the average one, otherwise some users could be disconnected all the time. The decomposition by the reliability properties is shown in Fig. 5.

We used PIA to perform the calculations and justify that the modelled system meets these reliability requirements under the identified cyber-attacks. The effect of cyber-attacks on the service provided by the system was measured using different rewards (utility function) linked to the supplied power. The length of a simulation run was selected be the equivalent of 10 years of operation. The details of our evaluation can be found in papers [13, 14]. Evidence Incorporation blocks are used to feed the results from PIA into the assurance case. PIA results returned in the form of JSON file were additionally processed using special aggregation functions (linked to the argument nodesof the blocks) to demonstrate that they indeed support the corresponding subclaims.

5 Findings and Discussions

Overall, we found that structuring case method with the use of CAE building blocks, has enabled us to gain a clear understanding of the key issues that need to be addressed, identify the factors having the major effect on the analysis, and choose the best approach to achieving confidence in the results.

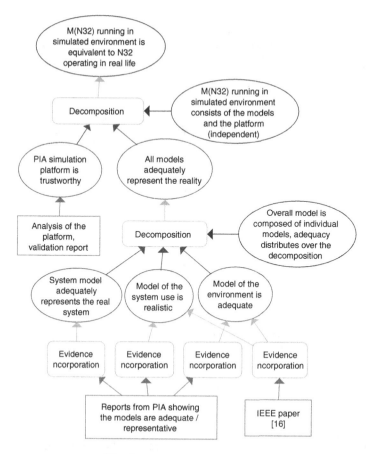

Fig. 4. Justification of the model

Some of the challenges and observations from our analysis are summarized below:

- Making environment and attacks explicit in the assurance case was essential for the analysis. As cyber-attacks have a great impact on the reliability, we needed to revisit the case study documents with the types of cyber-attacks toward the infrastructure. Some of the attack scenarios were identified by our in-house analysis and the assurance case challenged the justification of our decisions. Other sources discussing the plausible types of attacks also had to be reviewed to provide convincing evidence that they are relevant in a particular context and are indeed part of the security-threatened environment. We'll be continuing investigations into the specific adversary models that need to be considered. Ultimately, the critical properties will only be satisfied for the specific set of attacks so it is important to make an informed well-reasoned decision at this stage of assessment.
- Another crucial factor underpinning the success of analysis was the construction of an adequate model that represents the real system operating in its security-threatened environment. At this stage the assurance case required us to provide convincing

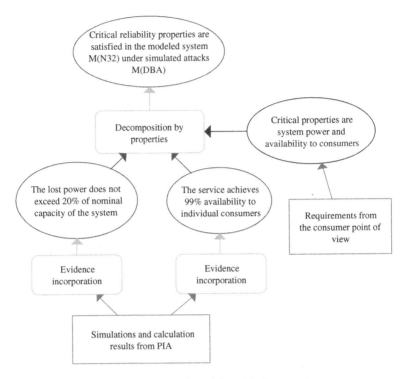

Fig. 5. Demonstration of the critical properties

evidence that the models of system, its usage and the environment are realistic. In doing so, it was identified that the usage model was not actually realistic and did not correctly represent the use of the system in real life. Specifically, the model of a load had a property defining the power consumed, and the property was set a constant value ignoring the natural fluctuations over time of the consumed power. In reality the power consumption is not constant and the model ideally should reflect this. The model is simplified since the fluctuations are managed by the power utilities, which are not part of the system model. Clearly, the model of the system must be scrutinized and the assumptions it is built upon – validated.

- In terms of the modelling platform (PIA tool), the assurance case also required us to conduct a thorough analysis and provide a validation report for PIA, which has been produced.
- The property evaluation part was substantial and took a considerable amount of time. The studied system is non-trivial, the model consists of more than 1500 state machines. With the chosen parameterisation we observed a significant number (~ 4000 to 32000) of events over a single simulation run of the system over 10 years of operation. Many of these events require power flow calculations, which take lots of time to complete. Similarly, following overloads or generator failures, active "control" is required to find a new stable system state, which is another time

consuming process. As a result, a single simulation run takes approximately 5 min to complete and obtaining results with high confidence requires a very large number of simulation runs.

6   Conclusions and Next Steps

In the paper we presented an approach to analysing critical reliability properties of a power transmission system under cyber-attacks using structured assurance cases and preliminary interdependency analysis method and tool. The paper is centred on the case, which articulates how one should address cyber-attacks and perform the validation of the model before the evidence in support is supplied by the modelling tool.

We believe the presented approach provides a good overview of the important concerns and efforts in assuring the reliability of any complex industrial systems. It discusses the need to explicitly identify adverse environment considering various types of cyber-attacks, justify that the system model can be trusted and show that the model has the required critical properties. Coupled with the PIA method and tool, the approach provides support addressing both aleatory and epistemic aspects of the integrated security and reliability analysis. It can be used for a wide variety of systems and infrastructures.

The future steps will be taken to develop an integrated tool support for the PIA and ASCE assurance case tools. In parallel, we are developing the CAE Building Blocks methodology and resources further, looking into the composite blocks and how these are defined, linking to challenge and review checklists generated from the blocks and more support for the formal aspects of assurance cases. In terms of justifying critical infrastructures properties we have indicated where the case presented in the case study could be expanded for a real industrial system. This is a very active and growing area with a number of research trends on argumentation, confidence and model based approaches and we plan to continue our research in this direction.

Acknowledgement. We acknowledge support from the Artemis JU SESAMO project (grant agreement number 295354), FP7 AFTER project (grant agreement number 261788), and the UK EPSRC funded Communicating and Evaluating Cyber Risk and Dependencies (CEDRICS) project, which is part of the UK Research Institute in Trustworthy Industrial Control Systems (RITICS).

References

1. Bloomfield, R.E., Netkachova, K.: Building blocks for assurance cases. In: IEEE International Symposium on Software Reliability Engineering Workshops (ISSREW) 2014, pp. 186–191 (2014). doi:10.1109/ISSREW.2014.72
2. Bloomfield, R.E., Bishop, P.G., Jones, C.C.M., Froome, P.K.D.: ASCAD – Adelard safety case development manual, London (1998)
3. ISO/IEC 15026-2:2011, Systems and software engineering — Systems and software assurance, Part 2: Assurance case (2011)

4. Bloomfield, R.E., et al.: Preliminary Interdependency Analysis (PIA): Method and tool support, p. 56. Adelard LLP (2010)
5. Bloomfield, R.E., Chozos, N., Nobles, P.: Infrastructure interdependency analysis: Requirements, capabilities and strategy. Adelard document reference: d418/12101/3, issue 1 (2009)
6. Toulmin, S.E.: The Uses of Argument. Cambridge University Press, Cambridge (1958)
7. Bishop P., Bloomfield, R.: A methodology for safety case development. In: Safety-Critical Systems Symposium 1998, Birmingham, UK, ISBN 3-540-76189-6 (1998)
8. Kelly, T.: The goal structuring notation–a safety argument notation. In: Proceedings of DSN 2004 Workshop on Assurance Cases (2004)
9. Hawkins, R., Kelly, T., Knight, J., Graydon, P.: A new approach to creating clear safety arguments. In: Dale, C., Anderson, T. (eds.) SSS 2011, pp. 3–23. Springer, Heidelberg (2013)
10. Littlewood, B., Wright, D.: The use of multilegged arguments to increase confidence in safety claims for software-based systems: a study based on a BBN analysis of an idealized example. IEEE Trans. Softw. Eng. **33**(5), 347–365 (2007). doi:10.1109/TSE.2007.1002
11. Denney, E., Pai, G.: A formal basis for safety case patterns. In: Bitsch, F., Guiochet, J., Kaâniche, M. (eds.) SAFECOMP. LNCS, vol. 8153, pp. 21–32. Springer, Heidelberg (2013)
12. Bloomfield, R.E., Bishop, P.G., Jones, C.C.M., Froome, P.K.D.: ASCAD – Adelard safety case development manual, London (1998)
13. Netkachov, O., Popov, P., Salako, K.: Model-based evaluation of the resilience of critical infrastructures under cyber attacks. In: Paper Presented at the 9th International Conference on Critical Information Infrastructures Security (CRITIS 2014), 13–15 October 2014, Limassol, Cyprus (2014)
14. Netkachov, O., Popov, P., Salako, K.: Quantification of the impact of cyber attack in critical infrastructures. In: Bondavalli, A., Ceccarelli, A., Ortmeier, F. (eds.) SAFECOMP 2014. LNCS, vol. 8696, pp. 316–327. Springer, Heidelberg (2014)
15. Assurance and Safety Case Environment (ASCE) Help File. Adelard LLP. http://www.adelard.com/asce/. Accessed 29 June 2015
16. Ten, C.-W., Liu, C.-C., Manimaran, G.: Vulnerability assessment of cybersecurity for SCADA systems. IEEE Trans. Power Syst. **23**(4), 1836–1846 (2008)

International Workshop on Next Generation of System Assurance Approaches for Safety-Critical Systems (SASSUR-2015)

Multidirectional Modular Conditional Safety Certificates

Tiago Amorim[1(✉)], Alejandra Ruiz[2], Christoph Dropmann[1],
and Daniel Schneider[1]

[1] Fraunhofer IESE, Kaiserslautern, Germany
{tiago.amorim,christoph.dropmann,
daniel.schneider}@iese.fraunhofer.de,
{tiago.amorim,christoph.dropmann,daniel.schneider}@tecnalia.com
[2] ICT-European Software Institute Division, TECNALIA, Derio, Spain
alejandra.ruiz@iese.fraunhofer.de, alejandra.ruiz@tecnalia.com

Abstract. Over the last 20 years, embedded systems have evolved from closed, rather static single-application systems towards open, flexible, multi-application systems of systems. While this is a blessing from an application perspective, it certainly is a curse from a safety engineering perspective as it invalidates the base assumptions of established engineering methodologies. Due to the combinatorial complexity and the amount of uncertainty encountered in the analysis of such systems, we believe that more potent modular safety approaches coupled with adequate runtime checks are required. In this paper, we investigate the possibility of an integrated contract-based approach covering vertical dependencies (between platform and application) and horizontal dependencies (between applications) in order to efficiently assure the safety of the whole system of systems through modularization. We integrate both concepts using state-of-the-art research and showcase the application of the integrated approach based on a small industrial case study.

Keywords: Safety · Assurance · Contracts · Multi-core · Conserts

1 Introduction

In recent years we have witnessed two different, very strong trends in the domain of embedded systems: collaboration between systems and more cores per chip.

The trend towards more collaboration has been prevalent for rather closed systems, such as communicating ECUs within a car, for over 20 years now. But roughly since the 2000s, it has been extended towards open systems such as dynamic compositions of different cars, traffic infrastructure, and Internet-based services. New computing paradigms have been coined along the way, most notably *pervasive computing, ubiquitous computing, ambient intelligence,* and *cyber-physical systems.* All these notions have in common that different types of systems from different manufacturers are integrated dynamically into so-called systems of systems, which can then render higher-level services based on their collaboration. This clearly bears huge potential for future applications and is bound to make a significant impact on our daily lives. However, from a safety perspective, this trend also brings huge challenges that could well prove to be a show stopper. One key challenge in this regard

© Springer International Publishing Switzerland 2015
F. Koornneef and C. van Gulijk (Eds.): SAFECOMP 2015 Workshops, LNCS 9338, pp. 357–368, 2015.
DOI: 10.1007/978-3-319-24249-1_31

is the uncertainty regarding dynamic compositions and reconfigurations, which can hardly be foreseen and analyzed at development time already. A corresponding solution idea is to shift parts of the safety certification activities into runtime, where all relevant information can be obtained and uncertainty can be resolved.

The other trend goes is about incrementing the number of CPU cores per chip. This trend has existed for about ten years and leads to higher computing power at lower cost. As a consequence, ECUs can host a higher number of applications at a time or applications that merely require much higher computing power. New kinds of applications are enabled that were previously unfeasible due to high hardware cost or lack of processing power. An example is camera-based recognition applications like those required for autonomous driving. However, from a safety perspective, the rise of multicore architectures has led to the problem of mixed criticalities. Different applications on a multicore processor share the same platform resources, resulting in potentially dangerous interdependencies and interferences. These need to be analyzed thoroughly, measures need to be introduced and their sufficiency needs to be shown. A particular challenge in this regard is cases where applications are developed by different parties or where there is a possibility of dynamic application downloads.

We expect future systems of systems to consist of different collaborating systems (i.e., entities consisting of hard- and software) that might in turn be built upon multicore technology and host several applications. Moreover, dynamic application updates are probably a feature future systems will possess. From a safety engineering perspective, we thus face uncertainties with respect to a system's environment (e.g., other collaborating systems; "horizontal dependencies") as well as regarding different applications of one system (i.e., via common shared resources; "vertical dependencies").

In this paper, we investigate the possibility of runtime safety support covering both horizontal and vertical dependencies. To this end, we will first elaborate these notions in more detail and provide a brief overview of related research. We will then go into a bit more detail regarding two specific approaches, each of which will be focused on regarding one of these two aspects. The main contribution of this paper is an initial concept regarding the integration of these two approaches, leading to the new notion of multidirectional modular conditional certificates. The concept is illustrated based on an industrial use case from the context of the EMC^2 project.

2   Related Research

In the automotive domain, ISO 26262 [7] is the functional safety standard. It demands that the safety requirements for a function and the functions be allocated to systems and subsequently to items. Some critical functions are supposed to work independently on a single core with their dedicated resources. When this is not the case, partitioning and shared resource techniques are used. Ruiz [9] state: "The safety assurance argument that these techniques should address is that the presented items of evidence should show sufficiently spatial and temporal independence between each partition." With the introduction of multi-core computers, multiple partitions may run concurrently on a single computing card, all accessing memory or I/O interfaces at the same time and needing to share processing time and resources in a 'safe' way.

Kotaba [8] analyzed the low-level temporal effect from sharing the on-chip resources that impact the determination of execution time. In the "multicore domain, the applications compete for resource access, typically arbitrated in a non-explicit manner by the specific hardware implementation. This causes non-deterministic temporal delays to the execution". They analyzed the effects and suggest mitigation techniques for resources such as system bus, bridges, memory bus and controller, memory (DRAM), shared cache, local cache, TLBs, addressable devices, pipeline stages, or logical units.

In SPEEDS [14] a formal meta-modeling language and the syntax of component contracts were developed and implemented. These contracts define the premises and promises of the component regarding its behavior in a specific way as well as an attribute designating its viewpoint. Another project that pursued this idea, CESAR [3], defined the CESAR Meta-Model (CMM), which includes the concept of 'rich' components that can be connected and integrated into hierarchies. Different kinds of rich components are possible depending on the perspective, such as operational actors, functions, logical components, or technical components. The CMM is based on the integration of component-based design with contracts based on input from the SPEEDS project, EAST-ADL2 (traceability, verification and validation) from the ATESST project, and its own CESAR Requirements Management Meta-Model (RMM). All these propose a metamodeling language for components dealing with safety-critical systems.

From another perspective, the FRESCOR project (Framework for Real-time Embedded Systems based on COntRACTS) [5] proposed contract-based resource management in distributed systems. It uses service contracts as a mechanism for dynamically specifying execution requirements. To accept a set of contracts, the system has to check as part of the negotiation whether it has enough resources to guarantee all the minimum requirements specified, while upholding guarantees on all previously accepted contracts negotiated by other application components. If successful, the system reserves enough capacity to guarantee the requested resources and will adapt any spare capacity available to share it among the different contracts that have specified their desire or ability to use additional capacity.

Sljivo [17] introduced the concept of weak/strong assumptions/guarantees when formalizing. They propose contracts in which all properties that an environment shall satisfy are defined separately from those required only in some contexts. This allows their contracts to be used for components and in different contexts.

Ruiz [10] propose "to formalized contracts through a well-defined and structured contract 'grammar' to support how users may systematically assure the safety of their system while integrating components through the definition of a BNF (Backus Normal Form or Backus–Naur Form) grammar". Ruiz proposes this grammar for design time contracts.

3 Use Case Description

In the context of the next generation of hybrid powertrains, our goal is to reduce the efforts and timing due to software updates in order to reduce time to market. This generation needs to satisfy the ISO 26262 compliance requirements such as the need to include "measures relating to detection, indication and control of faults in the system itself". This means that we need to provide corresponding capabilities for the diagnosis function. To achieve this in a safety-critical context, we propose the use of contract-based runtime assurance mechanisms for checking the safety of new updates in a standard and cost-efficient way.

In the figure below, the scenario for our use case is presented. The scenario represents the next-generation hybrid powertrains which is provided by AVL[1] and being framed under the EMC2[2] project. An electric motor is accessed by an accelerator pedal via a set of software applications. A brief overview of the technical background of the system is given in Fig. 1.

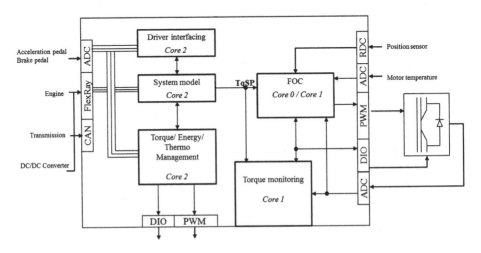

Fig. 1. Powertrain use case context

The **System Model** located on Core 2 is in charge of receiving data from the accelerator pedal and sends it to Field Oriented Control FOC and Torque Monitoring through the Torque Set Point signal.

The **Field Oriented Control (FOC)** component allocated in core 0 controls the speed of the electric motor (E-Motor) based on the Torque Set Point signal received from the system model. In addition, the FOC gets feedback from the electric motor (motor voltage, current, temperature, and rotor position) and communicates with the Torque Monitoring block regarding safety-related information.

Torque Monitoring performs a plausibility check of the Torque Set Point value based on the signals from the electric motor (voltage and current). It checks if the set value or the FOC violate the system safety by overloading the electric motor. In the case of a potential overload, the monitor sends safety-related information back to the FOC and disables the electric motor.

---

[1] http://www.avl.com/.

[2] http://www.artemis-emc2.eu/.

All these applications need to be safely integrated in order to provide a function that is critical for the vehicle. The objective of the use case is to integrate an update of the torque monitoring functionality into the powertrain system and to ensure that this update is safe and free from interferences with other functionalities. An upgraded functionality should undergo an impact analysis in order to be included. A quick and effective way to verify the impact of this upgrade is the use of a contract-based approach to verify the feasibility of this new development and the lack of unwanted interferences between applications through the platform.

4 Vertical and Horizontal Dependencies

The concept of vertical and horizontal interfaces was first introduced by Zimmer [16]. The authors distinguish between two types of interfaces: the vertical interface between the application and the underlying platform, and the horizontal interface between applications (regardless of whether they are running on the same platform or not).

A platform consists of components that provide function-independent services. It enables the hardware that runs the application and the required software to execute the applications independent of the hardware and according to the application's requirements. On the technical level, the vertical interface is not clearly separated into software and hardware relations. However, the overall viewpoint of our work is the software point of view. Implying that we consider the hardware as a resource used by the software, we do not focus on hardware-specific aspects such as manufacturing technology or special-purpose hardware components. Examples of platforms from the software point of view are AUTOSAR [2] and the ARINC 653 [1] Integrated Modular Avionics standard. Applications are software components that provide system-level functions to end users or other applications and are not related to services provided by the platform.

The vertical interfaces describe the safety-relevant relations between an application and a platform service. Platform services are typically developed for reuse, e.g., libraries, communication protocols, or operating systems. Platform developers do not know all future systems that a platform service will be a part of and they do not know in which way the service will be part of the application functionality. Therefore, it is impossible to perform a hazard and risk analysis for a standalone platform service. To overcome this challenge, we propose a vertical interface description according to [15] following a modular, contract-based approach for the specification of demands and guarantees to form a vertical safety interface. The demands describe the safety-related behavior of the platform as required for the safe execution of the application. Consequently, a demand is linked to a specific application. The guarantees, on the other hand, are linked to a specific platform and define the actual safety-related capabilities of the platform. Whether an application demand is satisfied by a service guarantee depends on the consumed service guarantees from other applications. Mitigation and arbitration are needed to realize safe use of the vertical interface and mitigate application demands and platform guarantees.

The horizontal interfaces describe relevant (e.g., safety-relevant) relations between applications that enable emergent functionalities that applications would not be able to perform on their own, such as Platooning of Autonomous Vehicles [4] and Tractor Implement Automation [6]. In horizontal relations, there exist the roles of service consumer (which establishes demands to be fulfilled by the consuming services) and service provider (which states guarantees for the provided services). An application can play both roles, being the consumer of some application services while being the provider of services for others. If the guarantees are fulfilled by the demands, the applications can function in the way they were designed; otherwise, the available system safety level will be below the designed level.

4.1 Vertical Safety Dependencies

In this subsection, we describe VerSaI, our approach for dealing with vertical safety dependencies. Zimmer [15] proposed a classification of safety-related demand-guarantee dependencies. The dependency classes are platform service failures, health monitoring, service diversity, and resource protection.

Platform service failures focus on the detection or avoidance of platform failure, e.g., a value failure of a service signal larger than a specified threshold must be detected within a defined period of time.

Health monitoring is the opposite of platform service failure. Application and execution failures get trapped and encapsulated by health monitoring. As an example, the platform has to detect and arbitrate an execution time overrun.

Service diversity, also called dissimilarity or independence, aims at reducing the likelihood of common-cause systematic failures in redundant components. Service diversity focuses on the independence of input services, communication links, and output services. An example is the need to develop the analog input channel that is used to read the accelerator pedal in a different way to avoid an analog input value failure as a common-cause failure.

Resource protection focuses on protection from interferences. We define interference as a cascading failure via a shared resource that potentially violates safety requirements. The interference propagates between several software components via a commonly used resource instead of a private resource for every software component, e.g., the torque mo.nitoring component must be protected from interferences via the analog-to-digital converter software component that is shared with the FOC.

The demands and guarantees are applied to a probability attribute. The attribute states the integrity achieved by a guaranty or requested by a demand. Examples are the automotive safety integrity levels (ASILs) or the design assurance levels (DALs) in avionics.

In the case of an open system like the hybrid powertrain, it is possible to integrate new applications, e.g. torque monitoring, during the product's lifetime. In such a scenario, we assume that the application developer has specified all the demands that are needed to guaranty safety from the application point of view and that the platform service developer has specified guarantees that can be given by the platform. Both guarantees and demands can be described using a semi-formal language such as VerSaI (Vertical Safety Interface) [15], which allows automated evaluation if demands and quarantines are compatible. Platform service failure, health monitoring, and service diversity are vertical dependency classes that arise even for a federated system (with separate platforms for applications).

We assume that for systems that integrate applications into a commonly used platform, especially in the context of mixed criticality, the resource protection class is of major interest. For this reason, besides the VerSaI guarantees and demands, we focus on an automated platform service interference analysis in combination with a protection assignment. This allows safe and automated integration of additional applications during a product's lifetime.

4.2 Horizontal Safety Dependencies

In this subsection, we describe ConSerts as a solution for horizontal dependencies. ConSerts stands for Conditional Safety Certificates. It is an approach presented in [11–13] that utilizes modular conditional certificates and operates between horizontal interfaces of systems. ConSerts are post-certification artifacts (i.e., certification has been conducted in the traditional way) equipped with variations points bound to formalized external dependencies that are meant to be resolved at runtime. This characteristic is what makes the certificates "conditional" and provides the flexibility in the certificates that is required to be useful for a sufficiently wide range of concrete integration scenarios. The conditional certificates must also be modular in order to conduct the certification process at the level of the units composing the targeted systems of systems.

The conditional certificates are to be evaluated automatically and autonomously by the system at the moment of integration at runtime, based on runtime representations of the certificates of the involved compositional units. This certificate evaluation can be realized off-board (performed by an extra system) and/or on-board (the systems support runtime evaluation). Once all conditions have been resolved and the evaluation is finished, an overall certificate variant can be determined for the actual composition that has been formed. In a sense, the final certification step has thereby been postponed to runtime and we can thus speak of "runtime certification".

Whenever the overall system composition changes or the system adapts itself, a re-evaluation of the conditional certificates must be conducted and the overall certificate for the composition must be updated. Such a re-evaluation might well be triggered by a minor dynamic adaptation in one of the subsystems or even an update, which, however, can easily trigger a chain reaction in related components leading to complex reconfiguration sequences. Therefore, there is a strong interdependency between dynamic adaptations and the dynamic evaluations of the conditional certificates. An adaptation might lead to an invalidation of the current certificate and thus to re-evaluation and the determination of a new one. This might then violate given top-level trust requirements, which might again trigger additional adaptations in order to regain sufficient trust guarantees (e.g., via graceful degradation, which could imply a loss of application features).

5 Multidirectional Modular Conditional Certificates

The vertical interface has direct influence on the performance of the application since it is the platform that provides the physical resources to run the application. If the required application demands are not completely fulfilled by the platform guarantees, the application cannot deliver its full capabilities with the designed confidence. Thus, this has a direct impact on the horizontal services guarantees provided by the application to other applications. In other words, the horizontal guarantees of the application are influenced by the fulfillment of its vertical demands.

The mediation of horizontal and vertical interfaces becomes highly relevant if different applications are integrated in the same platform, consequently influencing the horizontal guarantees provided by the application services. This occurs in the context of mixed criticality and dynamic updates where re-evaluation is required to assess whether the overall demands, both vertical and horizontal, are properly satisfied.

To address the aforementioned issues, we introduce Multidirectional Modular Conditional Certificates (M2C2), a runtime certification approach that addresses both vertical and horizontal interfaces. The approach is realized through the synergy between VerSaI (in the context of vertical interfaces) and ConSerts (in the context of horizontal interfaces).

In ConSerts, a service guarantee can be correlated to demands and their fulfillment by other application services' guarantees. In M2C2, the services are additionally influenced by the guarantees of the platform. This relation is illustrated in Fig. 2. During M2C2 contract resolution, the vertical application demands shall be fulfilled by platform guarantees before resolving the horizontal relations. If some of the vertical demands are not fulfilled, some of the application-service guarantees at the horizontal interfaces might not get validated.

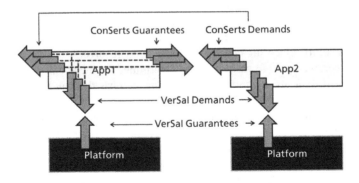

Fig. 2. Relations between ConSerts guarantees and VerSaI demands

Resolving vertical dependencies on a single application running on a platform is very straightforward. The platform guarantees and application demands are compared and either match or do not match. However, if a platform hosts more than one application (several single core platforms being combined in one multi-core), the applications might influence each other's behavior, even if there are no horizontal interfaces between them. Interferences as described in Sect. 4 can occur. To guarantee segregation between the integrated applications, the platform needs to allocate its resources consequently considering the tradeoff between the demands of each application and the required rendered services/safety levels.

In a situation where the vertical application demands cannot be satisfied for a given configuration of applications, a new configuration needs to be identified. This results in an iterative approach in which the platform resources are re-allocated to critical applications while non-critical or less critical ones get to share what is left. This can even lead to the removal of existing applications.

Besides the capability to address dependencies between applications as well as between applications and their platform, the M2C2 approach presented in this section exhibits two important synergies.

First, the combination of the horizontal and vertical contracts in one consideration allows additional flexibility. For instance, if the platform's guarantees are not sufficient, due to an accidental or intended alteration such as a partial platform service breakdown or an application download, the information can be propagated to the horizontal interface. Subsequently, the alteration propagates through the guarantee-demand relationships of affected applications, potentially resulting in an alteration of the "top-level" guarantees of the current overall system configuration. This kind of propagation could either be fostered by means of the Boolean logic employed by ConSerts or, alternatively, there might be a dedicated centralized mediator component as part of a corresponding runtime framework. This mediator would then be responsible for monitoring the established contracts and, in case of deviations, would calculate a new safe set of vertical and horizontal contracts based on the current conditions.

Second, as part of the vertical interface we want to detect and address all potential interferences between applications. Besides interferences, there are intended interactions between applications as well. The interference analysis can point out such intended interactions in addition and forward them as a warning to the horizontal interface. Hence, unconsidered interactions between applications can be revealed. For instance, in the use case from Sect. 3, the DIO (Digital Input/Output) is used by the torque monitoring and the FOC applications. This could either be intentional or an error in the integration design, e.g., if the FOC as a less safety-critical component could enable the motor when the torque monitor application tries to disable the motor.

6 Applying the M2C2 Framework to the Use Case

To provide a better understanding of the aforementioned approach, we will describe a practical application with the help of the use case scenario described in Sect. 3. The use case describes a processor with three cores running applications that control an electric powertrain. These applications are distributed among the cores and share several resources such as communications channels, which implies possible influences between those applications. Besides, some applications must interact with each other on the horizontal level and require (from its peers) services with a minimal integrity level. The M2C2 framework can be used to address these issues.

We assume that the vertical application demands are specified by the application developers and the platform guarantees are specified by the platform developer. An example is that the FOC and the Torque Monitoring applications specify demands regarding the analog-to-digital converter (ADC) service, which does, for instance, comply with the

AUTOSAR specification. Our vertical approach then consists of two steps. First, health monitoring and service diversity will be performed to examine if all application demands can be fulfilled by the ADC service guarantees. Second, the resource protection dependencies will be evaluated. Consequently, it will be evaluated if the shared use of the service is without interferences between the applications.

After the vertical dependencies have been assessed positively, the next step is the resolution of the horizontal dependencies. The System Model (SM), Torque Monitoring (TM), and Field Oriented Control (FOC) are the applications that participate in the presented use case and their relations are depicted with arrows in Fig. 3. Their certificates are defined with ConSerts, which is described using EBNF grammar in order to facilitate runtime resolution. An example of a service guarantee is *SystemModel.SMTorque (1): ASIL = c, Late {10 ms;}.ASIL.d.* This guarantee is bound (e.g., via the Boolean logic of ConSerts; cf. [13]) to a demand directed at the platform. The service in the example is implemented in ASIL c and guarantees that the application passes the signal in less than 10 ms with a confidence level of ASIL d. The demand representation has a similar format. The TM and FOC demands need to be lower or equivalent to the service guarantee provided by the SM. The same happens between TM and FOC and vice-versa (since they have a closed-loop relation and are provider and consumer of each other's services at the same time). Once all demands are fulfilled by the respective corresponding guarantees, the overall system can be considered as safe. Due to space and scope limitations, the syntax and semantics of the contracts will not be further detailed, for more information, the reader shall refer to [13] and [15].

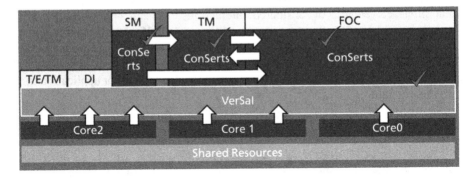

Fig. 3. M2C2 certificate verification applied to the use case (The direction of the arrows represents a guarantee (from) being provided to a demand (to)).

An overview of the M2C2 certificate assessment is illustrated in Fig. 3. Note that although the applications Torque/Energy/Thermo Management (T/E/TM) and Driver Interfacing (DI) do not participate in the horizontal interface assessment, they are considered in the vertical interface step. In case of a change in the initial application configuration, i.e. if new applications are added or applications are replaced by others with more functionality, a new assessment needs to take place to guarantee that the change will not jeopardize the intended integrity level.

7   Conclusions

In this paper, we presented an approach aimed at supporting systems that are able to assure dependability of the whole system of systems through modularization of safety assessment. The proposed Multidirectional Modular Conditional Certificates (M2C2) framework is a novel runtime certification approach because it addresses both vertical and horizontal safety interfaces. Vertical interfaces describe dependencies between applications and a platform and horizontal interfaces describe dependencies on the system level between applications or systems of systems. Besides a detailed discussion of horizontal and vertical aspects, we presented a first idea for merging ConSerts, an approach for the horizontal safety interface, and VerSaI, an approach for the vertical safety interface.

The resulting M2C2 framework allows negotiating whether a system consisting of applications integrated on common platforms is safe or not. In addition, the combination of the two perspectives allows mitigating interferences between applications and platforms at runtime in such a way that safety can be ensured in combination with maximal application service availability instead of a failsafe. The applicability of the framework ranges from applications running within a processor core (like the presented use case) to coarse-grained systems of systems (such as cyber-physical systems).

The work we presented in this paper is on a conventional level. As future work, we plan to refine the concepts regarding the mitigation and the implementation of the presented approach in a demonstrator to evaluate and demonstrate that M2C2 can be proposed. Considering other properties related to the certificates (such as security) is also a path to be explored. Another point that can be explored is strategies in case of the run time check failing completely. Some initial ideas are self-adaptation of the applications or graceful degradation.

Acknowledgment. The research leading to these results has received funding from the EMC^2 – 'Embedded Multi-Core systems for Mixed Criticality applications in dynamic and changeable real-time environments' project. This is an ARTEMIS Joint Undertaking project in the Innovation Pilot Programme 'Computing platforms for embedded systems' (AIPP5) under grant agreement n°621429.

References

1. ARINC 653, avionic application software standard interface, part 1 (2005)
2. Website of the AUTOSAR standard. http://www.autosar.org/
3. D_SP1_R3.3_a_M3 Meta-Model Concepts for RTP V; CESAR Project
4. Fernandes, P., Nunes, U.: Platooning of autonomous vehicles with inter vehicle communications in SUMO Traffic Simulator. In: International IEEE Conference on Intelligent Transportation Systems (ITSC), (2010)
5. Frescor project: Framework for real-time embedded systems based on COntRACTS 04 May 2015. http://www.frescor.org

6. Hoyningen-Huene, M., Baldinger, M.: Tractor-Implement-Automation and its application to a tractor-loader wagon combination. In: 2nd International Conference on Machine Control & Guidance, University of Bonn, Germany (2010)

7. International Organization for Standardization (ISO), ISO 26262 Road vehicles – Functional safety, ISO, November 2011

8. Kotaba, O., Nowotschy, J., Paulitschy, M., Pettersz, S.M., Theilingx, H.: Multicore in real-time systems – temporal isolation challenges due to shared resources. In: WICERT workshop (2013)

9. Ruiz, A., Habli, I., Espinoza, H.: Towards a case-based reasoning approach for safety assurance reuse. In: Ortmeier, F., Daniel, P. (eds.) SAFECOMP Workshops 2012. LNCS, vol. 7613, pp. 22–35. Springer, Heidelberg (2012)

10. Ruiz, A., Espinoza, H., Kelly, T.: Adequacy of contract grammars for component certification. In: SAFECOMP 2013 Fast Abstract. Toulouse, France, September 2013

11. Schneider, D., Trapp, M.: Conditional safety certificates in open systems. In: Proceedings of the 1st Workshop on Critical Automotive Applications: Robustness and Safety (CARS 2010) (2010)

12. Schneider, D., Trapp, M.: A safety engineering framework for open adaptive systems. In: Proceedings of the Fifth IEEE International Conference on Self-Adaptive and Self-Organizing Systems (SASO) (2011)

13. Schneider, D., Trapp, M.: Conditional Safety Certification of Open Adaptive Systems. ACM Trans. Auton. Adapt. Syst. vol. 8, p. 20, Article 8 (2013)

14. D.2.5.4 Contract Specification Language (CSL); SPEEDS Project; Deliverable; Rev. 1.0.1; April 2008

15. Zimmer, B.: Efficiently deploying safety-critical applications onto open integrated architectures. HRSG, Fraunhofer IESE, Kaiserslautern (2014)

16. Zimmer, B., Bürklen, S., Knoop, M., Höfflinger, J., Trapp, M.: Vertical safety interfaces – improving the efficiency of modular certification. In: Flammini, F., Bologna, S., Vittorini, V. (eds.) SAFECOMP 2011. LNCS, vol. 6894, pp. 29–42. Springer, Heidelberg (2011)

17. Sljivo, I., Carlson, J., Gallina, B., Hansson, H.: Fostering reuse within safety-critical component-based systems through fine-grained contracts. In: proceedings of the International Workshop on Critical Software Component Reusability and Certification across Domains (CSC 2013), (2013)

Approaches for Software Verification
of An Emergency Recovery System
for Micro Air Vehicles

Martin Becker$^{(\boxtimes)}$, Markus Neumair, Alexander Söhn,
and Samarjit Chakraborty

Institute for Real-Time Computer Systems, Technische Universität München,
Arcisstraße 21, 80333 Munich, Germany
becker@rcs.ei.tum.de

Abstract. This paper describes the development and verification of a competitive parachute system for Micro Air Vehicles, in particular focusing on verification of the embedded software. We first introduce the overall solution including a system level failure analysis, and then show how we minimized the influence of faulty software. This paper demonstrates that with careful abstraction and little overapproximation, the entire code running on a microprocessor can be verified using *bounded model checking*, and that this is a useful approach for resource-constrained embedded systems. The resulting Emergency Recovery System is to our best knowledge the first of its kind that passed formal verification, and furthermore is superior to all other existing solutions (including commercially available ones) from an operational point of view.

Keywords: Remotely-piloted aircraft systems · Multicopter · Safety · Parachute · Software verification · Formal analysis

1 Introduction

In the recent years, Micro Air Vehicles (MAVs) such as quadrocopters, hexacopters, etc., are a rapidly growing class of airspace users. As of January 2015, we estimate the number of light MAVs (< 5 kg) to be at least 1.6 million in *Europe*[1], possibly even one magnitude higher due to the plethora of manufacturers and custom builds. In comparison, this is more than quadruple the number of aircraft in general aviation *worldwide* [1], and soon, if not already, the daily flying hours will also catch up, thanks to a growing number of civil use cases.

However, in contrast to aircraft in general aviation, MAVs are usually not subject to in-depth safety considerations, but tend to have a high probability

---

[1] Based on the number of DJI sales and their growing business figures over the last years. This is also supported by the number of and growth rate of registered MAVs at the federal agencies around Europe, and their estimated number of unreported vehicles [18].

© Springer International Publishing Switzerland 2015
F. Koornneef and C. van Gulijk (Eds.): SAFECOMP 2015 Workshops, LNCS 9338, pp. 369–385, 2015.
DOI: 10.1007/978-3-319-24249-1_32

of failure. This comes from the nature of these systems: They are open for modifications, little analyzed, and often not fully understood by their operator. Together with the omnipresence of those vehicles, this results in a considerable potential of MAVs endangering their environment.

Whatever solution is chosen to increase the level of safety, it has to be tailored towards those low-cost, mass-market systems. Imposing certification rules on the entire MAV, such as DO-178C for civil A/C software, could eventually hold back a number of desirable use cases. For example, certification could require redundancy in the flight controls, which would decrease payload capacity and thus render some applications infeasible. Last but not least, low cost is also a key for those platforms, which generally contradicts a full-system certification.

In this paper, we describe our experiences in developing a light-weight recovery system which increases the operational safety of MAVs and is nevertheless amenable to certification, independently from the internal structure of the MAV. It is a hardware-software solution based on a parachute, which can bring down the MAV safely, avoiding loss of the MAV in case of malfunctions, and minimizing collateral damage. Our system is a "plug and play" solution, i.e., it can be retrofitted to existing MAVs with only one single interface (the power connector) and has little impact on the flight performance.

In the following we first explain the overall solution, and then focus on the verification of the embedded software, which is the most complex part, and meanwhile the main contributor towards the effectiveness of the proposed solution.

2   Related Work

MAV Safety Systems: In general, the safety systems available by today are either specific to the MAV brand, incomplete, or require radical modifications to the existing MAV. For example, there are MAVs that ship with a parachute system, such as the MCFLY-Helios [9], or others which can be extended with OEM parachute systems, such as the "DropSafe" for the *DJI Phantom* [8]. However, being tightly integrated with their specific MAVs, the trigger conditions are not made public, and there is no formal proof illustrating the increased overall safety. Moreover, they require CO_2 capsules and a backup battery, as opposed to our solution. Other available systems are "operated" solutions, such as the Opale [15], SKYCAT [17] or MARS [13] parachute systems. They only support a manual release, do not switch off the MAV propulsion and require, as the others before, a working power supply in case of emergency.

There are also more *local* approaches to increase the safety of subsystems, such as robust control algorithms by Mueller and D'Andrea [14]. Their algorithms can cope with partial loss of propulsion whilst keeping the MAV in a controlled flight. However, not only do they require a lot of insight into and modification of the MAV, they also demand significant non-local changes, as for example the provisioning of safety margins in the propulsion (e.g., more thrust per motor, higher peak current etc.). Eventually, those margins make the MAV inefficient under normal conditions, but still only cover a subset of all possible MAV failures.

The parachute solution that we propose offers similar operational limits than the mentioned automatic systems, but is MAV-independent and covers the maximum number of failure conditions among the mentioned solutions, and at a lower weight. Additionally, through the verification shown here, we have evidence that the overall MAV safety is indeed increased, as opposed to all other solutions.

Verification of Code Running on Microprocessors: Model-checking the entire C code running on microprocessors has been reported only a couple of times, e.g., with *cbmc* on an ATmega16 processor in [16] and on an MSP430 in [4], but either it failed because of state space explosion and missing support for concurrency, or succeeded only for smaller programs.

However, recent developments that turn concurrency into data nondeterminism [11], spot race conditions [20] and support for interrupts in *cbmc* [4] can solve the concurrency issues and make bounded model checking an interesting approach. In this paper we take together all these ideas, point out problem with those, and propose abstractions which mitigate the state space explosion, enabling a workflow which allows verifying an entire real-world program running on a microcontroller.

3   Challenges

The main design challenge for this system is to maintain a low weight, since this directly translates into flight time. This however means we can introduce redundancy only where inevitable for safety.

Second, to make the system work independently of MAV internals, it implies that the interface to the MAV must be minimalist. Standard approaches known from avionics like *triplex controllers* (see [2, p. 88]) with its internal data consolidation are too intrusive and therefore not an option.

The biggest challenge however, is deciding whether there is an emergency, and triggering the recovery independently of the pilot. A software implementation is the natural choice, since this allows for iterative development and parametrization for the specific MAV. This software is then *safety-critical*, since it directly influences whether crashes can be avoided or not. Through this, the quality of the software will drive the quality of the overall solution. That is why in this paper our main concern is a formal verification of the software, which is known to be challenging, especially because this software interacts with its physical environment.

4   Proposed Emergency Recovery System for MAVs

Our proposed Emergency Recovery System (ERS) is shown in Fig. 1, both on a quadrocopter and a hexacopter. It is a parachute system, designed to increase the overall safety of the MAV. In case of an emergency (what constitutes an emergency is described later), the ERS automatically turns off the propulsion and deploys a parachute. The technical specifications are given in Table 1.

Fig. 1. Prototypes of our *Emergency Recovery System* mounted on a hexacopter (left) and deployed on a quadrocopter (right).

Table 1. Specifications of the Emergency Recovery System.

Property	Value
total weight	320 g
input voltage	6...25.2 V (2...6 LiPo cells)
power consumption	<3 W depending on propulsion state
worst-case trigger time	≤140 ms
terminal speed & min. altitude	4.5 m/s within 10 m

No modifications to the existing MAV are required, e.g., neither altering the flight controller nor the propulsion system. Our system effectively acts as a power proxy between MAV battery and MAV. The only (necessary) interface for our ERS is the power connector, which is why we call it a "plug and play" solution. A second optional interface is for one RC channel, allowing the pilot to trigger the parachute manually.

4.1   Internal Structure

The ERS consists of the following three components, also illustrated in Fig. 2:

- **Emergency Detection Unit (EDU):** A Printed-Circuit Board (PCB) with sensors and a microprocessor running software to detect emergencies. In case it detects an emergency, it can trigger the ejection of the parachute.
- **Power Switch (PS):** A PCB with power electronics, acting as a proxy between the MAV's battery and the propulsion. In case of emergency, it cuts off the power.
- **Parachute Unit (PU):** This is a housing holding the parachute. It is also comprising an ejection sensor and an electro-magnetic (EM) lock, which, when opened or powerless, releases a compressed spring, which in turn ejects the parachute.

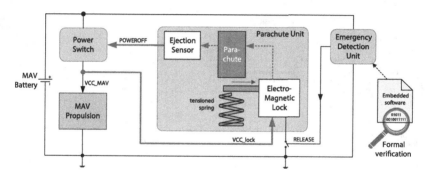

Fig. 2. Internal structure of our *Emergency Recovery System*: The *Emergency Detection Unit* on the top right is running the to-be-verified software.

Mode of Operation: The EDU features an Atmel ATmega 328p microprocessor (Harvard, 8 MHz, 32 kB Flash, 2 kB RAM, no caches), a barometer sensor and an accelerometer sensor. The embedded software evaluates those sensors periodically, and estimates the MAV's air state. When it detects emergency conditions, it triggers the parachute ejection by emitting a RELEASE signal, which opens the EM lock. This releases a compressed spring, which can now eject the parachute from its housing. Simultaneously, when the parachute is pushed out, an ejection sensor detects this and sends a POWEROFF signal to the *Power Switch*. This ensures, that the MAV's propulsion is deactivated as soon as the parachute is ejected.

Emergency Conditions: The root causes for failure in MAVs are wide-spread. Due to tight integration of functionality and – as explained before – the imperative minimalism in redundancy, even errors in non-critical components can evolve quickly into fatal failures. Therefore, it seems more efficient to apply a holistic monitoring, instead of monitoring single components. Accordingly, an emergency is considered as the MAV being *uncontrolled*, that is, when the pitch or roll angles exceed user-defined thresholds, or when the descent rate gets too high. These conditions cover the most important malfunctions, such as FCS failure (e.g., badly tuned controllers or error in software logic), electrical or mechanical failure of propulsion (propeller, ESC), loss of power and partially even human error (in the form of initiating an uncontrolled state).

5 System Level Failure Analysis

Although this paper focuses on software verification, we briefly explain the failure analysis at system level, to show the influence of the software on the overall safety.

We designed our ERS to make it fail-safe together with the MAV w.r.t. any *single-failure* event, i.e., a MAV equipped with our ERS can tolerate at least one statistically independent failure without leading to a crash. Towards that, we repeatedly conducted a Fault Tree Analysis during the design process of the ERS.

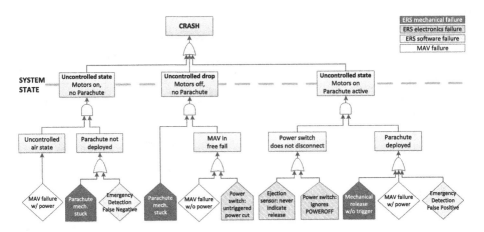

Fig. 3. Fault tree for the top event "crash", valid for any electric Micro Air Vehicle equipped with our Emergency Recovery System (Color figure online).

In Fig. 2 we highlighted a built-in *fail-safe loop* between power switch, EM lock, parachute and ejection sensor. It creates a circular dependency between its components. If any of them fails (e.g., broken power switch), then this also leads to the ejection of the parachute, thus covering failures that may occur in the ERS itself. The effects of different failure scenarios can be seen in the Fault Tree in Fig. 3.

Considered MAV Failures: The MAV was treated as a black box with two possible failures (grey in the figure) "MAV failure with power" and "MAV failure without power". The first one means, that the MAV is in an uncontrolled state but still powered (e.g., broken propeller and resulting loss of control), whereas the latter one means, that the MAV lost power (e.g., due to battery failure or electronic defects), which naturally results in an uncontrolled state as well. We are not concerned with the MAV being powered up in a controllable state (no error), or being in a controllable but unpowered state (impossible for multicopter configurations).

Influence of the Software: The Fault Tree is depicted in Fig. 3. It can be seen, that the three *uncontrolled* system states which lead to a crash, can only be reached if at least two failures occur at the same time. As indicated with the color coding, there are four categories of failures: *(a)* mechanical failure in ERS (red), *(b)* electronics failure in ERS (orange), *(c)* software failure in ERS (green) and *(d)* MAV failure (white). Although there are many kinds of errors possible in software, from a system point of view we are only interested in the two consequences depicted in the Fault Tree:

1. **Emergency Detection False Negative**: The embedded software does not trigger the emergency sequence despite emergency conditions.
2. **Emergency Detection False Positive**: The embedded software does trigger the emergency sequence without emergency conditions.

While both software failure events can have the same impact at system level (both can lead to crash if a second failure occurs), the case of a *False Negative* is practically more critical, since MAV failures with power are more likely than a second independent failure occurring in the ERS. Furthermore, the ERS runs self-checks during initialization, reducing the probability of being used in the presence of internal failure. For these reasons, our verification efforts that we explain in the next section, focused on (but were not limited to) finding defects that lead to False Negatives.

6   Software Verification

Safety-critical systems in general must be free of defects that can lead to errors in behavior. Here, traditional testing is not favorable, since only a full coverage of all possible executions could guarantee absence of defects, which implies modeling the system's environment in a test harness. That especially holds true for our ERS, where the functionality strongly depends on timing and the interaction with its environment. Testing specific cases would require simulating the environment, as well as the sensors and the microprocessor running the software. On top of that, in our system we cannot afford any redundancy due to weight reasons, which is why we need to identify all defects in the software.

Consequently, we aimed for a toolchain that supports formal verification of C code based on static analysis. While there are multiple tools that one could choose for that task (e.g., Frama-C [7], Astrée [6], BLAST [10], Polyspace, etc.), we have selected *cbmc* and related tools [5], because they support concurrency to some extent, are freely available (and thus can be extended if necessary) and also widely used. More model checkers for C code were compared in [3,16].

Software Structure: The software running on the EDU can be partitioned into four sequential parts:

1. **Initialization:** Initializes all sensors, and captures environmental conditions (e.g., pressure at ground level). When completed, the ERS switches to *self-check mode*.
2. **Self-Check:** To ensure that there is not already a failure in the ERS during start-up, we added built-in self tests covering the major subsystems of the ERS. When completed, the ERS switches to *detection mode*.
3. **Detection:** The software periodically reads all sensors and estimates the MAV's air state. If the emergency conditions apply, the EM lock is released and the software switches to *emergency handling mode*.
4. **Emergency Handling:** Current sensor data and decision conditions are written to EEPROM, to enable a post-flight analysis.

The sensors and actuators are connected to the microcontroller as depicted in Fig. 4 on the left. The interfaces impose some concurrency in the software, which is shown on the right. For example, the maintenance console and manual trigger signal both require interrupts (polling would be too slow), thus each introduces

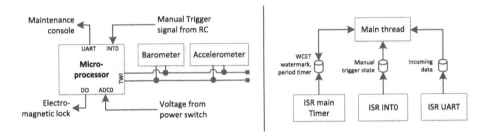

Fig. 4. Microprocessor with interfaces to its environment (left) and the resulting concurrency in the software (right).

one thread concurrent to the main program. Additionally, a timer interrupt is used to support a time-triggered execution of the detection loop, contributing one further thread.

Proper Timing: The mentioned concurrency poses the first verification task. To ensure that the detection loop always runs at the desired rate – which is important for correctness of computed data, e.g., the descent rate – we need to show that the required computations can be completed before the next period begins.

Towards that, the *worst-case execution time* (WCET) of the main loop must be determined. Here we took a dual approach: On one hand, we performed a static WCET analysis with a freely available analyzer tool [19], but we also monitor the execution time on the microprocessor with a *high watermark*.

For the static analysis we made the assumption that the sensors are healthy, and follow their datasheets' timing specification. The resulting WCET was 2.7 ms for the detection loop, which is well below the 5 ms-period in the EDU. However, interrupts also need to be considered. The *worst-case response time* (WCRT) is (in this context) the maximum amount of time that the detection loop needs to finish processing, under the preemption of interrupts. Only if the WCRT is less than the period, then it can be concluded that the timing is correct.

However, without further provisions the minimum inter-arrival time (MINT) for the event-based interrupts (manual trigger from RC, UART) have no lower bound, i.e., it would be possible that a broken RC receiver or UART peer could induce so many interrupts, that the detection could never execute, resulting in an unbounded WCRT. To avoid this situation, the inter-arrival times of all event-driven interrupts are also measured in the microcontroller. If an interrupt occurs more often than planned, the attached signal source is considered failing, and the interrupt turned off.

With these bounded MINTs and the WCET values from the static analysis, a standard response time analysis yielded a WCRT of 2.89 ms for the detection loop. Again, this is for the case of healthy sensors.

The purpose of the high watermark is to detect those cases when sensors are failing, but also to gain confidence in the above analysis. The response time of the detection loop is continuously measured using a hardware timer, and maximum values are written to EEPROM. With rising number of flying hours, the watermark should approach the WCRT. If it exceeds the statically computed WCRT, then a sensor failure is likely, which triggers the emergency sequence.

In practice, the watermark measurements were observed approaching the statically computed WCRT up to a few hundred microseconds with healthy sensors, thus giving confidence in the analysis. By construction of the software, it can be concluded that the timing of the detection loop is correct, unless the parachute is deployed. However, there are more timing-related issues to be considered, namely, the time-sensitive effects of interrupts upon the control flow in the main program. This was addressed later during the verification process.

Proper Logic: The ultimate goal of the software verification is to ensure that the emergency detection algorithm works as intended. As explained before, the main concern was to avoid False Negatives, i.e., the error that the embedded software does not trigger the emergency sequence, despite emergency conditions.

An obvious reason for such failure is, that the software is not running because it crashed or got stuck. This can be a consequence of divisions by zero, heap or stack overflow[2], invalid memory writes, etc. Note that a reboot during flight is not possible, since the initialization and self-checks need user interaction (open and re-close the ejection sensor to ensure it works correctly), and making them bypassable is not desirable for practical safety reasons. Therefore, crashes and stuck software have to be avoided.

The second reason for not recognizing an emergency is an incorrectly implemented detection algorithm. This entails both an error in decision taking (i.e., which sensor has to tell what in order to classify it as emergency), and also numerical problems (e.g., overflows) in data processing. Identifying these kinds of problems also decreases the number of False Positives.

The majority of those defects is checked automatically by *cbmc*, if requested during instrumentation. The correctness of the decision taking part, however, must be encoded with user assertions. Since our detection loop runs time-triggered, properties such as "latest 100 ms after free fall conditions are recognized, the parachute shall be deployed" can be encoded with some temporary variables. With that, verification of arbitrary properties of the decision algorithm follows the same workflow as the automatically instrumented properties, which is why we do not elaborate on the specific properties that were eventually verified, but rather show how we set up the workflow correctly.

6.1   Verification Workflow

The toolchain that we set up around *cbmc* is shown in Fig. 5. We start with a C program, written for the target. First, we run fast static checkers such as *splint* on the program, to identify and remove problems like uninitialized variables, problematic type casts etc. Not only does this help to avoid defects early during

---

[2] Heap was not used, and stack size was checked with *Bound-T*.

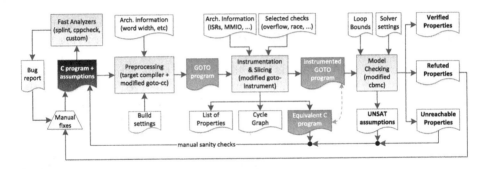

Fig. 5. Workflow for formal verification of the embedded software written in C.

development and thus to reduce the number of required verification runs later on, but also it complements the verification. For example, the semantics of an uninitialized variable depends on the compiler and the used operating system (if any); *cbmc*, however, regards these variables as nondeterministic and therefore overapproximates the program without a warning.

After passing the fast checks, the C code is given to *goto-cc*, which translates it into a *GOTO-program*, basically a control flow graph. During this process, all the macros in the C code are resolved by running the host compiler up to the preprocessing stage.

The *GOTO-program* is subsequently fed into *goto-instrument*, which adds *assert* statements according to user wishes. For example, each arithmetic multiplication can be checked for overflow, array bounds can be ensured, etc. Note that the original code may contain user-defined assert statements, which are preserved.

The resulting *instrumented GOTO-program* is finally handed over to *cbmc*, which performs loop unwinding, picks up all *assert* statements, generates VCCs for them and – after optional simplifications such as slicing – passes the problem to a solver back-end (we use *MiniSat2*; SMT solvers like *Z3* and *Yices*, are recent additions to *cbmc*).

After the back-end returns the proofs, *cbmc* post-processes them and provides a list of verified properties, and for each refuted one a counterexample. These lists can be used to fix defects in the original code, clearing the way for the next iteration.

6.2   Missing Architectural Information

A problem in static verification is implicit semantics that depends on the target, for example that certain functions are set up as interrupt service routines (ISRs) and thus their effect needs to be considered, although they never seem to be invoked. Another example is memory-mapped I/O, which may seem like ordinary reads from memory, but in fact could inject nondeterministic inputs from the environment.

Neglecting such context can easily lead to a collapsing verification problem and result in wrong outcomes. In our program, there were initially 351 properties, from which 349 were unreachable due to missing contextual information. Annotating all the necessary places manually is an error-prone labour, which bears the risk of having wrong or missing annotations and more importantly it is practically infeasible for our small program already. In the following we discuss how we addressed this problem.

Accounting for Interrupts: The preprocessed C code contains the ISR definitions, but naturally no functions call to them. The ISR is only called because its identifier is known to the cross compiler, and because particular bits are being written to registers at the start of the program; something that the model-checker lacks knowledge of. Consequently, it concludes that the ISR is never executed, and – through data dependencies – our detection algorithm seems to be never executed. This makes all properties within that algorithm unreachable and thus incorrectly evaluates them as "verified".

To overcome this, a nondeterministic invocation of the ISR must be considered at all places where shared variables are being evaluated, as described in [4]. This can be done with *goto-instrument* as a semantic transformation (flag--isr). Figure 4 shows the respective data that depends on interrupts in our case. Unfortunately, this technique not only grows the to-be-explored state space, but it even overapproximates the interrupts: The ISR could be considered too often in the case when the minimum inter-arrival time is longer than the "distance" of the nondeterministic calls (e.g., ISR for periodic timer overflow) that have been inserted. However, even if we would include execution time and scheduling information from parts of the main thread (to be computed by WCET and WCRT tools), the points in time where the ISR is called could be drifting w.r.t. to the main thread. This is true even for perfectly periodically triggered programs, solely due to different execution paths in the main thread.

Nondeterminism from Frequency-Dependent Side Effects: There exists another problem with interrupts that has not been addressed in [4] nor in goto-instrument. It stems from the frequency-dependent side effects of ISR invocation: In general, interrupts could also execute *more often* than the places where nondeterministic calls have been considered before. If there exist side effects other than changes to shared variables (i.e., if the ISR is non-reentrant in general), this can break the correct outcome of the verification. For example, ISRs that on each invocation increment some counter variable which is *not* shared with any other thread, could then in reality have a higher counter value than seen by the model checker[3]. In other words, all persistent variables that are manipulated by the ISR have to be modeled as nondeterministic, not only shared variables. In our case there were only three such variables (one was for the time-triggered release of the detection loop), which have been identified and annotated manually.

---

[3] A *lower* value is not possible, because all considered invocations are nondeterministic possibilities, and not enforced invocations.

Memory-Mapped I/O: All I/O variables (the sensor inputs) must be annotated to be nondeterministic. One option for that would be using the flag -nondet-volatile for *goto-instrument* to regard all volatiles as nondeterministic, however, this results in overapproximation for *all* shared variables (which are volatile as well), allowing for valuations which are actually infeasible due to the nature of the algorithms operating on the shared variable. Furthermore, this can override user-defined assumptions on the value domain of sensors, considering actually impossible executions and thus produce False Negatives on the verified properties.

In our case the microcontroller runs bare-metal code and uses memory-mapped I/O to read sensors, i.e., accesses show up in the preprocessed C code as dereferencing an address literal. In principle, it is therefore possible to identify such reads after the C preprocessing stage. However, in general it is a non-trivial problem to identify all these places, since indirect addressing is possible, which would require a full value analysis of the program to figure out whether the effective address is in the I/O range. At the moment we do not have a practical solution to this problem, which is why we instrumented all inputs manually. To support this process, we developed a *clang*-based [12] tool which generates a list of all dereferencing operations, suggesting the places that should be considered for annotating nondeterminism in the C code. Since we minimized the use of pointers to keep verification effort lower, the majority of the entries in this list is indeed reading input registers.

6.3   Preprocessing Against State-Space Explosion

After all architectural information has been added, the next big challenge is to verify the instrumented properties. A problem here is, that the state space grows rapidly from the architectural features, especially from the ISRs. In our case, the program has around 2,500 lines of C code, and running *cbmc* already fails for two reasons: (1) the program contains unbounded loops and (2) even if the loops were somehow bounded, there would be too many SAT variables to be considered (millions in our case).

Building Sequential Modes: The original structure of our program could not be verified, because the initialization and self-checks, were implemented as part of one hierarchic state machine, executed in main loop. The necessary loop unwinding then expanded the entire state machine as a whole. This resulted in too many SAT variables and could not be processed on our machine (we run out of memory after hours, having done only a fraction of the necessary unwinding).

To overcome this state space problem, we first partitioned our program into sequential modes, see Fig. 6. Each the initialization, the self-tests and the detection were refactored into their own loops, which take place one after another. Interrupts were enabled as late as possible, reducing the number of states to explore.

Assume-Guarantee Reasoning: However, at this point it turned out, that the initialization and self-checks still contributed too many variables for the program to be analyzed as a whole. As a countermeasure, the modes should now be analyzed independently and reasoning on the overall correctness should be done

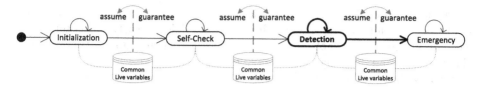

Fig. 6. Partitioning of software into strictly sequential modes, each verified individually and cascaded using *assume-guarantee* reasoning.

using *assume-guarantee* reasoning. Towards that, it was necessary to identify all possible program states between the modes, e.g., the detection mode can only be properly analyzed, if all possible program states after initialization and self-check are considered. One concrete example is, that the ERS determines the air pressure at ground level during the initialization, which is used later during detection. Verifying the detection mode thus involves considering all possible pressure levels, by assuming nondeterministic values for them.

To reduce the complexity of assume-guarantee reasoning, we first turned each mode into a potentially infinite loop which can only exit, if everything works as expected These "guards" reduce the number of program states to be considered for the postdecessor modes. For example, when analyzing the detection mode, we only need to consider program states corresponding to *successful* initialization and self-checks.

To construct the program states between modes, we identified all *live variables* between each two successive modes, i.e., all variables which are written in one mode and possibly being read in its successor modes. As this is another error-prone work that should not be done manually, we extended our *clang*-based tool to take this step automatically.

After having identified the live variables at the end of each mode, we instrumented them as illustrated in Listing 1: First, we added a nondeterministic assignment to each variable just before the new mode starts (line 6). This allows for *all* possible values, once the analysis on the new mode starts. Then, if due to some logical reason the value range could be limited, we used an **assume** statement to restrict analysis to this value range (line 7). However, to *guarantee* that the value domain is indeed complete, i.e., ensuring that no possible execution has been neglected, we added a matching **assert** statement at the exit of the predecessor mode (line 3).

Listing 1. Illustration of assume-guarantee reasoning using *cbmc* at the program point between two sequential modes X → Y, sharing one live variable **sharedvar**.

```
1  // end of mode X
   #ifdef ANALYZE_MODE_X
     assert(sharedvar > -10.f && sharedvar < 50.f);
   #endif
   #ifdef ANALYZE_MODE_Y
6    sharedvar = nondet_float(); // introducing nondeterminism
     assume(sharedvar > -10.f && sharedvar < 50.f);
   #endif
   // beginning of mode Y
```

A successful verification of the predecessor mode (here: X) means the asserts hold true, therefore *guarantees* that live variables indeed satisfy the assumptions we make at the beginning of the new mode (here: Y). Assume-guarantee reasoning therefore is sound. Finding the value ranges is currently done manually; in doubt one can omit the ranges, which leads to a safe over-approximation. However, tool support would be favorable, since tight ranges means no false alerts during verification.

In summary, this mode-building reduced the number of properties from 458 to below 250 in each mode, with 31 shared variables between them that were subject to assume-guarantee process (see Table 2).

Removing Dead Code: When going through the verification process shown in Fig. 5, it is desirable to entirely remove dead code (especially after mode-building and analyzing the modes separately), otherwise a lot of unreachable properties will be there, slowing down the analysis and cluttering the results. Although *goto-instrument* offers two slicing options, none of them removes dead code. This task is not trivial, since in our case the modes share code, e.g., both self-check and detection use a function that reads out the accelerometer. Again, we used our clang-based tool for this task, which operates on the C code that is equivalent to the GOTO-program and removes dead functions and variables (see Fig. 5).

Bounding Non-local Loops: A complexity-increasing problem for verification are nested, stateful function calls, as they occur in hierarchical state machines. Our program uses such hierarchical state machines to interact with the barometer and accelerometer peripherals. If one of the inner states has transition guards, then the *entire* hierarchy needs unrolling until these guards evaluate to true. In our case, we have guards like *waiting for ADC conversion to finish*. Unfortunately, hierarchic state machines are a popular design pattern in model-based design (e.g., Statemate, Stateflow, SCADE), which therefore needs to be addressed rather than avoided.

We found that some guards in the inner state machines can be removed safely, reducing costly unrolling. Assume that the guard will eventually evaluate to true (even if there is no upper bound on the number of steps it takes): If all *live* data that is written *after* this point is invariant to the number of iterations, then the guard can be removed. Consequently, such irrelevant guards can be identified by first performing an impact analysis (find all variables that are influenced by the guard), followed by a loop invariance test (identify those which are modified on re-iteration) followed by a live variable analysis on the result (from the influenced ones, identify those which are being read later during execution). If the resulting set of variables is empty, then the guard can be removed safely. This technique is of great help for interacting with peripherals, where timing may not influence the valuations, but otherwise contribute to state space explosion. The technique is easily extended, if there are multiple guards.

On the other hand, if a guard potentially never evaluates to true, e.g., due to a broken sensor, then there are two ways to treat this: If this is valid behavior, then this guard can be ignored for the analysis (no execution exists after it).

Table 2. Complexity of the verification before and after preprocessing. Unlike the full program, which cannot be analyzed, assume-guarantee reasoning between sequential modes *Initialization, Self-Check* and *Detection* was computationally feasible.

Mode →	Initialization	Self-Check	Detection	All
lines of code	1,097	976	1,044	2,513
#functions	36	29	43	94
#persistent variables	36	38	59	72
#live variables at exit	31	31	n.a.	n.a.
#properties	249	221	175	458
#VCCs	11,895	35,001	15,166	330,394
#SAT variables	5,025,141	8,616,178	6,114,116	n.a.
SAT solver run-time[a]	16 min	14 min	28 min	infeasible[b]

[a]On an Intel Core-i7 vPro at 2.8 Ghz and 4 GB RAM.
[b]Out of memory after 3 hours; #VCCs and SAT variables were still growing.

If it is invalid behavior, then the guard should be extended by an upper re-try bound and this new bounded guard can then be treated as explained above. After these transformations all state machines could be successfully unrolled.

6.4   Keeping Assumptions Sound

We made use of assumptions for limiting value domains where possible, and to perform assume-guarantee reasoning. Assumptions are a powerful tool in *cbmc*, however, it is easy to add assumptions which are not satisfiable (UNSAT). Those rule out *all* executions after the `assume` statement and thus might lead to wrong verification results.

Therefore, we have to ensure that the *composite* of all annotations is sound, otherwise the verification outcome may be wrong despite the individual annotations being correct. To check whether assumptions can be satisfied, we added a new check to *cbmc*, which does the following: It inserts an `assert(false)` after each assumption and subsequently runs the SAT solver on it. If the solver yields UNSAT for the assertion, it means it is reachable and thus the assumption is valid. If it yields SAT, then all executions were ruled out and thus the assumption is UNSAT and thus unsound. Finally, we warn the user for each UNSAT assumption.

6.5   Verification Results

With our extensions of existing tools we were able to set up a correct verification workflow for the software of the ERS. The complexity of the analysis (for each mode: run-time, number of variables etc.) is summarized in Table 2. During the process we identified several trivial and non-trivial defects, some of them were one deadlock in a state machine, multiple overflows in sensor data processing and even one timing-related error (barometer update took more steps than anticipated, which lead to wrong descent rate). Interestingly enough, during flight tests we sporadically experienced some of these errors, which by then could not be explained. One of the reasons for this is, that there was little information about these errors due to limited logging and debugging facilities on the microcontroller, and that we could not reproduce the environmental conditions in the lab.

7   Conclusion

In this paper we described our approaches in developing a safety-critical emergency recovery system for MAVs, in particular our efforts in applying methods and tools for formal verification of embedded software. This study has shown that formal verification of the entire, original software running on a microcontroller is possible, if appropriate preprocessing techniques are applied. The state space can be reduced to a size that can be covered by existing tools, but careful handling is necessary to obtain correct results. The efforts did pay off in our case. Not only could we identify defects in the software, but we obtained counterexamples for the defects, which can be the only useful source of debugging information for resource-constrained embedded systems.

As future work, we are planning to extend our clang-based tool to perform not only some, but all the steps we have taken automatically, as well as a complementary software supporting the described iterative workflow.

References

1. The 2013 General Aviation Statistical Databook and 2014 Industry Outlook. Technical report, General Association of Aviation Manufacturers (2014)
2. Abzug, M., Larrabee, E.: Airplane Stability and Control, 2nd edn. Cambridge University Press, New York (2005)
3. Beyer, D.: Status report on software verification. In: Ábrahám, E., Havelund, K. (eds.) TACAS 2014 (ETAPS). LNCS, vol. 8413, pp. 373–388. Springer, Heidelberg (2014)
4. Bucur, D., Kwiatkowska, M.: On software verification for sensor nodes. J. Syst. Soft. 84(10), 1693–1707 (2011)
5. Clarke, E., Kroning, D., Lerda, F.: A tool for checking ANSI-C programs. In: Jensen, K., Podelski, A. (eds.) TACAS 2004. LNCS, vol. 2988, pp. 168–176. Springer, Heidelberg (2004)
6. Cousot, P., Cousot, R., Feret, J., Mauborgne, L., Miné, A., Monniaux, D., Rival, X.: The Astreé analyzer. In: Sagiv, M. (ed.) ESOP 2005. LNCS, vol. 3444, pp. 21–30. Springer, Heidelberg (2005)
7. Cuoq, P., Kirchner, F., Kosmatov, N., Prevosto, V., Signoles, J., Yakobowski, B.: Frama-C: a software analysis perspective. In: Eleftherakis, G., Hinchey, M., Holcombe, M. (eds.) SEFM 2012. LNCS, vol. 7504, pp. 233–247. Springer, Heidelberg (2012)
8. Dajiang Innovation Technology: DJI DropSafe (2014). http://www.dji.com/product/dropsafe. Accessed February 2015

9. Drone Technology: RPAS MCFLY-HELIOS (2015). http://www.dronetechnology.eu/rpas-mcfly-helios/. Accessed February 2015

10. Henzinger, T.A., Jhala, R., Majumdar, R., Sutre, G.: Software verification with BLAST. In: Ball, T., Rajamani, S.K. (eds.) SPIN 2003. LNCS, vol. 2648, pp. 235–239. Springer, Heidelberg (2003)

11. Lal, A., Reps, T.: Reducing concurrent analysis under a context bound to sequential analysis. Form. Methods Syst. Des. **35**, 73–93 (2009)

12. Lattner, C.: LLVM and Clang: next generation compiler technology. In: The BSD Conference, pp. 1–2 (2008)

13. MARS Parachutes: M.A.R.S. 58 (2014). http://www.marsparachutes.com/mars-58/. Accessed January 2015

14. Mueller, M., D'Andrea, R.: Stability and control of a quadrocopter despite the complete loss of 1, 2, or 3 propellers. In: International Conference on Robotics and Automation (2014)

15. Opale Paramodels (2014). http://www.opale-paramodels.com/index.php/en/shop-opaleparamodels/rescue-systems. Accessed January 2015

16. Schlich, B., Kowalewski, S.: Model checking C source code for embedded systems. Int. J. Softw. Tools Technol. Transf. **11**, 187–202 (2009)

17. Skycat: SKYCAT Parachute Launcher (2015). http://www.skycat.pro/tech-specs/. Accessed March 2015

18. Steer Davies Gleave: Study on the Third-Party Liability and Insurance Requirements of RPAS. Technical report, European Commission (2014)

19. Tidorum Ltd.: Bound-T time and stack analyzer (2015). http://www.bound-t.com/. Accessed January 2015

20. Wu, X., Wen, Y., Chen, L., Dong, W., Wang, J.: Data race detection for interrupt-driven programs via bounded model checking. In: 2013 IEEE Seventh International Conference on Software Security and Reliability Companion, pp. 204–210 (2013)

The Role of CM in Agile Development
of Safety-Critical Software

Tor Stålhane[1][✉] and Thor Myklebust[2]

[1] Norwegian University of Science and Technology,
7491 Trondheim, Norway
stalhane@idi.ntnu.no
[2] SINTEF ICT, Strindveien 2, 7491 Trondheim, Norway
thor.myklebust@sintef.no

Abstract. Agile development is getting more and more used, also in the development of safety-critical software. For the sake of certification, it is necessary to comply with relevant standards – in this case IEC 61508 and EN 50128. In this paper we focus on two aspects of the need for configuration management and SafeScrum. First and foremost we need to adapt SafeScrum to the standards' needs for configuration management. We show that this can be achieved by relative simple amendments to SafeScrum. In addition – in order to keep up with a rapidly changing set of development paradigms it is necessary to move the standards' requirement in a goal based direction – more focus on what and not so much focus on how.

Keywords: Safety critical systems · Agile software development · Configuration management · IEC61508 · EN 50128

1 Introduction

It is always a challenge to change software – safety critical or not. In this paper we will discuss challenges related to changes and change processes when using agile development. We will do this from two perspectives – IEC 61508: 2010 (a generic standard often used in industrial automation) and EN 50128: 2011 (railway signalling systems). Change is always tightly connected to configuration management (CM) which is a well-known process. The challenge is more important for agile development that in any other development paradigm since agile development promises to "embrace change". The challenges related to CM will, however, increase when we use agile development since changes will be more frequent – possibly several changes included in each sprint. Changes during agile development come from several sources, e.g.:

- New requirements added after the development process has started
- Changes to existing requirements due to new knowledge or new customer needs
- New risk and hazards due to changes in the operating environment
- Refactoring – tidy up the code, which is important in agile development
- Not-accepted user story implementation from a sprint

© Springer International Publishing Switzerland 2015
F. Koornneef and C. van Gulijk (Eds.): SAFECOMP 2015 Workshops, LNCS 9338, pp. 386–396, 2015.
DOI: 10.1007/978-3-319-24249-1_33

All changes, irrespective of source, represent challenges for both the developers and for the system's integrity, e.g.:

- Testing. Which tests need to be re-run after the changes – the need for regression testing has to be evaluated
- Change impact analysis. How will the change affect system
  - Complexity – both IEC 61508 and EN 50128 require that the system complexity shall be controlled
  - Safety – which safety and hazard analyses should be checked or repeated

The CM process is well known and there is a plethora of tools available to support it. However, none of the proposed methods handle the problems pertaining to change impact analysis. Traditionally, the processes have been heavy on management and on documentation. None of these concepts fit well with agile development.

2   Related Works

First and foremost, there exist a well-known standard for CM – IEEE Std. 828 [10] which should be used as a reference document. When searching for existing work related to agile configuration management, we note that there exist few academic articles and that the few that exist mostly can be summarized in one sentence: "CM is important, also for agile development". If we look for papers on how to do CM during agile development, we find that the majority of relevant articles are published on blogs – e.g., [1, 2], although there are exceptions, e.g., [3, 4]. It is important to note the conclusion from [1]: "CM can be adapted to an agile iterative process without any problems" and the summary from [4]: "Modern CM tools can handle any number of configuration items without any problems and, therefore, controlling everything should be the tendency in agile methods".

In addition, there exist some books on the topic, e.g., [5–7]. The current conventional wisdom is best summed up in [1] – edited by the authors:

- Add support for parallel multiple development branches
- Avoid centralized Change Control Boards (CCB) that controls all changes. Control non-strategic decisions on changes in the distributed organization of Scrums. Reserve centralized decisions for changes that impact the whole program or organization.
- Let the agile team assumes the CM role instead of a dedicated Configuration Manager.
- Use automated tools – Automated continuous integration helps to reduce the integration and testing delays and allow quick feedback about the product quality.
- Continuously observe and adapt the CM tools and process.

3   Agile Development and SafeScrum

SafeScrum [8] is an adaptation of Scrum to make the development process comply with IEC 61508, EN 50128 and IEC 60880 – 2006, ed. 2. The main adaptations are shown in Fig. 1.

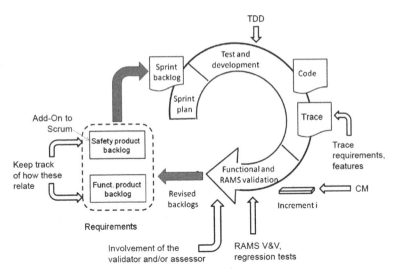

Fig. 1. The SafeScrum development process.

A complete description of Scrum and its development into SafeScrum can be found in [9]. The other important adaptation is the introduction of separation of concerns – see Fig. 2. The main message here is that SafeScrum cannot handle everything – we have decided to only handle software development, which is thus separated from the rest of the process described in IEC 61508 and EN 50128. The term "separation of concerns" stems from software design and we found this to be a useful and descriptive term when we designed the SafeScrum process.

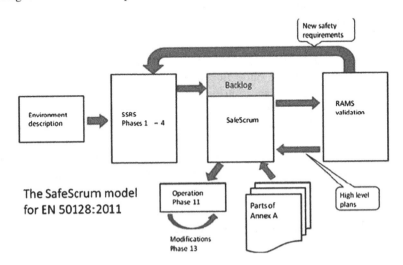

Fig. 2. Separation of concerns

SafeScrum gets its requirements from the system's SSRS and incorporate methods and techniques described in annex A, part 3 of the standard as required by the designated SIL. Each increment from SafeScrum goes through a RAMS validation and the result is either that it is OK, that it needs to be modified in another sprint or that it requires a new hazard analysis.

4 CM in Two Standards

4.1 CM in IEC 61508

The following sections of IEC 61508 are related to CM:

- Part 1 – Sects. 6.2.10 and 7.14.2.3. These two sections states that the project shall have a procedure for CM and the project needs configuration identification of items under test, the procedure applied for testing and the test environment
- Part 2 – Sects. 7.8.2.1 and D.2.1. These two sections are concerned with the CM of the complete E/E/PE system – hardware and software
- Part 3 – Sects. 6.2.3, 7.4.4.13, 7.4.4.15 – 17 and 7.8.2.8. Section 6.2.3 is the most important one since this section defines the requirements for the CM process to be used. We will look at this process in some more details below also because part 3 is the part of the standard that is concerned with software development. The other sections are concerned with CM history and CM for tools of categories T2 and T3
- Part 4 – 3.7.4 defines the term configuration data and also defines configuration baseline as "the information that allows the software release to be recreated in an auditable and systematic way
- Parts 5 and 6 – no relevant sections on CM
- Part 7 – appendix C.4.3 and C.5.24. The first of these two appendices state that the CM tools shall be certified and the second one describes the goals of CM

Part 1, part 2, part 4 or part 7 will have an impact on the chosen development method while part 3 is important. According to 6.2.3 Software configuration management shall:

(a) apply administrative and technical controls throughout the software safety life-cycle, in order to manage software changes and thus ensure that the specified requirements for safety-related software continue to be satisfied
(b) guarantee that all necessary operations have been carried out to demonstrate that the required software systematic capability has been achieved
(c) maintain accurately and with unique identification all configuration items which are necessary to meet the safety integrity requirements of the E/E/PE safety-related system. Configuration items include at least the following: safety analysis and requirements; software specification and design documents; software source code modules; test plans and results; verification documents; pre-existing software elements and packages which are to be incorporated into the E/E/PE safety-related system; all tools and development environments which are used to create or test, or carry out any action on, the software of the E/E/PE safety-related system

(d) apply change-control procedures:
- to prevent unauthorized modifications; to document modification requests
- to analyse the impact of a proposed modification, and to approve or reject the request
- to document the details of, and the authorisation for, all approved modifications;
- to establish configuration baseline at appropriate points in the software development, and to document the (partial) integration testing of the baseline
- to guarantee the composition of, and the building of, all software baselines (including the rebuilding of earlier baselines).

(e) ensure that appropriate methods are implemented to load valid software elements and data correctly into the run-time system

(f) document the following information to permit a subsequent functional safety audit: configuration status, release status, the justification (taking account of the impact analysis) for and approval of all modifications, and the details of the modification

(g) formally document the release of safety-related software. Master copies of the software and all associated documentation and version of data in service shall be kept to permit maintenance and modification throughout the operational lifetime of the released software.

The majority of these requirements will not be influenced by a choice of using an agile approach – in this case SafeScrum. Even most of the requirements in part 3, Sect. 6.2.3 will not be influenced by agile development. The mail challenges are point c and f. There is nothing there that cannot be fulfilled when using agile development but the resources needed may be large, depending on the tools used. It is thus important to agree on when we define a new configuration. This decision should be reached with the assessor – and may be with the customer – before development starts.

According to requirement 6.2.3 c, we need CM for the following documents: safety analysis and requirements, software specification and design documents, software source code modules, test plans and results, verification documents. We could for instance define configurations to be the result of:

- Each sprint. Use CM to recreate the status of the system after any chosen sprint.
- Separate CM-item sprints. The system's state can be recreated only to the states at these points
- The complete system. Only the final, delivered system can be recreated

4.2   CM in EN 50128

Even though both EN 50126 and EN 50128 also are relevant for railway applications, we have decided to only look at EN 50128 since we focus on software. The following sections in EN50128 are related to CM:

- Section 4 – requirement 4.1, which specifies that development environment shall contain a system for CM
- Section 5 – requirement 5.3.2.4, which specifies that the project shall have a CM plan, drawn up from the start of the project

- Section 6 – requirement 6.1.4.4 and 6.1.4.5 are related to tests. Requirements 6.5.3 and 6.5.4 handles quality assurance requirements, while requirements 6.6.2 and 6.6.3 handles change control. Each project needs a CM plan.
  - All software documents and deliverables shall be placed under CM control and changes to these documents shall be authorized and recorded. The CM system shall cover the software development environment used during a full lifecycle.
  - Each test specification shall document test environment, tools, configuration and programs, requirement and that we need to identify the configuration of all items involved in a test report.
  - All changes shall be done according to the CM plan and deliver a new CM record.
- Section 7 – requirements 7.4.4.2, 7.5.4.4, 7.6.4.5, 7.6.4.9 and 7.7.4.10
  - Requirement 7.4.4.2 requires that each component shall have a CM history attached
  - Requirement 7.5.4.4 requires that each component shall be under CM before we start *documented testing*
  - Requirements 7.6.4.5, 7.6.4.9 and 7.7.4.10 require that the software and hardware integrations shall identify the configurations of the elements involved and the validation report
- Section 8 has configuration requirements for configuration data of the system. In our opinion, this is outside the scope of this paper except for requirements 8.4.7.1 and 8.4.7.5 which requires that the configuration data shall be placed under configuration control
- Section 9 contains requirements for deployment and maintenance, which both are topics outside the scope of this paper. It is, however, important to note that requirement 9.1.4.8 opens up for incremental deployment

Note that EN 50128 does not mention regression testing. This should, however, be included in the next version of the standard.

4.3 Prescriptive vs. Goal Based Standards

The most convenient way to start this discussion is to use a definition of CM. In order not to favour any of the two standards that we discussed here, we will use the definition given by IEEE [12] which states that configuration management is the process of

- Identifying and defining the items in the system
- Controlling the change of these items throughout their lifecycle
- Recording and reporting the status of items and change requests
- Verifying the completeness and correctness of items

In order to make standards more robust when techniques and methods change, we work to make as many as possible of the standards goal-based. I.e., instead of saying what you shall do, we want to focus on what you shall achieve. To show what we mean, we will show a possible goal-based approach for some of the CM requirements for the two standards discussed above. The main goal for both standards is to be able to recreate a consistent set of documentation, code, test data and tools that is maintained throughout the development project. This goal alone covers IEC 61508, part 1, part 2 and part 7 plus EN 50128, Sects. 4, 5 and 6.

For IEC 61508, only part 3 is important, since it describes a set of concrete requirements to CM while part 4 only contains relevant definitions and parts 5 and 6 have no relevant sections pertaining to CM. A closer look at part 3, Sect. 6.2.3 shows that it only says that you should be able to recreate the complete project state at any defined time.

For EN 50128, Sects. 4 and 5 just say that a project shall have a plan and a system for CM. Section 6 adds that the CM shall cover the software development over a full lifecycle.

We have earlier stated that all the development requirements stated in annex A and B of IEC 61508 only contains sound software engineering practices. It would not be unreasonable to claim the same for the two standards' requirements for CM.

5   The SafeScrum Approach to CM

5.1   Some General Considerations

First and foremost: CM is more important when using an agile development approach then when using a waterfall process. There are several reasons for this:

- Builds baselines more frequent
- Have more frequent deliveries/releases
- Have more and more frequent changes

If we look at the table supplied by [4], we see that software CM is not a part of Scrum and thus needs to be added also to SafeScrum (Table 1).

Table 1. CM in agile development methods

Method	Software configuration management approach	Practices related to SCM
Adaptive Software Development	SCM not explicitly considered	–
Crystal family of methodologies	Tool viewpoint on SCM	–
Dynamic System Development Method	SCM explicitly considered	All changes during the development must be reversible
Extreme Programming	SCM partially considered	Collective ownership, small releases and continuous integration
Feature Driven development	SCM explicitly considered	Configuration management, regular builds
Pragmatic Programming	Tool viewpoint on SCM	Source code control
Scrum	SCM not explicitly considered	–

Note that [1] advices us to avoid a centralized Change Control Boards and to reserve centralized decisions for changes that impacts the whole program or organization. The rest should be handled by the SafeScrum team.

The term "component" is often used both in IEC 61508 and in EN 50128. From the definition given in EN 50128 – "…well-defined interfaces and behaviour with respect to the software architecture…" it is reasonable to interpret component as a functional unit – see IEC 61508-4, 3.2.3. Functional unit: entity of hardware or software, or both, capable of accomplishing a specified purpose.

5.2 Regression Testing

One important issue not explicitly related to CM but important for each change – which is the reason why we need CM – is regression testing. When we do test-first, e.g. TDD, we make a set of tests based on the current set of requirements (user stories) and develop software with the goal that the piece of code currently developed shall pass the tests. However, we will also have a lot of tests developed for previous requirements. In addition, the tests developed for a user story will in most cases depend on a set of stubs, fakes or mocks. It is not obvious that these tests can be run on any later version of the system without much ado. We see two practical ways out of this:

- Organize the user stories in such a sequence that we avoid – or at least minimize – the need for stubs, fakes and mocks. See for instance [11]
- Have two sets of tests – one for the total system and one for each increment. The first will be a system test that is increased for each sprint while the other one is a set of tests only relevant for the designated sprint – see Fig. 1. The system test could be maintained and run by the same persons who do the RAMS validation in the current SafeScrum model while the other tests could by the responsibility of the development team – see Fig. 2

Another important consideration is the need to retest only what was affected by the last sprint. To achieve this we will use two important mechanisms (1) connecting tests to user stories and (2) using the trace information. We need traces from user stories to code and from user stories to tests. This will give us information about which tests are related to which code units. We only need to retest components that are changed or receive input (directly or indirectly) from changed components. By having efficient tools for automation, it is possible to enable regression testing of relevant parts of the system, with increased frequency.

When developing safety-critical systems, changes may have effects that are outside the changed modules or components. This challenge is handled by change impact analysis. Even though this is important it is not part of CM. We have, however, discussed this problem and the suggested SafeScrum solutions extensively in [9]. The interested read should consult this paper and its references.

5.3 SafeScrum CM in IEC 61508 and EN 50128

The most important statement related to CM is that the Software Quality Assurance Plan, Software Verification Plan, Software Validation Plan and Software Configuration Management Plan shall be drawn up at the start of the project (i.e., outside SafeScrum) and be maintained throughout the software development life cycle. For

IEC 61508, this holds also for hardware and for tools of category T2 and T3 plus the documents listed in part 3, Sect. 6.2.3. The important thing for SafeScrum is to have a procedure at the start of each sprint where all plans are updated when necessary. This can be done either by the SafeScrum team itself as part of the sprint planning process or by the people who developed the plans, using information from the SafeScrum team.

EN 50128 also requires that all information related to testing – e.g., environment, tools and software – shall be included in CM. Note also that the standard requires all components to be under CM before we start documented testing. Testing done during development using e.g., TDD does not need to be included. In most projects, documented testing only includes integration testing and system testing.

The only part that we need to go through in some detail is IEC 61508, part 3, Sect. 6.2.3. This section specifies that we shall

- Have administrative and technical control throughout the lifecycles
- Apply the correct change control procedures and document all relevant information for later safety audits – i.e., that the CM job is done properly
- Have control over all identified configuration items
- Formally document the releases of safety-related software

An important challenge to the SafeScrum process is the first statement: administrative control throughout the lifecycles. For the other CM requirements, the challenge for SafeScrum is not to fulfil the requirements but to decide how often and under what circumstances. Most of the information needed for efficient CM is created automatically by tools. We suggest the following approach:

- Management decides at which milestones a new configuration should be defined. This is done before the project starts and is mentioned in the CM plan.
- The responsibility for managing the CM is normally assigned to the quality assurance department (QA).
- All code and data are tagged during check-in. The tags are administrated by the QA but used by the SafeScrum team.
- The QA and the SafeScrum team have regular meetings that focus on CM and other QA-related issues.

EN 50128 adds some requirements – all components shall have a CM history attached to it and that the validation report and configuration data shall be included in the documents under CM. In addition, the integrations shall identify the hardware and software components used. It is also worth mentioning that EN 50128 requires that each component shall be under CM before we start documented testing. Thus, the components need not be under CM during test-driven development.

To sum up; we have considered all requirements to CM in IEC 61508 and EN 50128. There are no practises in SafeScrum that prevent or hinder the use of standard CM methods and procedures. SafeScrum needs two add-ons (1) tagging of code and data at check-in and (2) regular meetings between the SafeScrum tam and the company's QA-department.

5.4 Threats to Validity

As always with this type of discussions, there are two threats to the validity of our discussions and conclusion: (1) have we understood the standards and (2) have we understood CM. We claim that we have understood

- The two standards, based on the practical experiences the two authors have with the standards – one is a certified assessor for EN 50128 while the other author has worked with IEC 61508 in industrial settings.
- CM, based on the practical experience of one of the authors with software development

6 Summary and Conclusions

We have had a detailed walk-through of the two standards IEC 61508 and EN 50128 with focus on CM and change management when we use an agile development process – in this case SafeScrum. The challenges related to CM increase when we use agile development since changes will be more frequent. There are just a few requirements in either of the standards that prevent the use of SafeScrum as is. The following changes (additions) are needed:

- A new process at the start of each sprint to do necessary updates to the CM plan when needed. The SafeScrum team should cooperate with QA in this process.
- A separation of testing into development tests – e.g., TDD – which is the responsibility of the SafeScrum team and system – and integration tests, which are the responsibility of the RAMS process
- All tools used, all documents generated and all plans should be under CM.
- An efficient tracing tool is needed, e.g., to keep track of the relationships between user stories, test cases and code

In addition we suggest changes to the two standards under discussion in order to make the requirements goal-based in order to be able to keep up with new ideas and concepts in software engineering.

Acknowledgements. This work was partially funded by the Norwegian Research Council under grant #228431 (the SUSS project).

References

1. Rey-Mermet, B.: Agile Configuration Management-overview, 23 May 2013. http://evocean.com/blog/agile-development/
2. Norin, J.: Lean Configuration Management. Evolving the CM Discipline Through the Agile Paradigm Shift. http://intellijens.se
3. Lindroth-Olson, Prentare, O.: What, When, Why and How. Introducing Software Configuration Management in Agile Projects, February 28 2012

4. Koskela, J.: Software configuration management in agile methods, 514th edn. VTT-publications, Espoo (2003)
5. Moreira, M.E.: Adapting Configuration Management for Agile Teams: Balancing Sustainability and Speed. Wiley. ISBN: 978-0-470-74663-9 October 2009
6. Jonassen Hass, A.M.: Configuration Management Principles and Practice. Addison-Wesley Professional
7. Black, R.: Managing the Testing Process: Practical Tools and Techniques for Managing Hardware and Software Testing, John Wiley and Sons (2002). ISBN 0471223980, 9780471223986
8. Stålhane, T., Myklebust, T., Hanssen, G.K.: The application of Safe Scrum to IEC 61508 certifiable software. ESREL, Helsinki (2012)
9. Stålhane, T., Hanssen, G.K., Myklebust, T., Haugset, B.: Agile Change Impact Analysis of Safety Critical Software, SASSUR. Florence, Italy (2014)
10. IEEE: Standard Glossary of Software Terminology. IEEE Std. 610. 12–1990
11. Bjerke-Gulstuen, K., Wiik Larsen, E., Stålhane, T., Dingsøyr, T.: High level test driven development – Shift Left: How a large-scale agile development project organized testing. XP2015, Helsinki, Finland
12. IEEE: Standard for Configuration Management in Systems and Software Engineering. IEEE Std. 828 - 2012

Is Current Incremental Safety Assurance Sound?

V. Cassano$^{(\boxtimes)}$, S. Grigorova, N.K. Singh, M. Adedjouma, M. Lawford,
T.S.E. Maibaum, and A. Wassyng

McMaster Centre for Software Certification, McMaster University, Hamilton, Canada
{cassanv,grigorsb,singhn10,morayoa,lawford,wassyng}@mcmaster.ca
tom@maibaum.org

Abstract. Incremental design is an essential part of engineering. Without it, engineering would not likely be an economic, nor an effective, aid to economic progress. Further, engineering relies on this view of incrementality to retain the reliability attributes of the engineering method. When considering the assurance of safety for such artifacts, it is not surprising that the same economic and reliability arguments are deployed to justify an incremental approach to safety assurance. In a sense, it is possible to argue that, with engineering artifacts becoming more and more complex, it would be economically disastrous to not "do" safety incrementally. Indeed, many enterprises use such an incremental approach, reusing safety artifacts when assuring incremental design changes. In this work, we make some observations about the inadequacy of this trend and suggest that safety practices must be rethought if incremental safety approaches are ever going to be fit for purpose. We present some examples to justify our position and comment on what a more adequate approach to incremental safety assurance may look like.

Keywords: Incremental design improvement · Incremental safety assurance

1 Introduction

Incremental design improvement, a.k.a. *normal* engineering design [23], has a long history and proven value as a way for constructing improved versions of artifacts. This engineering praxis caters for time and budget constraints, ensures an artifact's effectiveness, fitness for purpose, and the reliability of its production.

We consider that the same considerations guiding incremental design improvement have fostered a practice of incremental safety assurance which relies heavily on the reuse of existing safety artifacts, e.g., safety related evidence and arguments. However, in contrast to incremental design improvement, we argue that incremental safety assurance, as presently viewed and practiced, is not necessarily sound. An important reason for this is the global nature of safety as a property of a system. Focusing the safety assurance efforts in a localized fashion, e.g., on the slice of the system where the design change occurred, may ignore newly created global hazards or the re-emergence of those that are otherwise

© Springer International Publishing Switzerland 2015
F. Koornneef and C. van Gulijk (Eds.): SAFECOMP 2015 Workshops, LNCS 9338, pp. 397–408, 2015.
DOI: 10.1007/978-3-319-24249-1_34

mitigated. Complicating things further, safety artifacts cannot be straightforwardly composed, as the context and the assumptions in one safety artifact may undermine safety claims established in another. Though these considerations may seem well-known, that certain current safety practices fail to tackle them properly indicates that they are neither entirely understood nor easily dealt with.

In this paper, we put forward some observations on why incremental safety assurance, when understood from the perspective of incremental design improvement, is problematic, and in fact inherently deficient (that is the bad news!). Our discussion hinges on two main points: compositionality and the defeasibility of safety arguments, and locality and emergent properties. By elaborating on these points, we hope to bring to the foreground what we believe is an important issue of safety practice: the reuse of safety artifacts. While we believe that there is certainly great practical value in the reuse of safety artifacts, we offer a view of what a more sound approach to incremental safety assurance might look like (that is the good news!), this needs of a great deal of caution.

Structure of the paper: In Sect. 2, we explain what incremental safety assurance means from the perspective of incremental design improvement, commenting on its underlying philosophy and the necessity for its existence. In Sect. 3, we elaborate on our reservations about such an incremental approach to safety assurance. In Sect. 4, we substantiate our claims by providing examples from the automotive and medical domains. In Sect. 5, we discuss the challenges and opportunities presented by an incremental approach to safety assurance. In Sect. 6, we comment on some related work. In Sect. 8, we offer some conclusions and talk about our next steps.

2   Incremental Safety Assurance

When faced with a problem, engineers tend to build on experience, best practices, and already existing artifacts, analyzing their pros and cons in order to try to adapt them (incrementally) to the problem at hand. This approach is key for guaranteeing an artifact's reliability and the reliability of its production. This commonly accepted view of engineering praxis is, among other places, discussed by Vincenti in [23] under the name of *normal design*. In Vincenti's terms, a design is normal if both the *operational principle*, i.e., "how the device works", and the *normal configuration*, i.e., "the general shape and arrangement that are commonly agreed to best embody the operational principle", are known and used [23, pp. 208–209]. If either the operational principle or the normal configuration are largely unknown, or, if known, are left unused, then, the design is *radical* [23, p. 8]. Radical design is then to be thought of as based on engineering principles that are wholly different from those guiding normal design. This said, Vincenti remarks that "though less conspicuous than radical design, normal design makes up by far the bulk of day-to-day engineering enterprise" [23, p. 8].

The difference between normal design and radical design is easily illustrated in the automotive domain. A case can be made that majority of current vehicles are based on, reuse, or extend, design elements existing in other vehicles of the same kind, i.e., normal design. This applies both to the software and hardware components of a vehicle and enables the automotive industry to rely on well-tested systems while being up-to-date with technological advances. On the other hand, the development of an autonomous car would exemplify a radical design.

The inherent practicality of normal design, i.e., of incremental design improvement, has lead to its enduring prevalence. We consider that it is this prevalence, as well as the striving for efficiency and resource preservation, that has fostered an incremental approach to safety assurance. It is a given that designs often become more complex and sophisticated as they evolve from one version to the next. We are then naturally loathe to discard the immense amount of safety knowledge collected during the production of a previous version of the system, and documented in safety artifacts such as safety arguments, hazard analyses, test data, etc. In analogy with incremental design, it appears both reasonable and practical to take advantage of these safety artifacts and, whenever possible, e.g., if design changes are deemed "small" or systems are "sufficiently" similar, to reuse them so that safety engineers may focus their attention specifically on the effects of what has changed. This attempt to localize and focus safety assurance efforts by reusing safety artifacts is what we call an *incremental approach to safety assurance*, something that we further make clear in Sect. 4, where we present some real-life examples from the automotive and medical domains.

3 The Pitfalls of Incremental Safety Assurance

In this section we discuss some pitfalls associated with what we call an incremental approach to safety assurance. Our conclusion is that this approach to safety assurance cannot simply rely on principles analogous to those of incremental design improvement. If it does, it is unsound. This conclusion hinges on two main points. First, in contrast to what happens in incremental design improvement, safety assurance artifacts are not compositional. Second, while incremental design improvement is conducive to localization in terms of design parts, safety assurance requires a holistic view of the system. We elaborate on these points in Sects. 3.1 and 3.2, respectively.

3.1 Compositionality of Safety Artifacts

Regarding compositionality, the general idea of a safety argument provides us with a necessary context for discussion.

It is well-known lore that an argument is a series of assertions, in which the last element, the *conclusion, follows from* some foregoing assertions in this series, the *premises*. More precisely, from an inferential standpoint, to 'follow from' means that the conclusion is obtained from the premises by virtue of some judiciously chosen rules of inference. The bar against which an argument is then judged as being well-formed or not, i.e., right or fallacious, rests on an analysis of the properties that are satisfied by these rules of inference. In that respect, classical logical studies restrict their attention to the rules of inference of the propositional and the predicate calculus, or some of their variants, such as those dealing with modalities. Rules of inference of this sort, henceforth called classical, enjoy the desirable property of being definite, i.e., they are not subject to rebuttal. This entails that if a conclusion follows from some premises and some other conclusion follows from some other premises, then, both conclusions follow from the union of their sets of premises. In other words, if arguments are formulated in terms of classical rules of inference, then, they are *compositional*.

A safety argument is an argument whose main concern is the safety of an engineered artifact. Now, by looking at a safety argument, we can readily conclude that the rules of inference used in its formulation are far from being adequately captured as classical rules of inference (after all, we have yet to see definite safety claims). On the contrary, our view is that, whenever made explicit, safety arguments are formulated using defeasible rules of inference, i.e., rules of inference that are open to revision or annulment, e.g., as made precise in Toulmin's notion of a *rebuttal* [22]. This view of safety arguments makes them radically different from classical arguments; it makes them *non*-compositional. More precisely, as is well-known in the field of defeasible reasoning, in the presence of defeasible rules of inference, while a conclusion follows from some premises, and while some other conclusion follows from some other premises, neither of these conclusions may follow from the union of their sets of premises [11].

In short, the preceding discussion indicates that composing safety arguments incrementally suffers from the inherent problem that this composition step is clearly unsound. In consequence, if safety arguments are built resorting to defeasible rules of inference, then, their compositionality requires principles that are radically different from those underpinning what can be done incrementally.

3.2   Localization of Safety Assurance Efforts

Regarding localization, the general idea of a safety goal decomposition provides us with the necessary context for discussion.

In essence, safety goal decomposition involves the mapping of safety claims across different levels of the design hierarchy. At the highest levels of design, some general safety claims are made. At lower, more detailed, levels of design, these general safety claims are refined into more specific safety claims, e.g., as safety claims concerning design parts. Fundamental to the soundness of safety goal decomposition is the assumption that any refinement step encompasses a full knowledge of the design elements it involves, how these elements interact, how these interactions may fail, and what measures can be put in place so that safety claims are not violated. When looked at from this perspective, safety goal decomposition requires a holistic view of the design at hand.

This said, the design hierarchy reflected in safety goal decomposition has led some to believe that design parts may be straightforwardly replaced by others which are substantially equivalent in terms of the safety properties they satisfy. For us, this is a serious misconception. What the previous chain of reasoning fails to take into account is that safety claims are not obtained in a localized fashion, but instead are the result of a refinement mechanism which accounts for a holistic view of the design hierarchy. If any design part were to be replaced in any refinement step, not only would it be required to reassess the safety of the design parts involved in this refinement step, but also to reassess the safety of the design as a whole. The latter is largely due to the *emergent properties*, i.e., those arising from unexpected interactions between the replaced part and the rest of the system [17]. Because of their implications for safety, and given that they are not easily identified in the functional decomposition of a design, emergent properties are to be dealt with explicitly and seriously; failing to consider them is a serious omission in incremental safety assurance.

In short, safety assurance efforts cannot easily be limited to the modified design parts without considering a holistic view of the system. This means that, whether design parts and their corresponding safety artifacts may be replaced, or "plugged-in", modularly, without completely undermining what has thus far been deemed safe, requires principles that are radically different from those underpinning incremental design improvement. The approach is otherwise unsound.

4   Substantiating Our Claims

Focused on what we view are some of paradigmatic examples of safety gone wrong, in Sect. 4.1 we discuss the case of GM's faulty ignition switch, and in Sect. 4.2 we discuss the case of J&J's DePuy Orthopedics all-metal hip implants. We argue that these two real-life examples illustrate how what we call an incremental approach to safety assurance presents itself in practice.

4.1   Automotive Domain: The Ignition Switch Case

Not long ago, GM was faced with the recall of 2.6 million cars because of a defective ignition switch. The problem? The defective ignition switch would unintendedly move out of the "run" and into the "accessory" position during driving, leading to a partial loss of electrical power and turning off the car's engine. Why is this a problem? Under certain conditions, this accidental turn off of the car's engine resulted in an unfortunate series of events, which caused serious harm or death for car occupants; e.g., in a number of cases, this failure disabled the power steering, the anti-lock brakes, and the airbags, causing some fatal car crashes.

For us, GM's defective ignition switch problem is a glaring example of what may go wrong with an incremental approach to safety assurance. Why? GM found out that the problem with the ignition switch was the result of a new switch indent plunger that did not supply enough torque to keep the ignition from accidentally changing position [20]. It seems that, GM first became aware of the problem in 2001 and started to make incremental changes to the plunger part to address the issue in 2006 [13]. What went wrong with these changes? At least two things. First, our view is that when making the design change, GM engineers focused on meeting the specifications of an ignition switch, deeming unlikely that this would introduce any new system level hazards. In a sense, the emphasis was placed on the physical and structural aspects of the design of the ignition switch. Second, this seemingly physical modification had a bearing on the the overall safety of the car. Most likely, the software requirements at the conceptual level of the car assumed that the car is not in motion when the key is in "accessory" mode. If the car is assumed not to be moving when the key is in "accessory" mode, it is reasonable to deactivate the airbags in order to prevent unintended deployment (in a parked car the accidental deployment of airbags could seriously injure passengers as they enter or exit the car). With the defective ignition switch, the assumptions underlying these software requirements are undermined. It was indeed possible for the car to be in motion with the key in "accessory" mode, e.g., as a result of hitting a bump on the road. (To be noted, the latter did not occur in cars prior to the problematic ignition switch design, where more torque was required to change the key position, virtually eliminating the possibility of the key accidentally changing position).

Can safety be assured locally? Replacing an indent plunger, a seemingly local issue, has global safety implications, exactly because of the intervention of a software-based control system. Concentrating solely on the physical or the software based aspects of the ignition switch may miss the real safety consequences. What the defective ignition switch misses is a global impact analysis of the design changes. This may have allowed an assessment of which other elements might have been affected and what new hazards this design change could have introduced. But this is easier said than done. It was not trivial for GM engineers to link the infrequent cases of airbags not deploying in an accident after loss of power steering and power brakes to the defective ignition switch [4,24].

As a final remark, touching on the notion of what has been *proven in use* and its potential contribution to the safety of a newer car, the determination of what is safe is intrinsically an evolving notion. Namely, small design changes, such as changing an indent plunger, may have worked well in the past. Yet, in the past, losing power to the car may have not been considered to be a catastrophic failure. E.g., in the past, failure of power steering and brakes would still leave the driver with some measure of control via manual steering and the mechanical connection to the brakes. In this past, an engineer dealing with mechanical components may view the change of the key position as an undesirable event that could result in a hazardous situation, but the hazard 'loss of control leads to an accident' would have been seen as being mitigated by the manual system. Supporting these claims, at a lawsuit resulting from a fatal accident, an engineer testified that the car was "safe" because it "could still be maneuvered to the side of the road" [13]. People have different expectations nowadays.

4.2   Medical Domain: The All-Metal Hip Implant Case

The FDA 510(k) substantially equivalent (SE) criterion for clearance of a new medical device is another example of what may go wrong with an incremental approach to safety assurance. Why? By its definition, the SE criterion relies on a comparison of a to-be-marketed with an already marketed medical device. In essence, if changes in design are deemed to be "minor" or "small", inferences about the safety of the newer device can be made based on the safety artifacts of the device already marketed. Framed somewhat differently, the 510(k) SE criterion assumes that a small change in design will not likely bring about a major safety concern. As shown below, this assumption is, at least, problematic.

As reported in [12], in 2005, Johnson & Johnson's DePuy Orthopedics introduced a new all-metal design for their hip implants. A predecessor version of these hip implants was made of metal and plastic. The newer hip implants were cleared for market with the older hip implants being used as a predicate device using the 510(k) SE criterion. The new all-metal hip implants were cleared for market based on the fact that their predecessor had been cleared for market. No clinical trials nor additional tests were performed on the all-metal hip implants. Thus far, nothing seems to be wrong from an incremental safety assurance perspective (more so, a case can be made that the operational principle and the normal configuration are likely to be sufficiently similar, if not the same, for both the all-metal hip implant and its predecessor). The problem? It turned out that for the case of the all-metal hip implant "[t]he metal was eroding, releasing metallic particles into the blood and surrounding tissue of the joint and causing tremendous pain" [12]. This did not occur with the predicate device. It seems that drawing analogies between designs being substantially equivalent bears no obvious relationship to their safety. How can such a threat to safety be discovered if not by re-examining and carrying a thorough re-conceptualization of previously produced safety artifacts? Moreover, the all-metal hip implant is interesting for its ancestry, which can be traced back "more than five decades through a total of 95 different devices, including 15 different femoral heads and sleeves and 52 different acetabular components" [21]. It seems reasonable to assume that, even in the presence of impeccable initial safety artifacts, the compounded effects of design changes led up to a point where a new hazard was indeed present. This raises the question: do the small tweaks eventually get you?

5 Discussion

In hindsight, the threats to safety mentioned in Sects. 3 and 4 could have been mitigated with a proper preparation, revision, and perhaps re-conceptualization of the previously produced safety artifacts. Special attention must be given to impact that design changes may have on safety (potentially having to conduct new hazard analyses, reevaluate safety assumptions and the contexts in which these assumptions were made, etc.). Being able to count on a framework enabling the tracing of design changes to safety artifacts is a MUST, since it is precisely this framework that may enable the assessment of the effects of localized design changes on safety related artifacts. It is at this point where the notion of a safety case comes into play (a notion popular in some domains, but not so much in others). We believe that there is a version of incremental safety assurance that can take the necessary holistic view of safety assurance and perhaps offer a sort of middle ground between the present practices in many industries and the uneconomic approach of building all safety artifacts from scratch. Our hypothesis is that this middle ground would need an explicit safety case in terms of which to assess the impact that an incremental design change may have on safety. Such an explicit safety case may then lead to some ability to localize required changes to safety artifacts, yet not necessarily in the sense of localization to design parts. The moral of the story? Reuse of safety artifacts can only be sound if we are able to trace the global effects that design changes may have on the system.

This said, having a well-defined notion of a safety case is only a part of the big picture. As we have argued above, an incremental approach to safety assurance cannot be based on principles similar to those of incremental design improvement. We are of the view that reusing safety artifacts requires *rely/guarantee*-like engineering principles, as understood by the formal methods community [7]. Intuitively, these principles may be understood as: the guarantee properties of this safety artifact are met only if the *rely* properties of a safety artifact are met. How hazard analyses, safety related evidence and arguments, test libraries, etc., are to be dealt with in a rely/guarantee fashion is something largely to be explored.

In summary, while we acknowledge that there is great practical value in the reuse of safety artifacts, this has to be done with a great deal of caution. We take as foundational that any incremental approach to safety assurance cannot be based on those engineering principles underpinning incremental design. Insofar as its soundness is concerned, what is then needed are engineering principles allowing for an analysis of the effect that a design change may have on safety artifacts. Among many things, these principles must involve a careful and thorough review of the validity of safety arguments. This would enable us to identify whether a safety argument contains some fallacious inferential steps and to assess the degree of certainty of the safety claims it involves. As usually conveyed in safety discussions, we view a safety argument as a cornerstone in safety assurance. Without a safety argument that links safety evidence with safety claims, it is well-nigh impossible to establish either the relevance and the sufficiency of the provided evidence, or how this evidence contributes to the safety claims. For us, this needs, as a first step, a precise definition of a safety argument, i.e., there is a need of a logic for safety argumentation (this logic need not be a formal logic, but it must be a logic nonetheless). Moreover, it is our view that emergent properties require special attention in safety assurance, as these pose one of the greatest threats to safety being assured in an incremental fashion. All in all, what is needed is a framework allowing for safety artifacts to be traced back to the design parts under consideration, enabling an analysis of effect propagation of localized changes, such as those caused by the addition of a new functionality or the replacement of a design part. An explicit safety case is a first step in the right direction.

6   Related Work

The need for an explicit and properly defined safety case is well-recognized in the safety community. There is, however, some disagreement regarding what counts as a "properly" defined safety case. In this respect, we are pluralists: maybe there is no THE properly defined safety case, but properly defined domain specific safety cases. This said, we take as basic that a properly defined safety case shall consist of explicit safety goals, evidence of their fulfillment, acceptance criteria for the evidence, and a structured argument linking evidence to safety goals.

Among other places, the need for having an explicit safety case is commented on by Holloway in [15]. Holloway stresses that this is indispensable for evaluating the reasons why safety assurance practices in the aeronautics domain have thus far been adequate. Holloway makes this claim in reference to compliance with DO-178C, a standard which regulates the use of software on commercial airplanes, in an industry considered to be mature when it comes to safety matters. Our standpoint here is somewhat similar: without an explicit and adequate representation of a safety case, its analysis is close to impossible, as is the impact that design changes may have on safety. Works such as [2,3,8,19] also stress the importance of having an explicit representation of a safety case. However, in comparison to ours, these works are focused on what a safety case should look like, not on the problems with an incremental approach to safety assurance.

Particularly interesting in the context of incremental safety assurance is [18]. The authors of this work comment on how refinement, as understood by the formal methods community, allows for a much needed feature in incremental safety assurance: the introduction of more detail into the decomposition of safety goals. As a challenge of adopting such a technique for decomposing safety goals they point out that refinement leaves little room for revision. This is a consequence of refinement being conceived in a (logically) monotonic setting. The situation is radically different once one assumes safety properties are defeasible, as we have discussed in Sect. 3. In such a setting, the traditional ideas of refinement do not apply straightforwardly (e.g., it may be the case that refining a safety goal into two safety subgoals results in one of the subgoals undermining the other). Considering this phenomenon is crucial if safety assurance is to be thought of incrementally.

Works such as [1,6,9,14] are also related to incremental safety assurance. All of these works have in common with ours a discussion of safety being assured in an incremental fashion. However, in comparison with ours, their approach is presented from the point of view of techniques rather than principles. In that respect, they do not seem to discuss the issues that we have commented on in Sects. 3 and 4. Though they address and suggest a component based approach to safety assurance, they do not discuss how such components may be put together in a property preserving manner.

7   Some Final Remarks

Given that incremental design improvement is prevalent as an engineering practice, it is no surprise that matters related to the associated idea of incremental safety assurance appear in various safety standards and guidelines via the reuse of design elements.

The automotive domain incorporated the notion of *proven in use* in the recently published ISO 26262 standard for the functional safety of vehicles.

In ISO 26262 defines proven in use as "an alternate means of compliance [...] that may be used in the case of reuse of existing items or elements when field data is available" [16, Part 8, Clause 14]. ISO 26262 also introduces the concept of *safety element out of context* (SEOoC). A SEOoC is "intended to be used in multiple different items when the validity of its assumptions can be established during integration of the SEOoC" [16, Part 10, Clause 9]. Both 'proven in use' and SEOoC fall within an incremental approach to safety assurance under the assumption that they involve the reuse of the safety artifacts attached to a design element, with the purpose of contributing to the safety of a newly developed car.

The medical domain has its well-known 510(k) process. The US FDA defines the so called '510(k) program' as "a premarketing submission made to FDA to demonstrate that the [medical] device to be marketed is as safe and effective, that is, substantially equivalent (SE), to a legally marketed device that is not subject to premarket approval (PMA)" [5]. The SE condition indicates that the changes incorporated into the new medical device are somewhat "small" in relation to the already marketed medical device, from which the new device's safety follows. If looked at from this perspective, the FDA's 510(k) program is another instance of an incremental approach to safety assurance: small design changes cause no effect on the artifact's safety.

In avionics, an incremental approach to safety assurance may be seen as being present in the FAA's AC 20-148: Reusable Software Components [10]. In this advisory circular, the FAA comments that "because of economic incentives and advances in software component technology, software developers want to develop a *reusable software component* (RSC) that can be integrated into many systems' target computers and environments with other system software applications", all while still showing compliance with avionics safety regulations. As with ISO 26262's notion of a SEOoC, if we agree that a RSC involves the reuse of safety artifacts, then, it is more or less clear that this falls within the scope of what we call an incremental approach to safety assurance.

Following from the observations just made, to be noted is that, while the definitions and practices may vary across domains, a great deal of care should be taken so that these safety standards and guidelines are not undermined by the pitfalls and deficiencies that we discussed in Sects. 3 and 4.

8   Conclusions and Next Steps

Incremental design improvement, a.k.a. normal design, is a reliable and standard foundation for engineering practice. It is well understood, generally economic, and it supports the need and desire to see improvements in the artifacts that we use. When these are safety critical, the question becomes: how are safety related issues, arising due to changes in design, to be incorporated into the safety assurance scheme? We have argued that the obvious analogy to incremental design improvement encounters serious difficulties related to identifying new or re-emerging safety issues.

We have also discussed some of the principles and examples of an incremental approach to safety assurance. Resorting to the latter, we have shown that safety related issues were missed, leading to some catastrophic results. In our view, shared by some, the fundamental problem, the root cause of the mistakes, is that, even though design changes might be local, as in the ignition switch example, their effects on safety assurance are of a global nature. More generally, mistaking incremental design change for limited effects on safety has resulted in essential difficulties related to safety, and serious damage to people, completely undermining claims about safety. This has been worsened by the fact that the safety cases often remain implicit, making it very difficult to determine the global safety effects of the localized design change. Of course, we do recognize that when safety engineers have a great deal of experience, and they devote sufficient attention to the effects of design modifications on safety artifacts, things appear to run smoothly, even if approached incrementally. The problem is that this is difficult to evaluate externally, i.e., without the inside knowledge these safety engineers may have. If looked at from this perspective, rather than an engineering discipline, safety assurance becomes something that falls within the realm of obscurantism and practiced by safety gurus.

Conversely, our position is that, incremental safety assurance needs principles other than those underpinning incremental design improvement. These principles will define the basis for analyzing how incremental design changes impact existing safety artifacts. Thus, our recommendation goes beyond that of producing an explicit safety case. This said, safety cases are definitely necessary. It is with respect to them that the effects that design changes may have on safety may be tracked down more easily, establishing a foundation for eliciting sound engineering principles for incremental safety assurance. In any case, our proposal is not the one usually put forward in the context of safety assurance: start afresh from the ground up. We recognize that while perhaps viable in domains where changes in design seldom occur, this is economically and logistically infeasible when changes in design are frequent, as is the case in the automotive and medical domains. As future work, we need to rigorously develop and systematize our hypotheses, so that they can be evaluated in carefully conducted experiments.

Acknowledgments. The authors wish to acknowledge the support of the Automotive Partnership Canada, the Ontario Research Fund, and the Natural Sciences and Engineering Research Council of Canada.

References

1. Althammer, E., Schoitsch, E., Sonneck, G., Eriksson, H., Vinter, J.: Modular certification support - the DECOS concept of generic safety cases. INDIN **2008**, 258–263 (2008)
2. Birch, J., Rivett, R., Habli, I., Bradshaw, B., Botham, J., Higham, D., Jesty, P., Monkhouse, H., Palin, R.: Safety cases and their role in ISO 26262 functional safety assessment. In: Bitsch, F., Guiochet, J., Kaâniche, M. (eds.) SAFECOMP. LNCS, vol. 8153, pp. 154–165. Springer, Heidelberg (2013)
3. Birch, J., Rivett, R., Habli, I., Bradshaw, B., Botham, J., Higham, D., Monkhouse, H., Palin, R.: A layered model for structuring automotive safety arguments. In: European Dependable Computing Conference (2014)

4. Bunkley, N.: GM engineer says he didn't remember changing ignition switch part. Automotive News 28 May 2014. http://www.autonews.com/article/20140528/OEM11/140529859/gm-engineer-says-he-didnt-remember-changing-ignition-switch-part

5. Center for Devices and Radiological Health: Device approvals, denials and clearances 4 June 2014. http://www.fda.gov/medicaldevices/productsandmedical procedures/deviceapprovalsandclearances/default.htm

6. Conmy, P., Nicholson, M., McDermid, J.: Safety assurance contracts for integrated modular avionics. In: 8th Australian Workshop on Safety Critical Systems and Software (SCS 2003). vol. 33, pp. 69–78. Australian Computer Society (2003)

7. de Roever, W., et al. (eds.): Concurrency Verification: Introduction to Compositional and Non-compositional Methods. North-Holland, Amerstadam (2007)

8. Dittel, T., Aryus, H.-J.: How to "Survive" a safety case according to ISO 26262. In: Schoitsch, E. (ed.) SAFECOMP 2010. LNCS, vol. 6351, pp. 97–111. Springer, Heidelberg (2010)

9. Elmqvist, J., Nadjm-Tehrani, S.: Tool support for incremental failure mode and effects analysis of component-based systems. In: DATE 2008. pp. 921–927 (2008)

10. Federal Aviation Administration: Ac20-148: Software reusable components (2004)

11. Gabbay, D.M., Woods, J. (eds.): Handbook of the History of Logic: The Many Valued and Nonmonotonic Turn in Logic, vol. 8. North-Holland, Amsterdam (2007)

12. Groeger, L.: Four medical implants that escaped FDA scrutiny 30 April 2012. http://www.propublica.org/special/four-medical-implants-that-escaped-fda-scrutiny

13. Gutierrez, G., et al.: GM chose not to implement a fix for ignition problem. NBC News 13 March 2014. http://www.nbcnews.com/storyline/gm-recall/gm-chose-not-implement-fix-ignition-problem-n51731

14. Hatcliff, J.A.L.K., Lee, I., Macdonald, A., Anura, F., Robkin, M., Vasserman, E., Weininger, S., Goldman, J.: Rationale and architecture principles for medical application platforms. In: ICCPS 2012. pp. 3–12 (2012)

15. Holloway, M.: Making the implicit explicit. In: ISSC 2013. Boston (2013)

16. Internatiional Standard Organization: ISO 26262: Road vehicles - Functional safety (2011)

17. Johnson, C.W.: What are emergent properties and how do they affect the engineering of complex systems? Rel. Eng. & Sys. Safety 91(12), 1475–1481 (2006)

18. Lisagor, O., Kelly, T.: Incremental safety assessment: Theory and practice. In: Proceedings of 26th International System Safety Conference. Minneapolis (2008)

19. Palin, R., Ward, D., Habli, I., Rivett, R.: ISO 26262 safety cases - Compliance and assurance. In: Procedings of 6th IET International Conference on System Safety, pp. 1–6 (2011)

20. Spangler, T.: Delphi told GM Ignition Switch Didn't Meet Specs. Detroit Free Press, Michigan (2014). http://www.usatoday.com/story/money/cars/2014/03/30/gm-ignition-switches-recall-congressional-report/7085919/

21. Thompson, H.: Researchers say DePuy hip ancestry shows 510(k) flaws 19 February 2013. http://www.mddionline.com/article/researchers-say-depuy-hip-ancestry-shows-510k-flaws

22. Toulmin, S.E.: The Uses of Argument. Cambridge University Press, Cambridge (2003)

23. Vincenti, W.: What Engineers Know and How They Know It: Analytical Studies from Aeronautical History. The Johns Hopkins University Press, Baltimore (1993)

24. Wald, M., Vlasic, W.: 'Upset' GM engineer spoke in house inquiry. The New York Times 28 May 2014. http://www.nytimes.com/2014/05/29/business/upset-gm-engineer-spoke-in-house-inquiry.html?_r=0

Dependability Arguments Supported by Fuzz-Testing

Uwe Becker[(⊠)]

Systems Design, Draeger Medical GmbH,
Moislinger Allee 53-55, 23542 Luebeck, Germany
uwe.becker@draeger.com

Abstract. Today's situation in operating theaters is characterized by many different devices from various manufacturers. Missing standards for device intercommunication lead to the fact that inter-device communication in most cases is either difficult or even impossible. A system oriented approach with networked devices is envisioned to improve this heterogeneous situation. Every device in the operating theater shall be able to interchange data with every other device in the network. Even remote control of other devices shall be possible. Therefore, concepts for safe and secure dynamic networking of components in operation theaters and hospitals have to be provided. This paper will show methods to test such systems of systems and provide a way to increase the robustness of the interfaces. This will be part of the evidence described in multidimensional dependability arguments provided to certification authorities.

Keywords: Safety-critical medical devices · Systems of systems · Device interoperability · Robustness of interfaces · Dependability arguments · Fuzz-testing · Scenario-based testing

1 Introduction

In operation theaters and intensive care units many different devices from various different manufacturers are used. Some examples are camera systems, operation tables, endoscopes, infusion pumps, patient monitors, and other measurement devices. Today such solutions use proprietary protocols and interfaces. In most cases it is difficult to include devices from different manufacturers in the proprietary networks. Interoperability is only given if all devices are from the same manufacturer. For other devices a way has to be found to let them exchange data. In addition, to guarantee for interoperability, the hospital has to take the responsibility for the installation and manage possible risks appropriately.

To overcome the limitations mentioned, standardized interfaces and data structures are required. Interfaces and data structures have to be flexible enough to allow for additional functions, quality, and features for product diversification. This will lead to cost reduction both on the side of hospitals and on the side of manufacturers. Hospitals will be more flexible in buying new devices and delivering best possible treatment. Manufacturers can increase quality of treatment and even provide new therapies because they can include devices and access data they previously weren't able to access

© Springer International Publishing Switzerland 2015
F. Koornneef and C. van Gulijk (Eds.): SAFECOMP 2015 Workshops, LNCS 9338, pp. 409–420, 2015.
DOI: 10.1007/978-3-319-24249-1_35

or include. Though, there are still some standards missing, medical devices manufacturers have to react on this demand. They have to provide concepts for safe and secure dynamic networking of components in operation theater (OR) and hospital.

This paper will show methods to test such systems of systems and provide a way to increase the robustness of the interfaces. The rest of the paper will be organized as follows: The next chapter gives information on the state of the art, followed by an introduction to fuzz-testing. Examples show how the dependability of systems of systems is increased by the results obtained by fuzz-testing. The results provide evidence aggregated in dependability-arguments as shown in the chapter "Evaluation". The paper concludes with a short summary.

2 Testing Systems of Systems

System oriented approaches including software and IT applications require inter-operable data structures to guarantee that data can be exchanged without loss, providing additional benefit (semantic interoperability). Systems have to be reasonable mature before they are brought into a system of systems. For each system the individual features have to be tested first. This includes testing of combinations of related features and the required input variables. If this prerequisite is given, the end-to-end check on a benefit the system or program is supposed to deliver has to be done [8]. A scenario-based test approach should be used as it can help discover problems in the relationships among the features. In addition, scenario-based test approaches provide an early warning system for problems that may haunt the project later. The more complex a scenario is, the more likely it will show up compelling bugs because the tests provide more complex conditions than would otherwise have been tested. Nevertheless, it is essential that the tests are easy to evaluate. The more complex the test, the more likely will the tester accept a plausible-looking result as correct. Reports from IBM show that about 35 % of the bugs found in the field were bugs that had been exposed by tests but were not recognized as such by the testers [8].

Ryser and Glinz [9] convert natural language requirements and use-cases into statecharts thereby formalizing the scenarios. Some scenarios require certain prerequisites, e.g. the completion of another scenario or some other dependency. It is good practice not to test only the so-called "happy-day" scenario with all dependencies satisfied but also those with none or only a few of them fulfilled. This ensures that test cases for dependencies and interrelations between scenarios are obtained. Scenario-based testing is not suited for testing early or unstable code or systems. Each feature has to be tested in isolation otherwise the bugs they contain will block the scenarios.

3 Fuzz-Testing

Fuzz-testing is a test method that uses input values selected randomly or by heuristics. In general, each test-run would provide different input values to the system under test (SUT). The simplest type of test pattern generators (called "fuzzers") performs black box testing using random patterns. A large number of test pattern is generated to gain suitable test coverage. This kind of test pattern generators is very easy to use but can obviously find simple errors only. If the SUT requires the input to be protected by check-sums, encryption, and/or compression, simply providing random data at the inputs will not find any errors, since the SUT will assess the input being invalid and reject it. In order to generate sophisticated test pattern and to check test responses some information on the SUT is required. A model is required to both check test responses and generate test pattern for sophisticated protocols. Model-based fuzzers can cope with SUTs that require the input to be protected e.g. by check-sums. The model provides information on input ranges of variables and required sequences of operations. This is demonstrated on the protocol example below. Let the protocol have the structure: <*"command"*>, <*"device ID"*>, <*"string"*>, <*"check-sum"*>.

A stateful fuzzer is required to generate valid protocol packets with an appropriate check-sum. Providing random patterns, even with correct check-sum, may not find many errors because packets with unknown or invalid commands will be rejected. Depending on the command structure, this may result in most packets been rejected. A stateful, scenario-based fuzzer will provide packets with valid command, valid device ID, and appropriate check-sum. It will fuzz the string part of the protocol. This will provide packets with valid strings but also with empty ones, strings with many spaces, with spaces only, with special characters, etc. The random strings will show the robustness of the protocol implementation.

Fuzz-testing as such is not meant to supplant "more systematic testing". It rather is an additional tool for testing. Fuzz-testing can be automated to a high degree and can be applied to a wide range of problems [1]. Its use as black box testing approach is especially useful when evaluating proprietary systems. Fuzz-testing has become a crucial tool in security evaluation of software. Its effectiveness is based on how thoroughly the input space of the tested interfaces is covered. In addition, the effectiveness depends on how good the representative malicious and malformed inputs for testing each element or structure within the tested interface definition are (quality of generated inputs). Fuzzers should be model-based and stateful to insert malformed or unexpected data into quite specific areas of the input data stream.

4   System Testing and Optimization

Lot of work and research has been done on protocol testing and robustness testing for closed components [3, 6, 7]. Some effort has been spent on interoperability testing between two or more components. However, less work has been published on the robustness of concurrent and networked systems. The potential risk of being attacked makes the robustness of such systems become more and more important. One component can impact or even crash the whole system. In this paper robustness is defined as the degree to which a system will function correctly in the presence of invalid inputs, or stressful environmental conditions [4, 5]. In that sense, a robust system can be used without crashing even when it is used inappropriately. Testing for robustness [4, 7] tries to find inputs or behavior that possibly can jeopardize the system. In a system of systems (SoS) concurrent components are networked and work together as if they were a single component. Each component of the SoS has its own specification and is tested and approved separately. To increase the robustness of the SoS all components have to be analyzed together. To have the system operate in defined conditions, certain procedures have to be followed and certain conditions be fulfilled. Sometimes users do not follow the procedures required, thus introducing vulnerabilities. Therefore, to optimize the SoS as a whole, not only the internal communication but also the user interfaces and the operation procedures have to be tested and evaluated.

Until recently, in order to acquire certification, it was sufficient to argument development was done in an appropriate way according to certain prescriptive process-based standards. This included the adherence to defined processes, regular reviews, personnel competence, and a risk-management process [2]. Recent communication with certification authorities (e.g. the FDA) shows that now there is a preference for more than just safety arguments. Therefore, we propose five-dimensional dependability arguments which include safety but also other aspects such as security.

5 Dependability Arguments

There is a trend in the development of safety-critical software towards the use of safety cases [12]. Safety cases require evidence specifically tailored to the system and software development. Arguments based on safety only may not be enough to describe a system adequately. Especially networked systems require security cases as well. Therefore, dependability arguments consisting of the five dimensions "safety", "security", "dependability", "availability", and "resilience" are proposed:

Safety. It is the condition of being protected against types or consequences of failure, damage, error, accidents, harm, or any other event considered non-desirable.

Security. It is the degree of resistance to, or protection from, harm. It describes the degree of data protection and the ability of the system and its internal communication to withstand cyber-attacks.

Availability. It is the degree to which a system or subsystem is in a specified operable and committable state, i.e. a functioning condition, at any time.

Resilience. It is the ability to absorb or avoid damage without suffering complete failure.

Dependability. In general is a measure of a system's availability, reliability, and its maintainability. In this paper it means the readiness for and continuity of correct service as well as the degree of reliability of conveyed information. Dependability of a system defines the degree further decisions can depend on the information.

To increase robustness of the system a three step testing approach is proposed. Basis of the method proposed is fuzz-testing, a well-established method to check and improve robustness of communication interfaces. This testing method is also applied to improve the reaction of the system on situations where users do not follow the defined operating procedures. Information from test scenarios and previous tests is used to increase quality of generated inputs during fuzz-testing. In addition, formalized scenarios are (re)used in testing [8, 9]. Fuzzer frameworks or commercially available fuzzers usually are capable to use this information and to increase the quality of generated inputs with information from previous test-runs. After performing the tests according step 1 to step 3, information is obtained where the system of system, its internal communication, and the operation procedures involved show vulnerabilities. Fixing the vulnerabilities provides evidence for the dependability arguments.

Step 1 – Test the Interface Protocol Using Fuzz-Testing

In order to bring their medical devices to market, manufacturers test the external interfaces against internal or external (public) standards. Testing against the interface-standard will be comparable to tests against commercially available interfaces such as the USB interface for instance. The tests ensure that after connecting the device to the system it will function as desired. The device will just add its functionality to the system. However, to achieve full functionality it may be necessary, to have some kind of "driver", which provides information on how to handle the device and its data.

Conformity tests for many standards just require that devices adhere to a certain protocol. Proving that a certain piece of code or a device satisfies a given set of properties may not be enough to prove correctness or to guarantee that it will be reliable in any environment or under certain circumstances in the intended environment. There is no information about malformed or invalid datagrams and various other off-nominal conditions, which are of central importance in safety-critical systems [11]. The off-nominal conditions do not necessarily have to be huge impacts but rather be an aggregation of relatively small events. It turns out that in almost all cases where safety-critical systems fail, the cause is an unexpected combination of relatively low-probability events [14]. Therefore, in a first step the robustness of the interface shall be increased. This is done by fuzzing the protocol.

Fuzzing the protocol involves sending malformed packets and unexpected data at certain points in the protocol. With the information gained, the robustness of the protocol interface is increased against both other devices that do not function as expected and attack scenarios. The higher the robustness of the interface, the more increases the chance that the device continues to deliver its function even if another device in the system of systems is faulty or the connection between the devices is unreliable.

Step 2 – Test the User Interfaces Using Fuzz-Testing

Defined operation and handling of the user interface is expected and sometimes also required to perform certain operations or during special conditions of the system. Occasionally though, users may find the required value they are ought to set too high or otherwise inappropriate in the current situation. Sometimes it is just by the stress users feel in a certain situation that they select and change the setting of a parameter not expected to be changed at that moment.

Systems have to cope with such situations and such "unexpected" settings. Therefore, fuzz-testing of the user interfaces is proposed. It will provide valuable insight in the function and requirements of the user interface. Sometimes even hidden requirements or implicit assumptions made by programmers can be discovered with fuzz-testing. If users inadvertently change values because stress and misperception makes them select a certain value, there may be a way to change the layout of the user interface (e.g. placement of the value on the screen). Nevertheless, sometimes trade-offs have to be made at this point. It may be that increasing the robustness of the user interface would mean to compromise safety. As the latter is not an option, the dependability argument will have a smaller value for robustness than for safety.

Step 3 – Test System Operation Conditions Using Fuzz-Testing

Systems of systems increasingly become more complex and human-centered. Resilient systems need flexible adjustments. It turns out that in many cases human variability and flexibility is the core driver of the required adjustments. Therefore, it is extremely useful and should not be eliminated. In some cases, human variability may engender failure, in most cases, though, it ensures successful adjustment of the system to internal or external disturbances [10]. Human variability keeps the systems operating at the desired or at least at a satisfying level of performance [13]. The human intention to keep the systems running leads to the fact that the specified guidelines are not perfectly – or even not at all – followed. Tests for antifragile or resilient systems should take this into account instead of relying on fixed values in response to certain events. Responses to events are fuzzy values, at least as long as human beings are involved.

Having said this, it opens a different view on the often very stringent rules to be followed when operating a system of systems. In some cases it may be difficult to follow all the instructions specified. Even worse, instructions of different manufacturers may be in contradiction to each other. Therefore, fuzz-testing the operating guidelines is proposed to evaluate the consequences that arise from not perfectly following them. This includes different scenarios such as normal operation but special operations as well. When expanding the approach to other domains, operational procedures during disaster/disaster recovery may also be included (with simulated values only).

6 Evaluation

In this chapter some examples will be given to show how the method proposed will detect possible issues. The first example is based on the scenario that a therapy device shall forward its alarm condition to a device in the network such as a pager or the like. Let us assume that at first the communication is secured by a check-sum and that there is some kind of keep alive signal to ensure that the device in the network is available. The device sending the alarm information identifies itself by transmitting some information about its position and/or its associated patient. This patient related data has to be encrypted for security reasons and to ensure privacy. For safety and security reasons a patient ID is transmitted together with bed and room information.

Using the assumptions above, the second column of Table 1 below shows the values for the dependability argument prior to optimization using fuzz-testing. An average value of 5 is given to "safety", "security", and "dependability". There is no resilience (1) and availability is low (3). The next step is to fuzz-test the alarm annunciation interface and the complete transmission chain of the alarm from the device to the pager of the nurse. Based on the shortcomings and/or vulnerabilities found, mitigation measures will be implemented. Fuzz-testing is performed again after implementing the measures. The second testing step is done to check whether there are new or non-fixed vulnerabilities. If the test is passed without findings, the respective parameter is attributed with the highest value. The values to attribute the five dimensions of the dependability arguments are in the range between 1 and 10. A value of 1 indicates that the parameter is more or less not fulfilled, e.g. no protection against attacks. Whereas a value of 10 indicates that the parameter is covered by the measures implemented, e.g. the system is immune against the defined/considered attack scenarios.

Testing of the alarm annunciation revealed many shortcomings and vulnerabilities. When fuzzing the device identification it was found that every device could confirm alarms. If a hacker would be able to get into the network and receive an alarm packet he could confirm the alarm thus avoiding it to be conveyed to the nurse that ought to receive it. Thereby causing danger for the patient. Therefore, it was decided to include an authentication of the devices. In addition, only a defined set of devices was given the right to confirm alarms. Fuzzing the alarm information showed that every device was able to send every possible alarm with every possible alarm priority. If by an attack the priority of an alarm could be altered, this could also be dangerous for the patient. The decision therefore was that every device can only transmit a defined set of alarms with predefined priorities. The alarm priority information not only increases security but can also increase robustness against errors during transmission. The communication protocol was vulnerable against any kind of replay attack. To avoid this attack scenario, the communication should include some kind of time stamp and packet ID. The receiver should discard packets received twice or with unexpected time or packet IDs. The description of the alarm in the communication packet should consist of multiple bytes. To further secure the transmission, it should be checked if the device signaling the alarm is really capable of generating such alarms. The same holds for the answer on the alarm. The nurse receiving the alarm should confirm that she received it and will take appropriate action. The receiver of the confirmation should check if the sending device is capable and authorized to do so. It should reject packets from other devices. At this point it is not intended to define further actions e.g. by network administrators if it is for instance detected that a scale tries to confirm an alarm from an intensive care ventilator.

As explained above, fuzz-testing highlighted some weaknesses in the communication protocol. Any device could confirm or send an alarm. The transmission was not robust against transmitting wrong alarm information to mention just a few. The issues were resolved and the test was run again – now with the result that the transmission was robust against the issues mentioned. The latter test provides evidence that the communication is safe and secure. This information can be used to generate a dependability argument for safe alarm annunciation which is shown in Table 1 below. It shows which measures had been implemented (column 4) and how the values for the different dimensions of the dependability argument changed (column 3). A set of measures was defined to mitigate the vulnerabilities and shortcomings revealed by fuzz-testing. The effect on the communication was very positive as the rating for every dimension could be increased. Regarding the safety aspect the communication now covers the attack and failure scenarios (value "10"). Security was increased too, but to reduce the overhead it was decided not to cover all attack scenarios. The communication is still vulnerable to sophisticated attacks. Nevertheless, security is rated sufficiently high (value "7"). The degree the user can rely on the information received was increased to a sufficiently high value (value "7"). There are, though, some cases in which the information is not reliable. Resilience and Availability are rated to have reached the maximum possible values (value "10").

Table 1. Dependability argument "safe alarm annunciation" with optimization

Alarm annunciation is safe

Confirmed authenticated transmission of alarms

Parameter	Value		Measures	Comment
Safety	5	10	Check sum + answer back + keep alive signal + defined alarms with predefined priorities from defined devices only + transmission with time stamp, packet ID, and patient ID	The communication is safe. Safety is increased by checking the alarm source and priority (result from fuzz-testing)
Security	5	7	Patient data (patient ID) is encrypted, communication only with authenticated partners, only defined alarms (including priority) from defined devices + transmission with time stamp and packet ID + one packet for each alarm	Time stamp against replay attack. Robustness against attacks increased with information gained from fuzz-testing
Dependability	5	7	Receiver shows error if connection to sender is lost. Detection by use of a keep alive signal	User can rely on displayed alarm
Resilience	1	10	First alarm in network on different devices, then on nurse call interface, then locally + time-out before and after confirmation + Alarm shown after confirmation until alarm is off	Alarm will be announced even if some of the devices fail.
Availability	3	10	Alarm on different network devices + via nurse call interface (including in hallway) + local alarm to increase availability	The alarm will be available. Please note: This is for the alarm itself not for the alarm annunciators in the network.

The first example is based on a scenario in which a therapy device is source of information and transmits it into the network. The second example is based on a scenario in which a therapy device is the receiver of information transmitted from other devices within the network. When treatment is performed to a patient, any device around the patient (in the workplace) may sound an alarm e.g. caused by motion artifacts. The user expects to silence all devices at once by pressing the "alarm silence" button on the device nearest to her. In general, silencing an alarm is very sensitive and

Table 2. Dependability argument "safe remote alarm silence" with optimization

Remote alarm silence function is safe

Confirmed authenticated transmission of alarm silence

Parameter	Value		Measures	Comment
Safety	5	10	Confirmed transmission with check-sums. Multi-bit status, "Pairing" of devices to identify a workplace, Display shows "workplace alarm silence" functionality	Content of transmission protected against errors or changes
Security	5	10	Only from defined and authenticated devices, transmission with time stamp and packet ID. Only two defined states allowed, each alarm and each alarm silence request in a separate packet	Reduced attack surface by reduced number of states and authentication (result from fuzz-testing)
Dependability	5	10	Alarm silence set if all devices agree on "alarm silence". Device accepts new alarms of equal or higher priority. Signal is only available within a single workplace.	Signal is reliable. No alarm silence if signal is given too often (e.g. more than 10/minute) (result from fuzz-testing)
Resilience	1	3	Alarm silence set locally or based on status received from other devices in the workplace. Defaults to "no silence"	The remote alarm silence function still permits to issue a local alarm silence.
Availability	1	1	Only accepted if not longer than allowed by standards (e.g. 2 min). Does not change if alarm silence is already active, defined overall alarm behavior	Alarms have priority against convenience function. Standards may limit availability.

potentially may become of high risk for the patient because even alarms indicating a life threatening situation may be silenced.

Let us assume that at first the communication between the devices is secured by a check-sum and that there is some kind of keep alive signal to ensure that the devices in the network are available. The device sending the alarm silence information identifies itself by transmitting some information about its position and/or its associated patient. This patient related data has to be encrypted for security reasons and to ensure privacy. The patient ID is transmitted together with bed and room information.

Column 2 of Table 2 above shows the values of the dependability argument prior to optimization. An average value of 5 is given to "safety", "security", and "dependability". There is no resilience (1) and availability is very low (1). Fuzz-testing of the implementation has been done to improve the transmission of the alarm silence information. Again weaknesses in the initial protocol were discovered by fuzz-testing.

If the information is transmitted in a single bit only, it is relatively easy to change the information e.g. by influence of EMC. To mitigate this issue the alarm silence information has to be transmitted as multi-bit value. It turns out, that in the first implementation every device could send an alarm silence information. Therefore, two different measures have to be implemented. Only devices authenticated and allowed to do so are accepted as sender of alarm silence information. This is a necessary but not sufficient condition. It is required to introduce some kind of "pairing" to identify the devices of a single workplace. Only devices that are identified to be around the same patient as the receiving device are accepted as senders for alarm silence information. In addition, some of the weaknesses found are the same as those in example 1. Therefore, measures already implemented in example 1 are required here also.

A set of measures was defined to mitigate the vulnerabilities and shortcomings revealed by fuzz-testing. The measures implemented have very positive effect on the communication as the rating for most dimensions could be increased. Regarding the safety aspect the remote silence function now covers the attack and failure scenarios (value "10"). Security and the degree the devices can rely on the information received were increased too (value "10"). If the alarm silence information is received, it can be relied on. The communication of the information was immune to security breaches by the predefined attack scenarios. The value for "Resilience" could only be increased by a small value. The information is transferred more than once and there is the possibility to silence the device locally. Therefore, the parameter is attributed with the value "3". Availability could not be increased. On any error not positively covered, the remote silence functionality is lost and thus the parameter is still attributed with "1".

The five dimensions of a dependability argument may be in competition or even in contradiction to each other in the fulfillment of a certain safety-case. We see this as an advantage of the arguments proposed. Furthermore, it may happen that not all vulnerabilities found during fuzz-testing can be fixed. Some information may be very important but vulnerable. In such cases a trade-off between parameters has to be made. The trade-off is evident in the dependability argument by the values attributed to the parameters. Sometimes evidence from multiple teams with different backgrounds is required. One team may provide evidence for security; another team may provide evidence on safety and so on. The weights of the different dimensions in the argument show the point of view from which the evidence is made. More than one evidence may be given or even be required to adequately form the desired dependability argument, to satisfy a certain safety case, or to fulfill a certain sub-goal respectively.

Figure 1 shows the graphical representation of the two examples mentioned. Such graphical representation is also used to display the contribution of different dependability arguments in fulfilling sub-goals. A net-diagram with values between 0 and 10 turns out to be well suited for this purpose. The graphical representation is especially well suited to show how the respective arguments contribute to fulfill the goal. It also highlights trade-offs made between different dimensions of the various dependability arguments. If one would take the two dependability arguments from the examples as required to fulfill a certain sub-goal, one would identify a trade-off been made between

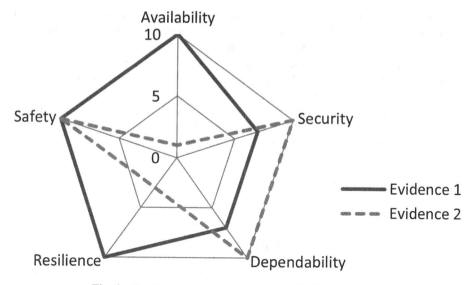

Fig. 1. Graphical representation of dependability arguments

safety and availability in the second dependability argument. The first parameter is attributed with the value "10" and the latter with the value "1" only.

7   Conclusion

There is a strong continuous development from autonomous devices and applications towards system oriented approaches including software and IT applications. In the near future complex and networked medical devices and medical procedures will inter-operate with each other. This interoperability demands for inter-operable data and data structures.

An overall test approach should exist that covers not only single devices but also systems of systems. In this paper we propose scenario-based fuzz-testing to fulfill this demand. Fuzz-testing is used to check the implementation of the communication interfaces and the user interfaces. This concept can easily be extended even for the procedures users have to follow when using the system of systems. The testing is used to gain information on vulnerabilities and other issues of different parts of the system. This information is used to improve the communication interfaces in a first step. In a second step user interfaces of the system of systems are improved. In a third and last step procedures users have to follow when operating the system are improved. These procedures are described in much the same way communication protocols are descri-bed. Therefore they are also optimized in the same way.

Networked systems of systems are not only required to be safe but also to be secure. In most cases users want them also to be available. This paper proposes multidimensional dependability arguments that include "safety", "security", "depend-ability", "availability", and "resilience". Each dimension is attributed with a value showing its degree of fulfillment in the respective argument. Scenario-based fuzz-testing and the implementation of identified optimization measures gives evidence required by the dependability arguments.

Future work will include identification of potential for further optimization of systems of systems according to the OR.net initiative. Optimizations will be in a way to increase safety, security, and customer satisfaction. At this point it is unclear which parameters the certification authorities will require for such systems of systems. It may be possible that only a subset of the parameters of the dependability arguments proposed will be made available for those certification authorities.

References

1. van Sprundel, I.: Fuzzing: Breaking software in an automated fashion. CCC congress (2005)
2. Stephenson, Z., Kelly, T., Camus, J.-L.: Developing an Argument for Def Stan 00-56 from Existing Qualification Evidence, Embedded Real-Time Software and Systems (2010)
3. Fu, Y., Koné, O.: Security and robustness by protocol testing. IEEE Syst. J. **8**(3), 699–707 (2014)
4. Castanet, R., Koné, O., Zarkouna, K.B.: Test de robustesse. In: Proceedings SETIT, pp. 100–111, March 2003
5. IEEE Standard Glossary of Software Engineering Terminology, IEEE Standard 610.12-1990, December 1990
6. Gotzhein, R., Khendek, F.: Compositional testing of communication systems. In: Uyar, M., Duale, A.Y., Fecko, M.A. (eds.) TestCom 2006. LNCS, vol. 3964, pp. 227–244. Springer, Heidelberg (2006)
7. Lei, B., Li, X., Liu, Z.: Robustness testing for software components. Sci. Comput. Program. **75**, 879–897 (2010)
8. Kaner, C.: An Introduction to Scenario Testing, Florida Tech, June 2003
9. Ryser, J., Glinz, M.: A scenario-based approach to validating and testing software systems using statecharts. In: 12th International Conference on Software and Systems Engineering and their Applications, ICSSEA 1999, Paris (1999)
10. Sujan, M.-A., Pozzi, S., Valbonesi, C., Ingram, C.: Resilience as individual adaptation: preliminary analysis of a hospital dispensary. In: CEUR Proceedings 4th Workshop HCP Human Centered Processes, February 10–11, 2011
11. Redin, R.M., Oliveira, M.F.S., Brisolara, L.B., Mattos, J.C.B., Lamb, L.C., Wagner, F.R., Carro, L.: On the use of software quality metrics to improve physical properties of embedded systems, Institute of Informatics, Federal University of Rio Grande do Sul
12. Waever, R., Despotou, G., Kelly, T., McDermid, J.: Combining software evidence-arguments and assurance, department of computer science. In: Proceedings of ICSE-2005
13. Arney, D., Goldman, J.M., Bhargav-Spantzel, A., Basu, A., Taborn, M., Pappas, G., Robkin, M.: Simulation of Medical Device Network Performance for an Integrated Clinical Environment, Biomedical Instrumentation & Technology, pp. 308–315, July/August 2012
14. Holzman, G.J.: Fault Intolerance, IEEE Software, pp. 16–20, November/December 2014

Author Index